Introduction to Computers and Information Technology

PREPARING FOR IC3 CERTIFICATION

Third Edition

SUZANNE WEIXEL

Boston • Columbus • Indianapolis • New York • San Francisco
Amsterdam • Cape Town • Dubai • London • Madrid • Milan • Munich
Paris • Montreál • Toronto • Delhi • Mexico City • Saõ Paulo • Sydney
Hong Kong • Seoul • Singapore • Taipei • Tokyo

330 Hudson Street, New York, NY 10013
Hardcover ISBN 10: 0-13-521015-1
Hardcover ISBN 13: 978-0-13-521015-4
1 2 3 4 5 6 7 8 9 10 12 11 10 09 08

Contents

To the Student

Using Your Text

This text is organized into three parts, with each part corresponding to one of the three IC3 certification exams:

- Computing Fundamentals
- Key Applications
- Living Online

Each part is organized into chapters, and each chapter is organized into lessons. Within the text you will find the following features.

CHAPTER OVERVIEW Each chapter begins with an introduction to concepts and a chapter outline.

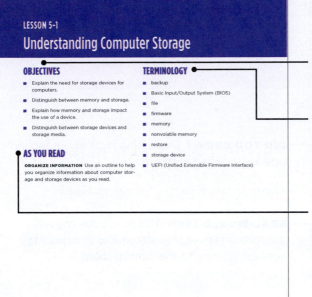

At the start of each lesson you will find helpful tools that guide you through the learning process.

OBJECTIVES Tasks you should be able to complete by the end of the lesson.

TERMINOLOGY Vocabulary terms you should know after you complete the lesson.

AS YOU READ Ideas for how you can best organize information for maximum learning.

Feature boxes are used throughout the text to enhance and support the content.

TECHNOLOGY@HOME
TECHNOLOGY@SCHOOL
TECHNOLOGY@WORK
These include relevant information on how you can use the technology that you are learning about. Each is followed by a prompt to think about how the topics apply to the real world.

IC3 CHECKPOINT Throughout the text, IC3 checkpoints identify the specific content you are expected to know for the IC3 certification exams.

LESSON 26-1 WHAT IS THE INTERNET?

Internet Management

Who owns the internet? The truth is that no specific organization or government does. Many organizations are responsible for different parts of the network. Here are some examples:

- The World Wide Web Consortium (W3C) is an international community of organizations, employees, and the public that develops standards for the web.

- Internet Engineering Task Force (IETF) is a large international community of network designers, operators, vendors, and researchers. This group is concerned with the future structure and smooth operation of the internet. Like many organizations that set computing standards, the IETF is "open," meaning any interested person can participate.

- Internet Corporation for Assigned Names and Numbers (ICANN) is a nonprofit corporation with a variety of responsibilities, including the management of **domain names**. The domain name is the part of an internet address that identifies the location where a web page is stored.

- Web Standards Project (WaSP) is a coalition that supports standards for simple, affordable access to web technologies.

FREEDOM OF THE INTERNET One advantage to the open quality of the internet is the ability to share information. Anyone can make an idea or opinion accessible to anyone else.

PITFALLS OF THE INTERNET However, there are pitfalls to this open organization. People can post whatever point of view or information they want, even if it is be misleading or false. It is up to the users of the internet to think critically about the information they read online. If you have a question about anything you find on the internet, ask an adult you trust about it.

DID YOU KNOW?
Did you know that you can get a traffic report about the internet? Like the traffic reports you may hear on television or on the radio during rush hour, the Internet Traffic Report monitors the flow of data around the world. Visit www.internettrafficreport.com to see how the traffic is in your neighborhood.

DID YOU KNOW? Interesting facts about technology are included in this feature.

REAL-WORLD TECH
VOTING ON THE INTERNET?

According to the Federal Election Commission, the internet is not ready for U.S. citizens to vote on it. Safeguarding the privacy, security, and reliability of the voting process is important to ensuring a free democratic election.

While there have been some experiments with internet voting, experts agree that it will be a long time before it is used in general elections. The internet, however, can improve some parts of the election process. For example, the technology is in place for secure overseas military voting. Also, registration databases and vote totals can be sent over the internet, saving time and money.

In what other ways might you use the internet to find out more about politics?

REAL-WORLD TECH This is a technology-awareness feature that introduces a technology concept relating to the current topic.

551

LESSON 11-4 BASICS OF DESKTOP PUBLISHING

CONNECTIONS

THE ARTS Desktop-publishing programs let you enhance a document in many ways. You can use color, large type, bold and italic type, drawings, and special effects to make the pages interesting. Experienced designers offer the following guidelines for using these tools:

- Use only a few fonts and choose appropriate ones for the task.
- Don't overuse color, bold, or italic type. Too much can make a document difficult to read.
- Use type size, space, and other elements to emphasize the most important parts of the document.
- Keep the reader in mind. Design a document so that it is easy to read and use.

PUBLISHING After the document is final, it is printed or published for online viewing. Sometimes, DTP documents are printed using desktop printers, or they may be sent to printers who print and

bind finished copies. For color documents, the DTP program can prepare color separations, which are separate versions of the document's pages. Each version contains a specific set of colors; each of which is applied in a separate pass through the printer. When the colors are combined, the full-color document is finished.

CAREER CORNER

Workers who do desktop publishing are called graphic designers. There are about 200,000 graphic designers in the United States.

Most work for companies, but about one third work for themselves.

The Bureau of Labor Statistics says that in the next few years the number of jobs for desktop publishers will grow by a huge amount—about 67 percent.

Interested students can take courses in design at some colleges and professional schools. Of course, experience in using computers is a great plus!

CONNECTIONS This cross-curricular feature explains how the technology covered in the chapter is used in other areas, including the arts, science, social studies, language arts, and mathematics.

CAREER CORNER This feature includes information on careers that use the technology being discussed in the chapter.

FIGURE 11.4.1 Designing a newsletter in Microsoft Publisher.

246

At the end of each chapter there are review questions and activities to help you check and assess your comprehension.

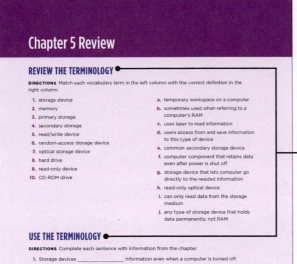

Chapter 5 Review

REVIEW THE TERMINOLOGY

DIRECTIONS Match each vocabulary term in the left column with the correct definition in the right column.

1. storage device
2. memory
3. primary storage
4. secondary storage
5. read/write device
6. random-access storage device
7. optical storage device
8. hard drive
9. read-only device
10. CD-ROM drive

a. temporary workspace on a computer
b. sometimes used when referring to a computer's RAM
c. uses laser to read information
d. users access from and save information to this type of device
e. common secondary storage device
f. computer component that retains data even after power is shut off
g. storage device that lets computer go directly to the needed information
h. read-only optical device
i. can only read data from the storage medium
j. any type of storage device that holds data permanently; not RAM

USE THE TERMINOLOGY

DIRECTIONS Complete each sentence with information from the chapter.

1. Storage devices _____ information even when a computer is turned off.
2. A _____ is a collection of related information or program code, which has been given a unique name.
3. The _____ is a set of programs that directs computer equipment to start up.
4. The purpose of _____ is to store data and program instructions needed by the CPU.
5. ROM is _____ **memory**, which means it stores its contents permanently, even when the computer is turned off.
6. _____ memory is used in ROM chips within your computer to store basic information about the computer's configuration.

104

REVIEW THE TERMINOLOGY AND USE THE TERMINOLOGY Exercises to check your understanding of vocabulary terms in the chapter.

CHAPTER 8 REVIEW

3. If a pop-up menu is context-sensitive, what is it related to?
   a. file format
   b. printer settings
   c. what you are doing
   d. operating system
4. Which of the following is NOT a system change most users should attempt?
   a. moving the operating system
   b. adding a scanner
   c. changing mouse settings
   d. removing a program
5. Along with the data itself, which of the following is saved with a file?
   a. login procedure
   b. code for the application that created it
   c. icon that describes it
   d. maintenance utility
6. Which of the following is one way that a file can be corrupted?
   a. by deleting it
   b. by appearing on the desktop
   c. by moving it to a new folder
   d. by storing it on a damaged disk

THINK CRITICALLY

DIRECTIONS Answer the following questions.

1. Why would you add or remove buttons from the Quick Access Toolbar at the top of an application window?
2. What is the biggest difference between a list box and a multiple selection list, when viewing a typical dialog box or pop-up menu?
3. What is the difference between "Sleep Mode" and "Hibernate Mode"? What is the benefit of using these features?
4. How might a malicious individual use social engineering to install malware and viruses on another user's computer? What might these programs be capable of, and what can be done to prevent this?
5. What would be a benefit to accessing and altering read/write permissions for a file or folder? Give an example.
6. Why would it be beneficial to share a link to a file or folder via a cloud service like Microsoft OneDrive?

EXTEND YOUR KNOWLEDGE

DIRECTIONS Choose and complete one of the following projects.

A. With a partner, interview three adult computer users: one who uses Microsoft Windows, one who uses a Macintosh, and one who has experience with both operating systems.
B. Prepare written questions related to ease of learning the operating system, ease of use, availability of programs, and overall satisfaction with the operating system, and take notes to record the answers. Add your findings to your own experiences and write a conclusion about the user preferences of the two major operating systems. Share your conclusion with a partner or with your class.

162

THINK CRITICALLY Short-answer questions to demonstrate your understanding of concepts.

EXTEND YOUR KNOWLEDGE Projects incorporating the skills you have learned in a fun and challenging activity.

CHAPTER 1 REVIEW

IC3 PREP

1. Which of the following are typical peripheral devices used with desktop computers? (select all that apply.)

   a. CPU   **b.** printer

2. Match the port type on the left with its purpose.

   1. Audio

   2. Ethernet

   3. Parallel

   4. Serial

   5. PS/2

   6. DVI

   7. VGA

   8. HDMI

   9. USB

   a. The most common networking technology used for local area networks.

   b. A standard connection interface that allows communication between computers and devices such as mice, printers, and smartphones.

   c. An older interface once used for connecting input devices such as a keyboard or a mouse.

   d. A digital cable standard for audio and video transmission found on most HD television sets.

   e. An interface used to connect a monitor or other display device to a computer.

   f. A bi-directional interface once commonly used for connecting devices such as a modem.

   g. An older interface used to connect any type of display device to a computer.

   h. Color-coded mini jacks used for microphones and headphones.

   i. An interface used to transfer multiple bits of data at the same time, which was once the most common way to connect a printer to a computer.

3. Which of the following are likely caused by hardware problems? (select all that apply)

   a. monitor is blank   **d.** keyboard does not respond to typing

   b. application will not open   **e.** Web page will not load in browser

   c. pointer does not respond to mouse

27

IC3 PREP At the end of chapters that include IC3 content, there are questions focused on what you are expected to know for the IC3 certification exams.

CHAPTER 2 REVIEW

IC3 PROCEDURES

LOGGING OUT OF AN OPERATING SYSTEM

   1. Select the **Start** button ⊞ on the taskbar.

   2. Select the **User Name** button near the top left of the Start menu.

   3. Select **Sign out**.

LOGGING OUT FROM AN ONLINE ACCOUNT

   1. Select the **Start** button ⊞ on the taskbar.

   2. Select the **Settings** icon ⚙

   3. Select **Accounts**, and select **Your info** if not already selected.

   4. Select **Sign in with a local account instead**.

   5. Enter your Microsoft account password and select **Next**.

   6. Enter a name for your new local account, a password, and a hint, Select **Next**.

   7. Select **Sign out and finish**.

MAINTAINING AND UPDATING ANTIVIRUS SOFTWARE

   1. In the Search bar on the Windows Taskbar, type **Windows Defender**.

   2. Select **Windows Defender Security Center**.

   3. Use the available options to verify the status of protection, update virus definitions, and run scans.

CONFIGURING FIREWALL SETTINGS

   1. In the Search bar on the Windows Taskbar, type **Firewall**.

   2. Select **Windows Firewall**.

   3. Use the available options to adjust settings, including selecting programs to allow or block.

CLEARING THE INTERNET BROWSING HISTORY

   1. Open the Microsoft Edge browser.

   2. Select the **Hub** icon ☆

   3. Select the **History** icon 🕓.

   4. Select **Clear all history**.

DELETING TEMPORARY FILES, COOKIES, SAVED PASSWORDS, AND WEB FORM INFORMATION

   1. Open the Microsoft Edge browser.

   2. Select the **More** icon ⋯, and select **Settings**.

   3. Under the **Clear browsing data** heading, select **Choose what to clear**.

   4. Select the items to clear.

   5. Select **Clear**.

66

IC3 PROCEDURES Step-by-step procedures are included at the end of chapters that cover specific skills you are expected to know for the IC3 certification exams.

Step-by-step procedures for applications and operating system skills are included.

Additional Microsoft Windows 10 Procedures

STARTING THE COMPUTER
Press the On switch.

SHUTTING DOWN THE COMPUTER
1. Click the Windows button on the Taskbar ⊞.
2. Click Power.
3. Click Shut down.

RESTARTING THE COMPUTER
1. Click the Windows button on the taskbar ⊞.
2. Click Power.
3. Click Restart.

LOGGING IN TO A USER ACCOUNT
Click the desired user account to log in as that user.

STARTING A PROGRAM
1. Click the Windows button on the Taskbar ⊞.
2. From the Start menu, click the program's tile or name.
    OR
1. Click the Windows button on the taskbar ⊞.
2. Begin typing the program name.
3. When the program name appears in the Search list, click the program name.
    OR
    Double-click the program icon on the desktop.
    OR
    Click the program icon on the Windows taskbar.

EXITING A PROGRAM
Click the **Close** button on the right side of the program's title bar.

USING THE MOUSE
- Click the left mouse button to execute a command.
- Click the right mouse button to open a shortcut menu.
- Hover the mouse pointer on an object to display a ScreenTip.
- Select an object and hold down the left mouse button to drag the object to another location.
- Spin the scroll wheel on the mouse to move through an open file.
- Double-click the left mouse button to open a file or application.

USING A TOUCH SCREEN
- Tap once on an item to open or select it.
- Press down and hold an item to select it, display a ScreenTip, or open a shortcut menu.
- Pinch or stretch an item to display different levels of information or zoom in or out.
- Drag across the screen to scroll.
- Swipe a short stroke to select an item.

USING THE KEYBOARD
- Use function keys as shortcuts for performing specified tasks.
- Use modifier keys (Alt, Shift, and Ctrl) in combination with other keys or mouse actions to select certain commands or perform actions.
- Use the number keypad to enter numeric data.

172

Preparing for the IC3 Certification Exams

ABOUT THE EXAMS

The IC3 Digital Literacy Certification program is designed to prepare you for career success in a technology-based world. The certification includes three exams. To receive IC3 certification, you must pass all three exams:

1. Computing Fundamentals, which covers the foundations of computing.

2. Key Applications, which covers skills for working with common application programs.

3. Living Online, which covers skills for working in an internet- or networked-based environment.

You are allowed 50 minutes for each exam. Computing Fundamentals and Living Online each have 50 questions. Key Applications has 45 questions. There is a total value of 1,000 for all three exams, and the passing score is 700.

The exams are administered online. They make use of the latest testing technologies, including the integration of both performance-based and knowledge-based testing. That means you will have the opportunity to answer concept-based questions in formats such as multiple choice, multiple select, matching, and labeling, as well as opportunities to show your mastery of skills using simulated application environments.

TEST-TAKING TIPS

- Before the exam begins, there will be instructions. Read them carefully and make sure you understand the exam process before you begin.

- Read each question and prompt carefully. Make sure you understand what is being asked before selecting an answer.

■ Pay attention to whether a question is multiple choice or multiple select. If it is multiple choice, there is only one correct answer. If it is multiple select, there may be more than one correct answer.

■ Watch for words such as NOT in a question or prompt. You may be asked to identify the answer that is NOT true, or NOT applicable.

■ You can skip questions. If there is time at the end, you can return to any question.

■ If you are faced with a question you do not know, skip it, and go back at the end if there is time.

■ In the simulations, if you do not immediately recognize the application or skill, do not panic! Most applications are similar. If you know how to complete a task in one application, you will be able to do it in a different application. For example, if you know how to change a profile picture in Skype, but are asked to change a profile picture in Twitter, look for commands that you would use in Skype. The steps will be similar.

■ In the simulations, you have the opportunity to clear your steps and start again, if necessary.

■ In the simulations, you may find that some commands do not function. If you select a command and nothing happens, you can be sure that command is not required to complete the steps. Try something else.

■ Application simulations may be used in all three exams, but most of them are in the Key Applications exam. There are not usually simulations for the database portion of the Key Applications exam.

PART 1
Computing Fundamentals

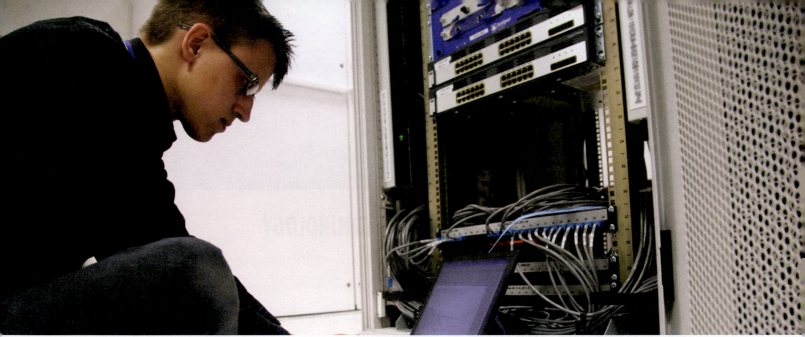

CHAPTER 1

Computer Basics

HOW DO COMPUTERS WORK?

The answer to this question can be very long and complicated, even though computers work in a fairly simple way. At its core, a computer contains a set of on/off switches; by turning these switches on and off very rapidly, the computer can represent information. Imagine a wall covered with a thousand lightbulbs, each with its own on/off switch. By turning switches on and off in a certain way, you could use the lights to spell words or create pictures. Computers work in a similar way.

But a computer cannot use its switches without instructions. That's where software and you, the user, come into play. By giving the computer instructions and data to work with, you and your software programs tell it how to work its switches—turning them on and off millions of times each second.

What Is a Computer?

OBJECTIVES

- Describe the four operations of computers.

- Contrast analog and digital computers.

- Explain why data and instructions for computers are coded as 0s and 1s.

- Explain the hexadecimal system of displaying color.

AS YOU READ

SEQUENCE INFORMATION Use a sequence chart to help you organize the four operations of computers as you read the lesson.

TERMINOLOGY

- bit

- byte

- computer

- data

- hexadecimal value

- input

- internet

- memory

- output

- processing

- program

- storage

Computer Basics

A **computer** is a machine that changes information from one form into another by performing four basic actions. Those actions are input, processing, output, and storage. Together, these actions make up the information processing cycle. By following a set of instructions, called a program, the computer turns raw data into organized information that people can use. Creation of usable information is the primary benefit of computer technology. There are two kinds of computers:

- Analog computers measure data on a scale with many values. Think of the scales on a mercury thermometer or on the gas gauge of a car.

- Digital computers work with data that has a fixed value. They use data in digital, or number, form. The computers that run programs for playing games or searching the **internet**, a global network of computers, are digital computers.

Input

Input is the raw information, or **data**, that is entered into a computer. This data can be as simple as letters and numbers or as complex as color photographs, videos, or songs. You input data by using a device such as a keyboard or digital camera.

BITS OF DATA Data is entered into a computer in a coded language. The building blocks of that language are units called **bits**. *Bit* is short for *binary digit*. Each bit is a number, or a digit. A bit can have only two possible values—0 or 1.

BITS INTO BYTES Every letter, number, or picture is entered into the computer as a combination of bits, or 0s and 1s. The bits are combined into groups of eight or more. Each group is called a **byte**. Each letter or number has a unique combination of bits. For instance, on most personal computers, the letter *A* is coded as 01000001. The number *1* is 00110001.

Even images are formed by combinations of bytes. Those combinations tell the computer what colors to display and where to put them.

HEXADECIMAL VALUES Color can be represented by a three-byte combination where each byte represents the red, green, or blue (RGB) component of the displayed color. The intensity of each component is measured on a scale from 0 to 256, since there are 256 possible combinations of 1 or 0 in each group of eight bits. To represent a color, the three-byte RGB codes are simplified into a 6-digit **hexadecimal value** where the first two digits represent the intensity of red, the second two are green, and the last two are blue.

A hexadecimal number has sixteen possible values, so the RGB values are assigned a number from 0 to 15. But since 10 through 15 are two digit numbers they are expressed with the letters A through F, where A equals 10 and F equals 15. In this way, the 256 possible combinations of each byte can be expressed in two digits. For example, the hexadecimal value for pure, intense red is FF0000 since red has the highest intensity and both green and blue are at zero. The hexadecimal for white is FFFFFF, or complete intensity of all three colors, and black is 0000000.

CONNECTIONS

MATH You ordinarily count using the decimal, or base 10, system. That system has 10 values, 0 through 9. You can express many numbers using those values by adding additional places—the 10s, the 100s, and so on. Each place is 10 times larger than the previous place. In a binary system, the quantity represented by each place is 2 times the previous quantity. In an 8-digit binary number, the places are the 1s, 2s, 4s, 8s, 16s, 32s, 64s, and 128s. The hexadecimal system is a base 16 system. The places for RGB code are the 1s and 16s. In the conversion from binary to hexadecimal, the first hexadecimal value is equal to the 1s, 2s, 4s, and 8s of the color's binary number.

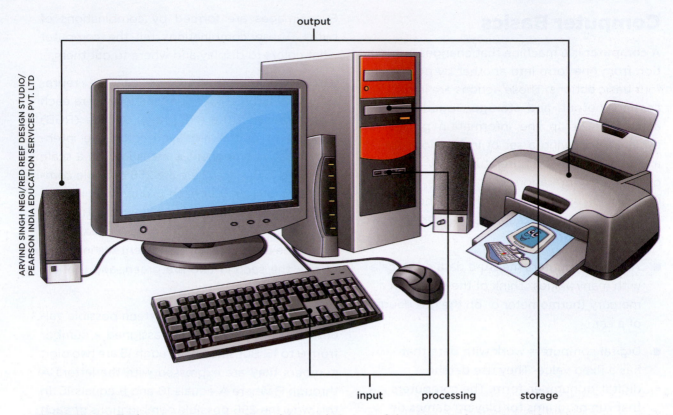

ARVIND SINGH NEGI/RED REEF DESIGN STUDIO/
PEARSON INDIA EDUCATION SERVICES PVT. LTD

FIGURE 1.1.1 Each computer component plays a role in one of the system's four primary functions.

Processing

The second step of the information processing cycle is called **processing**. In this step, the computer carries out a task using the data.

CODED INSTRUCTIONS What the computer does depends on the instructions, or **program**, given to the computer. The instructions are also written in binary code, using combinations of 0s and 1s. They might tell the computer to add two numbers, or they might have the computer compare two numbers to see which is larger.

SPEED OF PROCESSING Computers can process data very rapidly, performing millions of operations every second. The ability to process data with lightning speed is another reason computers are so valuable.

TECHNOLOGY@SCHOOL

In some schools, students' work is collected over the year in electronic portfolios. These portfolios reflect a range of the students' work on many projects during the school year. The computer's ability to store this information is perfect for portfolio work.

THINK ABOUT IT!

Think about how an electronic portfolio might be used. Which items below do you think could be in an electronic portfolio?

- multimedia presentations
- maps
- paper-and-pencil homework
- poetry
- lab report

REAL-WORLD TECH
ROBOTS AT WORK

Some output is very unusual. Computer-controlled robots work in some auto factories. Their output is cars. The robots are perfect for the tasks that take place on an assembly line. These tasks are done over and over again without change. For instance, robots weld parts together and paint car bodies.

NATALIYA HORA/SHUTTERSTOCK

What is a disadvantage to workers of bringing in robots to do tasks such as factory work? What can businesses and workers do to make that less of a problem?

Output

The third step, **output**, is the result of the computer's processing presented to the user. If the program tells the computer to add two numbers, the output stage displays the result. To create output, the computer takes the bytes and turns them back into a form you can understand, such as an image on the screen, a sound through a speaker, or a printed document.

Storage

The fourth operation is **storage**, which is the action by which a computer saves information. Without storage, all the work you do on the computer would be lost. Computers have temporary **memory** chips used to store data during the processing stage. When the computer is turned off, however, any data in that temporary memory is lost. By storing the data in a permanent form on a device such as a hard drive, you can access the information over and over. This is another great advantage of computers—what you do one day can be saved and reused on another day.

What Is Computer Hardware?

OBJECTIVES

- Summarize how processing and memory work together.

- Contrast primary and secondary storage.

- Identify types of ports and connectors.

- Explain how to connect a variety of peripherals to a computer.

- Describe how to connect using Wi-Fi.

AS YOU READ

COMPARE AND CONTRAST Use an outline to help you compare and contrast computer hardware as you read.

TERMINOLOGY

- Bluetooth

- central processing unit (CPU)

- circuit

- circuit board

- cloud storage

- connector

- device

- Digital Visual Interface (DVI)

- Ethernet

- hardware

- High-Definition Multimedia Interface (HDMI)

- IR wireless

- memory card

- optical storage device

- parallel port

- peripheral

- physical connection

- port

- random access memory (RAM)

- serial port

- Small Computer Systems Interface (SCSI)

- terabyte

- universal serial bus (USB)

- upload

- Video Graphics Array (VGA)

- volatile memory

- Wi-Fi

- wireless connection

What Is Hardware?

When you think about a computer, you probably picture its **hardware**, the computer's physical parts. You use hardware devices such as a keyboard or mouse to input data. The processor is a hardware **device** that turns the raw data into usable information. Hardware devices such as a monitor or a disk drive show output and store data for later access.

Inside the Case

Much of a computer's hardware is found inside the computer case, hidden from view. Most of this hardware is used for processing and storing data.

PROCESSING DEVICES Perhaps the most important piece of hardware in a computer is the **central processing unit**, or **CPU**. This is the device that processes data. The CPU is a small, thin piece of silicon attached to a **circuit board**. The CPU is covered with tiny electrical **circuits**, or paths along which an electrical current is carried. By moving data along these circuits in specific ways, the CPU can do arithmetic and compare data very quickly.

PRIMARY STORAGE Some hardware used to store data is inside the computer case near the CPU. The computer uses **random access memory**, or **RAM**, to store data and instructions while the computer is working. In this way, the CPU can quickly find the data it works with. This type of storage is called primary storage. RAM is **volatile memory**, which means data in RAM is lost when the computer is turned off.

SECONDARY STORAGE DEVICES Other pieces of storage hardware are secondary storage. The following devices let you store data permanently—even when the computer is turned off.

- Hard drives use a stack of disk platters to store large amounts of information permanently on the computer. External hard drives, which are plugged into the computer, are used to store backups of your data. They can be desktop or portable devices. They usually connect to the computer via a **universal serial bus**, or **USB**, port. A **port** is a connection between a computer and a device.

- Flash, jump, thumb, or pen drives—all names for the same kind of storage device—connect to the computer through a USB port. They hold anywhere from 4 gigabytes to more than a terabyte. (TB). A **terabyte** is about 1,000 gigabytes. A gigabyte (GB) is just over a billion bytes.

- Compact discs (CDs), digital video discs (DVDs), and Blu-ray Discs (BDs) are **optical storage devices**. You insert the CD or DVD into your computer through the disc drive. A CD can store 650 to 700 megabytes of data. DVDs can store anywhere from 4.7 gigabytes to double that amount if the DVD is double-sided. Blu-ray Discs hold from 25 gigabytes to 128 gigabytes.

- **Cloud storage** is online storage offered on various websites. Most of them will give you a few gigabytes for free, but then require you to pay for more space.

- **Memory cards** store data for mobile devices like smartphones and digital cameras. Some memory cards can store up to 2 terabytes.

RMIKKA/SHUTTERSTOCK

FIGURE 1.2.1 The CPU fits in a socket on a circuit board.

SECONDARY STORAGE CAPACITY Hard disk drives hold the most data. Many computers now have hard drives that can store more than 4 terabytes. Some external hard drives can store more than 30 terabytes. Thumb or flash drives hold the next largest amount of data, sometimes going over a terabyte. CDs and DVDs hold the least amount of data—from around 700 megabytes to almost 10 gigabytes. A megabyte (MB) is just over a million bytes, but still several hundred of them on a DVD can store entire encyclopedias, including images, maps, and sound.

Peripherals

For most desktop systems, input devices, such as the keyboard and mouse, are separate from the case. So are output devices, such as monitors and printers. Hardware that is separate but can be connected to the case is called a **peripheral**.

Printers, mice, and keyboards are typical peripheral devices that connect to desktop computers and laptops. Keyboards are also often used with tablets. Smartphones may connect as a device to a computer in order to transfer pictures or data files and they may also have peripherals of their own, such as a headset for hands-free use or speakers for playing music.

GRANT TERRY/SHUTTERSTOCK

FIGURE 1.2.2 Most computers feature a built-in hard drive. Some have capacities of 4 terabytes or more. Some external hard drives are able to store 30 terabytes of data.

Not all computers have all this equipment as peripherals. Apple's iMac® computers include the monitor as a physical part of the main system. Other computers may have built-in storage devices. Portable computers, such as laptops, have the keyboard, a touchpad, and a monitor all attached to the main unit.

IC3✔ Know which peripheral devices are typically used with desktop computers.

Device Ports and Connectors

Peripherals need to be connected to the computer so that data can be moved back and forth. Some use a **wireless connection**, such as radio waves, and some use a **physical connection**, such as a cable. Both wireless and physical connections require a plug, or **connector**. Most plugs join the computer at a port on the computer case, but some are installed internally.

Connectors can be unique for the peripheral. Monitors have specific plugs designed for transferring image data. Speakers and microphones have unique plugs as well. Many devices, such as keyboards, printers, and mice, use USB ports.

To connect a peripheral to a computer with a physical connection, identify the type of plug coming from the peripheral and locate the correct port on the computer. Attach the plug to the port and make sure the cable is secure at both the computer end and the peripheral end.

IC3✔ Know how to connect the following devices to a computer: camera, speakers, microphone, printer, USB devices, and external display monitor.

Each port is designed to accept a specific connector, so most connectors only fit into one type of port. That means you cannot plug a USB connector into an Ethernet port. Most ports are labeled with icons to identify the type, and some are color-coded to match the connector.

- **Serial ports** move data one bit at a time. For example, they connect computers to modems for internet access.

- **Parallel ports** move data in groups.

- Multiple device ports, such as **Small Computer Systems Interface (SCSI)** and Universal Serial Bus (USB) ports, connect several peripherals to a computer at one time. They all move data faster than serial ports can.

ETHERNET PORTS AND CONNECTORS **Ethernet** is the most common networking technology used for local area networks (LANs). To create the network, Ethernet cables plug into Ethernet ports on computers, LANs, and cable or DSL modems. An Ethernet port is usually labeled with an icon similar to the one on the right in Figure 1.2.3.

IC3✔ Understand the use of Ethernet ports.

FIGURE 1.2.3 Ports are usually labeled, making it easy to know what plugs in where.

USB PORTS AND CONNECTORS Universal Serial Bus (USB) is a standard connection interface that allows communication between personal computers and electronic devices. Almost all devices now can use a USB port, including printers, keyboards, mice, storage devices, cameras, smartphones, and fitness trackers. USB lets devices draw power from the connection so it can be used for charging. Adapters let you connect a USB port to A/C power. A USB port is usually labeled with an icon similar to the one on the left in Figure 1.2.3.

VIDEO PORTS AND CONNECTIONS There are three basic types of video ports and connectors, with HDMI being the most common.

- **High-Definition Multimedia Interface (HDMI)** is a digital cable standard for audio and video transmission. HDMI ports accept a connector with 19 wires—ten on one side and nine on the other. HDMI is found on most high-definition (HD) television sets, newer computers, projectors, Blu-ray players, and television devices such as Apple TV. HDMI cables can stream digital video and audio at the same time.

- **Digital Visual (or Video) Interface (DVI)** ports are used to connect a monitor or other display device to a computer. Most DVI connectors accept plugs with up to 24 pins. DVI with 24 pins supports 1920 x 1200

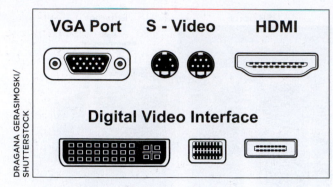

FIGURE 1.2.4 Common video ports.

HD video. If there are fewer pins, it means it supports lower resolutions. DVI is video only; it does not support audio. Although DVI may be available on some computers, it is being replaced by HDMI.

■ **Video Graphics Array (VGA)** is one of the oldest types of computer port. It was used to connect any type of display device to a computer, including monitors, projectors, and televisions. VGA is being replaced by DVI and HDMI but may still be available on some computers. A VGA port accepts a 15-pin connector. The pins are arranged in three rows with five pins on each row. The plug is often blue. VGA can support resolutions up to 640 x 480 in 16 colors.

AUDIO PORTS AND CONNECTORS Many audio devices can connect to USB ports. Some computers have a 3.5 mm audio jack for connecting headphones and speakers. It is usually labeled with an icon of headphones. There are also dedicated audio ports called mini jacks used for microphones and headphones. These ports are usually color-coded.

■ Pink or red indicates a line-in port that connects the sound card to a microphone.

■ Green indicates a line-out port that connects the sound card to speakers or headphones.

■ If there are orange and black line-out ports, they connect to surround sound speakers.

■ The blue line-in port may be used to connect a device that will play through your computer's speakers.

PARALLEL PORTS AND CONNECTORS A parallel port is usually the biggest port on a computer. It is shaped like a capital letter D and accepts a 25-pin parallel connector. Parallel ports can transfer multiple bits of data at the same time. Parallel ports were once the most common way to connect a printer to a computer. Now, most printers use USB connectors or are wireless.

SERIAL PORTS AND CONNECTORS Serial ports, also called COM ports, were once the most basic connector available for devices such as a modem. Now, devices that once used a serial port use a USB port. A serial port transmits the 8 bits in a byte of data one at a time. Serial ports are bidirectional, which means they can accept data as well as transmit it. Serial ports accept serial plugs that usually have 9 pins. One row

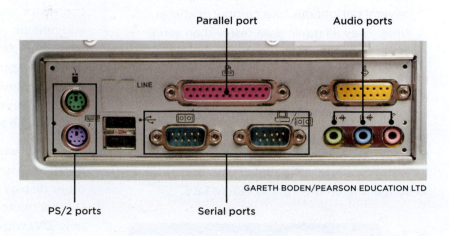

FIGURE 1.2.5 Ports may be color-coded, and labeled with icons.

GARETH BODEN/PEARSON EDUCATION LTD

has five pins and a second row has four. Some serial connectors have 25 pins.

PS/2 PORTS AND CONNECTORS A PS/2 port used to be the port of choice for connecting input devices such as a keyboard or a mouse to a personal computer. Now these devices usually use USB ports. PS/2 ports are round, and accept a 6-pin plug. PS/2 ports may be color-coded.

- Purple is used for connecting the keyboard.

- Green is used for connecting the mouse.

> **IC3✔** Know how to identify ports and explain their purpose.

Wi-Fi and Bluetooth Connections

Wi-Fi and **Bluetooth**™ are types of wireless technologies you can use to connect to devices and the internet. Bluetooth is used for communicating between devices that are less than 30 feet apart, while Wi-Fi is used for connecting to the internet. Wi-Fi signals can reach up to 300 feet.

You might use Bluetooth to connect a wearable fitness tracker to a computer so you can **upload** your daily activity statistics, to send photos from your smartphone to a computer, or to connect your tablet to a wireless speaker. You might use Wi-Fi to print a file when you are using your tablet in a conference room and the printer is in your office on the other side of the building, or to access the internet when you are at a coffee shop.

> **IC3✔** Know how to connect to a printer on a network.

To set up or connect to a Wi-Fi network, the computer must have an internet connection, a modem, a router, and a wireless network adapter card.

Bluetooth devices have built-in radio transmitters and receivers that enable wireless communication.

Operating systems today make it easy to establish Wi-Fi or Bluetooth communications. For example, in the Settings utility for Windows you can choose to add a Bluetooth or other type of wireless device. Windows prompts you through the steps to make the connection. To set up a Wi-Fi network in Windows, you set up a new network from the Network and Sharing Center. Windows prompts you through the necessary steps.

> **IC3✔** Know how to connect to a Wi-Fi network with Windows 10.

> **IC3✔** Know how to connect a device such as a printer to a Wi-Fi network with Windows 10.

IR Wireless

One of the earlier wireless technologies that allowed computers to exchange data is called **IR Wireless**. It uses infrared radiation to transmit data. Infrared is electromagnetic energy at a wavelength slightly longer than that of red light.

Some older notebook computers and handheld personal devices were equipped with infrared adapters, and had IR ports on the back or side. The infrared signals cannot penetrate walls, so IR devices have to be in the same room, within a few feet of each other to exchange data. This may seem like an inconvenience, but it provides security during the transmission.

Although IR Wireless has been replaced by the faster and more reliable Wi-Fi and Bluetooth technologies for data transfer, it is still used for other purposes, including television remote controls, home-entertainment control units, intrusion detectors, robot control systems, cordless microphones, and headsets.

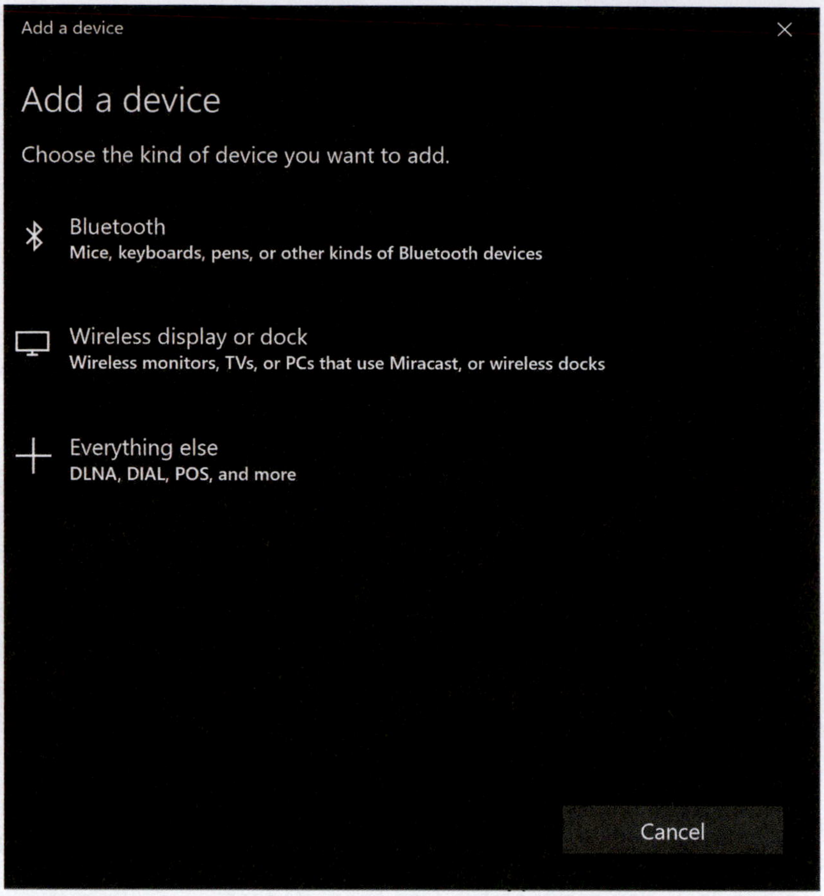

MICROSOFT CORPORATION

FIGURE 1.2.6 Windows includes a Settings utility for connecting a wireless device to a computer.

What Is Computer Software?

OBJECTIVES

- Explain the difference between system and application software.

- Describe what an operating system does.

- Explain what utility software does.

- Identify four types of application software and ways to obtain them.

AS YOU READ

CLASSIFY INFORMATION Use a concept web to help you classify different types of computer software as you read.

TERMINOLOGY

- application software

- apps

- download

- operating system (OS)

- software

- system software

- utility software

BLOOMICON/SHUTTERSTOCK

FIGURE 1.3.1 Operating systems that run on computers, tablets, and smartphones are examples of system software.

What Is Software?

Hardware includes all the physical pieces that make up a computer. However, hardware is useless without software. **Software** includes all of the programs that tell a computer what to do and how to do it. Think of a computer as a sports team. Hardware is the players, and software is the coach. No matter how talented the players are, the team will only perform properly if the coach gives it the right instructions.

Types of Software

Software is divided into two main types: system software and application software. **System software** includes programs that help the computer work properly. You are probably more familiar with **application software**, which are programs designed to help you do tasks such as writing a paper or making a graph. This type of software also includes programs that allow you to use the computer to listen to music or play games.

DID YOU KNOW?

One key to processor speed is its clock speed, the rhythm at which the processor works. Clock speed is measured in hertz (Hz). A Hz is a unit of frequency equal to one cycle per second. Most processor clock speeds are measured in Gigahertz (GHz). 1 GHz equals one billion cycles per second.

Clock speed is not the only thing to consider when you select a processor, however. Speed is also influenced by factors such as the amount of RAM, clock speed of the RAM, and the size of the cache.

System Software

There are two types of system software: operating systems and system utilities. Both help computers run smoothly.

OPERATING SYSTEMS The **operating system (OS)** lets the hardware devices communicate with one another and keeps them running efficiently. It also supports the hardware when applications programs are running. The two most widely used operating systems are macOS and Microsoft® Windows®.

SYSTEM UTILITIES Programs that help the computer work properly are called **utility software**. They usually do maintenance and repair jobs that the operating system cannot do itself. Some utility programs repair damaged data files or save files in certain ways so they take up less space. Others translate files created in one OS so they can be read and worked on in another.

Application Software

There are many different applications. They can be grouped into four main categories:

■ Productivity software helps people be more productive at work. People use these programs to write reports, prepare financial plans, and organize data.

■ Graphics software makes it possible to draw, paint, and touch up photos.

■ Communication software allows computers to connect to the internet and to send email.

■ Home, education, and entertainment software helps people manage their money or figure their taxes. Other products can be used to learn new skills or simply to have some fun.

CUSTOM SOFTWARE Some organizations need software programs to do very specific jobs. They hire people to write custom software designed to do those jobs. Because these programs are custom written, they are usually quite expensive.

OFF-THE-SHELF SOFTWARE Most people use software to do standard jobs. They might want to write letters or organize an album of photos. They can choose from many ready-made programs to handle these common tasks. These are called "off-the-shelf" programs because stores and companies that sell software online stock them. Most off-the-shelf software purchased online can be **downloaded** directly onto the buyer's computer. Because software publishers can sell many copies of this software, it is less expensive than custom software.

APPS The term **app** is an abbreviation for the term "application" usually used for programs developed specifically for smartphones, tablet computers, and other handheld devices. Apps are purchased from app stores, which are online portals where you select and download the programs. Basic versions of these apps are often free, although premium apps offering more features may cost anywhere from $0.99 to more than $200.00.

TECHNOLOGY@WORK

A software program's version is usually indicated by a number, such as "Version 4" or "Version 8.5." Software is upgraded to remove programming errors and to add new features. Some revisions are major, and the version number jumps from, for example, 9.0 to 10.0. Minor fixes typically change the number after the decimal point, such as 10 to 10.2.

THINK ABOUT IT!

For which items below would it be worthwhile for you to buy the new version of the program?

• a program you use all the time that is moving from 4.3 to 5.0

• a program you rarely use that is moving from 2.2 to 2.3

• a program you often use that is moving from 5.1 to 5.2

• a program you often use that is moving from 1.0 to 3.0

MICROSOFT CORPORATION

FIGURE 1.3.2 You can download apps from an app store such as Google Play.

What Is Troubleshooting?

OBJECTIVES

- Explain basic problem solving techniques.
- Describe how to determine if a problem involves hardware or software.
- Use proper terminology to describe problems.

AS YOU READ

IDENTIFY KEY POINTS As you read, use a conclusion chart to help you identify key points about troubleshooting.

TERMINOLOGY

- compatibility
- default factory settings
- device driver
- error message
- firmware
- full system restore
- hard reboot
- knowledge base
- malware
- platform
- reboot
- reformat
- restore
- restore point
- safe mode
- soft reboot
- troubleshooting
- update
- virus

Troubleshooting

Troubleshooting is the act of diagnosing and, hopefully, solving a problem. Knowing some basic problem-solving, or troubleshooting, techniques can help you keep your computer running properly. Before you begin troubleshooting, you will have to diagnose what type of problem your computer is experiencing. A good first step is to determine whether the problem involves hardware or software.

- If you are having trouble opening an application, programs are running slowly, or the computer is crashing or turning off unexpectedly while you are working, the problem is most likely with the software.

- If the monitor will not display an image or the pointer is not responding to the mouse movement, the problem is most likely with your hardware.

- Because the device hardware depends on software, sometimes the problem is with both the hardware and the software.

IC3 ✔ **Know how to determine if a problem is caused by hardware or software.**

There will always be some trial and error involved in troubleshooting while you determine the specific problem. It is a good idea to write down the steps you take so you can recreate them, and also write down any **error messages** displayed by your system. An error message is information displayed by your computer when something happens to prevent a command from executing, such as no communication between the processor and a device or a problem with the software code.

IC3 ✔ **Know basic problem-solving techniques.**

Basic Hardware Troubleshooting

Sometimes your hardware devices may experience problems. They may stop working or stop responding to commands. Hardware does wear out, so you may have to replace older, broken components, but you also may be able to use troubleshooting techniques to diagnose and solve hardware problems.

CABLES AND CONNECTIONS Many hardware problems occur when cables or wires become loose. When your monitor goes dark or your keyboard won't respond, turn the system off and check to make sure all cables are securely connected. Many computers are plugged into a power strip. Make sure the power strip is on. When you have reestablished all connections, turn your system back on and see if the problem is resolved.

REBOOT Many computer problems—such as a program freezing—can be solved by a simple **reboot**. When you reboot your computer, you turn it off and then on again. There are two kinds of reboots: A **hard reboot** is when you turn off all power by pushing the power button or unplugging your computer. A **soft reboot** is when you use the computer's own software to allow your computer to shut down properly. You can select the main menu and choose "shut down" or "restart."

Basic Software Troubleshooting

Most of the time your software programs will respond to your commands as intended. Sometimes there will be problems. Programs might seem slow or sluggish, applications might freeze in the middle of an important task, or you might not be able to launch an application at all.

PLATFORM CONSIDERATIONS A computing **platform** is the hardware, operating system, and **firmware** on which programs run. Firmware is the software that provides basic instructions

AUREMAR/123RF.COM

FIGURE 1.4.1 Tightening cables and connections can solve many basic hardware problems.

for controlling devices. Problems may occur if there is not **compatibility** between the programs and the platform. Compatibility is the ability of things to work together. If they are not compatible, they cannot work together.

Some software is only designed to run on certain operating systems. For example, you might have a game that can only run on a PC with Windows OS and will be unable to run on Macintosh or Linux systems. You might have a mobile device running Apple's iOS, which means you cannot run an app designed for a device that runs the Android operating system.

Documents and media files, such as videos or audio, can only be opened with certain programs. If you have media that won't play, you probably don't have the correct software on your computer. Likewise, a game might not run on your computer if your system is not compatible with the program.

Checking the application and system requirements of programs will allow you to verify that your platform meets the minimum operating criteria for the software.

Some software also requires specific hardware devices to run properly. For example, a device may require a connection to the internet in order to run an application. If the device is not

hard wired through an Ethernet port, or is not equipped with Wi-Fi, the software will not run.

IC3✔ **Know platform implications and considerations and the consequences of platform compatibility.**

UPDATES When manufacturers are aware of problems with software programs, they usually release an **update**. Updates are software that fix errors in the program as well as issues such as compatibility with hardware devices or security risks. Installing a software update may quickly resolve a problem. Companies usually make updates available to registered users free of charge. You can set your programs to automatically check for, download, and install updates, or to notify you when updates are available so you can download and install them manually. If installing an update does not solve a problem, you can try restoring the program defaults or uninstalling and reinstalling the program.

DEVICE DRIVERS **Device drivers** are the programs that enable peripherals and devices to communicate with the hardware through the operating system. If a device stops working, it may be because there is a problem with the driver. You can use a device management utility to check that the device is set up properly and that the driver software is installed and up-to-date. In Windows it is called Device Manager; on Mac systems, it is called Profile Manager. You can use these utilities to install or update the driver, rollback the driver to a previous version, disable the driver, or uninstall and reinstall it.

IC3✔ Know what drivers do and how to determine if a driver is compatible with a personal device.

VIRUSES AND MALWARE Malware is a program designed to damage your system. A virus is a type of malware designed to spread through a computer system or network. If all programs are running slowly, you may have accidentally downloaded a virus or other malware program. Run a virus scanner to identify and remove dangerous programs. Always have virus and malware detection software installed and up to date.

DISK SPACE The amount of storage space may seem like a hardware problem, but it will cause software to run slowly, and it will prevent you from saving your files or installing new programs. Your operating system has a utility to check the amount of used and available storage space. Another utility can recommend files to delete in order to free up additional space. In Windows, the program is called Disk Cleanup. It is found in the System settings. Another Windows utility, called Defragmenter, reorganizes the data stored on a hard disk to make more space available.

TASK AND PROCESS MANAGEMENT Most operating systems include a utility for monitoring tasks and processes currently running on your computer. On a Windows system, it is called Task Manager. You open it by pressing Ctrl + Alt + Delete and selecting Start Task Manager. On a Mac, it is called Activity Monitor. You open it from the Applications/Utilities folder. These

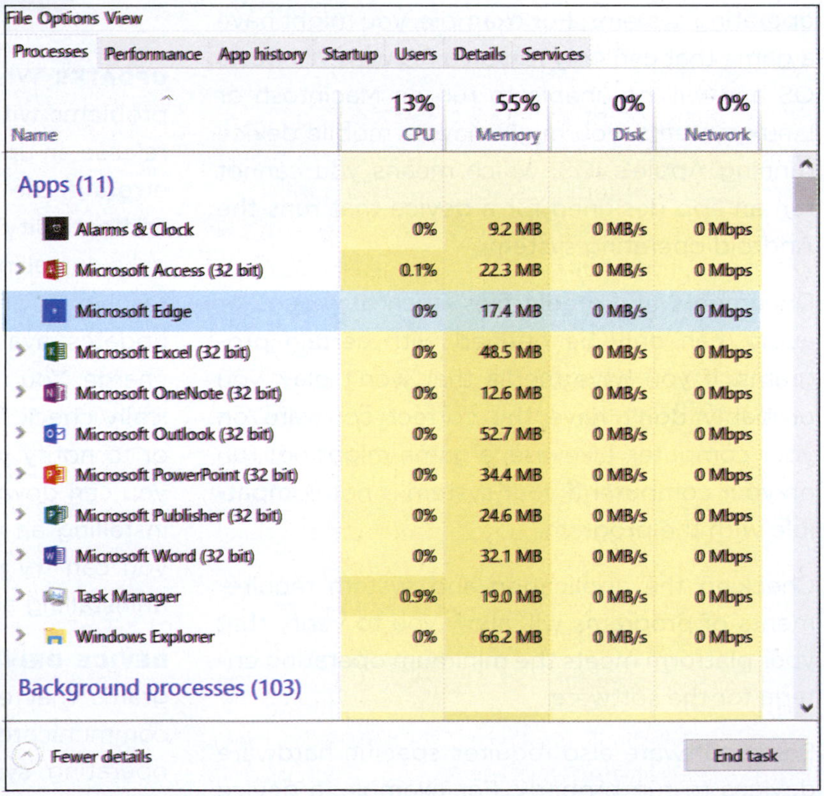

File Options View					
Processes Performance App history Startup Users Details Services					
Name		13% CPU	55% Memory	0% Disk	0% Network
Apps (11)					
Alarms & Clock		0%	9.2 MB	0 MB/s	0 Mbps
> Microsoft Access (32 bit)		0.1%	22.3 MB	0 MB/s	0 Mbps
Microsoft Edge		0%	17.4 MB	0 MB/s	0 Mbps
> Microsoft Excel (32 bit)		0%	48.5 MB	0 MB/s	0 Mbps
> Microsoft OneNote (32 bit)		0%	12.6 MB	0 MB/s	0 Mbps
> Microsoft Outlook (32 bit)		0%	52.7 MB	0 MB/s	0 Mbps
> Microsoft PowerPoint (32 bit)		0%	34.4 MB	0 MB/s	0 Mbps
> Microsoft Publisher (32 bit)		0%	24.6 MB	0 MB/s	0 Mbps
> Microsoft Word (32 bit)		0%	32.1 MB	0 MB/s	0 Mbps
> Task Manager		0.9%	19.0 MB	0 MB/s	0 Mbps
> Windows Explorer		0%	66.2 MB	0 MB/s	0 Mbps
Background processes (103)					
⟳ Fewer details					End task

MICROSOFT CORPORATION

FIGURE 1.4.2 Use the Task Manager in Windows to start and end a program or process.

programs show you the status of programs and processes currently running on your system. You can use them to start and end a program or process; enable or disable startup programs; and to identify and end processes that may be running in the background that you do not need.

SAFE MODE Most computers let you start in **safe mode**, which means they start with only a limited set of files and drivers, which are programs that allow the computer to communicate with devices such as printers and monitors. Safe mode lets you identify and fix problems with software that is interfering with the operating system and other components. You may be able to choose to start in safe mode with or without internet access.

SYSTEM RESTORE You can often use a utility to **restore** your system or personal device to the settings in effect before it stopped working. Windows comes with a Restore utility that automatically creates a **restore point** at specific intervals, such as each day when you start your system or when you install a new software program. You can also manually set a restore point.

The restore point identifies the configuration settings in effect at a specific point in time. If there is a problem, you can use the utility to revert back to a restore point before the problem occurred. Changes to your system settings since the date and time of the restore point are undone, including new software installation or modified system settings. Your data files remain unchanged. Reverting to a restore point is not the same as restoring data that you have previously backed up. Using a restore point restores system settings; it does not affect data files. If data files have been lost or damaged, reverting to a restore point will not solve the problem. You must restore the files from a backup to make them available again.

Another option is to use a system repair disk. With an operating system such as Windows, you can create a system repair disc or recovery drive that allows you to boot the computer and access troubleshooting tools.

You may also be able to perform a **full system restore** to reset a device to the **default factory settings**, which are the settings the device is built with. This should be a last resort, as it usually involves deleting all data stored on the device and reinstalling the operating system. If you must revert to the default factory settings, you should always create a full system backup first so you can restore your data once the reset is complete. Similarly, if you **reformat** a hard disk, you erase all data from the disk. Reformatting sets up a file system so the operating system can read data to and write data on a disk. In Windows 10, you use the Disk Management Utility to reformat a hard disk.

IC3✔ **Know how to complete a full system restore on a personal device.**

Getting Help

There are many methods of getting help for identifying and solving computer issues, including searching for information online, reading the documentation, using the built-in Help program, and contacting a technical support service.

DOCUMENTATION All your computer products—from your PC to your printer and software—come with product manuals. The manuals may be printed books but most likely they are available on the manufacturer's website. These manuals will always have a troubleshooting section.

HELP PROGRAMS Most software has a built-in Help program that provides information on how to use features and accomplish tasks. You can look in a table of contents or index or search the program for answers to specific questions. These Help programs often provide links to troubleshooter utilities that prompt you through a series of questions to diagnose a problem and offer suggestions for action you should take to correct the problem. For example, you can find Windows troubleshooters through the Control

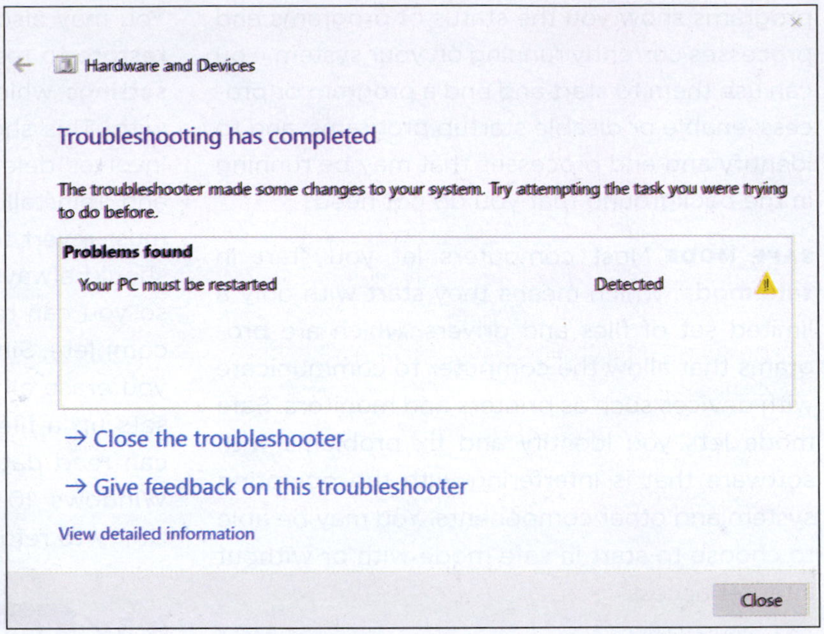

MICROSOFT CORPORATION

Hardware and Devices

Troubleshooting has completed

The troubleshooter made some changes to your system. Try attempting the task you were trying to do before.

Problems found	
Your PC must be restarted	Detected ⚠

→ Close the troubleshooter

→ Give feedback on this troubleshooter

View detailed information

Close

FIGURE 1.4.3 Use a trouble-shooter utility to diagnose and correct computer problems.

Panel. Open the Control Panel, and then select Find and fix problems.

TECHNICAL SUPPORT You can often find answers to questions and solutions to problems through technical support. If the product is still under warranty, or you are a registered user, you can often get help from the manufacturer's tech support team via email, through a knowledge base website, over the phone, or through an online live chat. A **knowledge base** is a collection of information about a specific topic. Most companies maintain a searchable knowledge base that is similar to a Help program. Other methods of obtaining technical support include online user forums and discussion groups where other users and product experts share information.

IC3✔ **Know how to use the correct terminology to identify and discuss troubleshooting.**

Chapter 1 Review

REVIEW THE TERMINOLOGY

DIRECTIONS Match each vocabulary term in the left column with the correct definition in the right column.

1. input
2. bit
3. byte
4. output
5. hardware
6. central processing unit
7. random access memory
8. peripheral
9. software
10. utility software

a. program that tells the computer what to do

b. group of 8 bits

c. area where data and instructions are stored while the computer is working

d. physical parts of a computer

e. raw data entered into a computer

f. program that does maintenance or repair tasks

g. part of a computer that processes data

h. basic unit of data a digital computer can understand

i. hardware separate but connected to the computer

j. the results of the computer's processing

USE THE TERMINOLOGY

DIRECTIONS Complete each sentence with information from the chapter.

1. A _____ is a connection between a computer and a device.

2. A _____ is about 1,000 gigabytes.

3. _____ is the most common networking technology used for local area networks (LANs).

4. Many devices such as keyboards, printers, and mice use _____ ports.

5. _____ ports move data one bit at a time. For example, they connect computers to modems for internet access.

6. _____ ports move data in groups.

7. _____ ports accept a connector with 19 wires—ten on one side and nine on the other.

8. Pink or red indicates a line-in port that connects the sound card to a _____.

9. A _____ port is shaped like a capital letter D and accepts a 25-pin parallel connector.

10. _____ is used for communicating between devices that are less than 30 feet apart.

11. _____ is a wireless technology used for connecting to the internet.

12. Knowing some basic _____ techniques can help you keep your computer running properly.

THINK CRITICALLY

DIRECTIONS Answer the following questions.

1. How do analog and digital computers differ?

2. What is the RGB hexadecimal value for a pure intense green? Explain your answer.

3. What are the differences between primary and secondary storage?

4. What is the difference between system software and application software? Give at least one example of each.

5. You purchased a new game for your computer that lets you play online with other people. You install the software but the feature for playing online won't work. What might be the problem?

EXTEND YOUR KNOWLEDGE

DIRECTIONS Choose and complete one of the following projects.

1. Look at a computer. Create a five-column chart. In the first column, list all the hardware that you can identify. In the remaining columns, state whether each item is used for inputting, processing, outputting, or storage. Examine how the different pieces are connected to the computer. What other hardware do you think the computer has that you cannot see? With your teacher's permission, unplug and replug all of the computer components, including external drives, a printer, mouse, keyboard, monitor, projector, and the power supply. Start the system. Record your observations. Discuss your findings with the class.

2. Using the internet or library resources, research at least three types of processing devices used in laptop computers. Keep track of your sources. Create a chart that compares and contrasts the price, top speed, and number of operations per second each one can perform. Determine which device would be most appropriate for working with text, graphics, and math. Write a brief summary explaining your findings, including a list of sources or bibliography. Read your summary out loud to a partner and listen as your partner reads his or hers out loud to you.

3. With your teacher's permission, practice the steps for the following procedures:

   ■ Connect a wireless device to a computer.

   ■ Connect a computer to a wireless network.

   ■ Start a computer in safe mode.

   ■ Open the Task Manager on your computer.

IC3 PREP

1. Which of the following are typical peripheral devices used with desktop computers? (Select all that apply.)

   a. CPU

   b. printer

   c. mouse

   d. keyboard

2. Match the port type on the left with its purpose on the right.

   1. audio

   2. Ethernet

   3. parallel

   4. serial

   5. PS/2

   6. DVI

   7. VGA

   8. HDMI

   9. USB

   a. the most common networking technology used for local area networks

   b. a standard connection interface that allows communication between computers and devices such as mice, printers, and smartphones

   c. an older interface once used for connecting input devices such as a keyboard or a mouse

   d. a digital cable standard for audio and video transmission found on most HD television sets

   e. an interface used to connect a monitor or other display device to a computer

   f. a bidirectional interface once commonly used for connecting devices such as a modem

   g. an older interface used to connect any type of display device to a computer

   h. color-coded mini jacks used for microphones and headphones

   i. an interface used to transfer multiple bits of data at the same time, which was once the most common way to connect a printer to a computer

3. Which of the following are likely caused by hardware problems? (Select all that apply.)

   a. monitor is blank

   b. application will not open

   c. pointer does not respond to mouse

   d. keyboard does not respond to typing

   e. web page will not load in browser

4. Match the troubleshooting term on the left with its definition on the right.

1.	error message	**a.**	starting a computer with only a limited set of files and drivers
2.	knowledge base	**b.**	turning off all power to the computer by pushing the power button or disconnecting the power cord
3.	reboot		
4.	hard reboot	**c.**	programs designed to damage your computer system
5.	soft reboot		
6.	safe mode	**d.**	information displayed by your computer when something happens to prevent a command from executing
7.	malware		
8.	update	**e.**	turning the computer off and then on again
9.	device driver		
10.	compatibility	**f.**	a collection of information about a specific topic
11.	restore point		

g. using the computer's own software to allow your computer to shut down properly

h. programs that enable peripherals to communicate with hardware

i. the configuration in effect at a specific date or time

j. able to work together

k. software that fixes errors, compatibility, or security problems

IC3 PROCEDURES

CONNECTING TO A WIRELESS NETWORK

1. Select the **Internet access** icon near the right end of the Taskbar.

If the icon is not visible, select the Show hidden icons arrow to display it.

2. Select the Wi-Fi network you want.

3. Select **Connect**.

4. Type the network password.

5. Select **Next**.

6. Select **Yes** if you want your device to be visible to other devices on the network.

OR

Select **No** if you do not want the device to be visible.

CONNECTING A PRINTER TO A WIRELESS NETWORK

1. Turn on the printer.
2. Select the **Start** button ⊞.
3. Select the **Settings** icon ⚙.
4. Select **Devices**.
5. Select **Printers & Scanners**.
6. Select **Add a printer or scanner**.
7. Select a printer from the results.
8. Select **Add device**.

STARTING A WINDOWS 10 COMPUTER IN SAFE MODE

1. Select the **Start** button ⊞.
2. Press and hold the **Shift** key.
3. Select the **Power** button ⏻.
4. Select **Restart**.
5. Select **Troubleshoot**.
6. Select **Advanced options**.
7. Select **Startup settings**.
8. Select **Restart**.

OPENING THE TASK MANAGER ON A WINDOWS COMPUTER

1. Press **Ctrl + Alt + Delete**.
2. Select **Task Manager**.

USING DEVICE MANAGER TO UPDATE DRIVERS

1. Right-click (or press, hold, and release) the **Start** button ⊞.
2. Select **Device Manager**.
3. Expand the category of the device to be updated.
4. Right-click the device to be updated and click **Update driver**.

REINSTALLING A DEVICE DRIVER

1. Right-click the **Start** button ⊞.
2. Select **Device Manager**.
3. Expand the category of the device to be reinstalled.
4. Right-click the device to be reinstalled and click **Uninstall device**.
5. If you are prompted to restart the computer, continue to step 6. If you are not prompted to restart the computer, skip to step 8.
6. Plug in the device and then restart the computer. The device will be detected and reinstalled after Windows restarts.

7. Follow any instructions on-screen to complete installation. Do not complete steps 8 and 9.

8. In Device Manager, in the **Action** menu, click **Scan for hardware changes**.

9. Follow the instructions on-screen.

CREATING A RESTORE POINT WITH WINDOWS 10

1. In the Search bar on the Windows Taskbar, type **Create a restore point**.

   If the Search bar isn't displayed, right-click (or press, hold, and release) the taskbar, select Cortana, and then select Show search box.

2. In the list of results, select **Create** a restore point.

3. In the System Properties dialog box, select the **Create** button [Create...].

4. Type a name for the restore point, and select **Create**.

5. Select **Close**.

REVERTING TO A RESTORE POINT WITH WINDOWS 10

1. Select the **Start** button ⊞, type **control panel**, and then choose it from the list of results.

2. Search Control Panel for Recovery.

3. Select **Recovery > Open System Restore > Next**.

4. Choose the restore point related to the problematic app, driver, or update, and then select **Next > Finish**.

CREATING A SYSTEM REPAIR DISC

1. Select the **Start** button ⊞, type **control panel**, and then choose it from the list of results.

2. Select **Backup and Restore (Windows 7)** in the System and Security section.

3. Select **Create a system repair disc** on the left-hand side.

4. Choose a location from the drop-down menu and select **Create**.

REFORMATTING A HARD DISK

WARNING This erases all data from the disk.

1. Press the **WIN** key ⊞ + **X** together.

2. Select **Disk Management**.

3. Locate the drive you want to format from the list at the top.

4. Right-click or tap-and-hold on the drive and choose **Format...**.

5. In the Volume label: textbox, enter a name. If this is a new drive, Windows will assign the volume label **New Volume**.

6. For File system: choose **NTFS** or the file system you want to use.

7. Set the Allocation unit size: to **Default** or the size you want to use.

8. Deselect the **Perform a quick format** check box.

9. Deselect the **Enable file and folder compression** check box.

10. Select **OK**.

11. Select **OK** to format the drive, erasing all data.

RESETTING A WINDOWS 10 COMPUTER TO FACTORY SETTINGS

1. In the Search bar on the Windows Taskbar, type **reset**.
2. Select the option **Reset** this PC.
3. Select the **Get started** button.
4. Choose an option for either keeping files or removing everything.
5. Follow the remaining prompts to initiate the reset.

CONNECTING PERIPHERALS TO A COMPUTER OR DEVICE

Connecting a Camera

1. Connect the camera to the USB port of the computer.
2. Turn the camera on.
3. If necessary, follow the Windows prompts to initialize the device and install the device driver.

Connecting a Speaker

1. Connect the speaker cable to the Speaker input port on a desktop.

   OR

   Connect the speaker cable to the headphones port on a laptop.
2. If necessary, follow the Windows prompts to initialize the device and install the device driver.

Connecting a Microphone

1. If the microphone has an analog cable, connect it to the microphone input on the desktop.

   OR

   For a laptop, use a microphone with a USB connection and connect to an available USB port.
2. If necessary, follow the Windows prompts to initialize the device and install the device driver.

Connecting a Printer

1. Connect the printer to the USB port of the computer.
2. Turn the printer on.
3. If necessary, follow the Windows prompts to initialize the device and install the device driver.

Connecting USB Devices

1. Connect the required device using an available USB port on your computer.
2. Be sure the device is powered on.
3. If necessary, follow the Windows prompts to initialize the device and install the device driver.

Connecting an External Display

1. If an HDMI connection is available, plug the monitor into this port.

   OR

   If an HDMI is not available, but a DVI port is, plug into this port.
2. If necessary, follow the Windows prompts to initialize the device and install the device driver.

GEORGE RUDY/SHUTTERSTOCK

CHAPTER 2
Understanding Computers

WORKING TOGETHER

Computers come in many different shapes and sizes. Some are large enough to fill a room. Others can be held in the palm of your hand. Whatever their size and capabilities, all these computers have something in common. They use electronic parts and instructions to perform specific tasks.

The electronic parts or components are called hardware. Hardware includes things like computer chips, circuit boards, hard drives, keyboards, monitors, and speakers. These hardware pieces, however, cannot perform the tasks by themselves. They require power and instructions. Electricity provides the power and software provides the instructions to work. Software programs unlock the potential of the hardware so that you can use the computer to do amazing things.

Exploring Computer Systems

OBJECTIVES

- Explain how input devices are suited to certain kinds of data.

- Distinguish between RAM and ROM.

- Explain how memory, storage, and processing speed impact usage.

- Identify an appropriate output device for different types of data.

- Explain Ohm's Law and its effect on electricity in a circuit.

- Summarize the tasks of operating systems.

- Identify two leading operating systems and explain why compatibility is an issue.

AS YOU READ

IDENTIFY INFORMATION Use an outline to help you organize details about devices used to perform computing functions as you read the lesson.

TERMINOLOGY

- alternating current (AC)

- circuit

- command

- computer system

- current

- direct current (DC)

- flash drives

- font

- handwriting-recognition software

- memory speed

- motherboard

- multicore processor

- Ohm's Law

- read-only memory (ROM)

- resistance

- screen-magnifier software

- speech-recognition software

- stylus

- transformer

- transistors

- touchscreen

- virtual memory

- voltage

Parts Make a Whole

It takes many different parts working together for a computer to do its job. A **computer system** includes several devices that perform the four basic functions of computing: input, processing, output, and storage.

Input Devices

Input means entering data, such as text, images, or sounds. Computer users can choose from several different input devices.

TEXT AND COMMANDS Perhaps the most basic input device is the keyboard. You can type on it to input text (letters, numbers, and symbols) and commands. Keyboards may be localized for a specific language, such as Arabic or Chinese. A **command** is an instruction for the computer to perform some action. For example, the Print command tells the computer to send the file you are working on to a printer. With **speech-recognition software**, users can input text by speaking into a microphone, and with **handwriting-recognition software**, users can input text by writing with a **stylus** directly on a device such as a tablet or screen. The software changes the words into digital data the computer can read. This software can be used by people with disabilities that prevent them from typing.

A mouse moves a pointer on the monitor, which allows you to move around a document, or to select commands. Some individuals cannot use a mouse. For them, keyboard equivalents for mouse commands provide access to the data. Adaptive devices can help users type without using their fingers on the keyboard. A trackball, touchpad, or trackpad function similarly to a mouse.

A **touchscreen** lets you input some commands by touching the monitor directly. There are also motion-recognition software programs that let you input some commands by moving your hand across the display or by looking at a location on the screen. A joystick, often used in computer games, is yet another input device.

THINK ABOUT IT!

Think about what would be harmed by a loss of power. Which kinds of data listed below would suffer from a loss of power?

- data on a hard drive
- data in ROM
- data on a DVD
- data on a cloud server
- unsaved data in RAM

IMAGES A mouse or stylus can also be used to input images by drawing in a graphics program. You can also input images using a digital camera or scanner, by importing them from a storage device or smartphone, or by downloading them from the internet.

SOUNDS Microphones can be used to input sounds. As with images, sounds stored on a storage device or on the internet can also be entered into the computer as input.

Processing Devices

Inside the computer, data travels from one device to another through the computer's **motherboard**. This board is covered with electrical circuits and switches, and it connects vital pieces of hardware such as the CPU and memory.

THE CPU The main processing device in a computer is the central processing unit, or CPU. The CPU is a chip that receives data from input devices and changes it into a form that you can use, such as text, pictures, or sounds. The processor also follows your commands to do something to that data, such as change a word or move a picture.

CPUs can carry out fewer than 1,000 instructions. However, they can perform millions of these operations every second. That ability is what makes computers able to work so quickly.

MULTICORE PROCESSORS **Multicore processors** have two or more CPUs so they can process data faster. Most personal computers have at least a dual core processor (two CPUs), and some have quad core processors (four CPUs). The more cores on the CPU, the higher the price. But, the improved processing speed may be worth it.

RAM The CPU temporarily stores the instructions and data it is using on chips called random access memory, or RAM. Once the computer is turned off, RAM no longer stores any data. Reading information from RAM takes very little time—just billionths of a second. Because programs today are complex, they need a large amount of RAM to run properly. The amount of time that it takes RAM to receive a request from the processor and then read or write data is called **memory speed**. Like CPU processing speed, RAM speed is measured in MHz.

ROM A second kind of memory is called **read-only memory**, or **ROM**. These chips contain the instructions that start the computer when you turn it on. The instructions in ROM typically do not change once this memory is placed on the motherboard.

CPU VS. RAM VS. HARD DISK Factors that impact computer performance include processing speed, memory speed and size, and storage device speed and size. Most important, however, is how well these three components work together. Even if you have the fastest, most efficient CPU available, it cannot process data quickly if there is not enough RAM available, or if the RAM speed is too slow. If there is not enough RAM to hold the data, the CPU uses virtual memory. **Virtual memory** is actually storage space on the hard disk that can function as memory when needed. The problem is that when the CPU needs virtual memory, it must keep accessing the disk. As a result, the computer can only perform as fast as the disk drive.

IC3 ✔ **Know the impact of memory and storage on usage.**

Output Devices

Output is the results of the computer's processing. The output that users see or hear can lead them to give the computer new instructions for processing their data.

A computer needs output devices to display the results of its processing. Text and images are displayed on a computer screen. They can also be printed by a printer. Sound data is sent to speakers inside, or connected to, the computer. You can also connect headphones to a computer to listen to sounds. Some output devices and features help make computers more accessible to users with disabilities.

FIGURE 2.1.1 The motherboard houses all the chips and circuits a computer needs in order to function.

ANDREYBRUSOV/SHUTTERSTOCK

TECHNOLOGY@WORK

Purchasing and maintaining a computer system is costly for both individuals and companies. It is important to research all available options to make sure the investment will pay off in terms of productivity, ease of use, and efficiency.

THINK ABOUT IT!

Although the decision-making process is similar for both individuals and companies, there are some differences. Rank the following factors in order from more important to less important for individuals and then for businesses. Are the rankings the same? Why or why not?

- How much does it cost?
- Is it easy to use?
- Does it work with existing software and hardware?
- Does it meet current needs?
- Will it meet future needs?
- Is it expandable?
- Is it easy to maintain?
- Is it durable?

MONITORS Both text and images are displayed on the monitor. **Screen-magnifier software** can make images on the monitor much larger for people who have difficulty seeing. The program enlarges the area where the cursor is. The user can also change the colors on the monitor to make text easier to see.

PRINTERS Another form of output for text and images is print. A high-quality output at a large font size may help some people with poor vision read printed text more easily. A **font** is a specific typeface with a certain size and style that is used for characters in a document or on a screen. Braille printers can also provide output in a format some people with visual disabilities can read.

SPEAKERS To hear recorded voices, sounds, and music, you need external speakers or headphones. Software lets you choose which recording to hear and adjust the volume. Windows has a feature called Show Sounds. When activated, this feature shows a visual symbol when it plays a sound and displays spoken words as text. This feature can help people who have hearing difficulties. Many programs can display audio as printed text so people with hearing difficulties can see the spoken words.

DIEGO CERVO/SHUTTERSTOCK

FIGURE 2.1.2 Headphones let you hear sounds output from the computer.

Storage Devices

Because memory is temporary, a computer needs a secondary location for storing data permanently. Devices such as hard disk drives, **flash drives**, CDs/DVDs, and online storage are all popular types of secondary storage.

Electricity Powers the Computer

All computer components are powered by electricity. When you plug the computer into an outlet, the electricity flows from the outlet to the circuits of the computer. A **circuit** is a network of electronic components. The computer circuits contain switches, or **transistors**, that use the electricity to complete tasks.

But how does the electricity get to your house? Power companies send electricity from a power plant to your house through power lines. Before the electricity goes into your house it travels into a **transformer**, which is a device that transfers electricity from one circuit to another. Wires, called windings, in the transformer lower the **voltage**, or electric pressure, of the electricity before it reaches your house.

The electricity flowing through your computer behaves in a constant fashion and follows scientific rules. **Ohm's Law** is a rule that describes how electricity will behave as it travels through circuits. Ohm's Law says that the **current**, or flow of electricity, through a wire is directly proportional to the voltage pushing electricity through the wire. Think of water moving through pipes. If you increase the pressure in the pipes, the water moves faster. Electricity acts in the same way. If you increase the voltage, the current moves faster.

Electronics in your house do not use a constant flow of electricity, called **direct current (DC)**. Instead, they use an **alternating current (AC)**. With AC current, the electricity briefly travels in one direction and then reverses direction. The back and forth happens very rapidly: over 50

STUART ATTON/123RF.COM

FIGURE 2.1.3 In transistors, three terminals are connected to an external circuit. Altering the current in one terminal changes the current in the other two. Many transistors together make up the integrated circuits used in modern electronics.

times a second! Computers plug into the same type of AC outlet that other appliances use, but once the current reaches the computer's power supply it is converted to DC. That's because the internal computer components require DC.

CONNECTIONS

MATH Ohm's Law can be summarized in the math equation:

$V = IR.$

This equation states that the voltage (V) equals current (I) multiplied by resistance (R). If you had a constant voltage but increased the resistance, the current would decrease. The equation shows that there is a direct relationship between voltage and current and an inverse relationship between current and resistance. Because this relationship is constant, it is possible to adjust one variable within the circuit by controlling the other two.

Give it a try: if you had a circuit with a voltage of 6 and a resistance of 2 what would the current be? The measurements for voltage is volts, resistance is ohms, and current is amps. Now what would happen if you kept the voltage at 6 volts but then changed the resistance to 3 ohms?

Ohm's law also says that if there is more **resistance** in a wire, the current will move more slowly. Resistance is caused by anything that obstructs or inhibits current. Think about when you have a clog in your pipe: the water pressure is still the same but less water can flow through. There are many different types of conductors, or materials that electricity flows through, and each creates a different amount of resistance. Length and width of wires can affect resistance as well. Resistance can be added to a circuit by using different materials or changing the thickness of the wires. Devices that add resistance to a circuit are called resistors. Computers use the relationship between voltage, resistance, and current in a circuit to control either the voltage or the current through the different components.

The total resistance of all resistors in a circuit depends on both their individual values and how they are connected. When resistors are in a series, or straight line, the current from the voltage source flows through them sequentially, or one after the other. So, the total resistance in the circuit is equal to the sum of the individual resistances. When resistors are placed parallel, with each resistor connected directly to the voltage source, each resistor gets the full voltage of the source. More current flows from the source, so the total resistance is lower. In fact, the total resistance in the circuit is equal to the sum of the inverse, or opposite, of each individual resistance.

DID YOU KNOW?

A digital multimeter (DMM) is a tool that can measure amps, volts, and ohms. It is used by technicians in most fields that involve electrical work including the computer industry because it can help diagnose electrical problems. In use, you connect the DIMM so it becomes part of the circuit, and the digital display shows the selected measurement.

Software Controls the System

Recall that the software that tells a computer how to do its work is the operating system, or OS. The OS does many different jobs:

- Working with peripherals: moving data and commands between the CPU and monitors, printers, and disk drives

- Managing data: finding the needed programs and files

- Using memory: storing data and programs in RAM or on the hard drive

- Coordinating data processing: doing many tasks at once without interfering with one another

- Providing the user interface: organizing and displaying the options you see on your screen when you turn on your computer

SYSTEMS COMPATIBILITY The two most popular operating systems are Microsoft® Windows® and macOS. Both use text and images to represent data and programs. macOS runs on Apple® computers.

For many years the two systems were not compatible, meaning that files saved in one OS had formats that could not be read by the other OS. Today, cross-platform compatibility, or the ability to use a file on any device no matter what operating system is being used, is important. Versions of many programs are written to run on many operating systems. For example, versions of Microsoft Office applications are available for PCs running Windows, Macs running macOS, mobile devices running iOS, and mobile devices running Android OS.

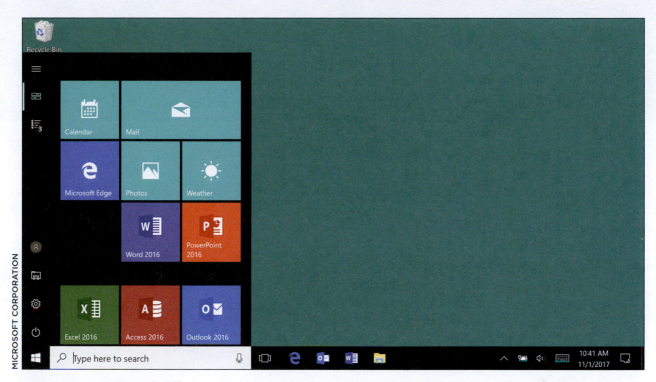

FIGURE 2.1.4 Microsoft Office applications available on the Start menu of a Windows 10 computer.

In addition, most programs include a Save As command that lets you save files in different formats, and an Open command that lets you open files saved in a different format. There are also utility programs that can translate files that previously may have been unreadable so they can be used on devices running a different OS.

Basic Programming Concepts

OBJECTIVES

- Explain the binary system used by computers.

- Describe how software is written and translated.

- Explain why Boolean Algebra is used in computers.

- Explain the function of algorithms and how they are used in programming.

- Identify the three components of structured programming.

AS YOU READ

OUTLINE INFORMATION Use an outline as you read to help you organize information about how software makes computers work.

TERMINOLOGY

- algorithm

- ASCII

- Boolean algebra

- character set

- compiler

- IF statements

- interpreter

- logic gate

- object

- object code

- object-oriented programming

- operator

- procedural programming

- programmer

- programming language

- source code

- subroutine

- Unicode

Software Provides Directions

How does a computer know what to do with data in digital form? Software gives it the instructions it needs. Experts called **programmers** write the instructions that become software. Programmers write these instructions, called **source code**, using a programming language.

TYPES OF PROGRAMMING There are two basic categories of programming, procedural and object-oriented. **Procedural programming** uses step-by-step instructions to tell a computer what to do. Procedural programming languages include C, Fortran, Pascal, and Basic. **Object-oriented programming** provides rules for creating and managing **objects**, which are items that include both data and how to process the data. Object-oriented programming languages include Java, Alice, Python, and VBScript. Some programming combines the two. C++ is an example of a **programming language** that uses both procedural and object-oriented programming.

COMPILERS AND INTERPRETERS Special programs called **compilers** translate the source code into binary form using only 0s and 1s. The result, called **object code**, can be read and acted on by a computer. Sometimes programs called **interpreters** are used to translate the source code directly into actions, bypassing the need for a compiler. Interpreters are able to immediately follow the instructions in the binary code while compilers must first wait and translate the binary. Even though the compilers take longer to get started, they are able to complete tasks much faster than interpreters.

REPRESENTING DATA Some programming languages require the programmer to assign a data type to variable data. Some common data types include string, which is a sequence of characters that does not contain numbers used for calculations; numeric, which is numbers or amounts that are used in calculations; character, which is text; integers, which represent whole numbers; and date, which is the method of coding dates.

Digital Computing

The computers widely used today are digital machines. Each piece of information used in the computer is identified by a distinct number. As a result, the computer acts on each piece of data by comparing its value to the value of other data or by performing a mathematical operation on it.

ANDREY POPOV/SHUTTERSTOCK

FIGURE 2.2.1 Programmers write the instructions that tell a computer what to do.

TECH@HOME

When you backup your data, you make copies of data stored on your computer's hard drive to an external hard drive, USB flash drive, online storage service, or CDs/DVDs. Using an external hard drive with backup software or an online service lets you backup automatically. If you use CDs/DVDs or flash drives, you must backup data on your own.

THINK ABOUT IT!

Before deciding *how* to backup your hard drive, think about *why* it is important to backup. Sequence the importance of backing up each item in the list below using a scale of 1 (lowest) to 5 (highest):

- a program you can download from the internet
- a report that you spent four hours on
- a file not used for a year
- photos of friends
- stored files of a game

THE BINARY WORLD Most computers are not just digital but binary, too. That is, they only recognize two possible values. Think of a television's power switch. It, too, is binary: The switch is either on or off. There are no other possibilities.

Computers break data into pieces called bits and give each bit a value of either 0 or 1. A byte is a group of bits—usually 8. Using 8 bits in different combinations, each byte can represent a different value. For example, one byte might be 00000000, another might be 01010101, and another might be 00110011. There are 256 possible combinations!

DATA IN BYTES Every piece of data that a computer works on, therefore, must be expressed in 0s and 1s and organized into bytes. These bytes can alone represent characters and numbers or be taken in combination to express more complex instructions like displaying color.

DIGITIZING TEXT Programmers use 0s and 1s arranged in 8-digit bytes to represent the letters of the alphabet and many standard punctuation marks. American Standard Code for Information Interchange (**ASCII**) is a common system, or **character set**, for coding letters that uses 8 bits. **Unicode**, which uses 16 bits, is another.

Programming Creates the Software

THE LANGUAGE OF COMPUTERS People communicate using words made up of 26 letters. Computers communicate using programs made up of two numbers—1s and 0s. No matter how complex, all computer tasks within a program are based on directions given in 1s and 0s.

To write computer code, programmers use math called **Boolean algebra**. Boolean algebra only has two values: true and false. This form of algebra is perfect for programming because binary also has two values. While using Boolean math in programming, 1 is true and 0 is false.

When you solve a math problem, you use an operation like addition or multiplication to find the relationship between two numbers. Boolean calculations are solved with the Boolean **operators** *AND*, *OR*, and *NOT*. These operators compare one or more Boolean values. When using the *AND* operator, if two values are true, then the solution is true; otherwise it is false. With the *OR* operator, if either of two values is true, then the solution is true. The *OR* operator is only false when both values are false. The *NOT* reverses a value from true to false.

Computers use physical devices consisting of a group of switches called a **logic gate** to perform Boolean equations. Using a combination of logic gates, programs direct the computer to perform more complex functions like computing advanced math or playing a song from an audio file.

DID YOU KNOW?

Boolean operators are used outside of algebra as well. When you use a search engine to search for information online you can use Boolean operators to fine-tune your search results.

- **If you search for George Washington *AND* the American Revolution, the search engine would display links to Washington's efforts during the revolution.**
- **If you search for George Washington *OR* the Revolution, the list includes links about Washington and links about the Revolution.**
- **If you search for George Washington *AND NOT* the Revolution, the list includes links to Washington's life outside the American Revolution.**

Charts called Truth Tables can be used as a quick reference to find the solutions to Boolean algebra problems. The values in the equation are X and Y. The solution is Z. For example, with the AND truth table, when X and Y equal 0, or false, then Z equals false. For the OR truth table only one variable needs to be true for the result to be true.

Programs Are Directions

Programs are a sequence of instructions that result in the computer performing a specific task. This linear sequence of instructions is called an **algorithm**. In a program, the algorithm is a designated sequence of calculations. The calculations are always done in the same order and steps are never skipped, so the result is always the same. Algorithms do not have to be a sequence of calculations. They can be a sequence of instructions that result in a predictable outcome, or solve a specific problem. When you bake a cake, the recipe is your algorithm. If you follow the recipe steps precisely and in the correct order, the result is a successful cake.

The Structure of a Program

There are three main components in programs: *sequence, decision,* and *loop*. Programs follow the same linear *sequence* of actions every time they run. If a program is solving the equation $2(x + 1)$, it always adds 1 then multiplies by 2. If it performs the operations in a different order—say, multiplies by 2 and then adds 1—the answer would not be correct. The computer ends each action with a *decision*. The decision is the choice the program takes at the end of each step. The decisions are determined with **IF statements**. An IF statement defines conditions that must be met for the program to move to the next step.

For example, *IF* you have finished adding the ingredients to the cake batter, *then* you can put the cake in the oven. Sometimes an action is repeated in a *loop,* or iteration, until a desired result occurs. You can illustrate the structure of an algorithm with a flowchart, using arrows to indicate the linear sequence, and the iterative loops.

SOLVING BOOLEAN ALGEBRA WITH TRUTH TABLES

AND			OR		
X	Y	Z	X	Y	Z
0	0	0	0	0	0
0	1	0	0	1	1
1	0	0	1	0	1
1	1	1	1	1	1

FIGURE 2.2.2 Examples of an AND Boolean truth table (left) and an OR Boolean truth table (right).

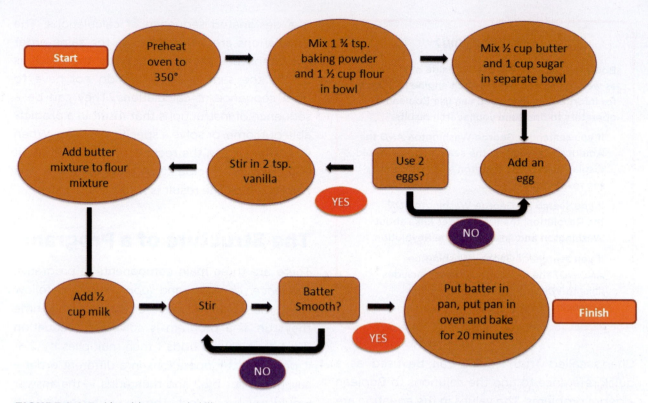

FIGURE 2.2.3 Algorithms can be illustrated using a flowchart, which has boxes connected with arrows, showing the order of steps. This flowchart shows the sequence of steps involved in following the steps in a cake recipe.

Some sequences are described in a single line of code called a **subroutine**. With a subroutine, a programmer can tell the computer to perform an entire sequence without having to type every step.

DID YOU KNOW?

Software is written in lines of code. Each line is an instruction or a comment. Operating-system software can take up a huge number of lines of code in different machines. Here are some comparisons:

- an ATM: 90,000 lines
- air traffic control: 800,000 lines
- Microsoft Windows 10: 50 million lines (estimated)
- all Internal Revenue Service programs: 100 million lines

Group and Individual Computing

OBJECTIVES

- Understand common hardware configurations.

- Compare and contrast different kinds of computers used in organizations.

- Compare and contrast different kinds of computers used by individuals.

AS YOU READ

COMPARE AND CONTRAST Use a Venn diagram to help you compare and contrast information about the types of computers as you read the lesson.

TERMINOLOGY

- computer configuration

- desktop computer

- emerging technology

- evolving technology

- handheld computer

- laptop

- mainframe

- notebook

- server

- smartphone

- supercomputer

- tablet computer

- workstation

A Dizzying Variety

Computers are available in a wide range of configurations, from huge machines as big as a room to devices so small they can fit in your pocket. A **computer configuration** refers to the hardware, software, and peripherals that comprise the computer. It includes memory, storage, processor, and both internal and external devices. Computers are usually configured based on the tasks for which they will be used and the environment where they will be used. Each type of computer is suited to handling a particular set of jobs in a particular setting.

IC3✔ Understand common hardware configurations.

Both the type of hardware and the type of software used in a particular configuration impact everything from where you can use the system to the type of documents you can create. For example, if you have a large desktop computer that you use for word processing or spreadsheet applications, you cannot take it with you when you travel. If you have a smartphone, you can take it with you when you travel, but it may be difficult to edit a report or update a spreadsheet on the small screen, not to mention the effect running such applications might have on the device battery.

IC3✔ Understand the implications of hardware selection for document usage.

When thinking about this great variety of computer configurations, it is helpful to look at them in two groups: those used by organizations and those used by individuals.

Computers for Organizations

Companies and other organizations use the full range of computers. Large organizations can afford the largest and most expensive machines, and such companies are more likely to need all the processing power that these huge machines have. Many companies also want some of their workers, such as salespeople, to have small **handheld computers**.

SUPERCOMPUTERS The largest and most powerful computers can process huge amounts of data very quickly. These superfast scientific computers are called **supercomputers**. Where most CPUs can perform millions of calculations a second, supercomputers can perform millions upon millions of calculations a second. The organizations using supercomputers do very complex work, such as forecasting the weather or creating detailed models of nuclear reactions.

TECHNOLOGY@SCHOOL

When computers are linked in a network, the network is set up to prevent people who have no right to be in the network from having access to the information. Typically, users use a password to gain access.

THINK ABOUT IT!

Think about the kind of information stored on a school network. Which informational items listed below do you think should have blocked access?

- class schedules
- students' grades
- students' health records
- sports team results
- scheduled school events

THE INTELLIGENT ROOM

VALERIE POTAPOVA/SHUTTERSTOCK

Some businesses are using a powerful new approach to working together called the Intelligent Room. The room looks like a normal conference room, but computer-controlled microphones and cameras placed around the room make sure that the speaker is always in view. This is especially helpful for videoconferencing, in which a video of a meeting in one room is sent to another group of workers in another room. Screens mounted on the wall can be used to display data from computers simply by touching the screen.

Why is the camera's ability to follow the speaker useful for videoconferencing?

Supercomputers are not only the largest and most powerful type of computer, they are also the most expensive. A single supercomputer can cost hundreds of thousands of dollars or tens of millions of dollars. They are also extremely rugged and dependable systems, so users can place constant heavy workloads on them.

MAINFRAMES The **mainframe** is another type of computer used by government agencies and large corporations. Mainframe computers are used in centralized computing systems as the storage location for all or most of the data. Other, less powerful computers connect to the mainframe so users can access the data. For example, airline company employees use mainframes to store and process reservations. In this way, reservations agents and travel agents all around the world can locate and use the same information at the same time. The trend now is to replace mainframes with servers. Even many government agencies have reduced the amount they rely on mainframes.

SERVERS Most organizations connect their computers together in a network. All the computers that are part of the network are connected to a computer called a **server**. The server stores data and programs that people on the network can use on their personal computers. A computer

SCANRAIL/123RF.COM

FIGURE 2.3.1 Some organizations use very large computer systems and house them in their own special environments.

connected to a network, called the host, uses a special program, called the client, to contact the server and get data from it. Unlike terminals, computers on a network can have their own disk storage, but the main source of data for the network is still the server. Servers can be host or client-based. If the server is host-based, the server runs the programs and receives directions from the client computers. In a client-based server the programs and processing are split between the client and host computers. The networking found in servers can also be found in peer-to-peer networks, where computers in a system share resources and there is no host computer.

Computers for Individuals

Most individuals do not need as much computing power as organizations do. They can use smaller—even mobile—devices for their computing needs.

WORKSTATIONS The most powerful and expensive personal computers are **workstations**. Architects, engineers, designers, and others who work with complex data use these machines for their power and speed.

CAREER CORNER

COMPUTER ENGINEER Designing compact, powerful machines like subnotebooks and PDAs is the work of computer engineers. They design and test components and then put them together to make sure they work properly. Engineers need to know software and programming as well as understand the workings of hardware. Demand for computer engineers is expected to be good in the coming years.

PERSONAL COMPUTERS Most individuals use personal computers to do everyday jobs more quickly and easily. **Desktop computers** are personal computers that are small enough to fit on or under a desk but too large to move around easily. Desktop computers may be connected to a network or they may be standalone, which means they are not connected to any network.

Small portable computers such as **laptops** and **notebooks** are as powerful as a desktop but can be easily carried around. They usually include an internal hard drive. They can connect to an AC power source or run on battery power. Laptops usually have a monitor, keyboard, and pointing device built-in, as well as ports and Wi-Fi for connecting to peripherals and the internet. Some, called all-in-ones, have touchscreens, as well.

IC3 ✔ **Distinguish between types of devices including servers, laptops, and desktops.**

TABLET COMPUTERS **Tablet computers** are small, portable computers that have a flat panel display. The display is usually a touchscreen, which can be used with a finger or a stylus. There is no external keyboard. They may have ports and usually allow wireless connection to peripherals and a network. The primary characteristic of a tablet is its small size. Most are about 6-inches wide by 8-inches tall and weigh less than 1 pound.

SMARTPHONES A **smartphone** is a telephone with computing capabilities. Most smartphones are mobile, or cellular. Smartphones provide internet access using 3G, 4G, or Wi-Fi technology. They run apps, which are small programs designed for one purpose, such as checking the weather, finding a nearby restaurant, or playing a game. Smartphones have built-in devices such as cameras, microphones, and speakers. They have internal storage for saving data such

FIGURE 2.3.2 Using a smartphone to pay in a retail store is an example of evolving technology.

S4SVISUALS/SHUTTERSTOCK

as pictures, music, contact information, and a calendar. Smartphones also have the capability to send and receive emails and text messages. Some smartphones have attached keyboards, but most use a pop-up keyboard on the touchscreen display.

EVOLVING AND EMERGING TECHNOLOGIES
Technology is always changing and adapting. As new needs are identified, technology is developed to meet those needs. As a technology becomes widely used, it may be modified to be more efficient or to meet a new or different need. A new, innovative technological development is called an **emerging technology**. Augmented reality, in which digital information is layered over someone's real-world view, is an emerging technology. An existing technology that changes to be more efficient or meet a different need is called an **evolving technology**. For example, using a smartphone to pay for products is one way existing technologies are evolving.

OBJECTIVES

- Recognize the requirements of cellular connections.

- Distinguish the capabilities and limitations of cellular phones, smartphones, and cellular tablets.

- Describe the purpose of a SIM card.

- Explain how mobile devices connect to networks.

- Identify the benefits and limitations of Wi-Fi and cellular connections.

- Identify elements of a cellular service contract.

AS YOU READ

SEQUENCE INFORMATION Use a column chart to help you compare and contrast types of mobile devices as you read.

TERMINOLOGY

- 3G

- 4G

- bandwidth limit

- cable modem

- cell site

- cells

- cellular network system

- cellular phone

- cellular service contract

- cellular service provider

- ebook

- ebook reader

- full-duplex

- hard-wired telephone

- mobile device

- mobile internet services

- Mobile Telephone Switching Office (MTSO)

- personal digital assistant (PDA)

- Public Switched Telephone Network (PSTN)

- subscriber identification module (SIM) card

- touchscreen

- wearable computer

- Wi-Fi

- wireless data plan

Mobile Devices

A **mobile device** is a wireless computer that is small enough to use when it is held in your hand. While all portable computers are mobile, including laptops and notebooks, the term generally refers specifically to smartphones and tablets.

FEATURES OF MOBILE DEVICES Mobile devices run on battery power, and the battery must be kept charged. They have operating systems designed specifically for mobile devices, such as Google's Android or Apple's iOS. Most mobile devices have a **touchscreen** interface that can be used with a hand or a stylus. They are primarily used for communication via email or messaging and for accessing the internet, but most can do many of the same things a personal computer can do.

TYPES OF MOBILE DEVICES The two main types of mobile devices are cell phones and tablets. **Ebook readers**, such as Amazon's Kindle, are also considered mobile devices, as are **personal digital assistants (PDAs)**. A smartwatch is a mobile device, or a **wearable computer**. Wearable computers are designed to be worn on the body, leaving the hands free for other tasks. They are usually intended for a specific purpose, such as inventory control or for monitoring body systems, such as heart rate. They may be worn on the arm or wrist or around the waist like a belt. Smartwatches are worn on the wrist and tell the time along with having the ability to run apps. Some wearable computers are worn as eyewear and can affect vision or display information.

Cell Phone vs. Smartphone

All smartphones are cell phones, but not all cell phones are smartphones. A cell phone is any mobile cellular device that can be used to make a phone call. Some cell phones can be used for sending and receiving text (SMS) messages as well. Most have built-in features such as a contact list for storing telephone numbers and a calendar. However, you cannot add programs or customize the built-in programs.

TECHNOLOGY@WORK

Communicating with cell phones can pose a major security risk. Wireless communication can be monitored by outsiders, who can intercept and overhear what is being said. Some employers prohibit the use of most wireless devices for company communication.

THINK ABOUT IT!

How might eavesdroppers use information collected from wireless communications to harm a company? Can you think of other risks posed by using cell phones?

CELL PHONE A cell phone actually is a type of radio. In fact, that's the definition: **cellular phones** are mobile phones that use radio waves to communicate. A cell phone is a **full-duplex** device. That means that you use one frequency for talking and a second, separate frequency for listening. Both people on the call can talk at once.

Early cellular phones were called radiotelephones and were used in ships at sea and in police cars. Radiotelephones were very useful during World War II, when they were used to send military information. For a while after that war, only a few people in a city could use radiotelephones at one time. New technology, however, soon increased the number of possible callers by adding more radio frequencies within each city.

IC3✔ Understand cellular phone concepts.

SMARTPHONE A smartphone is a cellular device that can do much more than make phone calls. Smartphones are, in effect, mobile computers. They have operating systems such as iOS or Android that make it possible to download and run mobile applications, or apps. You can use them to do many of the same tasks you do on a desktop, laptop, or tablet, including sending and receiving email, sending and receiving multimedia messages (MMS), managing a schedule, storing notes, using a word processing or spreadsheet program, uploading videos or pictures to social networking sites, streaming music and video, and playing games.

IC3✔ Be familiar with smartphones.

What Does "Cellular" Mean?

When you use a traditional analog landline phone, the call is connected through a wire. The wire from your house is connected to a telephone pole or buried cable in the local loop and from a local office to long-distance wires. Digital landline phones connect to a cable or fiber optic system through a router. Cell phones bypass part of the wired system, using a **cellular network system** instead.

LOCATING CELLS Cell phone network systems are divided into **cells**, or geographic areas to which a signal can be transmitted. Each cell has a **cell site**, also called a base station, for all the cellular phones in that area. Each cell site has a radio tower that receives radio signals from other towers and sends them on to still other towers. As a caller moves from one area to another, a new cell site automatically picks up the call to keep the signal strong and clear. Ultimately, the signal gets to individual cell phones.

MANAGING LOCATIONS Each geographic area is assigned to a central base station, or **Mobile Telephone Switching Office (MTSO)**. It, in turn, is connected to the standard **Public Switched Telephone Network (PSTN)** telephone system. The MTSO has several responsibilities:

- Directs cellular activities at base stations

- Locates cellular users in the area

- Tracks users as they roam, or move, from cell to cell

- Connects cellular phones to land-based phones

ESB PROFESSIONAL/SHUTTERSTOCK

FIGURE 2.4.1 Primarily due to their flexibility and ease of use, cell phones are replacing wired telephones as the communication system of choice.

How Cell Phones Work

When you turn on a cellular phone, it searches for a signal from the service provider's base station in the local area. When you place a call, the MTSO selects a frequency for your phone. It also selects and identifies a tower for you to use. Each tower sends and receives signals to and from the individual cell phones within its cell. The MTSO is connected to the local telephone network, usually by telephone cable. Cell phones are connected to the telephone network through the cell site.

RECEIVING A PHONE CALL When someone calls your cell phone, the **cellular service provider** locates the phone by cell. Moving from one cell into another, the phone transmits this information to the service provider's base station. The base station reports this information to the MTSO so it knows where to find you.

PLACING LONG-DISTANCE CALLS If you dial a long-distance number from your cell phone, the MTSO connects the call through a digital leased line. A digital leased line is a permanent connection that allows the MTSO to interact with long-distance providers.

Connecting a Smartphone to the Internet

When you want to do more than make a phone call with your cell phone, you must purchase a **wireless data plan** from your cell service provider so that your device can access **mobile internet services**. Most providers maintain their own cellular networks, which is why someone with a Verizon data plan may have a poor connection in a location where someone with an AT&T plan has a strong signal.

Cell phones connect to the internet using either Wi-Fi or a cellular network. They connect to other devices using Bluetooth.

CELLULAR NETWORKS Cellular networks are usually referred to as **3G** or **4G**. The major benefit of using a cellular network is that there is almost always connectivity available. Anywhere your cell phone has service you will be able to access the internet.

Drawbacks include the cost of the data plan as well as limitations imposed by the service provider. For example, just as many providers limit the amount of time, or minutes, you can spend on phone calls each month, they may limit the amount of data you can download each month. Often called a **bandwidth limit**, carriers track the number of gigabytes you download and charge extra if you exceed that limit. Cellular networks are also generally slower than other broadband internet connections.

WI-FI Most cell phones have built-in **Wi-Fi** adapters so they can connect to nearby Wi-Fi networks. Wi-Fi connections are usually faster than cellular networks, and usage is not counted toward your monthly bandwidth limit.

The major drawback of using Wi-Fi is that if there is no nearby Wi-Fi network, the phone will not have access. In addition, if the Wi-Fi network is secured, you will need the password in order to gain access.

ETHERNET Recall that Ethernet is the most common networking technology used for local area networks (LANs). Ethernet is a hard-wired network. To create the network, Ethernet cables plug into Ethernet ports on computers, LANs, and cable or DSL modems.

IC3✔ Know the difference between cellular, Wi-Fi, and wired networks.

FIGURE 2.4.2 Cell phones can connect to the internet using Wi-FI, like other devices on a home network.

MAXX-STUDIO/SHUTTERSTOCK

What's in a Cellular Service Plan?

In order to use a cell phone, you must have a cellular service provider. The provider is the company that maintains the cellular network your phone uses to make calls, send and receive messages, and access the internet. Most providers offer a variety of plans that include a set amount of voice minutes, text messages, and data amounts.

You can select the plan that best meets your needs. For example, if you use a lot of minutes and a lot of data, you might choose a higher cost plan that provides unlimited usage. If you talk a lot, but do not use the internet, you might choose a plan with a lot of minutes, but less data.

Unfortunately, many providers do not make it easy to find the best plan, but do make it easy to run up extra charges. For example, your plan might offer unlimited nighttime calling, but a limited amount of daytime minutes. And nighttime might start at 7 PM, or it might start at 9. Many providers also require you to agree to a multi-year **cellular service contract** in order to earn the lowest rates. However, if you change your mind, they charge a high cancellation fee.

In addition to the monthly fee for voice, text, and data, following are charges you might find on your monthly cellular bill:

- Taxes and fees, usually set by the government

- Overage fees, for minutes, texts, and data spent over the plan limit

- Roaming charges, for services used outside of your provider's regular service area

- International charges, if you use your phone outside the United States

- Hidden fees, usually for extra services you may or may not have agreed to

REAL-WORLD TECH
CELLULAR NETWORK TECHNOLOGY

PHANTHIT.MALISUWAN/SHUTTERSTOCK

1G, the first generation of cellular technology used an analog system. 2G, the second generation of cell phone technology, introduced a digital system. Digital phones work by converting voices into binary data and then compressing it for faster, more efficient transmission.

3G, or third generation, digital technology arrived in 2003. 3G increased transfer speeds enough to make it possible for cell phones to transmit multimedia such as music, photos, and videos, as well as voice. For example, a 2G network's fastest transmission speed is about 144 kilobits per second (kpbs), while a 3G network can transmit at up to 3 megabits per second (mbps).

4G is the next step up in transmission speed. There is no standard for calling a network "4G," so transmissions speeds vary widely depending on the service provider. Also, 4G service may not be available everywhere. 5G, the newest generation of cellular technology, promises faster mobile connections, but may not be available to most consumers until 2020.

TECHNOLOGY@HOME

Many of us use a combination of technologies to communicate at home. We use phones, computers, and televisions to send and receive messages.

THINK ABOUT IT!

Conduct a class survey to identify how many of each tool below your class uses at home. Write your own answers and then compare your responses with those of your classmates. What conclusions can you draw?

- analog telephones
- cell phones
- ISDN or DSL connections
- digital satellite systems
- cable systems
- wireless networks
- other

What Is a SIM Card?

Some cell phones need a **subscriber identification module (SIM) card** to work. A SIM card is a small piece of plastic with an integrated chip that fits inside the phone. The chip stores information used to verify that the owner is a network subscriber. When someone uses the phone, the information on the SIM card is transmitted to the network, and the network grants access. If the SIM card is not in the phone, access to the cellular network will be denied. The phone may still be able to access a Wi-Fi network, but will not be able to use the provider's cellular network.

Not all phones require a SIM card; it depends on the carrier and type of phone. Some SIM cards can be moved from one phone to another, as long as the phones use the same cellular network.

FIGURE 2.4.3 A SIM card is inserted into a cell phone to provide information confirming the phone owner's identity.

Where Else Is Cellular Technology Used?

Tablets such as the Microsoft Surface or Apple iPad may use cellular technology to access the internet. They usually have built-in Wi-Fi, like a cell phone. That way, they can connect to the internet wherever they are within range of a Wi-Fi network.

Cellular-enabled tablets can use the service provider's 3G or 4G network. In order to connect a cellular-enabled tablet using 3G or 4G, you must purchase a wireless data plan. Some providers offer plan bundles that you can use with a cell phone and a tablet, but some require a separate plan for a tablet, which means an additional cost. Still, for people who travel frequently or use a tablet in locations where Wi-Fi is not available, a cellular-enabled tablet may be worth the cost.

IC3 ✔ **Be familiar with cellular-enabled tablets.**

What Is a Hard-Wired Phone?

Unlike a cell phone, which uses radio waves for transmission, a **hard-wired telephone** is a phone that is connected directly to the wiring that transmits the audio from the caller to the recipient. The connection may be made at a phone jack, or it may be to a **cable modem**, which is the same modem that connects to broadband internet service. Traditional hard-wired landline phone services use twisted copper wires as the core of the cables that transmit the voice information, but newer, higher quality systems such as coaxial and fiber-optic cable are now available.

Like a cell phone, hard-wired telephone users rely on service providers for access to the telephone lines. For hard-wired phones, calling plans generally include local calling, optional long-distance, and add-on features such as caller ID, call waiting, and three-way calling. Many cable TV and internet providers also provide landline telephone service. These services may be bundled together by the provider.

One major benefit of a hard-wired phone is that it does not run on a battery and therefore does not need to be recharged. However, if service is provided by a cable or internet company, the phone may not work if the power is out. In an emergency, a 911 operator can identify your specific location based on a hard-wired phone, which is more reliable than a cell phone GPS location. Also, hard-wired phones usually have clearer sound than cell phones.

A personal digital assistant (PDA), is a small, highly portable handheld computer that can use Wi-Fi or Bluetooth for internet connectivity. Most PDAs provide all the features of a smartphone, without the phone. The devices may cost more than a smartphone to purchase, but they do not require an ongoing voice or data plan, so are usually less expensive in the long run. In addition, with the availability of internet telephone apps such as Skype, it is possible to make voice calls using some PDAs.

An ebook reader lets you shop for, download, and read **ebooks**, which are electronic versions of books, newspapers, magazines, websites, blogs, and more. Some ebook readers use Wi-Fi or Bluetooth and some also are cellular-enabled.

IC3 ✔ Understand the use of hard-wired phones.

Internet Connections

OBJECTIVES

- Explain the components required to connect to the internet.
- Define bandwidth.
- Identify and troubleshoot IP addresses.
- Distinguish between secured and unsecured networks.
- Explain how to secure personal information on a public computer.
- Discuss e-commerce.

AS YOU READ

SEQUENCE INFORMATION Use an outline to help you organize information about internet connections as you read.

TERMINOLOGY

- authentication
- bandwidth
- bits per second (bps)
- broadband
- browser history
- cache
- client
- client/server network
- cookies
- data network
- e-commerce
- encryption
- firewall
- IP address
- internet
- local area network (LAN)
- modem
- network interface card (NIC)
- router
- TCP/IP
- virtual private network (VPN)
- wide area network (WAN)

What Is a Network?

A network is a group or system of connected things. A computer network, which may be called a **data network**, is two or more computing devices connected to each other so they can share data, devices, and other resources. A network may be small, with just a few computers, or it may be large, with thousands of connected devices.

Home and many business networks are usually **local area networks (LANs)**. A LAN is a network in which all the workstations and other equipment are near one another. Most home networks are set up so family members can access the internet from different devices, such as a tablet, smartphone, laptop, and even the television. Each device can connect to every other device on the network. Businesses usually use a **client/server network**, in which one powerful computer, called the server, provides information and management services to the workstation computers, which are called the **clients**.

A **wide area network (WAN)** connects computers and other resources that are far apart. A business with offices in many places can use a WAN to link its LANs in different cities. Then, users from any of the locations can, with the proper permissions, access the network.

Connecting to the Internet

The **internet** is a worldwide network of computers connected to each other using wiring such as twisted pair telephone lines, coaxial cable, or fiber-optic cable, and wireless transmitters such as microwave, radio, or infrared signals. Communication on the internet depends on all connected devices using software called **TCP/IP (Transmission Control Protocol/Internet Protocol)**.

Internet service providers maintain the physical wiring for connecting to the internet. They install the cables that connect to homes and other buildings.

- For wired internet access, you physically connect the computing device using an Ethernet cable.

- For wireless internet access, you must have a wireless-enabled device such as a modem or router that is physically connected to the internet, usually with an Ethernet cable. That device, or access point, then transmits the signals to devices that have a wireless network adapter or built-in radio transmitters and receivers that enable wireless communication.

IC3✔ **Know the difference between a wired and a wireless internet connection.**

MODEM AND ROUTERS Modems and **routers** direct the input of data between multiple computers. Originally, modems were used to send computer data over telephone lines so computers could access the internet through dial-up. Modern modems can send information through cable, satellite, or DSL. The modem converts the data from analog format to the digital format a computer can understand, and then back to analog so it can be transmitted. Modem speed is measured in **bits per second (bps)**, which is the amount of data that can be sent in one second. Routers forward data from one source to another, such as between two computers or between a computer and the internet.

IC3✔ **Know the purpose of modems and routers.**

For internet access, a router is connected to a modem, usually using an Ethernet cable. The modem connects to an internet provider and the router directs the flow of data between the internet and computers.

IC3✔ **Know the role of a modem in connecting to the internet.**

IC3✔ **Know the role of a router in connecting to the internet.**

NETWORK INTERFACE Cards Some computers are designed with the ability to connect to networks. Others need a **network interface card (NIC)**, which handles the flow of data to and from the computer in both wired and wireless networks. If the network is put together by actual cables, those cables connect to the NIC. NICs often have a light that blinks green and amber to alert you to activity it's experiencing.

BANDWIDTH **Bandwidth** is the amount of data that can be sent through a modem or network connection. The more bandwidth, the faster the connection. It is usually measured in bits

per second (bps) or in megabits per second (Mbps). The more bandwidth, the more information can be transferred in a given amount of time. If you are online watching a movie on a tablet, while someone else in your family is online researching a topic for a report, and someone else is using IM to communicate with friends, you may notice a drop in speed or interruption in a download. That's because all the devices require a lot of bandwidth, but there is only a certain amount available.

IC3✔ **Know the role of bandwidth in relation to internet connection speed.**

BROADBAND **Broadband** is the general term for all high-speed digital connections that transmit at least 1.5 megabits per second (Mbps), though current broadband services usually transmit between 10 and 30 Mbps. Mobile phones use mobile broadband, which transmits around 10 Mbps. Many factors influence actual transmission speed, including the quality of the hardware devices, the distance from the modem or router, and the number of people using the service at the same time.

NORMAN CHAN/SHUTTERSTOCK

FIGURE 2.5.1 For wireless internet access you must have a modem (left) or router (right) that is physically connected to the internet.

IP Addresses

Each device that connects to the internet has to be uniquely identified. To do this, every computer is assigned a four-part number separated by periods called the **internet protocol (IP) address**. For example, the IP address for your computer might be 123.257.91.7. Any device with an IP address can communicate with any other device with an IP address over the internet. An IP address is usually automatically assigned by a Dynamic Host Configuration Protocol (DHCP) server. You can locate your computer's IP address and connection speed in the Network and Sharing Center in Windows and in the Network Utility on macOS.

IC3✔ Know how to define IP address.

IC3✔ Know how to find an IP address on a personal computer.

IC3✔ Know how to determine a connection speed.

DID YOU KNOW?

Some cities have municipal wireless networks. These networks provide wireless internet connectivity for all or parts of the city so that residents do not have to rely on commercial internet service providers (ISPs). The city manages the network, providing internet access at a lower cost. The networks use hundreds of wireless access points, such as routers, installed throughout the area to transmit and receive data from the internet.

Network Security

Both wired and wireless networks can be secured or unsecured. On an unsecured network, there are no barriers to access and anyone within the network can access information. The internet is an unsecured network.

UNSECURED NETWORKS These networks allow for free flow of information but leave little protection from hacking for the individual computers. They may be called public networks, although your home network may also be unsecured. An unsecured wireless network can be accessed by anyone within range of the wireless signal. It does not require a login or password and does not use encryption to protect data. Your neighbor may be able to access your unsecured Wi-Fi network. Someone outside your building might be able to read files, or access email, thereby learning personal information. Connecting to an unsecured network exposes your data and hardware devices to risks.

SECURED NETWORKS Secured networks limit access and protect the computers and users. One way secured networks prevent unauthorized access is by requiring users to enter an ID and password. Another way is by using a firewall. You can secure a wireless network by using an encryption protocol such as Wi-Fi Protected Access 2 (WPA2).

IC3✔ Know the risks and ramifications of connecting to a secured or unsecured network.

On a Windows computer, secure wireless connections are identified on the Internet Access menu. Select the Internet Access icon in the notification area of the taskbar. The word *secured* displays below all secured connections.

VIRTUAL PRIVATE NETWORKS A **virtual private network (VPN)** is a private, secure network set up through a public network. VPN users connect to an internet service provider (ISP) to access the private network with a user name and password. VPNs are a more secure way to log in to a private network from a computer on a public network. They are often used by employees working remotely who need access to the company's network.

IC3 ✔ Know what a virtual private network (VPN) is.

FIREWALLS A **firewall** is a filtering system that opens or blocks programs and ports to keep outside data from entering a network. Firewalls are usually located on a gateway, such as a router that lets a network access the internet. From that location the firewall can examine the packets trying to get into the network and determine whether or not to let them through. Some firewalls are built into a computer's operating system, such as Windows. You, or the system administrator, can control what the firewall blocks and what it lets through by maintaining lists of allowed or blocked programs and ports.

IC3 ✔ Know how to use a firewall and configure basic firewall settings.

Using Public Computers

Public computers are available in public places for anyone to use. You might find them in hotel lobbies or coffee shops. They are usually connected to unsecured or public networks. When you use the computers in your local library, you are using a public computer that other people use, too, putting your privacy at risk. The computers in your school or home, however, are private and usually require an ID and password for access.

When you visit a website, your browser saves information about the site to your computer. Stored information includes **cache**, **cookies**, **browser history**, and even passwords. Storing this information helps web pages load faster when you visit the same site again, or saves you the trouble of reentering a password. However, it also creates a security risk. Someone can check the cache or browser history and know which websites you visited. Cookies and saved password files can disclose your passwords or other private information you have typed into web forms.

To protect your information you can delete the cache, cookies, browser history, saved passwords, saved web form information, and other saved browser files. You should do this any time you use a public computer, and periodically on your own computer. If your computer ends up in the wrong hands, your private information

BELYJMISHKA/123RF.COM

FIGURE 2.5.2 Accessing the internet using an unsecured network can put your data at risk.

will not be as easily available. You should also log out of any websites or operating system accounts before closing or exiting the computer. If you fail to log out, the next person to use the computer has access to all the files and information associated with your account.

IC3✔ **Know how to find and clear browser histories, cache, and cookies.**

IC3✔ **Know how to log out of online and operating system accounts.**

Electronic Commerce

Electronic commerce, or **e-commerce**, is the use of telecommunications networks or the internet to conduct business. Thanks to the internet and affordable computers, e-commerce has become accessible to anyone who has an internet connection and a web browser. More and more internet users are researching products, shopping, opening bank accounts, and trading stocks online. Many businesses realize that they may lose customers if they do not have an online presence.

ONLINE SHOPPING When many people think of e-commerce, they think of shopping online. Online shopping has grown in popularity due to security features built into popular web browsers. Every year, online shopping gains in popularity, resulting in the closing of many actual stores and shopping malls.

A savvy e-commerce consumer knows how to use the power of the internet to research products and compare prices before buying. The buyer also knows how to make sure he or she is using a reputable website that will deliver the correct product in a timely manner. At many sites, buyers can read product reviews posted by other buyers. At other sites, they can find vendor and product ratings. Savvy e-commerce consumers also know not to give out personal or payment information without knowing that the website is secure and honest.

IC3✔ **Know how to be a savvy e-commerce consumer.**

SECURE ELECTRONIC TRANSACTIONS One of the keys to the growth of e-commerce is secure electronic transactions. Originally a standard that relied on digital signatures, secure electronic transaction now refers to a variety of measures online vendors use to secure online transactions so customers can bank and shop online without worrying that their private information will be misused, lost, or stolen, which could result in identity theft and fraud.

A secure website uses **encryption**—coding—and **authentication** standards to protect online transaction information. That means your personal information, including debit card numbers and personal identification numbers (PINs), are safe when you shop online. You can tell that you are viewing a secure website because the letters "https" display to the left of the website name in the Address bar of your browser. On an unsecured site, there is no "s." Also, a small lock icon displays in your web browser's status bar. You can double-click the lock icon to display details about the site's security system.

IC3✔ **Recognize a secure connection for e-commerce.**

Online payment systems, such as PayPal, Google Wallet, or Apple Pay, let you avoid repeatedly entering your credit card number and other personal data when making transactions online. To use PayPal, or any other secure online payment service, you sign up directly and provide your payment information only once. The service keeps your records secure and handles payments to online vendors for you, using only secure methods.

Chapter 2 Review

REVIEW THE TERMINOLOGY

DIRECTIONS Match each vocabulary term in the left column with the correct definition in the right column.

1. command
2. motherboard
3. read-only memory
4. programmer
5. compiler
6. supercomputer
7. algorithm
8. server
9. desktop computer
10. circuit

a. a sequence of instructions

b. instruction for the computer to do something

c. a network of connected electronic components

d. where the CPU is located

e. high-speed computer for complex work

f. another name for personal computer

g. set of chips that starts the computer when it is turned on

h. language that translates source code into binary form

i. writes instructions for a computer to follow

j. computer accessed by users on a network

USE THE TERMINOLOGY

DIRECTIONS Determine the correct choice for each of the following.

1. What would you most likely use a microphone to input?

   a. commands

   b. images

   c. sound

   d. text

2. Data from which part of a computer is lost when it is turned off?

   a. the CD-ROM

   b. the hard drive

   c. RAM

   d. ROM

3. Which is NOT a component in programs?

   a. loop

   b. choice

   c. sequence

   d. decision

4. Which is an example of a binary number?

   a. 10011001   **c.** 67439622

   b. −342   **d.** .0000002

5. Which of the following is NOT a task performed by operating systems?

   a. controlling a printer   **c.** coordinating how programs run

   b. managing memory   **d.** compiling a program

6. What kind of machine is more powerful than a server?

   a. desktop computer   **c.** mainframe

   b. portable computer   **d.** handheld computer

THINK CRITICALLY

DIRECTIONS Answer the following questions.

1. What are the functions of compilers and interpreters?

2. Explain the risks and ramifications of connecting to a secured or unsecured network.

3. Identify and explain the concept of an algorithm.

4. Explain how the following data types are used to represent variable data in software development: string, numeric, character, integer, and date.

5. List at least three object-oriented programming languages and three procedural programming languages. Explain how they are used in software development.

EXTEND YOUR KNOWLEDGE

DIRECTIONS Choose and complete one of the following projects.

1. Make a flowchart to illustrate a linear sequence of actions you do every day, such as getting ready for school or packing your lunch. Does your flowchart contain the main components of programs: sequence, decision, and loop? Create an IF statement for one step of your flowchart to illustrate the iterative instructions.

2. Collect three advertisements for home computer systems. List the components that are offered in each ad. Compare the three systems for their appropriateness for inputting and outputting text, images, and sounds. Compare their capacity to store data. Based on the features, write a brief explanation of which machine you think is best and why. Read your explanation out loud to a partner and listen as your partner reads his or hers out loud to you.

3. Work with a partner to practice using a digital multimeter (DIMM). Being sure to follow all safety protocols, use the DIMM to measure AC and DC voltages. Then, measure AC and DC current. Finally, measure the resistance of a circuit consisting of resistors. If possible, construct simple circuits on a breadboard or with a soldering iron.

IC3 PREP

1. For the line below, select whether the statement is True or False.

   An internet connection with more bandwidth is faster than an internet connection with less bandwidth.

2. Which of the following is not considered part of a hardware configuration?

   a. memory

   b. processor

   c. monitor

   d. color

3. Which of the following describes capabilities of a cell phone? (Select all that apply.)

   a. both people on the call can talk at once

   b. runs mobile apps

   c. uses radio waves to communicate

   d. can be used anywhere it can access the cellular network system

4. Which of the following can a cellular-enabled device use to connect to the internet? (Select all that apply.)

   a. Ethernet

   b. cellular data network

   c. Wi-Fi

   d. phone jack

5. Which of the following factors impact computer performance? (Select all that apply.)

   a. memory speed

   b. type of monitor

   c. storage capacity

   d. amount of RAM

6. Match the type of device on the left with its description on the right.

   1. server

   2. laptop

   3. desktop

   4. tablet

   5. smartphone

   a. portable computer as powerful as a desktop, with built-in monitor, keyboard, and pointing device

   b. telephone with computing capabilities

   c. personal computer too large to move around easily

   d. computer that stores data and programs that people on a network can access

   e. very small portable computer with a flat-panel touchscreen display and no keyboard

7. Fill in the blank:

   a. _____ forward data from one source to another.

   b. _____ convert data from analog format to digital format and then back to analog.

   c. Every computer is assigned a four-part number separated by periods called the _____.

   d. A _____ is a private, secure network set up through a public network.

IC3 PROCEDURES

LOGGING OUT OF AN OPERATING SYSTEM

1. Select the **Start** button ⊞ on the taskbar.
2. Select the **User Name** button near the top left of the Start menu.
3. Select **Sign out**.

LOGGING OUT FROM AN ONLINE ACCOUNT

1. Select the **Start** button ⊞ on the taskbar.
2. Select the **Settings** icon ⚙.
3. Select **Accounts**, and select **Your info** if not already selected.
4. Select **Sign in with a local account instead**.
5. Enter your Microsoft account password and select **Next**.
6. Enter a name for your new local account, a password, and a hint. Select **Next**.
7. Select **Sign out and finish**.

MAINTAINING AND UPDATING ANTIVIRUS SOFTWARE

1. In the Search bar on the Windows Taskbar, type **Windows Defender**.
2. Select **Windows Defender Security Center**.
3. Use the available options to verify the status of protection, update virus definitions, and run scans.

CONFIGURING FIREWALL SETTINGS

1. In the Search bar on the Windows Taskbar, type **Firewall**.
2. Select **Windows Defender Firewall**.
3. Use the available options to adjust settings, including selecting programs to allow or block.

CLEARING THE INTERNET BROWSING HISTORY

1. Open the Microsoft Edge browser.
2. Select the **Hub** icon ⭐.
3. Select the **History** icon 🕘.
4. Select **Clear all history**.

DELETING TEMPORARY FILES, COOKIES, SAVED PASSWORDS, AND WEB FORM INFORMATION

1. Open the Microsoft Edge browser.
2. Select the **More** icon ⋯, and select **Settings**.
3. Under the **Clear browsing data** heading, select **Choose what to clear**.
4. Select the items to clear.
5. Select **Clear**.

CHAPTER 3
Input/Output Basics

INPUT AND OUTPUT

If you think of the computer as a person, its brain would be the central processing unit, or CPU. Like a brain, a CPU receives and organizes data from many different sources into useful information.

Also, like a person, a computer needs more than just a brain to work properly. It needs a way to receive the unorganized data and to show the results of its processing of the data.

The brain receives data through the senses: sight, hearing, smell, taste, and touch. It shows the results of its processing of the data through speech, movement, and writing. The CPU receives its data from input devices such as the keyboard and mouse. It shows the results of its processing through output devices such as a monitor, printer, or speakers.

Basic Input Devices

OBJECTIVES

- Distinguish among four types of input.
- Compare and contrast basic input devices.
- Explain the purpose of scanners.
- Discuss the health risks of using some input devices.

AS YOU READ

ORGANIZE INFORMATION Use a concept web to help you organize information about basic input devices as you read.

TERMINOLOGY

- command
- data
- digital camera
- ergonomic
- game controller
- joystick
- pointer
- pointing device
- repetitive strain injury (RSI)
- scanner
- webcam

What Is Input?

Recall that input is any kind of information, or instructions, that is entered into a computer's memory. There are four basic types of input: data, software instructions, user commands, and responses.

DATA Words, numbers, images, and sounds that you enter into a computer are **data**. This is the raw material that a computer processes.

SOFTWARE INSTRUCTIONS To perform any job, a computer must follow instructions from a software program. Software typically is installed by downloading the program files from the internet or a removable drive such as a DVD. The program files are stored on a device such as an internal storage device or a network server. Launching a program moves it into the computer's RAM. That makes the program available to the CPU—and to you.

USER COMMANDS A **command** is an instruction that tells a software program what action to perform. For example, to open a program, save your work, or close a program, you must issue a command to the computer.

RESPONSES Sometimes a program asks you to enter information or make a choice so that it can carry out a command or process data. For example, if you try to close a program without saving your work, the program will ask if you want to save it. Before you can continue, you must input a response.

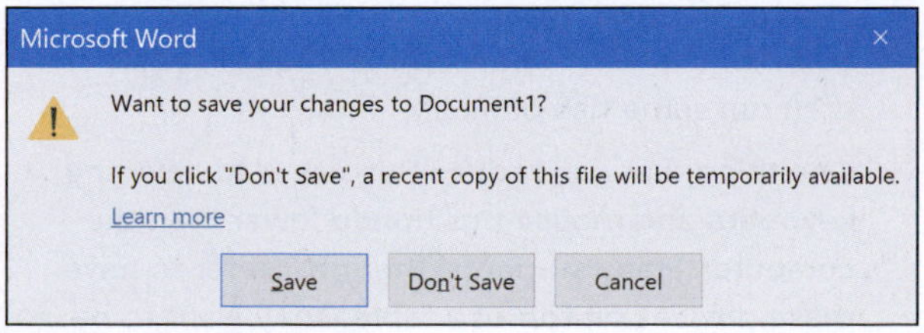

MICROSOFT CORPORATION

FIGURE 3.1.1 Responding to a prompt is one way to input instructions so the computer can complete a process.

What Is an Input Device?

An input device is any hardware used to input data. Recall that two common input devices are the keyboard and the mouse. A mouse is a type of **pointing device**. Moving the mouse over a surface moves a **pointer** on the screen. Notebook computers often use a touchpad, or trackpad, as the pointing device. It is built into the computer. Moving your finger on the touchpad moves the pointer. Smartphones, some computers, and tablets use touchscreens that allow you to move your finger directly on the screen. Some can sense motion and react to a hand moving in front of the screen or even respond to eye movements. There are also specialized input devices, such as digital cameras, for capturing and inputting photos and videos, microphones for inputting sound, and even global positioning systems (GPS) used to input maps and locations.

GAME CONTROLLERS A **game controller** is a handheld device that lets you input commands and interact with video and computer games. They usually have buttons, directional pads, and even motion sensors. A **joystick** is a lever that can be moved in all directions to move objects on the screen. It may be used with computer games, flight simulators, or virtual reality programs.

MICROPHONE To input sounds, you can use a microphone. Your computer must have a sound card installed in order to record and play back sounds. Many computers, including smartphones and tablets, use sound input for direction. Voice recognition programs, like Apple's Siri or Google's Voice, are used to start searches on smartphones. Smart speakers, such as Amazon's Echo and Google Home, respond to voice commands.

DIGITAL CAMERAS, WEBCAMS, AND SCANNERS **Digital cameras** connect to the computer by a cable or a wireless link to input photos. When you video chat with a friend, you're using a **webcam**, a small camera that attaches to the computer monitor, sits on your desk, or is built into the computer. Webcams usually come with software that enables you to record video, upload it to a social networking site, or stream the video on the web. Most smartphones and tablets have built-in cameras for still pictures and video. **Scanners** are devices that convert printed content into digital format so you can save it as a file on your computer. This is useful for archiving documents, such as medical records, and also so you can easily transmit the file. For example, you can scan a photo or report so you can send it to someone by email. Scanners are often built into printers, but there are stand-alone scanning devices.

IC3✔ **Know the purpose of a scanner.**

TECHNOLOGY@WORK

Some people have disabilities that prevent them from working a mouse with their fingertips. Adaptive technology includes devices for people who cannot use their hands to control an input device. For example, you can purchase a mouse that can be controlled with head movements, by foot, and even by mouth.

THINK ABOUT IT!

Which mouse actions do you think need to be considered in an adaptive input device for people with physical disabilities?

• select text

• scroll through a document

• create art in a drawing program

• click the mouse button to select a menu option

• cut text

Health Risks of Some Input Devices

When you use a keyboard or mouse a lot, you make the same hand movements over and over again. This can cause damage to nerves in the hand. The problem is called **repetitive strain injury (RSI)**. **Ergonomic** keyboards have been designed to reduce RSI. Some people who suffer from this problem use a mouse controlled by foot pedals or voice recognition software. Proper posture and lighting and limiting the amount of time you spend looking at a screen can help prevent health problems.

DMITRY MELNIKOV/SHUTTERSTOCK

FIGURE 3.1.2 Ergonomically designed keyboards, like this one with a sloped shape, can reduce the risk of repetitive strain injuries.

DID YOU KNOW?

You might think that repetitive strain injury only affects adults who work all day at a computer. Researchers are trying to find out if children can also be affected by repeated use of the keyboard and mouse. They have learned that children run some risk of injury.

One thing that can reduce this risk is to have the keyboard and mouse positioned lower than the computer. Many students, though, prefer to have these devices on top of a table. They want to be able to see the keys as they type!

Basic Output Devices

OBJECTIVES

- Distinguish among the four types of output.
- Compare and contrast basic output devices.
- Explain how visual display systems work.
- Compare touchscreen and non-touchscreen displays.
- Summarize printing technology.

AS YOU READ

OUTLINE INFORMATION Use an outline format to help you organize information about output as you read.

TERMINOLOGY

- cathode ray tube (CRT)
- dot matrix printer
- impact printer
- inkjet printer
- laser printer
- liquid crystal display (LCD)
- nonimpact printer
- output
- output device
- printer
- three-dimensional (3D) printer
- touchscreen

What Is Output?

After a computer has processed data, it provides the results in the form of **output**. There are four types of output: text, graphics, video, and audio.

TEXT Characters such as letters, symbols, and numbers are called text. To be considered text, the characters must be organized in a coherent way. For example, random letters on a page are not considered text, but paragraphs in a book report are text.

GRAPHICS Drawings, photographs, and other visual images are called graphics.

VIDEO Moving images are known as video. Images captured by a digital video camera, and which can be played on a computer, are one example of video. The use of animation is another example.

AUDIO Sound output is called audio. This includes music or speech that the computer plays through its speakers or headphones.

What Is an Output Device?

An **output device** is any piece of hardware that displays or plays back the result of computer processing in one of the four forms of output. For example, monitors and printers create a visual record of the processing completed by the computer.

Monitors

The computer displays information on a monitor, a hardware device that receives and shows images on a screen. The images the monitor displays change as the computer processes data.

LCDS Modern monitors use the **liquid crystal display (LCD)**. In an LCD, two transparent surfaces are placed on either side of a layer of cells containing tiny crystals. Electrical signals sent to the crystals cause them to form images on the surface.

THINK ABOUT IT!

Think about ways the SMART Board can be used at school. For which examples below do you think the SMART Board would be useful?

- solve math problems
- display reports
- play music
- meet in groups
- edit text

LCDs are very light and have a flat screen. They use little power and can even be operated using just batteries. Also, there are now two different techniques for producing color: thin film transistor (TFT) and passive matrix technology. TFT produces sharper color and images, so it is becoming the standard.

FAD82/SHUTTERSTOCK

FIGURE 3.2.1 This is an LCD monitor—an output device for displaying text and graphics.

CRTS An older type of monitor is the **cathode ray tube (CRT)**. In a CRT, the monitor receives electrical signals from the computer. The signals cause "guns" in the CRT to shoot a stream of electrons at the back of the screen. The electrons strike materials called phosphors, which begin to glow. The glowing phosphors appear as points of light on the screen.

Color monitors have three electron guns, each one shooting a beam of a different color: red, blue, or green. CRTs today are now capable of producing thousands of colors. Some of the first monitors and televisions were CRTs. However, these monitors are not only heavy and take up a lot of desk space, but they also heat up easily. CRTs use more electricity than LCDs. As LCDs became more affordable, companies stopped producing and selling CRTs in the United States.

TOUCH SCREEN MONITORS Touchscreen monitors, used on smartphones, tablets, and some computers, are designed to respond to input from a finger or stylus touching the screen. There are pros and cons of using a touchscreen, with the most important being personal preference. The trend is moving toward touchscreens, as many people find swiping with a finger easier, faster, and more intuitive than using a keyboard, mouse, or touchpad. Some problems are that the touchscreen may be less responsive than a pointer, or it might be easier to accidentally touch something you do not want to select.

FIGURE 3.2.2 Touchscreens are used for tablets, smartphones, and some notebook PCs.

Currently, there are two main types of touchscreens:

- Analog resistive touchscreens are made of two layers: usually one is glass and the other is plastic film. They are each covered with a grid of electrical conductors. When you touch the screen, there is contact between the grid on the glass and the grid on the film, creating a circuit. The monitor detects and responds to the change in electric current resistance at the spot of the touch.

- Projected capacitance (pro-cap) touchscreens also use two layers of conductors, but they rely on electrical capacitance, which is the build-up of electrons in an object. When you touch the top layer of the screen, the screen takes some electrons—or charge—from the other layer. The monitor responds to the change in the charge.

IC3 ✔ **Explain the pros and cons of using touchscreens compared to non-touchscreen devices.**

Printers

A **printer** makes a paper copy of the display shown on a monitor. The most common types of printers are **nonimpact printers**, which have made **impact printers** almost obsolete.

NONIMPACT PRINTERS Most computer users today use inkjet and laser printers to produce paper copies. **Inkjet printers** make images by spraying a fine stream of ink onto the paper. **Laser printers** use a powder called toner and operate like a copy machine. Heat fuses the toner to the paper to create the image. Laser printers create more crisp images than inkjet. Both inkjet and laser printers are available in all-in-one versions that add fax, copier, and scanner capabilities at a very low cost.

IMPACT PRINTERS **Dot matrix printers** are a kind of impact printer that uses hammers or pins to press an ink-covered ribbon. They are noisy and the image quality is poor, but some are still used in businesses to provide copies of multi-part forms, like invoices.

3D PRINTERS A newer printer technology involves three-dimensional printing. Three-dimensional objects can be modeled in software and then created using a **three-dimensional (3D) printer**. 3D printers interpret the model as 2 dimensional layers, which they output one on top of the other in an additive process to produce the 3D object. The output may be in a variety of materials, including plastic, metal, and wax. They read two-dimensional layers as build objects by slicing the digital model into thin layers and then printing the layers as sheets. These sheets are then joined together to produce the three-dimensional object.

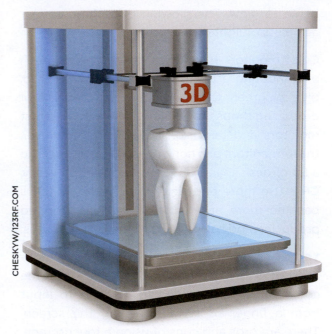

CHESKYW/123RF.COM

FIGURE 3.2.3 3D printers are used for product design in many industries ranging from footwear to medical devices.

REAL-WORLD TECH
E-CYCLING

You've probably noticed that your printer ink cartridges can be recycled at your local office supply stores. However, did you realize that you can recycle your old computer or other electronic equipment that still works? The best way to do this is to donate them to schools, other nonprofits,

OLIVIER VANBIERVLIET/SHUTTERSTOCK

or low-income families in need. To help you do this—and keep our country greener—the Environmental Protection Agency has a website that lets you find local programs, manufac-turer–retailer programs, and government supported donation and recycling programs:

http://www.epa.gov/osw/conserve/materials/ecycling/donate.htm

Chapter 3 Review

REVIEW THE TERMINOLOGY

DIRECTIONS Match each vocabulary term in the left column with the correct definition in the right column.

1. command
2. pointer
3. output device
4. digital camera
5. scanner
6. repetitive strain injury
7. touchscreen
8. liquid crystal display
9. impact printer
10. nonimpact printer

a. produces images by sending electrical signals to crystals

b. any piece of hardware that displays or plays back the result of computer processing

c. device with hammers or pins that strike a ribbon to leave ink on paper

d. lets you input printed images into a computer

e. a type of monitor designed to respond to input from a finger or stylus

f. follows a mouse's movements

g. device such as an inkjet or laser printer

h. takes photographs that a computer can read

i. condition caused by making the same movements again and again

j. instruction to a software program to take an action

USE THE TERMINOLOGY

DIRECTIONS Determine the correct choice for each of the following.

1. Which type of input provides answers to questions issued by programs?
   a. commands
   b. data
   c. responses
   d. software

2. Which device connects to a computer to input photos?
   a. keyboard
   b. digital camera
   c. joystick
   d. microphone

3. Which of the following devices can be designed to reduce the problem of RSIs?

    a. scanner

    b. digital camera

    c. monitor

    d. keyboard

4. What do output devices provide?

    a. data to be processed

    b. software code

    c. text and images only

    d. results of processing

5. Which of the following is a type of touchscreen?

    a. cathode ray tube

    b. analog resistive

    c. liquid crystal display

    d. thin film transistor

6. What kind of output device would NOT be used to output images?

    a. CRT

    b. LCD

    c. printer

    d. speaker

THINK CRITICALLY

DIRECTIONS Answer the following questions.

1. Why are microphones or digital cameras unlikely to cause the damage that is found in repetitive strain injury?

2. Identify the type and purpose of at least three specialized input devices.

3. What type(s) of monitor(s) do you use at school? What are the advantages and disadvantages of the different types of monitors?

4. What is the purpose of a scanner?

5. Why have nonimpact printers all but replaced impact printers?

EXTEND YOUR KNOWLEDGE

DIRECTIONS Choose and complete one of the following projects.

1. Open a word-processing program. Use the keyboard to input the definition of the word "Text" found on page 72. Input the paragraph a total of five times. Each time you do so, time yourself. With your teacher's permission, print the five paragraphs. Compare the five times. Determine whether you were able to type faster and more accurately with practice.

2. With your teacher's permission, practice disconnecting and connecting your computer system's input and output devices. For example, disconnect and connect the mouse, keyboard, and printer. Then, verify that the devices are working correctly by opening a word-processing document and typing a paragraph about the different input and output devices you are working with. Move around in the document using the keyboard and the mouse, and edit the paragraph to include an explanation of which device you think is easier to work with and why. With your teacher's permission, print the document. Read your paragraph to a partner or to the class and answer any questions.

IC3 PREP

1. Which of the following is a good reason to use a touchscreen? (Select all that apply.)

    a. more intuitive

    b. less responsive

    c. easier to make incorrect selections

    d. faster

2. A _____ is a device that converts printed content into digital format.

3. Which of the following is a purpose for a scanner? (Select all that apply.)

    a. capturing a video to upload to a website

    b. archiving medical records in digital format

    c. converting a printed photo to digital format so it can be sent by email

    d. sending a text message

CHAPTER 4

Understanding Specialized Input/Output

FROM TEXT TO MOVING PICTURES

Early personal computers could work with text and numbers. Today's computers can also handle different types of data, such as still images, sound, and video. Hardware makers have designed new devices to allow users to input data and output information in new ways.

These devices have taken computers from the still and silent world of text and numbers into a dazzling multimedia world of sound, images, and motion.

Specialized Input Devices

OBJECTIVES

- Explain how sound cards process sound.

- Compare and contrast traditional and digital cameras.

- Explain how cameras and phones are used to take pictures and transfer files.

- Identify files formats used to save scanned content.

AS YOU READ

ORGANIZE INFORMATION Use a concept web to help you organize information about devices used to input sound, still images, and video as you read.

TERMINOLOGY

- compress

- digital video camera

- fax machine

- optical character recognition (OCR)

- sound card

- video capture card

Inputting Sound

The microphone is the most basic device for inputting sound into a computer. You use it for all types of sound, including music, narration, and speech for voice recognition software. Microphones capture sounds in analog form—as a series of rapidly changing waves or vibrations. To be usable by a computer, sounds must be in digital form, that is, the waves must be converted to binary code (1s and 0s) that the computer can recognize. The sound card does this work. Typical formats for audio files include WAV, AIFF, MP3, and PCM.

A **sound card** is a circuit board that processes sounds in multiple ways. First, it digitizes sounds by changing them from analog to digital form. Then, it processes the digital sounds by following a set of built-in instructions. For example, it can prepare the digital sound files for use with voice recognition software. Sometimes the sound card reduces the size of sound files by compressing the data. That way, the files take up less space in memory. Finally, the sound card reverses the digitizing process so you can play analog sounds through the computer's speakers.

Inputting Still Images

You can input still images such as photos, drawings, or printed documents as digital files. If the image is already stored as a digital file, such as a picture you take with your smartphone, you can transfer it using either a wired or wireless connection. If the image is not a digital file, it must be converted using a device such as a scanner or digital camera.

DIGITAL CAMERAS A digital camera, like a traditional camera, takes pictures. Unlike a traditional camera, the pictures are stored as digital files.

In a traditional camera, light enters the lens and strikes a piece of film coated with chemicals that are sensitive to light. The chemicals produce an image on the film. In a digital camera, a computer chip takes the information from the lens and records it as pixels, or small dots, that form the image. A digital camera has memory to store the picture files. Almost all cell phones have a built-in digital camera. Digital pictures are stored on the phone's memory card and can be viewed on the device's screen or transferred to a computer or other device.

CONNECTIONS

THE ARTS A digital camera can take pictures that use from 4 to 20 million dots (pixels) to make the picture. The more dots it uses, the sharper the image is. But more dots also take up more space on the memory card where the pictures are stored in the camera.

Photographers can choose to take photos of lesser quality to save space. They can also delete photos from the camera's memory to make space for new ones.

FIGURE 4.1.1 A sound card handles the audio-processing tasks in a computer.

FIGURE 4.1.2 Digital cameras capture and store images electronically.

Some digital cameras store images on a memory card that can be removed. If a computer or device such as a tablet has the correct memory card port, the card can be inserted and the computer can open and input the picture files. Most digital cameras, including smartphones, can connect to a computer or tablet via a cable, usually USB, or wireless link, such as Bluetooth. When the camera is connected, the computer treats it like a disk drive and the picture files can be copied to the computer.

IC3✔ **Know how to use a digital camera or cell phone camera to take pictures, and how to transfer the picture files to a computer or tablet.**

SCANNERS Any printed document can be digitized by using a scanner. Scanners shine a light onto the material to be copied and change the image into pixels. This creates a digital image that can be input and saved as an image file. Scanners often come with software that lets you select the file format to use for saving the digital file. Common formats include PDF and image file formats such as JPG or PNG. Some software applications such as Adobe Acrobat include an option for importing data from a scanner.

Most scanners have **optical character recognition (OCR)** software. When you scan printed text using this software, the text is turned into a digital text file, not an image file. These types of files may be saved in TXT, DOC, or RTF format. In this way, you can input printed text, including handwriting, without having to type it.

There are different types of scanners:

■ With a sheet fed scanner, you insert the pages you want copied and the scanner pulls them through one at a time.

■ Flatbed scanners work more like copy machines. You lay material on a flat glass panel to make the copy. All-in-one printers have flatbed scanner capability.

■ Handheld scanners are portable models that you hold in your hand. They are useful for copying small originals.

IC3✔ **Know common file formats for scanned image files and scanned OCR files.**

FACSIMILE MACHINES A **fax machine**, or facsimile machine, scans printed documents and sends them over phone lines to another fax machine. Though fax machines are still used by some companies, many documents that were once sent as a fax are now sent online as image files or as email attachments.

TECHNOLOGY@WORK

Scientists use an input device called a sensor to record many different kinds of data. Sensors can detect physical phenomenon, such as humidity, air pressure, and temperature.

THINK ABOUT IT!

For which examples below could a sensor be used?

• weather forecasts

• climate control

• monitor of medical patients

• work by robots

Inputting Video

You can input and display full-motion video and animation on a computer. Like all other forms of input, the videos must be in digital format. Common video file formats include MP4, AVI, and FLV. **Digital video cameras** record moving images and save them as digital video files. Most smartphones can record video, too. Most digital video cameras and phones connect to your computer using a USB port so you can transfer the video files from one device to another. Some may have the ability to connect using wireless technology such as Bluetooth so you can transfer the files.

To convert analog videos to digital format, a computer needs a **video capture card**. Like a sound card, this type of circuit board changes video images into a digital file. These cards also **compress** files so they occupy less disk space. Compressing a file may affect the quality.

REAL-WORLD TECH
CROSSING THE LINE

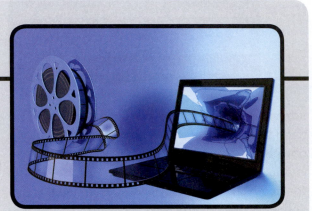

CYBRAIN/SHUTTERSTOCK

There is another use for video capture that is strictly illegal. Some computer users digitize movies, pay-per-view events, and television shows and post them on websites. People can visit the sites, download the shows, and watch them for free. This breaks copyright law, which protects the rights of people who create works of art, such as books, songs, and movies.

Why would the government pass laws to protect the rights of authors, songwriters, and movie directors regarding the sale of their works?

Specialized Output Devices

OBJECTIVES

- Distinguish among different video adapters.

- Compare and contrast different printers.

- Compare and contrast other output devices.

- Identify kinds of audio output.

AS YOU READ

GATHER INFORMATION Use a chart to help you gather information about output devices used for still images, video, and sound as you read.

TERMINOLOGY

- data projector

- high-definition television (HDTV)

- Musical Instrument Digital Interface (MIDI)

- Organic Light Emitting Diode (OLED)

- smart TV

- speech synthesis software

- thermal transfer printer

- video adapter

- video memory (VRAM)

- virtual reality

- Cave Automated Virtual Environment (CAVE)

Video Adapters

The images you see on your monitor are created by a **video adapter**. The adapter is a circuit board that receives data from an operating system or software application. It changes that data into electrical currents and sends them to the monitor. In a color monitor, the amount of current sent by the video adapter determines the color the monitor will produce. Like a sound card, a video adapter processes data so that the computer's CPU can take care of other jobs. It also has its own memory, called **video memory** or **VRAM**, to free up space in the computer's memory.

SPECIAL VIDEO ADAPTERS Some video adapters send images to the monitor very quickly. They are called video accelerators.

Most computers today have highly specialized video adapters, called 3D video adapters. Images on a monitor have only two dimensions—height and width. 3D video adapters add a third dimension to an image—depth.

DENIS DRYASHKIN/SHUTTERSTOCK

FIGURE 4.2.1 The video adapter card is installed on the motherboard. It processes video data for display on the monitor, allowing the CPU and RAM to handle other tasks.

TECHNOLOGY@HOME

Another new technology might help users of small video screens to see better in sunlight. **Organic Light Emitting Diode (OLED)** technology consumes less power and produces better displays than current LCD screens. OLED screens also have very good video quality—the manufacturers call it "full motion" video.

THINK ABOUT IT!

Think of the small display screens that you have seen in use. Think also of the lighting conditions in which they are used. Which of the following products do you think could best use OLED display?

- cell phone
- PDA
- tablet computer
- MP3 player, like an iPod

Outputting Images with Printers

Recall that image quality varies based on which type of printer is used to output an image. Both impact and nonimpact printers create images by printing tiny dots on the paper. Inkjet and laser printers have much higher print quality. Therefore, they are more often used for printing graphic images.

The best printer for printing color images is a **thermal transfer printer**. These printers use heat to transfer color dyes or inks onto paper. Thermal transfer printers do not make pictures out of tiny dots. Instead, the colors actually blend together on the paper. These printers only work with glossy paper.

Outputting Video

You can watch videos on your computer monitor, your tablet, or your smartphone. You can also use the following types of devices to output video.

DATA PROJECTORS You may be familiar with **data projectors**, which show a computer's video output on a projection screen so many people can view it at once. These projectors are often used to display presentations for educational or business meetings.

Digital light processing, or DLP, projectors use millions of tiny mirrors to create a very sharp image. That image is then projected through a lens and onto a screen. Because the image they produce is so sharp, DLP projectors can be used with large audiences. They can even be used in brightly lit rooms.

TELEVISIONS Some devices let you send video from a computer to a television. Many people find that their **high-definition television (HDTV)** makes an excellent output device. HDTV uses only digital audio and video and produces a much sharper image than regular television. Many new televisions are also able to access to the internet. These so-called **smart TVs** come with built-in Ethernet and Wi-Fi capability so they can connect through a local area network. You can use them to stream video, including movies and television shows, and also to access social media websites.

VIRTUAL REALITY HEADSETS A **virtual reality** headset, which has two LCD panels, is worn over the head. The computer sends video images to each panel. The person wearing the headset sees and reacts to the images as if in a three-dimensional space.

FIGURE 4.2.2 Virtual reality headsets output video images to simulate a three-dimensional experience.

A similar but larger device is the **Cave Automated Virtual Environment (CAVE)**. This is a room in which three-dimensional images are shown on the floor, walls, and ceiling. A person in the room wears 3D glasses. The glasses and images create the illusion of interacting in three-dimensions.

Outputting Sound

To output sound to headphones or speakers, your computer must have a sound card and speakers. The sound card changes digital sound files stored in the computer's memory into an electrical current. It sends that current to the speakers to produce audio output.

The sound a computer can produce depends on the computer's software. Two kinds of software allow audio output:

- **Speech synthesis software** allows the computer to read text files aloud.

- **Musical Instrument Digital Interface (MIDI)** software allows the computer to create music. With this software, you can send instructions to a digital musical instrument called a synthesizer. This device then sounds the notes it has been instructed to play.

DID YOU KNOW?

One new technology goes beyond headsets and CAVEs to combine computers and people. Army researchers are trying to develop a special suit. Run by computers and guided by the wearer, the suit will include simple machines such as pistons. If it works, the suit will greatly increase the speed and strength of the person wearing it. Having powerful arms, for example, could be helpful during rescue operations.

Chapter 4 Review

REVIEW THE TERMINOLOGY

DIRECTIONS Match each vocabulary term in the left column with the correct definition in the right column.

1. compress
2. fax machine
3. optical character recognition
4. digital video camera
5. video capture card
6. video adapter
7. VRAM
8. thermal transfer printer
9. speech synthesis software
10. MIDI

a. turns text into audio
b. prints high-quality output suitable for photos
c. software that lets the computer play like an electronic instrument
d. software that scans text and turns it into a digital file
e. memory on a video adapter
f. to make files smaller
g. captures still images, which are then shown rapidly
h. controls video output to the monitor
i. converts analog video into digital
j. scans documents and sends them over phone lines

USE THE TERMINOLOGY

DIRECTIONS Complete each sentence with information from the chapter.

1. To play sound that has been stored in a computer, it must be converted to _____ format.

2. Digital photos can be input from a camera by connecting the camera to the computer using a(n) _____ cable.

3. _____ software allows people to convert printed text into digital text files instead of retyping it.

4. Printed photos can be converted into digital format using a _____.

5. The amount of current that a video adapter sends to the monitor determines the _____ display on the monitor.

6. Three-dimensional graphics include height, width, and _____.

7. DLP projectors are better than LCD projectors for giving a presentation to many people because the _____ appear sharper.

8. Standard printers create output by printing tiny _____ on paper.

9. Virtual reality headsets and the room-sized _____ let users experience virtual three-dimensional environments.

10. Audio can be output to headphones or _____.

THINK CRITICALLY

DIRECTIONS Answer the following questions.

1. What is one advantage of having memory on a video card dedicated to displaying graphics?

2. Why are sound and graphics files compressed?

3. Suppose someone had to scan ten images. Which kind of scanner would require him or her to stay closer to the machine as it is working, a sheet fed or flatbed? Why?

4. Would a 3D graphics adapter be needed on a machine used mostly for word processing and spreadsheets? Why or why not?

5. Which kind of printer would be better for printing a report for school that included two or three photographs, an inkjet or a thermal transfer printer? Why?

EXTEND YOUR KNOWLEDGE

DIRECTIONS Choose and complete one of the following projects.

1. Divide a sheet of paper into two columns, creating a T-chart. Write the heading *Standard System* over the left column. Write the heading *Graphics System* over the right column. In each column, list the input and output components you would include if you were setting up these two computer systems. Include the types of output cards you would want. Assume that the standard system will be used for word processing and spreadsheet work. Assume that the graphics system will be used for high-quality photographs.

2. Find out what kind of sound your computer can output. If possible, output audio and then determine what kinds of software your computer used to output the sound. With a partner or as a class, discuss for whom audio output is an advantage and when this feature is a necessity.

3. Use a digital camera or cell phone to take at least five pictures. Transfer the picture files from the camera or phone to a computer or tablet. Use the pictures to make a presentation or photo album or, with your teacher's permission, print one of the pictures and share it with a partner or with the class.

IC3 PREP

1. For each line below, select whether the statement is True or False.

   a. A digital camera stores images as digital files.

   b. Only very expensive smartphones have built-in digital cameras.

   c. You can transfer image files from a digital camera to a computer using Bluetooth.

2. Which of the following are common file formats for scanned image files? (Select all that apply.)

    a. PDF

    b. MP3

    c. JPG

    d. TIF

    e. PNG

3. Which of the following are common file formats for scanned OCR files? (Select all that apply.)

    a. PDF

    b. DOC

    c. TXT

    d. TIF

    e. RTF

IC3 PROCEDURES

TRANSFERRING PICTURES FROM A CAMERA OR PHONE TO A COMPUTER OR TABLET.

1. Connect the camera or phone to the computer or tablet.

2. Turn on the phone or camera.

3. Open **File Explorer** .

4. Right-click the icon for the device where the pictures are stored.

5. Select **Import Pictures and Videos**.

6. Select **Import All New Items Now** and type description in the Add Tags box.

    OR

    Select **Review, Organize, and Group Items to Import**.

7. Select the **Next** button.

8. Adjust the time grouping, if necessary, to keep related photos in the same location.

9. Select other options, as necessary.

10. Select the **Import** button.

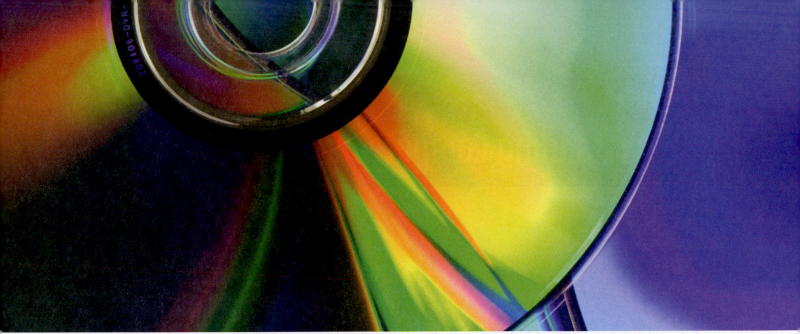

CHAPTER 5
Storage Basics

HOW DO COMPUTERS STORE DATA?

Computer storage is like the backpack you bring to school. Both store things until you are ready to use them. Your backpack stores books and school supplies; most computers store software and data.

Computer storage devices can store information for long periods of time. This lets you create a file today, save it, and then use it again in the future. In this chapter, you will learn why storage is necessary and how information is stored. You will also examine some of the storage devices you are likely to find on today's computers.

Understanding Computer Storage

OBJECTIVES

- Explain the need for storage devices for computers.

- Distinguish between memory and storage.

- Explain how memory and storage impact the use of a device.

- Distinguish between storage devices and storage media.

AS YOU READ

ORGANIZE INFORMATION Use an outline to help you organize information about computer storage and storage devices as you read.

TERMINOLOGY

- backup

- Basic Input/Output System (BIOS)

- file

- firmware

- memory

- nonvolatile memory

- restore

- storage device

- UEFI (Unified Extensible Firmware Interface)

Computer Storage Devices

A **storage device** is the computer's hardware component that retains data even after the power is turned off. The purpose of a storage device is to provide a location where you can store data so that it is available now and in the future.

Suppose you turned off your computer without saving your work to a storage device. All your work would be lost. Without storage devices, you would have to recreate all of your work every time you wanted to use it.

Why not keep all of a computer's software and data available at all times? Because no one needs to use every program or file every time they work on the computer. For example, you might be doing word processing today, but creating a computer drawing tomorrow. There is no need to have both programs open at the same time if you are not using both of them.

FILES A computer stores data and program instructions in files. A **file** is a collection of related information or program code, which has been given a unique name.

The type of file people most often use is called a document. A document can be any kind of file that a user can create, save, and edit. For example, you can use a word-processing program to create a letter, which is one type of document. A digital photo is another type of document.

CONNECTIONS

SCIENCE Nanotechnology is a field of science and technology that studies how to make things by arranging individual atoms and molecules. Nanotechnology has contributed to advances in computer technology.

For example, nanotechnology has made it possible for computer hard drives to hold ever larger amounts of data. They can do so because the parts that retrieve and record data—called the read/write heads—are made from an extremely thin layer of magnetic material. The material is less than one billionth of a meter thick, or close to 7,000 times thinner than a strand of a spider web.

SYSTEM STARTUP Computer storage devices are a key part of a computer's startup process. Without a storage device to hold startup information permanently, a computer would not know what to do when you turned it on.

When you start a computer, it looks for information that tells it what to do. The **Basic Input/Output System (BIOS)**, is a set of programs, called **firmware**, that tells the computer equipment how to start up. When a computer is built, the BIOS is set up with this basic information. The BIOS is permanently stored in special memory chips called read-only memory, or ROM. Usually the BIOS instructs the computer to look for the operating system. The operating system contains all the commands required to run the computer.

Desktop > Work in Progress		
Name	Type	Size
Current Projects	File folder	
Book Report Compressed.zip	Compressed (zipped) Folder	4,770 KB
IMG_1519.JPG	JPG File	3,888 KB
Data.xlsx	Microsoft Excel Worksheet	7 KB
Book Report Presentation.pptx	Microsoft PowerPoint Presentation	893 KB
New Microsoft Publisher Document.pub	Microsoft Publisher Document	59 KB
Book Report.docx	Microsoft Word Document	14 KB
Book Report Video.mp4	MP4 File	3,760 KB
audiobook.png	PNG File	12 KB

MICROSOFT CORPORATION

FIGURE 5.1.1 Every file stored on your computer has a unique name.

It provides the tools to operate the system and to run programs. Most Apple Macintosh computers and personal computers built to run Windows 8 and later use **UEFI (Unified Extensible Firmware Interface)** instead of BIOS. UEFI allows for faster startup, supports large capacity storage drives, and is more secure than BIOS.

Memory and Storage

When people talk about computer **memory**, they usually mean a set of chips that acts as a temporary workspace in the computer or other device. The purpose of this device memory, called random access memory, or RAM, is to store data and program instructions needed by the CPU.

RAM and ROM are different in two important ways. First, ROM is **nonvolatile memory**, which means it stores its contents permanently, even when the computer is turned off. Recall that RAM, on the other hand, is volatile memory and only stores its contents temporarily; if the computer loses power, RAM's contents are lost.

Second, because ROM stores instructions that are needed only by the computer, you seldom need to think about ROM or the information it holds. But RAM holds data and programs while they are being used. As you use the computer, you constantly work with the contents of RAM.

STORAGE VERSUS MEMORY New computer users sometimes get confused about temporary device memory (RAM) and permanent storage devices (disks and disk drives). They will say "memory" when they actually mean to say "storage." To avoid this problem, remember that RAM uses chips to temporarily store information. These chips depend on a constant supply of power to keep their contents; when the power is lost, the chips lose their contents. Storage uses different methods to store data permanently, so it isn't lost when the power is turned off.

Adding confusion, both are measured with the same units: bytes. One byte equals about 8 bits, or a single character. A kilobyte, or 1KB, is 1 thousand bytes. A megabyte, or 1MB, is 1 million bytes. A gigabyte, or 1GB, is 1 billion bytes. A terabyte, or 1TB, is 1 thousand billion bytes. A petabyte, or 1PB, is one million gigabytes.

IMPACT OF STORAGE AND MEMORY ON PROCESSING Recall that the amount of available memory and storage has a significant impact on how efficiently a device can process data. If there is not enough RAM for processing, the device must use virtual memory, which is dependent on storage space. If a device seems to be have trouble processing commands, chances are there is not enough RAM and disk space available. For example, if a program takes a long time to open or to save a file, you may need to install more RAM. If an error message displays telling you there is not enough storage space, you must free up additional disk space.

Disk space is used by files that you save and programs you install. It is also used by downloaded program files; offline, or cached, web pages; temporary internet files, including cookies; the files in your recycle bin or trash that you have not permanently removed; and operating system logs. Operating systems come with utilities you can run in order to free up disk space. For example, Windows comes with Disk Cleanup and the Disk Defragmenter.

Some activities that decrease available device memory include:

- Running multiple programs at the same time

- Leaving a device running for a long period of time without rebooting

- Running programs that use a lot of multimedia or 3D effects

- Undetected viruses or malware

- Programs running in the background

DID YOU KNOW?

Most computers only have enough RAM to store programs and data while a computer is using them. This is because RAM is relatively expensive to make and to buy.

As a result, makers of computers limit the amount of RAM in their machines to help lower initial computer costs and to allow users who want more RAM to purchase it separately.

You can increase available device memory by closing programs you are not using, rebooting the system, and using an antivirus and malware utility to detect and remove malicious software. You can identify and close or disable background programs using the Windows Task Manager or the Mac Activity Monitor. On some devices, you may be able to install additional RAM chips.

IC3✔ **Know the impact of memory and storage on usage.**

Storage Media and Storage Devices

Storage has two components: storage media and storage devices.

STORAGE MEDIA In terms of storage, a medium is an object that physically holds data or program instructions. Flash drives, hard disks, magnetic tapes, compact discs, DVDs, and Blu-ray discs are examples of storage media. (The word *media* is the plural of *medium*.) One important use of storage media is for making a **backup** of computer data. When you backup data you copy the data to a different location for safekeeping. If the original data is lost or damaged you can **restore** the data from the backup files.

IC3✔ **Understand backing up concepts.**

STORAGE DEVICES A storage device is a piece of hardware that holds the storage medium, sends data to the medium, and retrieves data from the medium. Hard drives, flash drives, and CD and DVD drives are all examples of storage devices.

FIGURE 5.1.2 A DVD is the storage media you insert into the DVD drive.

BRIAN A JACKSON/SHUTTERSTOCK

Classifying Storage Devices

OBJECTIVES

- Explain how computer storage devices are classified.

- Compare and contrast primary, secondary, and archival storage devices.

- Describe the categories of storage devices.

AS YOU READ

CLASSIFY INFORMATION Use a spider map to help you classify storage devices as you read.

TERMINOLOGY

- archival storage device

- DVD-RAM

- optical storage device

- primary storage

- random access storage device

- read-only device

- read/write device

- secondary storage

- sequential storage device

- solid state disk (SSD)

Hierarchy of Storage Devices

Computer storage devices are sometimes classified in a hierarchical structure—that is, primary or secondary.

PRIMARY STORAGE DEVICES The term **primary storage** is sometimes used to describe the main memory, or RAM, in a computer. This is because when the CPU needs data or instructions, it looks in memory before looking anywhere else.

Most knowledgeable computer users, however, avoid using the term *storage* when talking about RAM. This is because RAM works very differently from storage devices such as disks or flash drives. RAM also loses any data it contains when the computer is turned off, while disks and flash drives can hold data permanently.

SECONDARY STORAGE DEVICES The term **secondary storage** is sometimes used to describe devices that can store data permanently, such as a hard drive, flash drive, compact disc, DVD, or external hard drive. This is because the computer will look for data on one of these devices if the data is not in RAM.

Many kinds of secondary storage devices can hold much more data than a computer's RAM can. For example, while most of today's PCs come with 4 to 16 gigabytes of RAM, they have hard drives that can store a terabyte or more.

Because they can store data permanently (or until you erase it), secondary storage devices are sometimes called **archival storage devices**. This refers to the fact that you can store data on a drive or disk and then put it away for a long time, only using it again when you need it.

THINK ABOUT IT!

Rate the computer equipment that you think is most sensitive to mishandling and needs the most care. On a scale of 1 to 5, use 1 for most sensitive and 5 for least.

- CD-ROM/DVD
- flash drive
- hard drive
- power cord
- laser printer
- tablet

Categories of Storage Devices

Storage devices (but not RAM) are divided into three categories. Each category has two options based on the device.

READ-ONLY VERSUS READ/WRITE A **read-only device** can only read data from the storage medium. You cannot change the data on the medium or save new data onto it. A CD-ROM drive is an example of a read-only device, because it does not have the capability to write data onto a disc.

The media used with read-only devices come with data already saved on them. Music CDs or software programs on CDs are CD-Rs. Your CD-ROM drive will be able to play the music or read the program instructions from the disc, but you cannot change the disc's contents. Standard DVD players are another example of a read-only device.

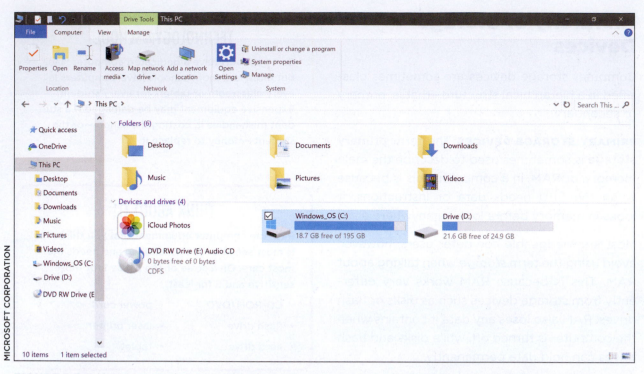

FIGURE 5.2.1 Use an operating system such as Windows to view a list of storage devices connected to your computer.

A **read/write device** not only can read data from the storage medium, but can write data onto the medium, as well. These devices let you read data, make changes to the data, and save new data onto the medium. Hard drives, USB flash drives, CD-Rewritable drives (CD-RW), and **DVD-RAM** drives are commonly used examples of read/write devices.

SEQUENTIAL VERSUS RANDOM ACCESS When equipped with a tape drive, business computers can store data on a long piece of tape, similar to an old-fashioned cassette tape. A tape drive is an example of a **sequential storage device**, which requires the computer to scan from the beginning of the medium to the end until it finds the data it needs. While cheaper and slower than other types of storage, the highest capacity tape cartridges can hold five terabytes of uncompressed data. Because it can take several minutes to locate data on a high-capacity tape, tapes are used chiefly by businesses that want to backup their computer systems—often after the business day is over.

> **TECHNOLOGY@HOME**
>
> You probably use a variety of data storage devices in your home. Some of these may be in a computer, while others are not.

> **THINK ABOUT IT!**
>
> Some of the devices listed below are based on read-only technology, while others are based on read/write technology. Which storage devices in the list do you think are based on read-only technology?
>
> - smartphone
> - CD-ROM drive
> - game console
> - DVD player

REAL-WORLD TECH
HIGH-CAPACITY PORTABLE STORAGE

Devices such as Apple's iPod Touch and the Sony Walkman function as both MP3 players and as high-capacity, portable storage devices. The iPod touch comes with up to 128 GB of storage. (This is enough for more than 18,000 songs or up to 64 hours of continuous video!) Smartphones, such as Apple's iPhone or Samsung's Galaxy, have as much as 256 GB of storage. In addition to storing music, pictures, and videos, these mobile devices store contact information, calendars, and documents. You can even connect them to other devices and the internet to download and upload files.

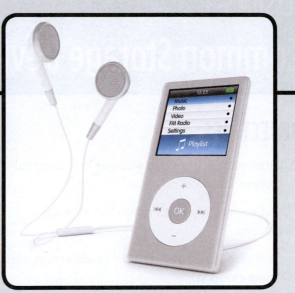

KSANDER/SHUTTERSTOCK

A **random access storage device** lets a computer go directly to the needed information. The device does not have to search the entire medium to find data. For this reason, random access storage devices are much faster, and more expensive, than sequential devices. A hard drive is an example of a random access storage device.

MAGNETIC STORAGE Magnetic storage devices are specially treated disks or tapes, such as those mentioned previously, that record information using magnetically sensitive materials. These devices use electricity to shift magnetic particles so they form a pattern that the computer reads and stores as information. Common magnetic storage devices include hard drives and tape drives.

OPTICAL STORAGE Other storage devices use laser beams to read information that has been stored on the reflective surface of a disc. These are called **optical storage devices**. Popular types of optical storage devices for computers include CD-ROM and DVD-ROM drives.

SOLID STATE STORAGE A **solid state disk (SSD)** stores data on an array of flash memory chips organized as a disk drive. SSDs can access data faster than optical drives because they can read data directly from a specific flash SSD cell location. Unlike magnetic and optical drives, SSDs have no moving parts, which makes them more durable and reliable. SSDs are also quieter than hard disk drives, and lighter, which makes them suitable for ultralight notebook computers.

Common Storage Devices

OBJECTIVES

- Differentiate between internal and external storage devices.

- List commonly used magnetic storage devices.

- Describe concepts relating to accessing and using cloud storage.

- Summarize optical storage options.

AS YOU READ

CLASSIFY INFORMATION Use a T-chart to help you classify information about magnetic and optical storage devices as you read.

TERMINOLOGY

- cloud storage

- collaborate

- download

- flash memory

- hard drive

- online storage

- shareable link

- share

- storage service provider (SSP)

- sync

- upload

Internal and External Storage Devices

Storage devices can be installed in your computer or connected to it. A storage device installed inside your computer is called an internal storage device. One that is positioned outside your computer is referred to as an external storage device.

Magnetic Storage Devices

The most common magnetic storage device installed in computers is a **hard drive**. You cannot see the hard drive because it is installed inside your computer. Often, a small flashing light on the front of a computer shows when the hard drive is in use. Hard drives hold a great deal of data, but they are not portable.

EXTERNAL MAGNETIC DEVICES Other forms of magnetic storage devices include a variety of USB external hard drives. These can hold up to as much as 4 terabytes of data, and they are portable. External drives communicate with the computer via a high-speed interface cable. By using the external hard drive with an automatic backup program, like the Mac's TimeMachine or Windows 10's File History, computer users have peace of mind. They know their data is always recoverable if their computer crashes or is hit by a virus.

LEFTERIS PAPAULAKIS/SHUTTERSTOCK

FIGURE 5.3.1 If you removed a PC's internal hard drive, you would see the actual magnetic platter, or disc, and the arm used to read and write data.

Cloud Storage

Many **cloud storage**, also called **online storage**, applications, such as Google Drive, Dropbox, Microsoft OneDrive, and Apple iCloud, are available where you can store files online on a network server at a remote location. Many programs, including Microsoft Office, come with free online storage space. You can also pay a **storage service provider (SSP)** for additional space.

IC3✔ | Identify a variety of online storage applications.

Cloud storage is used often in businesses to make files available to many employees on a secure storage location. It can also be used for storing backups of important data. For individuals, it provides storage space for backups and also for documents, photos, videos, and music that require more storage space than may be available locally. Some cloud storage locations are even customized for storing specific types of files. For example, Google Photos, SnapFish, and Shutterfly are used for storing, organizing, and sharing picture files.

CAREER CORNER

COMPUTER SECURITY SPECIALIST Today, security specialists are in demand to work with various computer storage systems, such as tape warehouses and online storage companies.

Computer security specialists study ways of improving the overall security of their systems. For example, some goals include improving recording or access time or the safety of the protected information in case of a natural disaster.

THINK ABOUT IT!

Think about why a business might need to store its backups at a completely different site. Which disasters listed below might destroy a backup if it were kept on-site?

- fire
- flood
- earthquake
- break-in
- tornado

CLOUD STORAGE ACCOUNTS In order to use cloud storage, you must have an account with the SSP. The account has a user name and password that you use to log in from any device with internet access. For example, to use Microsoft OneDrive you log in with your Microsoft account information. To use Google Drive, you log in with your Google account information. When you store files online, most applications let you **sync** that data with more than one device. That means that you can log in from your PC, smartphone, tablet, or other device to access data on a site such as OneDrive, your music on a site such as Apple iTunes, or photos on a site such as SugarSync. No matter which device you use to log in, you have access to the same files.

IC3 ✔ **Understand account management on the cloud.**

IC3 ✔ **Know how to sync files between devices using the cloud.**

BENEFITS OF CLOUD STORAGE Cloud storage offers many benefits including:

- It is expandable.
- It allows you to access your data from any location with an internet connection.
- It allows you to share files with others.
- You can sync data between devices using the cloud.
- Data stored in a remote location is protected if your computer is stolen or damaged.

IC3 ✔ **Know the benefits of using cloud storage.**

STORING AND ACCESSING DATA ON THE CLOUD To store the data, you log in to your account and then **upload** or save the files to the online storage location. Many applications let you select an online storage location in the Save As dialog box you use to save the file, if the device you are working on is connected to the internet. Usually there is a desktop, or device-based, interface with commands for creating and organizing folders, and for uploading and downloading files. You may be able to use your operating system's file management utility, such as Windows' File Explorer, to drag and drop or copy files from your local storage to the online storage location.

Accessing your storage account is not the same as accessing the internet. You can access the internet using a browser on any internet-enabled computer. Once a file is stored online, you access it by logging in to your account through the internet using a secure password. You can **download** the data to a local storage device, or work with the data without downloading so the online version of the file is the most up-to-date. Downloading may be as simple as using

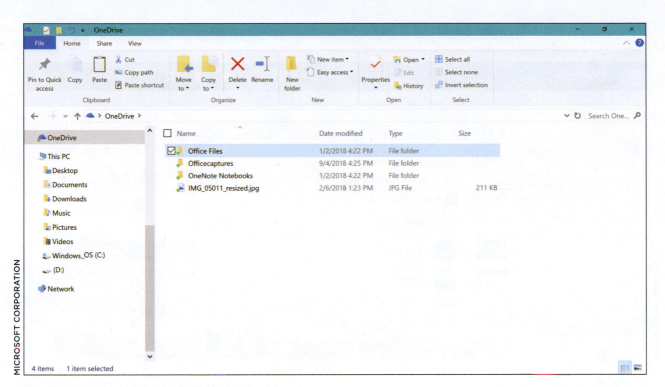

FIGURE 5.3.2 The Microsoft OneDrive Desktop App.

the File > Open command in an application such as Microsoft Word, or you may use the storage provider's interface to download files or folders.

IC3✔ Understand the difference between accessing the cloud and storing data on the cloud.

IC3✔ Know how to upload and download content from the cloud.

SHARING AND COLLABORATING USING THE CLOUD

When multiple users have access to the same online storage folder they can **share** files simply by uploading and downloading. For example, one person can create a Google Drive folder, upload files to it, and then share the folder with coworkers by sending an email invitation, or providing a **sharable link**, which is a direct link to the online file or folder. The person who created the folder can control permissions by allowing others to organize, edit, and add information, or limiting them to viewing only.

Storing a document on the cloud also makes it possible for multiple users to **collaborate** on the same version of the file instead of passing multiple versions of the file around to one another. Not only does everyone know that they are working with the most recent version of the document, many applications allow real-time editing of documents stored online. Users can see the edits and notes others are making as they occur.

IC3✔ Understand sharing and collaboration on the cloud.

Flash Memory Storage Devices

Flash media use a non-magnetic storage medium called **flash memory**. Flash memory is used in ROM chips within your computer to store basic information about the computer's configuration. It is also used in memory cards and memory sticks for digital cameras that require removable, reusable storage and in USB flash drives (also

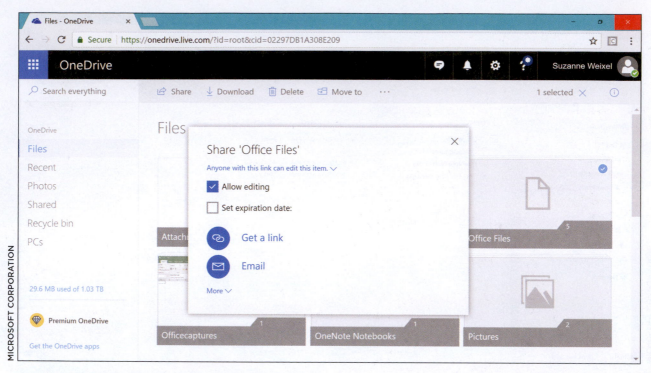

MICROSOFT CORPORATION

FIGURE 5.3.3 Sharing a OneDrive folder.

called jump, pen, and key drives). Flash drives connect to the computer through a USB (universal serial bus) port.

Most removable flash memory devices include a chip that stores data and a microcontroller that permits the operating system to communicate with the chip. As the technology of flash memory improves, the capacity of flash devices increases significantly. Early flash devices only held 32–256 MB, but capacities of up to 512 GB are now common. Flash drives with more than 1 TB

CHROMAKEY/SHUTTERSTOCK

FIGURE 5.3.4 A USB flash drive has a USB connector, a flash memory chip, a mass storage controller, and a crystal oscillator that allows the device to communicate with the computer.

are available but very expensive. The small size, increasing capacity, and ease of connection of these removable devices make them widely used.

Optical Storage Devices

Optical storage devices store data by etching tiny pits onto a disc. A laser then scans the disc and changes the data into a form the computer can work with. CDs, DVDs, and Blu-ray Discs are the most common types of optical storage media. On a PC, built-in CD or DVD drives have a button on the front that opens a tray on which you insert a CD or DVD. You push the button to close the tray so you can read the disc's contents. On Macs the built-in drive is simply a slot into which you insert a disc, and you can eject it electronically by moving the disc icon into the "trash." Many computers, particularly notebooks, no longer have built-in CD or DVD drives.

Standard CD-ROM and DVD drives can only read data stored on an optical disc. Only optical drives labeled CD-R, CD-RW, or DVD/CD-RW can be used to record data onto blank discs.

A standard CD can store 650 megabytes of data, or around 74 minutes of audio. Newer CDs can store 700 megabytes of data, or about 80 minutes of audio. DVDs can store about 4.7 gigabytes of data on each side. These discs are used for storing programs, games, data, and movies.

IC3✔ **Know how to compare storage capacities measured in bytes, KB, MB, GB, and TB.**

CAPACITIES OF TYPICAL STORAGE DEVICES	
Device	**Capacity**
Internal hard drive	500 GB–1 TB and more
External hard drive (USB connection)	500 GB–8 TB and more
MP3 player	16 GB–64 GB and more
Smartphones	256 GB and more
Flash memory cards and drives	4 GB–256 GB and more
CD-ROM	650 MB–700 MB
DVD	9.5 GB
Blu-ray disc	25 GB

MADTATYANA/SHUTTERSTOCK

FIGURE 5.3.5 DVDs can store about 4.7 GB on each side.

REVIEW THE TERMINOLOGY

DIRECTIONS Match each vocabulary term in the left column with the correct definition in the right column.

1. storage device

2. memory

3. primary storage

4. secondary storage

5. read/write device

6. random access storage device

7. optical storage device

8. hard drive

9. read-only device

10. firmware

a. temporary workspace on a computer

b. sometimes used when referring to a computer's RAM

c. uses laser to read information

d. users access from and save information to this type of device

e. common secondary storage device

f. computer component that retains data even after power is shut off

g. storage device that lets computer go directly to the needed information

h. a set of programs that tells the computer how to start

i. can only read data from the storage medium

j. any type of storage device that holds data permanently; not RAM

USE THE TERMINOLOGY

DIRECTIONS Complete each sentence with information from the chapter.

1. Storage devices _____ information even when a computer is turned off.

2. A _____ is a collection of related information or program code, which has been given a unique name.

3. The _____ is a set of programs called firmware that directs computer equipment to start up.

4. The purpose of _____ is to store data and program instructions needed by the CPU.

5. _____ is an alternative to BIOS that allows for faster startup and is more secure.

6. _____ memory is used in ROM chips within your computer to store basic information about the computer's configuration.

7. A hard drive is an example of a _____ storage device.

8. A _____ stores data on an array of flash memory chips organized as a disk drive.

9. A magnetic tape is an example of a(n) _____ storage device.

10. _____ lets you store data on a network server at a remote computer.

THINK CRITICALLY

DIRECTIONS Answer the following questions.

1. Which type of secondary storage device do you use most at school? Do you think this will change in the near future? If so, why?

2. What can you do with a CD-RW that you cannot do with a CD-R?

3. Why do you think computer hard drives locate information directly, rather than sequentially?

4. Explain the benefits of using online, or cloud, storage.

5. Explain the difference between accessing the cloud and storing data on the cloud.

EXTEND YOUR KNOWLEDGE

DIRECTIONS Choose and complete one of the following projects.

1. Look at your computer at school and find out how much memory it currently has. Next, use online documentation or other resources, such as the manufacturer's website, to compare your computer memory to the maximum amount of memory your computer can hold. Identify advantages to having more random access memory and compare this to the cost. As a class, conclude whether or not your school computers have sufficient memory to meet students' needs.

2. Go online and research storage service providers. Take notes and keep track of your sources as you work. Be sure to evaluate the information and only use it if it is accurate, relevant, and valid. What services and features do they offer? How do they protect the data they store? How easy is it for customers to access their data once they have given it to the service? Can customers share the stored data with other people? What fees do these services charge? Do you think such services can be useful to individuals as well as to companies? Discuss your findings with a partner, or as a class.

IC3 PREP

1. Which of the following is a safe way to make more device memory available for processing? (Select all that apply.)

   a. close unused programs

   b. disable the virus protection software

   c. empty the recycle bin

   d. install additional RAM

   e. download large images and videos to the local drive

2. Which of the following is an online storage application? (Select all that apply.)

   a. Google Drive

   b. Microsoft Office

   c. Apple iOS

   d. SugarSync

3. For each line below, select whether the statement is True or False.

    a. To use cloud storage, you must have an account with a storage service provider.

    b. You can only sync data from one device to your online storage account.

    c. Uploading is the way you move files from online storage to your local drive.

    d. You can access data stored online from any location with an internet connection.

    e. Using cloud storage lets a team collaborate on the same version of a document in real-time.

4. A direct link to an online file or folder is called which of the following:

    a. collaboration link   c. erasable link

    b. sharable link   d. downloading link

5. Put the following storage capacities into order from smallest to largest:

    _____ 90 GB

    _____ 85000 MB

    _____ 1 TB

    _____ 70,000 KB

IC3 PROCEDURES

UPLOADING CONTENT TO MICROSOFT ONEDRIVE

1. Select **File**.

2. Select **Save As**.

3. Select **OneDrive** .

4. Select the desired OneDrive folder in the right pane.

5. In the Save As dialog box, enter the file name.

6. Select **Save**.

DOWNLOADING CONTENT FROM MICROSOFT ONEDRIVE

1. Open **File Explorer** .

2. Select the **OneDrive** folder in the Navigation pane.

3. Double-click the files/folders to open.

SYNCHRONIZING FILES BETWEEN DEVICES USING MICROSOFT ONEDRIVE

On an Android Device:

1. On the computer, open a web browser and open your OneDrive, Dropbox, or Office 365 team site.

2. Upload the file.

3. Sign in to the Android device.

4. Tap **Open**, tap the service in which you saved the file, and find the file.

    OR

    If a file is open, select the **File** icon or menu, tap **Open**, tap the service in which you saved the file, and then find the file.

On an iPad or iPhone:

1. On the computer, open a web browser and open your OneDrive, Dropbox, or Office 365 team site.

2. Upload the file.

3. Sign in to your iPad or iPhone.

4. Tap and sign in to the service in which you saved the file.

5. Tap **Open** to find the file.

   OR

   If a file is open, tap **Back** and then tap **Open**.

On a Windows Mobile device

1. On the computer, open a web browser and open your OneDrive, Dropbox, or Office 365 team site.

2. Upload the file.

3. Sign in to your Windows Mobile device.

4. Tap the **Word**, **PowerPoint**, or **Excel** icon to open the app, locate your file, and tap to open it.

   OR

   If a file is open, tap the **File** tab or menu, tap **Open**, and locate your file.

CHAPTER 6

Understanding How Data Storage Works

WHY IS COMPUTER STORAGE IMPORTANT?

Once you understand the basics of computer storage, you can begin to understand why storage is so important. In fact, the true power of a computer is its ability to store data for future use. Without storage, a computer would be similar to a calculator; useful for a one-time task, but not much more than that.

In this chapter, you will examine how different types of storage devices work. You will learn more about the advantages and drawbacks of storage devices, and the steps you can take to protect your data.

Understanding Hard Drives and Flash Drives

OBJECTIVES

- Identify the parts of a hard drive.

- Explain the role platters play in storing information.

- Compare and contrast the access time of different storage devices.

AS YOU READ

ORGANIZE INFORMATION Use a concept web to help you organize key concepts related to hard-drive storage as you read.

TERMINOLOGY

- access time
- cylinder
- data loss
- flash memory
- metadata
- platter
- property
- read/write head
- sector
- solid state disk (SSD)
- storage media
- track
- USB flash drive
- writing
- write-protect switch

Parts of a Hard Drive

Recall that a hard drive is a storage device that is usually installed inside a computer, although some hard drives are external. Its main function is storing information. Several rigid disks, coated with a magnetically sensitive material, are enclosed with recording heads in a hard metal container that is sealed to protect it from dirt and other damaging items.

PLATTERS Inside the sealed container is a stack of metal disks, known as **platters**, that store information. The platters rotate around a spindle inside the sealed container. These platters are so close together that only a thin layer of air separates them. The platters are **storage media**, coated with a special material that allows information to be saved on them.

Each platter is divided into **tracks**, or a set of circles on the surface of the platter, on which the data is recorded. A **cylinder** is the same track location on all the stacked platters. Each track is divided into segments, called **sectors**.

The process of storing information on storage media is called **writing**. Information can also be deleted from the platters. This is done when you no longer need a file or want to make room for another one.

READ/WRITE HEADS A hard drive has a motor that spins the platters at a high speed. Usually these platters spin continuously when your computer is on. A small, needle-like component,

called the **read/write head**, travels back and forth across the surface of each platter, retrieving and storing data. Most hard drives have at least one head on the top and one on the bottom of each platter for storage on each side.

Storing Data on a Hard Drive

When a file is saved to the hard drive, the read/write head locates a spot on a platter. It then generates a magnetic field on the surface of the platter. The magnetic field records a string of 1s and 0s, or binary code, to generate the information a computer can read.

If the hard drive is damaged or if the read/write head changes the field in order to modify or delete the file, the magnetic field will not remain intact. A head crash, or the collision of a read/write head with the surface of the disk, could occur. If this were to happen, data could no longer be stored on the damaged sector of the drive.

Limitations of Hard Drives

The amount of information a hard drive can hold depends on several factors. One factor is the number of platters contained in the hard drive. The greater the number of platters, the more information a drive can store.

Another factor is the number of read/write heads. Generally, there is a read/write head for each side of each platter. However, sometimes one side of one platter will not have its own read/write head. That means information cannot be stored on that side.

EFFECTS OF PERFORMANCE The performance of your hard drive directly affects how fast your computer works. The faster the hard drive, the faster your computer will read and write data. Because the platters in a hard drive are rigid, they can spin at very high speeds. The platters in most hard drives can spin at a rate of 7,500 rpm (revolutions per minute), but some can spin at rates as high as 15,000 rpm.

SKALJAC/SHUTTERSTOCK

FIGURE 6.1.1 In a stack of platters, the same track creates a cylinder.

TECHNOLOGY@HOME

Natural disasters present a threat to computer information stored at home. Even if you backup your information using standard methods, back-ups typically are stored in the home and are likely to have suffered the effects of the disaster.

THINK ABOUT IT!

Choosing the right backup system can mean the difference between being able to retrieve lost information and never being able to find it. Which backup storage methods below might survive a fire at home?

- store in a home safe
- store in a drawer at work
- store next to the computer
- send as email attachments to a remote computer
- store on the hard drive in a different folder

HARD DRIVE SPEED A storage device's most important performance characteristic is the speed at which it locates the desired data. This is measured by its **access time**, the amount of time it takes for the device to begin reading the data. For hard drives, the access time includes the time it takes the read/write head to locate the data before reading begins.

The speed of storage devices varies considerably, but all storage devices are significantly slower than RAM. RAM speed is measured in nanoseconds, or billionths of a second. A storage device's speed is measured in milliseconds, or thousandths of a second.

HARD DRIVE CAPACITY The first PC hard drives held only about 10 MB of data and program instructions. Recent personal computers are available with hard drives with capacities up to 3 terabytes!

Alternative Storage Options

Manufacturers of computer chips are working to provide faster alternatives to magnetic storage.

SOLID STATE DISKS **Solid state disks** or drives, or SSDs, are a mass storage device similar to a hard disk drive. SSDs do not have any moving parts, like the hard drive's magnetic platters; they store data using flash memory. SSDs have better read performance because the data does not get fragmented into many locations, and, since they are not magnetic, SSDs do not lose data when next to a strong magnetic field.

SSDs do have disadvantages, though. They cost more per gigabyte, so people tend to buy SSDs with smaller capacity than most hard drives. Their limited number of write cycles means their performance declines over time. Yet, with improvements in SSD technology, these devices will advance, and their prices may come down.

FLASH MEMORY DEVICES Several types of storage devices using flash memory offer the speed of memory with the high capacity of a magnetic storage device. Flash memory drives work faster than magnetic drives, because they have no moving parts, and they do not require battery power to retain their data. Flash drives installed inside computers resemble magnetic hard drives in size and shape.

A **USB flash drive** is a portable, self-contained storage device that uses **flash memory**. In addition to portability, these drives offer the advantages of speed, capacity, and cost. A USB flash drive has a USB connector that plugs into the USB port on a computer; a flash memory chip that stores data; a USB mass storage controller that allows the computer to read, write, and erase data on the drive; and a crystal oscillator that controls the speed with which the drive works.

CONNECTIONS

MATHEMATICS In math class, you are accustomed to a system that combines ten possible digits, or numbers, in a certain order to represent larger numbers. In binary code, only 0 and 1 are used.

In math class, you carry a number over to the next column when numbers in a column add to 10 or more. With binary numbers, a number is carried if the items add to 2. In an eight-bit example, the number 35 would be written as 100011.

While numbers in math class refer to specific quantities, binary code numbers refer to specific actions. A 1 turns a circuit on, while a 0 turns a circuit off.

The electronic parts of the flash drive are protected by a hard plastic or metal case. The USB connector usually has a cover to protect it as well. Most USB flash drives have a light that comes on when the drive is plugged in. The drive may have a **write-protect switch**. When the switch is in the on position, the computer can read from the drive but cannot write to it or delete data from it.

Protecting Your Information

Computers store information about virtually every aspect of life. We use them to store school grades, lists of business contacts, names of registered voters, bank account balances, and many other kinds of crucial data. Since this information can be so important, computer users should be aware of data loss and protection.

DATA LOSS When a storage device experiences **data loss**, the data is damaged or made unusable. Storage devices and computers can also be lost, stolen, or destroyed, resulting in data loss. The data may be gone forever. It may be time-consuming or impossible to reconstruct the information that had been stored.

DATA PROTECTION One way to reduce the impact of data loss is to backup your data. Storing

information on removable storage media, which may be locked in high-security areas or stored at a different location, makes it difficult for people to steal the information, or to lose it due to a disaster such as fire, flood, or system failure. Many businesses use magnetic tape to backup large amounts of data, because it is relatively inexpensive and reliable. Some organizations hire storage service providers, or SSPs, to store data on off-site computers, and online storage is becoming increasingly popular.

Information can also be accidentally deleted, overwritten, or stolen by unauthorized users. One way to protect data is to apply password protection to a file or drive so only authorized users can access it, or to set a read-only property so the data may be read but cannot be changed. A **property** is a piece of data, sometimes called **metadata**, attached to or associated with a file, program, or device. Typical properties include name, type, storage location, and size. You can view and customize properties in the Properties dialog box.

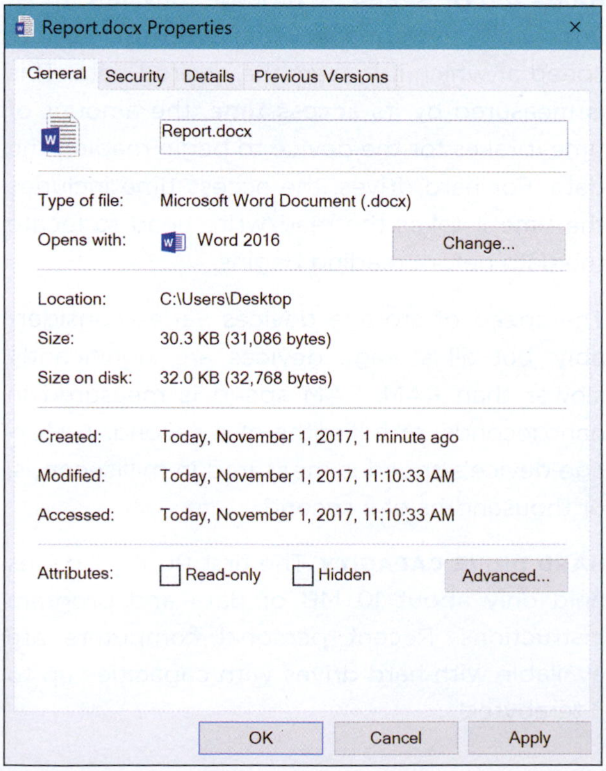

FIGURE 6.1.2 The Properties dialog box for a Microsoft Word document file.

Optical Storage Devices

OBJECTIVES

- Compare and contrast CD-ROM and DVD-ROM drives.

- Summarize how compact discs and digital video discs store data.

AS YOU READ

ORGANIZE INFORMATION Use a spider map to help you organize information about optical storage devices and how they work as you read.

TERMINOLOGY

- data transfer rate

- land

- laser sensor

- pit

CD-ROM and DVD-ROM Drives

Optical storage includes CD-ROM (compact disc read-only memory), DVD-ROM (digital video disc read-only memory), Blu-ray discs and similar storage devices. Optical storage media—the discs themselves—are easy to transport and can store large amounts of information. Many computers have built-in DVD or Blu-ray drives, or ports for connecting external drives. In part to distinguish optical media from magnetic media, some people prefer changing the spelling of disc (optical) to disk (magnetic).

COMPACT DISC MEDIA Optical drives are storage devices into which you insert a compact disc, or CD. When you look at an optical disc, it looks like a shiny, circular mirror. Optical discs are made up of three layers. The bottom layer is a clear plastic. The middle layer is a thin sheet of aluminum. The top layer is a lacquer coating that protects the disc from scratches and dust.

FIGURE 6.2.1 You can use a computer's built-in DVD or Blu-ray drive to install programs, watch movies, backup files, or play audio.

THINK ABOUT IT!

Which of the following businesses might need the storage capacity of DVDs to record their business transactions?

- graphic-arts firm
- insurance company
- dry cleaner
- auto repair shop
- grocery store

Reading Optical Information

All storage devices read information at a speed measured by the unit's **data transfer rate**, or the number of bits of data the device can transfer to memory or to another device in a single second. In DVD drives, the speed is measured in a multiple of 1,352.54 KB per second. A 2X drive transfers data at double speed, or 2,705.05 KB per second. Some drives transfer data at more than 21,000 KB per second.

LASER SENSORS Inside the optical drive is a **laser sensor**, which is a laser-operated tool that reads information. Optical drives read information by shining a laser on the disc in the drive. A laser sensor starts to read from the center of the disc's spirals and moves outward. The sensor notices changes in the physical properties of the disc and reads these changes as binary code: 0s and 1s.

LANDS AND PITS The surface of an optical disc stores data as a series of lands and pits. A **land** is a flat, reflective area on the surface of a disc. Lands reflect light from a laser's sensor and are recorded as a 1 by a computer. A **pit** is an indented area on the surface of a disc that scatters the light from a laser's sensor. Since no light is reflected by a pit, it is recorded as a 0. The binary code represents the information encoded on the surface of the disc.

Storing Optical Information

CD-ROM and DVD-ROM drives are read-only devices. CD-R, CD-RW, and DVD-RAM drives read *and* write information.

CD-R DRIVES These drives let you insert a blank recordable CD and then save data to it. After the information is stored, the disc's surface is changed so that the recorded information cannot be changed or erased.

CD-RW, DVD-RAM, AND DVD-R/RW Optical devices that let you record, change, or overwrite data multiple times are called read/write storage devices. For example, CD-RW, DVD-RAM, and DVD-R/RW drives provide read/write capabilities using erasable discs. The information on that disc can be deleted after it is written, and additional information can be added.

DID YOU KNOW?

In the first decade of this century, there was a battle for dominance between Blu-ray Disc™ or BD™ and HD DVD™ formats for DVD. At that time it was not known which of these formats would win out and be used by most high-definition DVD players.

In February 22, 2008, the battle ended when Toshiba announced it would stop manufacturing the HD DVD player. Both of the formats were invented to take the place of DVDs that didn't have enough storage for what is called "hi-def" video. Dual-layer BDs can hold up to 9 hours of HD video or 23 hours of standard definition (SD) video. Even though dual-layer HD DVDs held slightly more video than BDs, the Sony PlayStation 3 contained a BD player for primary storage, and that is how the war for market domination was won!

Storage Trends

OBJECTIVES

- List limitations of current storage technologies.

- Compare solid-state storage devices to magnetic and optical storage devices.

AS YOU READ

IDENTIFY KEY CONCEPTS Use a spider map to help you identify key concepts about future storage devices as you read.

TERMINOLOGY

- cloud computing

- data decay

- data integrity

- digital multilayer discs (DMDs)

- enterprise storage system

- friction

- holographic data storage system (HDSS)

- Redundant Array of Inexpensive Disks (RAID)

- slow retrieval

- storage area network (SAN)

- virtualization

Limitations of Storage Devices

All technologies change over time. Existing technologies evolve to become more efficient and meet changing needs, and new technologies emerge to solve problems and meet new needs. Technological breakthroughs have helped correct these common storage-device problems:

SLOW RETRIEVAL Tape devices are limited by **slow retrieval** speeds. Because devices must search from the beginning to the end of the tape to find the data, and magnetic tape cannot spin as fast as hard drives, it can take several minutes or even hours to locate information. Also, because tapes are usually stored in a remote location, you must first physically retrieve them.

DATA DECAY One limitation of current storage devices is the possibility of **data decay**, or the loss of information resulting from the gradual wearing down of a storage medium. Information stored on magnetic tapes and disks will, over time, become unusable. Air, heat, and humidity can break down the surface of magnetic storage media. As this breakdown occurs, the information stored may be lost. People once thought optical storage devices did not decay. However, studies have shown that user-recorded discs can lose information in as few as five to ten years. Factory-recorded, or pressed, compact discs may decay in 10 to 25 years. In addition to being vulnerable to gradual decay, magnetic storage devices can lose data in an instant if exposed to a strong magnetic field.

LLYA ANDRIYANOV/SHUTTERSTOCK

FIGURE 6.3.1 Time and environmental conditions can take their toll on any storage medium.

FRICTION As a magnetic tape travels through the tape heads, **friction** is created. This causes heat, which can stretch and burn a tape. Companies are trying to develop read/write heads that decrease this friction and preserve magnetic media.

Data Integrity

When information is stored, it must be maintained correctly. **Data integrity** means that stored information is usable and available in the location in which you expect to find it. Data integrity can be maintained using **Redundant Array of Inexpensive Disks (RAID)**.

RAID is a term used to describe a collection of drives or disks that run together to store data. For example, a computer using RAID may have two or more hard drives installed. The hard drives work together as one to read data from and write to the drive at the same time. This backup process ensures that copies of files can be retrieved in case one drive fails.

Enterprise Storage

Computers linked together by a cable or wireless medium are called networked computers. In a network environment, computers can share data using an **enterprise storage system**. This technology allows networked computers to access storage devices linked to the network, such as servers, RAID systems, tapes, and optical disc systems.

Cloud Computing

Cloud computing makes computers more efficient by using centralized storage, memory, and processing. **Cloud computing** uses the internet and central remote servers to host data and applications.

Virtualization

Like cloud computing, virtualization makes computers more efficient by using centralized storage, memory, and processing. **Virtualization** is when physical storage is pooled from multiple network storage devices into what seems to be one single storage device managed from a central console. Storage virtualization is usually used in a **storage area network (SAN)**, a network of storage devices that can be accessed by multiple computers. Many businesses use virtualization to consolidate many different servers onto one piece of physical hardware that then provides a simulated set of hardware to two or more operating systems. While cloud computing and virtualization are two distinct storage options, many cloud computing providers use virtualization in their data centers.

Future Trends

NEW MAGNETIC MEDIA In the future, by manipulating molecules and atoms, magnetic hard drives will store as much as 1 terabyte (TB) per square inch of disk space. That's an increase of 100 times the 10 gigabytes per square inch of current hard drives.

NEW OPTICAL MEDIA **Digital multilayer discs (DMDs)** contain multiple layers of a fluorescent material that stores information on each layer. A disc can hold up to 1 terabyte of data.

HOLOGRAPHIC MEDIA A **holographic data storage system (HDSS)** stores data in images called holograms on optical cubes the size of a sugar cube. These devices will hold more than 1 terabyte of storage and will be ten times faster than today's hard drives.

> ### TECHNOLOGY@WORK
>
> As more businesses use computers at work, the need for faster, more reliable, higher capacity storage devices is also on the rise.

> ### THINK ABOUT IT!
>
> Some businesses are storage-intensive while others require only basic components. The businesses listed below might benefit from a variety of storage technologies. Which would benefit more from new magnetic media? Which from DMD? Which from HDSS?
>
> - graphic-design company
> - school district
> - online catalog
> - hospital
> - airline

OLEKSIY MARK/SHUTTERSTOCK

FIGURE 6.3.2 Solid-state devices store large amounts of data, despite being very small.

Chapter 6 Review

REVIEW THE TERMINOLOY

DIRECTIONS Match each vocabulary term in the left column with the correct definition in the right column.

1. storage media
2. platter
3. writing
4. read/write head
5. access time
6. USB flash drive
7. SSD
8. data transfer rate
9. laser sensor
10. pit

a. amount of time it takes storage device to begin reading data

b. one of the disks in a hard drive

c. removable, portable storage device inserted into a USB slot

d. saving information on a storage medium

e. indentation on optical disc that does not reflect light

f. a mass storage device, similar to a hard disk drive that uses flash memory

g. needle-like device that retrieves and stores data on a magnetic disk

h. tool in optical drive that reads information

i. number of bits per second at which data is moved from a storage device to RAM

j. material that retains stored information saved by a computer storage device

USE THE TERMINOLOGY

DIRECTIONS Determine the correct choice for each of the following.

1. What type of media are used in a computer hard drive?
   a. magnetic
   b. optical
   c. solid state
   d. photo

2. What does the performance of a hard drive affect?
   a. if a read/write head can store data
   b. where a read/write head stores data
   c. how fast a computer reads and writes data
   d. the computer's memory

3. Which medium stores the least amount of information?

    a. DVD   **c.** hard drive

    b. CD   **d.** USB flash drive

4. Optical drives read information by using a _____.

    a. memory chip   **c.** laser sensor

    b. magnetic sensor   **d.** binary code

5. How many layers of material make up an optical disc?

    a. one   **c.** three

    b. two   **d.** four

6. Which of the following storage devices allow you to write data to a medium multiple times?

    a. CD-Rs   **c.** DVD-ROMs

    b. read/write storage devices   **d.** Blu-ray discs

THINK CRITICALLY

DIRECTIONS Answer the following questions.

1. Why are disks (and discs) considered secondary—and not primary—storage devices?

2. Why is it important to be sure data is protected and secure? Give an example of how you can keep your data safe.

3. What can happen if a read/write head is disturbed?

4. How are magnetic storage devices organized?

5. If USB flash drives and CD-Rs cost about the same per megabyte of storage, which do you think is more advantageous? Why?

EXTEND YOUR KNOWLEDGE

DIRECTIONS Choose and complete one of the following projects.

1. Find out the age and the storage capacity of the hard drive on the computer you use at school. By using computer ads or visiting a local retailer, find out what improvements have been made to hard drives currently on sale. What conclusions can you draw about today's computers?

2. Research evolving and emerging storage technologies. Take notes and keep track of your sources. What kinds of storage devices do you think computers will have in five to ten years? What trends, if any, do you predict? Present an oral report on the topic to your class.

SSUAPHOTOS/SHUTTERSTOCK

CHAPTER 7
Software Basics

WHAT IS AN OPERATING SYSTEM?

Have you ever wondered what happens when you turn on your computer? For many users, just seeing that the computer starts and that they can begin working is enough to meet their needs. But to become a more knowledgeable user, you should know how your computer works. One of the main behind-the-scenes contributors is the operating system.

The operating system is like the control center of your computer: it controls everything that happens with your computer. The operating system makes sure that files are stored properly on storage devices, software programs run properly, and instructions to peripherals are sent, among other jobs. Without an operating system, your computer would not be able to perform even basic tasks.

Introducing the Operating System

OBJECTIVES

- Explain what an operating system is and what it does.

- Identify types of operating systems.

- Explain the difference between an operating system version, update, and upgrade.

AS YOU READ

ORGANIZE INFORMATION Use a concept web to help you collect information about operating systems as you read.

TERMINOLOGY

- crash

- desktop

- graphical user interface (GUI)

- icon

- interface

- update

- upgrade

- versioning

What Operating Systems Do

An operating system (OS) is a set of instructions designed to work with a specific type of computer, such as Windows 10 for a PC or macOS for a Mac. The OS controls all the computer's functions. It also provides an **interface**, the on-screen tools you use to interact with the computer and your programs. The operating system performs several tasks:

- Manages the central processing unit (CPU) so that processing tasks are done properly

- Manages computer memory

- Manages files stored on the computer's disks

- Manages input and output devices

- Loads application programs into memory

AVOIDING CONFLICTS In most computers, especially personal computers, the operating system is stored on the hard drive. Before you can use the computer, a portion of the operating system must be loaded into memory. This is true of all programs; they may permanently reside on a disk but must be copied into RAM before you can use them.

Some operating systems enable a computer to run more than one program at a time. To do this, the operating system has to assign each program some space in RAM, and then protect that space. Otherwise, conflicts can occur when two programs try to occupy the same space in RAM. When this happens, one or both of the programs may **crash**, or stop working, until the conflict is resolved.

VERSIONING, UPDATES, AND UPGRADES When companies that develop operating system software add features, fix problems, or make improvements, they release new versions. Software **versioning**, as it is called, assigns numbers or names to each release so that developers, manufacturers, and users know exactly what operating system they are using. For example, release 1.0 might be the first version of the product. Release 1.1 might be an **update** that fixes problems such as bugs, security issues, and the ability to work with new hardware. Updates are usually delivered for free automatically over the internet. Release 2.0 might be an **upgrade** that introduces new features. Users wishing to upgrade must usually purchase the software.

IC3✔ Explain operating system versioning and the purpose of updates and upgrades.

Types of Operating Systems

All computers require an operating system. There are four kinds of operating systems.

REAL-TIME SYSTEMS Real-time operating systems are used to control large equipment, such as heavy machinery and scientific instruments, and to regulate factory operations. In order for these systems to run, they require very little user interaction.

SINGLE-USER/SINGLE-TASK SYSTEMS This kind of system lets one person do one task at a time. An example is the operating system that controls a handheld computer.

DID YOU KNOW?

If a printer or other device fails to respond to a request from the operating system, there is probably a problem with the connection, such as a loose cable or disabled network connection. If you try to print a document and nothing happens, check that the cables are correctly and firmly attached, the device is plugged in, and that the network is operating correctly. For a printer, of course, you should also check that there is paper in the paper feeder.

REAL-WORLD TECH
AN OPERATING SYSTEM—IN YOUR DOG?

Robots are devices that can move and react to input from sight, hearing, touch, and balance. How are those "senses" and those reactions controlled? Through an operating system, of course! Robots are used to explore outer space and to do factory jobs.

ILTERRIORM/SHUTTERSTOCK

Now, however, they're also available as pets. Some robotic "dogs" can learn their own name and your name. They can show joy, anger, and surprise through lights, sounds, and gestures.

For what purposes do you think robots would be useful or fun?

SINGLE-USER/MULTITASKING SYSTEMS A multitasking system allows the computer to perform several jobs, either one after the other or at the same time. For example, you could use your computer to write a letter as it downloads a video from the internet and prints a letter. Most desktop and laptop computers today use this kind of system. Windows and macOS are examples of this type of operating system.

MULTI-USER SYSTEMS These systems allow many individuals to use one large computer. The OS balances all the tasks that the various users ask the computer to do. UNIX® is an example of this type of operating system.

Operating Systems for Mobile Devices

Mobile devices such as smartphones and tablets are computers and therefore need an operating system to run properly. However, they cannot just use a PC's operating system, like Windows or Linux. Mobile operating systems have been designed to maximize the efficiency of a smaller touchscreen, limited memory, and limited storage capacity. They are optimized to use wireless networks and to provide access to the specific apps most people expect from their mobile devices. Smartphones actually contain two operating systems: one that supports the user's software and one that operates the phone's hardware. Three common mobile device operating systems are Apple's iOS, Microsoft's Windows Phone, and Google's Android.

The User Interface

The operating system's user interface lets you start programs, manage disks and files, and shut down the computer safely. To start the OS, you turn the computer on. During the startup procedure, the OS places part of itself into the computer's memory.

DESKTOP Nowadays, computer operating systems are based on visual displays. The **graphical user interface**, or GUI (*GOOee*), lets you use a pointing device to interact with the workspace on the computer screen, called a **desktop**.

TECHNOLOGY@SCHOOL

Fingerprint identification programs allow scanned fingerprints to be matched to electronic fingerprints stored in the computer.

THINK ABOUT IT!

For which activities below do you believe such a fingerprint identification system would be an advantage at school?

- paying for a school lunch
- checking out a library book
- taking attendance
- turning in homework
- accessing computer files

ICONS On the screen, pictures called **icons** or tiles represent resources on the computer, such as a program, a document, a hardware device, or a website. You select an icon or tile to perform an action, such as starting a program or opening a file.

OPTIONS You can use the operating system to customize some features of the desktop, such as the look of the background or the placement of the icons. You can also change how other components work, such as keyboard functions and the speed at which the cursor blinks on the screen. Use the documentation that came with your system or the Help program to explore these options.

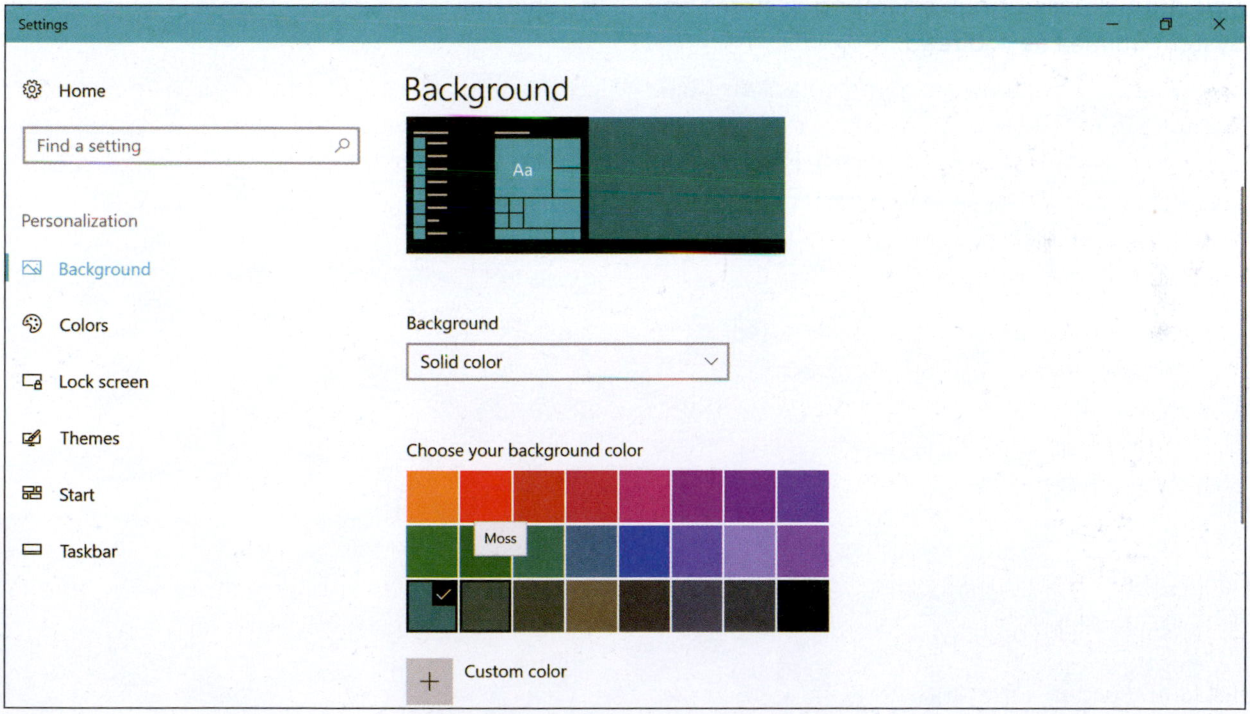

MICROSOFT CORPORATION

FIGURE 7.1.1 You can change the Background settings in Windows 10.

Operating Systems and Utilities

OBJECTIVES

- Examine different operating systems.

- Discuss the function of the file manager in an operating system.

- Describe how system utilities help operating systems function.

AS YOU READ

OUTLINE INFORMATION Use an outline to help you note details about operating systems and system utilities as you read.

TERMINOLOGY

- backup utility

- driver utility

- file compression utility

- install

- Plug and Play (PnP)

- reinstall

- system image

- uninstall

Popular Operating Systems

The first widely-used operating system for personal computers was called MS-DOS. It was developed in the early 1980s by Microsoft for IBM-compatible PCs. Now, three operating systems dominate the computer world—Microsoft Windows®, macOS, and UNIX. The computer you use at school or at home probably has a version of Windows or macOS installed. UNIX, and adaptations of it, is most often found running on large business or scientific networks.

MACOS X® In 1984, Apple® became the first computer maker to sell consumers a personal computer equipped with a GUI. *Macintosh* names both the computer and its operating system. Easy for beginners to use, some version of macOS runs all Macintosh computers.

MICROSOFT WINDOWS The Windows OS is currently the market leader, installed on more than 90 percent of personal computers. Early versions of Windows were based on MS-DOS. In fact, Windows 98 was the last version of Windows based on MS-DOS.

THINK ABOUT IT!

Which items below are represented by an icon on a home computer?

- music files
- email
- internet browser
- printer
- text files
- antivirus software

UNIX AND LINUX™ UNIX was one of the first operating systems ever written. It was designed to work on powerful business and scientific computers. Later versions of UNIX have been developed to work on personal computers.

One of these versions of UNIX is Linux. Linux works with an optional GUI and is very fast compared to other operating systems. It is also unique in that it is an open source operating

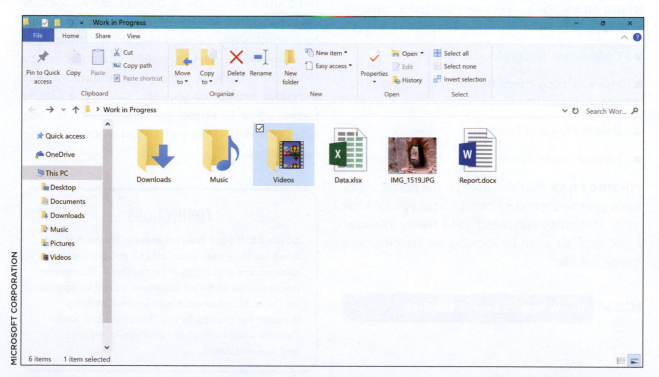

FIGURE 7.2.1 Use an operating system such as Windows to organize and manage files and folders.

system, in which the source code used to create it is available to the public. Programmers from across the globe constantly work on Linux to test and improve it. Linux is free and can be downloaded from the internet, but most users buy it with other features. Though Apple and Microsoft dominate the market of OS for personal computers, Linux claims a share of the web client OS market.

System Utilities: File Management

Utility software is a collection of programs that help you maintain and repair your computer. Today, many types of utilities are built into the operating system. Probably the most important utilities are file managers, which let you work with data stored on your computer.

ORGANIZING FILES The operating system, programs, and data are all stored in files, each with a name. Files can be grouped together into folders. Folders are also called directories. A folder can be divided into subfolders.

USING FILES You can use an operating system's file manager to perform several tasks:

- Create new folders or subfolders
- Move or copy items between folders or to other disks
- Delete files and folders
- Launch applications

FINDING FILES You can use the file finder utility from your operating system to help you look for a file. This utility can search for a file by its name, type, date, or even by looking for specific data inside the file.

 Know how to search for files.

System Utilities: Other Jobs

Your operating system probably has utilities that can help with routine maintenance and other jobs.

DRIVER UTILITIES A **driver utility** contains data needed by programs to operate input and output devices such as a mouse and printer. Operating systems that have **Plug and Play (PnP)** capability can automatically detect new PnP-compatible devices. Otherwise, you can download the files from the device manufacturer's website, or use the installation CD/DVD.

PROGRAM UTILITIES Before you can use a program, you must **install** it on your hard drive. In Windows, you can use the Add/Remove Programs utility to ensure that your program installs properly. You can use the same utility to **uninstall**, or remove, a program you no longer need, or to **reinstall** a program that is not working the way you want.

BACKUP UTILITIES **Backup utility** programs automatically copy data from the computer's hard drive to a backup storage device, such as an external hard drive or a CD. Operating systems usually include a backup utility such as Windows 10's File History. You can set the utility to automatically backup files on a schedule, or you can backup files manually. You can create a full system backup, which is sometimes called a **system image**, or you can select the files to backup. For example, you can select to only backup files that have changed since the previous backup.

CONNECTIONS

SCIENCE If your science teachers have not yet done so, they may soon add to your computer a microscope and a driver to control it. Computer microscopes allow an enlarged image to appear on the monitor or on a wall screen, making it easier for groups to see. Students can also capture images to study and use in reports and presentations.

Businesses and individuals routinely use backup utilities to ensure data is not lost if a computer or disk drive fails. You, too, should regularly backup your computer data. By maintaining a regular backup schedule and by keeping incremental versions of backed up files, you minimize the risk of losing data. Some operating systems, including Windows and macOS, automatically save previous versions of files that you change. You can open and save the previous version if the current version becomes damaged or unusable. This is another way of avoiding data loss.

IC3✔ **Know how to backup and restore files on a Windows 10 computer.**

FILE COMPRESSION UTILITIES **File compression utilities** are programs that reduce the size of files without harming the data. These programs make it easier to copy and transmit files because it is easier to transmit a smaller, compressed file.

Most email programs have size limits for transmitting and receiving messages. Operating systems such as Windows come with a built-in file compression utility you can use to compress—or zip—one or more files or folders. Select the items, select the Share tab, and then select Zip on the Ribbon. The zipped file has a .zip file extension.

IC3✔ **Know how zip (compress) files and folders.**

GLOBAL SETTINGS Operating systems also manage global settings for features such as privacy and storage. For example, global settings may be used to control access from outside sources, such as whether an online game can store a score on your computer.

IC3✔ **Differentiate between applications, operating system, and global settings.**

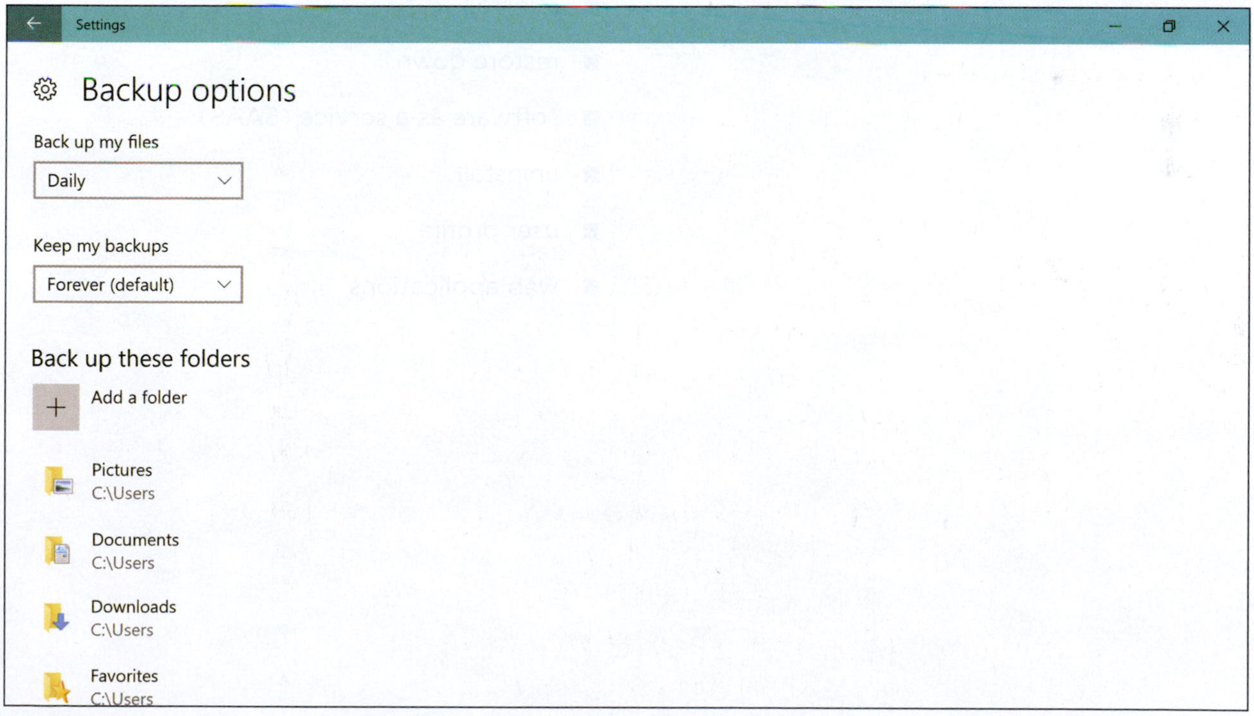

FIGURE 7.2.2 Use a backup utility such as Windows 10's File History to schedule automatic backups.

Application Basics

OBJECTIVES

- Explain how to install, uninstall, update, and repair applications.
- Demonstrate how to manage application windows.
- Explore software preferences.

AS YOU READ

IDENTIFY KEY POINTS As you read, use a conclusion chart to help you identify key points about application software.

TERMINOLOGY

- application software
- customer relationship management (CRM)
- default
- discussion board
- launch
- learning management system (LMS)
- local applications
- maximize
- minimize
- preferences
- reinstall
- restore down
- software as a service (SAAS)
- uninstall
- user profile
- web applications

What Is an Application?

Application software performs a specific job or task. There are thousands of applications available for everything from playing games to managing human resources information for large corporations. Some common types of application software include:

■ Word processors for writing letters and reports

■ Spreadsheets for working with numbers and doing math

■ Databases for storing and finding information

■ Presentation graphics for creating slide shows

■ Desktop publishing for creating printer-ready publications such as brochures, newsletters, and invitations

■ Telecommunications for using the internet and email

■ **Personal information manager (PIM)** programs for storing phone numbers and addresses and creating schedules

The type of application software you choose depends on what you want it to do, how much you are willing to spend, and how easy the programs are to learn. It also depends on whether the software is compatible with your device or computer system. You might want to match the software you use at home with the programs you use at school so you can work on documents in both locations.

Installing, Reinstalling, Uninstalling, and Updating Software

Before you can use an application you must set it up to run on your computer. Installing software makes a program ready for use. You install **local applications** on a local storage device such

as the hard drive on a PC or flash memory on a smartphone. Locally-installed applications may be called desktop applications, perpetual applications, or non-subscription applications. The installation process involves copying the program files from a location such as an installation disk or downloading them from the internet.

To delete a program that has been installed, you must run a special removal program to properly **uninstall** it. Otherwise, parts of the program can remain on the computer and may interfere with its operation. You can **reinstall** the program if you need it again, or run a repair utility to fix problems.

Recall that companies release software updates to keep the program current, fix errors, or resolve issues such as compatibility with hardware or security risks. Updates are usually available to registered users free of charge. You can set your programs to automatically check for, download, and install updates, or to notify you when updates are available so you can download and install them manually. In rare cases, the company might issue an update disk and provide the update files in a format that can be downloaded to storage media, such as a CD or DVD. In that case, you can use the storage media to update the software.

IC3✔ Know how to install, uninstall, update, and repair software using local media or the internet.

Web Applications

Web applications, which may be called online or cloud applications, are not copied to the local storage device. The files reside on a web server and the program runs in a web browser, such as Chrome or Edge. Some web applications may have an interface installed locally, but the program files remain stored on the server, and all processing occurs on the server.

Many web apps are available for a variety of platforms, such as smartphone, tablet, or PC. However, there may be slight variations in the interface and features depending on the platform on which you install the app. For example, a web app downloaded to a smartphone will be designed for the size and shape of the phone screen. A web app downloaded to a tablet will be designed for the size and shape of the tablet screen. Microsoft Word installed on your phone may not have all the features it has when you install it on your desktop PC.

Some common web apps include online email services, such as Gmail and Outlook on the web, social networking sites, such as Facebook and Twitter, and office applications, such as Google Docs, iWorks for iCloud, and Office Online. Businesses, such as a large insurance company, may have a cloud-based, database-driven **customer relationship management (CRM)** system for managing customer data and interactions. Examples include Insightly, Nimble, ProsperWorks, Apptivo CRM, Salesforce Sales Cloud Lightning Professional, and Zoho CRM.

Discussion boards, which allow registered users to exchange text comments, are also a type of web app. They may also be called web forums or message boards. Usually, they are focused on a specific topic and may even be set up by companies to make it easy for customers to comment, ask questions, and get help. For example, Microsoft has many discussion boards that Office users access to learn more about how to use their programs.

IC3 ✔ | Understand web app types, including online storage apps, online office apps, and CRM apps.

IC3 ✔ | Know the difference between apps designed to run in a browser or on a tablet, smartphone, or PC.

You must have an internet connection to use a web application. Most web applications require that you have a subscription for the service. This usually means that you pay an annual or monthly fee and set up an account with the vendor. You sign in to your account in order to access the program. This type of computing is often called **software as a service (SAAS)**.

IC3 ✔ | Know the difference between locally installed applications and software as a service.

A **learning management system (LMS)** is a type of web app used to deliver online education courses to students. It is also used to organize and manage the content, to track progress, and to generate reports. The LMS resides on a server either on a school's network or on the internet. Teachers, students, and administrators log in using a secure account.

IC3 ✔ | Know what learning management systems (LMS) do.

Managing Program Windows

When a computer is turned on, it typically starts its operating system. You can then **launch**, or start, any application installed on the computer. A launched application appears in a frame called a window. You can work in any size window, but it is usually best to **maximize** the window, or make it as large as it can be. To resize a window, you usually drag a window border or corner. In most programs, you can **restore down** a maximized window, which returns it to the size and position it had before you maximized it.

Sometimes you will want to use another program without closing the first one. You can resize the program window by dragging its borders, or **minimize** it to make it as small as possible so it remains out of the way while you use the other program. Programs running on a Windows system display buttons in the upper-right corner of the window for maximizing, minimizing, and restoring down the window. Minimized windows display as a button on the taskbar. You select the button to restore the minimized window to its previous size and position.

> **IC3✔ Know how to resize, maximize, minimize, and restore down a window.**

Setting Software Preferences

Software applications start using **default** settings. These are options preset by the software maker, based on what most users prefer. You can customize the program for the way you want to work by selecting **preferences** or options. Changing an option or preference replaces the default setting.

You can change such features as how the screen looks, how the spelling checker works, the frequency for automatically saving files, the preferred location for saving documents, and the way the document prints. You can choose to apply a preference to a current document only, or save it in the computer as a new default setting.

Many programs also allow you to reset the revised default settings back to their original settings. To set options in a Microsoft Office program, select File and then select Options.

> **IC3✔ Know how to set software preferences such as AutoSave, font sizes, print settings, and File Options.**

On a system shared by multiple people, each user account is associated with a **user profile**. The profile includes settings such as software preferences and operating system customizations. When the user logs in, the profile settings load, so the user sees the desktop picture he or she selected and the prefered color scheme, and programs run the way he or she wants. When another user logs in, the user's profile settings load.

> **IC3✔ Know how user profiles affect the operating environment.**

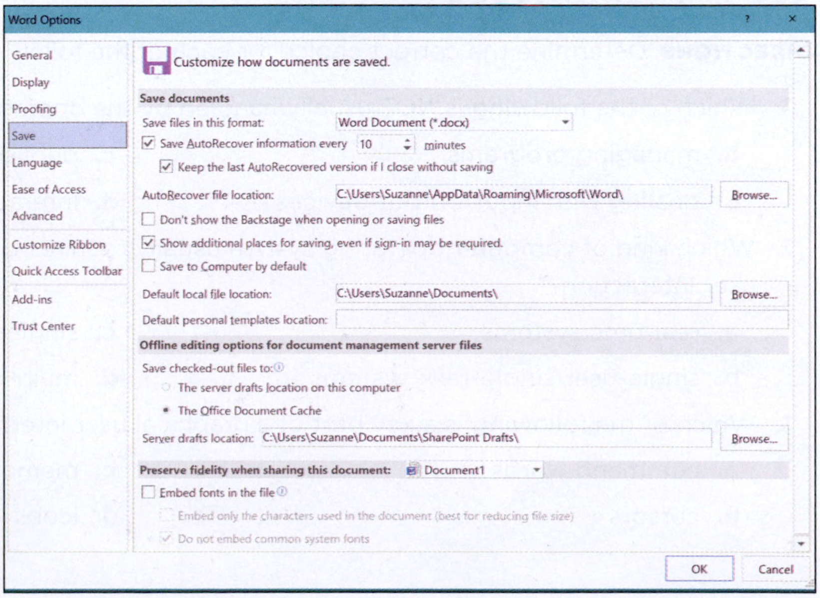

FIGURE 7.3.1 Use the Options dialog box to customize Microsoft Office application settings.

MICROSOFT CORPORATION

Chapter 7 Review

REVIEW THE TERMINOLOGY

DIRECTIONS Match each vocabulary term in the left column with the correct definition in the right column.

1. interface
2. crash
3. graphical user interface
4. desktop
5. icon
6. driver utility
7. Plug and Play
8. backup utility
9. file compression utility

a. area on a computer screen where you perform work

b. to stop working

c. program that controls input/output devices

d. picture that represents something on a computer

e. on-screen tools that let you use the computer

f. program that copies a file onto another medium

g. lets you use a mouse to work with the computer

h. capable of detecting compatible devices

i. reduces file size without harming data

USE THE TERMINOLOGY

DIRECTIONS Determine the correct choice for each of the following.

1. Which of the following is NOT usually handled by the operating system?
   a. managing programs
   b. dealing with input/output devices
   c. publishing web pages
   d. interacting with the user

2. Which kind of computer operating system usually requires the least amount of user interaction?
   a. real-time systems
   b. single-user/single-task systems
   c. single-user/multitask systems
   d. multi-user systems

3. Which of the following is a key part of a graphical user interface?
   a. command words
   b. cursors
   c. memory
   d. icons

4. Which operating system is found most often on large business and scientific computers?

   a. Microsoft Windows   c. UNIX

   b. macOS   d. Linux

5. Which of the following do operating systems, application programs, and user data have in common?

   a. They are all system utilities.   c. They are all created by the user.

   b. They are all Windows-based.   d. They are all stored in files.

6. What kind of utility is used to reduce the size of a file?

   a. driver utility   c. backup utility

   b. program utility   d. file compression utility

THINK CRITICALLY

DIRECTIONS Answer the following questions.

1. What are the major functions of an operating system?

2. What effect do you think the development of graphical user interfaces had on the number of people using computers? Why?

3. Pick one operating system component such as disk operations, GUI, or hardware drivers and explain its purpose.

4. What is the purpose of an operating system update?

5. Identify at least three reasons for backing up files.

6. What are some differences between a web app running on a tablet or smartphone, versus a local program on a desktop PC?

7. What are the benefits of storing software preferences for each individual user of a device?

EXTEND YOUR KNOWLEDGE

DIRECTIONS Choose and complete one of the following projects.

1. Go to Help in a Microsoft Windows operating system. Find out how it is organized, but make no changes to the system settings. Follow the same process on a Macintosh computer. Which Help section was easier to use? Provide reasons for your preference. Discuss your conclusions as a class.

2. Find ads in computer magazines or on the web that are sponsored by companies that sell backup and file compression utilities. Make a chart to summarize the features of three products in each category. Note which operating system each product works with and its price. Create a word-processing document in which you summarize your findings. Name and save the document using proper file management techniques. With your teacher's permission, print the document. Read it out loud with a partner or to the class.

3. With your teacher's permission, use the internet to research two or three operating systems for mobile devices. As you work, take notes and keep track of your sources. Evaluate the information you find and only use it if it is accurate, relevant, and valid. Create a column chart comparing and contrasting the operating systems. Share the chart with a partner or with the class.

4. Make a column chart to compare and contrast the benefits and limitations of backing up files to the cloud, a network share, a portable hard drive, a CD or DVD, a USB drive, and the local computer.

IC3 PREP

1. Which of the following operating system versions likely represents a major upgrade? (Select all that apply.)

   a. 2.0

   b. 3.1

   c. 5.0

   d. 1.1

   e. 4.0

2. What parameters can the file finder utility in your operating system generally use to search for a specific file? (Select all that apply.)

   a. file name

   b. file type

   c. date of last use/creation

   d. specific file data

   e. all of the above

3. For each line below, select whether the statement is True or False.

   a. A backup utility such as Windows 10's File History cannot be automated to backup files on a schedule.

   b. Some operating systems automatically save previous versions of files that you change.

   c. A full system backup is sometimes called a "system image."

   d. Maintaining a regular backup schedule of your computer data allows you to recover versions of files that have been corrupted or otherwise altered.

   e. Backup utilities are used only by large businesses, never individuals.

4. You have been instructed to compress several files into a zipped file on your Windows 10 device. Put the following steps in order for completing the process.

   a. Select the Share tab.

   b. Select the items to compress.

   c. Select Zip on the ribbon.

5. Which of the following is a reason to zip (compress) files? (Select all that apply.)

   a. to make transmitting the file faster

   b. to make it easier to find the file using the Search command

   c. to make the data in the file difficult for hackers to read

   d. to meet email size limits

6. For each line below, select whether the statement is True or False.

    a. Installing or reinstalling data for local applications can be done using files located on physical storage, or downloaded from the internet.

    b. It is always safe to delete a local application without running a removal program to uninstall it.

    c. You can often set programs to automatically check for, download, and install updates, or to notify you when updates are available to be manually downloaded and installed.

7. Which of the following are examples of web apps?

    a. Google Docs

    b. Outlook

    c. Microsoft Windows

    d. Zoho CRM

8. What are some true statements about software as a service? (Select all that apply.)

    a. You must set up some sort of account with the vendor of said service.

    b. Use of the software generally involves a recurring payment system.

    c. SAAS can almost always be used without connecting to the internet.

    d. SAAS applications generally run entirely off one's own device.

9. For each line below, select whether the statement is True or False.

    a. An application can be launched without turning on the computer it is on.

    b. You can restore a minimized window by selecting its button on the Windows taskbar.

    c. To resize a window, you usually drag a window's border or corner.

    d. Maximizing a window makes it fill the entire screen.

10. Which of the following are common examples of software preferences? (Select all that apply.)

    a. font size

    b. print settings

    c. save file preferences (save directory, file type, etc.)

    d. amount of installed RAM

IC3 PROCEDURES

CONFIGURING BACKUP SETTINGS ON A WINDOWS 10 COMPUTER

1. Select the **Start** button 🪟.

2. Select **Settings** ⚙.

3. Select **Update & Security**.

4. Select **Backup**.

5. Select **Add a drive**, and then choose an external drive or network location for your backups.

ZIPPING FILES AND FOLDERS IN WINDOWS 10

1. Open **File Explorer** 📁.

2. Click the file you want to compress to select it, or select multiple files.

3. Click **Share** and then click the **Zip** button.

4. Enter a new name for the zipped folder, if desired.

EXTRACTING COMPRESSED FILES

1. In File Explorer, click to select the zipped folder.

2. Click the **Compressed Folders Tools Extract** tab.

3. Click the **Extract all** button 🗄.

4. If necessary, select the file(s) you want to extract.

5. Click **Extract**.

SEARCHING FOR FILES AND FOLDERS

1. Open **File Explorer** 📁.

2. Select the drive or folder you want to search.

3. In the search box at the top right of the window, enter the name, or part of the name of the file or folder you want to find.

4. Press **Enter**.

MINIMIZING A WINDOW

Select the **Minimize** button − in the top right of the window.

OR

Press the **Windows** key and the down arrow key on your keyboard twice.

MAXIMIZING A WINDOW

Select the **Maximize** button ☐ in the top-right corner of a window that is not currently maximized.

OR

Press the **Windows** key and the up arrow key on your keyboard.

RESIZING A WINDOW

1. Position the mouse pointer over the window border.

2. Press and hold the left mouse button and then drag the border.

RESTORING DOWN A WINDOW

Select the **Restore Down** button ❐ in the top-right corner of a window that is currently maximized.

CONFIGURING PRINT SETTINGS FOR AN OFFICE APPLICATION

1. Start the Office application.

2. Select **File**.

3. Select **Print**.

4. Select the printer and other settings as desired.

5. Select **Print**.

CREATING A SYSTEM IMAGE

1. Select the Search bar on the Windows Taskbar.

2. Type **Control Panel** and select the top choice labeled **Control Panel**.

3. Select **Backup and Restore (Windows 7)** under the **System and Security** section.

4. Select **Create a system image** from the left-hand side.

5. Select the location where you would like to save the image, select **Next**.

6. Select **Start backup**.

INSTALLING A PROGRAM IN WINDOWS 10

1. Access the website in your browser and select the **Download** link.

   OR

   Insert the CD or DVD into your computer's storage drive.

2. When prompted, select **Run**.

3. Follow the prompts to complete the installation.

UNINSTALLING A PROGRAM IN WINDOWS 10

1. Select the Search bar on the Windows Taskbar.

2. Type **Uninstall**.

3. Select **Add or remove programs**.

4. Select the program to uninstall.

5. Select the **Uninstall** button.

6. Select **Uninstall**.

7. Follow the prompts to complete the process.

REPAIRING A PROGRAM IN WINDOWS 10

1. Select the Search bar on the Windows Taskbar.

2. Type **Repair**.

3. Select **Add or remove programs**.

4. Select the program to repair.

5. Select the **Modify** button.

6. Select **Repair**.

7. Select **Next**.

8. Follow the prompts to complete the process.

CHAPTER 8

Understanding Software

WHAT IS THE PURPOSE OF AN OPERATING SYSTEM?

When you use a computer program, most of the activity you see on the screen is conducted by the operating system. An application, such as a word processor, asks the operating system to perform actions, such as opening a file, printing a document, or showing a list of recently used documents.

To fulfill these requests, the operating system needs to know how to handle different file formats, or standards used to save data on a disk. Those formats determine how text documents, graphics, audio, and video files are stored and used. In this chapter, you will learn more about what the functions are that the operating system and its utilities perform, and how you use them.

Exploring the Operating System

OBJECTIVES

- Summarize the boot process.

- Describe the features of a graphical user interface.

- Use menus and dialog boxes.

- Explain how operating systems can be configured and changed.

AS YOU READ

ORGANIZE INFORMATION Use a concept web to help you collect information about operating systems as you read.

TERMINOLOGY

- boot

- check box

- CMOS

- dialog box

- drop-down menu

- hibernate mode

- list box

- lock screen

- monitoring software

- multiple selection list

- password

- pop-up menu

- power-on self test (POST)

- radio button

- Ribbon

- sleep mode

- social engineering

- system administrator

- task pane

- theme

- Trojan

- user account

- username

- user rights

- window

Loading the Operating System

The operating system, or OS, controls the computer and manages its work. The OS also provides an interface that enables you to interact with the computer.

THE BOOT PROCESS When you turn the computer on, you **boot** it. That is, you start the computer, and it responds by loading the operating system. If your computer is set to show it, the first thing you see is the BIOS screen. Recall that *BIOS* stands for basic input/output system, and it manages and configures the computer's hardware. This means that the computer will be able to accept input from the keyboard and display information.

THE POWER-ON SELF TEST As a computer boots, it performs a series of tests called the **power-on self test (POST)**. During POST, the BIOS or UEFI (Unified Extensible Firmware Interface) checks the major components of the system, such as its memory, keyboard, and hard drive. It does this in part by reading information stored on the **CMOS** chip. CMOS, which stands for Complementary Metal-Oxide Semiconductor, is a battery-powered memory chip on the motherboard that stores information about the computer components.

If there is a problem during start up, a written message or a sound alerts you. If this happens, the computer may need repair. If no problem is detected, parts of the operating system are loaded from storage into memory and take control of the computer.

THE LOGIN As the operating system starts, you may see a screen that asks you for a username and password. This is called the login screen. Businesses and schools often use this process to control who has access to the computer.

CONNECTIONS

THE ARTS CRT monitors can be damaged if the same image stays on the monitor for an extended period of time. A screen saver is a utility designed to protect the monitor by continuously changing the image it displays. Most screen savers use an animated effect, such as flying graphics or product logos, or imaginative shapes that build themselves piece by piece on the screen. On LCD monitors, screen savers are used for fun instead of for protection.

Screen savers are created by talented artists, using sophisticated digital drawing and animation tools. These artists need to know more than just how to draw; they need to know how to create effective, small-scale animations that will work under a specific operating system.

Exploring the GUI

When the operating system is loaded into RAM, it displays the desktop provided by the graphical user interface, or GUI. The desktop is where all work is done, including opening and closing programs, modifying system settings, and managing files. Icons on the desktop allow you to launch programs by selecting them. You also can select Start (on a PC) or Finder (on a Macintosh) and then the name of the program you want. A taskbar on the desktop identifies which programs or files are open. To switch back and forth among applications, just select what you want to work on next.

NAVIGATING WITH MENUS Recall that programs and documents display in **windows**, or rectangular, on-screen frames that can be opened, closed, resized, and rearranged. Each window displays commands and options that you select to tell the program what you want to do. Most programs use a combination of drop-down menus (sometimes called pull-down menus) and buttons to present commands. Sometimes menus have submenus with additional commands. In Microsoft Office, commands are on the **Ribbon**, a series of tabs at the top of the window. Each tab has a group of related commands for specific tasks. There is also a Quick Access Toolbar at the top of the application window. You can add and remove buttons so it displays commands you use frequently.

IC3✔ **Know how to add a command to the Microsoft Office Quick Access Toolbar.**

Pop-up menus, or lists of shortcut commands that appear when an area of the screen is selected or right-clicked or the mouse button is held down, can appear anywhere in a window. Pop-up menus can be context-sensitive, providing options that relate to tasks you are doing at that moment.

DIALOG BOX OPTIONS Sometimes when you choose a command, a **dialog box** or **task pane** displays. Dialog boxes and task panes provide options that let you customize the command. Often, you can set several options at the same time. Some of the ways you select options in a dialog box are:

- **Radio buttons**. Radio buttons which may be called option buttons, are small circles to the left of each item in a list of options. The selected item has a small dot inside the radio button. Only one option in the list can be selected.

- **Check box**. Check boxes are small squares to the left of each item in a list of options. Selected check boxes are marked with an X. Usually multiple options in the list can be selected.

- **List box**. A list box is a scrollable list of choices. You can select one item in the list. The selected item usually displays in a box at the top of the list.

- **Multiple selection list**. A multiple-selection list box is also a scrollable list of choices, but each choice has a check box. You can select multiple items in the list by selecting multiple check boxes.

DID YOU KNOW?

Today, a number of operating systems on computers and other devices use voice recognition, which allows you to say, for example, "Computer, start word processing," or "Computer, check email," and the computer will know what you mean. However, you must know the right commands. If you say, "Ditch that file," instead of "Delete that file," the computer will not know how to process the command.

- **Drop-down menu**. A drop-down, or pull-down menu, displays one option, with a downward pointing arrow or other icon next to it. When you select the icon, a menu drops down. When you select an option from the menu the menu closes, and the selected option displays.

IC3✔ **Know how to use menus and dialog boxes.**

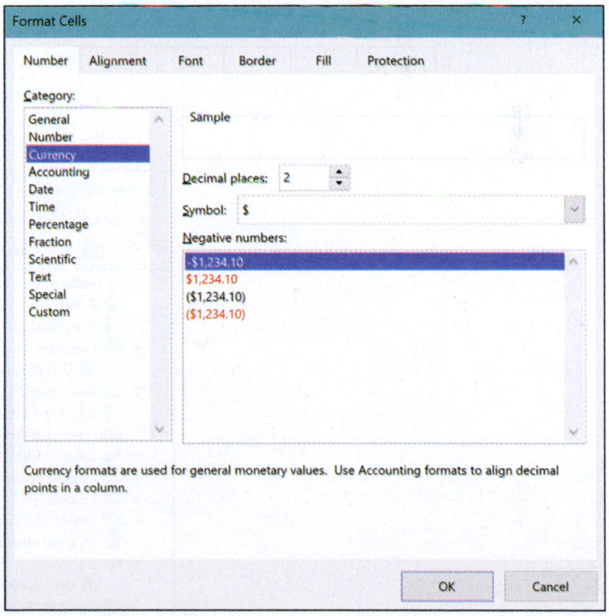

MICROSOFT CORPORATION

FIGURE 8.1.1 Many programs have dialog boxes you use to select options, such as number formats in a spreadsheet.

Exploring Configuration Options

Computer systems come in many different configurations. In order for an operating system to work correctly on every computer it must be flexible. The two most common tools an operating system uses to adapt to different requirements are drivers and system preferences.

- Drivers are software programs that let the OS work with different devices and peripherals. Some basic drivers for common devices such as a keyboard and a mouse are built into the operating system. Other drivers you install when you connect a device. The Windows Update feature in the Windows operating system keeps most drivers up-to-date by automatically downloading and installing compatible device drivers when they become available. You can also use the Windows Device Driver utility to check if a driver is compatible with a device, and to update it if necessary.

IC3 ✔ **Know how to use Device Manager in Windows 10 to check for and update compatible device drivers.**

- System preferences let the user select options for controlling and customizing options, such as the appearance of the user interface or how the computer will shut down. In Windows, you use the Control Panel to access the customization options. On a Mac, you use the System Preferences command.

POWER OPTIONS You can usually set options to control the way a computer uses power. This is particularly important when you use a system such as a tablet or notebook that relies on a battery. Using more power might increase performance, but it also drains the battery faster and costs more on your energy bill. Some operating systems, such as Windows, have built-in power plans designed for maximum performance, maximum energy conservation, or a balance.

POWER STATES You know your computer can be on or off. It can also be sleeping or hibernating. In **sleep mode**, which may be called standby, power is shut off to non-essential components. Some power is used and data remains in RAM. In

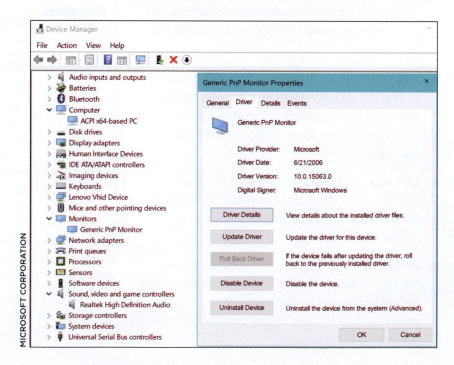

FIGURE 8.1.2 Use the Device Manager in Windows to manage device drivers.

MICROSOFT CORPORATION

OFFERING A FREE OPERATING SYSTEM

JAROSLAV MACHACEK/SHUTTERSTOCK

As discussed, the operating system Linux® is based on a powerful scientific system called UNIX®. Linux is freeware, or open-source software, which means programmers can freely modify its code. To help expand computer use in schools in Mexico, Miguel de Icaza, while still in his 20s, developed GNOME, one of the Windows-based, easy-to-use desktop graphical user interfaces for Linux.

What are some of the advantages and disadvantages of a freeware operating system?

hibernate mode, data from RAM is saved to the hard disk and then power is shut down.

Most operating systems let you select options for entering sleep mode or powering down the display after a set period of inactivity. On a tablet or notebook, you might also be able to change the function of the Power button. Options include doing nothing, powering down, sleeping, or hibernating. Some operating systems automatically lock the system after a set period of inactivity. A **lock screen** displays until you enter a password or PIN number to unlock the system to regain access. You can usually manually lock the system, as well. For example, in Windows, press Win Key + L to display the lock screen.

Changing system settings lets you customize your computer, but it can also cause your computer to malfunction. Most operating systems have a feature that lets you restore settings to a previous configuration.

IC3✔ Know how to configure power management and power settings.

FIGURE 8.1.3 The Power & Sleep Settings in Windows 10.

MICROSOFT CORPORATION

Settings

- ⚙ Home
- Find a setting
- System
  - 🖵 Display
  - 🖵 Notifications & actions
  - ⏻ Power & sleep
  - 🔋 Battery
  - 🖴 Storage
  - 📱 Tablet mode
  - 🗔 Multitasking
  - 🖥 Projecting to this PC

Power & sleep

Screen

On battery power, turn off after
3 minutes

When plugged in, turn off after
1 hour

Sleep

On battery power, PC goes to sleep after
30 minutes

When plugged in, PC goes to sleep after
1 hour

DESKTOP CHANGES Your operating system lets you change the desktop display. For example, in Windows 10 you use the Personalization settings. Among your choices are these:

- Change the background appearance of the desktop, sometimes called the wallpaper

- Select colors

- Change and manage the lock screen, which is where you enter a password or code to access your data and applications

- Select and manage **themes** and desktop icons

- Select options for the Start menu

- Select options for the Taskbar

- Display or hide the taskbar

IC3✔ | **Know how to personalize the Windows 10 desktop.**

Basic Security

There are certain basic steps businesses and individuals can take to protect a computer, data, and personal identity. One step is to manage user accounts to control which users have access to programs, files, and folders. Another step is to be aware of the basic threats to security, including viruses and malware.

USER CREDENTIALS One way to protect data is to set up **user accounts** that identify who can access a computer. Each user is assigned a **username** and a **password** that he or she must provide in order to gain access. Usually, the system's lock screen displays until the correct credentials are entered.

User accounts are set up using a system tool provided by the operating system. The **system administrator** is the person responsible for maintaining the computer system and for setting up user accounts. He or she has administrative rights, including permission to customize and configure all aspects of the system for all users, including setting or changing passwords,

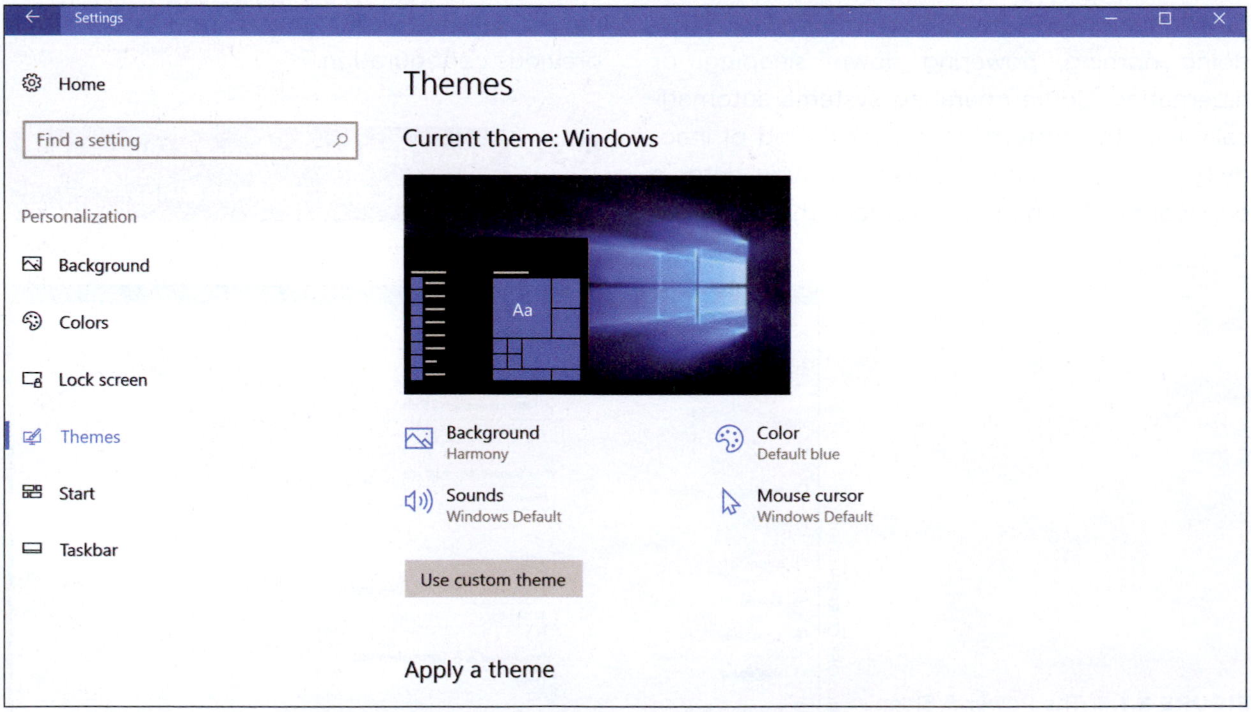

FIGURE 8.1.4 The Themes page of the Personalization Settings in Windows 10.

account permissions, and pictures associated with a user account. On your PC or other personal device, you are the system administrator.

A strong password is important for security because it makes it harder for criminals to access your data. Best practices for creating a password include the following:

- Do not use personal information such as family names, nicknames, or birth dates.

- Do use random passwords that have no meaning to you or anyone else.

- Use a combination of at least eight upper- and lowercase letters, numbers, and symbols. The more characters the better.

- Change your password every three or four months.

- Do not keep a record of your passwords on your computer or on a piece of paper near your computer.

- Never give out your passwords to anyone, and never type a password while someone is watching.

It can be difficult to remember all of your passwords, which makes it tempting to use the same password for all accounts. There are applications sometimes referred to as password managers where you can store your login information for all of your accounts. Windows comes with a utility called Windows Credential Manager that automatically logs passwords for websites and Windows accounts. You can access it from the User Accounts settings in the Control Panel.

IC3✔ **Know the purpose of a username.**

IC3✔ **Know the components of a good password.**

IC3✔ **Know basic account setting management.**

CONNECTIONS

SOCIAL STUDIES Adding new hardware to a classroom computer can create exciting possibilities. Think of a user account for a social studies teacher on a school district's network. If the hardware rights for the account allow the user to add hardware, the teacher might connect a large-screen monitor so a current event article downloaded from a history website could be displayed for the entire class to read at once. A map downloaded from the internet could also be displayed on the monitor. With installation rights, webcams, and a microphone, students could interview a political figure or complete a project with students in another city.

USER RIGHTS User accounts may also have specific **user rights** assigned to them by administrators to limit or allow access, including:

- File access rights that specify which files a user has permission to access and whether he or she can only read files or has access to read and write (edit) them

- Installation rights that specify whether a user can install or remove programs

- Hardware rights that specify whether a user can add or remove hardware

- Configuration rights that specify whether a user can change operating system settings

- Group policy rights that specify configuration and policy settings for a group of users on computers and mobile devices

IC3✔ **Explain rights and permissions, including administrative rights.**

BASIC THREATS One of the best defenses against security breaches is a strong offense. For example, always have virus and malware protection installed and up-to-date. Also, be aware of the ways criminals try to lure you into selecting a link that will install harmful programs such as

Trojans. A **Trojan** is a type of malware that hides inside a seemingly harmless program but once installed can wreak havoc. Trojans are known to collect personal information; change security settings without permission so unauthorized users have access; and even lock down the computer so you cannot use it. If they infiltrate a smartphone, they may hi-jack the messaging system to send text messages to premium numbers that can cost a lot of money.

Trojans are difficult to recognize. They use **social engineering** to trick you into selecting links or downloading files. **Social engineering** refers to ways of influencing someone to do something that may not be in their best interest. For example, you might receive a message that appears to come from a friend or business contact prompting you to download a photo. Because you trust the sender, you download the file.

IC3 ✔ Know how malware, viruses, and Trojans pose a threat to computers, data, and identity.

IC3 ✔ Know the purpose of social engineering, and how it can be used to install malware.

MONITORING SOFTWARE Businesses, schools, and individuals may choose to install **monitoring software** in order to keep track of all desktop and online activities that occur on a computer system. Monitoring, or surveillance, software logs all actions, such as web browsing, application use, uploads, and downloads. The system administrator sets rules, such as which websites are allowed and which are not, and the software issues an alert if a rule is broken. For example, a parent can use monitoring software to track whether a child is really doing homework, or just spending time on a social networking site. Similarly, an employer can use it to determine if an employee is working or shopping during office hours.

IC3 ✔ Know the implications of monitoring software.

LOGGING ON AND OFF To access your account, you log on to the system. When you are finished, you should always log off so no one else can access your data and account information. Most operating systems also let you switch users without logging off. This closes your account and switches to the account for the other user.

DID YOU KNOW?

Some devices, including cell phones, tablets, and eReaders, have an Airplane mode that turns off all cellular and data connections that might interfere with an airplane's sensors and other equipment. The device is on, just not able to connect to a network. You can read, watch videos, or listen to music stored on the device. You can also use cameras and play games that do not require internet access. If the airplane has Wi-Fi onboard, the flight crew will notify you after takeoff if you may turn Wi-Fi back on.

LESSON 8-2
Exploring System Utilities

OBJECTIVES

- Analyze file names and file formats.
- Explain cross-platform compatibility issues.
- Identify and discuss system maintenance utilities.

AS YOU READ

DRAW CONCLUSIONS Use a chart to help you draw conclusions about system utilities as you read.

TERMINOLOGY

- corrupted
- cross-platform compatibility
- directory
- disk scanner
- eBook
- eReader
- file extension
- file format
- file fragmentation
- file name
- hierarchical
- malware
- metadata
- path
- quarantine
- root directory
- subdirectories
- Trojan
- virus

Managing Files and Folders

Among the most important system utilities is the file manager, called File Explorer in Windows and Finder in macOS. This utility allows you to organize, view, copy, move, rename, and delete files.

DIRECTORIES AND FOLDERS Most operating systems manage file storage using a multilevel, or **hierarchical**, filing system called a **directory**. At the top is the main storage location, called the **root directory**. Root directories are labeled with letters followed by a colon. On most Windows computers, the root directory is C:, external hard drives may be D:, E:, and so on. Within the root are **subdirectories** called folders, which may contain subfolders and files. You can create, delete, copy, and move files and folders

NAVIGATING THE FILE SYSTEM You navigate through the file system by expanding and collapsing folders to show or hide their contents. You use a **path** to identify the specific location of a folder or file. The path lists each location in the directory hierarchy beginning with the root. Each specific location is separated by a \ character. So, the path **C:\Documents\Schoolwork\Report.doc** is the storage location for a document file named Report, stored in the Schoolwork subfolder, stored in the Documents folder, in the root directory C:.

Most operating systems come with some folders already set up. Windows comes with folders set up for each user, including folders for Documents, Pictures, and Downloads. Android devices have a Files or My Files folder with subfolders for Images, Downloads, Audio, Video, and so on. Use your file manager to identify and change the default storage locations. For example, to find the default Downloads storage location in Windows, open File Explorer, right-click the Downloads folder in the navigation pane on the left of the window, select Properties, and then select the Location tab. The path to the folder displays. For example, the default Downloads storage location for a user named Sam might be **C:\Users\Sam\Downloads**. The default Documents storage location for the same user might be **C:\Users\Sam\Documents**.

NAMING FILES AND FOLDERS When you create a new file or folder, you give it a **file name**. Using descriptive names helps you identify the contents and keep your data organized. For example, the name *2019 Annual Report* is more descriptive than *Report*. It also helps keep you from accidentally deleting or overwriting files and folders that have the same name. Most operating systems have specific file and folder naming conventions. They usually let you use file and folder names with up to 255 characters, including spaces and punctuation. You cannot use <, >, :, ", /, \, |, ?, or *.

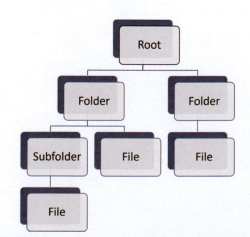

FIGURE 8.2.1 A hierarchical file system is like the roots of a tree extending out into folders, subfolders, and files.

FILE TYPE Some operating systems, such as Windows, automatically add a period and a file extension to file names. A **file extension** is a short series of letters that indicate the application used to create the file and the **file format**. The file extension determines the file type. For example, a Microsoft Word document has the extension .doc or .docx. You can set options to display file types when you view a file list. By default, the operating system uses the program associated with the file type to open the file. So, a file with an .xlsx extension opens in Microsoft Excel and a file with a .pdf extension opens in Adobe Reader or Acrobat.

IC3✔ | **Know the purpose of a file extension and be able to identify common file extensions.**

CROSS-PLATFORM COMPATIBILITY Recall that cross-platform compatibility is the ability to use a file on any device no matter what operating system is in use. This is possible because the OS associates files with specific programs, no matter what OS is being used. So, a word processing document created with a word processor on a macOS system can be opened on any device running the word processing application, such as a Windows notebook, iOS tablet, or Android OS phone.

COMMON FILE TYPE EXTENSIONS

Extension	File Type
.docx	Microsoft Word Document
.txt	Text Document
.xlsx	Microsoft Excel Document
.pptx	Microsoft PowerPoint Presentation
.wav	Waveform Audio File
.mp3	MP3 Audio File
.jpg	JPEG Image File
.pdf	Adobe Reader or Adobe Acrobat
.zip	Compressed File
.html	HTML File
.csv	Comma Separated Values Document

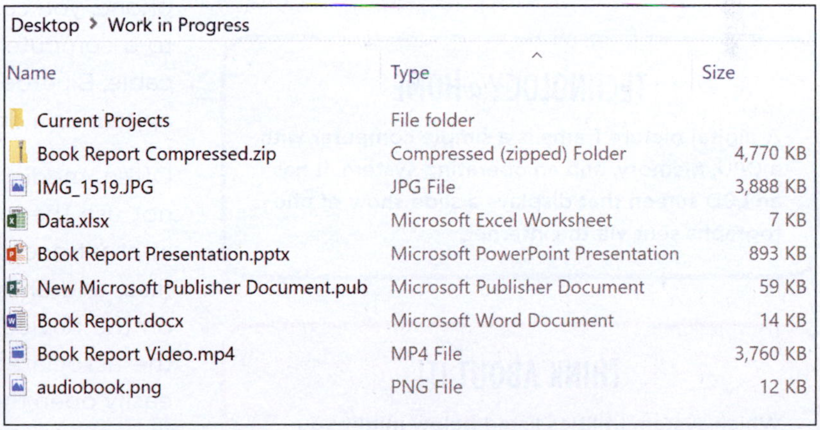

Desktop › Work in Progress		
Name	**Type**	**Size**
Current Projects	File folder	
Book Report Compressed.zip	Compressed (zipped) Folder	4,770 KB
IMG_1519.JPG	JPG File	3,888 KB
Data.xlsx	Microsoft Excel Worksheet	7 KB
Book Report Presentation.pptx	Microsoft PowerPoint Presentation	893 KB
New Microsoft Publisher Document.pub	Microsoft Publisher Document	59 KB
Book Report.docx	Microsoft Word Document	14 KB
Book Report Video.mp4	MP4 File	3,760 KB
audiobook.png	PNG File	12 KB

MICROSOFT CORPORATION

FIGURE 8.2.2 You can display file types when viewing files with Windows.

Managing Files and Folders

Operating systems include file management utilities for organizing, locating, and managing folders and files. For example, macOS has Finder, and Windows 10 has File Explorer. Versions of Windows prior to Windows 8 have a similar feature called Windows Explorer.

FILE AND FOLDER MANAGEMENT You use the file manager in your operating system to create, view, copy, move, rename, and delete files, folders, and subfolders. For example, you can open a file simply by double-clicking it in the file manager window. The operating system stores a lot of information called **metadata** with a file so it can find it when you need it. For you, the most important piece of information for identifying files and folders is the name. If you want to remember what a folder contains and what file you need, you should use logical, recognizable names that describe the contents.

IC3✔ Know how to create, view, copy, move, rename, and delete files, folders, and subfolders.

TECHNOLOGY@HOME

A digital picture frame is a simple computer with a CPU, memory, and an operating system. It has an LCD screen that displays a slide show of photographs sent via the internet.

THINK ABOUT IT!

Which system utilities listed below might you want to run when sending digital photos via the internet?

- file manager
- disk scanner
- disk defragmenter
- antivirus software

FILE PERMISSIONS Recall that file access rights specify which files and folders a user has permission to open, read, edit, and more. An operating system assigns default rights to new files and folders; usually the owner, who is the person who creates the file or folder, has full permission. The system administrator can set or change file permissions. In Windows, file permissions are set using the Security tab in the File Properties dialog box, which you open by right-clicking the file or folder, selecting Properties, and then selecting the Security tab. From there, select the Edit button to Allow or Deny specific permissions. Use the Advanced button for access to special permissions options.

IC3✔ Know how to identify, assign, and manage file rights and permissions.

MEDIA FILES On a computer, media files such as songs, videos, animations, and **eBooks**, are managed using the same tools as other types of files. You can move or copy them into folders, open them in an associated application, delete them, and rename them. If the media is stored online or on a device such as a tablet, **eReader**, or smartphone, you can transfer the files from the device to a computer. Connect the device using a USB cable, Bluetooth, or Wi-Fi. The device will usually appear as a drive in your file manager.

Often, media files are stored online so they do not use the local storage space. You must have internet access in order to play or manage the files, and an appropriate app must be installed on the device, such as iTunes or Google Play. If the associated application is installed, you can easily open the media file by double-clicking the file name in File Explorer, or by using the application's File > Open command.

IC3✔ Know how to manage electronic media such as videos, songs, and eBooks.

Using System Maintenance Utilities

Like any machine, a computer needs routine maintenance. System maintenance utilities do these jobs and more.

DISK MANAGEMENT Computer files can be **corrupted**, or damaged to the point at which data is unrecoverable, in different ways. One way is by being stored on a damaged part of the hard drive. Running a utility called a **disk scanner**, which checks magnetic disks for errors, can fix this problem. A disk scanner looks for and tries to correct irregularities on a disk's surface. You can use a disk cleaner utility to identify files such as cookies, offline web pages, and temporary files that you can delete to make more disk space available.

DISK DEFRAGMENTER As you add, move, and delete files on your computer, parts of files end up saved in different areas of the hard drive. **File fragmentation** occurs when a file is broken into pieces that are saved in different places on a hard drive.

File fragmentation reduces disk efficiency because the read/write head must travel longer distances to retrieve parts of a file that are scattered across a disk than if the files were stored close together. A disk defragmentation program can gather all the file pieces and place them together, thus improving the efficiency of the disk or hard drive.

VIRUS DETECTION Viruses and malware can enter your system through infected email messages, programs, and files. **Malware** is any type of software designed to damage or disable your computer system or data. A **virus** is a type of malware that can replicate, or copy, itself. A **Trojan**, or Trojan Horse, is a type of malware that allows unauthorized access to your computer. Antivirus and antimalware utilities constantly monitor your system for viruses and malware programs that can slow down processing or damage your data and devices. Once there, they can destroy or corrupt data. Antivirus programs check your computer's memory and disks looking for virus code. Most programs can also check email and files as they are downloaded to your computer from the internet. If the program discovers a virus, it alerts you and then attempts to **quarantine**, or disable, and remove the virus. Operating systems often come with an antivirus utility such as Windows Defender. You can also install a program such as Norton Security Backup or McAfee Internet Security.

Because new viruses and malware are introduced every day, it is important to install antivirus and antimalware program updates automatically whenever they become available. Most programs can be set to automatically check your system on a schedule, automatically install updates, and automatically remove or quarantine an infected file.

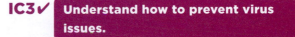

IC3 ✔ **Understand how to prevent virus issues.**

IC3 ✔ **Understand how to maintain and update antivirus software.**

BALEFIRE/SHUTTERSTOCK

FIGURE 8.2.3 Virus protection programs look for different types of viruses and malware that have infected your computer system.

Mobile Apps and Messaging Systems

OBJECTIVES

- Explain the purpose and benefits of mobile apps.

- Explain how to use personal messaging applications.

- Identify the capabilities and limitations of SMS and MMS.

- Describe the service requirements for instant messaging.

- Configure and use mobile device notifications.

- Configure and use voicemail.

- Explain file sharing options.

AS YOU READ

SEQUENCE INFORMATION Use an outline to help you organize information about mobile apps and messaging systems as you read.

TERMINOLOGY

- email attachment

- file compression

- File Transfer Protocol (FTP)

- instant messaging (IM)

- mobile apps

- Multimedia Messaging Service (MMS)

- notification

- outgoing voicemail message

- Short Message Service (SMS)

- text messaging

- tweet

- voicemail

Mobile Apps

Applications designed to download and use on a smartphone or tablet are called **mobile apps**. They are available for thousands of uses, from productivity suites to games. Most mobile devices come with a set of built-in mobile apps, such as a calendar, contact list, email client, and calculator. Additional apps can be downloaded from an app store. Among the benefits of mobile apps is the ease of using an app designed specifically for a mobile device and the ability to use many of the same apps you use on a computer on your mobile device.

Most mobile apps are installed directly on the mobile device. Some, such as Microsoft Office 365 Mobile, are cloud-based, which means the app can be accessed and used on any device while the program itself is stored and processed on an internet server. Many mobile apps are able to sync with the cloud and other devices registered to the same account so that your data can be accessed no matter whether you are working on your phone, tablet, notebook, or desktop.

Mobile apps have a range of uses from playing music to helping improve productivity. Some apps even track a user's health and exercise. Apps that use the internet can connect to a web browser, a user's email, or social media sites, such as Facebook and Twitter.

There are also reference apps you use to search for information; creation apps for drawing or creating images; and content apps for organizing data, like the contacts on your phone. Like computer applications, apps are written to run on a specific operating system so not all apps run on all mobile devices.

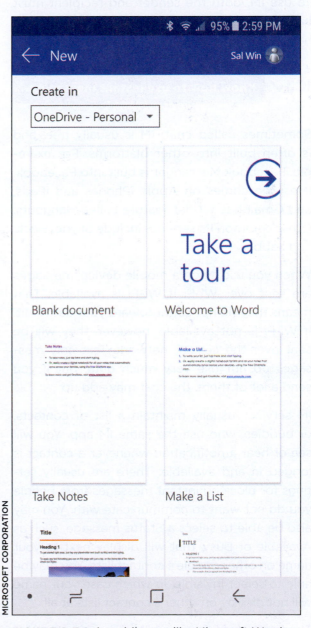

MICROSOFT CORPORATION

FIGURE 8.3.1 A mobile app like Microsoft Word 365 can be used to create and edit documents on a smartphone.

DID YOU KNOW?

Some apps on your device may have notification settings, as well. For example, you may be able to choose a ringtone or status bar notification for your calendar app. Configuring settings in a specific app depends on the type of device you are using. For example, on an iPhone or iPad, launch the Settings app, tap Mail, Contacts, Calendar, and select the options to use. On an Android phone, open the Calendar app, tap Menu, tap Settings, and then select the options to use.

Instant Messaging

Instant messaging (IM) started as a way for people to communicate in real time from computer to computer. Now, mobile devices with instant messaging (IM) apps installed are one way individuals and groups communicate with their contacts in real time from device to device. To use IM, both the sender and recipient must have accounts with the IM service provider, and have the app installed on their devices.

IC3✔ **Know how to use instant messaging.**

Sometimes called chat, IM is usually free, and is often built into other platforms. For example, Facebook Messenger is built into Facebook, iMessage comes on Apple iPhones and iPads, and Gmail has a Chat feature called Hangouts. Other common IM services include Skype, Slack, and Jabber.

When you use IM on a mobile device, messages are sent over Wi-Fi if Wi-Fi is available. That means they do not count toward your data limit. If Wi-Fi is not available, however, they will be sent over the cellular network. Text-only messages do not use very much data, but if you send a lot of them, the cost may add up.

IM services usually maintain a list of contacts, or buddies, who use the same IM app. You will see or hear a notification whenever a contact is logged in and available. There are usually settings for blocking instant messages from people you do not want to communicate with. You may also be able to select a Status message, such as Available or Busy, that will display next to your name on other people's contact lists. You may be able to select Invisible, in which case your name will not display on other's contact lists at all.

The basic steps for using IM are similar in most services: Open the app, select a contact, use the device keyboard to type a message and press Send or Enter. There is no limit to the length of the message. When you receive an IM, your device usually notifies you by making a sound or vibration. When you open the IM app, the message displays on the device screen.

Instant messaging services may also provide video calling, file sharing and device-to-device or device-to-phone calling. To use video calling, the device must have a working camera, microphone, and speaker.

GOOGLE IM SERVICES Google Hangouts is an IM app that comes built into the Gmail email program. You can use it on your computer, or download the Hangouts app on your mobile device and log in to it with your Google account. In addition to chatting, Hangouts provides video chat and screen sharing functionality.

SKYPE IM SERVICES Skype may be best known as a VoIP (Voice Over Internet Protocol) calling application, but it also lets you send instant messages to individuals or groups in your Contact list. Skype also supports video messaging. The Skype app can be installed on mobile devices or used from the outlook.com website.

FIGURE 8.3.2
Use an IM app such as Google Hangouts to chat with your contacts.

Text Messaging

Text messaging, or texting, allows you to use a smartphone or other mobile device to type a brief message and transmit it to another phone or as a group conversation to multiple phones. You must have a messaging app on your phone, but you can send messages to—and receive messages from—any cell phone number. You can even send texts to some landlines. A computer actually reads the message to you! The recipient does not have to use the same messaging app that you use.

Text messages are usually sent using a cellular network, but may use Wi-Fi if it is available. Cellular service plans may place a limit on the number of text messages you can send and receive, and may charge you if you exceed that limit.

SMS Text messages are sent using **Short Message Service (SMS)**. Texts are uploaded to the service's server and then downloaded to the recipient's device. Most text messages are limited to 160 characters in length. If you exceed that limit, the messaging app will usually break the message into two or more messages, sent separately.

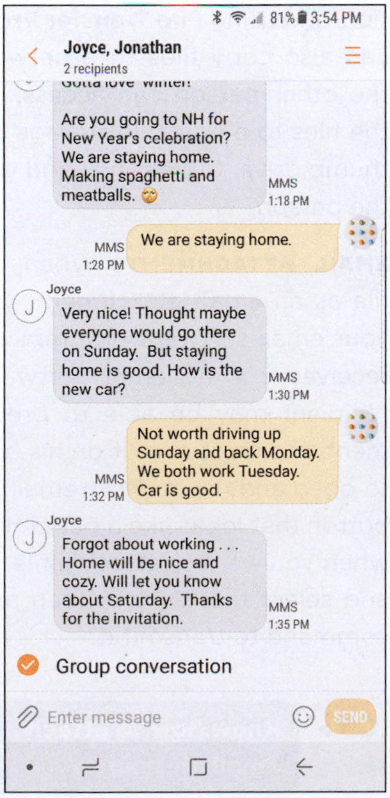

MMS Digital messages that include photos, audio, and videos are sent using **Multimedia Messaging Service (MMS)**. The process is basically the same as with SMS messages: the message is uploaded to a server and then downloaded to the recipient's device. There is not usually a size limit for an MMS message, but if it is too large the service may have trouble with the transmission, or the recipient may have trouble with the download. MMS messages usually use data and will count toward your cellular service plan's data limit. If you exceed the data limit, you will incur overage charges.

TWEETS A **tweet** is a form of text messaging that uses the Twitter app; you send the message to the Twitter website, where any registered user can read it. Twitter limits most messages to 140 characters. Twitter allows for short messages to be read by a much larger audience.

Configuring Notifications

Most cell phones and other devices display or play a **notification** when an event occurs. For example, the phone might pop-up a message to remind you of an appointment, play a tune to indicate an incoming call, or make a sound when a text message is received.

You can configure the settings on the device regarding when, where, and how to make notifications. For example, you can select the ringtone for incoming calls and the sound for text messages or for Outlook calendar reminders. Some devices let you customize the notifications for different contacts, so you know without looking whether a call is from your employer or your friend. You can adjust the volume of notifications, or select silent mode, which causes the device to vibrate instead of making a sound. You can even turn notifications off completely when you do not want to be distracted by your phone.

FIGURE 8.3.3 Text messages let you communicate phone-to-phone in real-time.

To configure notifications on most mobile devices, open the Settings app and locate the options for Sound. For some apps, you may use the Settings for the app itself.

IC3✔ Know how to configure notifications.

Using Voicemail

Cell phones, and most landline services, include **voicemail**, which allows callers to leave a spoken message if you do not answer after a set number of rings. Voicemail may be provided by the phone service provider, or you may install a voicemail app. Depending on the provider or the app, you have configuration options such as how many rings before answering and how long to store messages.

You can record an **outgoing voicemail message** instructing the caller that you are not available. When someone calls and you do not answer, the outgoing message plays. The caller then has the opportunity to speak a message that is recorded and stored until you delete it. You can listen to the message by accessing the voice mailbox.

IC3✔ Know how to configure and use voicemail.

On your personal phone, your outgoing voicemail message may be casual and even funny. In a business environment, it is important that your outgoing message is professional. This message may be the first contact a caller has with your business, and it is vital that you make a positive impression. A professional outgoing message should provide only the most essential information and be no more than 25 second long. Speak clearly so callers understand the message. Include the following:

- **Greeting** This should be short and simple, such as "hello."

- **Your name** Remember to speak clearly.

- **Your company name, department name, or both** This lets callers know they have reached the correct person.

- **Statement that you cannot take the call right now** You should not give a reason. Simply state that you are unavailable.

- **Invitation to leave a message** Ask callers to leave a name and phone number, and the reason for the call.

- **When to expect a return call** This courtesy lets callers know when to expect a call back.

- **Who callers can contact for immediate assistance (if applicable)** If there is someone covering for you while you are out, provide the name and phone number.

File Sharing

When you share files, you make them available to other people. Some common methods of file sharing are attaching files to an email message, uploading files to a shared online storage location, and using **File Transfer Protocol (FTP)**. You can also copy files to a network location that the other person can access, or you can copy the files to a portable storage device, such as a thumb drive, CD, or DVD and give the device to the person.

EMAIL ATTACHMENTS When you transfer a file as an **email attachment**, you send it using your email software program and the recipient receives it in his email software program. The recipient may be able to preview the attachment, but must save it on his computer in order to open and use it. Most email programs have a button that looks like a paperclip that you select when you want to attach a file. Then, you locate and select the file to attach and use the Send command to transmit it.

IC3✔ Know how to attach a file to an email message.

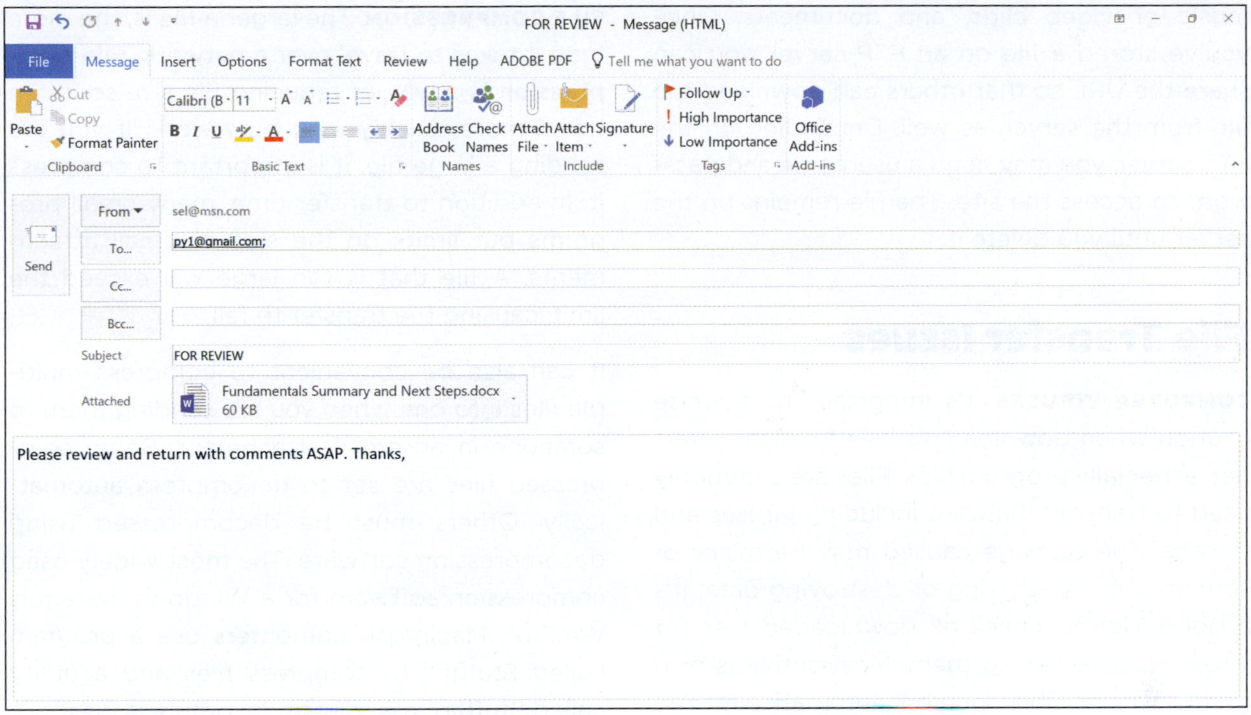

FIGURE 8.3.4 Attach a file to an email message to share it with the message recipient.

ONLINE STORED FILES Recall that you can share folders and files that are stored online with a cloud storage service such as Microsoft OneDrive or Google Drive. If you are the person who creates the folder or file, called the owner, you control who can access the data.

- A publicly shared folder is available to anyone. Anyone can access it, download it, and possibly even edit it.

- A shared link allows anyone with the link to access the data. The owner can send the shared link to the people he or she wants to invite. However, others may obtain the shared link and be able to use it to access the data. Shareable links are usually sent via email to the person or persons you want to share the file. It is also possible to copy and paste the shareable link, or to write it down manually and give it to someone. If someone else owns the file or folder, he or she can invite you to share it by sending the shareable link in an email message, or just giving you the link to enter in your browser's address bar.

- A shared folder can be accessed by anyone who has permission to open the folder. The owner or a system administrator is responsible for assigned access. Depending on the access level, someone may have permission to view, edit, or download the contents. Permissions can also be used to limit who can upload data to a shared folder.

IC3✔ **Know how to get a link to a file stored on Microsoft OneDrive.**

IC3✔ **Know the difference between publicly shared folders, shared links, and shared folders.**

FILE TRANSFER PROTOCOL With an FTP client, you can transfer files from an FTP server on the internet or on a local network to your computer in an operation called downloading. In uploading, you transfer files from the client to the server. FTP can transfer both text files and binary files. Binary files are program files, graphics, pictures, music or video clips, and documents. Once you've stored a file on an FTP server, you can share the URL so that others can download the file from the server, as well. Depending on the FTP server, you may need a username and password to access the site. The file remains on the server until you delete it.

File Transfer Issues

COMPUTER VIRUSES It's important to exercise caution when downloading files from the internet, especially program files. Files are commonly used to transmit malware including viruses and Trojans. The damage caused may be minor or serious, such as altering or destroying data. It's a good idea to check all downloaded files for viruses before saving them. Most antivirus programs will do this for you automatically. You should update your antivirus program regularly to be protected from the newest viruses. The Windows operating system helps by giving a security warning when a download is about to begin. You may want to review the advice provided by selecting the *What's the Risk?* link.

FILE COMPRESSION The larger a file is, the more time it takes to travel over a network. **File compression** is a way of reducing file size so it can travel more quickly over a network. If you are sending a large file, it is important to compress it. In addition to transfer time, many email programs put limits on the size of email attachments. A file that is too large will exceed the limit, causing the transfer to fail.

It can also be convenient to compress multiple files into one when you are sending them to someone in an email attachment. Some compressed files are set to decompress automatically. Others must be decompressed using decompression software. The most widely used compression software for a Windows system is WinZip®. Macintosh computers use a program called StuffIt™ to compress files and a utility called StuffIt Expander to decompress files.

IC3 ✔ **Explain the need for file compression/zipping when sharing files.**

Chapter 8 Review

REVIEW THE TERMINOLOGY

DIRECTIONS Match each vocabulary term in the left column with the correct definition in the right column.

1. boot
2. POST
3. window
4. drop-down menu
5. pop-up menu
6. dialog box
7. file extension
8. cross-platform compatibility
9. disk scanner
10. file fragmentation

a. to start the computer and load the operating system

b. option that appears when an item is selected from the menu bar

c. utility that looks for errors in magnetic media

d. a window that provides options for customizing a command

e. two to four letters that identify a file's format

f. series of tests run during the boot process

g. ability to share files across operating systems

h. shortcut command that appears anywhere in a window

i. frame that displays a document or file

j. having parts of files stored on different areas of a disk or hard drive

USE THE TERMINOLOGY

DIRECTIONS Determine the correct choice for each of the following.

1. Which of the following operating system processes checks system components such as the keyboard and monitor?

   a. POST
   b. BIOS screen
   c. GUI
   d. cross-platform application

2. At what point in the boot process can users be asked their username and password?

   a. at the control panel
   b. in a screen saver
   c. in a file manager
   d. at login

3. If a pop-up menu is context-sensitive, what is it related to?

    a. file format   **c.** what you are doing

    b. printer settings   **d.** operating system

4. Which of the following is NOT a system change most users should attempt?

    a. moving the operating system   **c.** changing mouse settings

    b. adding a scanner   **d.** removing a program

5. Along with the data itself, which of the following is saved with a file?

    a. login procedure   **c.** icon that describes it

    b. code for the application that created it   **d.** maintenance utility

6. Which of the following is one way that a file can be corrupted?

    a. by deleting it   **c.** by moving it to a new folder

    b. by appearing on the desktop   **d.** by storing it on a damaged disk

THINK CRITICALLY

DIRECTIONS Answer the following questions.

1. Why would you add or remove buttons from the Quick Access Toolbar at the top of an application window?

2. What is the biggest difference between a list box and a multiple selection list when viewing a typical dialog box or pop-up menu?

3. What is the difference between "Sleep Mode" and "Hibernate Mode"? What is the benefit of using these features?

4. How might a malicious individual use social engineering to install malware and viruses on another user's computer? What might these programs be capable of, and what can be done to prevent this?

5. What would be a benefit to accessing and altering read/write permissions for a file or folder? Give an example.

6. Why would it be beneficial to share a link to a file or folder via a cloud service like Microsoft OneDrive?

EXTEND YOUR KNOWLEDGE

DIRECTIONS Choose and complete one of the following projects.

1. With a partner, interview three adult computer users: one who uses Microsoft Windows, one who uses a Macintosh, and one who has experience with both operating systems. Prepare written questions related to ease of learning the operating system, ease of use, availability of programs, and overall satisfaction with the operating system. Take notes to record the answers. Add your findings to your own experiences and write a conclusion about the user preferences of the two major operating systems. Share your conclusion with a partner or with your class.

2. Explore the desktop on your computer. Identify the icons on the desktop and explain what each launches. Use the taskbar to identify files or programs that are open and the file formats they are in. How does the desktop help you manage your work on the computer? Using a text editor, word-processing application, or on paper, write a paragraph explaining the concept of a computer desktop. Then, write step-by-step instructions that someone could use to arrange items on the desktop. With your teacher's permission, print or publish the document and exchange it with a classmate. Read your classmate's work. As a class, discuss why step-by-step instructions are useful.

IC3 PREP

1. For each line below, select whether the statement is True or False.

   a. Drivers are software programs that let the OS work with different devices and peripherals.

   b. Most modern operating systems cannot automate the process of keeping drivers up-to-date on their host systems.

   c. Some basic drivers for common devices such as a keyboard and a mouse are built into an operating system.

2. Which of the following is a way a Windows desktop can be personalized?

   a. change the background, or "wallpaper"   c. select and manage themes

   b. display or hide the taskbar   d. change or manage the lock screen

3. For each line below, select whether the statement is True or False.

   a. A system administrator is a person responsible for maintaining the computer system and for setting up user accounts.

   b. To log in to a system with separate user accounts, you may need to provide a username and password.

   c. As a general rule, the longer a password is, the less secure it is.

   d. On your own PC or other personal device, you will typically be the administrator.

   e. A system administrator can set permissions for accessing and editing user files.

4. Which of the following is a typical use for monitoring software?

   a. an employer determining if an employee is working or shopping online during office hours

   b. a parent logging their child's web browsing history

   c. a teacher ensuring school computers are not being used to download music and movies

   d. an administrator setting a password

5. Match the file extension on the left to its corresponding file type on the right:

   Extension

   1. .txt
   2. .wav
   3. .mp3
   4. .jpg
   5. .pptx
   6. .docx
   7. .zip
   8. .xlsx

   File Type

   a. JPEG image flle
   b. text document
   c. Microsoft Excel document
   d. compressed file
   e. Microsoft PowerPoint presentation
   f. MP3 Audio file
   g. Microsoft Word document
   h. Waveform Audio file

6. What are some things you are able to accomplish with the use of a file manager? (Select all that apply.)

   a. copy a file
   b. create a new folder
   c. split a file into three equal parts
   d. rename a file
   e. view the contents of a folder

7. Which of the following is NOT a method of transferring videos, songs, and ebooks between two devices?

   a. USB cable
   b. Bluetooth
   c. Semaphore
   d. Wi-Fi or cellular data

8. For each line below, select whether the statement is True or False.

   a. Viruses and malware can enter your system through infected email messages, programs, and files.

   b. Antivirus and antimalware programs do not need updates to keep your computer healthy.

   c. Modern operating systems often come with an antivirus utility, such as Windows Defender.

   d. Antivirus programs can only check your computer files for viruses, not your emails.

9. Which of these is NOT necessary for two parties to set up and carry out a conversation over an Instant Messaging program? (Select all that apply.)

   a. both should be running the same IM application

   b. both should be using the same device to communicate

   c. both must be on a wired internet connection

   d. both must be using a device with a Windows operating system

10. You are using your email program and notice a small paperclip icon near the bottom of the message you are typing to your friend. What will selecting the icon most likely allow you to do?

    a. scan your computer for viruses
    b. attach a file to the email
    c. send your friend a paperclip
    d. compress selected files

11. Which of the following notification settings are you likely to find on a smartphone? (Select all that apply.)

    a. pop-up messages to remind you of an appointment

    b. alerts as to what number is calling you, and if they are in your contacts

    c. selecting a ringtone, either generally or on a per-contact basis

    d. status bar notification for your calendar app

12. For each line below, select whether the statement is True or False.

    a. A professional outgoing voicemail should provide only essential information.

    b. Voicemail is a feature of both landline phones and cell phones.

    c. It is not helpful to state your name at the beginning of a voicemail recording.

    d. When it comes to recording an outgoing voicemail, longer is always better.

13. What is the benefit of compressing/zipping files or folders before sharing them with others? (Select all that apply.)

    a. An unzipped folder may spill its contents during transfer.

    b. A compressed file has a smaller data footprint, and should transfer more quickly.

    c. A compressed file has a smaller data footprint, which should help if an email client has a restriction on transferring larger files.

    d. Unzipped files may not stay attached to an email message during transfer.

14. By default, where does a Windows device store files that a user named Rick downloads from the internet?

    a. C:\Users\Downloads   c. C:\Downloads\Default

    b. C:\Default\Downloads   d. C:\Users\Rick\Downloads

IC3 PROCEDURES

UPDATING DEVICE DRIVERS

1. Right-click (or press, hold, and release) the **Start** button ⊞.

2. Select **Device Manager**.

3. Expand one of the categories to find the name of your device, then right-click (or tap and hold) it, and select **Update Driver**. For graphics cards, expand the **Display adapters** category, right-click your graphics card and select **Update Driver**.

4. Select **Search automatically for updated driver software**.

5. If Windows doesn't find a new driver, you can try looking for one on the device manufacturer's website and follow their instructions.

CONFIGURING A SCREENSAVER ON A WINDOWS 10 COMPUTER

1. Enter **Screen Saver** in the Search box on the Windows taskbar.

2. Select **Turn the lock screen slideshow on or off**.

3. Scroll down the Lock Screen settings and select **Screen Saver Settings**.

4. Scroll down and select **Screen Saver Settings**.

5. From the Screen saver drop-down list, select a screen saver.

6. In the Wait box, enter a value for the number of minutes to wait before activating the screen saver.

7. Select the **On resume, display logon screen** check box, if desired.

8. Select **OK**.

OR

1. Right-click (or press, hold, and release) on the desktop.

2. Select **Personalize** to open Personalization settings.

3. Select **Lock screen** in the left pane.

4. Scroll down and select **Screen Saver Settings**.

5. From the Screen saver drop-down list, select a screen saver.

6. In the Wait box, enter a value for the number of minutes to wait before activating the screen saver.

7. Select the **On resume, display logon screen check box**, if desired.

8. Select **OK**.

CHANGING THE SCREEN RESOLUTION OF A WINDOWS 10 COMPUTER

1. Right-click (or press, hold, and release) on the desktop.

2. Select **Display settings**.

3. Select the **Resolution** drop-down arrow.

4. Select the desired screen resolution.

SETTING THE DESKTOP BACKGROUND OF A WINDOWS 10 COMPUTER

1. Select the **Start** button ⊞.

2. Select the **Settings** icon ⚙.

3. Select **Personalization**.

4. Select **Background**.

5. Select the **Background** drop-down arrow.

6. Select:

   ■ **Picture** and then select desired picture.

   ■ **Solid color** and then select desired color.

   ■ **Slideshow** and then select album where pictures are stored.

7. Set options for selected background type.

COPYING FILES AND FOLDERS

1. Open **File Explorer** 📁.

2. Browse to the drive or folder containing the file or folder you want to copy.

3. Select the files or folders you want to copy.

4. On the **Home** tab, select the **Copy** button.

5. Browse to the destination folder where you want to paste the files or folder.

6. On the **Home** tab, select the **Paste** button.

MOVING FILES AND FOLDERS

1. Open **File Explorer** 📁.

2. Browse to the drive or folder containing the file or folder you want to move.

3. Select the files or folders you want to move.

4. On the **Home** tab, select the **Cut** button.

5. Browse to the destination folder where you want to move the files or folder.

6. On the **Home** tab, select the **Paste** button.

RENAMING FILES AND FOLDERS

1. Open **File Explorer** 📁.

2. Select the file or folder to rename.

3. Right-click (or press, hold, and release) and select **Rename**.

4. Enter a new name.

5. Press **Enter**.

ADDING A COMMAND TO THE QUICK ACCESS TOOLBAR IN AN OFFICE APPLICATION

1. Select the Ribbon tab where the command to add displays.

2. Right-click (or press and hold) the command.

3. Select **Add to Quick Access Toolbar**.

IDENTIFYING THE DEFAULT FILE DOWNLOAD LOCATION

1. Open **File Explorer** 📁.

2. In the Navigation pane, right-click (or press, hold, and release) the **Downloads** folder.

3. Select **Properties**.

4. Select the **Location** tab.

DEFINING SEARCH OPTIONS

1. In the Search box on the Windows taskbar, enter **Indexing Options**.

2. In the list that displays, select **Indexing Options**.

3. Adjust settings as desired.

SETTING OR CHANGING ACCOUNT PERMISSIONS

1. Select the **Start** button ⊞.
2. Select the **Settings** icon ⚙.
3. Select **Accounts**.
4. Adjust settings as desired.

SETTING OR CHANGING A USER PASSWORD

1. Select the **Start** button ⊞.
2. Select the **Settings** icon ⚙.
3. Select **Accounts**.
4. Select **Sign-in options**.
5. Under Password, select **Change**.
6. Adjust as desired.

SETTING OR CHANGING A USER PICTURE

1. Select the **Start** button ⊞.
2. Select the **Settings** icon ⚙.
3. Select **Accounts**.
4. Select **Your info**.
5. Under Create your picture, select **Camera**, to use the device camera to capture a picture.

   OR

   Browse for and select a picture already stored on your device.

CHANGING PERMISSIONS FOR A SHARED FILE

1. Open **File Explorer** 📁.
2. Right-click (or press, hold, and release) the file or folder.
3. Select **Properties**.
4. Select the **Sharing** tab.
5. Select **Advanced Sharing**.
6. Select **Permissions**.
7. Select options as desired.
8. Select **OK**.

SWITCHING USER ACCOUNTS

1. Press the **Windows** key and **L** at the same time.
2. Select the account to use.

USING DROP-DOWN MENUS

1. Select the menu name to open a drop-down menu.

   OR

   Select the drop-down arrow to the right of the main menu name or on a command button ⌄.

2. Select the command you want to use from the drop-down menu.

USING RADIO BUTTONS

Select the radio button next to the option you want to use.

USING CHECK BOXES

1. Select the check box next to an option you want to use to display a mark in the box. Multiple selections are allowed.

2. Select a marked check box next to an option you do not want to use to clear the mark.

TRANSFERRING ELECTRONIC MEDIA FILES FROM A DEVICE TO A COMPUTER

1. Connect the device to the computer via the USB cable.

2. Turn the device on.

3. Once Windows recognizes the device, open **File Explorer** 📁.

4. Use the Copy and Paste or Move and Paste commands to transfer the files from the device to your computer.

OPENING ELECTRONIC MEDIA FILES

1. Open **File Explorer** 📁.

2. Navigate to the folder containing the media files.

3. Right-click (or press, hold, and release) and select **Open**.

   A compatible application must be installed on your system to open the file.

ATTACHING A FILE TO AN EMAIL MESSAGE IN OUTLOOK

1. Compose or open the email message.

2. On the Message tab, select the **Attach File** button 📎.

3. Select the file to attach from the Recent Items list, or browse to the location where it is stored, select it, and select **Insert**.

COPYING A FILE FROM A NETWORK SHARE

1. Open **File Explorer** 📁.

2. In the Navigation pane, select the network share.

3. Browse to the location where the file is stored.

4. Select the file to copy.

5. On the **Home** tab, select the **Copy** button 📋.

6. Browse to the destination location.

7. On the **Home** tab, select the **Paste** button 📋.

COPYING A FILE TO A NETWORK SHARE

1. Open **File Explorer** .

2. Browse to the location where the file is stored.

3. Select the file to copy.

4. On the **Home** tab, select the **Copy** button .

5. In the Navigation pane, select the network share.

6. Browse to the destination location.

7. On the **Home** tab, select the **Paste** button .

COPYING A FILE FROM A CLOUD STORAGE LOCATION

1. Open **File Explorer** .

2. In the Navigation pane, select **OneDrive** (or a different cloud storage location to which you have access).

3. Select the file to copy.

4. On the **Home** tab, select the **Copy** button .

5. Browse to the destination location.

6. On the **Home** tab, select the **Paste** button .

COPYING A FILE TO A CLOUD STORAGE LOCATION

1. Open **File Explorer** .

2. Browse to the location where the file is stored.

3. Select the file to copy.

4. On the **Home** tab, select the **Copy** button .

5. In the Navigation pane, select **OneDrive** (or a different cloud storage location to which you have access).

6. Browse to the destination location.

7. On the **Home** tab, select the **Paste** button .

COPYING A FILE FROM A PORTABLE STORAGE DRIVE

1. Connect the portable storage device to your system.

2. Open **File Explorer** .

3. In the Navigation pane, select the letter or name of the portable storage device.

4. Browse to the location where the file is stored.

5. Select the file to copy.

6. On the **Home** tab, select the **Copy** button .

7. Browse to the destination location.

8. On the **Home** tab, select the **Paste** button .

COPYING A FILE TO A PORTABLE STORAGE DRIVE

1. Connect the portable storage device to your system.
2. Open **File Explorer** 📁.
3. Browse to the location where the file is stored.
4. Select the file to copy.
5. On the **Home** tab, select the **Copy** button 📋.
6. In the Navigation pane, select the letter or name of the portable storage device.
7. On the **Home** tab, select the **Paste** button 📋.

LOCKING A COMPUTER

1. Press **Ctrl + Alt + Del**.
2. Select **Lock**.

   OR

   Press **Windows key + L**.

CREATING A FOLDER

1. Navigate to the location where you want to create the new folder.
2. Select the **Home** tab.
3. Select the **New folder** button 📁.
4. Type the name of the new folder and press **Enter**.

   OR

1. Right-click a blank area of the window.
2. Select **New** and then select **Folder**.
3. Type the name of the new folder and press **Enter**.

   OR

1. Select the **New Folder** button 📁 on the Quick Access Toolbar.
2. Type the name of the new folder and press **Enter**.

CREATING A FILE

1. Right-click the location in which you want to create the new file.
2. Select **New** on the shortcut menu.
3. Select the file type to create.
4. Type the file name.
5. Press **Enter**.

DELETING A FILE OR FOLDER

1. Right-click the file or folder you want to delete.

2. Select **Delete** on the shortcut menu.

3. Select **Yes** to confirm the deletion.

ADJUSTING POWER SETTINGS

1. Select the **Windows** button ⊞ on the taskbar.

2. Select **Settings**.

3. Select **System**.

4. Select **Power & sleep**.

5. Select **Additional power settings**.

6. Select desired options.

Additional Microsoft Windows 10 Procedures

STARTING THE COMPUTER

Press the **On** switch.

SHUTTING DOWN THE COMPUTER

1. Select the **Windows** button ⊞ on the taskbar.
2. Select **Power**.
3. Select **Shut down**.

RESTARTING THE COMPUTER

1. Select the **Windows** button ⊞ on the taskbar.
2. Select **Power**.
3. Select **Restart**.

LOGGING IN TO A USER ACCOUNT

Select the desired user account to log in as that user.

STARTING A PROGRAM

1. Select the **Windows** button ⊞ on the taskbar.
2. From the Start menu, select the program's tile or name.

   OR

1. Select the **Windows** button ⊞ on the taskbar.
2. Begin typing the program name.
3. When the program name appears in the Search list, select the program name.

   OR

   Double-click the program icon on the desktop.

   OR

   Select the program icon on the Windows taskbar.

EXITING A PROGRAM

Select the **Close** button on the right side of the program's title bar.

USING THE MOUSE

- Click the left mouse button to execute a command.
- Click the right mouse button to open a shortcut menu.
- Hover the mouse pointer on an object to display a ScreenTip.
- Select an object and hold down the left mouse button to drag the object to another location.
- Spin the scroll wheel on the mouse to move through an open file.
- Double-click the left mouse button to open a file or application.

USING A TOUCH SCREEN

- Tap once on an item to open or select it.
- Press down and hold an item to select it, display a ScreenTip, or open a shortcut menu.
- Pinch or stretch an item to display different levels of information or zoom in or out.
- Drag across the screen to scroll.
- Swipe a short stroke to select an item.

USING THE KEYBOARD

- Use function keys as shortcuts for performing specified tasks.
- Use modifier keys (Alt, Shift, and Ctrl) in combination with other keys or mouse actions to select certain commands or perform actions.

- Use the number keypad to enter numeric data.

- Use the Esc key to cancel a command.

- Use the Enter key to execute a command or to start a new paragraph when typing text.

- Use directional keys to move the insertion point.

- Use editing keys such as Insert, Delete, and Backspace to insert or delete text.

- Use the Windows key to open the Windows Start screen or in combination with other keys to execute certain Windows commands.

- Use the Application key to open a shortcut menu, or in combination with other keys to execute certain application commands.

NAVIGATING STORAGE LOCATIONS

- Select the **File Explorer** icon 📁 on the taskbar.

- Select an item in the window to select it.

- Double-click an item to open it.

- Use the **Back** ← and **Forward** → buttons to move through windows you have opened recently.

- Use the Quick Access menu to go directly to a window you have recently opened.

- Select a location in the Address bar to open it.

- Select an arrow between locations in the Address bar to display a menu, and then select a location on the menu to open it.

- In the Navigation pane, select a location to display its contents in the window.

DISPLAYING A SCREENTIP

Rest the mouse pointer on a window element.

CONTROLLING WINDOW SIZE AND POSITION

Closing a Window

Select the **Close** button ✕.

The Close button may be different in different types of windows but it will always have an X on it.

Moving a Window

Position the mouse pointer over the window's title bar, press and hold the left mouse button, then drag the window to the new position.

Displaying Open Windows Side by Side

1. Right-click a blank area of the taskbar.

2. On the shortcut menu, select **Show windows side by side**.

Cascading Open Windows

1. Right-click a blank area of the taskbar.

2. Select **Cascade windows**.

Changing the Active Window

Click in the window you want to make active.

CAPTURING A SCREEN IMAGE

1. Press **PrtScn** on your keyboard.

   *On a notebook computer, you may have to press **Fn** or the **Win** key at the same time.*

2. Position the insertion point in the file where you want to insert the image.

3. Select the **Paste** button 📋.

CAPTURING AN IMAGE OF THE ACTIVE WINDOW

1. Press **Alt + PrtScr** on your keyboard.

   *On a notebook computer, you may have to press **Fn** or the **Win** key at the same time.*

2. Position the insertion point in the file where you want to insert the image.

3. Select the **Paste** button 📋.

MANAGING THE DESKTOP

Viewing and Arranging Desktop Icons

1. Right-click the desktop and select **View**.

2. Adjust the view of desktop icons in any of these ways:

   - Deselect **Show desktop icons** to hide all icons.

   - Choose to display Large icons, Medium icons, or Small icons.

   - Select **Auto arrange icons** to have Windows arrange the icons, or deselect this option if you want to be able to drag icons to specific locations.

   - Select **Align icons to grid** to snap icons to a grid system so they maintain alignment with each other.

3. Select **Sort by** if desired and select a different sort order for icons.

   Icons are sorted by Name by default.

Sorting Desktop Icons

1. Right-click the desktop and select **Sort by**.

2. Select property to sort by.

Creating a Desktop Shortcut

1. Right-click the desktop and select **New**.

2. Select **Shortcut**.

3. Type the path to the program, file, folder, computer, or internet address, or select **Browse** and navigate to the desired location; select **OK** after selecting the desired object.

4. Select **Next**.

5. Type a name for the shortcut.

6. Select **Finish**.

Creating a Folder or File on the Desktop

1. Right-click the desktop and select **New**.

2. Select the item to create.

Deleting a Folder, File, or Shortcut from the Desktop

1. Right-click the item to delete.

2. Select **Delete**.

WORKING WITH FILES

Displaying File Extensions

1. Select **File Explorer** 📁 on the taskbar.

2. Select the **View** tab.

3. Select the **Options** button 📋 **Organize** in the toolbar.

4. In the Folder Options dialog box, select the **View** tab.

5. In the Advanced settings list, scroll down if necessary and clear the checkmark from **Hide extensions for known file types**.

6. Select **OK**.

Opening (Retrieving) a File

1. Select **File Explorer** 📁 on the taskbar.

2. Navigate to the location where the file is stored.

3. When the desired file displays in the file list, double-click the file to open the file and its application.

Saving a New File

1. Select **File**.

2. Select **Save As**.

3. In the File name box, type a file name.

4. Navigate to the location where you want to store the file.

5. Select **Save**.

Saving Changes to a File

1. Select **File**.

2. Select **Save**.

Printing a File

1. Display the location where the file is stored.
2. Right-click the file.
3. Select **Print**.

Displaying File Properties

1. Select **File Explorer** 📁 on the taskbar.
2. Navigate to the folder that contains the file.
3. In the file list, right-click the file and select **Properties**.
4. Select **OK** when finished.

Changing the Folder View

1. Navigate to a storage location.
2. Select the **View** tab.

Layout Group

Select one of the view options:

- Extra Large Icons
- Large Icons
- Medium Icons
- Small Icons
- List
- Details
- Tiles
- Content

ADDING A FILE TO A ZIPPED FOLDER

Adding a File to a Zipped Folder

1. In File Explorer, right-click the file you want to add to the zipped folder.
2. On the shortcut menu, select **Copy**.
3. Display the location containing the zipped folder.
4. Right-click the zipped folder.
5. On the shortcut menu, select **Paste**.

MODIFYING DISPLAY PROPERTIES

1. Right-click on the desktop, and select **Personalize > Themes > Themes settings**.
2. Select from these options:
   - Select **Desktop Background**, select the desired picture, and select **Save changes**.
   - Select **Color**, select a color for window borders from the gallery; then select **Save changes**.
   - Select **Screen Saver**, select a screen saver option, and select **OK**.
   - Select **Display** near the bottom of the left pane to modify Display settings; select **Apply** to apply the changes.
3. If desired, select **Save theme** to name and save personalized settings as a theme.

DISPLAYING SYSTEM INFORMATION

1. Select the **Windows** button ⊞ on the taskbar.
2. Select **Settings**.
3. Select **System**.
4. Select **About**.

ACCESSING THE COMMAND PROMPT

1. Select the **Windows** button ⊞ on the taskbar.
2. Type **Command Prompt**.
3. Select **Command Prompt**.

CHANGING SIMPLE SETTINGS

You may need permission from an administrator to make these changes.

Changing Date and Time

1. Select the **Windows** button ⊞ on the taskbar.
2. Select **Settings**.
3. Select **Time & Language**.

4. Select **Date and time**.

5. Toggle automatic options off or on.

6. If Set time automatically is set to off, select the Change button to set the date and time manually.

Changing Audio Settings

1. Select the **Windows** button on the taskbar.

2. Select **Settings**.

3. In the Find a setting box in the upper-right of the window, type **Adjust system volume**.

4. Select **Adjust system volume**.

5. Drag the sliders to set the volume.

Adjusting Firewall Settings

1. In the Search bar on the Windows taskbar, type **Firewall**.

2. Select **Windows Defender Firewall**.

3. Use the available options to adjust settings, including selecting programs to allow or block.

Modifying User Account Control Settings

1. Select the **Windows** button on the taskbar.

2. Select **Settings**.

3. Select **Accounts**.

4. Adjust settings as desired.

VERIFYING NETWORK CONNECTIVITY

1. Select the **Windows** button on the taskbar.

2. Select **Settings**.

3. Select **Network & Internet**.

4. Select **Wi-Fi**.

5. View the current active network connections.

PART 2
Key Applications

CHAPTER 9

Application Basics

WHAT IS APPLICATION SOFTWARE?

Application software is a type of program, such as word-processing or spreadsheet software, that directs a computer device to perform one or more tasks. Think about all the things a computer can help you do. You can write letters and reports. You can look up information, record songs, play games, chat with friends, and more. Application software makes it possible for your computer to perform such tasks.

There are many different types of application software (sometimes called applications), each best suited for a certain purpose. Some programs perform specific jobs. Others do many different tasks. Once you become familiar with application software, you can make choices to help your computer work faster and more efficiently.

Selecting Application Software

OBJECTIVES

- Identify widely used types of application software.

- Decide what kinds of applications will work best for you.

- Explain how to obtain apps.

- Describe the strengths and limitations of apps and applications.

- Identify different app genres.

- Recognize why some applications may only run on certain devices.

AS YOU READ

COMPARE AND CONTRAST Use a three-column chart to compare three different types of application software. Write each type as a column header and list the features below the header.

TERMINOLOGY

- application software

- apps

- cloud apps

- integrated software

- genre

- personal information manager (PIM) program

- pervasive computing

- productivity suite

- software as a service (SAS)

- stand-alone program

- web apps

Why Use Application Software?

Application software performs a specific job or task. For example, some applications help astronomers research stars. Others help doctors care for their patients. It is important to choose applications that can do the jobs you want done. Recall that some of the most common types of application software include:

- Word processors for writing letters and reports

- Spreadsheets for working with numbers and doing math

- Databases for storing and finding information

- Presentation graphics for creating slide shows

- Desktop publishing for creating printer-ready publications such as brochures, newsletters, and invitations

- Telecommunications for using the internet and email

- **Personal information manager** (PIM) programs for storing phone numbers and addresses and creating schedules

Types of Application Software

In addition to what they do and how much they cost, you can distinguish between different application programs by considering how they interact with other programs and hardware components, and how they are sold.

STAND-ALONE PROGRAMS Software that specializes in one task is called a **stand-alone program**. Because each program—such as a word processor, database, or spreadsheet—is dedicated to just one application, stand-alone programs can have many useful and advanced features. However, stand-alone programs may cost more than other forms of application software.

WHAT TO DO WITH APPLICATION SOFTWARE

Application	Purpose
Word processing	Create text-based documents such as reports and letters
Spreadsheet	Display and analyze business, personal, or financial data
Database	Store and organize information
Presentation	Create and deliver multimedia slide shows
Desktop-publishing	Create publications such as brochures and invitations
Email	Create, send, receive, and organize electronic mail messages

Because they focus on one kind of job, stand-alone programs usually have many very specialized features. Word processors, for example, give users tools to print labels and envelopes.

INTEGRATED SOFTWARE Multiple stand-alone programs might require too much memory in your computer or may cost too much. You might want to do more with the software than a stand-alone program is capable of handling.

Integrated software programs combine the basic features of several applications into one package. They are not as powerful or as complete as their stand-alone counterparts, nor do they specialize in one application. However, integrated software usually is less costly and is fairly easy to use. These programs let you do basic work in several applications such as word processors, databases, spreadsheets, graphics, and more.

People use integrated software programs because the applications work in similar ways. That is, you often can use many of the same commands. You also can use data from one program in another.

PRODUCTIVITY SUITES What if you need to use the advanced features of several stand-alone programs? You might select a productivity suite. Although one suite may differ from another, in general **productivity suites** combine several programs such as word-processing, spreadsheets, databases, and graphics. Like integrated software, the programs in productivity suites have a common look and feel. But productivity suites contain more than the basic software found in integrated programs. They contain the actual stand-alone programs with all their features.

Productivity suites generally cost more than integrated software, but usually they are cheaper than buying the stand-alone programs separately. Some common productivity suites include:

- Microsoft Office (with Word, Excel, PowerPoint, Outlook, and Access in the Windows version)

- Corel WordPerfect Office (with WordPerfect, Quattro Pro, Paradox, Corel Presentations, and Corel CENTRAL)

- Adobe Creative Suite (with Photoshop, Illustrator, InDesign, Dreamweaver, and Animate)

WEB APPLICATIONS Recall that **web apps**, which may be called online or **cloud apps**, are applications that reside on a web server and run in a web browser. You must have an internet connection to use a web application. Most web applications require that you have a subscription for the service. This usually means that you pay an annual or monthly fee and set up an account with the vendor. You sign in to your account in order to access the program. Recall that this type of computing is often called **software as a service (SAAS)**. For example, Microsoft offers a version of its Microsoft Office suite online, and Google offers Google Docs.

PERVASIVE COMPUTING **Pervasive computing**, also called ubiquitous computing, is when microprocessors are embedded in everyday objects, allowing them to communicate with users and other devices. Now that so many objects have embedded computer chips, applications are emerging that let users interact with their things. For example, applications make it possible for you to control everything from your home thermostat to your car's navigation system from your smartphone.

FIGURE 9.1.1 Applications make it possible for you to control objects in your home.

SCYTHERS/123RF.COM

OLEKSIY MARK/SHUTTERSTOCK

FIGURE 9.1.2 Computing devices usually come with some applications installed, and you can purchase more to meet your needs.

Which Type of Software Is Right for You?

The type of application software you choose depends on what you want it to do, how you will use it, how much you are willing to spend, and how easy the programs are to learn. It also depends on whether the software will work on your computer and how much space each program will take up on your hard drive. You might want to match the software you use at home with the programs you use at school or at work so you can work on documents in both locations.

While most computers are sold with some application software installed, your computer may not have the software you need. Your needs will also change over time. Consider how problems could arise if you use the wrong software product when you try to complete a specific task—like attempting to perform advanced mathematical calculations using a word-processing program. Whether you consider upgrading your existing software, buying new programs, or downloading free software from the internet, you should consider the following:

- Reviews of the software. Consumer reviews are usually a great source of information.

- User-friendliness. What kind of support is available? Is there live help included?

- Licensing agreements (see Lesson 9-2). Can you agree to the licensing requirements?

App Culture

With its iPhone, Apple Computer pioneered the development of **apps**, third-party software programs developed specifically for smartphones, tablet computers, and other handheld devices. Now, there are apps for laptops and other personal computers, as well. The distinction between applications and apps is blurring, but there are still some key differences.

Most *apps* are designed to perform one specific task, while an *application* does much more. For example, there is a Calculator app for Windows 10 which you can use to perform mathematical operations. If you want to also use functions, graphs, charts, data analysis, and other complex operations, you would use a spreadsheet application, such as Microsoft Excel.

OBTAINING APPS Apps usually take up very little storage space—anywhere from a megabyte to a few gigabytes. They are obtained from app stores, which are online portals, such as iTunes, the Microsoft Store, or Google Play. First you search the app store to find the app you want, and then use the Download or Install button to put it on your device. Some have web app versions that run in a browser.

Basic versions of apps may be free, or very inexpensive. Premium apps offering more features may cost anywhere from $2.00 to $200.00. Some so-called "free" games are designed so that the consumer can advance in the game faster if he or she pays a fee. These "free-to-play" games originally cost nothing but a player who is not careful can end up spending large amounts of money.

IC3✔ **Know how to obtain apps.**

APP GENRES There are many **genres**, or categories, of apps, including the following:

■ Productivity apps are designed to help users be more efficient at work, school, and at home. Examples include task management, calendars, timers, and document management.

■ Reference apps let users find information. Examples include maps, translators, dictionaries, and thesauruses.

■ Content apps organize and deliver content to your device. Examples include news feeds, radio streams, magazines, blogs, and podcasts.

■ Creation apps let you create and distribute content. Examples include photo and video creation and editing, word-processing, and blogging tools.

■ Social media apps are online communities that let you share content such as information, messages, photos, links, and videos with others. Examples include Facebook, Twitter, Instagram, and Snapchat.

■ Music apps let you organize and play music. Some, like Garageband, let you create and edit music files. Some, such as iTunes, are designed for purchasing individual songs to download and play on your device, and some, such as Spotify and Pandora, let you stream music over the internet. Some internet music apps are free but most require a subscription fee.

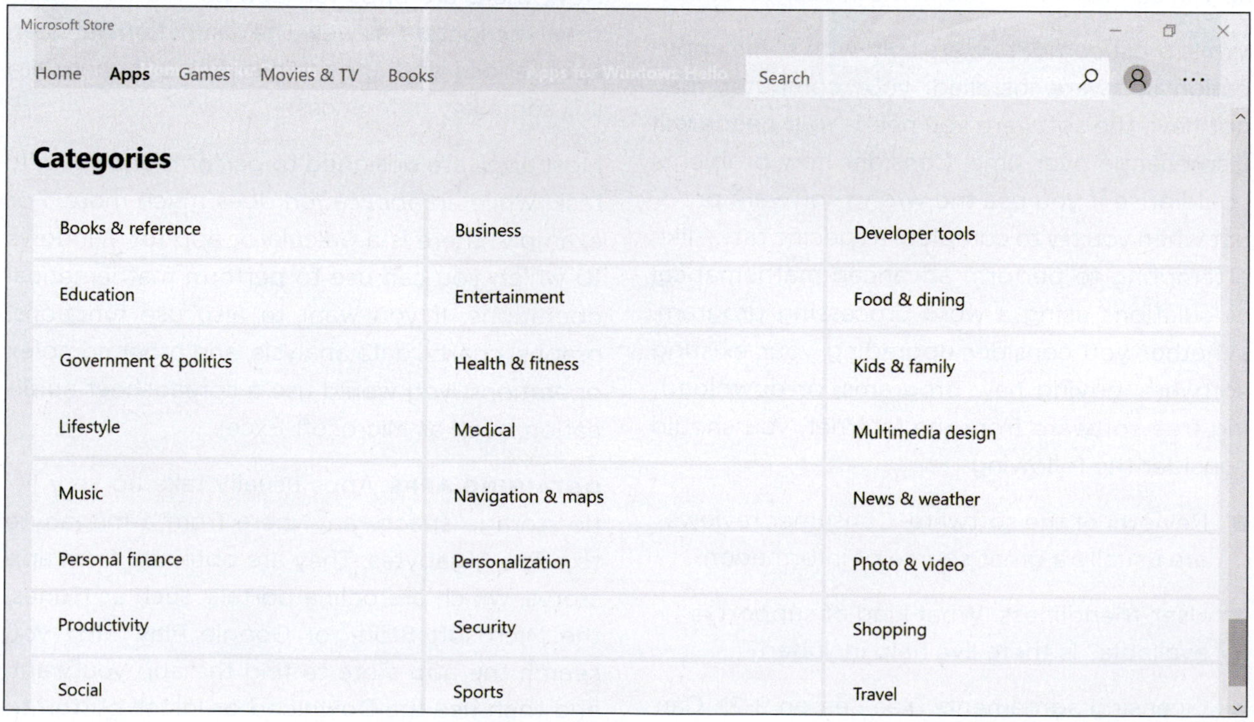

Microsoft Store				
Home	**Apps**	Games	Movies & TV	Books

Categories

Books & reference	Business	Developer tools
Education	Entertainment	Food & dining
Government & politics	Health & fitness	Kids & family
Lifestyle	Medical	Multimedia design
Music	Navigation & maps	News & weather
Personal finance	Personalization	Photo & video
Productivity	Security	Shopping
Social	Sports	Travel

FIGURE 9.1.3 Categories of apps in the Microsoft Store.

MICROSOFT CORPORATION

- Health apps are designed to help you monitor your health and well-being. The genre includes nutrition and fitness apps, such as heartrate monitors, calorie trackers, and pedometers.

IC3✔ Identify different genres of apps.

STRENGTHS AND LIMITATIONS OF APPS A well-designed app shows its strengths in the way it meets your needs. It should be easy to obtain, easy to use, and serve a specific purpose. It should run efficiently on your device, and contribute to your well-being. Many apps and applications have limitations that can outweigh the strengths.

- The cost may be high, making it a poor value and not worth purchasing.

- It may not deliver everything it promises, or may interfere with other apps you have installed.

- Some apps and applications only work on certain devices. They may be limited by operating system or device type. For example an app written for a tablet might not run properly on a smartphone or PC. An app written for an iPhone will not run on an Android or Windows phone. A browser app must run through a web browser. When selecting apps and applications, make sure it can run on your device.

IC3✔ Understand the strengths and limitations of apps and applications.

IC3✔ Understand that applications may only run on certain devices.

TECHNOLOGY@SCHOOL

There are many advantages to using the same software at school and at home. For example, some programs allow you to use one computer to access files stored elsewhere.

THINK ABOUT IT!

For which reasons listed below would it be helpful to have the same programs at school and at home?

- I can work on my school projects at home.
- I can practice using the programs that I need at school.
- I can email files to my teacher.

Obtaining Application Software Legally

OBJECTIVES

- Explain minimum system requirements.
- Compare legal types for application software.
- Explain the difference between proprietary and open-source software.
- Compare types of software licenses.
- Analyze how piracy affects makers and users of computer software.

AS YOU READ

ORGANIZING INFORMATION Make an outline of the lesson. Use Roman numerals for main headings. Use capital letters for subheadings, and use numbers for supporting details.

TERMINOLOGY

- commercial software
- creative commons
- freeware
- open-source software
- proprietary software
- public domain software
- shareware
- single-seat license
- single-user license
- site license
- software license
- software piracy
- system requirement
- volume license

Minimum System Requirements

Each software program has minimum **system requirements**. The computer must meet the minimum hardware and software needs of the program for it to work properly.

To get the most from your computer, it is important to choose software that will work with the following:

- your type of computer (Macintosh or PC compatible)

- microprocessor speed

- operating system (such as Linux, MacOS X, or Windows)

- available amount of memory (RAM)

- available hard drive space

- special equipment, such as speakers

Software that is not compatible with your system will not work. Worse, trying to install incompatible software may damage your computer. To avoid compatibility problems, double-check the system requirements before buying or installing any software program.

Legal Use of Application Software

Some application software is usually loaded on new computers. You can also obtain additional software in multiple forms.

COMMERCIAL SOFTWARE Companies own the copyrights to the application software they sell to the public. This prevents you from illegally copying it to sell it to others, giving it away, or sharing it. **Commercial software**, which may also be called **proprietary software**, is copyrighted software that you must buy before using. Usually,

you must agree to or sign a license. With commercial software, you are paying for the right to use the software, not necessarily for the right to the software's code. Software where the user doesn't gain access to the program's code is also called closed-source software.

SHAREWARE Proprietary software that you can use on a try-before-you-buy basis is called **shareware**. If you decide to keep using it, you must pay a registration fee. You are also allowed to copy shareware and give it to your friends. They must follow the same process to acquire the software.

FREEWARE Some companies give away their copyrighted software for free. This is known as **freeware**. The companies allow users to install the program as long as they do not resell it.

OPEN-SOURCE SOFTWARE **Open-source software** is a program, like proprietary software, and you may have to pay for it. However, unlike proprietary software, this kind of software makes the source code available to the public. The idea is that the software will improve and benefit from the innovations of users, who troubleshoot weak points and expand features. Critics, however, say that developers are not fairly compensated for their work (open source is not automatically "free") and also that the software development suffers if there is no central organizer.

CREATIVE COMMONS A **creative commons** license lets software copyright holders open some of their work for public use while letting them hold onto other parts of their work. As with open-source software, there are critics who complain that creative commons licenses eat away at intellectual property rights. Yet, several million pages of web content are made available by creative commons licenses, such as The Library of Public Science, Garageband.com, and Flickr, the photo sharing site.

PUBLIC DOMAIN SOFTWARE On occasion, program authors allow you to use programs, share them, give them away, or even alter them to meet certain needs. This is called **public domain software**. Beware: the quality of these programs can vary widely, and they may contain more errors than other types of software.

TECHNOLOGY@WORK

Shareware companies make money by collecting fees for the products they send out on a free trial basis.

THINK ABOUT IT!

Shareware has many advantages for its producers. Identify each benefit of shareware listed below as either true or false.

- A user might try shareware rather than opting to buy a commercial program.

- Shareware companies do not have to pay for distribution.

- Users who do not like the product still have to pay for it.

Software Licensing

Buying proprietary, copyrighted software comes with a **software license**, which allows the buyer to use and install the program, and sometimes entitles the buyer to receive free or reduced cost support and updates. Individuals might buy a **single-user license** for one copy of the program, or a **single-seat license** to install the program on a single computer. Organizations such as schools or businesses usually buy a **volume** or **site license**, which lets them install on multiple systems or a network for multiple users. Network licensing generally costs less per user and allows users to share resources.

SOFTWARE PIRACY People who copy copyrighted software to install on other computers, give away, or sell copyrighted software are guilty of violating federal copyright laws and stealing, called **software piracy**. Violating a copyright and pirating software are both morally wrong and illegal. These activities discourage the authors of good software from writing new and better programs because they may not get paid for their work. Pirated software cannot be registered, so users do not get the support services they may need.

MICROSOFT CORPORATION

> MICROSOFT SOFTWARE LICENSE TERMS
>
> WINDOWS OPERATING SYSTEM
>
> IF YOU LIVE IN (OR IF YOUR PRINCIPAL PLACE OF BUSINESS IS IN) THE UNITED STATES, PLEASE READ THE BINDING ARBITRATION CLAUSE AND CLASS ACTION WAIVER IN SECTION 10. IT AFFECTS HOW DISPUTES ARE RESOLVED.
>
> **Thank you for choosing Microsoft!**
>
> Depending on how you obtained the Windows software, this is a license agreement between (i) you and the device manufacturer or software installer that distributes the software with your device; or (ii) you and Microsoft Corporation (or, based on where you live or if a business where your principal place of business is located, one of its affiliates) if you acquired the software from a retailer. Microsoft is the device manufacturer for devices produced by Microsoft or one of its affiliates, and Microsoft is the retailer if you acquired the software directly from Microsoft.
>
> This agreement describes your rights and the conditions upon which you may use the Windows software. You should review the entire agreement, including any supplemental license terms that accompany the software and any linked terms, because all of the terms are important and together create this agreement that applies to you. You can review linked terms by pasting the (aka.ms/) link into a browser window.
>
> **By accepting this agreement or using the software, you agree to all of these terms, and**

FIGURE 9.2.1 Most software programs come with a license agreement, like the one shown here for Windows 10.

Getting Started with an Application

OBJECTIVES

- Describe how to launch a program.

- Explain how to create, open, save, and close a file.

- Explain how to exit an application.

AS YOU READ

DRAW CONCLUSIONS Use a conclusion chart to help you understand how to use application software as you read.

TERMINOLOGY

- command

- groups

- launch

- maximize

- menu bar

- minimize

- Ribbon

- scroll

- tab

- title bar

Launching an Application

To get started with an application program, you open it using the operating system on your computer. Most applications use similar commands to accomplish basic tasks, such as starting, exiting, and saving. Once you learn these tasks in one program, you can easily transfer the knowledge so you can use other programs, too.

STARTING A PROGRAM When a computer is turned on, it typically starts its operating system. You can then **launch**, or start, any application installed on the computer. You can launch an application in a variety of ways:

- Menu—In Windows, use the Start button to access a list of programs installed on the computer.

- Search—In Windows, type the program name in the Type here to search box on the taskbar. Select the program from the list that displays.

- Icon—Icons, which may be called tiles, are on-screen symbols that stand for a computer function or program. Select an icon to launch the program. Program icons can be pinned to your computer desktop, taskbar, or Start menu.

Exploring Application Windows

A launched application appears in a frame called a window. You can work in any size window, but it is usually best to **maximize** the window, or make it as large as it can be. Sometimes you will want to use another program without closing the first one. You can resize it or **minimize** it to make it as small as possible so it remains out of the way while you use the other program.

The largest portion of an application window is the space for your work. The rest of the window contains tools that you use to develop your files.

FIGURE 9.3.1 Programs can be pinned to the Windows 10 Start menu and taskbar.

MICROSOFT CORPORATION

TITLE BAR The top row of an application window is called the **title bar**. The title bar shows the program's name and, in some cases, the name of the document you are working on.

THE RIBBON In Microsoft Office, the **Ribbon** is the control center for using the application. The Ribbon has three parts:

- Tabs—Each **tab** contains important tasks you do within an application. For example, the Home tab in Excel offers formatting and formula options.

- Groups—Each tab contains **groups** of related tasks. For example, in Excel, the Number group on the Home tab offers number formatting options.

- Commands—A **command** is a button, a box for entering information, or a menu. For example, the % button in a spreadsheet program is the command for formatting a number as a percentage. Click, tap, or use your voice on a command to select it or use a shortcut key combination. For example, press and hold Alt and then press the shortcut key identified in the command name.

THE MENU A **menu bar** lists sets of commands. On a Macintosh, it appears at the top of the screen. In Windows applications that do not use a Ribbon, the menu generally appears under the title bar.

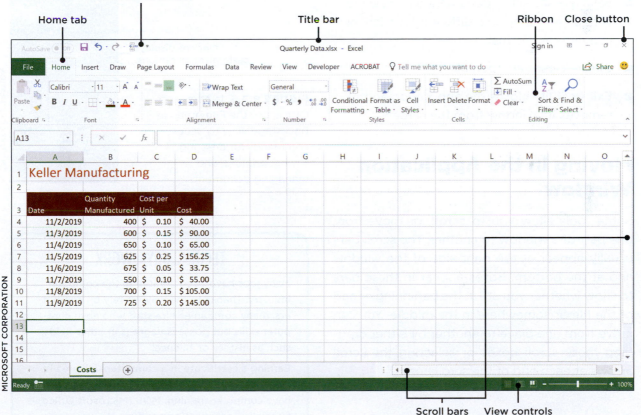

FIGURE 9.3.2 Applications in the Microsoft Office software suite share these basic elements.

Creating, Opening, Saving, and Closing

Application software lets you create new documents, save them for future use, or work on documents you have saved. You can close the application when you are done working. Most applications have a File menu that includes these commands:

- New—creates a file into which you can enter data

- Open—finds a document that was previously saved as a disk file and displays it in a window

- Save—saves the document in the current window to a disk file

- Save as—saves the document as a new file with a new name, in a different location, or in a different format

- Close—closes an open file

- Exit or Quit—closes the application and removes its window from the screen

Moving in the Application Window

Some tools allow you to **scroll**, or move from one part of a window to another. The scroll bars usually appear at the right side of the window and at the bottom. Boxes appear in these bars to show whether you are at the beginning or end of the file or somewhere in the middle. You can move from one place to another by either dragging these scroll boxes or selecting the scroll arrows at each end of the scroll bars.

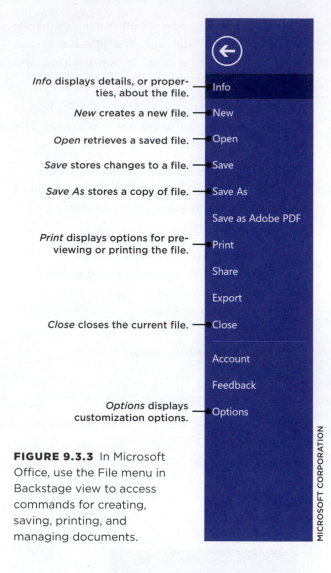

Info displays details, or properties, about the file. — Info

New creates a new file. — New

Open retrieves a saved file. — Open

Save stores changes to a file. — Save

Save As stores a copy of file. — Save As

Save as Adobe PDF

Print displays options for previewing or printing the file. — Print

Share

Export

Close closes the current file. — Close

Account

Feedback

Options displays customization options. — Options

MICROSOFT CORPORATION

FIGURE 9.3.3 In Microsoft Office, use the File menu in Backstage view to access commands for creating, saving, printing, and managing documents.

TECHNOLOGY@WORK

Many jobs have been created in the computer industry. Thanks to the way we rely on computers, many companies hire staff who have computer skills but possess degrees in other fields, such as history or science.

Earning a certificate in a computer skill area is one way to show today's companies that you have computer training. MOS (Microsoft Office Specialist) certification confirms the user is proficient with Microsoft Office programs such as Word, Excel, PowerPoint, or Access.

Chapter 9 Review

REVIEW THE TERMINOLOGY

DIRECTIONS Match each vocabulary term in the left column with the correct definition in the right column.

1. personal information manager
2. integrated software
3. productivity suite
4. shareware
5. freeware
6. public domain software
7. uninstall
8. maximize
9. apps
10. scroll

a. software that you can try before purchasing

b. uncopyrighted software that is given away without cost

c. software that stores phone numbers and creates schedules

d. combines several full-featured programs in one package

e. third-party software programs developed specifically for certain smart phones

f. to delete a program from the computer

g. combines basic features of several applications into one package

h. move from one place in a window to another

i. to make a window as large as possible

j. copyrighted software that is given away without cost

USE THE TERMINOLOGY

DIRECTIONS Determine the correct choice for each of the following.

1. Which of the following items is NOT an example of application software?

   a. spreadsheet

   b. database

   c. operating system

   d. word processor

2. Which of the following types of application software combines the basic features of several applications?

   a. stand-alone program

   b. integrated software

   c. productivity suite

   d. personal information manager (PIM) program

3. Which of the following types of software must be purchased in advance?

   a. commercial software

   c. freeware

   b. shareware

   d. public domain software

4. Which of the following types of software is available on a try-before-you-buy basis?

   a. commercial software

   c. freeware

   b. shareware

   d. public domain software

5. Which of the following features allows the user to launch an application?

   a. Help menu

   c. title bar

   b. menu bar

   d. desktop icon

6. Which of the following tools allows the user to move from one part of a window to another?

   a. scroll arrows

   c. scroll menu

   b. scroll icons

   d. scroll file

THINK CRITICALLY

DIRECTIONS Answer the following questions.

1. Compare and contrast open source and proprietary software. Why might a programmer choose to release software as open-source instead of as proprietary?

2. Why should you check a program's system requirements before purchasing it?

3. Why is it important to uninstall a program you no longer use?

4. What is the difference between the New and Open commands on the File menu?

5. Why does an application window include tools such as scroll bars, scroll boxes, and scroll arrows?

EXTEND YOUR KNOWLEDGE

DIRECTIONS Choose and complete one of the following projects.

1. The computer desktop shows many different types of icons. Icons can represent applications, files, or file folders. Experiment with a Macintosh or Microsoft Windows operating system. Make a three-column chart of the icons that appear on the desktop. Include a description of what happens when each icon is selected, and identify what type of file or program the particular icon represents.

2. Several types of application software are listed in this chapter. They include word processors, spreadsheets, databases, presentation graphics, telecommunications, and personal information managers. Using the internet or other resources, prepare a report that evaluates, compares, and contrasts at least two types of application software that you may use based on their appropriateness for a task, licensing agreements, and available support. As you work, take notes and keep track of your sources. Include a list of sources or bibliography with your report. Evaluate the information you find and only use it if it is accurate, relevant, and valid. Share your report with the class.

IC3 PREP

1. Which of these are valid locations from which one could purchase and download apps? (Select all that apply.)

   a. Google Play

   b. iTunes

   c. Bing

   d. The Microsoft Store

2. Which of these statements is NOT true of apps?

   a. In general, apps tend to take up very little storage space.

   b. Apps can cost money up front to purchase, or contain in-app purchases.

   c. Apps are a term used only for smartphone programs.

   d. An app is generally designed to do one specific task.

3. Match an app category on the left with an example of that category on the right.

   1. reference

   2. creation

   3. music

   4. productivity

   5. content

   6. social media

   7. health

   a. calendar

   b. maps

   c. podcasts

   d. word processor

   e. Instagram

   f. Spotify

   g. pedometer

4. For each line below, select whether the statement is True or False.

   a. An expensive app will always be a better product than an inexpensive or free one.

   b. An app purchased on an iPhone cannot run on an Android device.

   c. A developer can make claims about an app that do not live up to real-world usage.

   d. An app written for a tablet will always run properly on a smartphone.

5. What are some common methods that apps will use to charge users money? (Select all that apply.)

   a. an up-front purchase price

   b. a subscription service

   c. one or more in-app purchases

   d. charges based on app usage

IC3 PROCEDURES

STARTING AN APPLICATION

Select the program's icon on the Windows desktop.

OR

Select the program's icon on the taskbar.

OR

1. Select the **Start** button ⊞.

2. Select **All apps**.

3. Select the application to launch.

CREATING A NEW, BLANK FILE

1. Select **File**.

2. Select **New**.

3. Select the **Blank** file type icon.

OPENING A RECENTLY OPENED FILE

1. Start the application.

2. In the Recent list on the left, select the file.

   OR

1. At the bottom of the Recent list on the left side of the window, select the option to open other files.

2. In the file list on the right, select the file.

   OR

1. If the application is already open, select **File**.

2. Select the file in the list of files on the right.

OPENING AN EXISTING FILE

1. Start the application.

2. At the bottom of the Recent list on the left side of the window, select the option to open other files.

3. Select the storage location on the left, or select the **Browse** button and browse to the file's location.

4. Select the file and then select **Open**.

   OR

1. If the application is already open, select **File**.

2. Select **Open**.

3. Select the storage location on the left, or select the **Browse** button and browse to the file's location.

4. Select the file and then select **Open**.

SAVING A NEW FILE

1. Select **File**.

2. Select **Save As**.

3. Select the **Browse** button and browse to the location where you want to save the file.

4. Type the file name in the File name text box.

5. Select **Save**.

SAVING CHANGES TO A FILE

Select **Save** on the Quick Access Toolbar.

OR

1. Select **File**.
2. Select **Save**.

CLOSING A FILE

In the document window, select the **Close** button ☒ at the right end of the title bar.

OR

1. Select **File**.
2. Select **Close**.

EXITING AN APPLICATION

In the program window, select the **Close** button ☒ at the right end of the title bar.

OR

1. Select **File**.
2. Select **Exit**.

CHAPTER 10

Understanding Applications

HOW CAN AN APPLICATION HELP YOU?

Application software provides the tools you need to get a job done. When you select the right program for the job, you can accomplish the task quickly and efficiently. Applications are designed to meet different needs. Some are designed for one specific purpose, such as managing medical records or product inventory. Some are designed for multiple purposes, such as creating reports, letters, or memos.

In this chapter, you will examine application software more closely. You will learn more about types of applications and how to use an application program to complete a task.

Examining Types of Application Software

OBJECTIVES

- Compare and contrast horizontal and vertical applications.

- Describe the role of beta versions in the software-testing process.

AS YOU READ

ORGANIZE INFORMATION Use an outline to organize information about application software as you read.

TERMINOLOGY

- beta version

- copy protection

- horizontal application

- personal productivity program

- premium apps

- time-limited trial

- vertical application

Which Direction Is Right for You?

Application software can be classified as a stand-alone, integrated, or productivity suite program. These types of software differ in the number of tasks they perform. Another way to classify application software is based on whether it is developed for a few users with very specific needs or whether it appeals to many users with shared needs.

VERTICAL APPLICATION A **vertical application** is designed for a very limited purpose, such as restaurant management or medical billing. Although the software is very useful to one field or business, it is of little interest to others.

HORIZONTAL APPLICATION A **horizontal application** is a general-purpose program that meets the needs of many different users. It can be applied to many tasks. It also tends to be less expensive. It is likely that you will use horizontal, not vertical, applications for schoolwork you do on the computer. Horizontal applications are also used in many households to track finances and prepare tax forms.

Types of Horizontal Applications

Horizontal applications can be divided into several categories depending on the focus of the program.

PERSONAL PRODUCTIVITY PROGRAMS The most popular horizontal applications are known as **personal productivity programs**. They help people work more effectively and include common applications such as word processors and database systems.

MULTIMEDIA APPLICATIONS Some horizontal applications combine text, graphics, video, and sound. These include:

- Desktop publishing—to combine text and graphics to produce newsletters and brochures

- Graphics—to create and edit pictures

- Web page design—to create web pages using sound, graphics, animation, and text

INTERNET APPLICATIONS Some horizontal applications help computer users communicate over the internet, including:

- Web-browsers—to access data from the World Wide Web

- Email—to send and receive electronic messages

ONLINE OR MOBILE APPS Applications designed for use online are called online apps, web apps, or cloud apps, while those designed to download and use on a smartphone or tablet are called mobile apps. They are available for thousands of uses, from productivity suites to games. Some are free, and some, called **premium apps**, must be purchased.

TECHNOLOGY@SCHOOL

Most schools run horizontal applications to help students and staff perform everyday computing tasks. These commercial programs meet the needs of most computer users most of the time.

THINK ABOUT IT!

With permission, look at several computers at school, including one in the library and one for classroom use. Which of the following horizontal applications did you find?

- word processing
- spreadsheet
- database
- presentation graphics
- other

Apps have a range of uses from playing music to helping improve productivity. Some apps even track a user's health and exercise. Apps that use the internet can connect to a web browser, a user's email, or social media sites, such as Facebook and Twitter. There are also reference apps you use to search for information; creation apps for drawing or creating images; and content apps for organizing data, like the contacts on your phone. Like computer applications, apps are written to run on a specific operating system so not all apps run on all mobile devices.

Testing Software

Beta versions, or early working copies of application software, are often sent to selected users to test the program. They use it for a period of time and report errors or problems to the developer. Beta versions help ensure that the final software will work correctly and offer customers the best tools possible.

LIMITED TRIALS To protect their work and guard against illegal copying, companies may set their beta software to expire after a certain date. These **time-limited trials** stop working after a certain number of uses or days.

COPYRIGHT CONCERNS Developers sometimes add **copy protection**, a physical device or software tool to keep users from making unauthorized copies of the beta software. These copyright safeguards can protect the sellers' property from illegal copying—a serious crime. Copy protection prevents beta software, which is still in development, from being widely distributed.

REAL-WORLD TECH

PROTECTING DIGITAL MEDIA

ROBIN LUND/SHUTTERSTOCK

Copy protection extends beyond software. Any form of information that is stored digitally is at risk of being illegally copied, including CD music and DVD movies.

An early attempt by Sony Corporation to copy-protect CDs sold across Europe failed. It turned out that consumers could defeat the copy-protection method too easily.

Why do you think companies continue to research new and better ways to copy-protect their work from unethical and illegal duplication?

Application Documentation and Versions

OBJECTIVES

- Compare and contrast types of documentation.

- Explain the purpose of versions and version numbers.

- Describe why it is important to register your software.

AS YOU READ

CAUSE AND EFFECT Use a cause-and-effect chart to help you understand the results of various software elements.

TERMINOLOGY

- documentation

- End User License Agreement (EULA)

- knowledge base

- maintenance release

- product key

- troubleshoot

- version

Software Documentation

Most software packages provide directions on how to install the program, to use the application, and to **troubleshoot**, or correct, problems. These instructions, called **documentation**, are typically available in three forms:

- information on the publisher's website

- printed tutorials and reference manuals

- electronic help screens in the program or on CD-ROM

WEBSITES Software documentation is usually found on the software publisher's website. These sites can be searched for specific topics. They often include answers to users' frequently asked questions (FAQs) and give other helpful hints. They may include tutorials in video or text that help you learn how to use features. Downloadable files, sometimes called patches, may be available to fix, or patch, problems with the software. More so than other types of support, web documentation can be updated quickly by the publisher and shared with users who need it.

PRINTED DOCUMENTATION Installation instructions may be a single sentence printed on the software disk or CD. Other instructions may take the form of a booklet. Some programs include encyclopedia-type references that detail the software features.

ELECTRONIC HELP Application software sometimes provides reference materials in electronic form as part of the program, online, or on a CD or DVD. Opening the program's Help menu lets you troubleshoot problems as they happen and find out how to perform certain operations or tasks.

OTHER SOURCES If you need more information than is provided by the software's documentation, telephone or online support may be an option. Many software companies maintain an online **knowledge base** that users can search to find information and get help. There may be online communities or forums, which are discussion boards where users can post questions that other users or company employees can answer. In addition, many helpful application software references and tutorials are available in libraries, online, or at bookstores.

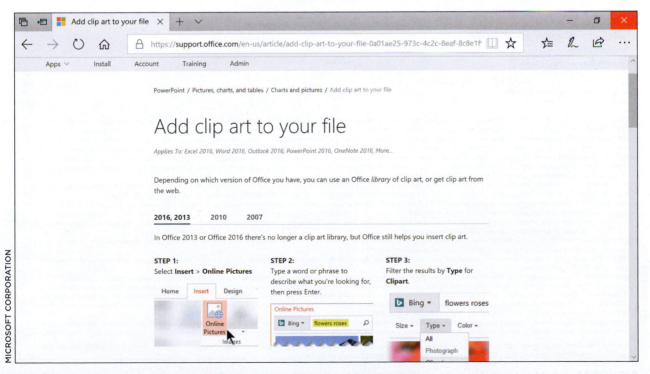

MICROSOFT CORPORATION

FIGURE 10.2.1 Most software programs provide online help and support.

TECHNOLOGY@WORK

There is a gradual but steady shift in most companies away from outputting files in hard copy (printed) to outputting soft copy (digital or electronic files). Digital output includes any information displayed on a computer, including application files, email attachments, and web pages.

THINK ABOUT IT!

Outputting files electronically is convenient, fast, and can save costs related to printing and mailing. It also poses some risks. Which of the following issues do you think poses the greatest risk to companies and individuals?

- lack of hard copy documentation
- risk of unauthorized access to data
- risk of loss or damage to data
- inability to open or read incompatible files

Versions of Software

Successful software can lead to multiple **versions**, or releases. Companies typically identify their new software with a version number. A version can be identified by the year it was released, such as Microsoft Word 2016. Sometimes the version number is a whole number followed by a decimal or a letter, such as 5.D or 6.22. Smaller numbers, such as 1.2 or 1.2a, indicate a **maintenance release**—a minor revision to correct errors or add minor features. A larger number indicates that the software has significant revisions with new features.

The version number may not be obvious when an application launches. However, most software manufacturers locate the version number somewhere in the program. Sometimes it is in the Help menu, where you can select the About command. In the Microsoft Office programs, Choose File > Account and then click the About button to view information about the software—including the license agreement and the version and revision numbers.

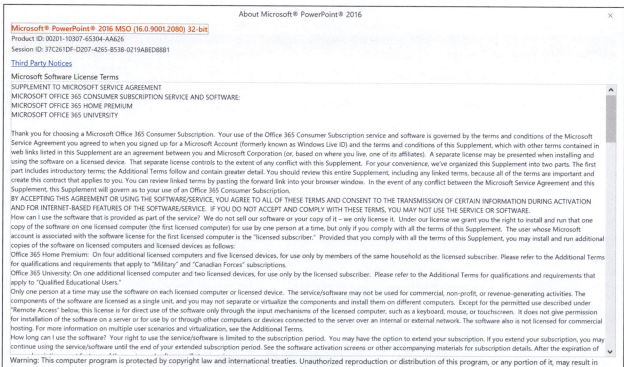

FIGURE 10.2.2 Microsoft PowerPoint 2016 license terms and version number.

MICROSOFT CORPORATION

Software Registration and Protection

When you install software, you are typically asked to register, or be recorded as the owner of your copy, with the publisher. Most registration is completed online as part of the program activation. You may be able to register by mailing a printed form. To activate the program, you usually enter a license number, called a **product key** or product code, and agree to an **End User License Agreement (EULA)**.

Registration allows you to use the software legally. Since the software company knows you have a legal copy of its product, it may offer services such as free technical support. The company may also send notices of new version releases or upgrades offered at no cost or at a discounted price.

Organizations that have many computers—such as schools, businesses, or government agencies—may purchase a site license instead of registering individual copies of the software. A site license, which may be called a multi-user or volume license, usually includes one product key for all users, and gives permission to install the software on a specific number of computers for the organization's internal use only. On the other hand, a single-user or single-seat license, provides one key per copy.

TECHNOLOGY@HOME

One type of software sees seasonal increase in sales. Every spring, many families purchase tax preparation software to assist in preparing annual federal tax returns to send to the Internal Revenue Service by the filing date in April.

THINK ABOUT IT!

Some revisions in tax preparation software are out of the control of the programmers. Of the reasons listed below for a revision, which do you think developers could not have predicted?

- bugs in the program
- changes in tax laws
- changes in the data user's input

Using Application Software

OBJECTIVES

- Identify features of an application window.

- Explain the purpose of Protected mode and read-only view.

- Explore program options and preferences.

- Identify and use common application features.

- Compare and contrast plain text and text with markup.

AS YOU READ

SUMMARIZE Use a chart to summarize the purpose of each common feature of application software as you read.

TERMINOLOGY

- application workspace

- command button

- default

- font

- menu

- multitask

- preference

- Print Preview

- Protected view

- Read-only view

- status bar

- tab

- tags

- title bar

- toolbar

- zoom

Working in an Application's Window

There are several common features you are likely to find in your application windows.

APPLICATION WORKSPACE The largest area of a program's window is called the **application workspace**. It displays the file in which you are working. You can enter text, graphics, or other data into the workspace. You also can locate and open a saved file into the application workspace. The workspace looks different depending on the application. For example, a word-processing application workspace looks like a page; a spreadsheet workspace looks like a grid of columns and rows.

TITLE BAR The **title bar** usually displays the name of the application and the name of the file you are in. If this is a new document, you will see a placeholder name, such as *Untitled* or *Document 1*.

TOOLBAR AND COMMAND BUTTONS Most applications have a **toolbar** or **command buttons** that you use to select a command. A toolbar is a row of icons or buttons. Selecting a toolbar icon or command button tells the application to execute that command. Microsoft Office applications display buttons on the Ribbon instead of on a toolbar.

Some applications have more than one toolbar. Many toolbars can be dragged to a different location, if desired, or even "floated" in the application workspace.

MENUS AND TABS **Menus** and **tabs** give you access to the program's commands. They present a list—or menu—of choices so you can select the one you need.

VIEWING A DOCUMENT Many programs let you change how a document is displayed in the application workspace. Changing the view can help you accomplish specific tasks. For example, you might change to **Print Preview** to see how a file will look when it is printed, or change to Draft view when you do not need to see features such as graphics or columns.

ADJUSTING THE DISPLAY You can adjust the display of the data in the workspace by using the **zoom** control. This option magnifies the view of the document. You typically can set it to any size you prefer between 10 percent and 500 percent. Zoom options do not affect the printing size, only how you see your document on the screen. A 100 percent magnification shows the document at the same size that a printed copy will be.

PROTECTED MODE Some programs automatically open certain files in Protected mode, or **Protected view**, which means most editing functions are disabled. For example, Microsoft Office programs open files downloaded from the internet or received as an email attachment in Protected view. Protected mode can help protect your computer from viruses and other malware. You can select the Enable Editing button to exit protected mode.

IC3✔ **Understand what Protected mode means.**

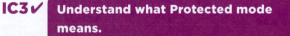

MICROSOFT CORPORATION

FIGURE 10.3.1 The Ribbon in Microsoft Office programs provides easy access to commands. Other programs may use toolbars or menus.

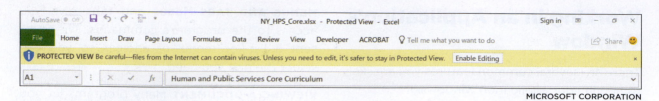

MICROSOFT CORPORATION

FIGURE 10.3.2 Microsoft Excel opens downloaded files in Protected view.

READ-ONLY VIEW Most programs let you set properties to open a document or file in **Read-only view**, which means you can read it but not edit it. Using Read-only view lets you protect the document from accidental or unauthorized changes.

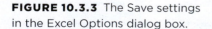

IC3✔ Know how to use Read-only view.

CHECKING YOUR STATUS Many software programs display a **status bar** below the application workspace. A status bar shows information about the program and other useful messages. For example, the status bar in Word displays the current page number, total page count, and the number of the line on which you are currently typing.

Setting Options and Preferences

Software applications start using **default** settings. These are options preset by the software maker, based on what most users prefer. You can customize the program for the way you want to work by selecting **preferences** or options. Changing an option or preference replaces the default setting.

You can change such features as how the screen looks, how spell check works, and the preferred location for saving documents. You can choose to apply a preference to a current document only, or save it in the computer as a new default setting. Many programs also allow you to reset the revised default settings back to their original settings. To set options in a Microsoft Office program, select File and then select Options.

FIGURE 10.3.3 The Save settings in the Excel Options dialog box.

MICROSOFT CORPORATION

Common Application Features

Most application programs have many of the same features and use the same or similar commands to accomplish tasks. This consistency makes it easy for users to quickly learn how to use different applications. Not only do almost all applications have these common commands, they use the same shortcut keystrokes. For example, Ctrl + S is the keyboard equivalent for the Save command in most programs. Ctrl + P is usually the keyboard equivalent for the Print command.

SELECTING In most applications, in order to work with content in a document you must select it. For example, you must select text in a document or a cell in a spreadsheet in order to delete it or format it. To select text in most programs, you drag across it with a pointer. To select a cell, you click it.

IC3✔ Be able to select text or cells.

CUT, COPY, AND PASTE When you want to move or copy selected content, you use the Cut, Copy, and Paste commands. Cut (Ctrl + X) deletes the selected content from its original location. Copy (Ctrl + C) leaves the original in place. The Paste command (Ctrl + V) inserts the cut or copied selection in a new location.

IC3✔ Know Copy, Cut, and Paste keyboard equivalents.

SPELL CHECK Most applications include a spell check feature you can use to identify and correct spelling errors.

IC3✔ Know how to use spell check.

REVIEWING Many programs have reviewing features for tracking and managing changes to documents. Reviewing features are often used for collaborating with others because you can see who inserted or deleted content, and you can communicate with others using comments.

IC3✔ Know how to use Reviewing features.

FIND AND REPLACE Most programs have tools for searching through a document to find specific information or formatting, and even for replacing the information with something else. These tools are generally referred to as Find and Replace features.

IC3✔ Know how to use Find/Replace features.

UNDO AND REDO Almost every program includes Undo and Redo commands. Undo lets you step back to undo previous actions. Redo lets you step forward to replace the actions you just undid. Some programs have a Repeat command that lets you repeat the previous action.

IC3✔ Be able to Redo and Undo.

DRAG AND DROP In addition to having Cut and Paste commands for moving content, most applications let you select, and then drag and drop the selected content to a new location. Drag and drop is often completed by holding down the mouse button while moving the pointer to the new location, and then releasing the mouse button.

IC3✔ Be able to drag and drop.

ZOOM Zoom tools let you change the magnification level of the content displayed on the screen. You can zoom in to a higher magnification to increase the size of the content on the screen, or zoom out to a lower magnification to decrease the size of the content on the screen. At a lower magnification, the content might be harder to read, but you will be able to see more at once.

IC3✔ Be able to use the Zoom feature.

CAREER CORNER

Software firms need employees with strong people skills as well as knowledge of the programs they develop. Customer-support technicians provide assistance to customers who need help with products. Sometimes help is offered by phone; other tech support is offered online.

Plain Text vs. HTML

Most applications support formatting such as colors and fonts for text, or shapes for images. Recall that a **font** is a specific typeface with a certain size and style used for displaying characters. For example, in Microsoft Word or Microsoft Excel, you can change the size of text and it is saved in the file. If you convert the file to another format, such as Adobe Acrobat .pdf, the formatting is retained.

However, not all files can store formatting commands. Plain text files, which have a .txt file extension, are created with a text-editing program such as Notepad. Plain text files can store only text, including numbers, symbols, and line breaks. They cannot save formatting options, such as fonts, colors, or text sizes. If you convert a Word document file to plain text, it loses its formatting.

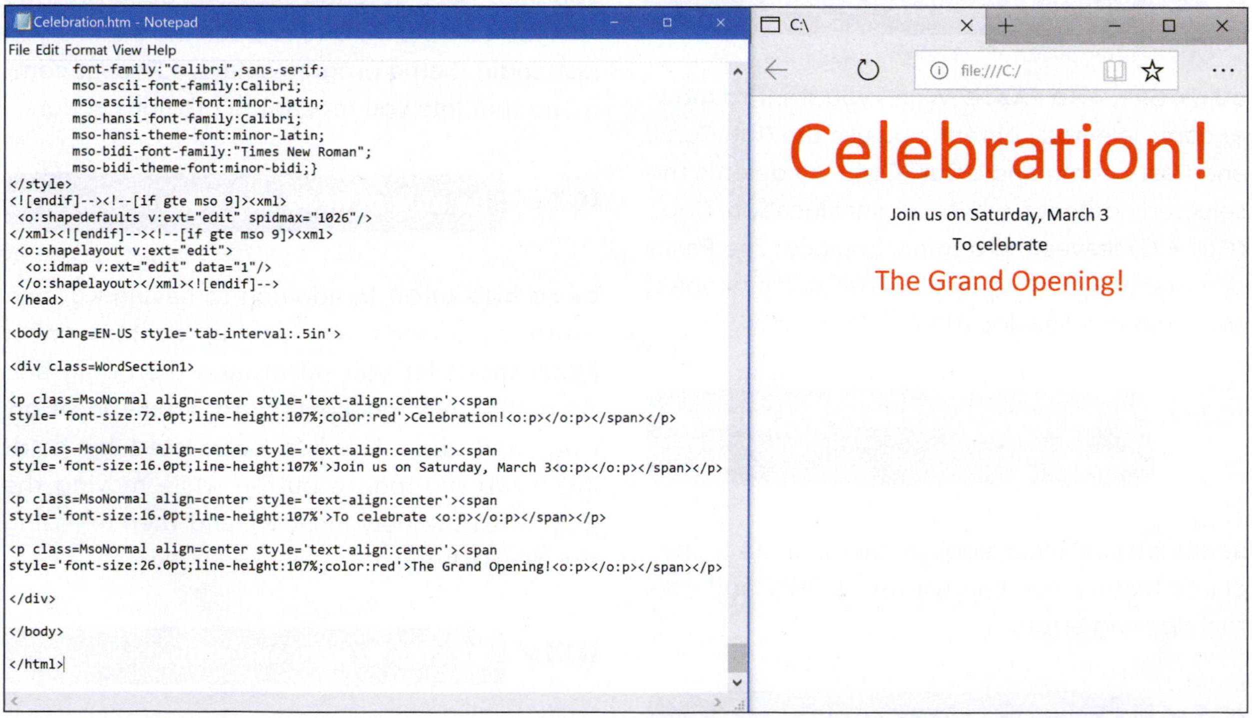

MICROSOFT CORPORATION

FIGURE 10.3.4 Compare the HTML text with markup file on the left with the same file displayed in a browser on the right.

Hypertext Markup Language (HTML) is a method of using codes, called **tags**, to define formatting and other properties for text. It is used to apply formatting to web pages and email templates. The tags, which are text characters surrounded by angle brackets, instruct an HTML-compatible program such as a web browser how to display the formatting. If you open the file in a text editor, you see only the plain text and the codes, which is sometimes called text with markup.

IC3 ✔ | **Understand the difference between plain text and HTML (text with markup).**

Working with Two or More Programs

The term **multitasking** means working with more than one computer application at the same time. Computer operating systems allow you to multitask by giving sections of memory to each application that is running. You can then switch among them as needed.

CONNECTIONS

LANGUAGE ARTS Settings in the Proofing section of Microsoft Word's Options can help you check and correct your spelling and grammar as you type. See which options are set as program defaults. Customizing these settings may enable you to write better and more clearly.

To multitask, open the desired programs, such as a word processor and a spreadsheet. Each application appears in a separate window. Select one window by selecting its button on the taskbar, and begin to work. You can move from one window to another. If you create a chart in a spreadsheet, you can cut or copy and paste it into the word processor. When you are done, exit each application to close your programs.

213

Chapter 10 Review

REVIEW THE TERMINOLOGY

DIRECTIONS Match each vocabulary term in the left column with the correct definition in the right column.

1. vertical application
2. horizontal application
3. beta version
4. copy protection
5. documentation
6. version
7. site license
8. application workspace
9. zoom
10. preference

a. permission to install software on multiple computers

b. main area of a program window

c. a program designed for a limited purpose

d. a general-purpose program that can be used by a variety of users

e. tool that keeps a user from making unauthorized copies of software

f. instructions that make using software easier

g. to change the size of the data on the screen

h. test copy of software that companies use to find errors

i. setting defined by the computer user

j. copy of software that may have new features

USE THE TERMINOLOGY

DIRECTIONS Determine the correct choice for each of the following.

1. Which of the following is an example of a vertical application?

    a. an internet browser

    b. a library card catalog

    c. a popular personal information manager

    d. an inexpensive spreadsheet

2. Which of the following is NOT an example of multitasking?

    a. switching from one program to another

    b. moving data to a different document

    c. keeping your desktop clear

    d. working in three or four applications at once

3. Software documentation can help you do which of the following?

   a. troubleshoot problems

   b. obtain a site license

   c. make an application vertical

   d. create a new version

4. Which of the following is NOT a characteristic of a maintenance release?

   a. minor revisions to existing features

   b. minor features added

   c. letter added to the version number

   d. significant improvements

5. Changing the zoom controls allows you to do which of the following?

   a. change the font of the data on the screen

   b. adjust the size of the data on the screen

   c. change the order in which the data is displayed on the screen

   d. adjust the document's margins

6. Which of the following menus would a word processor most likely have?

   a. Calculate

   b. Message

   c. Sound Controls

   d. Edit

THINK CRITICALLY

DIRECTIONS Answer the following questions.

1. What is the benefit of setting a document or file to "Read-only View" in its properties? How is this similar to "Protected mode"?

2. A project you're working on requires you to Paste (Ctrl + V) an image or text from one source to another. In what situation would you begin with using the Cut (Ctrl + X) command? What would be the benefit of using the Copy (Ctrl + C) command instead?

3. What are some benefits to editing a project with a word processor's Reviewing features?

4. Why might a user choose to upgrade to a newer version of a particular software application?

EXTEND YOUR KNOWLEDGE

DIRECTIONS Choose and complete one of the following projects.

1. Horizontal applications are popular types of software, such as word processors and internet browsers, with which most computer users work. Vertical applications are designed for more specific activities. Interview two adults who use computers for their jobs. Identify the types of applications they use at work. What programs do they use that are specific to their careers or businesses? How do they use popular applications differently? For both types of software, to what extent do licensing agreements and customer service/technical support influence their purchasing decisions? Create a Venn diagram comparing your findings.

2. Several types of documentation are listed in this chapter, including printed material, help screens, and websites. Using the internet or other resources, prepare a report that discusses documentation. Discuss the purpose of each type of documentation. How and when might you need to use each—now and in the future? What are some of the different features available in each type of documentation? Share your reports with the class.

IC3 PREP

1. You have received an email with an attached document you would like to edit, but when you open it you can only read and not edit the file. Why? (Select all that apply.)

    a. The document is being viewed in Protected mode on your system.

    b. The document contains a virus.

    c. The document was set to Read-only in its properties menu.

    d. The document was in the wrong font.

2. Which of these is NOT commonly coded into a modern word processor?

    a. Search

    b. Spell check

    c. AutoSum

    d. Find/Replace

    e. Zoom

3. You've just used your mouse to drag and drop an image into a document you're editing, but have realized that it is not the correct image! What are some solutions to this problem? (Select all that apply.)

    a. Select the image and use the Cut command.

    b. Use the Undo command.

    c. Close the document without saving and open it again.

    d. Use the Repeat command.

4. For each line below, select whether the statement is True or False.

    a. HTML files are able to store formatting options like fonts and text sizes.

    b. A Word document converted to a plain text file will retain any images stored among the text.

    c. HTML uses codes called "tags" to apply formatting in compatible programs like web browsers.

    d. Opening an HTML file in a text editor will show only plain text and code.

5. What would be the best program to use to view an HTML file?

    a. plain text editor

    b. web browser

    c. calculator

    d. word processor

6. Which tool lets you change the magnification level of the content on the screen?

    a. Magnify

    b. Zoom

    c. Scale

    d. Shrink

IC3 PROCEDURES

APPLYING AND REMOVING READ-ONLY VIEW

1. In File Explorer, browse to the file's location.

2. Right-click (or press, hold, and release) the file.

3. On the drop-down menu, select **Properties**.

4. Next to Attributes, select the **Read-only** check box to toggle the setting on or off.

5. A check mark in the box turns Read-only view on.

6. Select **OK**.

SELECTING TEXT

Mouse Selection Commands

- One word: Double-click word
- One sentence: Ctrl + click in sentence
- One line: Click in selection bar to the left of the line
- One paragraph: Double-click in selection bar to the left of the paragraph
- Document: Triple-click in selection bar
- Noncontiguous text: Select first block, press and hold Ctrl, then select additional blocks

Keyboard Selection Commands

- One character right: Shift + →
- One character left: Shift + ←
- One line up: ↑
- One line down: ↓
- To end of line: Shift + End
- To beginning of line: Shift + Home
- To end of document: Shift + Ctrl + End
- To beginning of document: Shift + Ctrl + Home
- Entire document: Ctrl + A

SELECTING NONCONTIGUOUS TEXT

1. Select the first block.

2. Press and hold the **Ctrl** key.

3. Select the next block.

SELECTING AND REPLACING TEXT

1. Select the text.

2. Enter the replacement text.

CANCELING A SELECTION OR COMMAND

- Click anywhere outside selected text to cancel the selection.
- Press **Esc** to cancel a command or close a dialog box.
- Click anywhere outside a displayed menu to close it without making a selection.

SELECTING IN A TABLE

1. Position the insertion point in the table.
2. Select the **Table Tools Layout** tab.
3. Select the **Select** button.
4. Select the element to select.

SELECTING A CELL IN A TABLE

1. Position the mouse pointer in the lower-left corner of the cell.
2. When the mouse pointer changes to a black, diagonal arrow ⬈ click to select the cell.

SELECTING MULTIPLE COMPONENTS IN A TABLE

To select contiguous cells, drag across them.

OR

1. Select the first cell.
2. Press and hold **Shift**.
3. Select additional cells.

   OR

1. To select noncontiguous cells, select the first cell.
2. Press and hold **Ctrl**.
3. Select additional cells.

SELECTING CELLS IN A WORKSHEET

Click or tap the cell to select.

OR

Drag across a range to select it.

OR

1. Select the first cell.
2. Press and hold the **Shift** key.
3. Select the last cell.

SELECTING NONCONTIGUOUS CELLS

1. Select the first cell.
2. Press and hold the **Ctrl** key.
3. Select the next cell.

MOVING A SELECTION

Using Drag-and-Drop

1. Select the text (including paragraph mark, if necessary) to move.

2. Move the mouse pointer anywhere over the selection.

3. Press and hold the left mouse button.

4. Drag to the desired location and release the mouse button.

Using Cut (Ctrl + X) and Paste (Ctrl + V)

1. Select the text (including paragraph mark, if necessary) to move.

2. Select the **Home** tab.

3. Select the **Cut** button ✄.

   OR

   Press **Ctrl + X**.

4. Position the insertion point where you want to move the text.

5. Select the **Home** tab.

6. Select the **Paste** button 📋.

   OR

   Press **Ctrl + V**.

Using F2

1. Select the text (including paragraph mark, if necessary) to move.

2. Press **F2**.

3. Position the insertion point where you want to move the text.

4. Press **Enter**.

COPYING A SELECTION

Using Drag-and-Drop

1. Select the text (including paragraph mark, if necessary) to copy.

2. Move the mouse pointer anywhere over the selection.

3. Press and hold **Ctrl**.

4. Press and hold the left mouse button.

5. Drag to the desired location and release the mouse button.

Using Copy (Ctrl + C) and Paste (Ctrl + V)

1. Select the text (including paragraph mark, if necessary) to copy.

2. Select the **Home** tab.

3. Select the **Copy** button 📑.

   OR

   Press **Ctrl + C**.

4. Position the insertion point where you want to copy the text.

5. Select the **Home** tab.

6. Select the **Paste** button 📋.

   OR

   Press **Ctrl + V**.

Using Undo (Ctrl + Z), Redo (Ctrl + Y), and Repeat (Ctrl + Y)

- Select the **Undo** button ↶ on the Quick Access Toolbar to reverse a single action or series of actions.

- Select the **Redo** button ↷ on the Quick Access Toolbar to reinstate any action that you reversed with Undo.

- Select the **Repeat** button ↺ on the Quick Access Toolbar to repeat the most recent action.

Using Find

1. Select the **Home** tab.

2. Select the **Find** button 🔎.

3. In the text box at the top of the Navigation pane, enter the text you want to find.

Using Find and Replace

1. Select the **Home** tab.

2. Select the **Replace** button.

3. In the Find and Replace dialog box, enter the text to find in the Find what text box.

4. Enter the replacement text in the Replace with text box.

5. Select the **Replace** button to replace each separate occurrence; Select **Replace All** to replace all occurrences.

CHECKING SPELLING

1. Select the **Review** tab.

2. Select the **Spelling** button.

3. In the Spelling task pane, select to **Change** or **Ignore** the suggestions.

4. Select **Close**.

   OR

1. Right-click (or press, hold, and release) a word that has been identified as misspelled.

2. On the shortcut menu, select the desired spelling.

ZOOMING USING THE SLIDER

- Drag the Zoom slider to the left to zoom out.

- Drag to the right to zoom in.

- Select the **Zoom Out** button ⊟ at the left of the Zoom slider to zoom out.

- Select the **Zoom In** button ⊞ to the right of the slider to zoom in.

ZOOMING USING THE VIEW TAB

1. Select the **View** tab.

2. In the Zoom group, select the desired zooming option.

    OR

1. Select the **View** tab.

2. Select the **Zoom** button 🔍.

3. In the Zoom dialog box, select the desired zooming option.

4. Select **OK**.

Additional Microsoft Office 2016 Common Procedures

VIEWING APPLICATION OPTIONS

1. With the application open, select **File**.
2. Select **Options**.
3. In the application's Options dialog box, select a category on the left and change options as desired.
4. Select **OK**.

USING THE RIBBON

- Select a tab on the Ribbon to display its commands.
- Point to a button on a tab to display its ScreenTip.
- Select a button on a tab to execute a command.
- Select a drop-down arrow on a button to display a gallery or menu of options.
- Select a group dialog box launcher to display a dialog box, task pane, or window where you can select additional or multiple options.
- Hide the Ribbon by selecting the **Collapse the Ribbon** button.
- Select any tab to expand the Ribbon temporarily.
- Select the **Pin the Ribbon** button to keep the Ribbon displayed.

CUSTOMIZING THE RIBBON

1. With the application open, select **File**.
2. Select **Options**.

   OR

1. Right-click anywhere on the Ribbon.
2. On the shortcut menu, select **Customize the Ribbon**.

3. In the application's Options dialog box, select **Customize Ribbon**.
4. Select options to customize the Ribbon as desired.
5. Select **OK**.

CUSTOMIZING THE QUICK ACCESS TOOLBAR

Adding Buttons to the Toolbar

1. Select the **Customize Quick Access Toolbar** button.
2. On the menu, select a button to add it to the Quick Access Toolbar.

   OR

1. Right-click a button on the Ribbon.
2. On the shortcut menu, select **Add to Quick Access Toolbar**.

Removing Buttons from the Toolbar

1. Select the **Customize Quick Access Toolbar** button.
2. On the menu, select a button with a check mark to remove it from the toolbar.

   OR

1. Right-click a button on the Quick Access Toolbar that you want to remove.
2. On the shortcut menu, select **Remove from Quick Access Toolbar**.

MOVING THE QUICK ACCESS TOOLBAR

1. Select the **Customize Quick Access Toolbar** button.
2. Select **Show Below the Ribbon**.

   OR

   Select **Show Above the Ribbon**.

SCROLLING

- Use the directional keys on the keyboard to scroll left and right or up and down.

- Drag a scroll box until you bring the desired portion of the file into view.

- Click a scroll arrow to scroll through the file in small increments.

- If your mouse has a scroll wheel, spin it to scroll up and down.

- If you use a touch screen, swipe to scroll in the desired direction.

APPLYING A THEME

These steps are written for Word and may vary in the other Office applications.

1. Select the **Design** tab.
2. Select the **Themes** button ⌷.
3. Select the desired theme from the Themes gallery.

WORKING WITH FONTS

Applying Font Styles

1. Select the **Home** tab.
2. Select the desired font style, as follows:

   Bold (Ctrl + B) ⌷

   Italic (Ctrl + I) ⌷

   OR

1. Select the **Home** tab.
2. Select the **Font** group dialog box launcher ⌷.
3. In the Font style list, select the desired style.
4. Click **OK**.

Changing the Font

1. Select the **Home** tab.
2. Select the **Font** button drop-down arrow ⌷.
3. Select the desired font.

   OR

1. Select the **Home** tab.
2. Select the **Font** group dialog box launcher ⌷.
3. In the Font list, select the desired font.
4. Select **OK**.

Changing the Font Color

1. Select the **Home** tab.
2. Select the **Font Color** button drop-down arrow ⌷.
3. Select the desired font color.

   OR

1. Select the **Home** tab.
2. Select the **Font** group dialog box launcher ⌷.
3. Select the **Font color** drop-down arrow.
4. Select the desired font color.
5. Select **OK**.

Changing the Font Size

1. Select the **Home** tab.
2. Select the **Font Size** button drop-down arrow ⌷.
3. Select the desired font size.

   OR

   Select the **Home** tab.

   - Select the **Increase Font Size** button ⌷ to increase the font size.

   - Select the **Decrease Font Size** ⌷ button to decrease the font size.

   OR

1. Select the **Home** tab.
2. Select the **Font** group dialog box launcher ⌷.
3. In the Size list, select the desired font size.
4. Select **OK**.

Applying Font Effects

1. Select the **Home** tab.
2. Select the **Font** group dialog box launcher.
3. Under Effects, select the desired effect.
4. Select **OK**.

Applying Underlines

1. Select the **Home** tab.
2. Select the **Underline** button drop-down arrow.
3. Select the desired underline style.

   OR

1. Select the **Home** tab.
2. Select the **Font** group dialog box launcher.
3. Select the **Underline style** drop-down arrow.
4. Select the desired underline style.
5. Select **OK**.

INSERTING OBJECTS

Inserting a Picture File

1. Select the **Insert** tab.
2. Select the **Pictures** button.
3. In the Insert Picture dialog box, navigate to and select the picture you want to insert.
4. Select **Insert**.

Inserting Clip Art

1. Select the **Insert** tab.
2. Select the **Online Pictures** button.
3. In the search box, type the name of the art you want to insert.
4. Select a picture in the task pane and then select **Insert** to insert it in the document.

Inserting a Shape

1. Select the **Insert** tab.
2. Select the **Shapes** button.
3. Select the desired shape from the gallery.
4. Click and drag to draw the shape as desired.

Inserting a Text Box

1. Select the **Insert** tab.
2. Select the **Text Box** button.
3. Select the desired style from the gallery.

   OR

1. Select the **Insert** tab.
2. Select the **Text Box** button.
3. Select **Draw Text Box**.
4. Click and drag to draw the text box as desired.

Inserting WordArt

1. Select the text.
2. Select the **Insert** tab.
3. Select the **Insert WordArt** button.
4. Select the desired style from the gallery.

Inserting a SmartArt Graphic

1. Select the **Insert** tab.
2. Select the **SmartArt** button.
3. Select the desired SmartArt from the Choose a SmartArt Graphic dialog box.
4. Select **OK**.

FORMATTING OBJECTS

Deleting an Object

1. Select the object to select it.
2. Press **Delete** or **Backspace**.

Resizing an Object

1. Select the object to select it.
2. Drag a sizing handle to adjust the size as desired.

   OR

1. Click the object to select it.
2. Select the **Drawing Tools Format** tab.
3. Use the **Shape Height** increment arrows and the **Shape Width** increment arrows to adjust the object's size.

Moving an Object

1. Position the mouse pointer over the selected object until the mouse pointer changes to a four-headed arrow ⊕.

2. Drag the object to the desired position and release the mouse button.

Applying a Style to a Picture

1. Select the picture to select it.

2. Select the **Picture Tools Format** tab.

3. Select the **More** button ⊽.

4. Select the desired style in the gallery.

Applying a Style to a Shape

1. Click the shape to select it.

2. Select the **Picture Tools Format** tab.

3. Select the **More** button ⊽.

4. Select the desired style in the gallery.

Applying a Border, Effects, and Layout to a Picture

1. Click the picture to select it.

2. Select the **Picture Tools Format** tab.

3. Click to apply the desired format, as follows:

   - **Picture Border** ✎
   - **Picture Effects** ◙
   - **Picture Layout** ▦

Applying a Fill, Outline, and Effects to a Shape

1. Click the shape to select it.

2. Select the **Drawing Tools Format** tab.

3. Click to apply the desired format, as follows:

   - **Shape Fill** ⬖
   - **Shape Outline** ✎
   - **Shape Effects** ◙

Wrapping Text Around an Object

1. Click the object to select it.

2. Select the **Drawing Tools Format** tab.

3. Select the **Wrap Text** button ▤.

4. Select the desired wrap option from the menu.

Cropping a Graphic

1. Click the graphic to select it.

2. Select the **Picture Tools Format** tab.

3. Select the **Crop** button ⊞.

4. Hover the mouse pointer over a cropping handle.

5. When the cropping pointer appears, click and drag to crop out the desired portion of the graphic.

   Use a corner handle to crop from two sides. Use a side or top handle to crop from the corresponding side.

6. When you're done cropping, select the **Crop** button ⊞ again to complete the crop.

Modifying a Picture

1. Click the picture to select it.

2. Select the **Picture Tools Format** tab.

3. Select an option to make the desired modification, as follows:

   - **Corrections** ☀ to adjust the contrast and brightness.
   - **Color** ▦ to change the color.
   - **Artistic Effects** ▦ to add special effects.
   - **Compress Pictures** ▣ to reduce the file size.
   - **Change Picture** ▦ to change to a different picture, preserving the formatting and size of the current picture.
   - **Reset Picture** ▦ to remove all formatting applied to the picture.

Changing the Direction of Text in a Text Box

1. Click the text box to select it.

2. Select the **Drawing Tools Format** tab.

3. Select the **Text Direction** button ▥.

4. Select the desired rotation option.

Adding Text to a Shape

1. Right-click the shape.
2. Select **Add Text** on the shortcut menu.
3. Type the text and apply formats as desired.

Grouping Objects

1. Click an object to select it.
2. Hold down **Shift** to select other objects to include in the group.
3. Select the **Picture Tools Format** tab.
4. Select the **Group Objects** button.
5. Select **Group** on the menu.

Positioning an Object

1. Select the **Picture Tools Format** tab.
2. Select the **Position** button.
3. Select the desired position from the gallery.

   OR

1. Select the **Picture Tools Format** tab.
2. Select the **Align Objects** button.
3. Select the desired alignment option from the menu.

   OR

1. Click the object to select it.
2. Press the up, down, left, or right arrow keys to nudge the object in the desired direction.

Rotating an Object

1. Click the object to select it.
2. Position the mouse pointer over the object's rotation handle so it resembles a circular arrow.
3. Drag to rotate the object as desired.

   OR

1. Click the object to select it.
2. Select the **Picture Tools Format** tab.
3. Select the **Rotate Objects** button.
4. Select the desired rotation option from the menu.

Layering Objects

1. Click an object to select it.
2. Select the **Picture Tools Format** tab.
3. Select the **Bring Forward** button or the **Send Backward** button to layer it with other objects.

Duplicating an Object

1. Select the object.
2. Press **Ctrl + C**.
3. Press **Ctrl + V** to paste a duplicate copy.

   OR

1. Select the object.
2. Hold down **Ctrl** and drag to place the duplicate in the desired location.

Aligning and Distributing Objects

1. Select the objects you want to align and distribute.

   Hold down **Ctrl** to select multiple objects.
2. Select the **Drawing Tools Format** tab.
3. Select the **Align** button.
4. From the menu, select the desired option.

USING OFFICE HELP

1. Select the **File** tab.
2. Select the **Help** button in the upper-right corner.
3. At the Support-Office.com page, click in the search box, type the topic for which you need help, and press **Enter**.

   OR

1. In an open Office application, click in the **Tell me what you want to do** box to the right of the Ribbon tabs.
2. Type a topic or query.

   OR

1. Press **F1** to open the Help Viewer.
2. Enter the topic for which you need help in the search box, or use the Top categories list to search for a topic.

VIEWING FILE PROPERTIES

1. Select **File**.

2. On the Info tab, review the file properties listed on the right.

USING ACCESS KEYS

- Press **Alt** to activate access keys.

- Press the keyboard character to execute the desired command.

USING THE MINI TOOLBAR

1. Select text you want to format.

2. On the Mini toolbar, select the desired formatting options.

USING A SHORTCUT MENU

1. Right-click an object or selected text.

2. From the shortcut menu, select the desired option.

USING DIALOG BOX OPTIONS

- Use a list box to display a list of items from which a selection can be made.

- Use a palette to select an option, such as a color or shape.

- Use a drop-down list box to either type a selection in the text box or select from a drop-down list.

- Click a check box to select an option. A check mark indicates the option is selected.

- Select a command button to execute a command. An ellipsis on a command button means that clicking it will open another dialog box.

- Select a tab to view additional pages of options.

- In the Preview area, you can preview the results of your selections.

- Use increment boxes to type a value, or use increment arrows to increase or decrease the value.

- Use a text box to type variable information.

- Use an option button to make one selection from a group.

DISPLAYING TASK PANES

Select a dialog box launcher ⌐ on a tab to open a task pane.

FORMATTING TEXT

Formatting Selected Text

1. Select the text to format.

2. Select the **Home** tab.

3. Select the desired formatting options.

Formatting New Text

1. Select the **Home** tab.

2. Select the desired formatting options.

3. Enter the text.

CHANGING THE VIEW

Word, Excel, and PowerPoint

Select the **View** shortcut buttons on the status bar.

OR

Select the **View** tab and select options as desired.

Access

Use the **Views** button to switch between an object's views.

USING MULTIPLE PROGRAM WINDOWS

- Select a button on the taskbar to display the desired window.

- Select a group button on the taskbar and select the desired window to display.

- Tile windows to see all of them at the same time. Right-click on a blank area of the taskbar. From the shortcut menu, select the desired tiling option.

Arranging Multiple Files within Word, Excel, and PowerPoint

1. Select the **View** tab.

2. Select the desired window arrangement option.

CHAPTER 11
Word Processing Basics

WHAT IS WORD PROCESSING?

In 1968, IBM first used the term *word processing*. The term described machines that could be used to type a document, remember the typist's keystrokes, and produce more than one copy. With this new tool, workers saved time.

That was just the beginning. Today's word-processing programs do much more. Suppose you were writing something by hand and made a mistake or changed your mind about what you wanted to say. If you were using a pen, you would probably cross out the words you wanted to change. Doing that leaves the page messy, though. With word-processing software, you can change the text and still create neat pages. You can even save what you typed and use it again a day, a week, or even a year later.

Creating a Document

OBJECTIVES

- List the four basic functions of word-processing programs.
- Create and save a word-processing document.
- Use templates to increase productivity.

AS YOU READ

ORGANIZE INFORMATION Complete a spider map to help you organize basic facts about word processing as you read.

TERMINOLOGY

- AutoCorrect
- AutoSave
- insertion point
- pagination
- scrolling
- template
- word-processing program
- word wrap

Functions of Word-Processing Programs

Word-processing programs are used for creating and printing almost any kind of text-based documents such as letters, reports, and brochures.

Word-processing programs have four functions:

- Writing—entering text and symbols into a document

- Editing—revising or reorganizing the text

- Formatting—changing how the text looks on the page

- Publishing—producing a final version either by printing, or preparing for digital viewing

These tasks do not need to be done all at once or even in the order shown here. Whatever the order, these four functions are at the heart of word processing.

Printing

Editing

Formatting

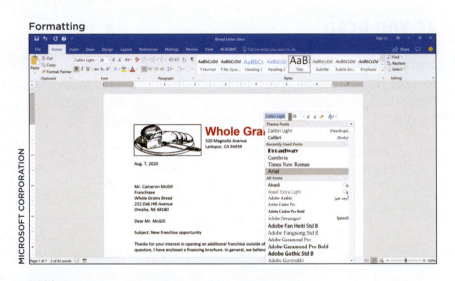

Writing

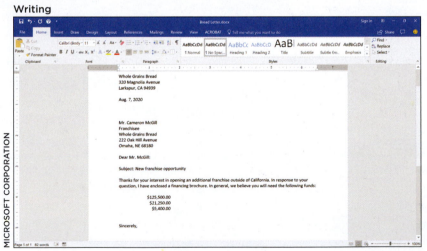

FIGURE 11.1.1

The four main functions of a word-processing program.

CAREER CORNER

COPY EDITOR Copy editors check documents for correct spelling, grammar, and consistency of style. Although some copy editors work on hard copy, or paper, most edit soft copy, or electronic files. Among the problems they look for are inconsistent or wrong formats, such as incorrect em dashes, en dashes, and spacing, or unacceptable hyphenation generated by the word processor.

Working with a Word-Processing Document

When you start a word-processing program, it may display a new blank document, or it may display a page where you can select an existing document, or create a new document.

CREATING A DOCUMENT A new, blank word-processing document looks like a blank piece of paper on the screen. The program is ready for you to start writing. You can create another new document at any time. For example, in Microsoft Word you create a new document by selecting the File tab, selecting the New command, and selecting Blank Document. Most word-processing programs allow you to create a new document using shortcut keys. For example, in a Windows-based program press Ctrl + N (hold the Ctrl key and press N). In MacOS, press Command + N.

SAVING A DOCUMENT To make sure the document you create is available for use in the future, you must save it. The first time you save a document you use the File > Save As command. In Microsoft Word, you then select a storage location to open the Save As dialog box. In other programs, it may open as soon as you select File > Save As. In the Save As dialog box, you give the document a name, select a file type, and select a storage location. Once you have used the Save As command, you can use the Save command to save subsequent changes, or the

Save As command to save a copy of the document with a different name, storage location, or file type.

By default, files are saved in the current document file type, such as .docx if you are using Microsoft Word. You can select from a list of compatible file types from the Save as type drop-down list in the Save As dialog box. For example, you can save the file in text format (.txt) or as a .pdf file. You can even choose to save the document in an older, or legacy, version of your current program, such as .doc for older versions of Word.

IC3✓ Create and save files.

TEMPLATES Most word-processing programs also allow you to create new documents using document templates. A **template** is a file that already includes layout, formatting, prompts, and some text suitable for a specific document type. For example, an invitation template might include a festive graphic, prompts for entering a date, time, and location, and a layout designed for printing on invitation cards. When you create a document using a template, your document includes all the settings already in the template. You can use built-in templates that come with your program, look for templates online, or create and save your own templates for future use.

Using templates can save time and increase productivity because you do not have to design or format the document. Another benefit is that using templates can give your documents a similar look and feel, which can help customers identify your business by brand.

To create a document based on a template in a Microsoft Office application, select File > New, and then select the document category to view the available templates. When you find one you like, select it and select Create. Replace the sample text and fill in the blanks to complete your document.

If you have a document you would like to use as a template in the future, you can use the File > Save As command and select the document template format from the Save as type list in the Save As dialog box. In Word, the document template file type has a .dotx file extension, and the template is saved by default in the Custom Office Template folder.

IC3✔ **Use word-processing templates to increase productivity.**

INSERTION POINT The **insertion point** shows where the text you type will appear. It moves as you type.

SCROLLING As you write, you might want to reread or change something you wrote earlier. That is made easy by **scrolling**—using the mouse or keyboard to move through the document.

You can scroll up or down by using the mouse to click the scroll bar or drag the scroll box at the right of the document window. Many mouse devices have scrolling wheels. You can also use the Up and Down arrow keys or the Page Up, Page Down, Home, and End keys to move around in the document.

Time-Saving Features

Most word-processing programs have features to help you write, edit, and save your work.

- With **word wrap**, the program automatically starts a new line, or "wraps" the text, when the current line is full. If you wish to force text onto a new line, press Enter or Return.

- When a page is full, the **pagination** feature automatically starts a new page. You can also force a new page by inserting a special character, called a page break.

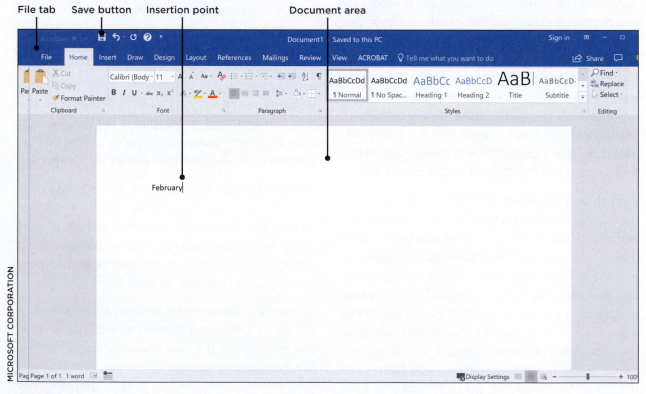

FIGURE 11.1.2 Microsoft Word is an example of a typical word-processing program.

- The **AutoCorrect** feature fixes common spelling mistakes as they are typed. You can turn off this feature or modify it to accept unusual words that you often use.

- The AutoRecover or **AutoSave** feature automatically saves a document as often as you want. If the computer shuts down accidentally, you can retrieve the most recently saved version.

- Spell Check identifies spelling and grammar errors and suggests corrections. You can select a suggestion, ignore the error, or type the correction yourself.

Typing Standards for Word-Processing Documents

As you write, keep in mind three standards of style to make your work look professional.

Two standards are met automatically by many programs. They change two hyphens (--) to an em dash (—). They also convert quotation marks to curly quotation marks, or "smart quotes."

The other standard is not automatic—you have to remember to do it. This standard is to type one space, not two, between sentences.

TECHNOLOGY@SCHOOL

Some students sharpen their word-processing skills by writing to pen pals in other countries.

THINK ABOUT IT!

Before writing a letter, think about the topics you could cover. Which items listed below would you discuss in a pen-pal letter?

- your family
- your school
- your hometown
- your math class
- your favorite movie

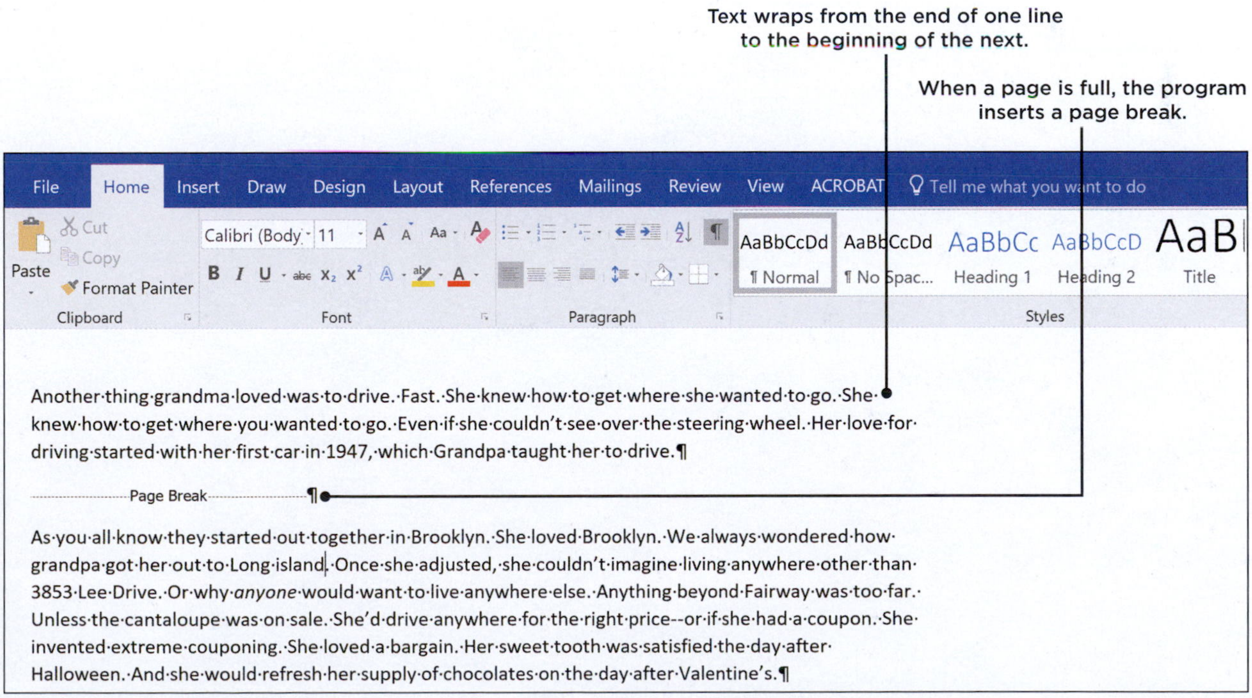

Text wraps from the end of one line to the beginning of the next.

When a page is full, the program inserts a page break.

FIGURE 11.1.3 Word wrap and pagination are two time-saving features found in most word-processing programs.

MICROSOFT CORPORATION

Basic Document Editing

OBJECTIVES

- Identify files that can be opened and edited with a word processor.

- Explain the purpose of the Clipboard.

- Demonstrate how to cut, copy, and paste text.

- Use Undo and Redo.

- Identify reasons for using mail merge.

AS YOU READ

IDENTIFY CAUSE AND EFFECT Complete a cause-and-effect chart to help you identify what happens when word-processing functions are applied as you read.

TERMINOLOGY

- Clipboard
- Copy
- Cut
- data source
- mail merge
- Paste
- Redo
- select
- Undo

Opening a Document for Editing

Editing can take place at any time after you have created the document. You can go back and edit text you recently entered, or you can edit a document you created, saved, and closed. To do so, you open the file so you can work on it again. You use a word-processing program's Open command to open a file, or you can use your operating system's file management features to find and open files wherever they are stored.

Word-processing programs can open and edit compatible files, which usually have file extensions such as .doc, .docx, .txt, or .rtf. Some word-processing programs, including Microsoft Word, are also compatible with .html, .pub (Microsoft Publisher), and .pdf (Adobe Acrobat) files.

Word-processing programs make editing easy. You can add words simply by typing them. You can delete characters by pressing the Delete or Backspace keys. Powerful features in these programs help you do even more.

IC3 ✔ **Understand which file types are compatible and/or editable with word processors.**

Selecting Text

To change text already entered in a document, you first must **select** it. Then, you can delete it, move it, copy it, or change its formatting. To select text, click and drag over the text you want. Most programs also let you select text by using the keyboard. You hold down the Shift key while you use the arrow keys and other keys to select the text. Selected text is highlighted on the screen; that is, it appears with a different background color. To help you select just the text you need, use the Show/Hide command to display nonprinting characters, such as paragraph marks, tabs, and spaces.

Cutting, Copying, and Pasting

Two common reasons for selecting text are cutting and copying. Both actions place the text in the Clipboard.

THE CLIPBOARD The **Clipboard** stores cut or copied text while you work. Once you close the program or shut down the computer, items on the Clipboard are no longer available. Some programs store only one item at a time, so cutting or copying new text replaces what was held before. Some programs can hold many items on the Clipboard.

■ The **Cut** command removes the selected text from a document and places it on the Clipboard.

■ The **Copy** command places a duplicate of the selected text on the Clipboard.

PASTING Use the **Paste** command to insert an item copied or cut to the Clipboard. Simply place the insertion point where you want the item to appear. Then, select the Paste command on the Clipboard group of the Home tab or press Ctrl + V. The copied item or text appears where you want it.

MOVING Moving a sentence from the middle of a paragraph to the beginning can be done by selecting and dragging it. You can use Cut and Paste to move that sentence farther—for

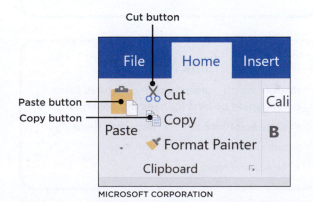

MICROSOFT CORPORATION

FIGURE 11.2.1 The Cut, Copy, and Paste buttons are located in the Clipboard group in Microsoft Word.

example, to another page—or to move text or a graphic from one document to another. You can even open a new window, paste the text you cut from another document, and save the pasted text as a new document.

COPYING Copying and pasting saves time when you need to repeat some text. You can also copy and paste to bring a graphic from one document into another.

Undoing and Redoing

Word-processing programs have commands that can undo or cancel an edit. If you delete a word by mistake, you can use the **Undo** command to put it back. Many programs also have a **Redo** command. You can use this feature to put a change back in effect after cancelling it with Undo.

MICROSOFT CORPORATION

FIGURE 11.2.2 The Undo and Redo commands are on the Quick Access toolbar in Microsoft Office programs.

TECHNOLOGY@WORK

Businesses sometimes use text called boilerplate. This is text that is used exactly the same way in many places to make certain that wording or features stay consistent in the same document or in many documents.

THINK ABOUT IT!

Identify which word-processing features listed below would be best for handling boilerplate.

- Copy and Paste
- Cut and Paste
- Select and Move
- Undo and Redo
- Templates

TECHNOLOGY@HOME

The Copy command isn't suitable if the copied text will change.

THINK ABOUT IT!

Think about what the Copy command does. For which items below would the copy command be useful? For which would it not be useful?

- the delivery address for letters to different people
- the cook's name on the top of recipe cards
- the title of a CD in a list of CDs
- a paragraph to appear in two different letters

Merging

Most word-processing programs have a **mail merge** feature you can use to generate customized form letters, mailing labels, envelopes, and even emails. You create a word-processing document that includes the content you want everyone to receive and then merge it with a **data source** of customized information, such as names and addresses.

LESSON 11-3

Basic Document Formatting

OBJECTIVES

- Identify and use basic formatting skills.
- Adjust margins, page sizes, and page orientation.
- Recognize and explain page layout concepts.

AS YOU READ

SUMMARIZE Complete a summary chart to help you identify different features that can be formatted as you read the lesson.

TERMINOLOGY

- alignment
- default
- font
- font color
- font size
- font style
- footer
- header
- indentation
- landscape orientation
- leading
- line spacing
- margins
- newspaper-style columns
- orientation
- page layout
- paper size
- paragraph spacing
- point
- portrait orientation
- sans serif font
- section
- serif font
- tabs

Appearance Is Important

A document's formatting—its appearance—is sometimes as important as its contents. Word-processing programs include many preset formats, called **defaults**. The program applies these formats automatically, unless you change them. For example, the default font in Microsoft Word is 11-point Calibri, but you can change to a different font or font size whenever you want.

You can format four distinct parts of a document: characters, paragraphs, sections, and pages.

Formatting Characters

Character formatting lets you change the look of text. It is usually used to improve the appearance and readability of the text on the page. It can also set a tone by providing a visual clue about the content of the document.

- The **font** is the family of characters used. A font is a set of characters with a certain style, or appearance.

- **Font size** is the height of characters, measured in points. One **point** equals 1/72 inch.

- **Font color** is the color used to display the font.

- **Font styles** are characteristics such as bold and italic.

There are four general categories of fonts. **Serif fonts**, such as Times New Roman, have serifs, or flourishes, projecting from the ends of the characters. They are easy to read and are often used for document text. **Sans serif fonts**, such as Arial, do not have serifs, and are often used for headings. Script fonts are used to simulate handwriting. Decorative fonts have embellishments such as curlicues.

Most word-processing programs have built-in lists of fonts, font sizes, font colors, and font styles. You may select them from a drop-down menu or in a dialog box. For example, in Microsoft Word the font options are on the Home tab of the Ribbon and in the Font dialog box. You can change character formatting before you type so the new text

CATEGORIES OF FONTS		
Category	**Description**	**Example**
Serif	Serifs, or decorative flourishes, project from the ends. Easy to read in print. Often used for paragraph text.	Times New Roman Cambria
Sans Serif	No serifs. Often used for headings. Easy to read on a screen.	Arial Tahoma
Script	Simulate handwriting. Characters appear connected or almost connected. Formal script fonts are usually neat and flowing. Informal script fonts are usually messy and more natural.	Edwardian Script ITC Mistral
Decorative	Artistic. May have embellishments, such as curlicues. Also called ornamental or display fonts.	Jokerman Chiller

displays the selected options. Or, you can select existing text and apply the formatting.

IC3 ✔ **Know how to perform basic formatting skills.**

Formatting Paragraphs

A paragraph is any text that ends with the press of the Enter key. Whenever you press Enter, you create a paragraph. You can change many paragraph formats, including:

- **Alignment**—This is the way a paragraph lines up between the page's left and right margins. There are four types of paragraph alignment: left, in which all lines are even with the left margin; right, in which all lines are even with the right margin; center, in which all lines are centered between the left and right margins; and justified, in which space is added between words so that lines are even with both the left and right margins.

IC3 ✔ **Know how to align text in paragraphs.**

- **Line spacing**—This is the amount of space between the lines of text in a paragraph. It is sometimes called **leading** (pronounced ledding).

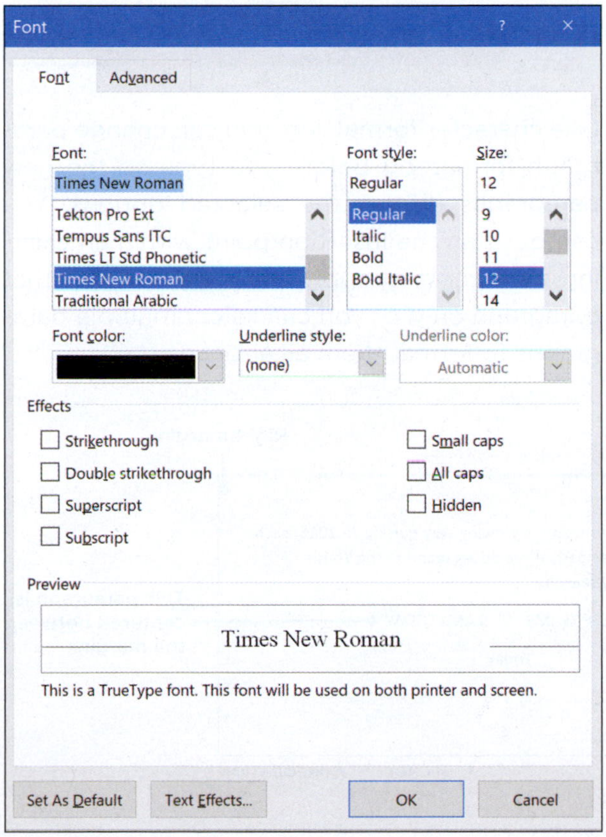

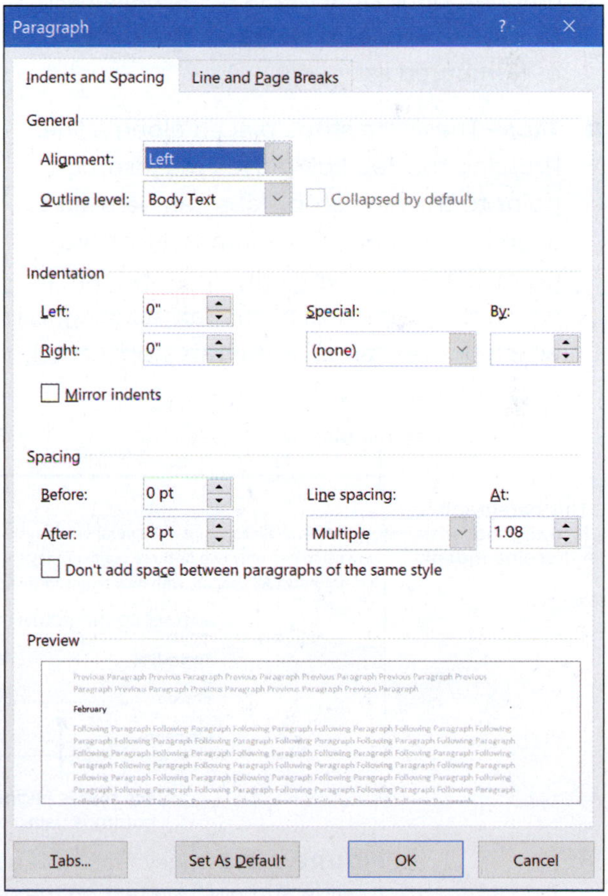

FIGURE 11.3.1 Use the Font dialog box (left) to apply character formatting. Use the Paragraph dialog box (right) to apply paragraph formatting.

- **Paragraph spacing**—This is the amount of space between the last line of one paragraph and the first line of the next paragraph.

- **Indentation**—This is added space between a margin and the text. There are four basic types: left, which indents all lines from the left margin; right, which indents all lines from the right margin; first line, which indents the first line of the paragraph from the left margin by a specified amount; and hanging, which indents all lines except the first from the left margin by a specified amount. Hanging indents are usually used to align multiple lines of text in a bulleted or numbered list.

- **Tabs**—These are stops placed along a line. Pressing the Tab key moves the insertion point to the next stop. Tabs can be used to align text in tables or columns. Most programs have four types of tab stops: left, in which the text starts at the tab stop; right, in which the text ends at the tab stop; center, in which the center of the text is aligned with the tab stop; and decimal, in which decimal points in the text are aligned with the tab stop.

In most word-processing programs you may select paragraph formatting options from a drop-down menu or in a dialog box. For example, in Microsoft Word, paragraph formatting options are on the Home and Layout tabs of the Ribbon and in the Paragraph dialog box. In addition, some paragraph formatting can be applied using the horizontal ruler displayed across the top of the page. For example, you can create a tab stop by clicking the horizontal ruler at the point where you want to place the tab stop. You can change a paragraph's indentation by dragging indent markers left or right across the ruler.

Like character formatting, you can change paragraph formatting before you type so the new paragraphs display the selected options. You can position the insertion point within an existing paragraph to apply the formatting to that paragraph only, or you can select multiple paragraphs to format them all at once.

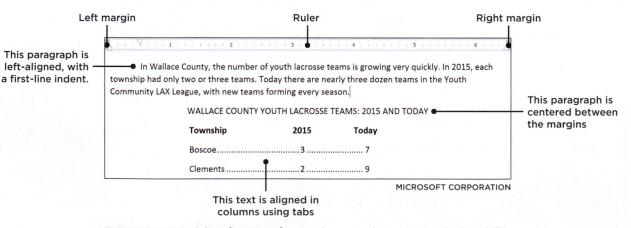

Left margin   Ruler   Right margin

This paragraph is left-aligned, with a first-line indent.

In Wallace County, the number of youth lacrosse teams is growing very quickly. In 2015, each township had only two or three teams. Today there are nearly three dozen teams in the Youth Community LAX League, with new teams forming every season.

WALLACE COUNTY YOUTH LACROSSE TEAMS: 2015 AND TODAY

This paragraph is centered between the margins

Township	2015	Today
Boscoe	3	7
Clements	2	9

MICROSOFT CORPORATION

This text is aligned in columns using tabs

FIGURE 11.3.2 A key feature of a word-processing program is the ability to align and position text on the page.

Formatting Pages

Page layout affects how and where text is positioned on the page. Page layout is often used to make a document look professional and appealing, and also to make it easier for the reader to locate and understand the information in the document. The main features in page layout are:

■ **Orientation**—Text can be printed in one of two directions, or orientations. In **portrait orientation**, text is printed down the page's long edge, creating a page that is taller than it is wide. In **landscape orientation**, text is printed down the page's short edge, creating a page that is wider than it is tall.

IC3✔ Know page layout concepts: orientation.

■ **Margins**—Margins are the space between the edges of the page and the text. This open space frames the page and can make the text easier to read. You can set the Top, Bottom, Left, and Right margins by selecting from a built-in list of common margins widths, or you can set custom margins.

IC3✔ Know page layout concepts: margins.

■ **Paper size**—Various sizes of paper can be used to create documents. This is sometimes called page size. You can select from a built-list of common paper sizes, or you can set a custom size.

IC3✔ Know how to adjust margins, page sizes, and page orientation.

COLUMNS By default, documents have one column which extends from the left margin to the right margin. You can divide the document into two or more **newspaper-style columns**. The text flows from the bottom of the column on the left to the top of the column on the right. Other ways to create columns in a document include using tabs and inserting a table.

MICROSOFT CORPORATION

FIGURE 11.3.3 Word-processing programs let you print documents in landscape (left) and portrait (right) orientations.

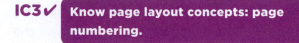

IC3 ✔ Know page layout concepts: columns.

HEADERS AND FOOTERS This is information placed at the top of every page—the **header**—or at the bottom—**footer**. Headers and footers are often used to display page numbers, the date, or the file name, because they display on every page. Options are usually available for having different headers and footers for odd and even pages, and for the first page.

PAGE NUMBERS Page numbers help readers identify where they are in a document. Most word-processing programs let you automatically insert page numbers. They are usually placed in the header or footer but can be put at any location.

IC3 ✔ Know page layout concepts: page numbering.

In most word-processing programs, page layout options can be found on a menu or in a dialog box. For example, in Microsoft Word 2016, most page layout options are on the Layout tab of the Ribbon and in the Page Setup dialog box.

Formatting Sections

In some word-processing applications, a **section** is part of a document that contains specific format settings. A document begins as one section, but you can insert section breaks to divide the document into more than one section. You can format each section in its own unique way. For example, in most newsletters, the first section is one column, so the title spans the width of the page, but the next section is two or more columns, allowing more articles to fit on the page. You can also have different headers and footers in each section. For example, you might define each chapter as a section, so the specific chapter name can display in the footer.

Basics of Desktop Publishing

OBJECTIVES

- Describe the benefits of creating documents in a desktop-publishing program.

- Compare word-processing and desktop-publishing programs.

- Summarize the basic steps in desktop publishing.

AS YOU READ

ORGANIZE INFORMATION Complete a sequence chart to help you organize basic facts about desktop publishing as you read the lesson.

TERMINOLOGY

- desktop-publishing

- frame

- layout

- master page

Publishing from a Desktop

Desktop-publishing (DTP) programs are used to create high-quality publications that look as if they were produced on a printing press. They can be used to do some of the same tasks as word-processing programs, but they greatly expand design options so you can create high-quality documents.

Word-processing and DTP programs complement each other. In fact, they are often used together. Text is frequently created and edited in a word processor, and then that text is brought into a DTP program to be formatted for publishing.

BENEFITS OF DTP Desktop-publishing software gives you tools you can use to produce the files for large projects, such as books, magazines, and other complex printed materials. DTP software also gives you more control over the final product than you would have if you hired a professional contractor or other "outside" source.

DRAWBACKS OF DTP Desktop publishing is not without its problems. Often it is a team effort, which means that the work of writers, editors, artists, and layout specialists has to be carefully coordinated. These complex programs can also be more difficult to learn than word-processing software.

Creating a Document with Desktop Publishing

Most word-processing programs include basic desktop publishing features. However, dedicated desktop-publishing programs such Microsoft Publisher and Adobe® InDesign®, provide tools for generating professional publications.

DESIGNING THE LAYOUT The most important task—and the one that is done first—is designing the document **layout**. A designer plans how

each page will look by creating a **master page**. This provides the pattern for all the pages to follow and sets the basic features of the document's look, including:

- Page size and margins

- Number of columns, width of columns, and space between columns. The columns on the master page create areas called **frames**. Frames are simply empty containers that will eventually hold text or graphics. They will be filled as you add text and images to the document.

- Type font, size, and treatment for all the major elements that will be repeated in the document, such as titles, headings, text, and headers and footers

- Rules that will be followed in placing, sizing, and treating images

ENTERING TEXT Text can be placed in the frames by typing, but is usually created and edited in a word-processing program. Then, that text is imported or copied into the DTP frames, filling as many pages as needed.

If the writer has formatted the text by using styles in the word processor, the DTP software may be able to use those styles to identify and format different parts of the document automatically.

IMPORTING GRAPHICS Images are usually imported or placed in the document once the text is in place. Tools in the program make it possible to adjust the size of images, set the distance between text and the image, and even change the image rotation.

CHECKING AND REVISING DTP documents are often published several times before they are finished. Editors review these versions, called proofs, to make sure that no text has been lost and that the text reads correctly. Designers check design elements. Then DTP users make changes to the document.

CONNECTIONS

THE ARTS Desktop-publishing programs let you enhance a document in many ways. You can use color, large type, bold and italic type, drawings, and special effects to make the pages interesting. Experienced designers offer the following guidelines for using these tools:

- Use only a few fonts and choose appropriate ones for the task.
- Don't overuse color, bold, or italic type. Too much can make a document difficult to read.
- Use type size, space, and other elements to emphasize the most important parts of the document.
- Keep the reader in mind. Design a document so that it is easy to read and use.

PUBLISHING After the document is final, it is printed or published for online viewing. Sometimes, DTP documents are printed using desktop printers, or they may be sent to printers who print and bind finished copies. For color documents, the DTP program can prepare color separations, which are separate versions of the document's pages. Each version contains a specific set of colors; each of which is applied in a separate pass through the printer. When the colors are combined, the full-color document is finished.

CAREER CORNER

Workers who do desktop publishing are called graphic designers. There are about 200,000 graphic designers in the United States.

Most work for companies, but about one third work for themselves.

The Bureau of Labor Statistics says that in the next few years the number of jobs for desktop publishers will grow by a huge amount—about 67 percent.

Interested students can take courses in design at some colleges and professional schools. Of course, experience in using computers is a great plus!

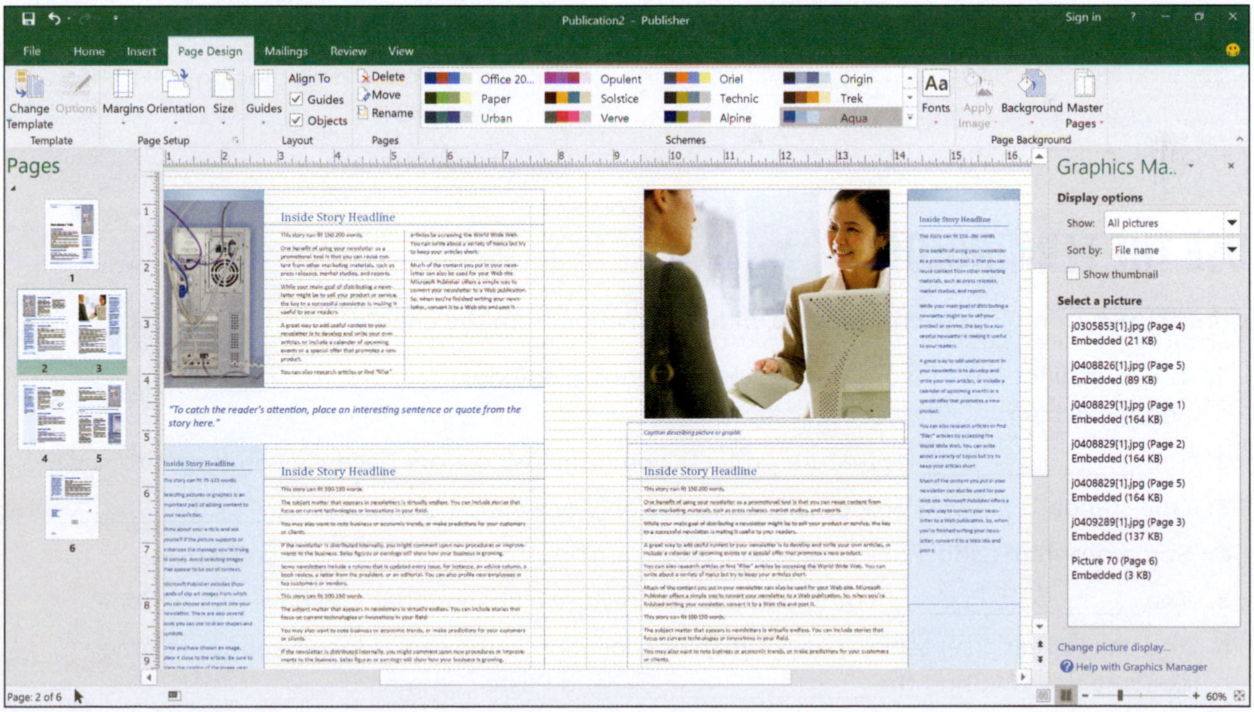

FIGURE 11.4.1 Designing a newsletter in Microsoft Publisher.

Chapter 11 Review

REVIEW THE TERMINOLOGY

DIRECTIONS Match each vocabulary term in the left column with the correct definition in the right column.

1. insertion point
2. word wrap
3. pagination
4. AutoCorrect
5. select text
6. Clipboard
7. default
8. section
9. page format

a. features that identify how and where text is positioned

b. a separate part of a document with its own formatting

c. area where cut or copied text is temporarily stored

d. fixes common spelling mistakes as they are typed

e. shows the place in a document where text will be added or deleted

f. automatically moves text to a new line

g. the automatic division of a document into pages

h. action made on a block of text before changing it

i. preset formats

USE THE TERMINOLOGY

DIRECTIONS Complete each sentence with information from the chapter.

1. The four functions of word processing are writing, editing, _____, and publishing.

2. The _____ feature protects you from losing work because you forgot to save.

3. One standard of word processing is to have only one space after each _____.

4. Some programs add extra characters, called a(n) _____, to a file name.

5. The _____ command lets you restore a change that you have just undone.

6. You can repeat a sentence in more than one location in the same document—or in other documents—by using the _____ and Paste commands.

7. _____ programs are used to create high-quality publications that look as if they were produced on a printing press.

8. One _____ equals 1/72 inch.

9. Indentation refers to the _____ between a margin and the text in a paragraph.

10. An example of a(n) _____ is a page number that appears at the bottom of every page in a report.

THINK CRITICALLY

DIRECTIONS Answer the following questions.

1. What are margins, and how is their adjustability in a word processor useful?

2. What is the benefit to breaking up a page of a document into more than one column of text?

3. What is the difference between landscape and portrait orientation?

4. What is the difference between a serif font and a sans serif font? Give examples of each.

EXTEND YOUR KNOWLEDGE

DIRECTIONS Choose and complete one of the following projects.

1. Open a word-processing program and type these directions in full. Add the heading *Formatting Sample* above the first line of text. Then do the following: (1) Copy your text and paste the copy below the first paragraph; (2) Format the text by changing fonts and type size; (3) Change the page to landscape orientation; (4) Apply a page background; (5) Add a header; and (6) Print your document. Remember to save your file.

2. Open a word-processing program. Choose one of the menus on the menu bars or Ribbon tabs. Write down the items listed on the menu or the groups listed on the tab. Choose two of the menu items or one of the groups. Look up the commands in the Help system. Take notes on what you read. Make a presentation to the class describing which actions result from choosing each command. Identify a way that someone could use the commands in working on a document.

3. With your teacher's permission, conduct research on different word-processing programs. Record your findings in a chart so you can compare and contrast the available features. Use critical-thinking skills to select the program you think would be best for creating documents for business communication. Explain your selection to a partner or to the class.

IC3 PREP

1. What are some ways to create a new, blank document in a word processor? (Select all that apply.)

   a. Open a new instance of the word processor itself and select Blank document.

   b. Select the File > New command.

   c. Use the appropriate keyboard shortcut (typically Ctrl + N or Command + N on a Mac).

   d. Select the Insert > Blank Document command.

2. For each line below, select whether the statement is True or False.

   a. To make sure the document you create is available for use in the future, you must save it.

   b. In the Save As dialog box, you can give files a name, select a file type, and select a storage location.

   c. Once you have used the Save As command, you can use the Save command to save subsequent changes.

   d. The Save As command can be used to save a copy of a document with a different name, storage location, or file type.

3. What are some ways word-processing templates increase productivity? (Select all that apply.)

   a. You can create and save a document you would like to use as a template in the future.

   b. Templates can give your documents a similar look and feel, which can help customers identify your business by brand.

   c. Templates can be built into a word processor, or easily shared and obtained online.

   d. Templates usually require no further work to put out a finished product.

4. Which of these is NOT a good fit for using a template?

   a. business newsletters

   b. novella

   c. invitation cards

   d. resume

5. Which of these file types is NOT compatible and/or editable with word processors?

   a. .doc

   b. .jpeg

   c. .txt

   d. .docx

6. What are some ways in which character formatting can be changed? (Select all that apply.)

   a. selecting a different font

   b. changing the font color

   c. applying a bold or italic style

   d. changing the indentation

7. What is the main difference between serif and sans serif fonts?

   a. serif fonts are larger than sans serif fonts

   b. serif fonts have extra flourishes projecting from the ends of the characters

   c. serif fonts and sans serif fonts are the same

   d. serif fonts look like handwriting

8. When you alter the horizontal alignment of text in a word processor, what are you doing to that text?

   a. selecting how the text lines up between the page's left and right margins

   b. selecting how high or low the text appears on the page

   c. selecting whether the text is correct or incorrect

   d. selecting the size of the text on the page

9. You are writing a draft of a paper for school and want to leave room for teacher feedback. What formatting options can you use to add room for anticipated notes? (Select all that apply.)

   a. line spacing

   b. font style

   c. paragraph spacing

   d. indents

10. Which of the following is a way to adjust the tab stop values in a document? (Select all that apply.)

    a. using the markers on the ruler at the top of the window

    b. selecting paragraph formatting options from a drop-down menu or in a dialog box

    c. manually adding space with the space bar to every line

    d. setting the horizontal alignment to center

11. Fill in the blanks: In _____ orientation, a page that is taller than it is wide. In _____ orientation, a page that is wider than it is tall.

    a. wide; narrow

    b. portrait; landscape

    c. alpha; beta

    d. standard; skewed

12. Which of the following are settings often used for preparing documents for printing?

    a. setting margins to adjust the amount of space between the edges of the page and the text

    b. setting the document to be saved as a template

    c. setting the orientation that makes the most sense for your project

    d. setting the proper page size to ready your work for printing

13. Fill in the blanks: Information at the top of every page in a document is called a _____ ; information at the bottom of every page is called a _____ .

    a. header; footer

    b. upper; lower

    c. beginning; end

    d. greeting; farewell

14. What would NOT be a suitable piece of information to place in the header or footer of a typical document?

    a. the page number

    b. an inspirational quote

    c. the date

    d. the file name

IC3 PROCEDURES

CREATING A DOCUMENT

1. Select **File**.
2. Select **New**.
3. Select **Blank Document**.

SAVING A WORD DOCUMENT AS A PDF

1. Select **File**.
2. Select **Export**.
3. Select **Create Adobe PDF**.
4. Select the **Create Adobe PDF** button.
5. In the Save Adobe PDF File As dialog box, enter the file name and select the location where you want to save the file.
6. Select **Save**.

OR

1. Select **File**.

2. Select **Save As**.

3. Select the **More options** link.

4. In the Save As dialog box, enter the file name and select the location where you want to save the file.

5. Select the **Save as type** arrow.

6. Select **PDF**.

7. Select **Save**.

SAVING A DOCUMENT IN A DIFFERENT FILE TYPE

1. Select **File**.

2. Select **Save As**.

3. Select the **More options** link.

4. In the Save As dialog box, select the **Save as type** arrow.

5. Select the desired file type.

6. Enter the file name and select the location where the file will be saved.

7. Select **Save**.

8. Select **OK** in the File Conversion dialog box, if necessary.

OR

1. Select **File**.

2. Select **Export**.

3. Select **Change File Type**.

4. Select the file type.

5. Select **Save As**.

6. Enter the file name and select the location where the file will be saved.

7. Select **Save**.

8. Select **OK** in the File Conversion dialog box, if necessary.

CREATING A DOCUMENT BASED ON A TEMPLATE

1. Select **File**.

2. Select **New**.

3. Select the desired template.

   OR

   a. Type a keyword or phrase into the Search for online templates box.

   b. Press **Enter**.

   c. Select a template.

4. Select **Create**.

SAVING A WORD DOCUMENT AS A TEMPLATE

1. Select **File**.

2. Select **Save As**.

3. Select the **More options** link.

4. In the Save As dialog box, select the **Save as type** arrow.

5. Select **Word Template**.

6. In the Save As dialog box, enter the template name and select the location where the file will be saved, if necessary.

7. Select **Save**.

APPLYING FONT STYLES

1. Select the **Home** tab.

2. Select the desired font style, as follows:

   - **Bold** (**Ctrl + B**) $\boxed{B}$

   - **Italic** (**Ctrl + I**) $\boxed{I}$

   OR

1. Select the **Home** tab.

2. Select the **Font** group dialog box launcher $\boxed{\scriptsize\lrcorner}$.

3. In the Font style list, select the desired style.

4. Select **OK**.

APPLYING A FONT

1. Select the **Home** tab.

2. Select the **Font** button drop-down arrow $\boxed{\text{Times New Ro} \blacktriangledown}$.

3. Select the desired font.

   OR

1. Select the **Home** tab.

2. Select the **Font** group dialog box launcher $\boxed{\scriptsize\lrcorner}$.

3. In the Font list, select the desired font.

4. Click **OK**.

CHANGING THE FONT COLOR

1. Select the **Home** tab.

2. Select the **Font Color** button drop-down arrow $\boxed{\underline{\mathbf{A}} \blacktriangledown}$.

3. Select the desired font color.

   OR

1. Select the **Home** tab.

2. Select the **Font** group dialog box launcher $\boxed{\scriptsize\lrcorner}$.

3. Select the **Font color** drop-down arrow.

4. Select the desired font color.

5. Click **OK**.

CHANGING THE FONT SIZE

1. Select the **Home** tab.

2. Select the **Font Size** button drop-down arrow 12 ▾ .

3. Select the desired font size.

   OR

1. Select the **Home** tab.

2. Select the **Font** group dialog box launcher ⊡ .

3. In the Size list, select the desired font size.

4. Click **OK**.

ALIGNING TEXT HORIZONTALLY

1. Select the **Home** tab.

2. In the Paragraph group, select the desired alignment button:

   - **Align Left** ☰
   - **Center** ☰
   - **Align Right** ☰
   - **Justify** ☰

APPLYING A HANGING INDENT

1. Select the **Layout tab**.

2. Select the **Paragraph** group dialog box launcher ⊡ .

3. Select the **Indents and Spacing** tab.

4. Select the **Special** drop-down arrow.

5. Select **Hanging**.

6. Use the **By** increment arrows to adjust the indent on the hanging indent, if desired.

SETTING TABS USING THE HORIZONTAL RULER

1. To select a tab type, click the **Tab** selector box at the left end of the horizontal ruler until the tab you want to use displays, as follows:

   - **Left** ∟
   - **Right** ⌐
   - **Center** ⊥
   - **Decimal** ⊥
   - **Bar** ∣

2. Click at the position on the horizontal ruler where you want to set the tab.

SETTING TABS IN THE TABS DIALOG BOX

1. Select the **Home** tab.
2. Select the **Paragraph** group dialog box launcher ⬚.
3. Select the **Tabs** button.
4. Enter the tab stop position in the **Tab stop position** text box.
5. From the Alignment option, select the desired tab type.
6. Select **Set**.
7. Select **OK**.

SETTING PARAGRAPH SPACING

1. Select the **Layout tab**.
2. Use the **Spacing Before** box increment arrows to set the spacing before the paragraph.
3. Using the **Spacing After** box increment arrows to set the spacing after the paragraph.

   OR

1. Select the **Layout tab**.
2. Select the **Paragraph** group dialog box launcher ⬚.
3. Select the **Indents and Spacing** tab.
4. Under Spacing, enter the desired spacing in the **Before** and **After** boxes.
5. Select **OK**.

SETTING LINE SPACING

1. Select the **Home** tab.
2. Select the **Line and Paragraph Spacing** button ⬚.
3. Select the desired line spacing option from the menu.

   OR

1. Select the **Home** tab.
2. Select the **Paragraph** group dialog box launcher ⬚.
3. Select the **Indents and Spacing** tab.
4. Select the **Line spacing** drop-down arrow.
5. Select the desired spacing option from the menu.
6. Click **OK**.

FORMATTING TEXT IN COLUMNS

1. Select the text or click in the section of text that you want to format in columns.
2. Select the **Layout tab**.
3. Select the **Columns** button ⬚.
4. From the gallery, select the desired number of columns.

SETTING COLUMN WIDTH

1. Select the **Layout tab**.
2. Select the **Columns** button.
3. Select **More Columns**.
4. In the Columns dialog box, set the column width and spacing as desired.
5. Select **OK**.

INSERTING A COLUMN BREAK

1. Position the insertion point where you want to insert the break.
2. Select the **Layout tab**.
3. Select the **Breaks** button.
4. From the Breaks gallery, select **Column**.

INSERTING PAGE NUMBERS

1. Select the **Insert** tab.
2. Select the **Page Number** button.
3. On the menu, select the desired location for the page number.
4. From the gallery, select the desired format for the page number.

SHOWING OR HIDING THE RULER

1. Select the **View** tab.
2. Select the **Ruler** check box.

   A check in the check box indicates the ruler is displayed.

SELECTING A PRESET MARGIN

1. Select the **Layout tab**.
2. Select the **Margins** button.
3. On the menu, click the desired margin setting.

SETTING CUSTOM MARGINS

1. Select the **Page Layout** tab.
2. Select the **Margins** button.
3. On the menu, select **Custom Margins**.
4. In the Page Setup dialog box, under Margins, set the margins as desired.
5. Click **OK**.

SELECTING A PAPER SIZE

1. Select the **Layout tab**.
2. Select the **Size** button .
3. Select the desired page size.

SETTING PAGE ORIENTATION

1. Select the **Layout tab**.
2. Select the **Orientation** button .
3. On the menu, select the desired orientation.

OPENING A COMPATIBLE FILE

1. Select **File**.
2. Select **Open**.
3. Select the storage location on the left, or select the **Browse** button and browse to the file's location.
4. Select the **File type** drop-down arrow and select the compatible file type.
5. Select the file and then select **Open**.

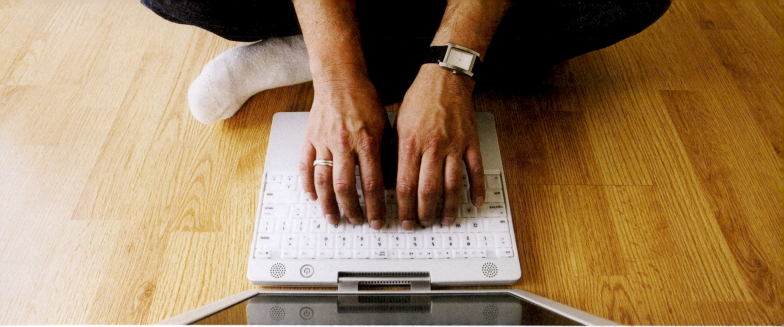

CHAPTER 12
Using a Word-Processing Application

WHAT DOES WORD PROCESSING DO?

In 1875, Mark Twain sent his publisher a historic manuscript. It was the first time that an author submitted a manuscript that had been written using a typewriter. At the time, it was a major technological accomplishment. Now, more than 125 years later, word-processing software does far more than a typewriter ever could. As discussed in Chapter 11, you can format text, add graphics, and even print documents in color.

In this chapter, you learn more about the word-processing tools you can use to create neat and professional documents. You learn how to select a view, how to insert pictures and symbols, and how to prepare a document for publication. Finally, you explore the options for collaborating with others to improve your work.

Viewing a Document

OBJECTIVES

- Compare different document views in a word-processing program.

- Describe the benefits of using split windows.

- Explain how to use a document pane to move through a document.

AS YOU READ

COMPARE AND CONTRAST Complete a conclusion chart to help you compare the different ways of viewing a word-processing document as you read.

TERMINOLOGY

- document map

- Draft view

- Outline view

- pane

- Print Layout view

- Read mode

- synchronous scrolling

- thumbnails

- Web Layout view

Changing Views

Word-processing software lets you look at your documents in several different views. Not all programs have the same View options.

DRAFT VIEW The most basic view, called Normal view or **Draft view**, shows text in the correct font and has character formatting like bold and italic. The basic view does not display certain parts of a document, such as margins, headers and footers, or columns.

PRINT LAYOUT VIEW The **Print Layout view** shows how a document will look when it is printed. This view may be called Page Layout view, Layout view, or Page view. It includes all text, graphics, margins, and other elements that will appear on the printed page. In this view, you can edit headers and footers, change margins, and work with columns and graphics.

WEB LAYOUT VIEW Some word-processing programs have a **Web Layout view**, which shows how a document will appear when published on the World Wide Web.

OUTLINE VIEW An **Outline view** reveals the structure of a document. It breaks down the document into its major headings, subheadings, and text. You can choose to view only the main headings, both the headings and subheadings, or everything, including the entire text. This view is useful when editing a large document. Some programs let users rearrange large amounts of text simply by dragging outline headings from one place to another.

READ MODE In **Read Mode**, the view is customized for reading rather than for writing. It fits the page to the current device, lets you zoom in and out on objects such as images and graphs, and lets you watch embedded videos.

RULER SETTINGS Some views display a horizontal ruler—a guide at the top of the document window, showing you where each paragraph's tab stops and indents are located. In Word's Page Layout view, you also see a vertical ruler on the left side of the screen. You can use rulers to set margins, tabs, indents, and other paragraph formats.

MICROSOFT CORPORATION (SCREENSHOT); MAGGY MEYER/SHUTTERSTOCK (CLIP ART)

FIGURE 12.1.1 A Word document in Print Layout view.

CHANGING VIEWS To change from one view to another, you usually use the commands on the View menu. Some programs, such as Microsoft Word, also have small icons representing different views on the status bar. Select an icon to change the view.

Zooming In and Out

The Zoom feature changes the size of the text displayed on the screen. While larger text is more readable, smaller text allows you to see more of the document onscreen at once. But only at 100 percent will you have an accurate picture of the text as it will appear when it is published.

Multiple Views of the Same Document

Some word-processing programs allow you to split the document window into two sections, or **panes**. This split screen lets you view two parts of a document at the same time. You can scroll through each pane separately to display any part of the document. This feature makes it easy to move or copy text from one part of a large document to another. You can also use this feature to compare discussions of the same topic in two different parts of a document.

CONNECTIONS

LANGUAGE ARTS A writing style is a set of guidelines for the language, punctuation, and formatting of a document. There are a number of accepted styles, but many teachers prefer the Modern Language Association (MLA) style. Some examples of MLA style rules include double-spaced lines, 1″ margins on all sides, and in-text citations of sources. Other commonly used styles include the *Chicago Manual of Style*, which does not require in-text citations, and American Psychological Association (APA) style, which is usually preferred for papers written about the social sciences. Before writing a research paper, ask your teacher which style you should use.

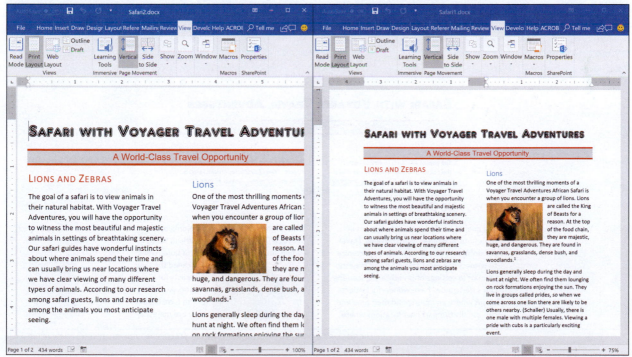

MICROSOFT CORPORATION (SCREENSHOT); MAGGY MEYER/SHUTTERSTOCK (CLIP ART)

FIGURE 12.1.2 Use Zoom controls to change the magnification of a document display. The document on the left is at 100%; the one on the right is at 75%.

Viewing Multiple Documents at the Same Time

Some word-processing programs allow you to display more than one document window at the same time. You may be able to arrange all open documents within the program window, working in each one independently while being able to view them all. You may also be able to view two documents side by side, and use **synchronous scrolling** to move up and down through them both at the same time. Viewing side by side is useful for comparing two versions of the same document.

Using the Navigation Pane

In some word-processing programs, such as Microsoft Word, you can use the Navigation pane to find and go to a heading, page, or any key term. If text is formatted as a heading, it will display in a list in the Navigation pane. This list is sometimes called a **document map**. Select a heading in the Navigation pane to quickly move the insertion point to its location in the document. The Navigation pane may also include options for viewing icons representing each page, called **thumbnails**. Select a thumbnail to display that page. Finally, the Navigation pane may include a Search box. When you type a word or phrase, all occurrences will be highlighted in the document and listed in the Navigation pane.

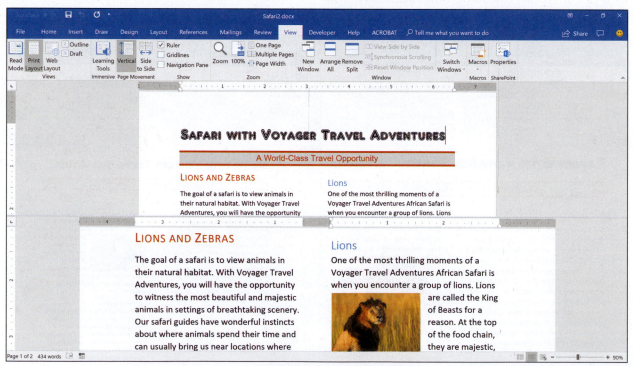

MICROSOFT CORPORATION (SCREENSHOT); MAGGY MEYER/SHUTTERSTOCK (CLIP ART)

FIGURE 12.1.3 Some programs let you split a document so you can see different sections at the same time using different views.

OBJECTIVES

- Identify the advantages of using keyboard shortcuts.
- Explain how to insert special characters or symbols.
- Demonstrate how to insert pictures.
- Describe uses for the Find and Replace features.

AS YOU READ

ORGANIZE INFORMATION Complete a spider map to help you organize details about different editing features as you read.

TERMINOLOGY

- clip art
- crop
- Find and Replace
- function key
- graphics
- keyboard shortcut

Keyboard Shortcuts

Usually, you move the insertion point and select commands using the mouse. Sometimes you may find it easier and faster to keep the fingers of both hands on the keyboard. You may be able to use the keyboard to type, issue commands, and select options quicker than you can move a mouse through a series of menus.

Most programs offer **keyboard shortcuts**, which are combinations of keys that can execute commands. Usually, issuing these commands requires pressing the Control (Ctrl) key in Windows or the Command key in Macintosh in combination with some other key. Ctrl + C, for example, is a Copy shortcut on Windows computers. Some of the shortcuts use a **function key** from the row of keys at the top of the keyboard that are labeled F1, F2, and so on.

COMMON KEYBOARD SHORTCUTS

Command	Windows	Macintosh
Boldface	Ctrl + B	Command + B
Italic	Ctrl + I	Command + I
Underline	Ctrl + U	Command + U
Cut	Ctrl + X	Command + X
Copy	Ctrl + C	Command + C
Paste	Ctrl + V	Command + V
Undo	Ctrl + Z	Command + Z

DID YOU KNOW?

There are ways other than a keyboard to enter text into a document. For example, you can create digital text using speech-recognition software, a stylus pen on a tablet, or an optical scanner.

For some, these technologies provide opportunities beyond those available using a keyboard. Students with disabilities or with auditory or tactile learning styles may find these options enhance their academic skills.

Using Special Characters and Symbols

Most word-processing programs allow you to insert special characters and symbols. These are symbols and characters that cannot be created simply by pressing one key. Common symbols can be made using a combination of keys. For example, in some programs you can type (c) to make the copyright symbol ©.

There are too many special characters to have keyboard shortcuts for all of them. Many word-processing programs provide a dialog box that displays all the characters they offer. In Word, to choose a symbol, select the Insert tab of the Ribbon and select the Symbol command in the Symbols group. You can select symbols and special characters from a variety of built-in fonts.

Inserting Graphics

Graphics are drawings, photographs, charts, and other objects that you can insert into a document. Some graphics, like charts and graphs, are informative. Others are decorative. Most word-processing programs have tools for using shapes to create graphics and for inserting graphics already stored in digital format. For example, you can insert a digital photo you took with your smartphone, or a drawing you find on online. Usually, use the Insert > Pictures command to locate and insert a picture file you have stored on your computer, or the Insert > Online Pictures to browse the program's collection of **clip art**. Always obey copyright laws when using pictures that were created and are owned by someone else. Request permission and give credit to the owner before sharing or publishing the document.

Once you insert a picture into a document, you can format it. You can resize it, move it, and apply effects such as shadows and borders. You can even **crop** it to hide parts you don't want to show. You can rotate it around an axis point. Most word-processing programs have basic tools for editing graphics. However, for more advanced work with graphics, it is a good idea to use a dedicated graphics program, such as Adobe Illustrator or Photoshop.

Finding and Replacing

Suppose you had written an essay about President George Bush. After finishing, you realized you had to make clear that you were writing about George W. Bush and not his father, George Herbert Walker Bush, who also had been president. You can use a powerful word-processing feature to search your essay for every time the name *George Bush* appears. You can even use the program to automatically replace every occurrence of *George Bush* with *George W. Bush*.

USING FIND AND REPLACE The **Find and Replace** (or search and replace) feature lets you:

- Locate a word or combination of words

- Change those words to other words

- Search for text characters, including spaces, punctuation, and symbols

- Search for text that is formatted a certain way

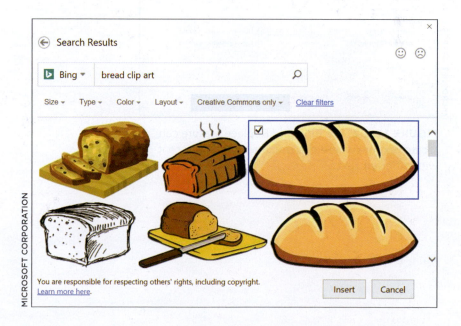

MICROSOFT CORPORATION

FIGURE 12.2.1 Most word-processing programs, such as Microsoft Word, provide access to online clip art galleries.

In most programs, you select the command for Find and Replace, and then use a dialog box to enter the text to find and the replacement text.

CAUTIONS Use the Find and Replace feature very carefully. The feature looks for a specific set of letters, not just the word containing that set of letters. Suppose you type *his* as the search term and *hers* as its replacement. Since the program will replace every instance of *his* with *hers*, it will change *history* to *herstory* and *this* to *thers*.

You can avoid this problem by making sure you search for the word *his*, not just the letters *his*. The dialog box typically has an option for searching only for the whole word. Be sure to choose this option to avoid such errors.

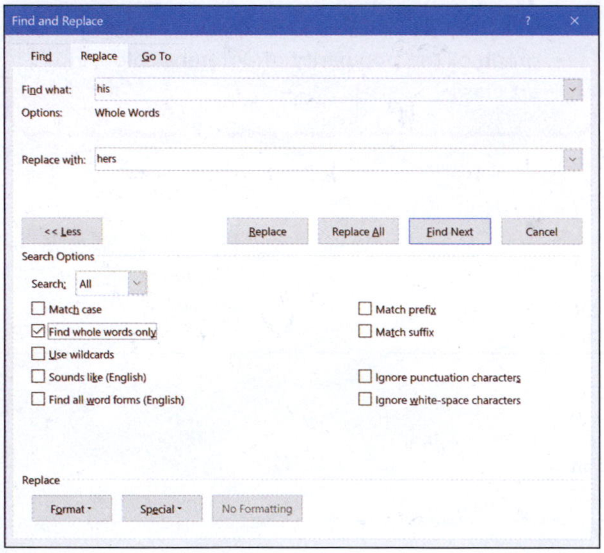

TECHNOLOGY@WORK

Some businesses mail the same letter to many different customers. In these letters, all the text is exactly the same. Only the name and address changes.

THINK ABOUT IT!

Think about a word-processing feature that automatically makes the changes needed in these letters. Which features listed below would be useful for this purpose?

- changing document views
- formatting text
- inserting special characters
- Find and Replace
- Merge

MICROSOFT CORPORATION

FIGURE 12.2.2 The Find and Replace feature can locate text anywhere in a document and replace it with different text.

Formatting and Printing

OBJECTIVES

- Demonstrate how to use styles to format a document.
- Explore how tables can be used to display information.
- Compare print options.

AS YOU READ

OUTLINE INFORMATION Complete an outline to help you identify different ways of creating a professional-looking word-processing document.

TERMINOLOGY

- cell
- column
- gutter
- Print Preview
- row
- style
- style sheet
- table

Applying Styles

A **style** is a set of formats that is applied all at once. You can apply styles to text and to objects. For example, you can apply a style to a heading to quickly format the heading with a set of formats, such as bold, large font size, and an underline. You can apply a style to a picture to change the border or shape, or to add effects. Using styles to apply consistent formatting gives your document a professional look.

USING STYLES Styles can be applied to selected characters or to paragraphs. Character styles include font formatting, such as font, font size, and font style. Paragraph styles include font formatting and paragraph formatting, such as alignment, line spacing, and tabs.

Most programs have a set of built-in styles called a **style sheet** for quickly formatting common document elements, such as headings and titles. Document templates usually have built-in style sheets for the selected document type. In Microsoft Word, styles display on the Home tab of the Ribbon and in the Styles task pane.

You can select a style and type new text, or you can apply a style to existing text. To apply a character style, select the characters and then select the style. To apply a paragraph style, place the insertion point in a paragraph or select multiple paragraphs, and then select the style.

CREATING AND MODIFYING STYLES You can create your own styles by formatting text and saving the formatting as a new style. In Word, just right-click the formatted text, select Styles, and select Create a Style. Enter a name for the new style, and then select OK.

When you modify an existing style, all text formatted with that style changes to match the modifications. In Word, right-click the style name on the Ribbon and select Modify. Then, select the changes in the Modify Style dialog box, and select OK. Or, position the insertion point in formatted text, right-click the style name on the Ribbon, and select Update *style name* to Match Selection.

IC3 ✔ **Know how to alter text and font styles.**

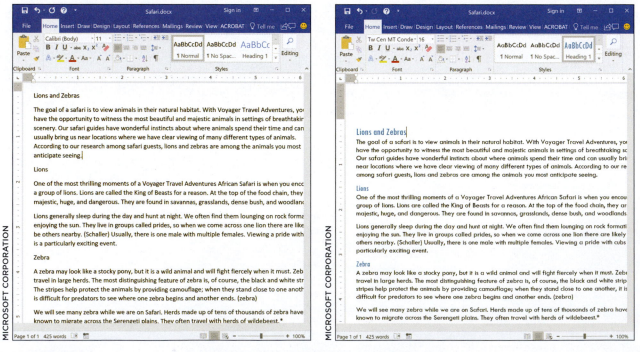

FIGURE 12.3.1 A document before (left) and after (right) styles were applied.

Presenting Information in Tables

Word-processing programs have tools for organizing content into easy-to-read tables and lists. A **table** is comprised of a series of vertical columns and horizontal rows. You enter content in the **cell** at the intersection of a **column** and **row**.

INSERTING A TABLE In some programs, you insert tables by using the Insert menu. Others have a special Table menu. In Word, the Tables group is on the Insert tab of the Ribbon. You can insert a blank table by dragging across the grid to select the number of columns and rows. You can also use the Convert Text to Table command to format selected text as a table. The text must include characters that mark where to start a new column or row. For example, a tab might mark where to start a new column, and a paragraph mark might mark where to start a new row.

IC3 ✔ Know how to use tables.

FORMATTING A TABLE Once you create a table, you can apply paragraph and character formatting to text in the table to improve its appearance and make it easier to read. For example, you can apply the bold font style and change the alignment to center to make column labels stand out. Tables are inserted using a basic grid, but you can add formatting such as colors, borders, and shading to the table design. To apply a set of formats all at once, you can select from a gallery of built-in table styles.

You can alter the layout of a table by inserting and deleting columns and rows. In Microsoft Word, on the Table Tools Layout tab you can select from a variety of alignment options. For example, you can change the text direction from horizontal to vertical, sort rows into alphabetical or numerical order, and adjust the cell margins, which is the distance between the text and the border of the cell. There are also nine options for aligning text in a table cell that combine horizontal alignment, such as left, right, and center, with vertical alignment, such as top, middle, and bottom.

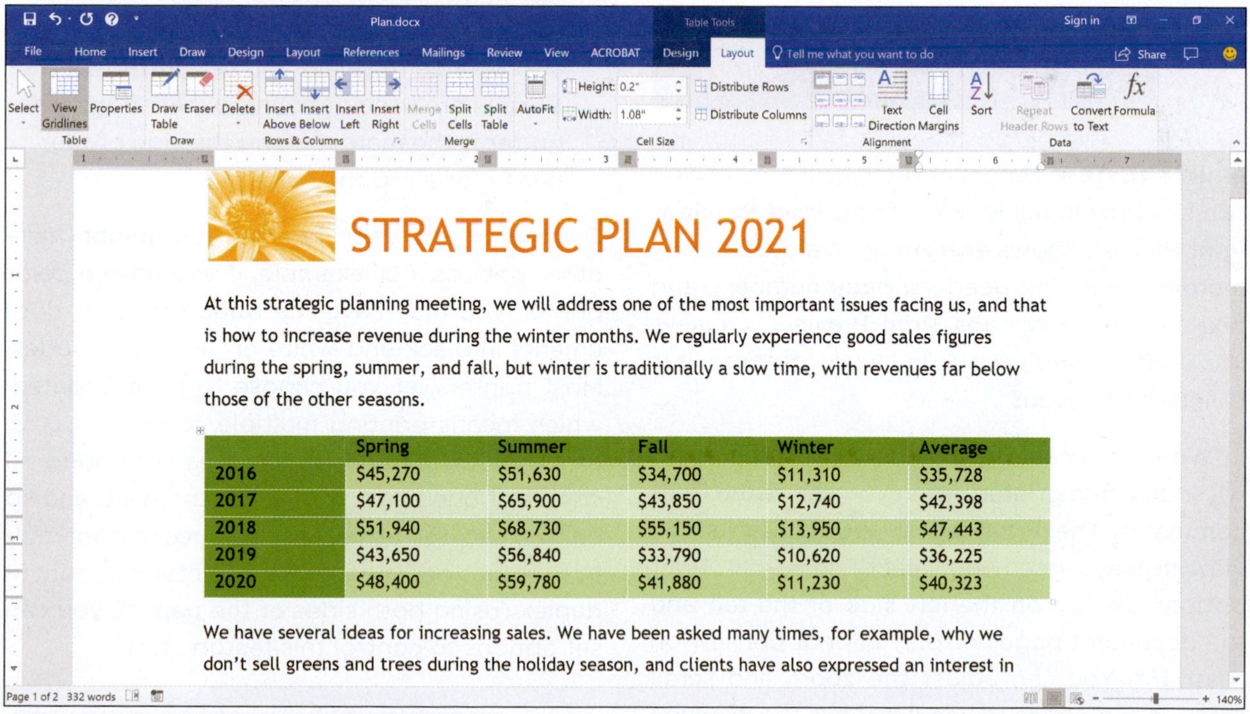

STRATEGIC PLAN 2021

At this strategic planning meeting, we will address one of the most important issues facing us, and that is how to increase revenue during the winter months. We regularly experience good sales figures during the spring, summer, and fall, but winter is traditionally a slow time, with revenues far below those of the other seasons.

	Spring	Summer	Fall	Winter	Average
2016	$45,270	$51,630	$34,700	$11,310	$35,728
2017	$47,100	$65,900	$43,850	$12,740	$42,398
2018	$51,940	$68,730	$55,150	$13,950	$47,443
2019	$43,650	$56,840	$33,790	$10,620	$36,225
2020	$48,400	$59,780	$41,880	$11,230	$40,323

We have several ideas for increasing sales. We have been asked many times, for example, why we don't sell greens and trees during the holiday season, and clients have also expressed an interest in

MICROSOFT CORPORATION

FIGURE 12.3.2 Insert and format a table in a word-processing document to present information in columns and rows.

For example, you can select Align Bottom Left to align text with the left cell margin horizontally and the bottom cell margin vertically.

IC3✔ **Know how to align text in tables.**

CREATING LISTS When you don't need multiple columns, you can format text as a bulleted or numbered list. Use numbers when the order matters, like for directions. Use bullets when the order does not matter. Most programs have commands that quickly apply list formatting.

Publishing a Document

Although many documents are designed to be viewed on a monitor, people often print the reports, greeting cards, letters, and posters they create. To quickly print a document you usually choose File > Print > Print, select a Print button, or use the Ctrl + P shortcut key combination. You can also preview the document before printing, and select print options.

IC3✔ **Know how to print a word-processing document.**

PRINT PREVIEW Before printing a document, you can see how it will look by using **Print Preview**. Print Preview shows everything in a document—margins, graphics, headers, page numbers, and text. In some programs, Print Preview is a view, like Draft or Web Layout. In Microsoft Word, it is called Print Layout.

In Word, you can also see how your document will look when printed when you select the Print command. The Print tab in Word's Backstage view displays when you select File > Print. Print options display on the left side of the tab and the document pages display in print preview on the right. You can adjust the zoom and scroll through the pages to see if it looks the way you want. If not, you can leave the Backstage view and adjust the layout and formatting.

PRINT OPTIONS Most programs have a Print dialog box or tab that gives you several options:

- Printer—If the computer is connected to more than one printer, you can choose which one to use.

- Page range—You can choose to print every page in the document, the current page, or a group of pages.

- Number of copies—You can print one copy of the document, hundreds of copies, or any number in between.

- Print quality—You may be able to print in a faster "draft" mode or in a slower, high-quality mode.

- Orientation—You can select Portrait (the height of the page is greater than the width) or Landscape (the width of the page is greater than the height).

- Paper Size—You can select from a list of standard paper sizes, such a 8.5" x 11", or you can set a custom size.

- Margins—You can select from standard margin widths or set custom margins. You may also be able to select and set **gutter** widths. Gutters are used in bound publications. The gutter is the margin along the side of the page closest to the binding.

Depending on your printer, you might have other options. For example, if you have a color printer, you may have the option to print documents in black-and-white or grayscale modes. Most printers let you choose to print Collated, which means printing multiple copies in 1, 2, 3, order; or Uncollated, which means printing all copies of one page, then all of the next, and so on. You can also usually scale pages to print multiple copies per sheet. If your printer can print in duplex (using both sides of the paper), you can set options to control this feature, too.

IC3✔ **Know how to use and configure print views.**

GLOBAL PRINTING OPTIONS Many programs let you set options to control how printing is handled in all documents, not just the document you are printing at the moment. Options might include printing drawings, background colors, or images, or updating fields or linked data before printing. In Microsoft Word, these options are on the Display tab of the Word Options dialog box. Select File > Options and then select Display in the left pane of the dialog box. The Printing options are listed at the bottom of the page. Select a checkbox to enable the feature or clear the checkbox to disable the feature.

Sharing and Exporting Documents

Printing is not the only way to make a document available for people to see and read. Most word-processing programs have commands for exporting the document into a different file format so it can be opened by someone who does not have the same program.

For example, in Microsoft Word, when you select File > Export, you can choose to convert the file into Adobe PDF format or to create a PDF/XPS document. These options ensure that the formatting of the original document will be retained, so others will see it as you intend. You can also choose from a long list of compatible file formats, including .rtf, .mht or .mhtl, or .txt.

Select File > Share to share your document electronically. You can save it to a cloud storage location, such as Microsoft OneDrive, so others can access it. You can share it as an attachment to an email message. You can even post it to a blog on a supported blogging site, such as WordPress or TypePad. Finally, use the Present Online command to upload the document to a server and send a link to others so they can view it in a web browser.

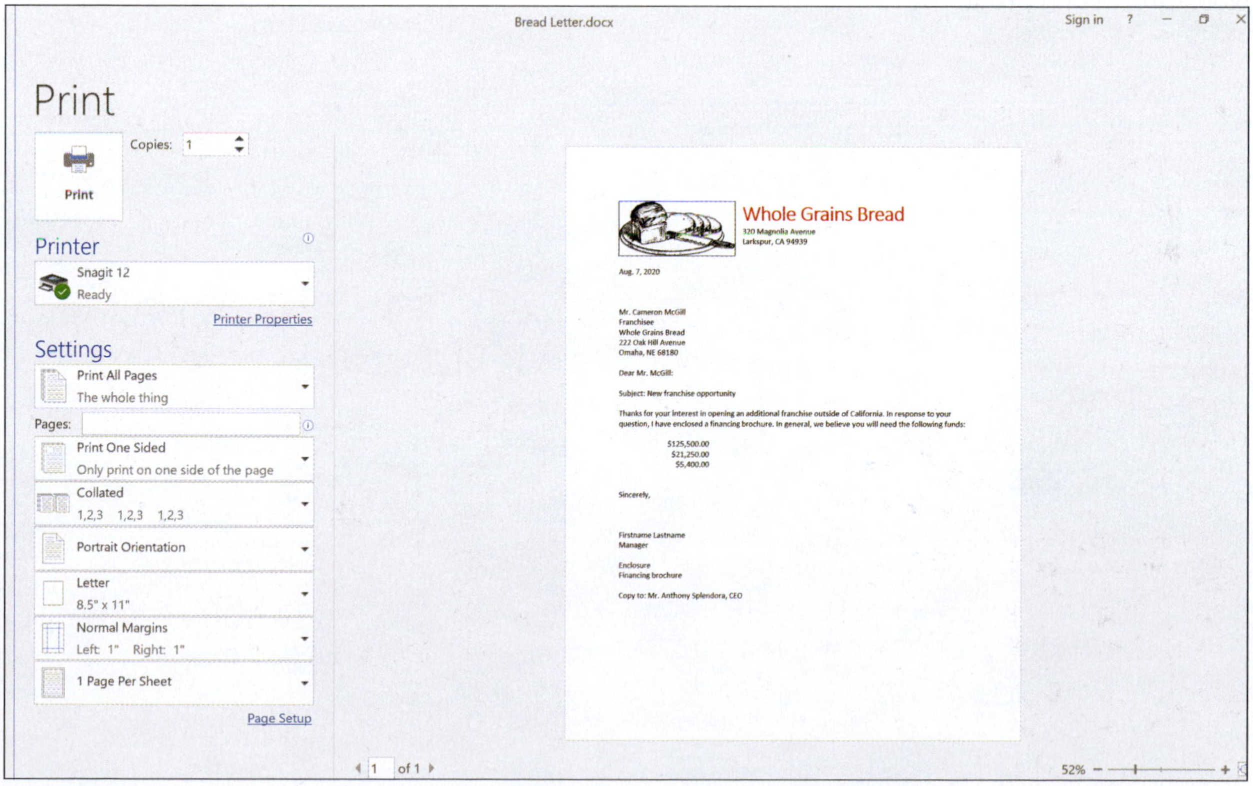

FIGURE 12.3.3 Many programs let you select options for printing in a Print dialog box or on a Print tab.

LESSON 12-4
Making and Tracking Edits

OBJECTIVES

- Explain how to check spelling, grammar, and style.

- Describe the benefits of tracking editing changes.

- Outline the steps for adding comments to a document.

AS YOU READ

ORGANIZE INFORMATION Complete a chart to help you organize basic facts about checking tools and workgroup editing functions in word-processing programs.

TERMINOLOGY

- grammar check

- spell check

- style check

- Track Changes

Tools for Correcting Errors

Most word-processing programs offer tools to help with your writing. These tools check spelling, grammar, and writing style.

SPELL CHECK Spell check matches each word in the text against a word list built into the program and gives you options for correcting a misspelling. You can accept one of the spellings or ignore the suggested change. You can also add a word to the word list so the program will accept it in the future. You can use spell check in two ways:

- Check spelling as you type. The program highlights possible errors as they occur. In some programs, you can select the error to find different spellings and then quickly choose one.

- Check a word, a selection, or a whole document. As each possible spelling error is displayed, you decide whether to keep the original spelling or change it.

THINK ABOUT IT!

Think about situations in which the translation feature might be used. Which examples listed below do you think could safely be translated by computer?

- a government document
- a movie review
- a newspaper article
- a letter from a lawyer
- a person's medical records

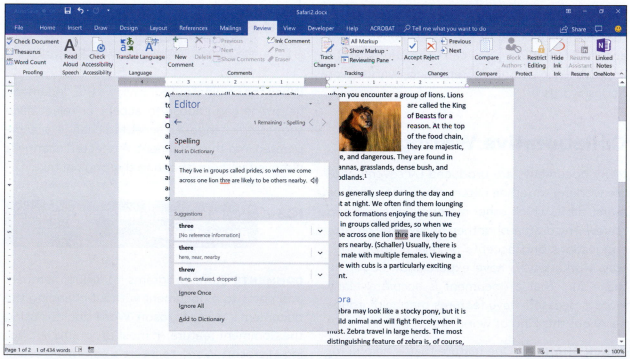

MICROSOFT CORPORATION (SCREENSHOT); MAGGY MEYER/SHUTTERSTOCK (CLIP ART)

FIGURE 12.4.1 Use spell check to check spelling in a document.

Spell check is useful, but it accepts any word that is spelled correctly—even if it is used incorrectly. You need to proofread your documents carefully even if you use spell check.

GRAMMAR AND STYLE CHECK You can run grammar and style checks as you type, or you can check a selection or the entire document at once. Either way, the program highlights potential errors. You can examine each one and accept or ignore the suggested correction.

Grammar check features look for problems such as errors in the use of verb tenses, pronouns, punctuation, and capitalization. For instance, the program would suggest fixing the sentence "He had ran yesterday." The grammar check also finds sentence fragments (incomplete sentences) and run-on sentences (two sentences joined together incorrectly).

Style check features suggest ways to improve the writing style in a document. They let you know whether a sentence is unclear or too wordy or long. They offer alternatives to the use of contractions or language that is too informal.

Most programs also include a Thesaurus feature that lets you look up definitions, synonyms, and antonyms for words. You can use a thesaurus to improve your writing by replacing overused or boring words.

Collaborative Writing

Many documents are produced by several people working together. Often, one person creates a first draft, which other members of the group review. The draft author then reviews the group's suggestions and accepts or rejects them. This way, workers who have expert knowledge can make sure that a document is accurate. Many word processors have features that help groups carry out this kind of work.

TRACK CHANGES One feature that is helpful for working in groups is called **Track Changes** in Microsoft Word. A similar feature in WordPerfect is the red-line method of document review. This feature marks each editing change made by each member of the group. This is done by adding specific markup formatting to the document at the point where the changes were made.

- Inserted text is shown in a specific color assigned to each group member.

- Deleted text is not removed but appears in the assigned color with a line running through the words.

- In some programs, special boxes name the person who made the change.

In Word, you turn Track Changes on or off by selecting the Review tab of the Ribbon and then selecting Track Changes. You can control how the program displays the tracked changes. For example, you can choose to show all markups, or you can select some markups, such as comments, insertions and deletions, or formatting. To select the markup options to show, select the Show Markup button on the Review tab, and select the options you want. You can also use the Track Changes Options dialog box.

IC3 ✔ **Know how to turn on and off change tracking features.**

When the original author reviews the document, he or she can choose to accept or reject each suggested change. An accepted change is incorporated into the document. A rejected change is removed without affecting the original text.

IC3 ✔ **Know how to accept or reject proposed changes.**

COMMENTS Some programs let group members add notes to a document without changing the document's text. Microsoft Word does so using the Comment feature. In most programs, including Microsoft Word, to insert a comment, select Review and then select New Comment. A special pane appears at the bottom or edge of the screen, ready for you to type your comment.

Several people can add comments to a document, and the program tracks each person's comments. That way, the author can see who added what remarks to the document. People can reply to comments to provide feedback. Comments can be hidden or deleted, and a comment's text can be formatted and edited just like normal text.

DOCUMENT PROTECTION Most programs let you protect a document from unauthorized changes. Protection options range from allowing users to read but not edit or format a document to allowing only those with a password to open the document.

THINK ABOUT IT!

You can help yourself create error-free documents by practicing enunciation and reading skills for use with speech-recognition programs, and digital penmanship for use with handwriting-recognition programs. Work with your teacher to create a plan for developing these skills. It will help you improve academically in all areas.

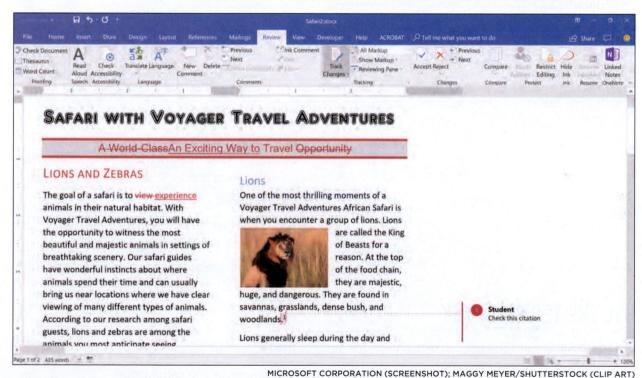

MICROSOFT CORPORATION (SCREENSHOT); MAGGY MEYER/SHUTTERSTOCK (CLIP ART)

FIGURE 12.4.2 Use the commands on the Review tab of the Ribbon in Microsoft Word to turn on and manage the Track Changes and Comments features.

Chapter 12 Review

REVIEW THE TERMINOLOGY

DIRECTIONS Match each vocabulary term in the left column with the correct definition in the right column.

1. Print Layout view
2. Web Layout view
3. pane
4. document map
5. keyboard shortcut
6. function key
7. Find and Replace
8. paragraph
9. style sheet
10. Print Preview

a. text in a document up to a forced new line

b. screen that shows a document's text and a list of its headings

c. feature that finds a word and puts another in its place

d. document display that shows how page elements will look when published on the web

e. print feature that shows everything in a document as it will look when printed

f. holds formats for all elements in a document

g. document display that shows how page elements will look when printed

h. a special key labeled F1, F2, and so on

i. combination of keys that carry out an action

j. partial window seen in split screen

USE THE TERMINOLOGY

DIRECTIONS Determine the correct choice for each of the following.

1. Which feature allows you to look at two parts of a document at the same time?
   a. side-by-side pages
   b. split screen
   c. Document view
   d. Outline view

2. Which of the following keys is used in many keyboard shortcuts?
   a. Backspace
   b. Delete
   c. Escape
   d. Control

3. In word processing, what determines the end of a paragraph?

    a. 20 lines of text   **c.** a forced new line

    b. 400 words of text   **d.** a forced new page

4. By choosing "Whole Word" when searching, what will you replace?

    a. every case where the letters appear   **c.** all paragraphs with those letters

    b. those letters and no others   **d.** the letters only when they make a word

5. How does a document look in Print Preview?

    a. as it appears when printed   **c.** as it appears on the monitor

    b. as it appears on the web   **d.** as it appears in computer code

6. Which options are provided in the Print dialog box?

    a. bold or italic type   **c.** size of paper

    b. number of copies   **d.** inserting graphics

THINK CRITICALLY

DIRECTIONS Answer the following questions.

1. What is the benefit of a word processor that is able to track changes in a document? Would this be more useful for single users, or collaborative groups?

2. What is the difference between using the mouse to carry out basic commands and using keyboard shortcuts? Which do you think is easier? Why?

3. Explain the process for inserting special characters.

4. When might you use the Insert > Picture command and when might you use the Insert > Online Pictures command?

5. Suppose you want to create a table to keep track of your test scores in math class. Explain how you would design your table, including an example.

EXTEND YOUR KNOWLEDGE

DIRECTIONS Choose and complete one of the following projects.

1. Open a word-processing program and create a new document. Locate the AutoCorrect settings and add a word to the list. Input any two paragraphs from this chapter. After you input the text, change the font of the paragraphs. Create a left tab setting for the paragraphs and indent the first lines using that setting. Type "Formatting Practice" as the title at the top, and center that line. Adjust the page setup to use different margins. Add a header at the top of the page that displays your name and the date. Check and correct the spelling. Review and save your document. Then, print it for your teacher to review.

2. Working with a partner or small group, develop and conduct a survey you can use to learn how many of your classmates use the following computer programs at home: word processing, spreadsheet, database, graphics, email, games, and web browser. Create a word-processing document. Type the first program type, press Tab, and type the number of classmates who use that program. Press Enter and repeat for each of the program types. Select all of the information and convert it to a 2-column table. Challenge yourself by sorting the table into alphabetical order by program name. Format the table with a table style. With your teacher's permission, print the document.

IC3 PREP

1. For each line below, select whether the statement is True or False.

   a. Styles can be applied to text, but not objects.

   b. Most programs do not have a set of built-in styles called a style sheet for quickly formatting common document elements.

   c. In Microsoft Word, styles display on the Home tab of the Ribbon and in the Styles task pane.

   d. Character styles include font formatting, such as font, font size, and font style.

   e. Styles can be applied to selected characters or to paragraphs.

2. You have been instructed to alter an existing text style in Microsoft Word. Put the following steps in order.

   a. Select Update *Style name* to Match Selection.

   b. Alter the text formatted with a current style.

   c. Select the altered text.

   d. Right-click the style name on the Ribbon.

3. Which of these methods are correct ways to create a table in Microsoft Word? (Select all that apply.)

   a. On the Insert tab of the Ribbon, drag across the grid to select the number of columns and rows.

   b. Use the Convert Text to Table command to format selected text as a table.

   c. Create patterns of rectangles with the Shape tool.

   d. Select the Table command on the Home tab of the Ribbon.

4. Fill in the blank: The spaces that make up the rows and columns of a table are commonly known as _____.

   a. rectangles   c. cells

   b. data entry points   d. check boxes

5. How many options are there for aligning text in a table cell?

   a. three   c. six

   b. four   d. nine

6. What is NOT a common way to print a word-processing document?

   a. Select a Print button.

   b. Use the Ctrl + Alt + Delete shortcut.

   c. Select File, then Print from the drop down menu.

   d. Use the Ctrl + P shortcut.

7. How does a document look in Print Preview?

   a. as it appears when printed   c. as it appears on the monitor

   b. as it appears on the web   d. as it appears in computer code

8. Which options are provided in the Print dialog box? (Select all that apply.)

   a. bold or italic type   c. size of paper

   b. number of copies   d. inserting graphics

9. Which of these tracking features can be toggled in Word? (Select all that apply.)

   a. Comments   c. Insertions and deletions

   b. Margins   d. Formatting

IC3 PROCEDURES

INSERTING A PICTURE FILE

1. Position the insertion point where you want to insert the image.

2. On the Insert tab, select the **Pictures** button.

3. Browse to the location where the image file is stored.

4. Select the image and select **Insert**.

INSERTING AN ONLINE PICTURE

1. Position the insertion point where you want to insert the image.

2. On the Insert tab, select the **Online Pictures** button.

3. In the search box, type a keyword, and then press **Enter**.

4. In the list of results, select the picture to insert.

5. Select **Insert**.

CROPPING A GRAPHIC

1. Select the graphic to select it.

2. Select the **Picture Tools Format** tab.

3. Select the **Crop** button.

4. Hover the mouse pointer over a cropping handle.

5. When the cropping pointer appears, click and drag to define the area you want to keep.

   Use a corner handle to crop from two sides. Use a side or top handle to crop from the corresponding side.

6. When you are finished cropping, select the **Crop** button again to remove the edges outside the defined area.

PRINTING A FILE

1. Select **File**.
2. Select **Print**.
3. Select the **Print** button.

PREVIEWING AND PRINTING A FILE

1. Select the **File** tab.
2. Select **Print**.

   In Backstage view, print settings display on the left, and a preview of the file displays on the right.

3. Use the **Next Page** and **Previous Page** arrows under the preview to view other pages.
4. Use the **Zoom** controls under the preview to adjust the preview magnification.
5. Select the **Print** button.

CHANGING PRINT OPTIONS

1. Select the **File** tab.
2. Select **Print**.
3. In the **Copies** box, enter the number of copies.
4. Under Printer, select the printer to use.
5. Under Settings, select options:
   - **What to print**
   - **Pages to print**
   - **One sided or two sided printing**
   - **Collated or Uncollated**
   - **Landscape or Portrait orientation**
   - **Page Size**
   - **Margin width**
   - **Pages per sheet**
6. Select the **Print** button.

CREATING A TABLE

1. Select the **Insert** tab.
2. Select the **Table** button.
3. Select **Quick Tables**.
4. From the gallery, select the desired Quick Table.

   OR

1. Select the **Insert** tab.
2. Select the **Table** button.
3. Position the mouse pointer on a cell to highlight the desired number of rows and columns.

4. Select to insert the table.

   OR

1. Select the **Insert** tab.

2. Select the **Table** button ▦.

3. Select **Insert Table**.

4. In the Insert Table dialog box, set the number of rows and columns and the AutoFit options as desired.

5. Select **OK**.

ENTERING TEXT IN A TABLE

Click in a cell and type the entry.

OR

Press **Tab** or an arrow key to move to a cell and type an entry.

CONVERTING TEXT TO A TABLE

1. Select the text to convert.

2. Select the **Insert** tab.

3. Select the **Table** button ▦.

4. On the menu, select **Convert Text to Table**.

5. In the Convert Text to Table dialog box, set options.

6. Select **OK**.

SETTING ALIGNMENT IN A TABLE CELL

1. Select the cell(s) in which you want to set the alignment.

2. Select the **Table Tools Layout** tab.

3. Select from the alignment options, as follows:

   - **Align Top Left** ▤
   - **Align Top Center** ▤
   - **Align Top Right** ▤
   - **Align Center Left** ▤
   - **Align Center** ▤
   - **Align Center Right** ▤
   - **Align Bottom Left** ▤
   - **Align Bottom Center** ▤
   - **Align Bottom Right** ▤

APPLYING A BUILT-IN STYLE

1. Position insertion point within the text to format.

2. Select the **Home** tab.

3. Select the desired style from the Styles gallery.

279

CREATING A CUSTOM STYLE

1. Format text.
2. Select the formatted text.
3. On the Mini toolbar, select **Styles**.
4. Select **Create a Style**.
5. Type a style name.
6. Select **OK**.

MODIFYING A STYLE

1. Select the **Home** tab.
2. Select the desired style from the Styles gallery.
3. Select the text and modify the formats as desired.
4. With the text still selected right-click the style in the Styles gallery and click **Update** *style name* **to Match Selection**.

TURNING TRACK CHANGES ON OR OFF

1. Select the **Review** tab.
2. Select the **Track Changes** button .

ACCEPTING OR REJECTING CHANGES

1. Select the **Review** tab.
2. Select the **Next** button to move to the next tracked change in the document.

    OR

    Select the **Previous** button to move to the previous tracked change.
3. Select the **Accept** button to accept the change.

    OR

    Select the **Reject** button to reject the change.

ACCEPTING ALL CHANGES

1. Select the **Review** tab.
2. Select the drop-down arrow on the **Accept** button .
3. Select **Accept All Changes**.

    OR

    Select **Accept All Changes and Stop Tracking**.

REJECTING ALL CHANGES

1. Select the **Review** tab.
2. Select the drop-down arrow on the **Reject** button .
3. Select **Reject All Changes**.

    OR

    Select **Reject All Changes and Stop Tracking**.

Additional Microsoft Word 2016 Procedures

SHOWING OR HIDING NONPRINTING CHARACTERS

1. Select the **Home** tab.
2. Select the **Show/Hide ¶** button ¶.
3. Select the **Show/Hide ¶** button ¶ again to toggle off.

CHANGING THE VIEW

1. Select the **View** tab.
2. Select the desired View button:
   - **Read Mode**
   - **Print Layout**
   - **Web Layout**
   - **Outline**
   - **Draft**

   OR

   Select a **View** button on the status bar:
   - **Read Mode**
   - **Print Layout**
   - **Web Layout**

SWITCHING BETWEEN OPEN DOCUMENTS

Click in the document window you want to make active.

OR

Select the program's taskbar button and select the document you want to make active.

OR

1. Select the **View** tab.
2. Select the **Switch Windows** button.
3. Select the document you want to make active.

ARRANGING MULTIPLE DOCUMENTS

1. Open all documents.
2. Select the **View** tab.
3. Select the **Arrange All** button.

CLOSING A DOCUMENT

Select the **Close** button ✕.

OR

1. Select **File**.
2. Select **Close**.

ENTERING TEXT AND DATA

Typing in a Document

- Press **Enter** to start a new paragraph.
- Press **Backspace** to delete one character to the left of the insertion point.
- Press **Del** to delete one character to the right of the insertion point.
- Press **Esc** to cancel a command or close a dialog box.

Using Overtype Mode

1. Right-click the status bar.
2. Select **Overtype** on the shortcut menu.

   A check mark next to the command on the shortcut menu indicates it is selected.

3. Select **Insert** on the status bar to change to overtype mode.

FINDING AND REPLACING

Using Find

1. Select the **Home** tab.
2. Select the **Find** button.

281

3. In the text box at the top of the Navigation pane, enter the text you want to find.

   Word displays a list of occurrences in the Navigation pane.

Using Advanced Find

1. Select the **Home** tab.
2. Select the **Find** button drop-down arrow 🔍.
3. Select **Advanced Find**.
4. In the Find and Replace dialog box, enter the text to find in the Find what text box.
5. Select **Find Next**. A message box appears when all occurrences have been found.

Using Find and Replace

1. Select the **Home** tab.
2. Select the **Replace** button 🔤.
3. In the Find and Replace dialog box, enter the text to find in the Find what text box.
4. Enter the replacement text in the Replace with text box.
5. Select the **Replace** button to replace each separate occurrence; select **Replace All** to replace all occurrences.

CHANGING CASE

1. Select the text whose case you want to change.
2. Select the **Home** tab.
3. Select the **Change Case** button Aa▾.
4. On the menu, select the desired case option.

APPLYING TEXT EFFECTS

1. Select the text.
2. Select the **Home** tab.
3. Select the **Text Effects** button A▾.
4. Select the desired effect from the gallery.

USING THE FORMAT PAINTER TO COPY FORMATS

1. Select the text whose format you want to copy.
2. Select the **Home** tab.
3. Select the **Format Painter** button 🖌.
4. Select the text to which you want to apply the copied format.

COPYING FORMATTING TO MULTIPLE SELECTIONS

1. Select the text whose format you want to copy.
2. Select the **Home** tab.
3. Double-click the **Format Painter** button 🖌.
4. Select the text to which you want to apply the copied format, and repeat for additional blocks of text.

HIGHLIGHTING TEXT

1. Select the text you want to highlight.
2. Select the **Home** tab.
3. Select the **Text Highlight Color** drop-down arrow 🖍▾.
4. Select the desired highlight color.

   OR

1. Select the **Home** tab.
2. Select the **Text Highlight Color** drop-down arrow 🖍▾.
3. Select the desired highlight color.

   The mouse pointer changes to the Highlight Text pointer 🖊.

4. Drag across the text you want to highlight.
5. Select the **Text Highlight Color** button 🖍▾ again to turn off the feature.

CLEARING FORMATTING

1. Select the **Home** tab.
2. Select the **Clear All Formatting** button 🧹.

REVEALING FORMATTING

1. Select the formatted text.

2. Select the **Home** tab.

3. Select the **Styles** group dialog box launcher ⬙.

4. In the Styles task pane, select the **Style Inspector** button 🗛.

5. In the Style Inspector task pane, select the **Reveal Formatting** button 🗛.

Aligning a Document Vertically

1. Select the **Layout** tab.

2. Select the **Page Setup** group dialog box launcher ⬙.

3. Select the **Layout** tab.

4. Select the **Vertical alignment** drop-down arrow.

5. Select the desired alignment from the menu.

6. Select **OK**.

SETTING INDENTS

Adjusting the Left Indent by 0.5"

1. Select the **Home** tab.

2. Select the indent option as follows to adjust the indent by 0.5":

   - **Decrease Indent** button ⬅
   - **Increase Indent** button ➡

Setting a Left or Right Indent Precisely

- Select the **Layout** tab.

- Use the **Indent Left** box increment arrows to set the left indent.

- Use the **Indent Right** box increment arrows to set the right indent.

Setting Indents Using the Paragraph Dialog Box

1. Select the **Layout** tab.

2. Select the **Paragraph** group dialog box launcher ⬙.

3. Select the **Indents and Spacing** tab.

4. Under Indentation, use the **Left** and **Right** increment arrows to set the left and right margins, respectively.

5. If desired, select the **Special** drop-down arrow to set the indent on the first line.

6. Select the **By** increment arrows to adjust the indent on the first line, if desired.

Using the Horizontal Ruler to Adjust and Clear Tab Stops

- Position the insertion point in the line of text for which the tab has been set.

- To clear a tab stop, drag the tab stop off the horizontal ruler.

- To adjust a tab stop, drag it to the desired position on the horizontal ruler.

Selecting a Tab Leader

1. Select the **Home** tab.

2. Select the **Paragraph** group dialog box launcher ⬙.

3. Select the **Tabs** button.

4. In the Leader area, select the desired leader style.

5. Select **OK**.

6. In the document, press **Tab** to advance to the tab stop and insert the selected leader.

WORKING WITH BREAKS

Inserting a Hard Page Break

1. Position the insertion point where you want to insert the page break.

2. Select the **Insert** tab.

3. Select the **Page Break** button 🗂.

   OR

1. Select the **Layout tab**.

2. Select the **Breaks** button 🗂.

3. From the Breaks gallery, select **Page**.

Deleting a Hard Page Break

1. Position the insertion point on the page break.

2. Press **Delete**.

Inserting a Section Break

1. Position the insertion point where you want to insert the break.

2. Select the **Layout** tab.

3. Select the **Breaks** button ⊞.

4. From the Breaks gallery, select the desired break type.

Deleting a Section Break

1. Position the insertion point on the section break.

2. Press **Delete**.

INSERTING SYMBOLS

1. Position the insertion point where you want to insert the symbol.

2. Select the **Insert** tab.

3. Select the **Symbol** button Ω.

   If the symbol you want displays in the Symbols gallery, select it to insert it in the document.

4. Select **More Symbols**.

5. In the Symbol dialog box, select a font, if necessary, and then select the desired symbol.

6. Select **Insert**.

INSERTING SPECIAL CHARACTERS

1. Position the insertion point where you want to insert the character.

2. Select the **Insert** tab.

3. Select the **Symbol** button Ω.

4. Select **More Symbols**.

5. In the Symbol dialog box, select the **Special Characters** tab.

6. Select the desired character.

7. Select **Insert**.

CREATING LISTS

Creating a Bulleted List

1. Select the **Home** tab.

2. Select the **Bullets** button drop-down arrow ▤▾.

3. Select the desired bullet style from the Bullet Library.

   OR

1. Select the **Home** tab.

2. Select the **Bullets** button drop-down arrow ▤▾.

3. Select **Define New Bullet** on the menu.

4. In the Define New Bullet dialog box, select the **Symbol** button, **Picture** button, and/or **Font** button to define a new bullet.

Creating a Numbered List

1. Select the **Home** tab.

2. Select the **Numbering** button drop-down arrow ▤▾.

3. Select the desired numbering style from the Numbering Library.

Changing an Item Level in a Numbered List

1. Select the **Home** tab.

2. Select the **Decrease Indent** button ⇤ to promote the item one level, or select the **Increase Indent** button ⇥ to demote the item one level.

Creating a Multilevel List

1. Select the **Home** tab.

2. Select the **Multilevel List** button ▤▾.

3. Select the desired numbering style from the List Library.

Changing the Bullet or Number Formatting

1. Right-click the bullet or number.

2. On the shortcut menu, select **Font** or **Paragraph** to open the corresponding dialog box and change formats as desired.

Changing the Page Number Format

1. Double-click in the header or footer containing the page number.
2. On the Header & Footer Tools Design tab, select the **Page Number** button ⊞.
3. On the menu, select **Format Page Numbers**.
4. In the Page Number Format dialog box, set the formatting as desired.

WORKING WITH HEADERS AND FOOTERS

Typing in the Header or Footer

1. Double-click in the header or footer area to make it active.
2. Type the header or footer information.
3. Double-click in the main document area to make it active.

   OR

   Select the **Close Header and Footer** button ⊠.

Inserting a Header or Footer

1. Select the **Insert** tab.
2. Select the **Header** button ⊡.

   OR

   Select the **Footer** button ⊡.
3. Select the desired style.
4. Type and format the header or footer information.
5. Select the **Header & Footer Tools Design** tab.
6. Select the **Close Header and Footer** button ⊠.

Modifying a Header or Footer

1. Select the **Insert** tab.
2. Select the **Header** button ⊡ or select the **Footer** button ⊡.
3. Select **Edit Header** or select **Edit Footer**.
4. Modify the header or footer information.

5. Select the **Header & Footer Tools Design** tab.
6. Select the **Close Header and Footer** button ⊠.

Balancing Columns

1. Position the insertion point at the end of the text in the last column on the page.
2. Select the **Layout tab**.
3. Select the **Breaks** button ⊞.
4. From the Breaks gallery, select **Continuous**.

Applying a Page Background

1. Select the **Design** tab.
2. Select the **Page Color** button ⊡.
3. Select the desired color from the color palette.

   OR

   Select **Fill Effects** on the menu.
4. In the Fill Effects dialog box, select the gradient, texture, pattern, and picture formats as desired.
5. Select **OK**.

Inserting Dropped Capitals

1. Select in the paragraph where you want to insert the dropped capital.
2. Select the **Insert** tab.
3. Select the **Drop Cap** button ⊞.
4. From the menu, select the desired format.

Customizing a Dropped Capital

1. Select in the paragraph where you want to insert the dropped capital.
2. Select the **Insert** tab.
3. Select the **Drop Cap** button ⊞.
4. From the menu, select **Drop Cap Options**.
5. In the Drop Cap dialog box, select the desired position for the drop cap.
6. Under Options, set the desired font, lines to drop, and distance from text.
7. Select **OK**.

Enhancing a Paragraph with Borders

1. Position the insertion point in the paragraph to which you want to add a border.
2. Select the **Design** tab.
3. Select the **Page Borders** button ⬜.
4. In the Borders and Shading dialog box, select the **Borders** tab.
5. In the Style list box, select the desired line style for the border.
6. Select the **Color** drop-down arrow and select the desired color for the border.
7. Select the **Width** drop-down arrow and select the desired line width for the border.
8. In the Setting list, select the desired effect for the border.
9. Select **OK**.

Enhancing a Paragraph with Shading

1. Position the insertion point in the paragraph to which you want to add shading.
2. Select the **Design** tab.
3. Select the **Page Borders** button ⬜.
4. In the Borders and Shading dialog box, select the **Shading** tab.
5. Select the **Fill** drop-down arrow and select the desired color for the shading.
6. Under Patterns, select the **Style** drop-down arrow and select the desired pattern for the shading.
7. Under Patterns, select the **Color** drop-down arrow and select the desired color for the pattern.
8. Select **OK**.

INSERTING THE DATE AND TIME

1. Select the **Insert** tab.
2. Select the **Date & Time** button 🖳.
3. In the list of Available formats, select the desired format.

Select the **Update automatically** check box if you want the date and time to update automatically every time you save or print the document.

4. Select **OK**.

SORTING PARAGRAPHS

1. Select the **Home** tab.
2. Select the **Sort** button 🔽.
3. In the Sort Text dialog box, select the **Ascending** button or the **Descending** button.
4. Select **OK**.

DRAWING A TABLE

1. Select the **Insert** tab.
2. Select the **Table** button ⊞.
3. Select **Draw Table**.

   The mouse pointer changes to ✎.

4. Drag to create table cells as desired.

CHANGING TABLE STRUCTURE

Viewing Gridlines

1. Click in the table to select it.
2. Select the **Table Tools Layout** tab.
3. Select the **View Gridlines** button ⊞.

Selecting in a Table

1. Click in the table.
2. Select the **Table Tools Layout** tab.
3. Select the **Select** button ⬈.
4. Select the desired selection on the menu.

Selecting a Table

To select the table, select the **Table Selector** button ⊞ that appears outside the upper left corner of the table.

Selecting a Row

1. To select a row, position the mouse pointer outside the table, to the left of the row.
2. When the mouse pointer changes to ⬈, click to select the row.

Selecting a Column

1. To select a column, position the mouse pointer outside the table, just above the column.

2. When the mouse pointer changes to ⬇, click to select the column.

Selecting a Cell

1. To select a cell, position the mouse pointer outside the cell, at the bottom left corner.

2. When the mouse pointer changes to ⬈, click to select the cell.

Selecting Multiple Components in a Table

- To select contiguous cells, drag across them.

  OR

  Select the first cell and press and hold **Shift** to select additional cells.

- To select noncontiguous cells, select the first cell and press and hold **Ctrl** to select additional cells.

Inserting Rows and Columns

1. Click where desired in the table.

2. Select the **Table Tools Layout** tab.

3. Select the options, as follows:

   - **Insert Above** ▦
   - **Insert Below** ▦
   - **Insert Left** ▦
   - **Insert Right** ▦

Deleting in a Table

1. Click in the cell, row, or column to be deleted.

2. Select the **Table Tools Layout** tab.

3. Select the **Delete** button ▦.

4. Select the desired option to delete on the menu.

Deleting a Table

1. Click in any cell of the table.

2. Select the **Table Tools Layout** tab.

3. Select the **Delete** button ▦.

4. Select **Delete Table** on the menu.

Merging Cells

1. Select the cells to merge.

2. Select the **Table Tools Layout** tab.

3. Select the **Merge Cells** button ▦.

   OR

1. Select the **Table Tools Layout** tab.

2. Select the **Eraser** button ▦.

   The mouse pointer changes to ▦.

3. Click on a cell divider to merge the cells.

Splitting Cells

1. Select the cell to split.

2. Select the **Table Tools Layout** tab.

3. Select the **Split Cells** button ▦.

4. In the Split Cells dialog box, set the number of columns and rows for the split cell.

5. Select **OK**.

FORMATTING A TABLE

Applying a Table Style

1. Click in the table to select it.

2. Select the **Table Tools Design** tab.

3. Select the **Table Styles More** button ▦.

4. Select the desired style.

Applying Formats to Cell Contents

1. Select the text to be formatted.

2. Select the **Home** tab.

3. Apply formats from the Font and Paragraph groups as desired.

Applying Cell Borders

1. Select the cell(s).

2. Select the **Table Tools Design** tab.

3. Select the **Line Style** button ▭.

4. From the Line Style gallery, select the desired line style.

5. Select the **Line Weight** button ▭.

6. From the Line Weight gallery, select the desired line weight.

7. Select the **Pen Color** button drop-down arrow 🖊.

8. From the palette, select the desired color.

9. Select the **Borders** button drop-down arrow ⊞.

10. From the Borders gallery, select the desired border style.

Applying Cell Shading

1. Select the cell(s).

2. Select the **Table Tools Design** tab.

3. Select the **Shading** button drop-down arrow 🎨.

4. From the color palette, select the desired shade.

Setting Column Width and Row Height

1. Select a cell in the column or row you want to adjust.

2. Select the **Table Tools Layout** tab.

3. Select the **AutoFit** button 🖽.

4. Select the desired option from the menu.

   OR

1. Rest the pointer on the column divider or row divider.

2. Drag to the desired width or height.

   OR

1. Select a cell in the column or row you want to adjust.

2. Select the **Table Tools Layout** tab.

3. Select the **Table Row Height** ⇕ increment arrows or the **Table Column Width** ⬌ increment arrows to adjust the size as desired.

   OR

1. Select the **Table Selector** button ⊞ to select the table.

2. Select the **Table Tools Layout** tab.

3. Select the **Distribute Rows** button ⊟ to distribute the rows evenly, or the **Distribute Columns** button ⊞ to distribute the columns evenly.

USING MAIL MERGE

1. Select the **Mailings** tab.

2. Select the **Start Mail Merge** button 📄.

3. Select **Step by Step Mail Merge Wizard**.

4. In the Mail Merge task pane, select **Next: Starting document**.

5. Select **Next: Select recipients**.

6. Under Use an existing list in the task pane, select **Browse**, and then navigate to and open the file.

7. In the Mail Merge Recipients dialog box, select **OK**.

8. Select **Next: Write your letter** at the bottom of the task pane.

9. Click to place the insertion point in the letter where you want to insert the address block field.

10. In the task pane, select **Address block**. Select **OK**.

11. Insert other merge fields as desired.

12. Select the **Mailings** tab.

13. Select the **Preview Results** button 🔍 to preview a copy of the merged letter.

Merging to a New Document

1. Select the **Mailings** tab.

2. Select the **Finish & Merge** button 📄.

3. On the menu, select **Edit Individual Documents**.

4. In the Merge to New Document dialog box, select **OK**.

CREATING A NEW ADDRESS LIST

1. Select the **Mailings** tab.

2. Select the **Select recipients** button 📋.

3. Select **Type a New List**.

4. In the New Address List dialog box, type the address of the first recipient.

5. Select **New Entry** to complete the entry and move to a new row to enter another recipient, if desired.

6. When you have entered all the recipients, select **OK**.

7. In the Save Address List dialog box, enter a name for the list and select the location where you want to save the file.

8. Select **OK**.

USING AN EXISTING DATA SOURCE

1. Select the **Mailings** tab.

2. Select the **Select Recipients** button.

3. On the menu, select the desired type of data source.

Adding Records to the Data Source

1. Select the **Mailings** tab.

2. Select the **Edit Recipient List** button.

3. In the Data Source box, select the data source you want to edit.

4. Select **Edit**.

5. In the Edit Data Source dialog box, select **New Entry**.

6. Enter new recipients as desired.

7. Select **OK**.

USING AN EXCEL FILE AS A DATA SOURCE

1. Select the **Mailings** tab.

2. Select the **Select Recipients** button.

3. On the menu, select **Use an Existing List**.

4. Navigate to and open the desired Excel file.

5. In the Select Table dialog box, select the sheet to be used as the data source.

6. Select **OK**.

Matching Fields to a Data Source

1. Select the **Mailings** tab.

2. Select the **Match Fields** button.

3. In the Match Fields dialog box, match the fields in the data source as desired.

4. Select **OK**.

CREATING AN ENVELOPE

1. Select the **Mailings** tab.

2. Select the **Envelopes** button.

3. In the Delivery address box, type the name and address to which the envelope will be sent.

4. Select the **Omit** check box if there is a return address printed on your envelopes already, or if you plan to use return address labels.

5. Click in the Return address box and type the return address.

6. Select **Print**.

7. Select **No** to continue without making the return address the default.

STARTING A LABELS MAIL MERGE

1. Select the **Mailings** tab.

2. Select the **Start Mail Merge** button.

3. Select **Labels**.

4. In the Label Options dialog box, select the **Label vendors** drop-down arrow and select the desired label type.

5. In the Product number list, select the desired label size.

6. Select **OK**.

Arranging the Labels

1. Select the **Mailings** tab.

2. Select the **Address Block** button.

3. In the Insert Address Block dialog box, verify that the Insert recipient's name is in the desired format. Verify that the **Insert postal address** check box is selected and that the **Only include the country/region if different than** option button is selected. Verify that the **Format address according to the destination country/region** check box is selected.

4. Select **OK**. The <<AddressBlock>> merge block is inserted in the first cell.

5. Select the **Mailings** tab.

6. Select the **Update Labels** button ⬚ to copy the layout from the first cell to the remaining cells.

Previewing and Printing the Labels

1. Select the **Mailings** tab.

2. Select the **Preview Results** button ⬚ to preview the labels.

3. If necessary, make adjustments to the label arrangement and formatting.

4. Select the **Mailings** tab.

5. Select the **Finish & Merge** button ⬚.

6. Select **Print Documents**.

7. In the Merge to Printer dialog box, select **OK**.

USING LANGUAGE TOOLS

Correcting Spelling as You Type

1. Right-click the misspelled word.

   A red wavy line under a word indicates a possible spelling error. A blue wavy underline indicates a possible word choice or grammatical error.

2. Select the desired option on the shortcut menu.

Correcting Grammar as You Type

1. Right-click the text marked with the blue, wavy underline.

2. Select the desired option on the shortcut menu.

Checking Spelling and Grammar

1. Select the **Review** tab.

2. Select the **Spelling & Grammar** button ⬚.

3. Select options to correct or ignore errors identified in the Spelling or Grammar task pane.

Using the Thesaurus

1. Right-click the word for which you want to find a synonym.

2. On the shortcut menu, select **Synonyms**.

3. On the submenu, select the desired synonym.

   OR

1. Select the word for which you want to find a synonym or antonym.

2. Select the **Review** tab.

3. Select the **Thesaurus** button ⬚.

4. In the Thesaurus task pane, select the desired synonym or antonym.

USING CONTENT CONTROLS

1. Select a content control to select it.

2. Type replacement text as desired.

Removing a Content Control

1. Right-click the content control.

2. On the shortcut menu, select **Remove Content Control**.

MANAGING DOCUMENT PROPERTIES

1. Select **File**.

2. On the Info tab, in the Preview pane under Properties, review the document's properties or click available content controls as desired.

3. If desired, select **Show All Properties** to display all properties.

Viewing a Properties Dialog Box

1. Select **File**.

2. On the Info tab, in the Preview pane, select **Properties**.

3. Select **Advanced Properties** to display the document's Properties dialog box.

4. Add or modify properties as desired.

5. Select **OK** to close the dialog box.

Printing Document Properties

1. Select **File**.
2. Select **Print**.
3. Under Settings, select the top button.
4. On the menu, select **Document Info**.
5. Select the **Print** button 🖨.

MANAGING SOURCES AND CITATIONS

Inserting Citations

1. Position the insertion point where you want to insert the citation.
2. Select the **References** tab.
3. Select the **Style** button drop-down arrow 📇.
4. On the menu of available citation styles, select the desired style.
5. Select the **Insert Citation** button 📑.
6. From the menu, select **Add New Source**.
7. In the Create Source dialog box, select the type of source and enter the source information.
8. Select **OK**.

Creating a Reference Page

1. Position the insertion point at the end of the document and insert a hard page break.
2. Select the **References** tab.
3. Select the **Bibliography** button 📖.
4. From the gallery, select the desired format.

WORKING WITH COMMENTS

Inserting a Comment

1. Select the text on which you want to comment.
2. Select the **Review** tab.
3. Select the **New Comment** button 🗨.
4. Type the comment in the comment balloon.

Displaying or Hiding the Reviewing Pane

1. Select the **Review** tab.
2. Select the **Reviewing Pane** button 🗔.

Editing a Comment

1. Position the insertion point within the comment text.
2. Edit text.

Moving through Comments

1. Select the **Review** tab.
2. Select the **Next** button ➡.

   OR

   Select the **Previous** button ⬅.

Deleting a Comment

1. Select the comment to delete.
2. Select the **Review** tab.
3. Select the **Delete** button ✖.

Deleting All Comments

1. Select the **Review** tab.
2. Select the **Delete** button ✖ drop-down arrow.
3. Select **Delete All Comments in Document**.

PROTECTING A DOCUMENT

Encrypting with Password

1. Select the **File** tab.
2. On the Info tab, select the **Protect Document** button 🔒.
3. Select **Encrypt with Password**.
4. In the Encrypt Document dialog box, enter the desired password.
5. Select **OK**.
6. In the Reenter password box, type the password again.
7. Select **OK**.

Open an Encrypted and Password-Protected Document

1. Open the protected document.
2. In the Password dialog box, type the password.
3. Select **OK**.

Stop Protection

1. Select the **Review** tab.

2. Select the **Restrict Editing** button 🔒.

3. In the Restrict Editing task pane, select **Stop Protection**.

4. Select **Save As**.

5. In the Save As dialog box, enter the file name and select the location where you want to save

SAVING A WORD DOCUMENT AS A WEB PAGE

1. Select **File**.

2. Select **Save As**.

3. Navigate to the location where you store files.

4. Select the **Save as type** button.

5. Select **Single File Web Page**.

6. Change the page title as desired.

7. Enter a file name for the page.

8. Select **Save**.

Changing a Web Page Title

1. Select **File**.

2. Select **Save As**.

3. Navigate to the location of your file.

4. Select the **Change Title** button.

5. In the Enter Text dialog box, type the title text.

6. Select **OK**.

7. Select **Save**.

SENDING A WORD DOCUMENT AS AN EMAIL ATTACHMENT

1. Select **File**.

2. Select **Share**.

3. Select **Email** 📧 and then select **Send as Attachment**.

4. Enter the email information as necessary.

5. Select **Send**.

WORKING WITH HYPERLINKS

Inserting a Hyperlink

1. Select the text or object to hyperlink.

2. Select the **Insert** tab.

3. Select the **Hyperlink** button 🌐.

4. In the Insert Hyperlink dialog box, locate and select the hyperlink destination.

5. Select **OK**.

Creating a Hyperlink to a Website

1. Select the **Insert** tab.

2. Select the **Hyperlink** button 🌐.

3. In the Insert Hyperlink dialog box, type the website address in the Address text box.

4. Select **OK**.

Testing a Hyperlink

Hold down the **Ctrl** key and select the hyperlink.

Editing a Hyperlink

1. Right-click the link.

2. On the shortcut menu, select **Edit Hyperlink**.

3. Edit the link as desired.

4. Select **OK**.

Removing a Hyperlink

1. Right-click the link.

2. On the shortcut menu, select **Remove Hyperlink**.

CREATING A BLOG

Starting a Blog Post

1. Select **File**.

2. Select **New**.

3. Select **Blog Post**.

4. Select **Create**.

5. Register your blog service if desired.

6. Type the blog text.

Registering a Blog Server

You must have a blog account in order to register a blog server.

1. In your blog file, select the **Blog Post** tab.
2. Select the **Manage Accounts** button.
3. In the Blog Accounts dialog box, select **New**.
4. In the New Blog Account dialog box, select the **Blog** drop-down arrow and select your provider.
5. Select **Next**.
6. Enter your user name and password, and select **OK**.
7. Select **Yes** to confirm.
8. At the message that the registration was successful, select **OK**.
9. Select **Close**.

SELECTING OBJECTS

1. Select the **Home** tab.
2. Click **Select** and then click **Selection Pane**.
3. Select the desired object in the Selection Pane.

MODIFYING A TEXT BOX

Changing the Font

1. Select the text box to select it.
2. Select the **Home** tab.
3. Select options to apply the desired font formatting.

INSERTING A CAPTION

1. Click to select the object to which you want to add a caption.
2. Select the **References** tab.
3. Select the **Insert Caption** button.
4. In the Insert Caption dialog box, select options as desired.
5. Select **OK**.

INSERTING A FILE IN A DOCUMENT

1. Select the **Insert** tab.
2. Select the **Object** button drop-down arrow.
3. On the menu, select **Text from File**.
4. In the Insert File dialog box, navigate to the file you want to insert and select it.
5. Select **Insert**.

CHECKING THE WORD COUNT

1. If the word count is not automatically displayed on the status bar, right-click the status bar.
2. On the shortcut menu, select **Word Count** to display the number of words in the status bar.

   Selecting text will display the word count for the selection as well as the entire document.

CREATING A TABLE OF CONTENTS

1. Select the **References** tab.
2. Select the **Table of Contents** button.
3. From the gallery, select the desired style.

Updating a Table of Contents

1. Make changes to the document's headings as desired.
2. Click anywhere within the table of contents.
3. Select the **References** tab.
4. Select the **Update Table** button.
5. In the Update Table of Contents dialog box, click to select the desired update option.
6. Select **OK**.

INSERTING AN ONLINE VIDEO

1. Select the **Insert** tab.
2. Select the **Online Video** button.
3. In the Insert Video dialog box, search for or select a video.
4. Select **Insert**.

Formatting a Video

1. Select the video file to format.
2. Select the **Picture Tools Format** tab.
3. Apply formatting options as desired.

COPYING DATA FROM A WEB PAGE TO A WORD DOCUMENT

Copying Text

1. Display the web page in a browser.
2. Select the text you want to copy.
3. Press **Ctrl + C**.
4. Click in the Word document where you want to paste the copied text.
5. Press **Ctrl + V**.

Copying Graphics

1. Display the web page.
2. Right-click the graphic you want to copy.
3. On the shortcut menu, select **Copy**.
4. Click in the Word document where you want to paste the graphic.
5. Press **Ctrl + V**.

SAVING A DOCUMENT TO THE ONEDRIVE

1. Select **File**.
2. Select **Save As**.
3. Select **OneDrive** ☁ in the Save As list.
4. Select the desired OneDrive folder in the right pane.
5. In the Save As dialog box, enter the file name as desired.
6. Select **Save**.

View and Edit a Document on the OneDrive

1. Sign in to your OneDrive account.
2. Open the document you want to view or edit.
3. Select **Edit Document**.
4. Select either **Edit in Word** or **Edit in Browser** (to edit in Word Online).

S.DASHKEVYCH/SHUTTERSTOCK

CHAPTER 13

Spreadsheet Basics

WHAT IS A SPREADSHEET?

Suppose you want to keep track of all your grades in one of your classes so you could calculate your final average for the class. Or, maybe you want to analyze the results of a science experiment, and then create a chart to illustrate the data. Or, you might want to create a team roster that includes contact information and pictures of every player and coach. A spreadsheet program is the tool for the job.

Spreadsheets store data in horizontal columns and vertical rows, like a table. They include features for setting up calculations, automatically creating charts and graphs, and performing analysis. You can format the table and the data; print the spreadsheet; export the data; and insert graphics. In other words, spreadsheets are a versatile software tool that you will find useful for many purposes.

Exploring Spreadsheets

OBJECTIVES

- Explain the purpose of spreadsheet software.

- Identify and describe parts of a worksheet.

- Define common spreadsheet terminology.

AS YOU READ

ORGANIZE INFORMATION Use a concept web to help you organize basic facts about spreadsheets as you read the lesson.

TERMINOLOGY

- active cell
- cell
- cell address
- cell identifier
- column
- comma-separated values
- contiguous
- formula
- formula bar
- frame
- function
- navigation
- noncontiguous
- range
- sheet tab
- spreadsheet
- row
- tab-delimited text
- workbook
- worksheet

Spreadsheet Basics

A **spreadsheet** is a program that processes information that is set up in columns and rows, like a table. Spreadsheets can be used to:

- Enter numbers and text in easy-to-read rows and columns

- Perform calculations and show the result

- Update calculations when values change

- Create charts to display data

- Create models and simulations

- Make predictions using inputs and reviewing results

- Analyze trends and forecast possibilities

These features make spreadsheets perfect for tracking information that involves numbers. Suppose you work at a company that needs to decide what price to charge for a product. You can create a spreadsheet that shows how much profit your company will make by charging several different prices. The spreadsheet finds the results quickly. Those results can be used to set a price.

Parts of a Worksheet

When you use a spreadsheet program, data is stored in a **worksheet**, which is a grid made of vertical columns and horizontal rows. Each **column** is labeled with a letter of the alphabet, starting with A on the left-most column. Each **row** is labeled with a number, starting with 1 at the top of the sheet.

IC3✔ Understand common spreadsheet terms: worksheet, column, and row.

At the intersection of each column and row is a rectangular area called a **cell**. You enter data in the cells. Each cell in the grid is identified by a unique name—its **cell address**. The address is the letter of the column and the number of the row that intersect to make the cell. For example, the cell at the intersection of column C and row 3 is cell C3.

IC3✔ Understand common spreadsheet terms: cell.

Most worksheets look similar. The parts of a worksheet (shown in Figure 13.1.2) include:

FRAME The **frame** forms the top and left borders of the worksheet. It includes the column and row headings.

ACTIVE CELL The **active cell** is the cell currently in use. A rectangle appears around this cell to highlight it and make it easy to spot.

CELL IDENTIFIER Located in the upper-left corner, just above the frame, the **cell identifier** is an area that shows the cell address of the cell that is active.

FORMULA BAR The **formula bar** displays data as you type, or the content of the active cell.

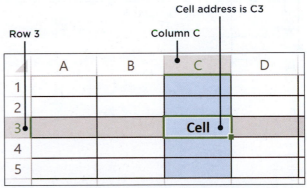

MICROSOFT CORPORATION

FIGURE 13.1.1 A worksheet includes rows and columns, which create a grid of cells that store data.

SCROLL BARS Scroll bars that you can use to move up, down, left, or right in the worksheet display on the worksheet's right and bottom edges.

SHEET TABS A spreadsheet file, which may be called a **workbook**, may have one or more worksheets. On the same line as the horizontal scroll bar are tabs that show all the worksheets in the workbook. Click a **sheet tab** to display that worksheet.

STATUS BAR The status bar displays below the scroll bar at the very bottom of the worksheet. Information about the worksheet or the current action display on the status bar. It may also be where the View buttons and Zoom bar are located.

Navigating in a Worksheet

Navigation is the way you scroll through a workbook and change the active cell. You can move down through the rows, across through the columns, and even change to a different sheet tab.

Use the Home, End, Page Up, and Page Down keys, along with the scroll bars or swipe movements with a touchscreen to scroll up, down, left, or right within the worksheet. Use the Tab key to move one cell to the right or the arrow keys to move one cell at a time in any direction, or touch a cell on a touchscreen to make it active. Use the Go To command to jump to any cell, or use the Search or Find feature to locate a cell with specific content.

IC3 ✔ **Understand common spreadsheet terms: navigation.**

Selecting Cells

Select a cell to make it active. For example, click it with a mouse pointer, or tap it on a touchscreen. A bold border around the cell indicates it is active. You can also select a **range**, which is a group or block of cells. The range is identified by the first cell, a colon, followed by the last

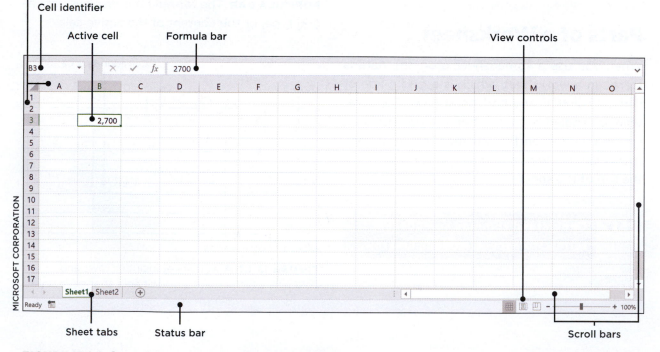

MICROSOFT CORPORATION

Frame
Cell identifier
Active cell
Formula bar
View controls
B3
2700
2,700
Sheet tabs Status bar Scroll bars
Sheet1 Sheet2
Ready

FIGURE 13.1.2 Spreadsheet programs share basic elements.

cell. So, if you select cells A1, A2, A3, and A4, the range identifier is A1:A4. Only the first cell in a range is active. All other cells in the selection appear highlighted.

IC3✔ **Understand common spreadsheet terms: range.**

A range may be **contiguous**, which means the cells are in one block, or **noncontiguous**, which means the cells are in two or more separate blocks. To select multiple cells in a range, select the first cell, then drag to select additional cells. You can also select the first cell, press and hold the Shift key, and then select the last cell. To select cells that are not adjacent to one another, press and hold the Ctrl key while selecting.

To select an entire column, click the column letter in the worksheet frame. To select an entire row, click the row number in the frame.

FORMULAS A **formula** is a mathematical expression that calculates the data in a spreadsheet cell. To enter a formula, you must first type a character that instructs the program that you are entering a formula, not text. In Excel, the character is an equal sign. The formula displays in the formula bar but the result of the formula displays in the active cell. A simple formula might add the numbers in two cells. For example, the formula =A1 + A2 sums the values in cells A1 and A2. =A1 x A2 multiples the value in A1 by the value in A2.

> **DID YOU KNOW?**
>
> A spreadsheet can hold a great deal of information. Microsoft Excel, for instance, can hold:
>
> - 16,384 columns
> - Over 1 million rows
> - As many worksheets as your computer's memory can keep open
>
> If you filled every column and row on just one worksheet, you would have filled 16,384,000,000 cells!

Spreadsheet programs come with built-in **functions**, which are predefined formulas for a wide range of calculations. For example, the SUM function is a basic formula for adding values; the PMT function calculates the payment for a loan based on the number of payments and the interest rate.

Opening and Saving Files

As with all application program files, you must save a spreadsheet file to store the data for future use. Once a file is saved, you can open it in your spreadsheet program to use at any time.

Spreadsheets can work with data saved in a variety of compatible file types. The default file type for Excel is .xlsx, but it can open and save in many other formats, including the format for older Excel versions (.xls), **comma-separated values** files (.csv), and **tab-delimited text.**

Entering and Editing Data

OBJECTIVES

- Describe types of data you can enter in a worksheet.

- Describe ways to edit and format data in a worksheet.

- Use a spreadsheet to create a chart.

- Evaluate the benefit of printing options.

AS YOU READ

SEQUENCE STEPS Use a sequence chart to help you sequence the steps in working with spreadsheets as you read the lesson.

TERMINOLOGY

- banded columns

- banded rows

- chart

- criteria

- filter

- header row

- label

- label prefix

- print area

- sort

- table

- truncated

- value

Entering Data

Type to enter data into the active cell. Data can be labels, values, or dates and times. Press Enter, tab to the next cell, or select the Enter button on the formula bar to enter the data in the cell.

IC3✔ Know how to enter data in a spreadsheet.

VALUES A **value** is a number, such as a whole number, a fraction, or a decimal. The program automatically formats values to align to the right in a cell. If a value is too large for the width of the cell, you may see a set of symbols such as ###### or *******. You can change the column width so that the full number shows. For example, drag the right edge of a column on the worksheet frame to the right to increase the width of the column.

LABELS A **label** is text or a combination of numbers and text. Labels are typically used for headings or explanations. By default, labels are aligned to the left in a cell. Labels that are too wide will overlap into the next cell to the right—if that cell is empty. If that cell already stores data, the label in the first cell will appear cut off, or **truncated**. Again, you can widen the column to display the entire label.

TECHNOLOGY@HOME

Many people use spreadsheets at home to track monthly income and expenses. They can set up a worksheet to show regular monthly costs. Then, they only need to copy and paste it on other blank worksheets to create budgets for other months.

THINK ABOUT IT!

Before you set up a budget, think about which expenses arise each month. Which items listed below do you think would be a regular monthly expense?

- housing payment
- vacation
- telephone
- holiday presents
- food
- magazine subscription

DATES AND TIMES Spreadsheets store dates and times as codes. They recognize entries and apply custom number formats according to the default setting. For example, if you type 9-5-20 in a cell, Excel will recognize it as September 5, 2020, and change the formatting to the default for dates, such as 09/05/2020.

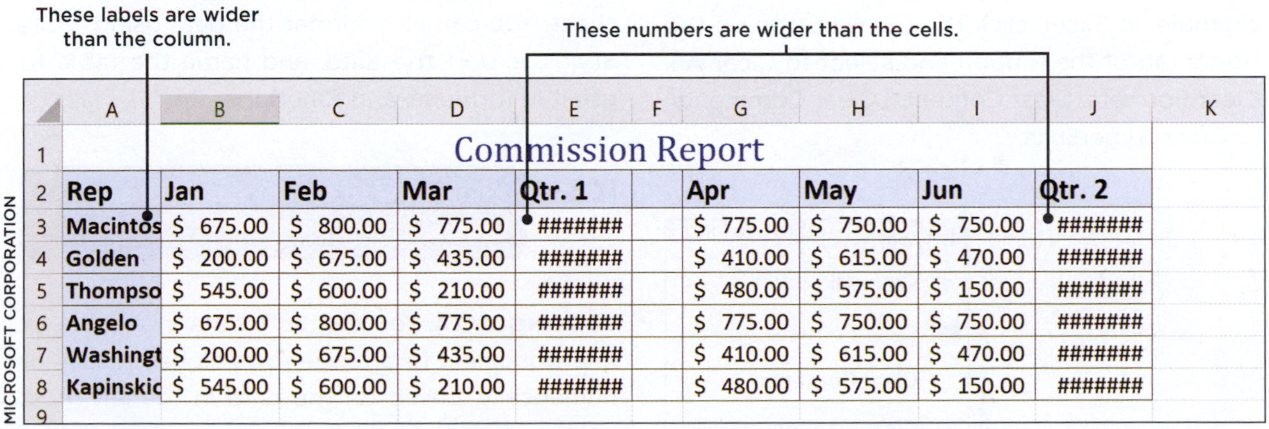
These labels are wider than the column.
These numbers are wider than the cells.
MICROSOFT CORPORATION

	A	B	C	D	E	F	G	H	I	J	K
1				Commission Report							
2	Rep	Jan	Feb	Mar	Qtr. 1		Apr	May	Jun	Qtr. 2	
3	Macintos	$ 675.00	$ 800.00	$ 775.00	#######		$ 775.00	$ 750.00	$ 750.00	#######	
4	Golden	$ 200.00	$ 675.00	$ 435.00	#######		$ 410.00	$ 615.00	$ 470.00	#######	
5	Thompso	$ 545.00	$ 600.00	$ 210.00	#######		$ 480.00	$ 575.00	$ 150.00	#######	
6	Angelo	$ 675.00	$ 800.00	$ 775.00	#######		$ 775.00	$ 750.00	$ 750.00	#######	
7	Washingt	$ 200.00	$ 675.00	$ 435.00	#######		$ 410.00	$ 615.00	$ 470.00	#######	
8	Kapinskic	$ 545.00	$ 600.00	$ 210.00	#######		$ 480.00	$ 575.00	$ 150.00	#######	
9											

FIGURE 13.2.1 If symbols display, resize the cell to fit the data.

Editing Data

You can easily change data already stored in a cell to correct an error or reflect new information in a spreadsheet.

EDITING CELL DATA To replace the entire contents of a cell, simply make the cell active and enter the new data. To edit data, select the cell that stores the data you want to change. Then, click within the formula bar to place the insertion point where you want to make the change. Press Backspace or Delete to remove characters, or type to add them. Press Enter to place the edited information in the cell.

MOVING OR COPYING DATA To move data from one cell to another, select the cell and drag its contents to the new cell, or use the Cut and Paste commands. To copy information, select the cell and then select the Copy command. Select the new destination location, and then select the Paste command. You can also select some of the data within a cell or in the formula bar to cut or copy.

IC3✔ Know how to cut, copy, and paste data.

DELETING DATA To delete the entire contents of a cell, select the cell and press Delete. In some programs you can use the Clear command. For example, in Excel, click the Clear button on the Home tab of the Ribbon and select to Clear All, Clear Formats, Clear Contents, Clear Comments, or Clear Hyperlinks.

MICROSOFT CORPORATION

FIGURE 13.2.2
The Clear drop-down menu in Excel 2016.

Organizing Data

When data in a spreadsheet is organized, it makes it easy to read and analyze. Most spreadsheets provide the following tools for organizing data.

TABLES A **table** in a spreadsheet is a range of cells you can work with separately from other data in the worksheet. You select the range and use a command to identify it as a table. For example, in Excel you select the Insert > Table command. In Excel, you can recognize a table because it has filter arrows in each cell in the **header row**, which is the top row containing column labels. It may also have **banded rows**, which means shading is applied to every other row, or **banded columns**, which means shading is applied to every other column, to help distinguish the table data.

Once data is identified as a table, you can use tools such as sorting and filtering to manage the data without affecting other data in the worksheet. You can also format the data using Table Styles, export the data, and name the table to use it in formulas and functions.

IC3✔ Know how to create spreadsheet tables.

SORTING DATA You can **sort** data in a table or in a worksheet to arrange rows alphabetically or numerically, based on the data in the left-most column. For example, you might sort a contact list alphabetically by name, or an expense sheet numerically by date. Most spreadsheets include commands for quickly sorting rows in ascending order, from smallest to largest, or in descending order, from largest to smallest. In Excel, the Sort commands are on the Sort & Filter button on the Home tab of the Ribbon. All rows adjacent to the active cell are included in the sort, or you can select the rows you want to sort. You can also use a custom sort to sort based on data in a different column, or to use more than one column to define the sort. For example, you could sort that contact list by last name and then by city.

FILTER DATA You can **filter** data to show only the rows that match the **criteria**, or specifics, that you select. For example, you might filter a contact list to show only rows that have Texas in the State field. You can also filter by color, if cells have shading, and by cell contents. For example, you can filter to display only expenses that are greater than $100.00 or that are between $75.00 and $100.00. To filter, you must display the filter arrows on the header row. They display by default in a table, or you can select the Filter command. In Excel, the Filter command is on the Sort & Filter button on the Home tab of the Ribbon. When you click the filter arrow, a menu of filtering options displays.

IC3✔ Know how to filter and sort data.

THINK ABOUT IT!

Think about other ways charts could be used at school. For which items listed below do you think graphed test results would be useful?

- to show parents how well their children are doing
- to show students which skills they need to work on
- to track students' mastery of curriculum concepts

Creating Charts

With a spreadsheet program, you can create charts, which are also called graphs. A **chart** is a graphical representation of data. Usually, it is easier to interpret the data and analyze trends when it is displayed as a chart.

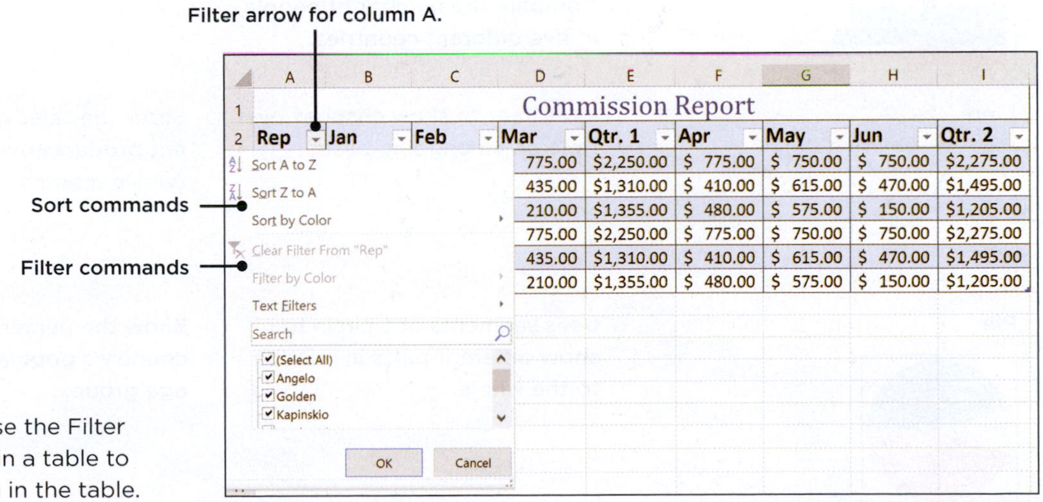

Filter arrow for column A.

Sort commands

Filter commands

FIGURE 13.2.3 Use the Filter drop-down arrow in a table to sort and filter data in the table.

MICROSOFT CORPORATION

Most programs come with a selection of chart types. It is important to select the right type of chart to properly display the data. Some common chart types include bar, column, pie, and line.

■ Select a bar chart to compare values, such as how many students there are in each grade in a school. Bars extend horizontally from the left edge of the chart, representing each category of data.

■ A column chart is also used to compare values, but the columns that represent each category of data extend vertically up from the bottom of the chart.

■ Select a pie chart to show how parts relate to the whole. Each slice of the pie represents a percentage of the whole. For instance, a pie chart would show what percentage of all students are in each grade.

■ Select a line chart to show change over time, such as the number of students in a grade each year. Each line represents a category.

Each chart type usually has subtypes, such as a clustered column chart, a 3-D pie chart, or a stacked line chart. You can apply a chart style, select a chart layout, and customize chart elements, such as the title, legend, and labels.

IC3 ✔ **Know how to use and create charts.**

COMPARING TYPES OF CHARTS

Chart Type	Use	Example
Column	Uses vertical bars to show changes over time emphasizing fixed points in time.	Compare the number of people in a country in five different years.
Bar	Uses horizontal bars to show different amounts of the same item. Compare the number of people in five different countries.	Compare the number of people in five different countries.
Line	Uses lines to show changes over time on an ongoing basis.	Show the sales of several different products over the period of twelve months.
Pie	Uses segments of a circle to show different parts in relation to the whole.	Show the percentage of a country's population in different age groups.

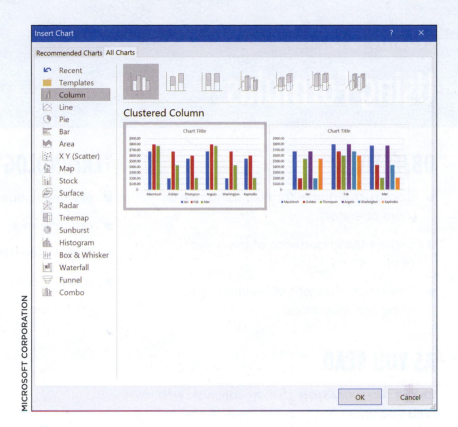

MICROSOFT CORPORATION

FIGURE 13.2.4 The Insert Chart dialog box in Excel 2016.

Previewing and Printing a Worksheet

Before you print, preview your worksheet to make sure the data displays the way you want. Most spreadsheets have options for controlling the way the sheet prints. The options may be in the Print dialog box, the Page Setup dialog box, or, in Excel, on the Print tab of Backstage view.

For example, you can specify a portion of a worksheet called a **print area** before you select the command to print. Headings for columns and rows by default only print on the first page, but you can choose to print the headings on every page. You can also add headers and footers, change the page margins, set the page size, scale content, which means adjust the size of the worksheet by a percentage so it fits on the page better, and switch from portrait to landscape orientation.

Using Formulas

OBJECTIVES

- Construct a simple formula using one or more operators.

- Explain the importance of the order of operations.

- Evaluate the benefit of building formulas using cell references.

AS YOU READ

ENTER INFORMATION Use a concept web to help you understand how to enter formulas in a worksheet as you read the lesson.

TERMINOLOGY

- arithmetic operators

- cell reference

- formula identifier

- order of operations

Entering Formulas in Worksheets

The power of a spreadsheet is its ability to use formulas to represent data in different cells. Recall that a formula is a mathematical expression which calculates the data in a spreadsheet cell.

ENTERING FORMULAS To enter a formula, select the cell where you want the result of the formula to display, type the **formula identifier**, which is the character that indicates to the program that you are entering a formula, and then type. In Excel and AppleWorks, that character is an equal sign (=). In Quattro Pro and Lotus 1-2-3, formulas start with a plus (+) or minus (–) sign. When the formula is complete, press Enter, tab to the next cell, or select the Enter button on the formula bar to complete the entry. The formula displays in the formula bar when the cell is active, and the result of the formula displays in the cell.

SIMPLE FORMULAS Most formulas use the basic **arithmetic operators** for calculation:

- addition (+)
- subtraction (–)
- multiplication (*)
- division (/)

Entering simple formulas is like writing a math problem. To add 5 and 2, you use the addition operator. In Excel, you would enter =5+2. To divide 5 by 2, you use the division operator. In Excel you would enter =5/2.

IC3 ✔ Be able to create simple formulas.

Complex Formulas

You can enter more complex formulas as well. Formulas can include many numbers, such as =1+2+3+4+5. When numbers are used repeatedly in multiplication, the exponentiation (^) operator may be used. With exponentiation, the

The formula displays in the Formula bar.

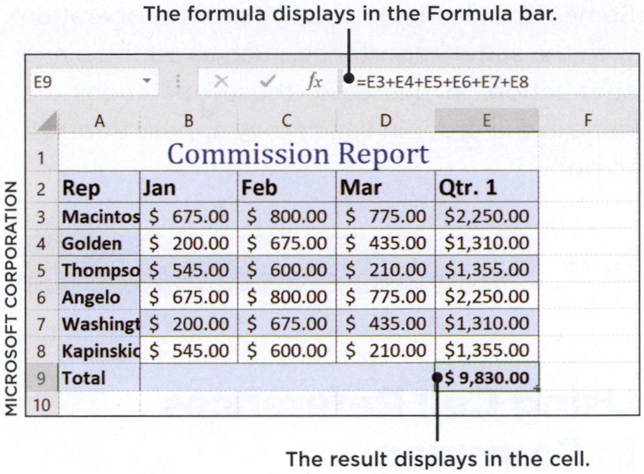

FIGURE 13.3.1 Using a formula in a worksheet.

The result displays in the cell.

raised, or superscript, number identifies how many times the normal-sized number is used as a factor in multiplication. For instance, 2^2 is 2^2; 2^3 is 2^2^2.

Complex formulas can also include more than one mathematical operator. If a formula includes more than one operator, it is important that the program knows which operation to complete first. For example, if you enter the formula 2+2+2*10, should the program add 2 and 2 and 2 and then multiply the total by 10, which would result in 60, or should it add 2 plus 2 and add that total to the result of 2 times 10, which would result in 24?

When there is more than one operator, the program uses the **order of operations**, which is a rule that specifies to complete the operations in order from most to least important.

EVALUATING THE ORDER OF OPERATIONS Operations within parentheses are considered the most important and are therefore processed first. Exponentiation comes next, followed by multiplication or division, then addition or subtraction. So, if you enter =(2+2)+(2*10), the result will be 24. If you enter (2+2+2)*10, the result will be 60. Use the sentence, "Please excuse my dear Aunt Sally" to remember the order. The first letter of each word (P-E-M-D-A-S) matches the first letter of each operation in the correct order.

Some formulas have more than one operation with the same importance, such as addition and subtraction. In this case, those operations are done in the order in which they appear from left to right.

IC3✔ **Understand operators.**

Using Cell References in Formulas

One of the benefits of using a spreadsheet for calculations is that the formulas can include cell references. A **cell reference** is the cell address that stores the data you want to use in the calculation. For example, if you want to find the result of the formula =5*3, in cell A5, you can select A5 and enter =5*3. If the value 5 is already entered in cell A2, and the value 3 is entered in cell A3, you could select A5 and enter =A2*A3. The benefits of using cell references instead of values include avoiding errors and updating results based on changes.

AVOIDING ERRORS You might accidentally type the wrong value and not realize it, as the formula does not always show in the cell. If you insert a cell reference, however, the formula will always use the correct value.

UPDATING RESULTS A value in a formula never changes. The formula =5*3 will always produce 15. But if you use a cell reference, the formula uses whatever value is entered in the cell. If the cell value changes, so will the result calculated by the formula. By using cell references, you make sure that your worksheet remains up-to-date even if the data changes.

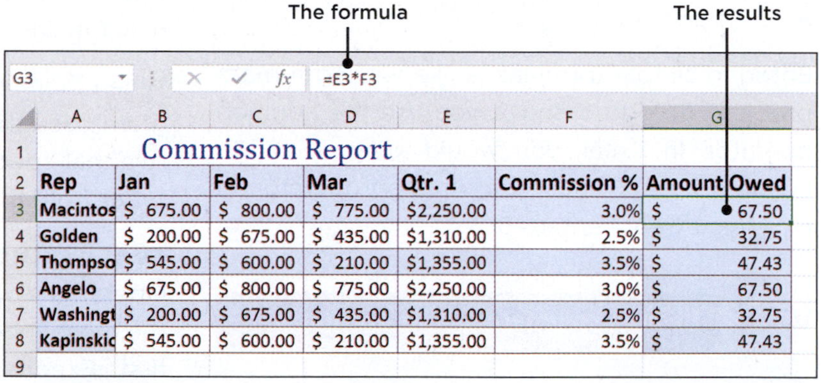

The formula — The results

G3			f_x	=E3*F3			
	A	B	C	D	E	F	G
1		**Commission Report**					
2	Rep	Jan	Feb	Mar	Qtr. 1	Commission %	Amount Owed
3	Macintos	$ 675.00	$ 800.00	$ 775.00	$2,250.00	3.0%	$ 67.50
4	Golden	$ 200.00	$ 675.00	$ 435.00	$1,310.00	2.5%	$ 32.75
5	Thompso	$ 545.00	$ 600.00	$ 210.00	$1,355.00	3.5%	$ 47.43
6	Angelo	$ 675.00	$ 800.00	$ 775.00	$2,250.00	3.0%	$ 67.50
7	Washingt	$ 200.00	$ 675.00	$ 435.00	$1,310.00	2.5%	$ 32.75
8	Kapinskic	$ 545.00	$ 600.00	$ 210.00	$1,355.00	3.5%	$ 47.43
9							

MICROSOFT CORPORATION

FIGURE 13.3.2 This formula multiplies the contents of cell E3 by the contents of cell F3.

Integrating Spreadsheet Data

OBJECTIVES

- Explain benefits of integrating data.

- Contrast embedding and linking data.

- Summarize how to import data from a word-processing program into a spreadsheet.

AS YOU READ

COMPARE AND CONTRAST Use a Venn diagram to compare and contrast ways to integrate data as you read.

TERMINOLOGY

- comma-separated values

- destination file

- embed

- export

- import

- link

- parse

- source file

- tab-separated values

Integrating Data

Most spreadsheet programs include tools for integrating data with documents created with other applications. For example, you might want to integrate Excel data with a Word document or a PowerPoint presentation. Most spreadsheet programs let you **import** and **export** data for integration. Bringing information, such as a table from a Word document, into a worksheet is called importing. Exporting is when data is saved in a format that can be used in another application.

USING STRENGTHS When you integrate data, you use the strengths of each program and then integrate the results. For example, suppose you are writing a report about the American economy. A word processor is appropriate for entering and formatting text. But, if you want to include a chart that shows the growth of the economy in one period, it makes sense to use the powerful charting features of a spreadsheet. Then, you can import that chart into your word-processing document.

SAVING TIME Importing data from another program also can save you time. Suppose you had created a worksheet containing the data on American economic growth before you started writing your report. Instead of typing the data again, it is much easier to simply copy it from the spreadsheet into the other application.

Ways to Share Data

There are two basic methods of sharing data between applications. In one you **embed** the data. In the other, you **link** it. In both, the file that contains the original data is called the **source file**, and the file where you place the shared data is called the **destination file**.

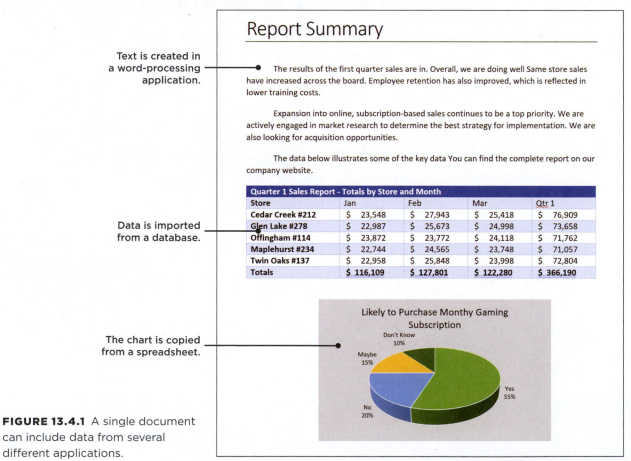

Text is created in a word-processing application.

Data is imported from a database.

The chart is copied from a spreadsheet.

Report Summary

The results of the first quarter sales are in. Overall, we are doing well Same store sales have increased across the board. Employee retention has also improved, which is reflected in lower training costs.

Expansion into online, subscription-based sales continues to be a top priority. We are actively engaged in market research to determine the best strategy for implementation. We are also looking for acquisition opportunities.

The data below illustrates some of the key data You can find the complete report on our company website.

Quarter 1 Sales Report - Totals by Store and Month				
Store	Jan	Feb	Mar	Qtr 1
Cedar Creek #212	$ 23,548	$ 27,943	$ 25,418	$ 76,909
Glen Lake #278	$ 22,987	$ 25,673	$ 24,998	$ 73,658
Offingham #114	$ 23,872	$ 23,772	$ 24,118	$ 71,762
Maplehurst #234	$ 22,744	$ 24,565	$ 23,748	$ 71,057
Twin Oaks #137	$ 22,958	$ 25,848	$ 23,998	$ 72,804
Totals	$ 116,109	$ 127,801	$ 122,280	$ 366,190

Likely to Purchase Monthy Gaming Subscription

Don't Know 10%
Maybe 15%
Yes 55%
No 20%

FIGURE 13.4.1 A single document can include data from several different applications.

MICROSOFT CORPORATION

FIGURE 13.4.2 In Windows applications, you can use the Paste Special dialog box to link data between documents.

EMBEDDING The simplest way to integrate data is to copy the data in the source file and paste it into the destination file using the Copy and Paste commands. This process is called embedding. For example, you could select a chart in a spreadsheet, and choose the Copy command. Then, position the insertion point in a word-processing document, and choose the Paste command. The chart displays in the word-processing document.

Embedding is useful if you do not need to keep the pasted data up-to-date. Even if the data in the spreadsheet changes, the data pasted in the document will not change.

LINKING There is a way to export data that keeps objects up-to-date. This is called linking. To link data, you begin in the same way—by copying the data from the source. However, instead of using the Paste command in the destination, you use Paste Special.

When you choose the Paste Special command, a Paste Special dialog box displays. In that box, click the button for Paste Link. Then, select the type of object you want. When you click OK, the object displays in your destination file. Any changes you make to the source data will be updated in the destination file as well.

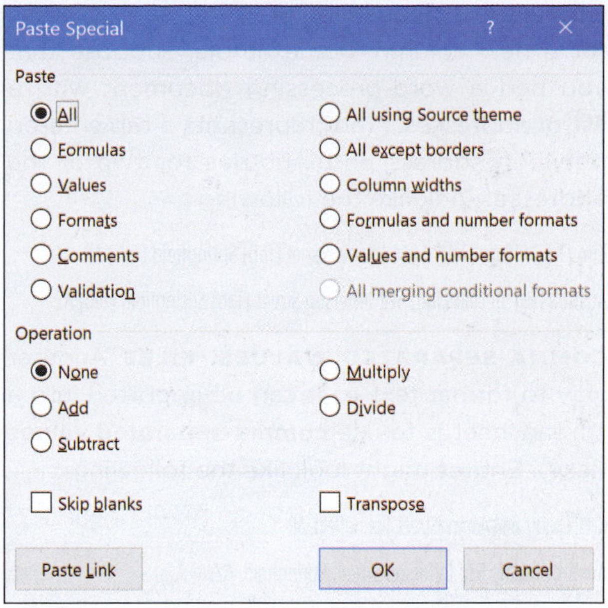

Importing Compatible File Type Data into a Spreadsheet

You can use embedding and linking to copy data from other files into a spreadsheet. If the data is in a spreadsheet file format, such as .xlsx or .xls, it is pasted into the spreadsheet cells. If it is formatted as a table or a list, it will be pasted into corresponding spreadsheet cells.

However, when plain text from a word-processing file is imported or pasted into a spreadsheet, it will all be placed in one cell unless the spreadsheet program receives instructions on how to split the data into rows and columns. To identify where to split the text, the program uses a **parse** feature.

Importing text files works best if the text is formatted in a way that lets the spreadsheet program identify where to break for each column. You can do this using commas or tabs.

TAB-DELIMITED TEXT FILES Tab-delimited text files, or **tab-separated values** files (.tsv), are text files that have tab characters at every point where the spreadsheet program should break for a new column. For example, suppose that you had a word-processing document with a list of addresses. [Tab] represents a tab entered between address parts. Entries for two of the addresses look like the following:

Kim [Tab] Chang [Tab] 4444 Adams Street [Tab] Springfield [Tab] AR

Austin [Tab] Sinclair [Tab] 522 Jefferson Street [Tab] Springfield [Tab] AZ

COMMA-SEPARATED VALUES FILES Another way to format text so it can be imported into a spreadsheet is to use **comma-separated values** (.csv). Entries might look like the following:

Kim, Chang, 444 Adams Street, Springfield, AR

Austin, Sinclair, 522 Jefferson Street, Springfield, AZ

To import the data into Excel, select the Data tab and then select From Text/CSV in the Get & Transform Data group. The program displays a dialog box showing how it will break up the data. In this example, it would convert the tabs or commas into column breaks. The result would be a spreadsheet with two rows and five columns—one each for first name, last name, street address, city, and state.

IC3 ✓ **Understand compatible spreadsheet file types.**

Exporting Data from a Spreadsheet

In addition to embedding and linking spreadsheet data into other types of documents, you can export data by saving a workbook in a different file format. Most spreadsheets support a variety of file types, including text (.txt), CSV (.csv), Portable Document Format (.pdf), Extensible Markup Language (.xml), and even web page (.html). Once you export the file, you can open it with any program that is compatible with the new file format. For example, you can open a .csv file using WordPad or Notepad.

To export a spreadsheet file into a different file format you can use the Save as type option in the Save As dialog box, or the File > Export command.

In Excel, select the File tab on the Ribbon and then select Export. Select the Change File Type option to display common file types. You can also click the Save as Another File Type option. When you select Save As, the Save As dialog box opens. Give the file a name and select a storage location. When you select the Save button, the program exports the data to the selected file format.

Alternatively, select File > Save As. Select the link for More options to open the Save As dialog box. Open the Save as type drop-down menu and select the file format you want to use, and then name and save the file.

Column1	Column2	Column3	Column4	Column5
Kim	Chang	444 Adams Street	Springfield	AR
Austin	Sinclair	522 Jefferson Street	Springfield	AZ

MICROSOFT CORPORATION

FIGURE 13.4.3 Excel converts commas in a .csv text file or tabs in a .tsv text file into column breaks.

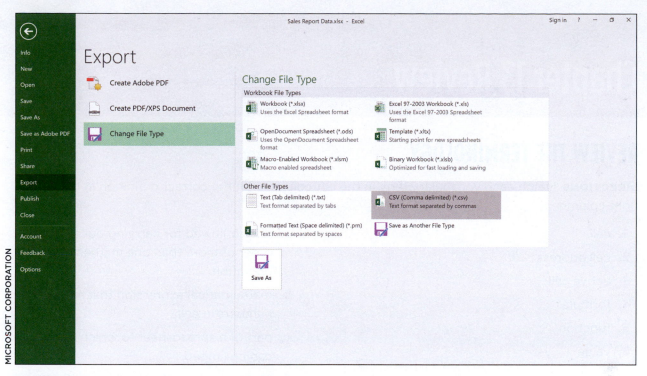

FIGURE 13.4.4 Use the File > Export command to export data from an Excel worksheet.

Chapter 13 Review

REVIEW THE TERMINOLOGY

DIRECTIONS Match each vocabulary term in the left column with the correct definition in the right column.

1. cell
2. cell address
3. active cell
4. formula
5. function
6. value
7. label
8. destination
9. print area
10. order of operations

a. rules followed for carrying out the order of more than one mathematical operation

b. mathematical expression that might link numbers in cells

c. part of a spreadsheet to which printing can be limited

d. place where a column and row meet

e. number in a cell

f. file where you paste shared data

g. highlighted cell in use, where data or a formula will be entered or edited

h. text or text and numbers in a cell

i. shortcut to a formula that is used frequently

j. identifies each individual cell

USE THE TERMINOLOGY

DIRECTIONS Determine the correct choice for each of the following.

1. Tables in spreadsheets are better than tables in word processors because they
   a. use numbers only.
   b. will have unchanging formats.
   c. can be easily updated.
   d. have accurate data.

2. All changes to values, labels, or formulas in a spreadsheet are made in the
   a. formula bar.
   b. cell.
   c. frame.
   d. function line.

3. Values, by default, are aligned
   a. to the left.
   b. to the right.
   c. centered in the cell.
   d. at the top of the cell.

4. How does an Excel spreadsheet know that =10/12 is a formula and not the date October 12?

   a. The formula identifier (=) signals it.

   b. The division (/) sign signals it.

   c. Dates cannot be shown that way.

   d. It would not know.

5. Operations are carried out in the following order:

   a. A-D-E-M-P-S

   b. M-D-E-P-S-A

   c. P-M-D-A-S-E

   d. P-E-M-D-A-S

6. It is best to write formulas using cell references so that a spreadsheet

   a. has no hidden information.

   b. has all correct values.

   c. can be updated easily.

   d. can be more easily graphed.

THINK CRITICALLY

DIRECTIONS Answer the following questions.

1. Explain how to input data into an active worksheet cell. What are some types of data that can be entered?

2. What is a spreadsheet table? How do you create a spreadsheet table in Excel?

3. Describe the function of a comma-separated value (.csv) file.

4. What type of graph would be best for showing how much a child grew in inches over the years? Why?

5. Look at the formulas =B1/B2+B3 and =B1/(B2+B3). Would these formulas give the same result? Why or why not?

EXTEND YOUR KNOWLEDGE

DIRECTIONS Choose and complete one of the following projects.

1. Open a spreadsheet program and create a new worksheet. Place the title "Cupcake Café Sales" in cell A1. Enter the days of the week in cells A2 to A8. Enter the following values in cells B2 to B8: $10,000; $11,500; $13,000; $9,500; $12,000; $13,000; $8,000. Write a formula that places a total in B9. Create a chart that compares sales for each of the seven days. Save the file, and, with your teacher's permission, print it. Then, save it in comma separated value (.csv) format.

2. Think of three ways spreadsheets could be used. Identify one use that is suitable for each of the following people: a 12-year-old student; a 35-year-old businesswoman; and a 70-year-old man. Describe each use, and explain how it is suitable to the person's age. If possible, create one of the spreadsheets using made-up data.

IC3 PREP

1. Fill in the blank: Spreadsheet programs store data in a _____, a grid made of vertical columns and horizontal rows.

   a. cloud

   b. worksheet

   c. file

   d. folder

2. Fill in the blank: Spreadsheet columns are labeled with _____; spreadsheet rows are labeled with _____.

    a. words; phrases
    b. ones; zeros
    c. letters; numbers
    d. names; places

3. Which of the following are valid cell addresses? (Select all that apply.)

    a. C3
    b. B128
    c. Z4
    d. 2A

4. Which of the following are ways to navigate within a spreadsheet program? (Select all that apply.)

    a. Typing to enter or change data in an active cell.
    b. Using the Go To command to jump to any cell.
    c. Changing to a different sheet tab.
    d. Using the arrow keys to move between rows and columns.

5. For each line below, select whether the statement is True or False.

    a. A worksheet cell must be selected to be considered active.
    b. A range is a group or block of cells.
    c. A range of cells must be contiguous.
    d. While all cells in a range are highlighted, only the first cell is active.

6. Which of these are NOT valid ways to select a range of cells?

    a. Select the first cell, then drag to select additional cells.
    b. Select the first cell, press and hold the Shift key, and then select the last cell.
    c. Double-click the worksheet tab.
    d. Select the column letter or row number to select all of that column or row.

7. For each line below, select whether the statement is True or False.

    a. To replace the entire contents of a cell, simply make the cell active and enter the new data.
    b. Data in a cell must be copied in its entirety; portions of a cell's data cannot be selected once entered.
    c. To move data from one cell to another, select the cell and drag its contents to the new cell, or use the Cut and Paste commands.
    d. Click within the formula bar to make changes to the contents of an active cell.

8. Which of the following are NOT possible using the filter and sorting functions of a spreadsheet program?

    a. Sorting a contact list alphabetically by name, and then by city.
    b. Filtering by color, if cells have shading.
    c. Sorting an expense sheet numerically by date.
    d. Sorting multiple worksheets by relative size.
    e. Filtering to display only expenses that are between $75.00 and $100.00.

9. Match the chart type in the left column with its description in the right column.

   1. Pie chart
   2. Column chart
   3. Line char
   4. Bar chart

   a. horizontal blocks representing different amounts of the same item

   b. vertical bars showing changes over time, representing fixed points in time

   c. using segments to show different parts in relation to a whole

   d. showing change over time, on an ongoing basis

10. Which of the following are valid formulas within a spreadsheet program? (Select all that apply.)

    a. =5+2
    b. =46
    c. =13/3
    d. =6*7+7
    e. =Eight-Three

11. Complex formulas in a spreadsheet program will always follow the order of operations; place the following operators in the order they would be carried out.

    a. exponents
    b. addition
    c. operations within parentheses
    d. division
    e. subtraction
    f. multiplication

12. Which of the following are compatible means of importing worksheet data into a new or existing project? (Select all that apply.)

    a. text files with comma or tab separated values
    b. existing spreadsheet files (.xls or .xlsx)
    c. a .doc or .docx file containing bulleted lists
    d. data already formatted as a table or list

IC3 PROCEDURES

NAVIGATING A WORKSHEET

- Click to make a cell active.
- Press **Ctrl + Home** to return to cell A1.
- Click the up or down scroll arrows on the vertical scroll bar to scroll one row up or one row down.
- Click the right or left scroll arrows on the horizontal scroll bar to scroll one column right or one column left.
- Click above or below the scroll box on the vertical scroll arrow to scroll one screen up or one screen down.
- Click to the left or right of the scroll box on the horizontal scroll arrow to scroll one screen left or one screen right.
- Drag the scroll box on either scroll bar to bring the desired portion of the worksheet into view.
- Use the mouse wheel to scroll up or down in the worksheet.

CHANGING THE VIEW

1. Select the **View** tab.

2. Select a View button:
   - **Normal**
   - **Page Break Preview**
   - **Page Layout**
   - **Custom Views**

   OR

   Select a View icon on the status bar:
   - **Normal**
   - **Page Layout**
   - **Page Break Preview**

SHOWING AND HIDING WORKSHEET ELEMENTS

1. Select the **View** tab.

2. Select to mark the check box for **Ruler**, **Gridlines**, **Formula Bar**, and **Headings**.

   A check in the check box indicates the element is displayed.

SAVING A NEW WORKBOOK

1. Select **File**.

2. Select **Save As**.

3. Select the **Browse** button and browse to the location where you want to save the file.

4. Type the file name in the File name text box.

5. Select **Save**.

SAVING CHANGES TO A FILE

Select **Save** on the Quick Access Toolbar.

OR

1. Select **File**.

2. Select **Save**.

SAVING EXCEL DATA IN CSV FILE FORMAT

1. Select **File**.

2. Select **Save As**.

3. Select the **More options** link.

4. Browse to the location where you want to save the file.

5. In the File name box, enter the name for the file.

6. From the Save as type drop-down list, select **CSV (Comma delimited)**.

7. Select **Save**.

   OR

1. Select **File**.

2. Select **Export**.

3. Select **Change File Type**.

4. Select **CSV (Comma delimited) (*.csv)**.

5. Select **Save As**.

6. Enter the file name and select the location where the file will be saved.

7. Select **Save**.

   Select **Don't Show again** *in the* **Possible Data Loss** *warning bar, if necessary.*

SAVE A WORKBOOK AS A TAB-DELIMITED TEXT FILE

1. Select **File**.

2. Select **Save As**.

3. Select the **More options** link.

4. Browse to the location where you want to save the file.

5. In the File name box, enter the name for the file.

6. From the Save as type drop-down list, select **Text (tab delimited)**.

7. Select **Save**.

   OR

1. Select **File**.

2. Select **Export**.

3. Select **Change File Type**.

4. Select the **Text (Tab delimited) (*.txt)**.

5. Select **Save As**.

6. Enter the file name and select the location where the file will be saved.

7. Select **Save**.

CHANGING THE ACTIVE WORKSHEET

Click the sheet tab of the sheet you want to display.

CLOSING A WORKBOOK

1. Select **File**.

2. Select **Close**.

ENTERING DATA

- Select the cell and enter the data.

- Press **Enter** to complete the entry and move to the cell below.

- Press **Tab** to complete the entry and move to the cell to the right.

- Press an arrow key to complete the entry and move to the cell in the desired direction.

EDITING DATA

- Select the cell and enter new data to replace the existing entry.

- Double-click in the cell and move the insertion point as necessary to edit the data.

- Select the cell, click in the formula bar, and move the insertion point as necessary to edit the data.

CLEARING CELL CONTENTS

1. Select the desired cell(s).

2. Select the **Home** tab.

3. Select the **Clear** button.

4. On the menu, select the desired clear option.

SELECTING A CONTIGUOUS RANGE

1. Select the cell in the top-left corner of the range.

2. Drag to select the remaining cells to include in the range.

   OR

   Press and hold **Shift** and use the arrow keys to extend the selection as desired.

   OR

   Press **Shift** and click the cell that's at the lower-right corner of the range.

SELECTING A NONCONTIGUOUS RANGE

1. Select the section of the range using one of the methods previously described.

2. Press and hold **Ctrl**.

3. Select addition sections of the range.

DEFINING A RANGE NAME

1. Select the range you want to name.

2. Select the **Name Box**.

3. Type the desired range name and press **Enter**.

   OR

1. Select the range you want to name.

2. Right-click the selected range.

3. Select **Define Name** on the shortcut menu.

4. In the New Name dialog box, type the desired range name in the Name text box.

5. Select **OK**.

   OR

1. Select the range you want to name.

2. Select the **Formulas** tab.

3. Select the **Define Name** button.

4. In the New Name dialog box, type the desired range name in the Name text box.

5. Select **OK**.

CUTTING AND PASTING DATA

1. Select the cells you want to cut.

2. Select the **Home** tab.

3. Select the **Cut** button ✄.

   OR

   Press **Ctrl + X**.

4. Position the insertion point where you want to move the text.

5. Select the **Home** tab.

6. Select the **Paste** button 📋.

   OR

   Press **Ctrl + V**.

COPYING AND PASTING DATA

1. Select the cells you want to copy.

2. Select the **Home** tab.

3. Select the **Copy** button ⧉.

   OR

   Press **Ctrl + C**.

4. Position the insertion point where you want to insert the text.

5. Select the **Home** tab.

6. Select the **Paste** button 📋.

   OR

   Press **Ctrl + V**.

CREATING A TABLE

1. Select a cell in the range of data that will make up the table.

2. Select the **Insert** tab.

3. Select the **Table** button ▦.

4. In the Create Table dialog box, verify the range containing the table data.

5. Select **OK**.

APPLYING A TABLE STYLE

1. Select any cell in the table.

2. Select the **Home** tab.

3. Select the **Format as Table** button ▨.

4. Select the desired table style.

   OR

1. Select any cell in the table.

2. Select the **Table Tools Design** tab.

3. Select the Table Styles **More** button ⊡.

4. Select the desired table style.

CONVERTING A TABLE TO A RANGE

1. Select any cell in the table.

2. Select the **Table Tools Design** tab.

3. Select the **Convert to Range** button ▣.

4. Select **Yes** in the dialog box to confirm the conversion.

SORTING ROWS

1. Select a cell in the column by which you want to sort.

2. Select the **Data** tab.

3. Select the **Sort A to Z** button ↓ to sort in ascending order, or the **Sort Z to A** button ↓ to sort in descending order.

FILTERING ROWS

1. Select anywhere in the range you want to filter.

2. Select the **Data** tab.

3. Select the **Filter** button ▽.

4. Select the arrow next to the heading of the column you want to filter.

5. From the menu, select the filter you want to apply.

SORTING A TABLE

1. Select the down arrow on the desired table column header.

2. From the menu, select the desired sort option.

   OR

1. Select the **Data** tab.

2. Select the **Sort** button ▦.

3. In the Sort dialog box, set the sort options as desired.

4. Select **OK**.

FILTERING A TABLE

1. Select the down arrow on the desired table column header.

2. From the menu, select to mark the desired column entries you want included in the filter.

CREATING A CUSTOM SORT

1. Select a cell in the column by which you want to sort.
2. Select the **Data** tab.
3. Select the **Sort** button.
4. In the Sort dialog box, in the Sort by box, select the first column by which you want to sort.
5. Select the **Sort On** arrow to specify the type of sort.
6. Select the **Add Level** button to add sort levels.
7. Specify the type of sort for each column.
8. Select **OK**.

REMOVING A SORT

After applying a sort, select the **Undo** button on the Quick Access Toolbar to remove the sort.

REMOVING A FILTER

1. Select any cell in the list.
2. Select the **Data** tab.
3. Select the **Filter** button.

CREATING A CHART

1. Select the range of data you want to chart.
2. Select the **Insert** tab.
3. Select the desired chart category button.
4. In the gallery, select the chart style.

DELETING A CHART

1. Select the chart.
2. Press **Delete**.

APPLYING A CHART LAYOUT

1. Select the chart.
2. Select the **Chart Tools Design** tab.
3. Select the **Quick Layout** button.
4. Select the desired layout from the gallery.

APPLYING A CHART STYLE

1. Select the chart to select it.
2. Select the **Chart Tools Design** tab.
3. Select the **Chart Styles More** button.
4. Select the desired style from the gallery.

ENTERING A FORMULA

1. Select the cell.
2. Type **=**.
3. Type the formula.
4. Press **Enter**, **Tab**, or an arrow key to complete the entry.

   OR

   Click the **Enter** button ☑ on the formula bar.

USING PARENTHESES IN A FORMULA

- Excel calculates the part of the formula enclosed in parentheses first.
- When there are multiple nested pairs of parentheses in a formula, Excel calculates from the innermost pair to the outermost.

EDITING A FORMULA

- Select the cell and type a new formula to replace the existing formula.
- Double-click in the cell and move the insertion point as necessary to edit the formula.
- Select the cell, click in the formula bar, and move the insertion point as necessary to edit the formula.
- Select the cell, press **F2**, and move the insertion point as necessary to edit the formula.

ENTERING A CELL REFERENCE IN A FORMULA

1. Select the cell.
2. Type **=**.
3. Begin entering the formula.
4. At the location where you want to enter a cell reference, type the cell or range reference.

   OR

   Select the cell or range to reference.

   You may select a cell or range on any worksheet.
5. Continue entering the formula until it is complete.
6. Press **Enter**, **Tab**, or an arrow key to complete the entry.

   OR

   Click the **Enter** button ☑ on the formula bar.

CHAPTER 14

Understanding Spreadsheets

WHAT DO SPREADSHEETS DO?

For many years, businesses tracked financial data on large pieces of paper called ledgers. For instance, a business owner might list each worker's weekly pay, then add the numbers to find the total weekly payroll. The process could take many hours. If there were any changes, a lot of work would have to be redone.

Today's businesses use spreadsheet programs to do this work automatically. Someone enters information into an electronic table, instead of on a paper ledger. Then, the spreadsheet program makes the calculations. If information changes, as when a new employee is added, the program returns a new result. These programs can save hours of work, and the calculations are often more accurate than those done by hand.

Using Functions in a Worksheet

OBJECTIVES

- Explain the purpose and usage of functions.
- Write a spreadsheet function using the correct syntax.
- Summarize how to copy a function.
- Contrast relative and absolute references.

AS YOU READ

SUMMARIZE INFORMATION Use a summary chart to help you summarize information about using functions in a worksheet as you read the lesson.

TERMINOLOGY

- 3-D reference
- 3-D workbook
- absolute reference
- argument
- keyword
- nest
- relative reference
- syntax

Spreadsheet Functions

Recall that a function is a commonly used formula built into a program. Spreadsheets offer many different functions. Some are general, like the functions to add or average a range of numbers. Some have specialized uses, like those designed for engineering, statistics, or financial work.

Some of the most commonly used spreadsheet functions are:

- Average—averages a group of numbers

- Count—counts the number of cells that contain values

- Maximum—finds the largest value in a set of values

- Minimum—finds the smallest value in a set of values

- Sum—adds a group of numbers and displays the total

IC3✔ Understand functions.

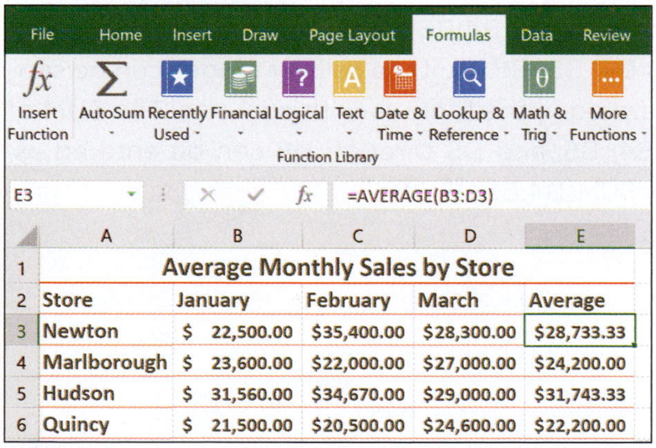

FIGURE 14.1.1 Insert the Average function to find the average of a range of numbers.

MICROSOFT CORPORATION

CONNECTIONS

MATH Spreadsheets are handy for doing conversions. Suppose you need a table that shows how ounces convert to grams.

In a worksheet, type the word Ounces in cell A1, and type Grams in cell B1. Type the numbers 1 through 10 in cells A2 through A11. In cell B2, type the formula =A2*28.35 and press Enter. Because one ounce equals 28.35 grams, the answer 28.35 appears in cell B2. Copy the formula into cell B2 and paste it into cells B3 through B11. The spreadsheet automatically converts the rest of the list for you!

ENTERING FUNCTIONS Each function has its own **syntax**, or rules that define the layout, order, and content that must be used to enter a function. Function syntax has three parts:

- The formula identifier, which is the symbol that identifies the entry as a formula or function. In Excel, the identifier is an equal sign.

- A **keyword**, which is the function's name, such as SUM or AVERAGE.

- An **argument**, which is data the function must use. This is often a reference to a cell or a range of cells but may be a number, date, table name, range name, or other data. A function's arguments are usually enclosed in parentheses.

Most spreadsheet programs prompt you through the process of entering a function, so that you use the correct syntax. For example, in Excel, you can select a function to open the Function dialog box, which will prompt you to select arguments as necessary.

IC3✔ Recognize the syntax of functions.

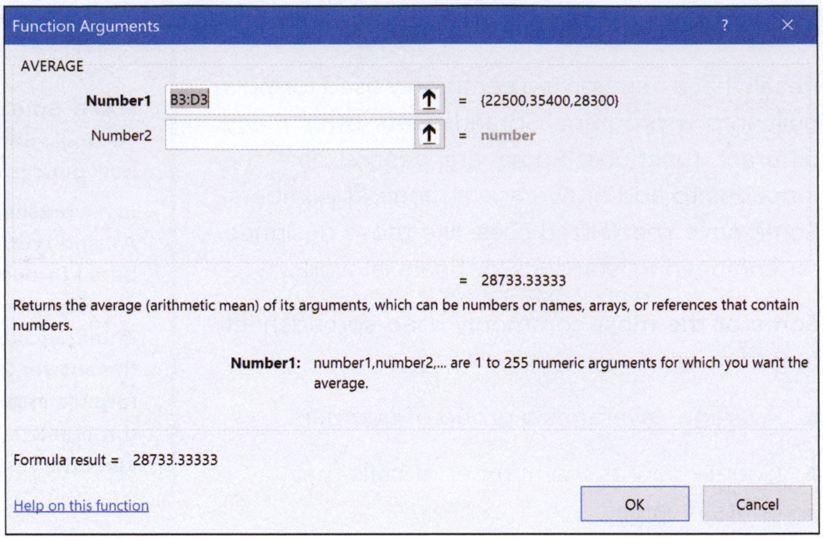

MICROSOFT CORPORATION

FIGURE 14.1.2 The Function Arguments dialog box for the AVERAGE function.

LOGICAL FUNCTIONS Most spreadsheets let you create formulas using an IF function. These formulas perform a calculation only *if* certain conditions are met. For example, you could apply a 10% discount if the total is less than 100, and a 15% discount if it is greater than 100. Using IF functions is useful for forecasting, because you can compare one possible outcome with another.

LOOKUP TABLES Lookup functions let you locate information in a table column or row based on specific data, such as the cost of a product.

NESTING FUNCTIONS You can even **nest** functions. When you nest a function, you include it within another function.

USING A RANGE IN A FUNCTION Often the argument includes a cell range, or a group of cells. A range can include cells from one column or one row, but it also can combine cells from more than one of either.

To include a cell range in a function—or to any formula—you don't need to name every cell in the range. Instead, name the cell in the range's upper-left corner, and then name the cell in the range's lower-right corner. Depending on the program you use, you must separate the ranges' cell addresses with either a colon (:) or two periods (..).

For example, using the SUM function to add the values in cells B4, B5, and B6 would look like this: =SUM(B4:B6). This is the same as entering: =B4+B5+B6. Multiple cells or ranges can be separated in the formula with commas. The SUM of B4, B5, and D5 through D8 can be entered as: =SUM(B4:B5,D5:D8).

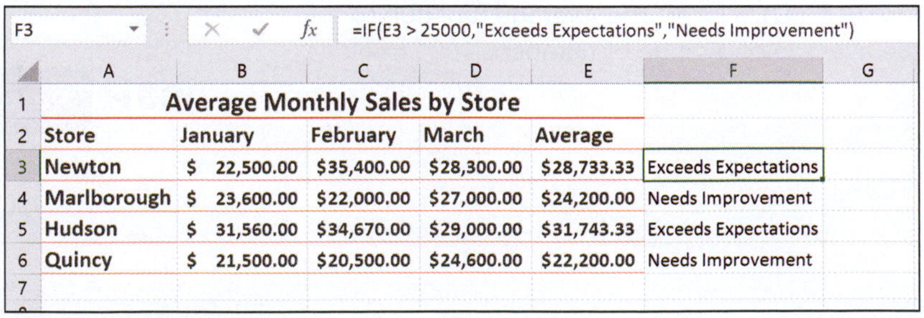

F3 =IF(E3 > 25000,"Exceeds Expectations","Needs Improvement")

	A	B	C	D	E	F	G
1	Average Monthly Sales by Store						
2	Store	January	February	March	Average		
3	Newton	$ 22,500.00	$35,400.00	$28,300.00	$28,733.33	Exceeds Expectations	
4	Marlborough	$ 23,600.00	$22,000.00	$27,000.00	$24,200.00	Needs Improvement	
5	Hudson	$ 31,560.00	$34,670.00	$29,000.00	$31,743.33	Exceeds Expectations	
6	Quincy	$ 21,500.00	$20,500.00	$24,600.00	$22,200.00	Needs Improvement	
7							

MICROSOFT CORPORATION

FIGURE 14.1.3 This IF function displays Exceeds Expectations if the value is greater than 25000 and Needs Improvement if the value is not greater than 25000.

> **CAREER CORNER**
>
> **COST ESTIMATOR** Spreadsheet functions are valuable to people who do cost estimating. Many such people work in the construction or repair industries. They have to estimate the cost of workers' labor and of materials and equipment in putting up houses, schools, and other buildings. They can use formulas and functions to find the cost of materials according to the size of the structure being built.

Relative and Absolute References

Usually, formulas (including functions) use relative cell references. A **relative reference** automatically changes when it is copied or moved so that it uses cell addresses that are specific to its new location. That means you only need to enter the formula in one location, and then copy or move it to use it someplace else.

USING AN ABSOLUTE REFERENCE When you do not want the reference to change if the cell is copied or moved, you must use an **absolute reference**. You should use an absolute reference when your formula or function must always refer to a specific cell or range. To enter an absolute reference, you type a dollar sign ($) character to the left of the column letter and/or row number in the range address.

Suppose, for example, in cell D6 you enter the function =SUM(D1:D5). If you move the function to cell E6, the relative references change and the function becomes =SUM(E1:E5). If you want the function to use the values in cells D1:D5, no matter where you move it, you enter =SUM($D$1:$D$5); the absolute references will not change even if you move the function.

TYPES OF ABSOLUTE REFERENCES You can create three types of absolute cell references by typing a dollar sign in front of the column letter, the row number, or both, as follows:

- $A$1 uses absolute references for both column and row; neither changes when the formula is copied or moved.
- A$1 uses a relative reference for the column and an absolute reference for the row; only the column changes if the formula is copied or moved.
- $A1 uses an absolute reference for the column and a relative reference for the row; only the row changes if the formula is copied or moved.

3-D References

In a **3-D workbook**—one that uses multiple worksheets in the same file—you can include a **3-D reference** in your formulas and functions. A 3-D reference refers to a cell or range on a specific worksheet. That means you can include a reference to a cell on Sheet2 in a formula entered on Sheet1. To enter a 3-D reference, type an exclamation point (!) character between the worksheet name and the cell reference. For example, =SUM(Sheet2!D1:D5) totals the values in D1:D5 on Sheet2; =SUM(Sheet3!D1:D5) totals the values in D1:D5 on Sheet3.

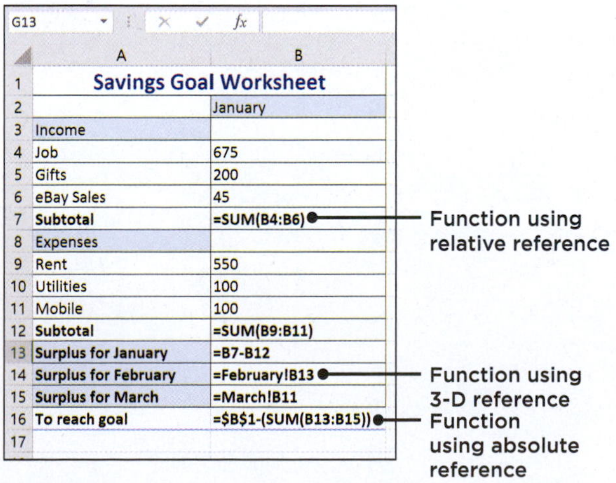

MICROSOFT CORPORATION

FIGURE 14.1.4 Examples of a relative cell reference, a 3-D reference, and an absolute cell reference.

Automatic Spreadsheet Features

OBJECTIVES

- Explain how to use a template.

- Explain how to use the automatic entry feature.

- Differentiate between series increments and decrements.

- Identify advantages of using the automatic fit and formatting features.

- Summarize the advantages of using macros.

AS YOU READ

ORGANIZE INFORMATION Complete a concept web to identify and organize information about automatic features of spreadsheets as you read the lesson.

TERMINOLOGY

- AutoComplete

- AutoFill

- AutoFit

- conditional formatting

- data series

- decrement

- increment

- macro

- template

- theme

Working with Spreadsheet Templates

Recall that a template is a file that already includes layout, formatting, prompts, and some content suitable for a specific document type. For example, a calendar template might have columns labeled with days of the week, and an invoice template might include a cell for entering addresses, a placeholder for a company logo, and formulas for totaling costs. When you create a spreadsheet using a template, your worksheet includes all the settings already in the template. You can use built-in templates that come with your program, look for templates online, or create and save your own templates for future use.

Using templates can save time and increase productivity because you do not have to design or format the spreadsheet yourself. Another benefit is that using templates can give your spreadsheets a similar look and feel, which can help customers identify your business by brand.

To create a document based on a template in a Microsoft Office application, select File > New, and then select the document category to view the available templates. When you find one you like, select it and select Create. Replace the sample text and fill in the blanks to complete your spreadsheet.

If you have a document you would like to use as a template in the future, you can use the File > Save As command and select the document template format from the Save as type list in the Save As dialog box. In Excel, the document template file type has an .xltx file extension, and the template is saved by default in the Custom Office Template folder.

IC3 ✔ Use spreadsheet templates to increase productivity.

Automatic Data Entry

With the automatic data entry feature (often called **AutoFill**), you can enter many kinds of data series in a set of cells. A **data series** is a

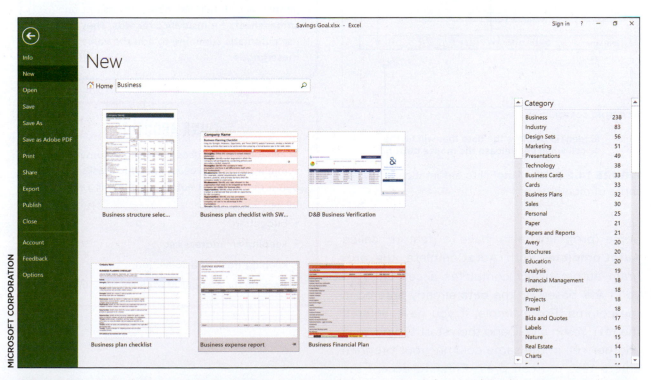

FIGURE 14.2.1 On the New tab in Backstage view in Excel, you can search for templates by category and type.

set of data that changes by a constant value. The series *2005, 2006, 2007, 2008* increases by one. The series *10, 8, 6, 4* decreases by two. The number by which each value increases is called the **increment**. If a series decreases, the value by which it becomes smaller is called the **decrement**. Some data series are text, such as the days of the week. Dates can also be entered as a series.

To use AutoFill, you only need to enter the first one or two values in the series. Then, move the mouse to the lower-right corner of the first cell until a small plus sign or arrow appears. Drag across a row or down a column until you reach the last cell in the series. The data in the series appears in the cells. In some programs you can use the Fill options. In Excel, the Fill command is in the Editing group on the Home tab of the Ribbon.

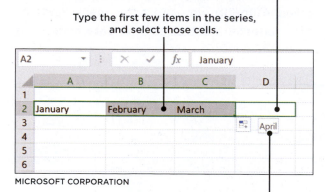

MICROSOFT CORPORATION

ScreenTip displays the data that will fill the cell when you release the mouse button.

FIGURE 14.2.2 Use AutoFill to automatically fill in a series of months.

Some programs also have a feature called **AutoComplete**. With AutoComplete, the program automatically completes a cell entry as you type, based on the data already entered in the column. For example, if you have entered the text *Yes* in a cell, and then start typing *Ye* in another cell in the same column, your program enters *Yes*. You can press Enter to accept the entry, or keep typing to change it.

Automatic Summing

A common calculation in spreadsheets is totaling a series of numbers. The automatic sum function—called SUM or AutoSUM—makes this action easy. A toolbar button with the symbol Σ controls the function. Use the following steps:

- Choose the Location—First, select the cell where you want the total to display and make it active. If you are totaling a column, choose the cell below the last number. If you are totaling a row, choose the cell to the right of the last number.

- Insert the Function—Select the Σ AutoSum button.

- Complete the Formula—In some programs, the total automatically displays. In others, a formula displays and you must select Enter to accept it.

TECHNOLOGY@HOME

The automatic sum feature can come in handy for some home users of spreadsheets. Some people record their valuable possessions on spreadsheets for insurance records. They can use automatic summing to add the value of these goods.

THINK ABOUT IT!

Think about other uses for which automatic summing might be used. For which tasks listed below do you think automatic summing would be suitable?

- budgeting
- keeping an address list
- keeping track of a collection
- tracking the amount of exercise done in a week

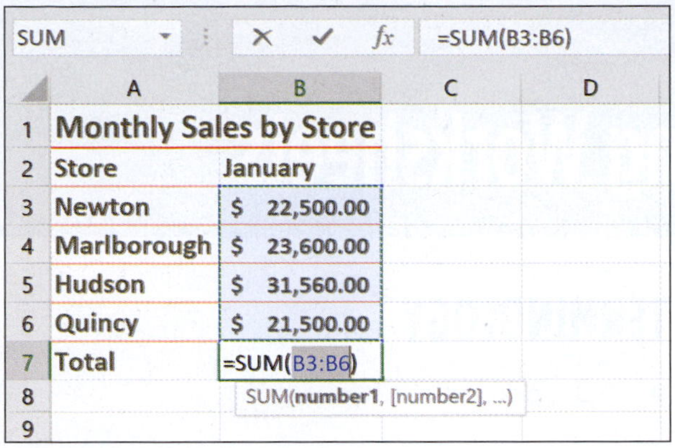

FIGURE 14.2.3 Insert the SUM function to total numbers in a worksheet.

Automatic Formatting

Some automatic features affect the appearance of the worksheet. They include automatic fit and formatting features.

FITTING DATA IN A CELL Recall that if the data in a cell is too long to fit in a column, you can change the column width by dragging the right edge of the column border in the frame. But, suppose you enter other data that requires you to repeat this step several times. You can choose the program's automatic fit feature to automatically adjust the column to fit the longest data in that column. Simply double-click the right edge of the column heading in the frame, or select the Format > AutoFit command, and the column automatically adjusts to fit the longest entry. **AutoFit** is available for rows, as well.

FORMATTING WORKSHEETS You can make many formatting enhancements to worksheets. Some spreadsheet programs offer an automatic formatting feature. This feature allows you to apply preset formats to an entire worksheet or to a selected part of a worksheet. For example, in Excel you can apply a **theme**, which is a collection of formatting settings for an entire worksheet, including colors, fonts, and effects, or use styles. In Quattro Pro, click the Format menu and select Speed Format. Then, select the format you want to apply. Most spreadsheets also include commands for conditional formatting.

Conditional formatting applies formatting only to cells in which the data meets certain criteria. For example, you might apply shading to cells with a value greater than 100.

Using Macros

A **macro** is a set of mouse actions, keystrokes, or commands that you can record and store for future use. Once a macro is recorded, you can use it whenever you want to repeat the task. Macros save the time and effort of repeating a series of instructions. The program carries out the macro much faster than you could perform the task yourself. Also, using macros ensures that steps are done exactly the same way each time.

TECHNOLOGY@SCHOOL

Automatic charting features let you quickly turn data into an easy-to-read graphic. Some social studies teachers have their students research details and statistics on the countries or time periods they study. By creating charts from the data they collect, students can compare information.

THINK ABOUT IT!

Some spreadsheet data may be easier to analyze in a chart than on a worksheet. Which topics below would be easier to interpret in a chart?

- area of forest
- population of cities
- climate by month
- forms of government
- main products grown in different states

Formatting and Managing Worksheets

OBJECTIVES

- Demonstrate how to modify borders, fill color, text color, and alignment.

- Compare different data types and number formats.

- Explain how to insert or delete columns or rows.

- Explain how to modify cell sizes.

- Discuss merging and unmerging cells.

- Manage multiple worksheets in the same spreadsheet file.

AS YOU READ

ORGANIZE INFORMATION Complete a main idea/detail chart to help you learn the options for formatting spreadsheets as you read.

TERMINOLOGY

- 3-D workbook

- borders

- cell style

- data type

- merge

- Merge and Center

- shading

- sheet tab

- text orientation

- unmerge

Formatting a Worksheet

Apply formatting to improve the appearance of a worksheet and make it easier to read. Usually, to apply formatting to an entire cell or a range, you select it and then select the formatting options to apply. You can even apply formatting to cells that do not contain data. When you do enter data, it picks up the cell formatting. You can also format part of the data in a cell. Select the cell and then select the data to format in the Formula bar.

Many programs, including Excel, have a Format Cells dialog box that includes all the options for applying formatting. Right-click any cell in an Excel worksheet and select Format Cells to open the dialog box, or select Format > Format Cells on the Home tab of the Ribbon.

FORMATTING DATA You can format labels or values the same way you do in a word-processing document. Formatting options may be on a menu or in a dialog box. For example, in Excel, you can do the following using buttons in the Font and Alignment groups on the Home tab of the Ribbon:

- Change the font
- Change the font size
- Change the font style
- Change the font color
- Set the horizontal and vertical alignment
- Set the **text orientation**, which is the rotation of text within a cell, usually to fit in a narrow column.

BORDERS AND FILLS To help cells stand out, apply shading and borders. **Shading** is color applied to fill a cell. **Borders** are the visible gridlines that define columns, rows, and cells. In Excel, the Borders and Fill color buttons are in the Font group on the Home tab of the Ribbon.

IC3✔ **Know how to modify borders, fill color, text color, and alignment.**

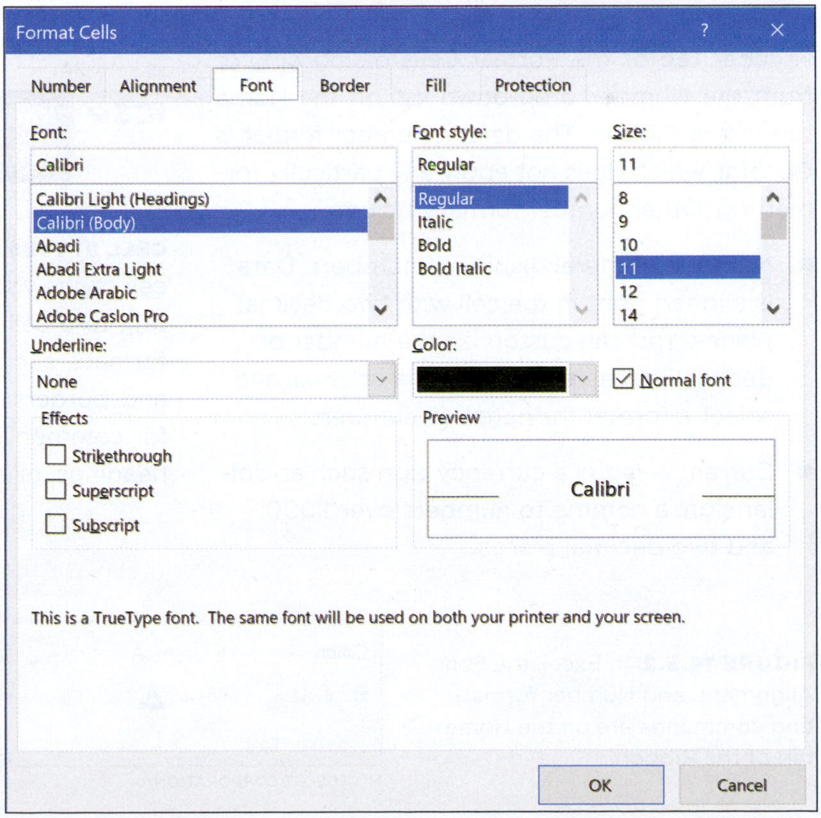

FIGURE 14.3.1 The Font tab of the Format Cells dialog box in Excel.

MICROSOFT CORPORATION

TECHNOLOGY@WORK

Some spreadsheet programs let you display worksheets from different files at the same time. Simply open the files and select Arrange in Excel or Tile Top to Bottom or Tile Side to Side in Quattro Pro.

THINK ABOUT IT!

Think about the advantages of viewing worksheets from different files at the same time. For which examples listed below would this feature be useful?

- move data from one file to another
- work on a worksheet on a different tab
- insert cell references in another file
- copy cells from one part of a worksheet to another

NUMBER FORMATS Number formats, such as percent, currency, decimal, or fraction, define the **data type** and the formatting of the data in a cell. Data types include text, number, date, and time. In Excel, you can select Number formats on the Number tab of the Format Cells dialog box, or from the Number drop-down list on the Home tab of the Ribbon. The default number format is General, which does not apply any particular formatting. Other number formats include:

- Number—general display of numbers. Data is aligned right in the cell with two decimal places. You can customize the number of decimal places, select to use a comma, and select a format for negative numbers.

- Currency—adds a currency sign such as dollar sign, a comma to numbers over 1,000, and two decimal places.

- Accounting—similar to currency, but currency signs and decimal points are aligned in columns.

- Comma—shows two decimal places and a comma for numbers over 1,000.

- Percentage—multiplies the number in the cell by 100 to calculate the percentage and adds a percent symbol to the result.

- Decimals—includes number of decimal places chosen.

- Date—provides a list of different date format types.

- Time—provides a list of different time format types.

- Text—treats the entry as text even when there are numbers entered.

- Special—includes formats for postal codes, phone numbers, and social security numbers.

- Custom—includes formats for some specific number types and lets you customize them to suit your own needs.

IC3✔ **Know how to apply data types and number formats.**

CELL STYLES Most programs come with built-in cell styles you can use to quickly apply formatting to a cell or range. A **cell style** has a set of formats, such as a font and font style, shading, and borders. In Excel, cell styles are designed for commonly-used purposes, such as for titles, headings, or calculations.

FIGURE 14.3.2 In Excel, the Font, Alignment, and Number formatting commands are on the Home tab of the Ribbon.

Calibri	11	A A				Wrap Text	Accounting
B I U						Merge & Center	$ · % ·
Font			Alignment				Number

MICROSOFT CORPORATION

MICROSOFT CORPORATION

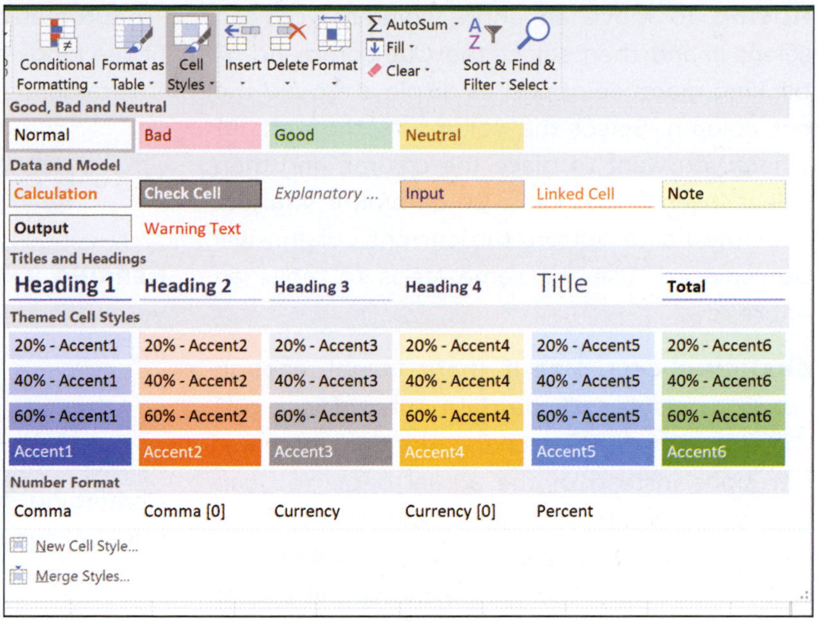

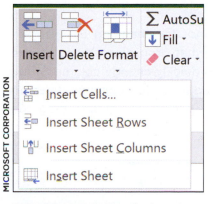

FIGURE 14.3.3 The Cell Styles gallery in Excel.

Adjusting Columns and Rows

You can modify a worksheet by inserting, deleting, moving, and resizing columns and rows. You can also **merge** multiple cells into one cell, or **unmerge** cells that have been merged, which means to divide them back into their original structure.

INSERTING To add columns or rows, go to the Insert menu and select Insert Sheet Column or Insert Sheet Row. The existing columns will move to the right of the active cell, and rows will move down to make room for the new column or row. If you select multiple columns or rows first, that is the number of columns or rows that will be inserted. You can also use the Insert command to insert cells. The program will prompt you to select whether to shift existing cells up, down, left, or right to make space for the new cells. Be careful when inserting cells. Shifting existing cells can result in data displaying in the wrong column or row.

MICROSOFT CORPORATION

FIGURE 14.3.4 Use the Insert command on the Home tab of the Ribbon to insert new rows, columns, cells, or sheets.

DELETING To delete a column or row, click the heading in the worksheet's frame. In the Edit menu, select Delete. If there is data already entered, it will be deleted as well.

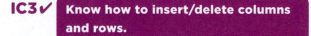

IC3✓ **Know how to insert/delete columns and rows.**

MOVING To move an entire column, you can select it and then select the Cut command. A blinking marquee of dashes displays around the cut column. Select the column to the right of where you want to place the column and then select Insert > Cut cells. Be careful! If you just click the Paste button, the current column will be replaced. Use the same steps to move an entire row.

CHANGING CELL SIZE If there is not enough space to display all the data entered in a cell, the program displays characters such as number signs instead of the actual data. You can change the width of columns and the height of rows. When you increase the width of a column or the height of a row, you increase the size of the cells, making more space to display data. When you decrease column width or row height, you decrease the size of the cells.

In Excel, commands for changing cell size are found on the Format drop-down menu on the Home tab. Or, to quickly change column width, drag the right edge of the column's heading left or right. To change row height, drag the lower edge of the row's heading up or down.

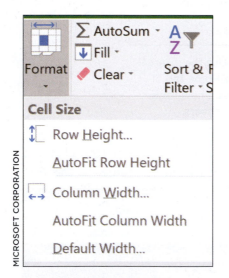

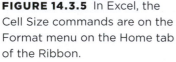

FIGURE 14.3.5 In Excel, the Cell Size commands are on the Format menu on the Home tab of the Ribbon.

To automatically adjust the column or row to fit the longest entry, double-click the border on the frame.

IC3✔ Know how to modify cell sizes.

MERGING AND UNMERGING Merge cells when you want to create one larger cell by combining two or more regular cells. If the cells already contain data, only the data in the upper-left cell is retained; the data in the other cells is deleted. You can unmerge merged calls, as well. Unmerging divides a merged cell back into the original number of cells. When you unmerge, existing data displays in the top-left cell.

Most programs have a **Merge and Center** command that lets you merge selected cells and center the data at the same time. This is useful for formatting headings and titles. Commands for merging and unmerging are usually part of the alignment settings. In Excel, they are in the Alignment group on the Home tab of the Ribbon, and on the Alignment tab of the Format Cells dialog box.

IC3✔ Know how to merge and unmerge cells.

Using Multiple Worksheets in a File

In most spreadsheet programs, a workbook file can contain more than one worksheet. Recall that each worksheet is represented by a sheet tab in the lower-left corner of the worksheet. Select a tab to switch to that worksheet. Recall that a workbook with multiple sheets is sometimes called a **3-D workbook**, because having these extra worksheets is like working in three dimensions; you can store data not only in columns and rows but also on different sheets.

NAMING WORKSHEETS By default, the original worksheet in a workbook is named Sheet1. Each sheet you add is named consecutively: Sheet2, Sheet3, and so on. To rename a sheet, right-click the sheet tab, select Rename, and type a new name, or double-click the tab and type a new name. Sheet tab names can help identify the data stored on each sheet.

ADDING AND DELETING WORKSHEETS To add another worksheet to a file in Excel, click the New sheet button to the right of the sheet tabs. Or, right-click on a worksheet tab, and select Insert from the pop-up menu. To delete a worksheet, right-click on the tab, and select Delete from the pop-up menu.

MOVING WORKSHEETS You can move a worksheet within a workbook or from one workbook to another. There are two ways to do this:

■ Pop-up Menu—Select the sheet that you want to move by clicking the sheet tab. Then, right-click to display the pop-up menu and select Move or Copy Sheet. A dialog box asks you to select the file (or workbook) and the new location.

■ Click and Drag—Click the sheet tab and then drag it to its new location in the same file or in a new one. To move a worksheet to a different file, that file must be open. As you drag, the mouse changes to a small sheet and an arrow guides you.

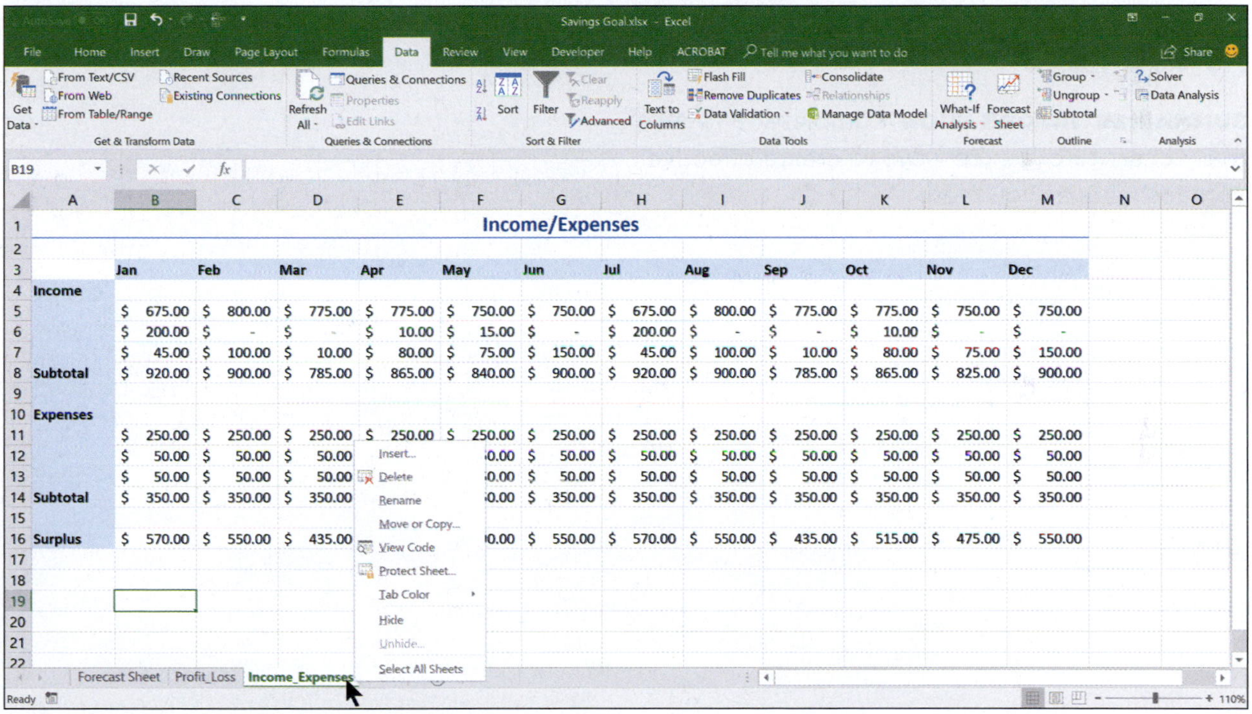

FIGURE 14.3.6 Right-click a sheet tab in Excel to display a menu of sheet tab options.

MICROSOFT CORPORATION

OBJECTIVES

- Outline the steps in designing an effective spreadsheet.

- Explain reasons for protecting spreadsheets.

- Describe how to hide cells and columns.

- Explain how a spreadsheet can be used as a simple database.

TERMINOLOGY

- database

- field

- password

- protect

- record

AS YOU READ

SUMMARIZE INFORMATION Complete a summary chart to organize ways to create effective spreadsheets as you read.

Planning Is Important

Almost anyone can create a worksheet. But someone who simply enters labels, values, and formulas might create a worksheet that contains errors. Effective worksheets require careful planning before any data is entered. Here are some suggestions to help you create an effective and error-free spreadsheet:

IDENTIFY THE PURPOSE OF THE WORKSHEET What are you trying to accomplish by creating the worksheet?

THINK ABOUT THE END PRODUCT What results do you want to report? What individual values do you expect in columns or rows? Do you need summary statistics such as totals or averages?

IDENTIFY WHAT DATA IS NEEDED What information will you need? How will it be gathered? Who will put it into the worksheet? How will its accuracy be checked?

THINK ABOUT WHAT FORMULAS ARE NEEDED How will you convert your input data into final results? Do you want intermediate results to appear in the worksheet or only final answers? What formulas or functions will you need? How will you test the accuracy of the formulas?

USE CELL REFERENCES IN FORMULAS How will you write formulas? Remember that it is better to write formulas that refer to cells rather than to values.

IDENTIFY CELLS TO PROTECT FROM REPLACEMENT What data and formulas should not be changed? You want to protect the data in these cells from being replaced.

PLAN HOW TO ENHANCE THE WORKSHEET Which cells are most important? Use formatting—typefaces, alignment, border, shading, and color—to make those cells stand out.

PROTECT DATA AND FORMULAS You can **protect** cells in order to prevent errors and avoid unauthorized changes to data.

Protecting Data

Spreadsheet programs let you lock one or more cells, a worksheet, or all the worksheets in a file. Often users protect an entire worksheet and unlock only the cells they allow to be changed. These might include cells that will hold the values that formulas use or data like names and addresses. The rest of the worksheet remains locked until protection is removed.

In Excel, select the Review tab, Changes group, and choose the Protect Sheet command. In Quattro Pro, you select Sheet from the Format menu. In Apple's Numbers click on the Inspector button and then use options in the document inspector to apply password protection.

Some programs also allow you to assign a **password**, or coded access word. Then, only people who know the password can open the file or save changes to it.

Another feature that can help protect data and formulas is the Hide option. By hiding certain cells or columns in a worksheet, you discourage other users from changing the information in them.

MICROSOFT CORPORATION

FIGURE 14.4.1 The Protect Sheet dialog box in Excel.

Using a Spreadsheet as a Database

A **database** is a collection of information organized so that it is easy to locate, analyze, and manipulate the specific data you need. A spreadsheet, like a database, organizes information in a table comprised of columns and rows. Each row is one **record** in the database. Each column is one **field**, or specific element of information.

Database applications, such as Microsoft Access, are complex programs with tools for managing very large files in sophisticated ways. When you want to work with a simple list of data, you might find that a spreadsheet program provides all the tools you need. You can enter, store, sort, filter, find and replace data in your spreadsheet, making it suitable for creating and working with a simple database.

IC3✓ Understand how a spreadsheet can be used as a simple database.

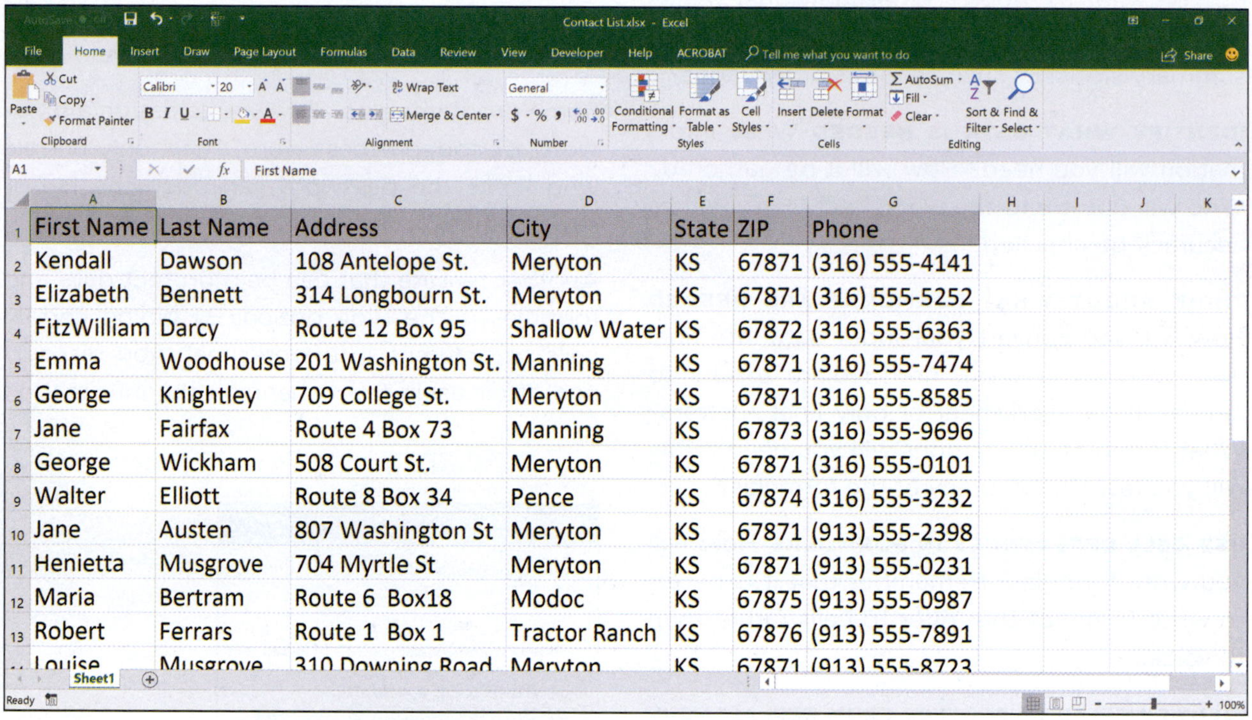

FIGURE 14.4.2 A contact list is a simple database you can store in a spreadsheet.

Chapter 14 Review

REVIEW THE TERMINOLOGY

DIRECTIONS Match each vocabulary term in the left column with the correct definition in the right column.

1. range
2. worksheet tab
3. data series
4. increment
5. decrement
6. syntax
7. keyword
8. argument
9. relative reference
10. absolute reference

a. function name

b. set of data that changes by a constant value

c. rules for writing a function

d. value by which numbers in a series decrease

e. value by which numbers in a series increase

f. cell reference that does not change

g. cell reference that does change

h. lets you access worksheets in a spreadsheet file

i. group of cells that might include cells from different columns and rows

j. reference to cells or range to be acted on by a function

USE THE TERMINOLOGY

DIRECTIONS Complete each sentence with information from the chapter.

1. To select a column, click on the _____.

2. In a spreadsheet, to record results for a race timed to the second and the tenth of a second, use the format _____.

3. To delete a column or row, highlight it, go to the _____, and choose Delete.

4. The automatic fit feature helps you when making a spreadsheet by automatically _____ a column.

5. The _____ feature formats spreadsheets so the data is clear and easy to read.

6. Both a(n) _____ and a line chart can display changes in data over time.

7. Column charts use _____ to display data.

8. _____ are ready-made formulas built into a spreadsheet.

9. A(n) _____ reference is automatically updated to reflect its new location if you move it.

10. The cell reference _____ shows an absolute reference for the column A1.

THINK CRITICALLY

DIRECTIONS Answer the following questions.

1. What is a spreadsheet template, and how can it be used to increase productivity?

2. How is a spreadsheet able to function as a simple database? What would be the benefit versus using a database application?

3. How would you write a reference to the cells in columns U through W and rows 17 through 25?

4. How would you write a function to add values in the cells D7 to D20? What built-in function could you use?

EXTEND YOUR KNOWLEDGE

DIRECTIONS Choose and complete one of the following projects.

1. Open a new workbook. Title it "Town Population Growth" in cell A1. Use the AutoFill feature to fill in the years from 2011 to 2020 in cells A2 to A11. Enter these values in cells B2 to B11: 15,000; 15,700; 16,500; 17,200; 18,000; 18,700; 19,300; 20,300; 21,700; 22,900. If you make an error, use the Undo command and try again. Create a line chart of the data. Save the file, and, with your teacher's permission, print it. Copy the data from B2:B11 to C2:C11. Change the value in cell C5 to 17,000. Delete row 2. Create a column chart of the new data. Insert a new column A. Apply the Long Date format to cell A1 and enter today's date. Apply the Time format to any blank cell and enter the current time. Save the file, and, with your teacher's permission, print it. Which type of chart is more effective for this data? Explain.

2. Use the internet or the library to learn how spreadsheets have changed the way people do business. In what ways are spreadsheets used in businesses today? Was the same work done in the past? How is it different to do the work now? As you work, take notes and keep track of your sources. Evaluate the information you find and only use it if it is accurate, relevant, and valid. Prepare and deliver a presentation to summarize your findings. Include a slide that lists your sources.

IC3 PREP

1. Which of the following are commonly used formulas in spreadsheet programs? (Select all that apply.)

   a. Average—averages a group of numbers

   b. Minimum—finds the smallest value in a set of values

   c. Metric—converts numbers to their metric values

   d. Sum—adds a group of numbers and displays the total

2. Put the following elements in order to construct a valid worksheet function.

   a. the keyword (the name of the function being called)

   b. an argument (the data a function must use, usually in parentheses)

   c. the formula identifier (in Excel, an equal sign)

3. Which of the following is NOT a type of formatting you can apply to worksheet data?

   a. changing the font

   b. setting horizontal and vertical alignment

   c. changing the shape of the cells

   d. setting the color of the cell borders or fills

4. Match the data type in the column on the left with its effect on the data in the column on the right.

   1. currency

   2. date

   3. text

   4. percentage

   5. time

   a. provides a list of different time format types

   b. adds a currency sign, a comma to numbers over 1,000, and two decimal places

   c. provides a list of different date format types

   d. multiplies the number in the cell by 100 to calculate the percentage and adds a percent symbol to the result

   e. treats the entry as text even when there are numbers entered

5. What is important to keep in mind when inserting new columns or rows into an existing worksheet, or deleting them? (Select all that apply.)

   a. Existing data may subsequently be displayed out of order.

   b. Existing cell data will be deleted from a deleted column or row.

   c. Existing data may be shifted in a random direction.

   d. The number of resulting cells may be randomized.

6. What are some valid methods of changing a cell's size in Excel? (Select all that apply.)

   a. Using the Format drop-down menu on the Home tab.

   b. Use the Zoom buttons.

   c. Drag the right edge of the column's heading left or right, or the lower edge of the row's heading up or down.

   d. Double-click the border on the column frame.

7. For each line below, select whether the statement is True or False.

   a. When cells are merged, only the data in the upper-left cell is retained; the data in the other cells is deleted.

   b. Merged cells cannot be unmerged.

   c. The Merge and Center command is commonly used to format headings and titles.

   d. Unmerged cells display their existing data in the bottom-left cell.

IC3 PROCEDURES

CREATING A NEW WORKBOOK FROM A TEMPLATE

1. Click **File**.

2. Click **New**.

3. In the Suggested searches list, click the desired category.

4. Click the desired template.

5. Click **Create**.

6. Personalize the information as desired and then save the workbook file.

SAVING A WORKBOOK AS A TEMPLATE

1. Select **File**.

2. Select **Save As**.

3. Select the **More options** link.

4. In the Save As dialog box, select the **Save as type** arrow.

5. Select **Excel Template**.

6. In the Save As dialog box, enter the template name and select the location where the file will be saved, if necessary.

7. Select **Save**.

USING AUTOSUM FUNCTIONS (SUM, AVERAGE, MAX, MIN, AND COUNT)

1. Select the cell in which you want to enter the function.

2. Select the **Home** tab.

3. Select the **AutoSum** drop-down arrow Σ AutoSum ▾ .

4. Select the desired function from the menu.

5. Verify the range.

6. Press **Enter**.

APPLYING A FONT

1. Select the text or cells to format.

2. Select the **Home** tab.

3. Select the **Font** button drop-down arrow | Times New Ro ▾ |.

4. Select the desired font.

   OR

1. Select the text or cells to format.

2. Select the **Home** tab.

3. Select the **Font** group dialog box launcher ⬚.

4. In the Font list, select the desired font.

5. Select **OK**.

CHANGING THE FONT SIZE

1. Select the text or cells to format.
2. Select the **Home** tab.
3. Select the **Font Size** button drop-down arrow ⌊12 ▾⌋.
4. Select the desired font size.

OR

1. Select the text or cells to format.
2. Select the **Home** tab.
3. Select the **Font** group dialog box launcher ⌐.
4. In the Size list, select the desired font size.
5. Select **OK**.

APPLYING FONT STYLES

1. Select the text or cells to format.
2. Select the **Home** tab.
3. Select the desired font style, as follows:
   - **Bold (Ctrl + B)** ⌊B⌋
   - **Italic (Ctrl + I)** ⌊*I*⌋

OR

1. Select the text or cells to format.
2. Select the **Home** tab.
3. Select the **Font** group dialog box launcher ⌐.
4. In the Font style list, select the desired style.
5. Select **OK**.

CHANGING THE COLOR OF TEXT IN A CELL

1. Select the text or cells to format.
2. Select the **Home** tab.
3. Select the **Font Color** button drop-down arrow ⌊A ▾⌋.
4. Select the desired font color.

OR

1. Select the text or cells to format.
2. Select the **Home** tab.
3. Select the **Font** group dialog box launcher ⌐.
4. Select the **Color** drop-down arrow.
5. Select the desired font color.
6. Select **OK**.

SETTING HORIZONTAL AND VERTICAL ALIGNMENT

1. Select the cells to format.

2. Select the **Home** tab.

3. Select the alignment to apply:
   - Top Align ▤
   - Middle Align ▤
   - Bottom Align ▤
   - Align Left ▤
   - Center ▤
   - Align Right ▤

WRAPPING TEXT IN CELLS

1. Select the cells to format.

2. Select the **Home** tab.

3. Select the **Wrap Text** button ▤.

APPLYING CELL STYLES

1. Select the cells to format.

2. Select the **Home** tab.

3. Select the **Cell Styles** button ▤.

4. From the gallery, select the style to apply.

APPLYING BORDERS

1. Select the cells to format.

2. Select the **Home** tab.

3. Select the **Borders** drop-down arrow ▤.

4. Select the Border option to apply.

   OR

1. Select the cells to format.

2. Right-click the selection.

3. Select **Format Cells**.

4. Select the **Border** tab.

5. Under Style, select the border line style.

6. Select the **Color** drop-down arrow and select the border color.

7. Select a **Presets** button.

   OR

   Select one or more **Border** buttons.

8. Select **OK**.

APPLYING FILLS

1. Select the cells to format.
2. Select the **Home** tab.
3. Select the **Fill Color** drop-down arrow.
4. Select the fill color to apply.

   OR

1. Select the cells to format.
2. Right-click the selection.
3. Select **Format Cells**.
4. Select the **Fill** tab.
5. Under Background Color, select the fill color.
6. Select **OK**.

APPLYING NUMBER FORMATS AND DATA TYPES

1. Select the cells to format.
2. Select the **Home** tab.
3. Select the **Number Format** drop-down arrow.
4. From the gallery, select the desired format.

INSERTING A COLUMN

1. Select the heading of the column that will be to the right of the new column.
2. Select the **Home** tab.
3. Select the **Insert** button drop-down arrow.
4. Select **Insert Sheet Columns**.

INSERTING A ROW

1. Select the heading of the row that will be below the new row.
2. Select the **Home** tab.
3. Select the **Insert** button drop-down arrow.
4. Select **Insert Sheet Rows**.

DELETING A COLUMN OR ROW

1. Select the heading of the column or row that you want to delete.
2. Select the **Home** tab.
3. Select the **Delete** button.

CHANGING COLUMN WIDTH

1. Position the mouse pointer on the right border of a column header.
2. When the pointer changes to ⊹, drag to the desired width as indicated in the ScreenTip.

   OR

1. Select the **Home** tab.
2. Select the **Format** button ⊞.
3. Select **Column Width** on the menu.
4. In the Column Width dialog box, enter the desired width.
5. Select **OK**.

CHANGING ROW HEIGHT

1. Position the mouse pointer on the bottom border of a row header.
2. When the pointer changes to ⬍, drag to the desired height as indicated in the ScreenTip.

   OR

1. Select the **Home** tab.
2. Select the **Format** button ⊞.
3. Select **Row Height** on the menu.
4. In the Row Height dialog box, enter the desired width.
5. Select **OK**.

MERGING AND CENTERING ACROSS CELLS

1. Select the cells that you want to merge and center.
2. Select the **Home** tab.
3. Select the **Merge & Center** button ⊞.

MERGING ACROSS CELLS

1. Select the cells that you want to merge.
2. Select the **Home** tab.
3. Select the drop-down arrow on the **Merge & Center** button ⊞.
4. Select **Merge Across**.

MERGING CELLS

1. Select the cells that you want to merge.
2. Select the **Home** tab.
3. Select the drop-down arrow on the **Merge & Center** button ⊞.
4. Select **Merge Cells**.

REMOVING A MERGE

1. Select the cells that you want to unmerge.
2. Select the **Home** tab.
3. Select the drop-down arrow on the **Merge & Center** button ⊞.
4. Select **Unmerge Cells**.

RENAMING A WORKSHEET

1. Double-click the Sheet tab of the worksheet to rename.
2. Type the new name.
3. Press **Enter**.

   OR

1. Right-click the Sheet tab of the worksheet to rename.
2. Select **Rename**.
3. Type the new name.
4. Press **Enter**.

   OR

1. Select the Sheet tab of the worksheet to rename.
2. Select the **Home** tab.
3. Select the **Format** command.
4. Select **Rename Sheet**.
5. Type the new name.
6. Press **Enter**.

ENTERING AN ABSOLUTE CELL REFERENCE

Type a dollar sign (**$**) before the column letter and a dollar sign (**$**) before the row number of the cell reference.

OR

Press **F4** to insert the dollar signs.

Additional Excel 2016 Procedures

HIDING THE RIBBON

1. Double-click the selected tab to hide the Ribbon.
2. Double-click the tab to redisplay the Ribbon.

SPLITTING A WORKSHEET INTO PANES

1. Select the cell to the right and below where you want the split to occur.
2. Select the **View** tab.
3. Select the **Split** button.

Removing a Split

1. Select the **View** tab.
2. Select the **Split** button.

SWITCHING BETWEEN OPEN WORKBOOKS

1. Select the **View** tab.
2. Select the **Switch Windows** button.
3. Select the desired workbook.

   OR

   Hover the mouse pointer over the Excel button on the taskbar, and select one of the other open workbooks.

ARRANGING MULTIPLE WORKBOOKS

1. Select the **View** tab.
2. Select the **Arrange All** button.
3. In the Arrange Windows dialog box, select the desired arrangement.
4. Select **OK**.

USING FIND AND REPLACE

1. Select the **Home** tab.
2. Select the **Find & Select** button.
3. On the menu, select **Replace**.
4. In the Find and Replace dialog box, enter the text or values you want to find in the Find what box.
5. Enter the replacement text or values in the Replace with box.
6. Select the **Options** button to further specify the search.
7. Select **Find Next** to find each occurrence and then **Replace** to replace each occurrence. Select **Replace All** to replace all occurrences.
8. Select **Close**.

CHECKING THE SPELLING IN A WORKSHEET

1. Select the **Review** tab.
2. Select the **Spelling** button.
3. Misspelled words are displayed in the Spelling dialog box, where you can choose to ignore or change them.

ENTERING DATES

Press **Ctrl + ;** to insert the current date in the mm/dd/yyyy format.

OR

1. Select the **Home** tab.
2. Select the **Number Format** drop-down arrow.
3. From the gallery, select **Short Date** or **Long Date**.

COPYING FORMATS

1. Select the cell whose formats you want to copy.

2. Select the **Home** tab.

3. Select the **Format Painter** button ⬚.

4. Select the cell to which you want to copy the formats.

    OR

1. Double-click the **Format Painter** button ⬚.

2. Select each cell to which you want to copy the formats.

3. Press **Esc**.

INSERTING COMMENTS

1. Select the cell where you want to insert the comment.

2. Select the **Review** tab.

3. Select the **New Comment** button ⬚.

4. Type the comment text.

Deleting a Comment

1. Select the cell containing the comment.

2. Select the **Review** tab.

3. Select the **Delete** button ⬚.

RESOLVING A #### ERROR MESSAGE

Double-click the right border of the column header to resize the column to the longest entry.

OR

1. Select the **Home** tab.

2. Select the **Format** button ⬚.

3. Select **AutoFit Column Width** on the menu.

WORKING WITH RANGES

Filling Range Cells with the Same Entry

1. Select the range.

2. Type the entry.

3. Press **Ctrl + Enter**.

Filling a Range with a Series

1. Select the cells with the series starting value(s).

2. Select the **Home** tab.

3. Select the **Fill** button ⬚.

4. Select **Series** on the menu.

5. In the Series dialog box, specify if the series will fill a row or column, the type of series, and the step and stop values.

6. Select **OK**.

Making a Range Entry Using a Collapse Dialog Box Button

1. In the dialog box, select the **Collapse Dialog** button ⬚, which normally appears at the end of the text box in which you are to enter the range address.

2. In the worksheet, select the range.

3. Select the **Collapse Dialog** button ⬚ to redisplay the dialog box.

USING AUTOFILL

Using AutoFill to Complete a Series

1. Select the range that will begin the series.

2. Select the **AutoFill** handle ⬚ and drag to the desired cell to complete the series.

Using AutoFill to Create a Trend

1. Select the range that will begin the series.

2. Right-click the **AutoFill** handle ⬚ and drag to the desired cell to complete the series.

3. When you release the mouse button, select the desired trend on the shortcut menu.

Using the Fill Button to Create a Linear Trend

1. Select the range that will begin the series.

2. Select the **Home** tab.

3. Select the **Fill** button ⬚.

4. Select **Series**.

5. In the Series dialog box, select **Rows** or **Columns** for the direction to fill.

6. Select the **Linear** type of series.

   Enter a step and stop value if desired.

7. Select **OK**.

EDITING A FORMULA

- Click in the cell and type a new formula to replace the existing formula.

- Double-click in the cell and move the insertion point as necessary to edit the formula.

- Select the cell, click in the formula bar, and move the insertion point as necessary to edit the formula.

- Select the cell, press **F2**, and move the insertion point as necessary to edit the formula.

USING FORMULAS

Copying a Formula Using the Fill Handle

1. Select the cell.

2. Drag the fill handle ⊞ to copy the formula to the desired cells.

Creating a 3-D Reference in a Formula

1. Select the cell where you want to enter the formula.

2. To enter a cell reference or range from another worksheet, select the sheet tab, select the cell or range of cells, and press **Enter**.

   OR

   Type the sheet name and cell reference or range address directly in the formula using the following guidelines:

   - Use an exclamation point (!) to separate the sheet name(s) from the cell reference(s).

   - Use a colon (:) between sheet names to indicate a range of worksheets.

   - Use single quotation marks to surround a sheet name that contains a space.

Displaying and Hiding Formulas

1. Select the **Formulas** tab.

2. Select the **Show Formulas** button 🖾.

3. Select the **Show Formulas** button 🖾 again to hide formulas.

   OR

   Press **Ctrl + `** to toggle formulas on and off.

Printing Formulas

1. Select the **Formulas** tab.

2. Select the **Show Formulas** button 🖾.

3. Select **File**.

4. Select **Print**.

5. In the Backstage view, select the **Print** button 🖨.

WORKING WITH FUNCTIONS

Entering a Function

1. Select the cell in which you want to enter the function.

2. Type **=**, the function name, and then **(**.

3. Type the range address or drag over the range on which you want to perform the function.

4. Type a **)**.

5. Press **Enter**.

Inserting Other Functions

1. Select the cell in which you want to enter the function.

2. Select the **Formulas** tab.

3. Select one of the function category buttons and select the desired function from the menu.

   OR

   Select the **More Functions** button 🔲, point to a category, and select the desired function.

PREVIEWING AND PRINTING A WORKSHEET

Previewing and Printing a File

1. Select **File**.
2. Select **Print**.
3. Check the preview in the Backstage view.
4. Select the **Print** button 🖶.

Changing Print Options

1. Select **File**.
2. Select **Print**.
3. In the Copies box, type the number of copies to print.

   OR

   Click the increment arrows to set the number of copies to print.
4. Under Settings, specify the page setup options as desired.

Printing a Selection

1. Select the range you want to print.
2. Select **File**.
3. Select **Print**.
4. In the Backstage view, under Settings, select the first drop-down arrow.
5. Select **Print Selection**.
6. Select the **Print** button 🖶.

FORMATTING WORKSHEETS

Selecting a Preset Margin

1. Select the **Layout** tab.
2. Select the **Margins** button 🗔.
3. Select the desired margin setting.

Setting Custom Margins

1. Select the **Layout** tab.
2. Select the **Margins** button 🗔.
3. Select **Custom Margins**.
4. Under Margins, set the margins as desired.
5. Select **OK**.

Selecting a Paper Size

1. Select the **Layout** tab.
2. Select the **Size** button 🗔.
3. Select the desired page size.

Setting Page Orientation

1. Select the **Layout** tab.
2. Select the **Orientation** button 🗔.
3. Select **Portrait** or **Landscape**.

Scaling to Fit

1. Select the **Layout** tab.
2. Select the **Scale to Fit** dialog box launcher 🗔.
3. In the Page Setup dialog box, on the Page tab, select the **Fit to** button.
4. Adjust the Fit to settings as desired.
5. Select **OK**.

INSERTING A BUILT-IN HEADER OR FOOTER

Using the Insert Tab

1. Select the **Insert** tab.
2. Select the **Header & Footer** button 🗔.
3. Click in the placeholders and type the desired header or footer text.

   OR

   From the menu of built-in headers or footers, select the desired format.

   OR

1. Select the **Header & Footer Tools Design** tab.
2. Select an element to insert it as desired.

Using Page Layout View

1. Switch to Page Layout view, if necessary.
2. Select a placeholder in either the header or footer area.
3. Select the **Header & Footer Tools Design** tab.

4. Select the **Header** button ▯ or the **Footer** button ▭.

5. Select the desired built-in option from the menu.

Using the Page Setup Dialog Box

1. Select the **Layout** tab.

2. Select the **Page Setup** dialog box launcher ▣.

3. In the Page Setup dialog box, select the **Header/Footer** tab.

4. Select the **Header** drop-down arrow or the **Footer** drop-down arrow.

5. Select the desired header or footer.

6. Select **OK**.

INSERTING A CUSTOM HEADER AND FOOTER

Using Page Layout View

1. Switch to Page Layout view, if necessary.

2. Select the desired placeholder in either the header or footer area.

3. Type the desired text in the placeholder.

OR

Select the **Header & Footer Tools Design** tab.

4. Select a button to insert the desired element.

Using the Page Setup Dialog Box

1. Select the **Layout tab**.

2. Select the **Page Setup** dialog box launcher ▣.

3. In the Page Setup dialog box, select the **Header/Footer** tab.

4. Select the **Custom Header** button or the **Custom Footer** button.

5. In the Header dialog box or the Footer dialog box, type the desired text or use the buttons to enter information in the Left section, Center section, and Right section boxes as desired.

6. Select **OK**.

Changing the Font of a Header or Footer

1. Switch to Page Layout view.

2. Select the text in the header or footer section whose font you want to change.

3. Select the **Home** tab.

4. Use buttons in the Font group to change the font and other formatting as desired.

WORKING WITH EXCEL TABLES

Inserting a Total Row

1. Select any cell in the table.

2. Select the **Table Tools Design** tab.

3. Select the **Total Row** check box.

Converting a Table to a Range

1. Select any cell in the table.

2. Select the **Table Tools Design** tab.

3. Select the **Convert to Range** button ▦.

4. Select **Yes** in the dialog box to confirm the conversion.

Sorting in a Table by Formatting

1. Select the arrow next to the heading of the column by which you want to sort.

2. From the menu, select **Sort by Color**.

3. Select the desired cell or font color.

WORKING WITH CHARTS

Resizing a Chart

1. Click the chart to select it.

2. Position the pointer on a corner handle.

3. When the pointer changes to ⤢, drag to the desired size.

Resizing a Chart Element

1. Click the chart to select it.

2. Select the chart element you want to resize.

3. Drag a corner sizing handle to resize the element as desired.

Moving a Chart Element

1. Click the chart to select it.
2. Select the chart element you want to move.
3. Position the mouse pointer on the border of the element.
4. When the pointer changes to 🔀, drag the element to the desired location.

Deleting a Chart Element

1. Click the chart to select it.
2. Select the chart element you want to delete.
3. Press **Delete**.

Changing Chart Text

1. Select the placeholder for the chart text you want to change, or click within a placeholder and select the text.
2. Edit the text as desired.

   OR

1. Click the chart to select it.
2. Select the **Chart Elements** shortcut button ➕.
3. Select **Data Labels**, **Axis Titles**, or **Chart Title** from the Chart Elements list.
4. Select the arrow and select the desired option.

Changing Data Series Orientation

1. Click the chart to select it.
2. Select the **Chart Tools Design** tab.
3. Select the **Switch Row/Column** button 📊.

COPYING FORMULAS CONTAINING A RELATIVE REFERENCE

1. Select the cell containing the formula you want to copy.
2. Select the **Home** tab.
3. Select the **Copy** button 📋.

   OR

   Press **Ctrl + C**.

4. Select the cell where you want to paste the copied formula.

5. Select the **Home** tab.
6. Select the **Paste** button 📋.

   OR

   Press **Ctrl + V**.

COPYING A FORMULA USING AN ABSOLUTE REFERENCE

1. Select the cell containing the formula you want to copy.
2. Enter a dollar sign (**$**) before both the column letter and row number of the cell you want to make an absolute reference.

   OR

   Press **F4** to insert the dollar signs.

3. Copy the formula using the procedures discussed above.

INSERTING AND DELETING CELLS

Inserting Cells

1. Select the cell that will be below the inserted cell.
2. Select the **Home** tab.
3. Select the **Insert** button 📊.

Deleting Cells

1. Right-click the cell you want to delete.
2. Select **Delete**.
3. In the Delete dialog box, specify the direction in which you want cells to shift.
4. Select **OK**.

APPLYING CONDITIONAL FORMATTING

1. Select the range to which you want to apply the conditional formatting.
2. Select the **Home** tab.
3. Select the **Conditional Formatting** button 📊.
4. Point to the desired type of conditional format.
5. From the format's gallery, select the desired style.

Modifying a Rule

1. Select the **Home** tab.

2. Select the **Conditional Formatting** button 📊.

3. Select **Manage Rules**.

4. In the Conditional Formatting Rules Manager dialog box, select the **Edit Rule** button.

5. Modify the rule as desired.

6. Select **OK**.

7. Select **OK**.

SAVING A WORKBOOK AS A PDF OR XPS FILE

1. Select **File**.

2. Select **Export**.

3. Select **Create PDF/XPS Document**.

4. Select **Create PDF/XPS**.

5. Browse to the location where you want to save the file.

6. In the File name box, enter the name for the file.

7. From the Save as type drop-down list, select either **PDF** or **XPS Document**.

8. Select **Publish**.

INSERTING PICTURES

1. Select the cell where you want to insert the picture.

2. Select the **Insert** tab.

3. Select the **Pictures** button 🖼.

4. In the Insert Picture dialog box, navigate to the location where the picture is stored.

5. Select the picture and select **Insert**.

INSERTING AN ONLINE PICTURE

1. Select the cell where you want to insert the picture.

2. Select the **Insert** tab.

3. Select the **Online Pictures** button 🖼.

4. In the Insert Pictures search box, type the keyword(s) for the clip art you want to insert.

5. Press **Enter**.

6. Select the desired image and select **Insert**.

Customer

Customer_ID
Name
Surname
Address
Age
Postal Code
Email
Gender
Event_ID
Invoice_ID
Order_ID

Invoice_ID
Price
Tax
Date
Due Date
Total

Product

Product_ID
Material_ID
Type
Availability
Stock
Subcontractor_ID

Order

Order_ID
Order_Type

Material

Material_ID
Material_Type

CHAPTER 15

Database Basics

WHAT IS A DATABASE?

What do the following things have in common: a contact list, a catalog of books, and a student roster? For one thing, each is a collection of information. When that information is stored in a format that can be searched, sorted, filtered, and used to generate reports, it is called a database.

A database can exist on paper or on a computer. Imagine a database with millions of pieces of information written on paper! Now, imagine a database of that size stored in a database application program. When a worker must find the account number for a customer, do you think it would be faster and easier to use the paper database, or the computerized database with tools for searching, sorting, and filtering?

The Essentials of a Database

OBJECTIVES

- Describe the basic organization of a database.

- Explain the use of tables and fields in a database.

- Recognize types of data and metadata.

AS YOU READ

ORGANIZE INFORMATION As you read the lesson, use a concept web to help you organize basic facts about databases.

TERMINOLOGY

- data

- database

- data mining

- datasheet

- data type

- field

- form

- garbage in, garbage out (GIGO)

- metadata

- object

- properties

- record

- table

Database Organization

A **database** is a collection of information organized so that it is easy to locate, analyze, and manipulate the specific data you need. But, what makes up a database? How is one organized? Picture a file cabinet in a company's human resources office. Inside the cabinet there are folders for each employee. Inside each folder there are pieces of paper about that employee. On each piece of paper there are specific details, such as hiring date, emergency contact information, salary history, and so on.

A database has a similar structure as the file cabinet. Instead of folders, a database has one or more tables. Instead of pieces of paper, the database has records. Instead of written bits of information, there are fields.

TABLES In a database, **objects** are the elements used to store, enter, and manage data. The most common object is a table. A database **table**, like a spreadsheet, is a grid of columns and rows into which you enter data. Sometimes, a table is called a **datasheet**. Most databases have one or more tables, just as a file cabinet holds many folders. Each table contains a collection of related data. Although databases can store data in one large table, it is more typical to divide databases into smaller tables. For example, your school's database might contain one table for students and one for staff.

RECORDS Each table row stores related information about one individual or item. Each of these units is called a **record**. For your school's student database, each unit of information, or record, stores information about one student.

FIELDS Each table column stores a specific piece of information, such as last name or date of birth. Each of these units is called a **field**. Each field is set up so that only a certain type of information, called the **data type**, is permitted in that field. For example, a Phone field only accepts entries for telephone numbers.

DID YOU KNOW?

Many government agencies store personal information about people in databases. You have legal rights to the information that pertains to you. If you find incorrect information, the agencies are required by law to amend your records.

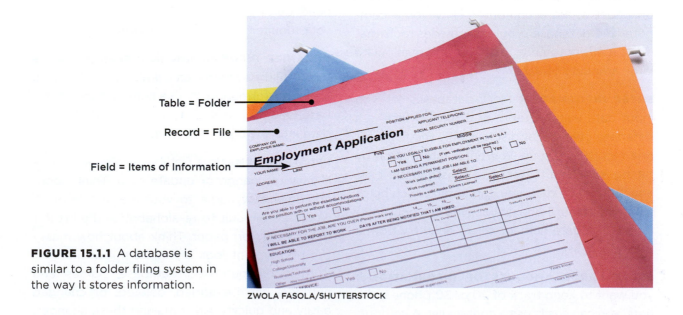

Table = Folder
Record = File
Field = Items of Information

FIGURE 15.1.1 A database is similar to a folder filing system in the way it stores information.

ZWOLA FASOLA/SHUTTERSTOCK

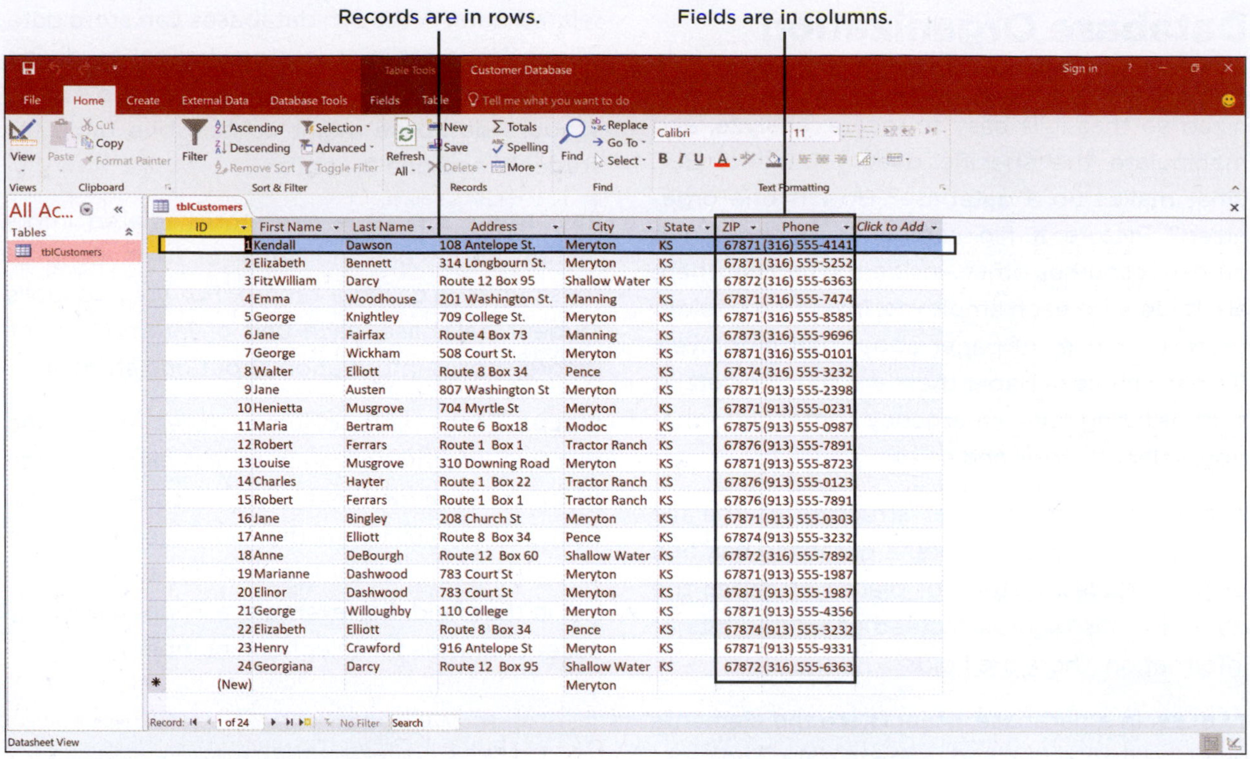

Records are in rows.　　　Fields are in columns.

FIGURE 15.1.2 A Customer table can be set up with fields for contact information such as first name, last name, address, and telephone number.

Advantages of a Database Program

Smaller databases might just as easily be kept on paper as on a computer. However, a computerized database program provides tools that make it easier to enter, manage, and manipulate large amounts of data.

ENTER INFORMATION Most databases let you input data using a table or a **form**, which is a database object that displays only the fields for one record at a time. You enter information by typing in a field. Often, rules restrict the type and amount of data you can enter, which helps minimize errors. For example, you can only enter a date in a date field, or select an entry from a drop-down list.

STORE LARGE AMOUNTS OF INFORMATION If you want to keep track of 20 or 30 phone numbers, you can easily use a contact list. A computerized database, however, can hold thousands, or even millions, of telephone numbers.

FIND INFORMATION QUICKLY A computerized database can save you time in finding information. Powerful **data mining** tools let you search through large amounts of data to find what you need quickly, and then let you easily change your requirements to find something else.

ORGANIZE INFORMATION IN DIFFERENT WAYS Paper filing systems can limit your ability to arrange information. With a computerized database, you can easily sort, re-sort, and filter the data into any order you need.

UPDATE INFORMATION Database software makes it easy to change or update data. Think about adding a new name to your address book. It would be difficult to re-alphabetize the list if it existed only on paper. Think about how messy the book might look after just a few changes. With a computerized database, names and numbers can be added, deleted, or changed easily and quickly. After making these changes, you have an easy-to-read, updated version of the database.

Describing the Data

Data, which is the plural of the word datum, are facts or figures about something. They are bits of information presented without any context or explanation. In order to make sense out of the data, it must be processed or organized in some way. With a database, you enter bits of data into individual fields, but the fields are organized into records, tables, forms, and reports so that you can analyze and interpret it.

IC3✔ Understand what data is.

Bits of information about the data entered in database fields are called **metadata**. Metadata, which is sometimes called **properties**, is data about the data. Metadata is not the data entered in a field. It is data generated by the program to describe the information stored in the database.

For example, metadata includes the data type and number of characters for a field; the name of every table; the name and storage location of the database file itself; and the date and time when the file was last modified. Metadata makes it possible for a program to organize and manage large quantities of information, and makes it easier and faster to search for a specific record, or organize records based on criteria. In Microsoft Access, you can view the metadata for a table and for fields in that table using Design View. In Design View, the Property Sheet pane lists the metadata for the table and the Field Properties panel lists the metadata for the selected field. Select View > Design View to change to Design View.

IC3✔ Know what metadata is.

Accuracy Is Vital

Databases can be useful tools at home and at work. They also have many different uses at school. Administrators can use them to track student performance, payroll, and supplies. Teachers can use them to record students' test scores and attendance. Students can use them to organize their grades or search for information for a project.

REAL-WORLD TECH
PRESERVING ANCIENT ART

Databases are often put to unexpected uses. Because databases can record and store large amounts of information, organizations have come up with creative ways to use them. For example, a database was designed for New Mexico State University to store aerial views of 1,500-year-old American Indian rock art. This database will help preserve a natural art form that is vanishing due to erosion and vandalism.

ZBRAMWELL/SHUTTERSTOCK

How might you use a database to record information about the culture of your family or your community?

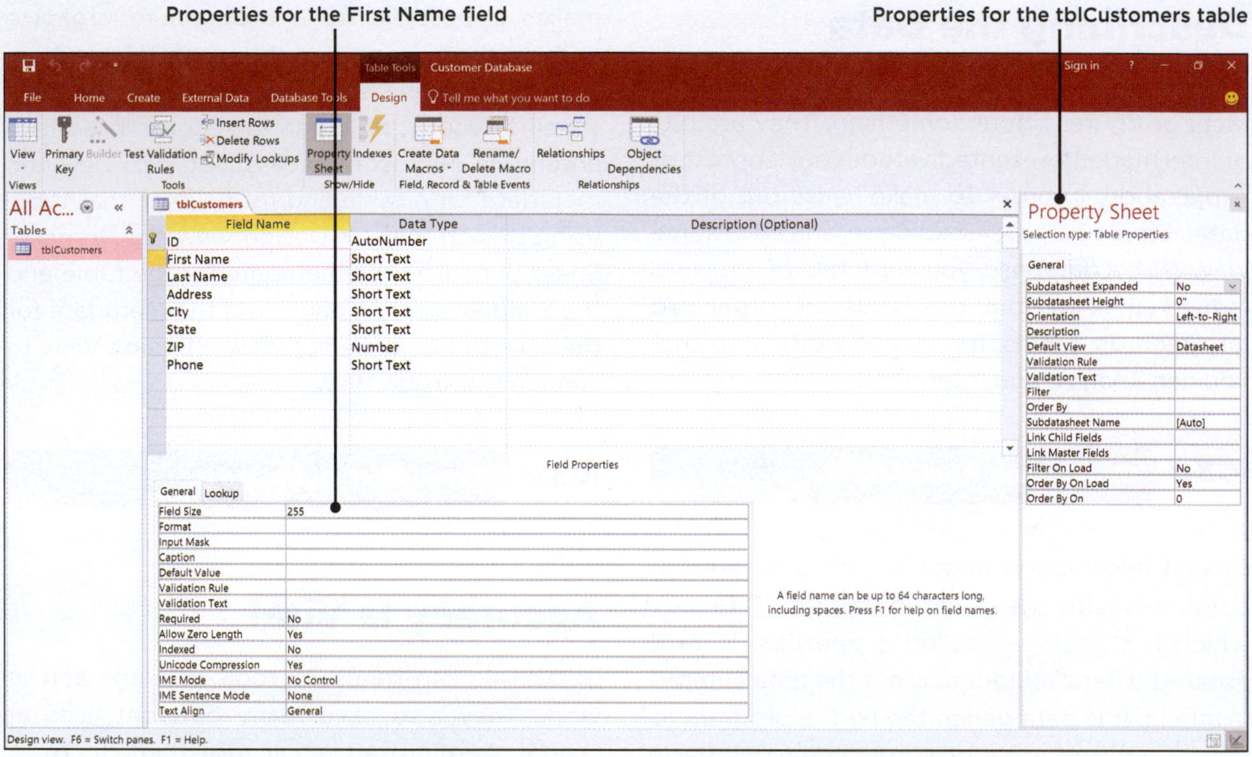

Properties for the First Name field

Properties for the tblCustomers table

FIGURE 15.1.3 Use Design View in Access to view the metadata, or properties, for a table and fields.

However, databases are useful only if they are accurate. In other words, databases are only as good as the data they contain. The acronym *GIGO* explains this principle. **GIGO** is short for "**garbage in, garbage out**." It means that if the information placed in a database is wrong, anyone using that information will get the wrong results. When adding information to a database, it is very important to do so accurately and to check your entries.

Types of Database Programs

OBJECTIVES

- Summarize the purpose of a database management system.

- Compare and contrast types of database management programs.

- Evaluate the characteristics of a well-designed database.

AS YOU READ

OUTLINE As you read the lesson, use an outline to help identify types of database management systems and characteristics of good design.

TERMINOLOGY

- database management system (DBMS)

- flat-file database

- key field

- object-oriented database

- relational database

- sort

Database Management Systems

A **database management system (DBMS)**, is software used to manage the storage, organization, processing, and retrieval of data in a database. There are several kinds of database management programs, including flat-file databases, relational databases, object-oriented databases, and multimedia databases.

FLAT-FILE DATABASES A **flat-file database** allows you to work with data in only one table. A computerized address book is one example. In flat-file databases, records can be retrieved randomly. That is, you can look for just one name on a list. You can also retrieve an entire table and **sort** the data, which means to arrange it in a specific order. You might sort to find all the people living in the same town, for example.

Flat-file databases have a limitation. The data in one table cannot be linked to the data in another table. That might not be a problem with a simple address book. However, many businesses and other large organizations use databases in more complex ways, and they need added flexibility.

RELATIONAL DATABASES A **relational database** can use data from several tables at the same time. This is because the tables are linked by a **key field**. A key field is field that is found in each table. For example, a part number field might be in a Products table, a Supplier table, and a Customer Order table. When there is a key field in multiple tables, you can create a relationship between the tables so that you can analyze and report on all the information at the same time.

A relational database is more complex than a flat-file database program. It also requires more skill to use and costs more. However, its greater power makes it more useful. Microsoft Access is a relational database.

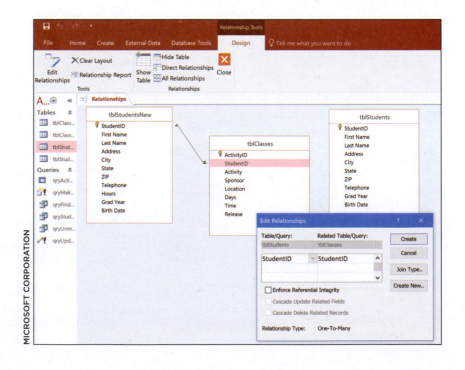

MICROSOFT CORPORATION

FIGURE 15.2.1 Creating a relationship between tables with Microsoft Access.

DID YOU KNOW?

A natural language database allows you to ask for data using the same standard language you would use when addressing another person.

To create a relationship between tables in an Access database, make the Database Tools tab on the Ribbon active and select the Relationships button. Select the tables and/or queries you want to relate and then select Add. Drag a line from the key field in one table to the key field in another table. Select options in the Edit Relationships dialog box, and select Create.

Think about a relational database a school might have. One table might hold all students' schedules. Another might have all their grades. Yet another table might include their addresses and phone numbers. All the tables can be linked by a key field: each student's name or student identification number. By using key fields, administrators can create a report about a particular student using data from all available tables.

Businesses can link their relational databases by customer names and numbers. Companies use these databases for many purposes, including storing customer information, such as name, address, and telephone number; seeing where to ship goods the customer buys; issuing bills for purchases and receipts for payments made; and tracking what customers have bought over time and using that information to tailor ads and promotions.

IC3✔ Know basic concepts of a relational database: tables, fields, and data.

OBJECT-ORIENTED DATABASES Another type of DBMS is called an **object-oriented database**. Instead of using tables, these databases represent data in objects, such as documents, video clips, and audio clips. Each object contains both that data and the program needed to display that data, including showing a graphic or playing a sound.

MULTIMEDIA DATABASES Traditional databases can store all kinds of text and numerical data. Today's computers also often deal with pictures, sounds, animation, or video clips. Multimedia professionals use databases to catalog media files, such as art, photographs, maps, video clips, and sound files. Media files themselves generally are not stored in databases because they are too large. Instead, a multimedia database serves as an index to all the separately stored files. Users can search through the index and then locate the particular file they want.

Well-Designed Databases

For databases to be effective, they need to be planned carefully. There are three basic characteristics of good database design.

ENSURING DATA SECURITY The same features that make databases efficient tools make them vulnerable to invasions of privacy. Personal information can be misused. Requiring users to input a password before they can access data is one way of keeping a database secure.

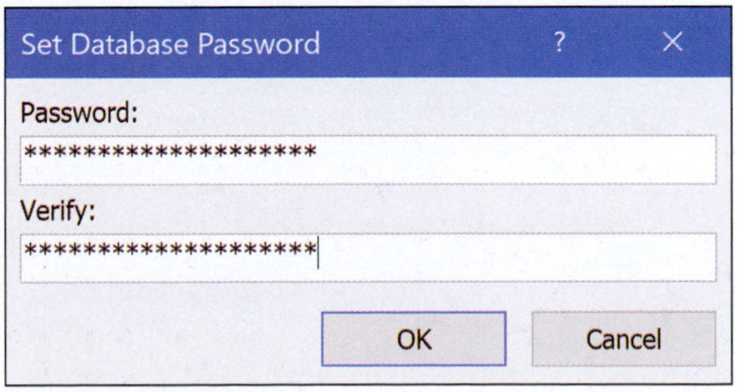

MICROSOFT CORPORATION

FIGURE 15.2.2 Setting a password that users must enter is one way to protect data.

PRESERVING DATA INTEGRITY The accuracy and validity of the information gives a database its data integrity. Errors make the database less accurate and less useful. Steps can be taken during design and data entry to help protect against errors. For example, double checking all typed entries is an obvious first step. Selecting the correct data type and length for a field helps avoid incorrect entries.

AVOIDING DATA REDUNDANCY Repeating the same data in many tables wastes space by requiring a computer to store the same information more than once. It also increases the amount of work needed to update records because the data needs to be changed in more than one place. That, in turn, increases the chance of errors and slows down searches for data. Properly designing a database so that data is stored in only one table and then linked to other tables helps avoid data redundancy. It also makes the data available for use in various ways.

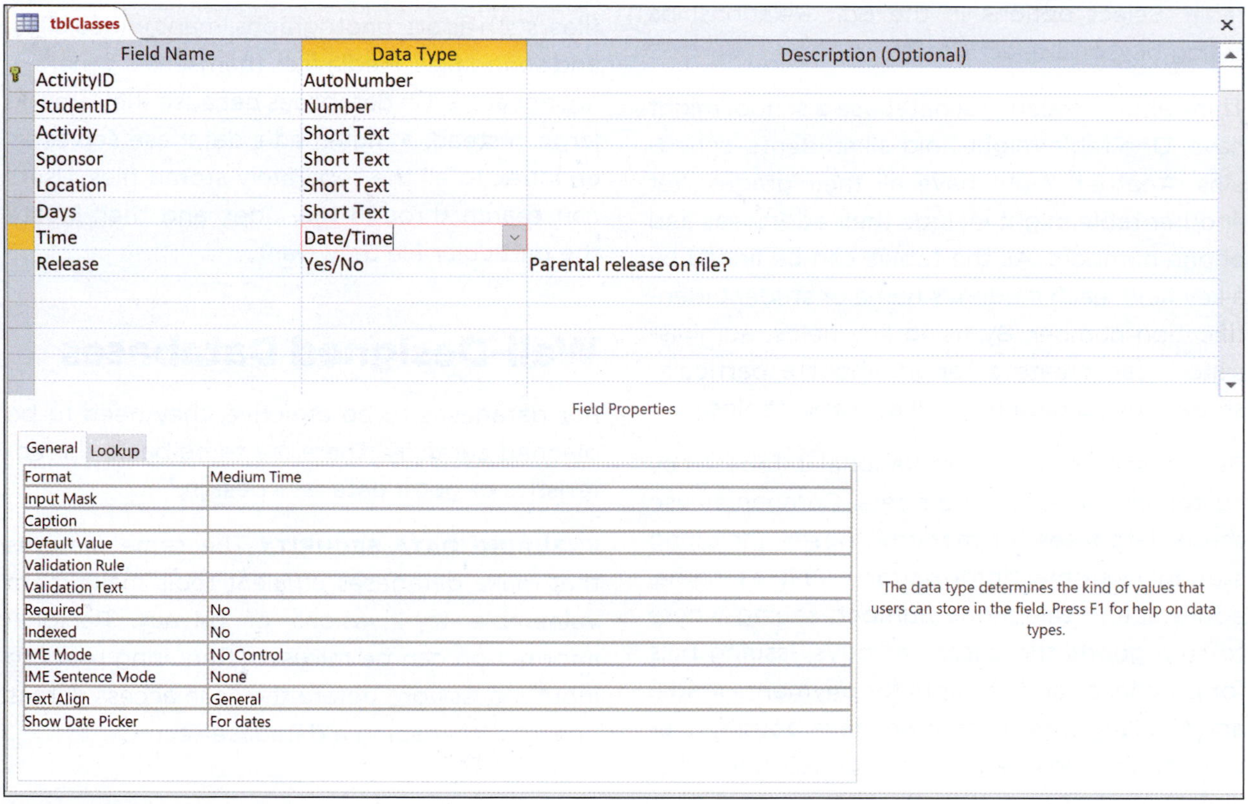

tblClasses			✕
Field Name	**Data Type**	**Description (Optional)**	
ActivityID	AutoNumber		
StudentID	Number		
Activity	Short Text		
Sponsor	Short Text		
Location	Short Text		
Days	Short Text		
Time	Date/Time		
Release	Yes/No	Parental release on file?	

Field Properties

General | Lookup

Format	Medium Time
Input Mask	
Caption	
Default Value	
Validation Rule	
Validation Text	
Required	No
Indexed	No
IME Mode	No Control
IME Sentence Mode	None
Text Align	General
Show Date Picker	For dates

The data type determines the kind of values that users can store in the field. Press F1 for help on data types.

MICROSOFT CORPORATION

FIGURE 15.2.3 Assigning the correct data type and setting field properties can help avoid data entry errors.

Database Techniques

OBJECTIVES

- Give examples of how to manage information in databases.

- Compare and contrast browsing, sorting, and querying data in a database.

- Describe the features of a report template.

AS YOU READ

SUMMARIZE As you read the lesson, use a chart to help you summarize techniques for using databases effectively.

TERMINOLOGY

- ascending order

- browse

- descending order

- information overload

- query

- report

- report template

Information Management

Computers can produce too much information, or **information overload**. Database creators can help manage data using techniques such as summarizing, filtering, and sorting.

- Summarizing information so that database users are not overwhelmed by details

- Filtering data in reports to include only what is necessary to meet specific user needs

- Sorting and grouping data in a specific order so that it is easier to view and understand

Locating Records in a Database

Entering data into a database is of little use if you cannot retrieve the information when you need it. One way to find data is to **browse**, or look through, all the records. You can browse through a table or use a form to display each record on a separate screen. Most database programs provide keyboard commands and other tools, such as scroll bars and navigation buttons that help users browse through records.

If you know some of the data in a record you want to locate, you can use the Find command to locate it quickly. In Microsoft Access, select the Find command on the Home tab of the Ribbon to open the Find and Replace dialog box. There, you enter data you know is entered in the record, specify whether to look in the current field or the whole document; whether to match the content in an entire field or just part of the field; and whether to search all records or just the previous or next records. You can also select whether or not to match the case. When you select Find Next, the program highlights the next record that matches your criteria. Using Find can greatly reduce the time it takes to locate or review specific records.

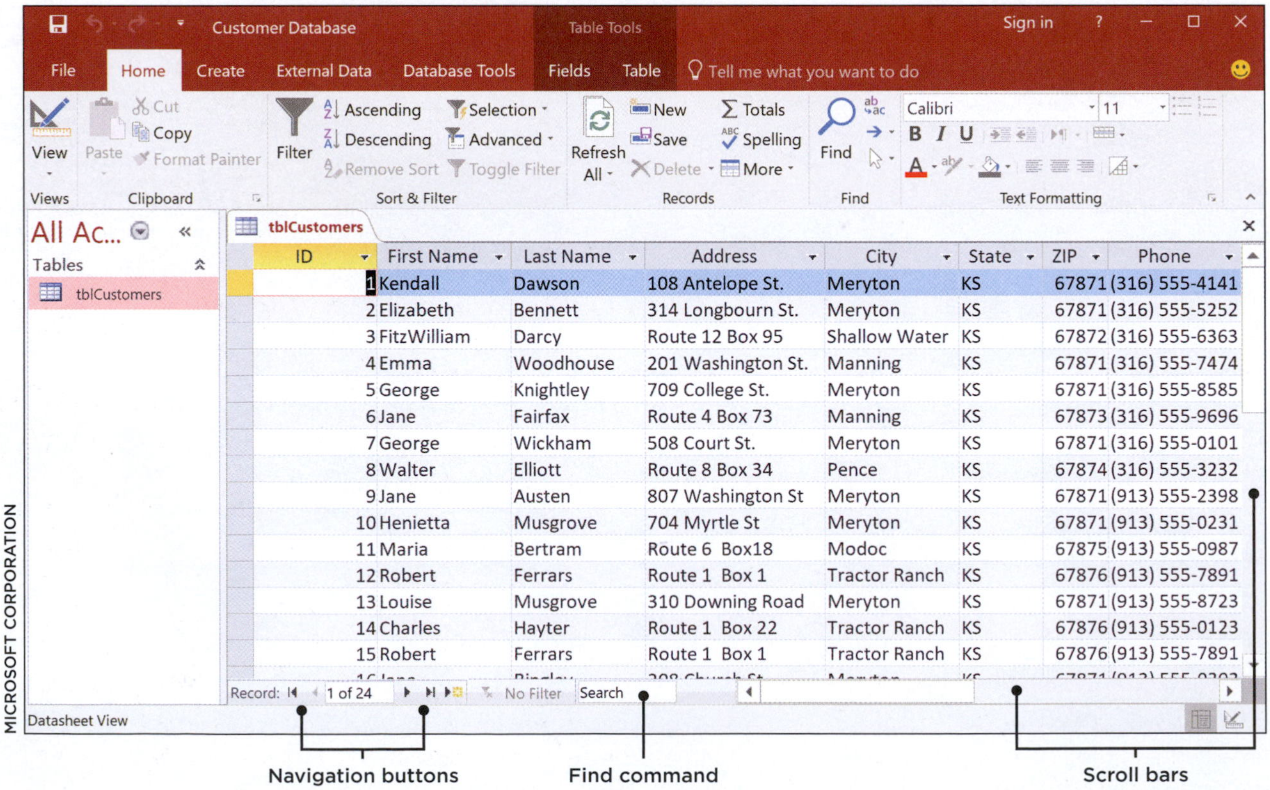

FIGURE 15.3.1 Navigation buttons and other tools allow users to move quickly through a large database table.

Sorting Data

Sorting records in a database is one way to keep the data organized, making it easier to find what you need when you need it.

TYPES OF SORTING Databases sort data based on the content in one or more fields. There are three types of sorts:

- Alphabetical sorting of letters and symbols
- Numerical sorting of numbers and values
- Chronological sorting of dates and times

Data can be sorted in **ascending order**, in which values increase, such as A, B, C or 1, 2, 3. It can also be sorted the opposite way, in **descending order**. In this order, values decrease. Letters are listed C, B, and A, and numbers are sorted 3, 2, and 1.

SINGLE AND MULTIPLE SORTS A basic sort uses a single field, such as last name. In Access, to sort a table based on a single field, click in the field by which you want to sort and select the Ascending or Descending button in the Sort & Filter group on the Home tab of the Ribbon. To sort based on multiple fields, such as last name and then by first name, you use a query.

TECHNOLOGY@WORK

A database report must contain basic information so that workers can access and use it correctly.

THINK ABOUT IT!

Think about what kind of information a report should have. Which of the fields below do you think a hospital's medical staff would want in a report about patients?

- patient's name
- special dietary needs
- room number
- attending doctor
- diagnosis
- medicines prescribed

Querying Data

Another tool for finding and displaying specific information is a query. A **query** is an object based on a set of rules that defines which records and which fields in those records should display on-screen. A query does not change the data entered in the database tables; it just specifies how to display the data.

StudentID	First Name	Last Name	Birth Date
1	Kendall	Dawson	3/25/1998
2	Elizabeth	Bennett	12/29/1997
3	FitzWilliam	Darcy	6/12/1996
4	Emma	Woodhouse	8/4/1998
5	George	Knightley	2/7/1997
6	Jane	Fairfax	11/20/1996
7	George	Wickham	9/22/2000
8	Walter	Elliott	7/4/1996
9	Jane	Austen	4/3/2000
10	Henietta	Musgrove	9/22/1996
11	Maria	Bertram	2/3/1998
12	Robert	Ferrars	4/9/2000
13	Louise	Musgrove	8/3/1998
14	Charles	Hayter	1/8/1997
15	Robert	Ferrars	5/11/1997
16	Jane	Bingley	4/15/1998
17	Anne	Elliott	2/4/2000
18	Anne	DeBourgh	1/4/2000
19	Marianne	Dashwood	6/8/2000
20	Elinor	Dashwood	7/8/1998
21	George	Willoughby	7/2/1997
22	Elizabeth	Elliott	7/4/1996
23	Henry	Crawford	7/6/1997
24	Georgiana	Darcy	12/29/2000

StudentID	First Name	Last Name	Birth Date
9	Jane	Austen	4/3/2000
2	Elizabeth	Bennett	12/29/1997
11	Maria	Bertram	2/3/1998
16	Jane	Bingley	4/15/1998
23	Henry	Crawford	7/6/1997
3	FitzWilliam	Darcy	6/12/1996
24	Georgiana	Darcy	12/29/2000
19	Marianne	Dashwood	6/8/2000
20	Elinor	Dashwood	7/8/1998
1	Kendall	Dawson	3/25/1998
18	Anne	DeBourgh	1/4/2000
8	Walter	Elliott	7/4/1996
17	Anne	Elliott	2/4/2000
22	Elizabeth	Elliott	7/4/1996
6	Jane	Fairfax	11/20/1996
12	Robert	Ferrars	4/9/2000
15	Robert	Ferrars	5/11/1997
14	Charles	Hayter	1/8/1997
5	George	Knightley	2/7/1997
10	Henietta	Musgrove	9/22/1996
13	Louise	Musgrove	8/3/1998
7	George	Wickham	9/22/2000
21	George	Willoughby	7/2/1997
4	Emma	Woodhouse	8/4/1998

StudentID	First Name	Last Name	Birth Date
24	Georgiana	Darcy	12/29/2000
7	George	Wickham	9/22/2000
19	Marianne	Dashwood	6/8/2000
12	Robert	Ferrars	4/9/2000
9	Jane	Austen	4/3/2000
17	Anne	Elliott	2/4/2000
18	Anne	DeBourgh	1/4/2000
4	Emma	Woodhouse	8/4/1998
13	Louise	Musgrove	8/3/1998
20	Elinor	Dashwood	7/8/1998
16	Jane	Bingley	4/15/1998
1	Kendall	Dawson	3/25/1998
11	Maria	Bertram	2/3/1998
2	Elizabeth	Bennett	12/29/1997
23	Henry	Crawford	7/6/1997
21	George	Willoughby	7/2/1997
15	Robert	Ferrars	5/11/1997
5	George	Knightley	2/7/1997
14	Charles	Hayter	1/8/1997
6	Jane	Fairfax	11/20/1996
10	Henietta	Musgrove	9/22/1996
8	Walter	Elliott	7/4/1996
22	Elizabeth	Elliott	7/4/1996
3	FitzWilliam	Darcy	6/12/1996

FIGURE 15.3.2 Sorting lets you organize data so it best suits your needs. The records on the left are sorted in ascending order by StudentID. The records in the middle are sorted in ascending order by Last Name. The records on the right are sorted in descending order by Birth Date.

In Access, you create a query by selecting a table or tables to use and then selecting the fields to display. You can further define the query by entering criteria to match in each field. For example, you could specify to only display records with a purchase date before January 1, 2019, and/or only records for products costing between $10.00 and $25.00. You can also select one or more sort fields in the query. When you run the query, the program displays only the records that match the specified criteria.

Generating Reports

To display and analyze information in a database, you can create a report based on a table or a query. A **report** is a database object that displays data from a table or query in an easy-to-read format. Reports can display data in columns, as labels, or as single records. Reports may be printed on paper or displayed on-screen so that people can read them and interpret the data.

Reports are really just a format and a layout; the data is stored in the database. When you generate the report to view or print, the program uses the data currently available. If you save the report and generate it again later, the data will show updates made to the database.

SPECIFYING DATA FOR A REPORT A report can include data from tables and queries. You select an object and then select the fields from that object to include in the report. You can also choose whether or not to group or sort the data in the report.

DESIGNING A REPORT In most databases, users design a **report template**, which is a format that controls how the data will be displayed. Most report templates include many common features.

- A report header that appears at the beginning of a report, such as the report title

- A report footer that appears at the end of a report, such as summary totals or averages

- A page header that appears at the top of each page, such as field headings

- A page footer that appears at the bottom of each page, such as the date the report was printed and the page number

- The arrangement of the data that you want the report to include

REVIEW THE TERMINOLOGY

DIRECTIONS Match each vocabulary term in the left column with the correct definition in the right column.

1. database
2. record
3. field
4. data type
5. GIGO
6. database management system
7. flat-file database
8. relational database
9. key field
10. ascending order

a. smallest part of a database; holds an individual piece of data

b. term that stresses the importance of inputting accurate data

c. examples are A, B, C and 1, 2, 3

d. organized collection of information stored on computer

e. database that allows you to work with data in only one table

f. part of a database that holds data about a particular person or item

g. software used to manage the storage, organization, processing, and retrieval of data in a database

h. database in which shared key fields link data among tables

i. limited kind of information that can be entered into a field

j. element that links tables

USE THE TERMINOLOGY

DIRECTIONS Complete each sentence with information from the chapter.

1. Some databases have only one _____, but others can hold several, each containing a set of related data.

2. Database programs are superior to paper databases in part because the information can be _____ in different ways.

3. GIGO is a reminder that a database is of poorer quality if the _____ is not accurate.

4. The kind of database that stores and opens programs for images, video clips, and audio clips is a(n) _____.

5. A multimedia database is similar to a book _____.

6. Protecting sensitive data by requiring users to input a(n) _____ is one way to aim for data security.

7. Data _____ is usually undesirable because it wastes space and introduces the possibility of errors.

8. One way that databases can be used to reduce information overload is to _____ information so that users are not overwhelmed by details.

9. Dates and times are sorted in _____ order.

10. You can create multiple _____ to tailor the reports generated from a database.

THINK CRITICALLY

DIRECTIONS Answer the following questions.

1. What is data, and how is it different from metadata?
2. What is the difference between a flat-file database and a relational database?
3. What can you do to try to ensure the accuracy of the data you enter into a database?
4. Identify and explain the purpose of fields in a database.
5. Identify and explain the purpose of records in a database.

EXTEND YOUR KNOWLEDGE

DIRECTIONS Choose and complete one of the following projects.

1. Select a magazine in your school library, and create a database of the articles featured in that issue. Include such fields as author, title, topic, and starting page number. Add another field for date of the issue, and add some records from another issue of the same magazine. Create a report that displays the data you input. With your teacher's permission, print your report. Then, find another way of presenting the data, and, with your teacher's permission, print that report. Save your database.

2. In small groups, make an appointment to visit a local business. Interview the owner or a key employee about the databases that the business uses. Find out what tables, records, and fields the databases have. Ask how the databases are used. Prepare a brief report summarizing your findings. Present it to the class. Read your report out loud to a partner and listen while your partner reads his or her report out loud to you.

IC3 PREP

1. For each line below, select whether the statement is True or False.

   a. The most common object used in a database is a table.

   b. A database table is a grid of columns and rows into which you enter data, much like a spreadsheet.

   c. Most databases store data in one large table, rather than multiple smaller tables.

2. Fill in the blanks: Each table row is known as a _____; each table column is considered a _____.

    a. record; field   **c.** subject; data

    b. horizontal; vertical   **d.** letter; number

3. In a table of students, which of these would be potential categories in a Field unit? (Select all that apply.)

    a. student name   **c.** number of students

    b. date of birth   **d.** grade point average

4. Put the following steps in order for creating a relationship between tables in an Access database.

    a. Select options in the Edit Relationships dialog box, and then select Create.

    b. Make the Database Tools tab on the Ribbon active and then select the Relationships button.

    c. Drag a line from the key field in one table to the key field in another table.

    d. Select the tables and/or queries you want to relate and then select Add.

5. What type of database does Microsoft Access specialize in?

    a. flat-file database   **c.** object-oriented database

    b. relational database   **d.** multimedia database

IC3 PROCEDURES

STARTING ACCESS AND CREATING A NEW DATABASE

1. Select the **Start** button ⊞ on the Taskbar.

2. Begin typing *Access*.

3. Select **Access 2016** in the Search list.

4. In the Access Welcome screen, click **Blank database**.

5. In the File Name box, type the name of the new database.

6. Select the **Browse** button 📁 and navigate to the location where you want to save the file.

7. Select **Create**.

CREATING A NEW, BLANK DATABASE

1. Select **File**.

2. Select **New**.

3. Select **Blank database**.

4. In the File Name box, type the name of the new database.

5. Select the **Browse** button 📁 and navigate to the location where you want to save the file.

6. Select **Create**.

SAVING CHANGES TO A DATABASE

Select the **Save** button 🔲 on the Quick Access Toolbar.

OR

1. Select **File**.
2. Select **Save**.

SAVING A COPY OF A DATABASE

1. Select **File**.
2. Select **Save As**.
3. Select **Save Database As**.
4. In the Save As dialog box, navigate to the location where you want to save the file.
5. In the File name box, type the database file name.
6. Select **Save**.

CREATING A FIELD IN A TABLE

1. In the open table, at the top of the right-most column, select **Click to Add**.
2. Select the desired field type.
3. Type the field name and press **Enter**.

ADDING RECORDS TO A TABLE

1. Select the first field in the row.
2. Type the field entry.
3. Press **Tab** to move to the next field.
4. Repeat to complete all fields for the record.

CHANGING A FIELD DATA TYPE

1. In Datasheet view, select the field to change.
2. Select the **Table Tools Fields** tab.
3. Select the **Data Type** drop-down arrow Data Type: Short Text ▾.
4. On the menu, select the desired field type.

EDITING FIELD DATA

1. Double-click the field.
2. Type to replace the existing data.

   OR

1. Click the field.
2. Position the insertion point and make edits, as necessary.

ADDING A RECORD USING A FORM

1. In Form view, select the **New (blank) record** button ▶ at the bottom of the form.

2. Type the data in the first field.

3. Press Tab.

4. Type the data in the second field.

5. Repeat until record is complete.

CHAPTER 16

Understanding Databases

WHAT MAKES INFORMATION VALUABLE?

Just because information can be stored in a database does not make it valuable. And yet, information is one of the most valuable commodities. Businesses collect, use, and sell information about customers, locations, products, and more. The right information makes it possible for companies to identify trends, target marketing, and track usage.

To be valuable, information must be easy to locate and retrieve; free of errors; relevant to your purpose; reliable; secure; clear and understandable; up-to-date; and verifiable.

Creating an Effective Database

OBJECTIVES

- Describe the parts of a data structure.

- Explain how the structure of a database influences its effectiveness.

- Sequence the steps in creating a data structure.

- Compare and contrast data types.

TERMINOLOGY

- data structure

- field name

- field sequence

- field size

- field width

AS YOU READ

IDENTIFY DETAILS As you read the lesson, use a main idea chart to help you identify important details for creating databases.

Creating a Data Structure

All structures have an underlying frame that determines their size, shape, and general appearance. Databases also have a framework, called a **data structure**. It defines the fields in the database and controls the data that each record will contain.

PARTS OF A DATA STRUCTURE A data structure has four parts:

- The **field sequence** is the order in which the fields will appear in each record.

- The **field name** is a unique identifier for each field, such as "Last Name" or "Class."

- Data type specifies the kind of information the field will contain; for example, numbers, date, text, or hyperlink.

- The **field width**, or **field size**, is a limit on the size of the field, which is typically the number of characters in the largest expected data value. For example, a field width for a U.S. state in an address might be two characters. The field for a phone number might be 10 or 14 characters.

CUSTOMIZING DATA STRUCTURE Most database programs in use today allow you to design a data structure from scratch and define your fields. Many programs also have predesigned database structures that can be customized.

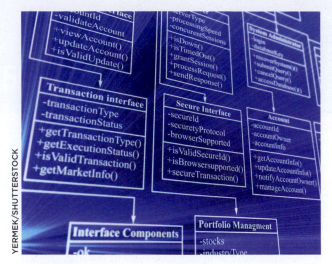

YERMEK/SHUTTERSTOCK

FIGURE 16.1.1 Taking the time to set up a data structure is the first step in creating an effective database.

BENEFITS OF GOOD DESIGN Well-designed data structures can improve database effectiveness. They set up the proper amount of space for the data you will collect. They also enable you to gather the data you need and organize data so that it can be searched efficiently. Poorly designed data structures result in databases that take up unnecessary disk space. They might exclude data that you need. These problems make it more difficult to retrieve the data you need in a meaningful way.

Designing the Data Structure

Generally, a database is used by many people—not just the person who designed it. Users should find the database easy to understand and its tools easy to use. The database should be set up to encourage accurate, efficient data entry and to provide reliable results when running queries and reports. A data structure is usually designed in four steps:

1. Identify the database. You can choose an existing database in which to place the tables or you can create a new database that will contain all the tables, forms, and reports you create.

2. Create the tables. Create each new table to be included in the database, giving each an appropriate name that identifies the data it will store.

3. Identify each field. As you create a table, specify the name, data type, and field size of each field in the table. Many database programs allow you to enter additional properties, or metadata, for fields. Including the following:

   - Default values are used automatically if no data is entered in the field.

   - Input masks are formats that standardize the way data looks, such as dashes between the different parts of all phone numbers.

   - Prompt captions are messages that appear on-screen to help the person entering data understand the content of the field.

   - Validation rules are limits that determine what data is acceptable for a field. For instance, a field for test scores could be limited to values between 0 and 100.

4. Save the data structure. You can always modify a structure later, if you wish. You can add or delete fields, rearrange their order, or modify the field properties. You can also add new tables and make changes to existing ones.

Common Data Types

Assigning a data type to a field is a basic step in creating an efficient database. It helps protect data integrity by limiting the data that can be entered. There are several common data types:

- Text—letters, numbers, and special characters. This is used for a name or an address, for example.

- Number—numeric data that can be used in calculations, such as values that are totaled or averaged.

- Logical—data with only two possible values, such as "yes/no" or "true/false." This might be used to indicate whether a student is male or female.

- Currency—consists of number fields with special formatting to reflect the fact that they represent sums of money. This could be used for billing information.

- Date/time—used to indicate a date or time of day.

- Memo—allows for an unlimited amount of text information. This type is used for notes.

- AutoNumber—automatically assigns a number to each record in the table. This could be used for assigning an identification number to each student, for instance.

- Object—any non-text object. This type is used for an image, sound, or video.

- Hyperlink—connects to a web address.

FIGURE 16.1.2 AutoNumber, Short Text, Number, and Date/Time are just some of the field data types you can assign in Microsoft Access.

Field Name	Data Type	Description (Optional)
StudentID	AutoNumber	
First Name	Short Text	
Last Name	Short Text	
Address	Short Text	
City	Short Text	
State	Short Text	
ZIP	Number	
Telephone	Short Text	
Grad Year	Number	Expected year of graduation.
Birth Date	Date/Time	

MICROSOFT CORPORATION

Maintaining an Efficient Database

OBJECTIVES

- Describe techniques for maintaining data.

- Compare two methods of processing records.

- Explain how adding and deleting data contributes to the efficiency of a database.

AS YOU READ

OUTLINE As you read the lesson, use an outline to help you organize basic information about maintaining databases.

TERMINOLOGY

- batch processing

- data access page

- data maintenance

- form

- online analytical processing (OLAP)

- online transactional processing (OLTP)

- transactional processing

Data Maintenance

You can make sure that a database continues to operate efficiently by performing regular **data maintenance**. This includes tasks such as adding new records, modifying existing records, and deleting those you no longer need. You can modify databases in other ways, too. You might change the reports the database uses. You also might update the structure of the database to reflect your needs.

ADDING DATA Adding records to a database is a common action. When new students enroll at a school, for example, their records must be added to student tables.

MODIFYING DATA Data already stored in a database can be modified or edited to reflect changing conditions or to correct a data entry error. For instance, when a student moves, the school's database can be updated to reflect the new address. If a grade is entered incorrectly, the student's record must be corrected.

DELETING, MOVING, AND LINKING RECORDS Sometimes a record is removed from a database. For instance, a customer might cancel an account with a business. Although you can remove records that are no longer needed, records are typically moved from an active table into an inactive table. For example, when you graduate, your records will probably not be deleted from your school's database but will be moved to a graduate table. The main database might retain only your name, ID number, and graduation date. These will be linked to the complete record in the graduate table.

Linking is done for two reasons. First, it keeps the information available in case it is needed again. Second, it reduces the space and processing time needed when using the active records in the database.

Using Forms

Recall that a **form** is a database object that displays the data for one record at one time. Forms are used for entering, editing, and displaying data. It is generally easier for a user to enter data in a form than to enter it in a table. With only one record displayed, it is more obvious what needs to be entered and where. A form might also include questions or prompts to instruct users on what to enter in each field. Forms are usually based on one table, but they can be created to include fields from multiple tables.

CREATING A FORM Most database programs have tools for automatically creating a form based on the current table. In Access, select the Create tab on the Ribbon and then select Form. The program creates a form that includes all the fields in the table in the default order. Customize it using the Form Layout Tools.

Select Form Wizard on the Create tab if you want the program to prompt you through the steps of creating a form, or Form Design or Blank Form if you want to create a form from scratch. Once you create a form, right-click the form tab to save it and give it a name.

ENTERING DATA IN A FORM When you create a form, you arrange the selected fields in the order in which you want them filled in. Each field includes a label that displays the field name. To enter the data, you type in the first field, and then press Tab to move to the next field.

Database forms may be similar to printed forms used to gather the same information. For example, employees might fill out an emergency contact form, and then someone enters the information into the database system. Increasingly, online database forms are replacing printed forms. That way, the information does not have to be entered twice, and there is less room for error.

IC3 ✔ **Know basic concepts of a relational database: forms.**

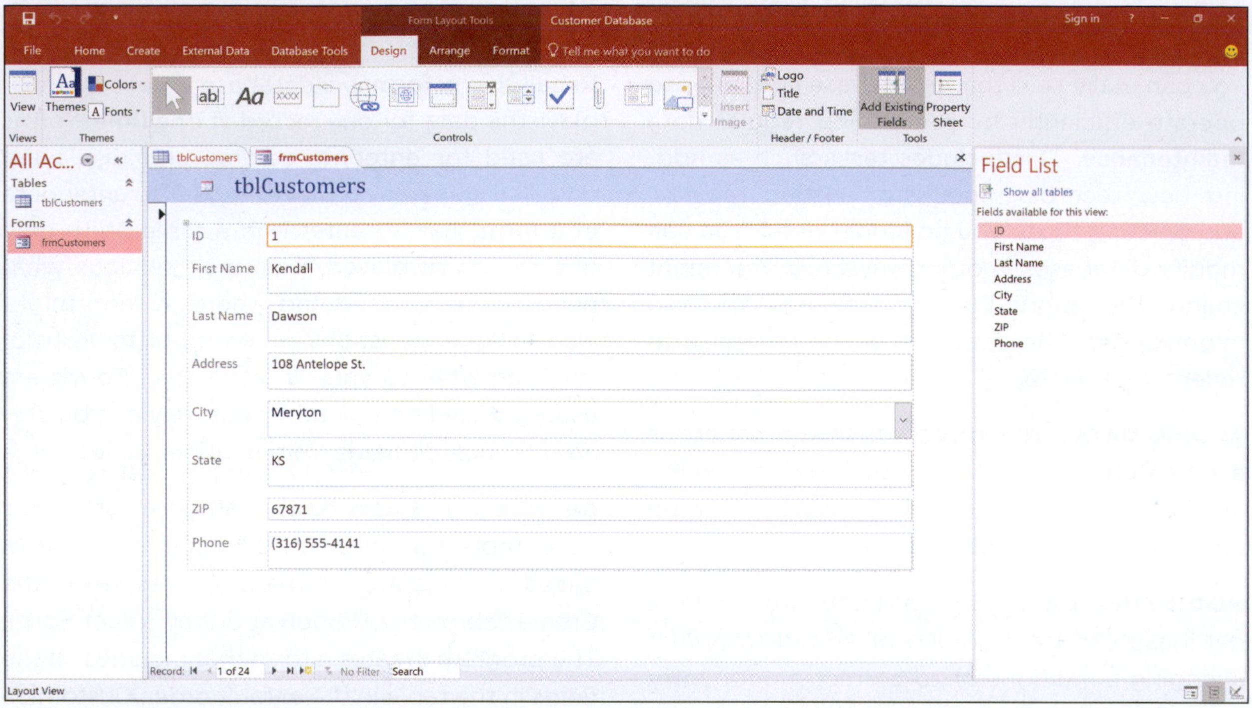

FIGURE 16.2.1 Select Create > Form in Access to create a form with all the fields from the current table.

MICROSOFT CORPORATION

TECHNOLOGY@WORK

Businesses want their databases to be kept up-to-date so they can be more efficient. Suppose a business sends bills to all its customers. If some are sent to the wrong address, payments may be delayed.

THINK ABOUT IT!

Which reasons listed below would require a company to access up-to-date database records?

- send bills
- pay employees
- check inventory
- ship goods
- send catalogs

HOW WEBSITES USE DATABASES Many websites are designed to collect data that can be stored in a database. The site may collect the data so it can customize the information it displays to a particular user, or it may collect the data to use for marketing, or even to sell to other companies. That's why an advertisement for something you just looked at in Amazon might pop up when you log in to your newsfeed site.

Websites use many methods to collect data, including online forms. Whenever you fill out a form on a website, the data is entered into a database. That includes registration forms, contest entry forms, and forms requesting additional information.

Websites use other methods to collect and store data, as well. They can track your browsing history, identify your location using your IP address

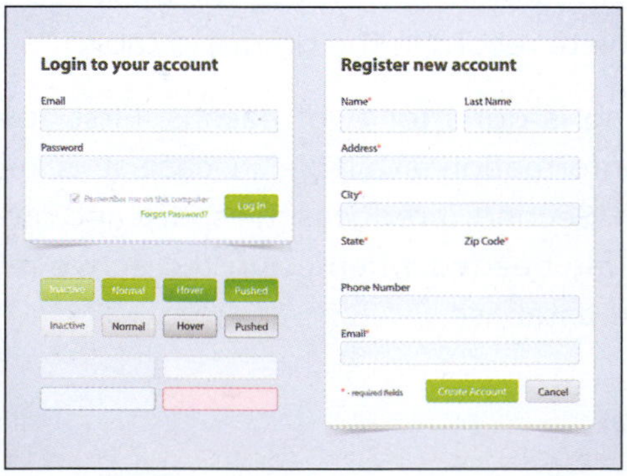

ANGELSID/SHUTTERSTOCK

FIGURE 16.2.2 Websites collect data such as registration information and usage history.

or GPS setting, mine your address book or contact list, and even track tagged photos. They can store all the data they collect in their databases.

As the creator of a database, you might want to provide a portal from a web page to your database. When you want to be able to access a database from the internet, you can create a type of form called a data access page. A **data access page** is basically a form in HTML format so it can be viewed and used in a web browser.

IC3✔ Understand how websites utilize databases.

Keeping a Database Current

Databases typically provide for two methods of updating data: batch processing and transactional processing. People choose a processing method based on how important it is for the data to be completely up-to-date. Batch processing was more common in the past. Most databases today use transactional processing.

BATCH PROCESSING In **batch processing**, the data is recorded as events take place, but the database itself is not updated until there is a group, or batch, of data ready to process. Each batch is processed all at once, typically when the computer is idle, such as in the late evening—this frees up memory for more extensive programs and also speeds up productivity.

Batch processing is used for tasks where updating a large database might take several hours. For example, credit card companies store customers' transaction data to be sent out in batches at the end of the month; otherwise, you'd get a paper bill for every single transaction. Batch processing is not appropriate, however, in situations where data must always be kept as current as possible.

TRANSACTIONAL PROCESSING Databases that require immediate updating of data use **transactional processing**. In this method, the database is updated as events take place. For example, airline reservation systems cannot wait hours to have their records updated. They must have each new reservation entered right away. A form of transactional processing called **online transactional processing (OLTP)**, provides for immediate approval of internet credit card purchases 24 hours a day.

ANALYTICAL PROCESSING Some databases use analytical processing to compare information from multiple sources at the same time. To analyze many types of data, queries are made using multiple dimensions. For example, when you compare two sets of data, such as the price of different types of pens and the number of pens sold, you are using two dimensions. If you include the total profit made from selling each set of pens, you are adding a third dimension. A form of analytical processing called **online analytical processing (OLAP)** is often used in business. OLTP databases are used for storing current information, like airline reservations, while OLAP databases are used for storing large amounts of historical information to be used for business analysis, such as profits over multiple years.

TECHNOLOGY@SCHOOL

Schools update their databases at least once a year. Each year, a new set of students enters the school. Another set leaves, and yet other students move to a new grade.

THINK ABOUT IT!

Which fields listed below do you think would be affected by the movement of students from grade to grade?

- lists of students by homeroom
- course names
- student emergency health contacts
- teachers' addresses
- school calendar
- parents' and guardians' names and addresses

Using Queries and Filters

OBJECTIVES

- Explain how queries make a database easier to use.

- Compare and contrast SQL and QBE.

- Compare and contrast a query and a filter.

AS YOU READ

SUMMARIZE As you read the lesson, use a chart to help you summarize details about queries.

TERMINOLOGY

- filter

- query

- Query by Example (QBE)

- query language

- Structured Query Language (SQL)

- syntax

Working with Queries

In a large database, it is inefficient to look through every record to find what you need. Many database programs have a search feature that lets you quickly locate only those records that match your search. To carry out this search, you create a query. Recall that a **query** is an object based on a set of rules that defines which records and which fields in those records should display on-screen. A query looks a lot like a table, but it is very different. You use a table to enter, store, and validate data. A query is a tool for finding, displaying, and manipulating the data stored in one or more tables.

CREATING A QUERY You can create a query and use it once, or you can save it to use again. Queries can also be used to maintain databases. For example, you may be able to use a query to update or even delete records in the database.

Most database programs, including Microsoft Access, have tools that prompt you through the steps in creating a query, or you can create one from scratch in Design View. In Access, select Query Wizard on the Create tab of the Ribbon to have the program prompt you through the steps; select Query Design to design the query yourself.

EXAMPLES OF QUERIES You can write queries to find subsets of any data entered in a database. Here are a few examples:

■ In a database of collector series baseball cards, you can find all new players whose careers started between 2010 and 2015 by including the word *rookie* in the query.

■ In an airline database, you can find the least expensive seat from Fort Worth to Houston on a weekday evening.

■ In a business database, you can find all customers who have not purchased anything in more than two years and then move these names to an inactive table.

IC3✔ | **Know basic concepts of a relational database: queries.**

Query Languages

However, the examples above are not expressed in a form that the database can understand. Databases use a special **query language** in which queries are written in ways similar to

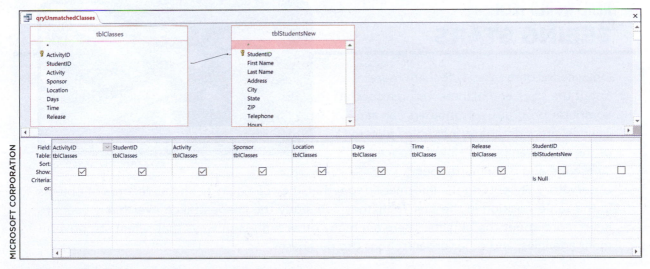

FIGURE 16.3.1 Creating a query in Microsoft Access.

mathematical equations. This language uses precise **syntax**, or rules, to correctly combine specific elements, such as statements, allowing you to specify exactly what you want to search for.

SQL A popular database query language is **Structured Query Language (SQL)**. SQL is written using elements, including queries, expressions, clauses, predicates, and statements. Most SQL queries start with a SELECT command. This tells the database to identify selected records that match given criteria. The SQL query also identifies the files and fields from which the data is to be selected.

For example, an SQL query to find the names and class schedules of all students in the seventh grade who have an average better than 85 looks like this:

SELECT: Name, Class
FROM: Student
WHERE: Average>85
AND: Grade=7

QBE Many database programs allow users to avoid typing SQL queries by providing a **Query by Example (QBE)**, feature that lets you provide

an example of what you are seeking. You typically identify a field and then type the condition that explains the acceptable data limits. For example, the query for the student list might look like this:

FIELD	Name	Class	Average	Grade
FILE	Student	Student	Student	Student
SHOW				
CRITERIA			>85	=7

QUERY OPTIONS Queries can search by complete data fields or parts of them. Database programs typically offer these search options:

- *Whole field* queries allow you to look for items that match the entire data value. For example, you can search for all records with a first name of "Martin."

- *Part of field* is a query that allows you to look for data that matches any part of a data value. For example, you can search for a date that includes March 2005 or a city that starts with "New."

REAL-WORLD TECH
SEEING STARS

LEXAARTS/SHUTTERSTOCK

One use for databases is to learn more about the stars and planets. Using a special computer program, astronomers can send queries into a database that holds pictures of the sky taken by the Hubble Space Telescope and by an earthbound observatory. By putting the information together, they can quickly find all records of objects in the same position in the sky. Then, they can study the images taken over many years to learn more about the objects. There are many other high-tech ways that scientists, government agencies, and other organizations use databases.

What databases can you think of that your local government agencies might maintain?

- *Sounds like* queries allow you to look for data values that are similar to the search word. For example, if you look for "Smith," you might also find "Smyth" or "Smythe."

- *Match case* is a kind of query in which you look for data that matches the capitalization exactly as written. In this case, a search for "PowerPoint" would not find "Powerpoint," "POWERPOINT," or "powerpoint."

Using Filters in a Database

A **filter** is a tool that lets you temporarily display only records that meet specific criteria. For example, if you plan to review or edit only the records of seventh-grade students, you could apply a filter to the database to display only records that have 7 entered in the Grade field. All other records are hidden from view.

A filter is similar to a query in that it limits the data displayed based on criteria. However, a filter is not as flexible as a query, and you cannot save it for reuse. With a filter, you choose the field on which you want to base the filter, and then you must select from a menu of filter types available for that field. You cannot customize the criteria the way you can with a query. Like a query, a filter does not affect the actual data stored in the database; it just limits what is displayed.

You can apply a filter to a table, form, query, or report. When you no longer need the filter, you can simply remove it to display all records. If you think you will want to use a filter again, you can save it as a query.

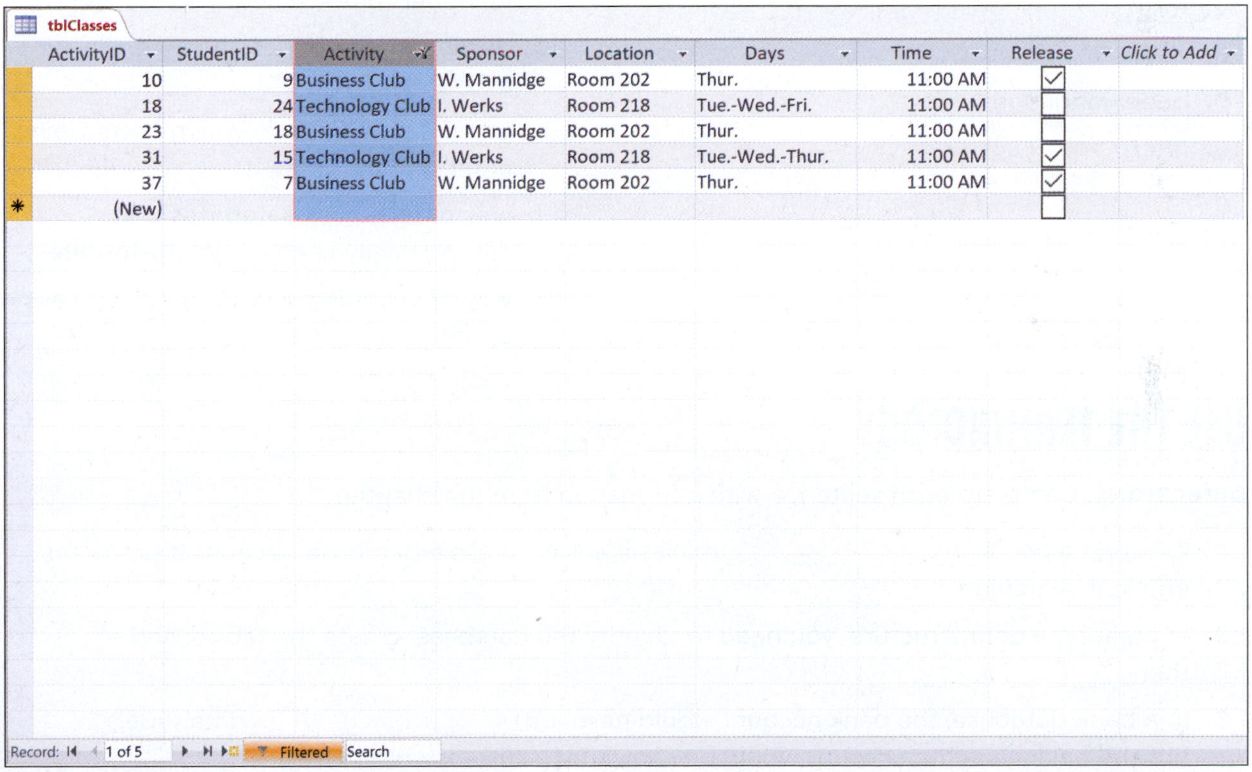

	ActivityID	StudentID	Activity	Sponsor	Location	Days	Time	Release	Click to Add
	10	9	Business Club	W. Mannidge	Room 202	Thur.	11:00 AM	✓	
	18	24	Technology Club	I. Werks	Room 218	Tue.-Wed.-Fri.	11:00 AM		
	23	18	Business Club	W. Mannidge	Room 202	Thur.	11:00 AM		
	31	15	Technology Club	I. Werks	Room 218	Tue.-Wed.-Thur.	11:00 AM	✓	
	37	7	Business Club	W. Mannidge	Room 202	Thur.	11:00 AM	✓	
*	(New)								

Record: 1 of 5   Filtered   Search

FIGURE 16.3.2 This table is filtered by the Activity field to show only students in the Business Club or the Technology Club.

MICROSOFT CORPORATION

389

Chapter 16 Review

REVIEW THE TERMINOLOGY

DIRECTIONS Match each vocabulary term in the left column with the correct definition in the right column.

1. data structure
2. field name
3. field width
4. batch processing
5. transactional processing
6. online transactional processing
7. form
8. query
9. query language
10. filter

a. special way of phrasing queries
b. provides approval of internet credit card purchases
c. request to search for data
d. way of limiting records being searched
e. the way a database is organized
f. identifier for each field
g. maximum number of characters in a field
h. on-screen window in which users view, enter, and edit data
i. way of changing databases that automatically keeps them up-to-date
j. way of changing databases that delays updates for a time

USE THE TERMINOLOGY

DIRECTIONS Complete each sentence with information from the chapter.

1. Creating a good _____ makes it easier to use a database because it promotes efficient searching.

2. In creating a data structure, you need to identify the database, create the tables, and then _____ .

3. In a bank database, the bank account would have a(n) _____ data type, but the balance in the account would be shown by a currency data type.

4. If a company sends weekly bills to clients, it would be reasonable for the company to use _____ processing.

5. Records can be modified in a table or by using a data _____ .

6. Moving outdated information into a(n) _____ file keeps the database smaller and easier to use.

7. Making a(n) _____ is an efficient way to find complex information in a database.

8. A query made with _____ tries to identify selected records that meet particular criteria.

9. To limit a query to only those records that match the entire value, you would choose the _____ option.

10. _____ work by temporarily hiding some records from a search.

THINK CRITICALLY

DIRECTIONS Answer the following questions.

1. What is the role of data structure in designing a database?

2. How do data types for each field affect a database?

3. Identify and explain the purpose of a query language.

4. Identify and explain at least two elements of a query language.

5. Describe the process of constructing a query to find the records for all freshmen in a school. Then, describe the process for finding records for all freshmen whose last names begin with the letter M.

EXTEND YOUR KNOWLEDGE

DIRECTIONS Choose and complete one of the following projects.

1. With your teacher's permission, use the internet to research the new-car inventory of an auto dealership. Review the dealer's database, or plan one of your own on paper that could be used to store information about the new cars in stock. Define or identify the fields and the report layout. Write a sample query, and share it with your class.

2. With your teacher's permission, use the internet to learn about database security issues. As you work, take notes and keep track of your sources. Prepare a summary of problems and possible solutions. Include a list of sources or a bibliography. Read your summary out loud to a partner.

3. Spreadsheets and databases are similar in many ways. For example, they both organize data in columns and rows. Create a spreadsheet file and enter contact information for at least five people. Include first name, last name, and email address. Save the spreadsheet. Start a database program and import the spreadsheet records to create a new table. Write a paragraph comparing the two programs, and discuss it with a partner or as a class.

IC3 PREP

1. Why are database forms replacing printed forms as a tool for collecting information? (Select all that apply.)

   a. Information entered directly into the database only has to be entered once.

   b. This is untrue; printed forms are increasingly used to collect information.

   c. There is less room for error if information is only entered once.

   d. Printing costs have become prohibitively expensive.

2. For each line below, select whether the statement is True or False.

   a. Many websites are designed to collect data that can be stored in a database.

   b. Websites never use the data they collect for marketing purposes.

   c. When you fill out forms on the web, that information is being stored in a database.

   d. In addition to information entered in forms, websites can track your browsing history, or identify your location using your IP address or GPS setting.

3. Which of these are valid examples of using queries to find subsets of data in a database? (Select all that apply.)

   a. In an airline database, finding the least expensive seat from Fort Worth to Houston on a weekday evening.

   b. In a business database, finding all customers who have not purchased anything in more than two years.

   c. In a library database, finding the books that have been made into movies.

   d. In a database of collector series baseball cards, finding all new players whose careers started between 2010 and 2015.

4. In Microsoft Access, which command lets you design a query yourself?

   a. Create > Query Wizard

   c. Create > Query Design

   b. Create > Query Blank

   d. Create > Query Format

5. For each line below, select whether the statement is True or False.

   a. A form is a database object that displays the data for multiple records at a time.

   b. It is generally easier for a user to enter data in a form than to enter it in a table.

   c. Each form includes a label that displays the field name.

   d. Forms can include fields from multiple tables.

   e. In Microsoft Access, use the Create > Form Wizard to automatically create a form that includes the fields in the table in the default order.

IC3 PROCEDURE

CREATING A RELATIONSHIP BETWEEN DATABASE TABLES

1. Select the **Database Tools** tab.

2. Select **Relationships**.

3. In the Show Table dialog box, select each table to use and then click **Add**.

4. Drag a line from the key field in one table to the key field in another table.

5. Select options in the Edit Relationships dialog box.

6. Select **Create**.

Additional Access 2016 Procedures

CHANGING THE VIEW

Collapsing and Expanding the Navigation Pane

1. In the database window, select the **Shutter Bar Close** button « to collapse the Navigation pane.
2. Select the **Shutter Bar Open** button » to expand the Navigation pane.

Changing the View of the Navigation Pane

1. If necessary, select the **Shutter Bar Open** button » to expand the Navigation pane.
2. Select the **down arrow** button ⊙ at the top of the Navigation pane.
3. On the menu, select the desired view option.

Opening and Closing the Field List

1. Open a form or report in Layout view or Design view.
2. Select the **Form Design Tools Design** tab.
3. Select the **Add Existing Fields** button.
4. Select the **Close** button × to close the Field List task pane.

OPENING A DATABASE

Opening a Recently Used Database

1. Select **File**.
2. Select **Recent**.
3. Select the desired database to open it.

   OR

1. From the Access Welcome screen, select **Open Other Files**.
2. On the Open menu, select **Recent**, if necessary.
3. From the Recent list, select the desired file.

Opening a Saved Database

1. Select **File**.
2. Select **Open**.
3. In the Open dialog box, navigate to the file you want to open and select it.
4. Select **Open**.

Opening a Database Exclusively

1. Select **File**.
2. Select **Open**.
3. Navigate to and select the file to open.
4. Select the **Open** button drop-down arrow.
5. Select **Open Exclusive**.

CLOSING A DATABASE

1. Select **File**.
2. Select **Close**.

MANAGING TABLES

Saving and Closing a Table

1. Right-click the table tab.
2. On the shortcut menu, select **Close**.

   OR

   Select the **Close** button × in the upper-right corner of the datasheet.
3. In the message box, select **Yes** to save the table.
4. In the Save As box, type the table name.
5. Select **OK**.

Opening a Table

In the Navigation pane, double-click the table.

Renaming a Table

1. In the Navigation pane, right-click the table you want to rename.
2. On the shortcut menu, select **Rename**.
3. Type the new table name and press **Enter**.

Creating Additional Tables

1. Select the **Create** tab.
2. Select the **Table** button ▦.

SELECTING RECORDS

- Select the record selector to select the desired record.
- To select multiple records, select the record selector of the first record, hold **Shift**, and select the record selector of adjacent records.
- Press **Ctrl + A** to select all records.

DELETING RECORDS

1. Select the record selector of the record you want to delete.
2. Press **Delete**.
3. In the message box, select **Yes** to confirm the deletion.

MANAGING FIELDS IN DATASHEET VIEW

Making a Field Required

1. In Datasheet view, select in the desired field.
2. Select the **Table Tools Fields** tab.
3. Select the **Required** check box.

Making a Field Unique

1. In Datasheet view, select in the desired field.
2. Select the **Table Tools Fields** tab.
3. Select the **Unique** check box.

Adding a Field by Right-Clicking

1. Right-click the field header that will be to the right of the new field.
2. On the shortcut menu, select **Insert Field**.

Adding a Field from the Ribbon

1. Click in the field that will be to the left of the new field.
2. Select the **Table Tools Fields** tab.
3. Select the button for the desired field type.

Renaming a Field

1. Double-click the field column heading.
2. Type the new name for the field and press **Enter**.

OR

1. Right-click the field column heading.
2. On the shortcut menu, select **Rename Field**.
3. Type the new name for the field and press **Enter**.

Moving a Field

1. Select the column heading of the field you want to move.
2. Click and hold the mouse button down and drag the field to the desired location.

Deleting a Field

1. Select the column heading of the field you want to delete.
2. Select the **Table Tools Fields** tab.
3. Select the **Delete** button ▣.
4. In the message box, select **Yes** to confirm the deletion.

Hiding and Unhiding Fields

1. Right-click the column heading of the field you want to hide.
2. On the shortcut menu, select **Hide Fields**.
3. To unhide a column, right-click the column heading of any field.
4. On the shortcut menu, select **Unhide Fields**.
5. In the Unhide Columns dialog box, click to select the field you want to unhide.
6. Select **Close**.

Changing Table Field Widths

1. Position the mouse pointer on the right border of the column heading.

2. When the pointer changes to ⬌, drag the column to the desired width.

   OR

   Double-click the right border of the column heading.

   OR

1. Right-click the column heading.

2. On the shortcut menu, select **Field Width**.

3. In the Column Width dialog box, enter the desired width.

4. Select **OK**.

Freezing/Unfreezing Fields

1. Select the fields you want to freeze.

2. Right-click the selected fields.

3. On the shortcut menu, select **Freeze Fields**.

4. To unfreeze the fields, right-click the column heading of a field.

5. On the shortcut menu, select **Unfreeze All Fields**.

WORKING WITH TABLES IN DESIGN VIEW

Opening a Table in Design View

1. Right-click the table name in the Navigation pane.

2. On the shortcut menu, select **Design View**.

   OR

1. With the table open in Datasheet view, right-click the table tab.

2. On the shortcut menu, select **Design View**.

Creating a Table in Design View

1. In the open database, select the **Create** tab.

2. Select the **Table Design** button.

3. Set the field names, data types, and field properties as desired.

Setting a Primary Key

1. Open the table in Design view.

2. Select the field you want to set as the primary key.

3. Select the **Table Tools Design** tab.

4. Select the **Primary Key** button 🔑.

Inserting a Field

1. In Design view, select the field selector of the field that will follow the new field.

2. Select the **Table Tools Design** tab.

3. Select the **Insert Rows** button.

Moving a Field

1. In Design view, select the field selector to the left of the desired field.

2. Holding the mouse button down, drag the field selector to the desired location in the field list.

Deleting a Field

1. In Design view, select the field selector of the field you want to delete.

2. Select the **Table Tools Design** tab.

3. Select the **Delete Rows** button.

Changing a Field's Data Type

1. In Design view, select the **Data Type** drop-down arrow of the desired field.

2. On the menu, select the desired data type.

Modifying a Field's Properties

1. In Design view, select the field selector of the field whose properties you want to modify.

2. In the Field Properties pane, modify the properties as desired.

PREVIEWING A DATASHEET

1. Select **File**.

2. Select **Print**.

3. Select **Print Preview**.

PRINTING A DATASHEET

1. Select **File**.
2. Select **Print**.
3. Select **Print**.
4. In the Print dialog box, select options as desired.
5. Select **OK**.

MODIFYING DATABASE PROPERTIES

1. Select **File**.
2. On the Info tab, select **View and edit database properties**.
3. In the Properties dialog box, modify properties as desired.
4. Select **OK**.

PROTECTING A DATABASE

Setting a Database Password

1. Open the database exclusively.
2. Select **File**.
3. On the Info tab, click **Encrypt with Password**.
4. In the Set Database Password dialog box, type the password in the Password box.
5. Type the password again in the Verify box.
6. Select **OK**.

Opening a Password-Protected Database

1. Open the database exclusively.
2. In the Enter database password dialog box, type the password.
3. Select **OK**.

Removing the Password from a Database

1. Open the database exclusively.
2. Select **File**.
3. On the Info tab, select **Decrypt Database**.
4. In the Unset Database Password dialog box, type the password.
5. Select **OK**.

CREATING A SIMPLE QUERY

1. In the open database, select the **Create** tab.
2. Select the **Query Wizard** button.
3. In the New Query dialog box, select **Simple Query Wizard**.
4. Select **OK**.
5. In the Simple Query Wizard dialog box, select the **Tables/Queries** drop-down arrow.
6. Select the table or query on which the new query will be based.
7. Select fields from the Available Fields list box to move to the Selected Fields list box.
8. Select **Next**.
9. Enter the title for the query.
10. Select **Finish**.

CREATING A QUICK FORM

1. In the Navigation pane, select the table on which you want to base the form.
2. Select the **Create** tab.
3. Select the **Form** button.

SORTING

Sorting Records in a Table

1. With the table open in Datasheet view, select in the field by which you want to sort the records.
2. Select the **Home** tab.
3. Select the **Ascending** button to sort in ascending order or the **Descending** button to sort in descending order.

Removing a Sort

1. Select the **Home** tab.
2. Select the **Remove Sort** button.

Sorting Using Multiple Fields

1. With the table open in Datasheet view, arrange the fields in the order you want to sort them so they are adjacent to each other.
2. Select the fields by which you want to sort.
3. Select the **Home** tab.
4. Select the **Ascending** button [A↓] to sort in ascending order or the **Descending** button [Z↓] to sort in descending order.

FILTERING

Filtering by Selection

1. With the table open in Datasheet view, select the field value for which you want to filter.
2. Select the **Home** tab.
3. Select the **Selection** button [▼].
4. On the menu, select the desired filter option.

Removing a Filter

1. Select the **Home** tab.
2. Select the **Toggle Filter** button [▼].

WORKING WITH QUERIES

Creating a Query in Design View

1. In the database window, select the **Create** tab.
2. Select the **Query Design** button [▦].
3. In the Show Table dialog box, select the table or query on which the new query will be based.
4. Select **Add**.
5. In Query Design view, drag fields from the table window to the grid as desired.

   OR

   Click in the Field row in the query grid, select the drop-down arrow, and select the field to add.

   OR

   Double-click a field in the table field list to add it to the grid.

Removing Fields from the Query

1. In the query grid, select anywhere in the field's column that you want to remove.

   OR

   In the query grid, click on the thin gray bar above the desired field to select the column.
2. Select the **Query Tools Design** tab.
3. Select the **Delete Columns** button [✗].

Running a Query

1. In Query Design view, select the **Query Tools Design** tab.
2. Select the **Run** button [!].

Saving a Query

1. In Query Design view, select the **Save** button [💾] on the Quick Access Toolbar.
2. In the Save As dialog box, type the query name.
3. Select **OK**.

Printing a Query

1. With the query open in Datasheet view, select **File**.
2. Select **Print**.
3. Select the **Print** button [🖶].
4. In the Print dialog box, set the print options as desired.
5. Select **OK**.

Creating a Multi-Table Query

1. In the database window, select the **Create** tab.
2. Select the **Query Design** button [▦].
3. In the Show Table dialog box, double-click the tables on which the new query will be based.
4. Drag fields from the table windows to the grid as desired.

Sorting Query Results

1. Open the query in Design view.

2. In the query grid, select in the **Sort** row for the field on which you want to sort.

3. Select the drop-down arrow and select **Ascending** or **Descending**.

Reordering Fields in a Query

1. Open the query in Design view.

2. In the query grid, select the gray bar above the field you want to move.

3. Drag the field to the desired location.

Using All Fields of a Table

1. In the database window, select the **Create** tab.

2. Select the **Query Design** button 🖼️.

3. In the Show Table dialog box, double-click the table on which the new query will be based.

4. In the table window, double-click the asterisk (*) at the top of the table field list.

Changing a Column Name

1. Open the query in Design view.

2. In the query grid, click in the **Field** row of the column you want to rename.

3. Position the insertion point to the left of the current field name.

4. Type the new name followed by a colon (:).

Specifying Criteria in a Query

1. Open the query in Design view.

2. In the query grid, click in the **Criteria** row for the desired field.

3. Type the criteria as desired.

Filtering by an Undisplayed Field

1. Open the query in Design view.

2. In the query grid, click in the **Criteria** row for the desired field.

3. Type the criteria as desired.

4. Select the field's **Show** box to deselect it.

Filtering for Null Values

1. Open the query in Design view.

2. In the query grid, click in the **Criteria** row for the desired field.

3. Type **Is Null**.

USING WILDCARDS AND OPERATORS IN A QUERY

Using Wildcards

1. Open the query in Design view.

2. In the query grid, click in the **Criteria** row for the desired field.

3. Type the criteria, using the asterisk (*) wildcard character to specify any number of characters, or the question mark (?) wildcard character to specify a single character.

Using the Like Operator

1. Open the query in Design view.

2. In the query grid, click in the **Criteria** row for the desired field.

3. Type **Like**, followed by the criteria as desired.

Using the Between . . . And Operator

1. Open the query in Design view.

2. In the query grid, click in the **Criteria** row for the desired field.

3. Type the criteria in the format **Between** criteria **and** criteria.

Using the In Operator

1. Open the query in Design view.

2. In the query grid, click in the **Criteria** row for the desired field.

3. Type the criteria in the format **In (criteria)**.

Using the Or Operator

1. Open the query in Design view.

2. In the query grid, click in the **Criteria** row for the desired field.

3. Type the criteria in the format criteria **Or** criteria.

Using a Comparison Operator in a Query

1. Open the query in Design view.

2. In the query grid, click in the **Criteria** row for the desired field.

3. Type the criteria with comparison operator as desired.

USING CALCULATED FIELDS IN A QUERY

1. Open the query in Design view.

2. In the query grid, click in a blank column and type the field name followed by a colon (:).

3. Select the **Query Tools Design** tab.

4. Select the **Builder** button.

5. In the Expression Builder, select from the Expression Elements, Expression Categories, and Expression Values as desired.

6. If necessary, delete the Expr text.

7. Select **OK**.

CREATING A FORM

Creating a Form in Layout View

1. In the Navigation pane, select the table on which you want to base the form.

2. Select the **Create** tab.

3. Select the **Blank Form** button.

4. Drag the fields from the field list to the form layout as desired.

Creating a Form in Design View

1. Select the **Create** tab.

2. Select the **Form Design** button.

3. Select the **Form Design Tools Design** tab.

4. Select the **Add Existing Fields** button.

5. In the Field List pane, select **Show all tables**.

6. Expand the fields of the table that you want to add to the form.

7. Double-click the desired fields to add them to the form.

MANAGING RECORDS IN A FORM

Navigating Records in a Form

Select the navigation buttons as follows:

- **First record**
- **Previous record**
- **Next record**
- **Last record**

Deleting a Record from a Form

1. In Form view, click in the record you want to delete.

2. Select the **Home** tab.

3. Select the **Delete** button.

4. On the menu, select **Delete Record**.

5. In the message box, select **Yes** to confirm the deletion.

CREATING AND VIEWING A TABULAR REPORT

1. In the Navigation pane, select the table on which you want to base the report.

2. Select the **Create** tab.

3. Select the **Report** button.

4. Select the **Report Design Tools Design** tab.

5. Select the **View** button drop-down arrow.

6. Select **Report View**.

Creating a Report in Layout View

1. Select the **Create** tab.

2. Select the **Blank Report** button.

3. Select the **Report Layout Tools Design** tab.

4. If necessary, select the **Add Existing Fields** button.

5. In the Field List pane, select **Show all tables**.

6. Expand the fields of the table that you want to add to the report.

7. Double-click the desired fields to add them to the report.

Deleting Fields from a Report Layout

1. In Layout view, select the field you want to delete.
2. Select the **Report Layout Tools Arrange** tab.
3. Select the **Select Column** button ⊞.
4. Press **Delete**.

Changing Field Widths in a Report

1. In Layout view, select the field whose width you want to change.
2. Position the mouse pointer on the right edge of the selected field.
3. When the pointer changes to ↔, drag to the desired width.

Creating a Report Using the Report Wizard

1. Select the **Create** tab.
2. Select the **Report Wizard** button ▤.
3. In the Report Wizard dialog box, select the table on which you want to base the report.
4. Select fields in the Available Fields list box and move them to the Selected Fields list box.
5. Select **Next**.
6. Select a grouping field if desired.
7. Select **Next**.
8. In the next dialog box, set a sort order if desired.
9. Select **Next**.
10. In the next dialog box, select the desired layout and orientation for the report.
11. Select **Next**.
12. In the next dialog box, enter the title for the report.
13. Select **Finish**.

PREVIEWING AND PRINTING A REPORT

1. With the report open, right-click its tab.
2. On the shortcut menu, select **Print Preview**.
3. Select the **Print Preview** tab.
4. Select the **Print** button 🖶.

OR

1. With the report open, select **File**.
2. Select **Print**.
3. Select **Print**.
4. In the Print dialog box, set print options as desired.
5. Select **OK**.

OR

1. With the report open, select **File**.
2. Select **Print**.
3. Select **Quick Print**.

WORKING WITH REPORT SECTIONS

Selecting Sections of a Report

1. Open the report in Design view.
2. Select the bar of the section you want to select.

Resizing a Section

1. Select the bar of the section you want to resize.
2. Position the pointer on the top border of the bar.
3. When the pointer changes to ⊥, drag to the desired size.

Moving a Control Between Sections

1. Open the report in Design view.
2. Select the control you want to move.
3. Press **Ctrl + X**.
4. Click where you want to move the control.
5. Press **Ctrl + V**.

MODIFYING A REPORT

Adding Page Number Codes

1. Open the report in Design view.
2. Select the **Report Design Tools Design** tab.
3. Select the **Page Numbers** button ▣.
4. In the Page Numbers dialog box, set the form, position, and alignment of the page numbers as desired.
5. Select **OK**.

Sorting Report Data

1. Open the report in Layout view.
2. Select the **Report Layout Tools Design** tab.
3. Select the **Group & Sort** button ▣.
4. In the Group, Sort, and Total pane, select **Add a sort**.
5. On the pop-up menu, select the field you want to sort by.
6. Click to select the sort order (with A on top or with Z on top).

Grouping Report Data

1. Open the report in Layout view.
2. Select the **Report Layout Tools Design** tab.
3. Select the **Group & Sort** button ▣.
4. In the Group, Sort, and Total pane, select **Add a group**.
5. On the field list that opens, select the desired field on which you want to group records.

WORKING WITH PRINT PREVIEW AND REPORT VIEW

Opening Print Preview

1. Select the **Home** tab.
2. Select the **View** button drop-down arrow.
3. Select **Print Preview**.

Opening Report View

1. Select the **Home** tab.
2. Select the **View** button drop-down arrow.
3. Select **Report View**.

SLAVEN/SHUTTERSTOCK

CHAPTER 17
Digital Graphics Basics

WHAT IS A GRAPHIC?

The word *graphic* generally refers to a picture, or image, that represents an object. A photograph, a painting, an abstract poster, a chart, and a stick figure drawn on a chalkboard are all examples of graphics. A *computer graphic*, which may be called a digital graphic, refers to an image created or modified using computer hardware and software. Computer graphics include drawings, shapes, geometric designs, photos, engineering drawings, and even maps. They might combine any or all of these items, as well as text and color.

Computer graphics can be realistic or abstract. They can stand alone as art or information, or be used to illustrate documents and webpages. They can be displayed on a monitor or printed. In other words, computer graphics are an art form as well as a way to communicate thoughts and ideas.

Digital Graphics and Their Uses

OBJECTIVES

- Identify two different types of graphics and explain the differences between them.

- List the advantages of each type of graphic.

- Differentiate between draw and paint programs.

AS YOU READ

COMPARE AND CONTRAST As you read this lesson, use a Venn diagram to show the similarities and differences between raster graphics and vector graphics.

TERMINOLOGY

- bitmap

- bitmapped graphic

- digital graphics

- draw program

- image editor

- paint program

- pixel

- raster graphic

- resolution

- vector graphic

Types of Digital Graphics

The most common ways to create **digital graphics**—images created or modified using computer hardware and software—is using a graphics program, by scanning printed content, or by using a digital camera. These graphics may stand on their own, or be inserted into a different application file using the Insert Picture or Insert Clip Art command. In the application, you can usually modify them to suit your needs. For example, you can crop unwanted areas, change the height, width or scale, and position them on the page.

There are hundreds of different uses for computer graphics. However, they fall into only two categories: raster graphics and vector graphics.

RASTER GRAPHICS A **raster graphic**, which is sometimes called a **bitmapped graphic** or **bitmap**, is an image formed by a pattern of dots. Imagine a sheet of graph paper with each of its squares filled in with a certain color to make a picture. If seen from far enough away, the picture will look clear, and the squares won't be noticed. But up close, you can see the individual squares of the graph paper.

Raster graphics are composed of tiny dots of different colors. Each single point in the image is a **pixel**, short for "picture element." The smaller the pixels in the image, the smoother it will look. The more colors in the image, the brighter and sharper the image will look.

Some common raster file formats include:

- Graphics Interchange Format (GIF)

- Joint Photographic Experts Group (JPG)

- Portable Network Graphics (PNG)

- Windows Bitmap (BMP)

Some formats are used for images on web pages, while others are used for icons and images in the operating system. In Windows, these same abbreviations are used as the file extensions. A file ending in *.gif*, for example, is in the GIF file format.

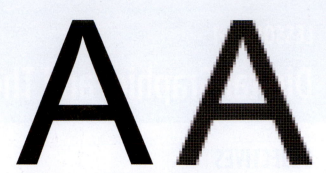

FIGURE 17.1.1 When viewed on the screen, vector graphics (left) look sharper than raster graphics (right).

Raster graphics are preferred for some types of images. They often are used for photos or images that require backgrounds.

VECTOR GRAPHICS A **vector graphic** is an image that is created using paths or lines. A vector image tells the computer where a line starts and where it ends. It allows the computer to figure out how to connect the two points. The lines can form shapes, which may be filled with a color or pattern.

Encapsulated PostScript, or EPS, is one of several formats commonly used for vector art. EPS files contain the information that a printer needs in order to print a graphic correctly. The information is combined with a small sketch of what the graphic should look like. The sketch inside an EPS file allows you to preview an image on-screen. This way, you can be sure the image is correct before printing it.

Size, Resolution, and Dots per Inch

Two basic qualities affect how every raster image will appear. Size, the height and width of the graphic, is normally measured either in pixels or in inches. **Resolution** tells how many pixels are in a certain piece of an image. Resolution also determines the quality of the computer image. Resolution is usually measured in dots per inch, or dpi. An image that is 1 inch square at 72 dpi will contain a total of 5,184 pixels (72 × 72). Generally, the higher the resolution, the sharper the image will look.

REAL-WORLD TECH
PIXAR STUDIOS

SUNLIGHT789/123RF.COM

Pixar, also known as Pixar Animation Studios, is a part of The Walt Disney Company responsible for such computer animated films as *Toy Story, Monsters, Inc.*, and *Coco*. These films were created using computers.

Pixar films are known for their realistic cartoon characters. Some aspects of creating these characters involved technology similar to the draw and paint programs and image editors discussed in this lesson. After final drawings or clay models of the characters were approved, 3D models were designed on computers. Next, designers considered movements and expressions. They looked at photos of live actors in various positions and with different expressions to get an idea of how each figure should move. Animators then used Pixar's animation software to make the images come to life with movements and expressions.

Vector graphics are created using lines or paths rather than pixels, so the number of dots per inch is not a concern when changing the size of vector graphics. If a raster image is enlarged to twice its normal size, it will look fuzzy and jagged. A vector image can be enlarged to any size and keep its quality.

TECHNOLOGY@SCHOOL

Students can use graphics to enhance reports, newsletters, websites, and even spreadsheets. It is also possible to include graphics in HTML-supported email messages.

THINK ABOUT IT!

A high resolution means a higher quality image and a larger file size. Which resolution would you choose for a graphic you plan to print? What if you plan to send the image via email?

- 2,500 pixels
- 22,500 pixels
- 10,000 pixels

Graphics Programs

Different programs allow you to create, edit, and view different graphic file types. Choosing the right program depends on which type of graphic you are working with and what your needs are.

PAINT PROGRAMS A **paint program** allows you to create a new raster image. Paint programs also allow you to open a raster image, view it on-screen, and make changes to it. Microsoft Windows comes with a basic paint program called Paint.

DRAW PROGRAMS A program that allows you to create and edit vector images is called a **draw program**. Since draw programs focus on vector images, they make editing easy. You can change the size of an image or add color to it. Many application programs, including Microsoft Word and PowerPoint, come with built-in basic drawing tools that you can use to create simple drawings in your documents. More complex programs, such as Adobe® Illustrator® and CorelDRAW®, have sophisticated tools for creating and editing graphics.

IMAGE EDITORS An advanced paint program is called an **image editor**. Image editors are designed for editing raster images. They are also often used for adding special effects to photographs. Adobe® Photoshop® and Adobe® Photoshop Elements® are examples of popular image editors. You can also use built-in picture editing tools in some programs, including Microsoft Word and PowerPoint.

TECHNOLOGY@WORK

Computer graphics designers develop images for many purposes, including websites, publications, advertising, and games.

THINK ABOUT IT!

Using the right design program is important for designers. Consider the following tasks. Which would need to be completed by a draw program?

- view a raster image
- add color to a vector image
- add effects to a raster image
- change the size of a vector image

MICROSOFT CORPORATION

FIGURE 17.1.2 Microsoft Word has built-in picture editing tools for editing raster images.

Exploring Graphics Programs

OBJECTIVES

- Identify the main sections of a graphics application window.

- List the different tools available in paint and draw programs.

- Determine when to use the tools in a paint or draw program.

AS YOU READ

SUMMARIZE INFORMATION Make a table that lists tools used in paint and draw programs on the left. On the right, include the type of program(s) each tool is used in.

TERMINOLOGY

- color palette
- Eyedropper
- graphics tablet
- inking
- Selection tool
- stylus
- workspace

Exploring the Application Window

Although the tools in paint and draw programs vary, most will include a workspace, toolbars, and color palettes.

WORKSPACE Most of the screen is devoted to the **workspace**, the blank, white area which contains the graphic. This area is sometimes called the drawing area or canvas.

TOOLBARS A toolbar is a bar across the top or down the side of a window. It contains icons that link to the program's tools. By clicking an icon, you can create, edit, add, or remove information within the graphic. Toolbars usually appear, or are docked, on the edges of the screen. They also can be moved around, or floated, to fit your preferences. In some programs toolbars are called panels.

COLOR PALETTES The display of color options in paint and draw programs is called the **color palette**. These options allow you to choose background, foreground, fill, and line colors. Most programs also allow you to change and customize the color palette.

Paint Program Tools

In paint programs, the following tools are used to place and remove color in the workspace.

PENCIL The Pencil tool is used for freehand drawing. Clicking and dragging this tool across the workspace leaves a trail of the selected color. This tool is used to draw fine details. Only the color or thickness of the line drawn can be changed.

BRUSH The Brush tool works like the Pencil tool, but it makes a broader stroke of color. Often, the shape of the brush can be changed to create different shapes of colors. For instance, the brush can be large and square or small and circular.

LINE AND SHAPE The Line tool allows you to draw a line and use the toolbar to change its color and width. Various shapes, such as rectangles and ovals, also can be drawn using tools on the toolbar. Shape tools allow you to create shapes in three different forms: Outline, Filled with Outline, and Filled without Outline.

EYEDROPPER The **Eyedropper** tool allows you to select a specific color from anywhere on the screen. You place the eyedropper over the desired color and click. That color becomes the selected color and can be used elsewhere in the image.

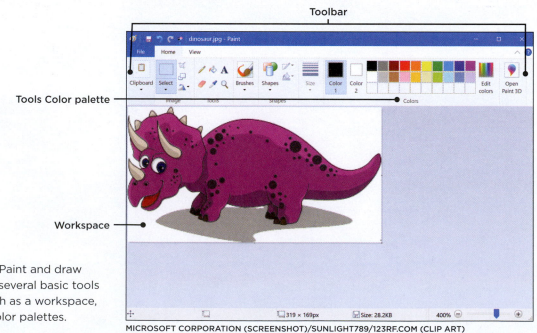

FIGURE 17.2.1 Paint and draw programs have several basic tools in common, such as a workspace, toolbars, and color palettes.

MICROSOFT CORPORATION (SCREENSHOT)/SUNLIGHT789/123RF.COM (CLIP ART)

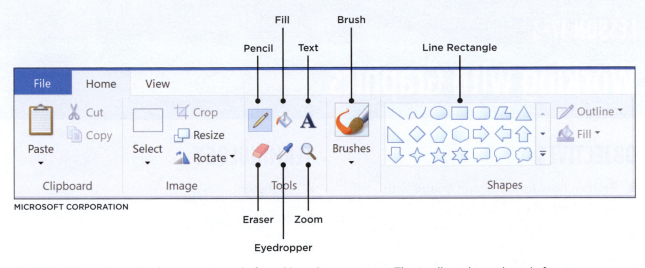

FIGURE 17.2.2 Some tools are commonly found in paint programs. The toolbar shown here is from Microsoft Paint.

ERASER The Eraser tool removes color from an image. It is used by clicking the tool and dragging the eraser across the image. The area touched with the eraser becomes the background color.

Draw Program Tools

The Line and Shape tools in draw programs are similar to those in paint programs, but with one important difference. In a draw program, you can change lines and shapes without affecting other elements of the graphic. In paint programs, it is hard to change one part of a graphic without altering other parts that are close to it. A **Selection tool** allows you to select a portion of an image to be enlarged, moved, or edited.

Interacting with the Program

Unlike a word-processing document or a spreadsheet, you cannot simply type to create and edit graphics. Instead, you must use input devices suitable for drawing. With a traditional monitor, you can use a mouse to select, drag, and draw. With a touchscreen monitor, you can use your finger or a stylus to draw directly on the screen. A **stylus** is a pen-shaped tool designed specifically for drawing or writing on a screen.

A **graphics tablet** is a specialized hardware device designed for creating digital graphics by drawing or **inking**. Inking is the task of finishing and enhancing preliminary drawings, usually for comics or animation. With a graphics tablet, the user moves a stylus or other pointing device over the drawing surface. The tablet senses the movement of the stylus and moves the pointer on the screen, mimicking the image that is being drawn on the tablet. The skills for writing with a stylus on a tablet are quite different than writing with a pen, and can take some time to master. Some tablet computers combine the features of a graphics tablet with the functions of a personal computer.

CAROL.ANNE/SHUTTERSTOCK

FIGURE 17.2.3 An interactive pen display combines the capabilities of a graphics tablet with an LCD monitor, so you can draw and choose commands directly on the screen by using a special pen.

Working with Graphics

OBJECTIVES

- Explain how to modify an image with special effects.
- Recognize clip art.
- Describe how graphics can be converted from one format to another.
- Explain how to import or insert a graphic into a document.

AS YOU READ

ORGANIZE INFORMATION As you read this lesson, make an outline. Use Roman numerals for main headings. Use capital letters for subheadings, and use numbers for supporting details.

TERMINOLOGY

- alignment
- balance
- clip art
- color
- contrast
- copyright
- emphasis
- export
- grouping
- harmony
- import
- intellectual property
- layering
- line
- proportion
- proximity
- repetition
- shape
- space
- texture
- trace
- ungrouping
- unity
- variety

Adding Effects to Graphics

To create a new graphic, start with a blank workspace (sometimes called the background or canvas). If you are modifying an existing graphic, import it into the program you want to use. For example, use the File > Open command, or the Import > File command.

If you are creating the graphic in a paint program, use the paint tools to add color and form to the image. If you are creating the graphic in a draw program, use the Line and Shape tools to add to the image.

Special effects and editing tools can be used to modify an image. For example, cropping removes the edges of the image. To crop, select the area you want to keep, and then select the crop command. In some programs, you select the entire image, select crop, and then drag crop handles to remove the edges you want to discard.

IC3✔ Know how to crop an image.

Other ways to modify or enhance a graphic include:

- Scaling changes the dimensions.
- Flipping an image turns it upside down.
- Mirroring the image makes it flip from left to right, as if it were being viewed in a mirror.
- Stretching makes the image appear longer in one direction than the other, as if it were drawn on a sheet of rubber that was stretched out.
- Skewing tilts the image horizontally or vertically.
- Inverting reverses the colors in the graphic. In a black-and-white graphic, all the white dots will turn black, and all the black will turn white. In a color graphic, each color will change to its "opposite" color. For example, yellow will become dark blue.

Understanding the Principles of Design

An effective graphic uses the basic principles of design, including contrast, balance, and proportion.

CONTRAST **Contrast** uses differences in shape and color to create a comparison. Different sized objects and opposite colors can distinguish one part of the graphic from another.

BALANCE The way objects are arranged is called **balance**. Symmetrically arranged objects are evenly balanced, while asymmetrically arranged objects are unevenly balanced.

MICROSOFT CORPORATION (SCREENSHOT)/
SUNLIGHT789/123RF.COM (CLIP ART)

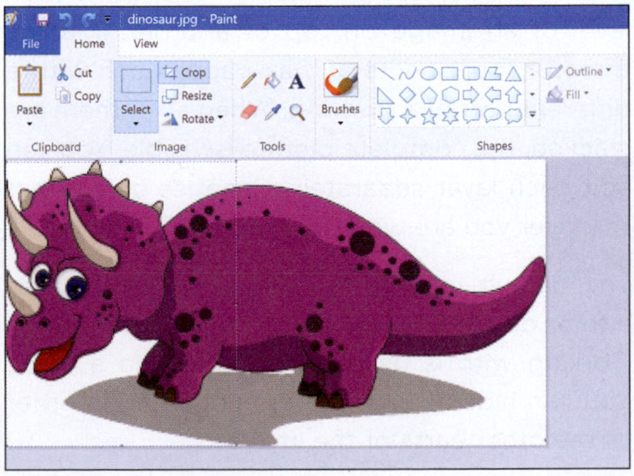

MICROSOFT CORPORATION (SCREENSHOT)/
SUNLIGHT789/123RF.COM (CLIP ART)

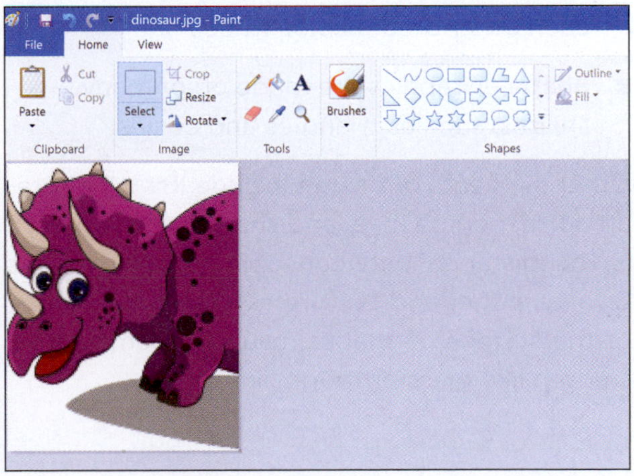

FIGURE 17.3.1 An image in Microsoft Paint with an area selected for cropping (left) and the same image after cropping (right).

PROPORTION The size and location of one object in relation to other objects in the graphic is called **proportion**.

Other principles of design include **repetition** in which a color, shape, or pattern is repeated throughout the graphic; **emphasis**, which creates a focal point; **proximity**, in which the closeness between objects indicates a relationship; **unity**, in which objects in the image establish a connection through style or color; **harmony**, which is when the elements of the graphic come together as a complete idea; **alignment**, which is the placement of text and objects so they line up within a space, and **variety**, which creates visual interest by using different colors and shapes.

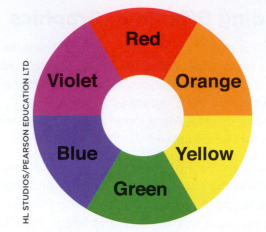

FIGURE 17.3.2 Violet and orange are analogous to red on the color wheel. Red and green are complementary.

HL STUDIOS/PEARSON EDUCATION LTD

Understanding the Elements of Design

Many different elements are present in an effective graphic, including color and shape.

- **Color**—The use of color has a direct effect on the appearance of a graphic. Each individual color has its own hue, value, and saturation. Hue is the base color, like blue or red. Value is the color's brightness; adding black or white to the color changes the value. Saturation is the colors intensity. Colors are also related to each other. Analogous colors are on either side of a color on the color wheel. Complementary colors are opposite each other on the color wheel.

- **Shape**—Graphics are made up of many shapes, such as triangles and circles.

Other elements of design include **lines** that create form, perspective, and shapes; **space**, which is the distance between objects in a graphic or on a page; and **texture**, which is the quality of the surface of shapes, causing them to look smooth like glass or rough like sand.

Combining Images

You can **import**, or bring data into, a graphics file from another program. Once imported, the image can then be modified or expanded. Copy and Paste commands may be used to import content, or you may use an Insert or Place command.

You can also **export** data from a graphics file by saving it in a different file format. When you export a graphic, you must consider how it will be used, and select an appropriate format that balances quality and file size.

LAYERING IMAGES Raster graphics use layers, or stacks of information, to create a graphic. A powerful process known as **layering** stacks each level of an image on top of another. Imagine three or four sheets of wax paper, each with a different part of a drawing. When all of them are stacked, the complete picture is visible. You can edit each layer separately. Changes only affect the layer you are working on.

The default layer is the background. You can add or delete layers as needed. The layer you're working with is usually highlighted in a color. You can hide a layer you are not using in order to see other parts of the image.

GROUPING IMAGES Grouping is the process of combining separate vector images into one image. Once the images are grouped, they can be moved or resized as a single unit. To group images, select all of the desired items and then select the Group command. **Ungrouping** is the process of separating combined images into individual images. To ungroup an image, select a grouped image and then select the Ungroup command.

Working with Clip Art

It is not always necessary to create an image from scratch. Instead, you can start with clip art. **Clip art** includes graphics files, videos, audio, and animations that come with a program or that you download from the internet.

RASTER CLIP ART Clip art in a raster format (such as GIF, JPG, or PNG) can be imported into a paint document. The art then can be edited like any other raster graphic.

VECTOR CLIP ART Vector art can be imported into a draw program and modified. If the image is complex, it can be ungrouped. Its individual parts can then be edited or moved.

COPYRIGHT LAWS When you use clip art created by someone else, it is important that you obey all copyright laws and usage requirements. **Copyright** laws protect individuals and companies from the theft or misuse of their **intellectual property**, such as creative, literary, or artistic work. It is a crime to copy this kind of work without the permission of the person who owns the copyright to it. Penalties include paying a large fine and possibly jail time. Some clip art images are available for use under a Creative Commons license, which is a type of copyright license that allows usage under certain conditions.

Even if a clip art website advertises free clip art files, there may be usage requirements. For example, it may be free to use for a school project, but not for use on a blog or social media page. Read the requirements carefully before downloading and using clip art files.

FIGURE 17.3.3 When you search for clip art with Microsoft Bing, by default only graphics available under a Creative Commons license display.

MICROSOFT CORPORATION

Converting Graphics

If you want to use a graphic that is in a format your program does not support, you may have to convert it. You can use a file conversion program, or open the file and use the Save As command to save it in a different file format. File conversion is also required if you want to change a vector graphic to a raster graphic, or vice versa.

VECTOR-TO-RASTER GRAPHICS Vector graphics must be changed to pixels before the image can be edited in a paint program.

RASTER-TO-VECTOR GRAPHICS Converting raster graphics to vectors requires a special process called **tracing**. Tracing requires special software and can be complicated when an image has a lot of color and detail.

Integrating Graphics with Other Programs

Once you have saved a digital image, you can use it to enhance a document in a different application. For example, you can insert an image to use on the cover of a report you created with a word-processing application, or you can insert a chart to illustrate a concept in a PowerPoint presentation.

To insert a graphic into a program, use the File > Import or Insert > Pictures command. For example, in a Microsoft Office application, select the Insert tab and then select Pictures. Navigate to the location where the graphics file is stored, select it, and then select Insert. Use the commands on the Picture Tools tabs to size, position, and format the graphic.

IC3✔ Be able to import and insert images into documents.

FIGURE 17.3.4 Insert clip art to illustrate a report in Microsoft Word.

Chapter 17 Review

REVIEW THE TERMINOLOGY

DIRECTIONS Match each vocabulary term in the left column with the correct definition in the right column.

1. raster graphic
2. vector graphic
3. resolution
4. paint program
5. color palette
6. Eyedropper
7. graphics tablet
8. import
9. layer
10. clip art

a. the number of pixels in a certain image that affects its visual quality

b. images that can be downloaded for use in a graphics program

c. images created using lines or paths

d. tool that captures and uses color from one portion of an image in another

e. input device for creating graphics

f. stacks of information on top of one another to form a more complete image

g. image created using pixels, or series of dots

h. allows you to modify raster graphics

i. brings information into a file from another file

j. the display of color options in paint and draw programs

USE THE TERMINOLOGY

DIRECTIONS Complete each sentence with information from the chapter.

1. Sets of dots that make up an image are called _____.

2. A(n) _____ allows you to create and edit vector graphics.

3. Advanced paint programs that allow you to edit and add effects to a raster graphic are _____.

4. The area of the screen where images are created and edited is the _____.

5. The set of color options in a particular paint or draw program shown in small boxes on the screen is called the _____.

6. In a draw program, a(n) _____ allows you to pick a certain portion of an image to work on.

7. A common input device in a graphics program is the _____.

8. The process of formatting data so that it can be used in another application is _____.

9. Combining separate images to form a single image is called _____.

10. The process of converting pixels to lines or paths is known as _____.

THINK CRITICALLY

DIRECTIONS Answer the following questions.

1. What would be some good uses for saved digital images when it comes to enhancing documents in other applications? Give examples.

2. When editing graphics, why is it important to consider the file format in which an image is created?

3. How do toolbars in draw and paint programs help you to edit and add effects to images?

4. Why are exporting and importing important functions for working with graphics?

5. How are layering and grouping similar? How are they different?

EXTEND YOUR KNOWLEDGE

DIRECTIONS Choose and complete one of the following projects.

1. Create a comic strip using vector or raster graphics. You may create your own images or edit clip art. Your comic strip should have at least four frames. Be sure to use the different tools and colors in the program. With your teacher's permission, print your comic strip to show to the class, or show it on a monitor or with a projector.

2. Newspapers and magazines often use graphics to capture the readers' attention or to make a point. Find three graphics (including photos with special effects) in newspapers or magazines. Next, create a three-column chart. On the chart, paste each image, identify each source and page number, and categorize the graphic as raster or vector. Present your chart to the class.

IC3 PREP

1. What is the crop tool used for in graphics editing?
   a. removing the edges of an image
   b. changing the color of an image
   c. copying an image
   d. creating a new image layer

2. Which of the following are ways in which a graphic can be modified? (Select all that apply.)
   a. cropping
   b. flipping
   c. wobbling
   d. skewing

3. Put the following steps for importing an image into a Microsoft Office document into the correct order.
   a. Select Insert.
   b. Navigate to the location where the graphics file is stored.
   c. Select the Insert tab, and then select Pictures.
   d. Select the desired image file.

IC3 PROCEDURES

CROPPING AN IMAGE IN MS PAINT

1. Start Paint.

2. Select **File** > **Open**.

3. Browse to the location where the image file is stored.

4. Select the image and select **Open**.

5. On the Home tab, select the **Select** drop-down arrow .

6. Select an option under Selection Shapes:

   - **Rectangular selection**

   - **Free-form selection**

7. Click and drag across your image to select the area of the image you want to keep.

8. On the Home tab, select the **Crop** button .

INSERTING AN IMAGE INTO AN MS OFFICE DOCUMENT

1. In the MS Office Document, position the insertion point where you want to insert the image.

2. On the Insert tab, select the **Pictures** button .

3. Browse to the location where the image file is stored.

4. Select the image and select **Insert**.

   OR

1. In the MS Office Document, position the insertion point where you want to insert the image.

2. On the Insert tab, select the **Online Pictures** button .

3. In the search box, type a keyword, and then press **Enter**.

4. In the list of results, select the picture to insert.

5. Select **Insert**.

CHAPTER 18

Understanding Digital Graphics

GRAPHICS IN THE REAL WORLD

Graphics make up everything you see on your computer screen. The images and even the letters in a word-processing document are kinds of graphics.

When working with computer graphics, there are many things to keep in mind. How many colors will an image need? How will those colors look? Will the image appear fuzzy and bumpy or smooth and sharp? How much space will it take to store the image on the computer? Can it be viewed on the internet? How fast will images be transmitted? Graphics software helps computer users create, change, and refine the words and images we see onscreen.

Preparing Computer Graphics

OBJECTIVES

- Compare and contrast lossless and lossy compression.

- Explain the effect of color on computer memory.

- Name and describe the four basic color modes.

AS YOU READ

ORGANIZE INFORMATION As you read this lesson, create an outline to help you organize the information on preparing computer graphics.

TERMINOLOGY

- color depth

- compress

- lossless compression

- lossy compression

File Compression and Graphics

Graphics files can be very large. When they are stored on the computer, the images are often **compressed**, or saved in a format requiring less space. This saves disk space and decreases the time it takes to send images via the internet.

When a file is compressed, the program performing the compression replaces certain pieces of information with shorter codes. This makes the file smaller.

LOSSLESS COMPRESSION In **lossless compression**, information is removed in such a way that all of it can later be fully restored without introducing errors. This process results in a perfect copy of the file that is about one third of the original size. Lossless compression is a good choice for reducing files with graphics, text, or computer code.

LOSSY COMPRESSION In **lossy compression**, some information is permanently removed from the file in such a way that it cannot be restored to its original state. Lossy compression can reduce a file to one fiftieth or less of its former size. It is best for reducing the size of video and audio files.

Color Depth

The more colors or shades of gray an image contains, the sharper and more detailed it will look. The number of colors that can be displayed on a monitor at one time is the **color depth**. Most modern computer monitors can display millions of colors. Because the computer must store more bits of information for each color pixel, more memory is needed to store colors than to store black and white alone.

Color Modes

Color modes determine which and how many colors are available for creating computer graphics.

BITMAP MODE When it comes to color modes, bitmap refers to a 1-bit, or black-and-white, image.

| Bitmap | Grayscale | RGB | CMYK |

FIGURE 18.1.1 An image's color mode determines how many colors display.

TONO BALAGUER/SHUTTERSTOCK

REAL-WORLD TECH
OFFSET PRINTING

The printing technique known as offset printing involves spreading ink on a metal plate with etched images on it. The plate is then pressed against another surface, often a rubber sheet. This transfers the ink onto the new surface, but the image now appears backward. Finally, the new surface is pressed against paper. This reverses the ink image from the surface onto the paper.

The equipment used and the cost of setting up the printing press are quite expensive. Therefore, offset printing is usually done to print a large quantity, or print run.

What types of printed materials that you read might have been printed using an offset process?

BOBBY DRAGULESCU/SHUTTERSTOCK

GRAYSCALE MODE When working in grayscale mode, the computer can display 256 different shades of gray to represent the colors, shades, and textures in an image.

RGB MODE Look closely at a television picture, and you may notice that it is made up of tiny clusters of dots. Each cluster has one red, one green, and one blue dot. When these three colors are combined in various ways, they produce different colors.

RGB mode allows each of these three colors to have 8 bits of information, resulting in 256 different shades each of the colors red (R), green (G), and blue (B). Color computer monitors use RGB color to display graphics, so RGB mode is used to design on-screen graphics such as those for the internet.

CMYK MODE In CMYK mode, a combination of four colors in different densities produces other colors. Variations of cyan (greenish-blue), magenta (purplish-red), yellow, and black (known as K) are combined to produce new colors.

CMYK mode is used to design graphics that will be printed on a printing press. Each of the four color values in a CMYK graphic is assigned to one of the four inks. These inks are then used on the printing press to print a full-color piece.

But what if you wanted to display a CMYK graphic on a monitor? To view a CMYK graphic on the screen, the computer has to convert it to RGB. This is why printed graphics may look different from an on-screen preview of the image.

Resolution Issues

When creating or modifying graphics, it is important to work with the proper resolution. A graphic's resolution should be determined by the planned output method, or how that graphic will be displayed.

If a graphic is to be viewed onscreen only, the resolution need not be higher than 72 dpi or 96 dpi. A 300-dpi graphic looks the same on-screen as a 72-dpi version of the same file. Increasing the dpi does not improve onscreen appearance. Because a 72 or 96-dpi file is smaller, it will display more quickly.

If a graphic will be printed, the resolution should be as high as the device on which it will be printed. For an image to look its best on a 300-dpi printer, it should be created at 300 dpi.

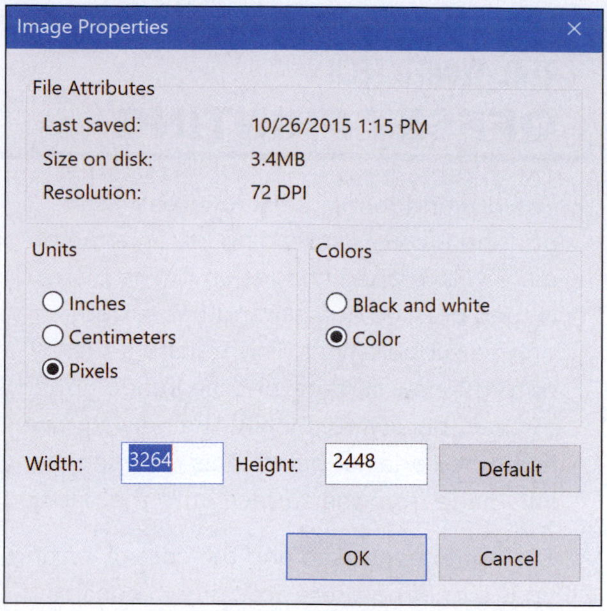

MICROSOFT CORPORATION

FIGURE 18.1.2 In Paint, you can check a graphic's resolution in its Properties dialog box.

DID YOU KNOW?

In Adobe® Photoshop® and other graphics programs, RGB mode assigns a value to each pixel. The values range from 0 to 255, for a total of 256 colors.

Black (no color) is assigned the value of 0, and white (full color) is given a value of 255. Since RGB mode is based on three colors, one value needs to be assigned to the red, another to the green, and another to the blue to make another color. For example, one shade of bright red is made using a value of 246 for red, 20 for green, and 50 for blue. The three values are programmed into the computer using the hexadecimal value system for color so the desired color displays onscreen or in print.

Exploring Image Editing Programs

OBJECTIVES

- Identify two different ways to bring existing images into a computer.

- Summarize how filters improve the look of an image.

- Compare and contrast image editor selection tools.

AS YOU READ

IDENTIFY KEY CONCEPTS As you read this lesson, use a concept web to help you identify tools used to edit images.

TERMINOLOGY

- filter

- Lasso

- Magic Wand

- Marquee

Input Devices for Graphics

While it is possible to create graphics from scratch using paint or draw programs, there are many times when existing images must be imported for use in a graphics program. There are two main input tools that let you digitize images so you can import them into the computer: scanners and digital cameras.

SCANNERS Recall that a scanner is a device that copies and changes a printed image into a digital format that a computer can process and store. A scanner is similar to a copy machine. It divides the image into boxes and assigns each box a value representing its "darkness" or color. Scanners consist of a light source, a lens, and a light sensor that translates optical impulses into electrical impulses. A flatbed scanner has a reader, which is the part that actually "sees" the image, sitting under a pane of glass. The image is placed face down on the glass so the reader can scan it and digitize it. Flatbed scanners are now routinely included in all-in-one printers. A handheld scanner is one that a person holds and moves across the image to digitize it.

DIGITAL CAMERAS A digital camera stores images digitally instead of on film. A computer chip in the camera changes light patterns from the captured image into pixels, which the camera can store. The image, or photo, can then be downloaded to the computer for storage or for printing. There is a wide variety of quality and type of digital cameras available. Professional photographers might spend thousands of dollars while a hobbyist might spend hundreds. Luckily, smartphones come with built-in cameras for capturing digital images in a quality suitable for printing or uploading.

Filters in Image Editors

Image editors are used to edit raster images—often, high-resolution images such as digital photographs. Image editors usually offer a variety

PTNPHOTO/123RF.COM

KLETR/SHUTTERSTOCK

FIGURE 18.2.1 A flatbed scanner (top) lets you digitize printed documents, such as photos. A digital camera (bottom) stores images digitally instead of on film.

of **filters**, preset features that apply specific effects to the image. Many filters are designed to improve photos, some to apply a tone or mode, and some are just for fun. Common filters include sharpening, blur, and noise filters.

SHARPENING FILTERS Image editors often contain several sharpening filters. One type of sharpening filter more clearly defines the edges of an image. It does this by finding a line of pixels that runs together as one color and is next to other pixels of other colors. The filter increases the color differences between the line of pixels of one color and those of nearby colors, making the edges more distinct.

BLUR FILTERS There are also many kinds of blur filters. A blur filter softens the look of an image by making hard edges look blurrier. They can be used to apply this effect to all or part of an image.

Using both sharpening and blurring techniques at the same time can add depth to an image. One way to do this is to apply sharpening effects to the area of an image that extends toward the viewer. Then, blur the areas farther away from the viewer. This produces a three-dimensional, or 3D, effect.

NOISE FILTERS Filters designed to add or remove roughness from an image are called noise filters. Two types of noise filters are the despeckle and median filters. They determine the edges of an image and leave them alone. Then, they smooth out other areas with less difference in color. This is often done to remove moiré patterns, or unwanted patterns of dots, that show up in some scanned photos.

Image Editor Selection Tools

One powerful feature of an image editor is its ability to work with certain pixels in an image while leaving other pixels unchanged. This is done using a selection tool, a graphics tool that allows you to choose one part of an image or the objects that make up an image. For instance, you can use a selection tool to choose eyes in an image of a face. Three common selection tools are:

- Marquee tool
- Lasso tool
- Magic Wand tool

TECHNOLOGY@HOME

A filter is an effect that can be applied to an image. Most graphics programs include filters and they can be fun and useful for home-computer projects. You can touch up images for holiday cards, party invitations, and even personal photographs.

THINK ABOUT IT!

The right filter is needed to gain a desired effect. For each of the following items, determine whether an image should be edited with a Sharpening tool, a Blur tool, or a Noise tool.

- make edges look crisp
- soften hard edges
- remove a pattern of dots
- add a textured look

PMPHOTO/SHUTTERSTOCK

FIGURE 18.2.2 The image on the left has no filter applied. The image on the right has a blur filter applied, to create a softer, or slightly fuzzy, effect.

MARQUEE The rectangle selection tool is sometimes called the **Marquee** tool. It works just like the Rectangle tool that allows you to draw a box in Word. But instead of drawing a box, the Marquee selection tool highlights a simple shape.

LASSO The **Lasso** tool in an image editor is used to select complex, or freehand, shapes. It is well suited for selecting images that share colors with nearby pieces of an image.

MAGIC WAND Perhaps the most powerful selection tool is the **Magic Wand**, which selects all touching pixels of a similar color. If you select a red pixel, then all red pixels that are connected with it will automatically be selected. The Magic Wand can be adjusted for small or wide ranges of color. For instance, if set for a small range, the wand will select only exact matches. But if set for large ranges, it will select similar shades of the selected color.

TECHNOLOGY@SCHOOL

Selection tools can be useful when working on images for the school paper or to touch up yearbook photos.

THINK ABOUT IT!

For the following shapes, identify the right tool to use to highlight an image of each—Marquee tool, Lasso tool, or the Magic Wand.

- shape of a tree outside a classroom window
- color blue in a textbook cover lunchbox
- red stripes in the American flag

MICROSOFT CORPORATION (SCREENSHOT)/AFRICA STUDIO/SHUTTERSTOCK (CLIP ART)

FIGURE 18.2.3 Use the Marquee or Rectangular Selection tool to select part of an image.

Draw and Animation Features

OBJECTIVES

- Describe four advanced tools in draw programs.

- Summarize the process of computer animation.

- Explain how animation is viewed on a computer.

AS YOU READ

SHOW CAUSE AND EFFECT Use a cause-and-effect chart to help you understand how advanced drawing tools create graphics.

TERMINOLOGY

- Align

- animation

- Distribute

- frame

- frame rate

- grid

- order

- player software

- tween

Advanced Draw Program Tools

Draw programs provide a number of tools to help you work with images.

ALIGN TOOL The **Align** tool moves parts of an image and determines how the parts will be placed in relation to one another. It can be helpful for lining up objects of different sizes. To use this tool, select several objects in the graphic—such as lines or shapes—and then open the tool. You can arrange objects to make the tops, bottoms, sides, or middles of the objects align with one another.

DISTRIBUTE TOOL The **Distribute** tool moves objects to distribute, or space, them from each other. The two kinds of distribution are fixed amount and within bounds. Fixed amount distribution puts a uniform distance between objects. For instance, you might want to put an inch of space between several objects. Within bounds distribution leaves the outermost objects exactly where they are and evenly spaces all the other selected objects between them.

ORDER TOOL Sometimes objects in an image overlap, or lay partially on top of one another. When this happens, certain objects may be blocked from view. The **Order** tool changes the position in which objects are stacked and rearranges them to avoid this problem. Objects can be moved to the bottom, the top, or the side of a stack.

GRID TOOL Many graphics programs offer a **Grid** tool to align images properly. Grids work just like a sheet of graph paper, by showing squares on the computer screen. For objects to align, they must begin in the same column on the grid.

Many graphics programs offer a feature called snap-to-guides or snap-to-grids. When this feature is turned on, objects are automatically moved to the nearest grid line. This helps ensure that every object is in a perfectly aligned position.

Animating Images

When two or more graphics are displayed one after the other, they can appear to be in motion. **Animation** is the process of quickly showing many images of an object to make it appear as if it is moving.

ANIMATING BY HAND Before computers, animation was done by hand, or with cameras. Sometimes, artists drew by hand each **frame**, or individual still image in a sequence. The frames would then be flipped to simulate motion. Other times, sophisticated film cameras took one still picture at a time and sequenced them quickly to mimic movement. The more frames displayed per second, the more convincing the animation looked. The speed at which a frame moves, measured in number of images per second, is called the **frame rate**.

ANIMATING ON A COMPUTER In computer animation, frames are created and then rapidly displayed to create the impression of motion. There is, however, a key benefit to computer animation. **Tweening** is the ability of a graphics program to determine in between frames, so you do not need to draw every one. You just draw the starting and ending frames, and the computer draws those in-between frames in sequence.

Software for Viewing Animation

Player software, a program that interprets the information in an animation file, must be installed in order to view animated graphics on a computer monitor. Player software usually can tell the computer how to interpret and convert animated graphics into images it can display.

PLAYER SOFTWARE VLC media player, developed by the VideoLAN project, is a free, open-source player for media and streaming media. It is available for desktop systems running Windows, Linux, and MacOS as well as for mobile devices running Android, iOS, and Windows Phone.

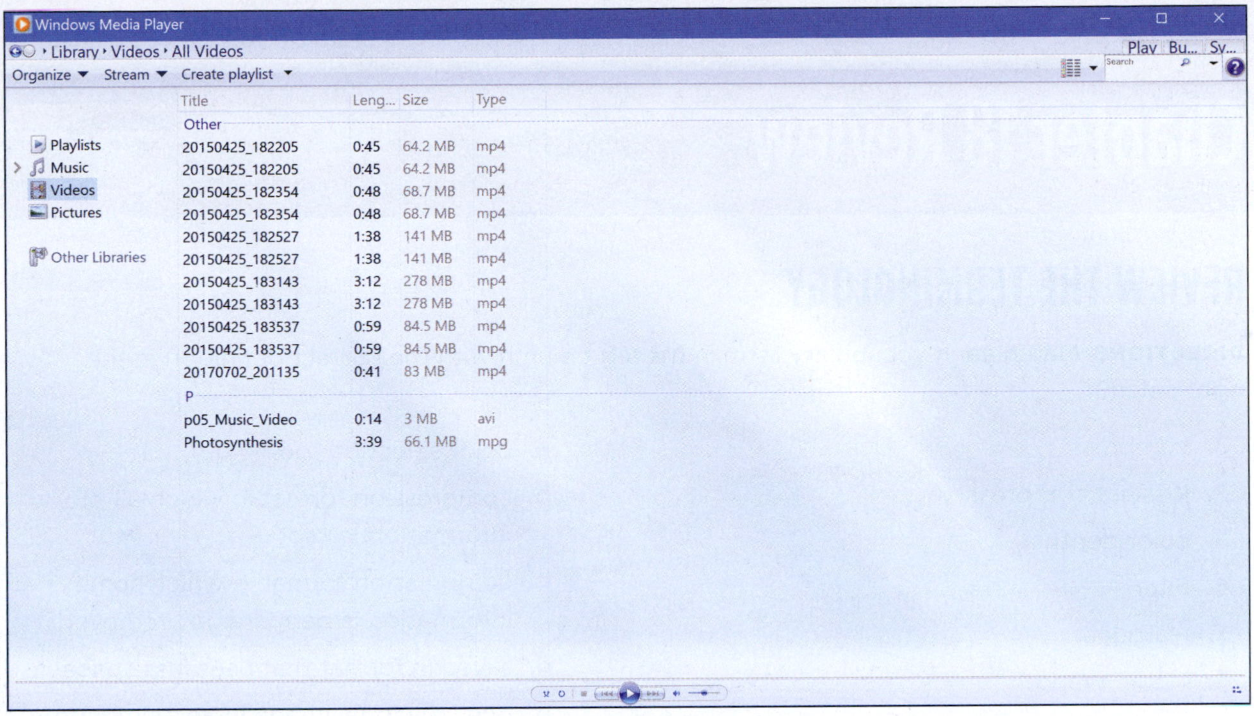

FIGURE 18.3.1 Windows 10 comes with Windows Media Player, which you can use to play music and videos, or display pictures.

Adobe's Flash Player is player software that allows a web browser to view vector animation. For many years, Flash was one of the most commonly-used player programs, but has recently been overtaken by other software.

Created by Apple Computer, Quick Time Player is commonly used for bitmapped animation. It provides the continuous flow of information needed to display movies, live action, and animation. Although it was created for use on Apple computers, versions are available for older Windows systems.

Part of Microsoft Windows, Windows Media Player was first introduced in 1991. It is used for playing, viewing, and organizing media files, such as videos, animations, and still images. To open Windows Media Player on a Windows 10 device, enter Media Player in the search box on the toolbar and then select the Best Match entry for the Windows Media Player Desktop app.

DIGITAL MEDIA SERVICES Digital media services and apps, such as Apple iTunes and Microsoft Windows & TV, let you rent or purchase videos or music and then play them. These services also offer features for storing media on cloud servers, as well as for organizing and cataloging media files.

Chapter 18 Review

REVIEW THE TERMINOLOGY

DIRECTIONS Match each vocabulary term in the left column with the correct definition in the right column.

1. compress
2. lossless compression
3. color depth
4. filter
5. Marquee
6. Magic Wand
7. lossy compression
8. frame
9. tween
10. player software

a. color selection tool

b. compression format in which all information is kept

c. compression format in which some information is permanently removed

d. saved in format that uses less space

e. one individual image in an animation

f. image editor feature that changes appearance of an image

g. program that converts animation files for viewing

h. colors shown on a monitor at one time

i. to generate middle frames of animation by computer

j. rectangle selection tool

USE THE TERMINOLOGY

DIRECTIONS Determine the correct choice for each of the following.

1. Which color mode is based on a combination of three colors to make new colors?
   a. bitmap
   b. grayscale
   c. RGB
   d. CMYK

2. If a graphic is to be printed, how high should its dpi rating be set?
   a. 72 dpi
   b. higher than output device
   c. lower than output device
   d. same as output device

3. Which filter will make an image's edges look softer?
   a. sharpen
   b. blur
   c. noise
   d. despeckle

4. Which tool is good for selecting complex shapes of whatever color you point out?

    a. Marquee   **c.** Magic wand

    b. Lasso   **d.** Distribute

5. Which tool is used to move objects so they line up in a certain way?

    a. Align   **c.** Order

    b. Distribute   **d.** Grid

6. Which player software views vector and bitmapped images?

    a. Flash Player   **c.** QuickTime Player

    b. RealPlayer   **d.** Vector Player

THINK CRITICALLY

DIRECTIONS Answer the following questions.

1. Why do graphics files often need compression?
2. Why is RGB mode used to design computer graphics?
3. What input devices allow graphics in other formats to be digitized?
4. How has tweening changed the animation process?
5. What is one advantage of vector animation?

EXTEND YOUR KNOWLEDGE

DIRECTIONS Choose and complete one of the following projects.

1. Experiment with the toolbars in an image editor to see what each tool does. Then, use a scanner or digital camera to capture an image and save it on your computer. Edit the image, using several of the tools. With your teacher's permission, print the images and present both your original and edited images to the class. Explain which tools you used to achieve the effects shown.

2. Several tools for working with graphics are discussed in this chapter. Research other tools for applying special effects to graphics, such as tools that let you create drawings that look like they were created using actual ink, watercolor, acrylic, or oil paint. Create a chart identifying these tools and explaining how they are used. Use a graphics program to create drawings or shapes using the tools to illustrate your chart. Read your chart out loud to a partner and listen while your partner reads his or hers out loud to you.

3. As a class, discuss how graphics can be used to make a publication look better and also to help convey a message. Select a topic that interests you and have it approved by your teacher. Then, use graphics software to create an image that could be used on a web page about your topic. Make sure the image would both enhance the appearance of the page and convey a message about the topic. As a class, display and discuss the images.

TORIA/SHUTTERSTOCK

CHAPTER 19

Presentation Basics

WHAT ARE PRESENTATIONS?

A presentation is a visual or multimedia display. Every day, presentations are shown on monitors in classrooms, at meetings, and to online audiences. They help people teach ideas, sell products, and share information with others.

Before computers, creating a professional presentation took a lot of time and involved many people. First, an artist would create graphics. Next, the graphics and wording would be organized for logical flow and visual appeal. Then, this information was transferred onto transparencies or slides. Now, thanks to presentation software, many people create presentations more quickly. Knowing how to use presentation software is an important skill in today's world.

Exploring Presentation Software

OBJECTIVES

- Identify the benefits of presentation software.

- Identify two options for creating a new presentation.

- Describe six views in PowerPoint.

AS YOU READ

ORGANIZE INFORMATION Use a concept web to help you organize ways to create and view presentations as you read.

TERMINOLOGY

- AutoContent wizard

- Master views

- Normal view

- Notes page

- Notes Page view

- Outline view

- presentation

- presentation software

- presenter

- Reading view

- Slide

- Slide show

- Slide Show view

- Slide Sorter view

- template

- theme

- thumbnails

- wizard

Introducing Presentation Software

Presentation software is the application you use to organize and display a sequence of ideas using text, graphics, sound, animation, and video. The content is arranged on separate pages. Each page is called a **slide**. Each slide can contain one or more main points. Information about each main point is organized into a list of short, easy-to-read bullet items and illustrated with graphics, such as drawings, tables, and pictures. The completed file, called a **presentation** or **slide show**, can be published for display on a monitor or screen to an audience of one or more, or printed for distribution. Sometimes, there is a **presenter**, or live person speaking and controlling the presentation. Other times, the presentation can be viewed and controlled by the audience.

IC3✔ Identify presentation software options: presentations.

CREATING A NEW PRESENTATION There are many programs, such as Corel Presentations and Apple's Keynote, that are specifically designed for creating, saving, editing, and producing presentations. The most common presentation software is Microsoft PowerPoint. With PowerPoint, you have two options for designing and creating a new presentation:

- template

- blank presentation

TEMPLATE Recall that a **template** is a file that already includes layout, formatting, prompts, and some content suitable for a specific document type. For example, you might select a marketing template, or a training template. You can use built-in templates that come with your program, look for templates online, or create and save your own templates for future use.

After choosing a template, you enter the information on the slides in the template placeholders. You can also change the look and feel of the template by selecting a theme or manually

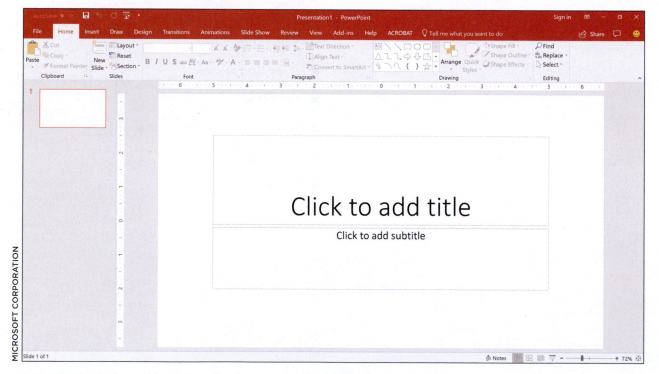

FIGURE 19.1.1 A new, blank presentation starts with one blank title slide.

adjusting the settings, such as the colors. A **theme** is a collection of formatting settings such as color scheme, fonts, and effects.

Using templates can save time and increase productivity because you do not have to design or format the presentation yourself. Another benefit is that using templates can give your presentations a similar look and feel, which can help customers identify your business by brand.

To create a document based on a template in a Microsoft Office application, select File > New, and then select the document category to view the available templates. When you find one you like, select it and select Create. Replace the sample text and fill in the placeholders to complete your presentation.

If you have a file you would like to use as a template in the future, you can use the File > Save As command and select the document template format from the Save as type list in the Save As dialog box. In PowerPoint, the document template file type has a .potx file extension, and the template is saved by default in the Custom Office Template folder.

IC3✔ Be able to use templates.

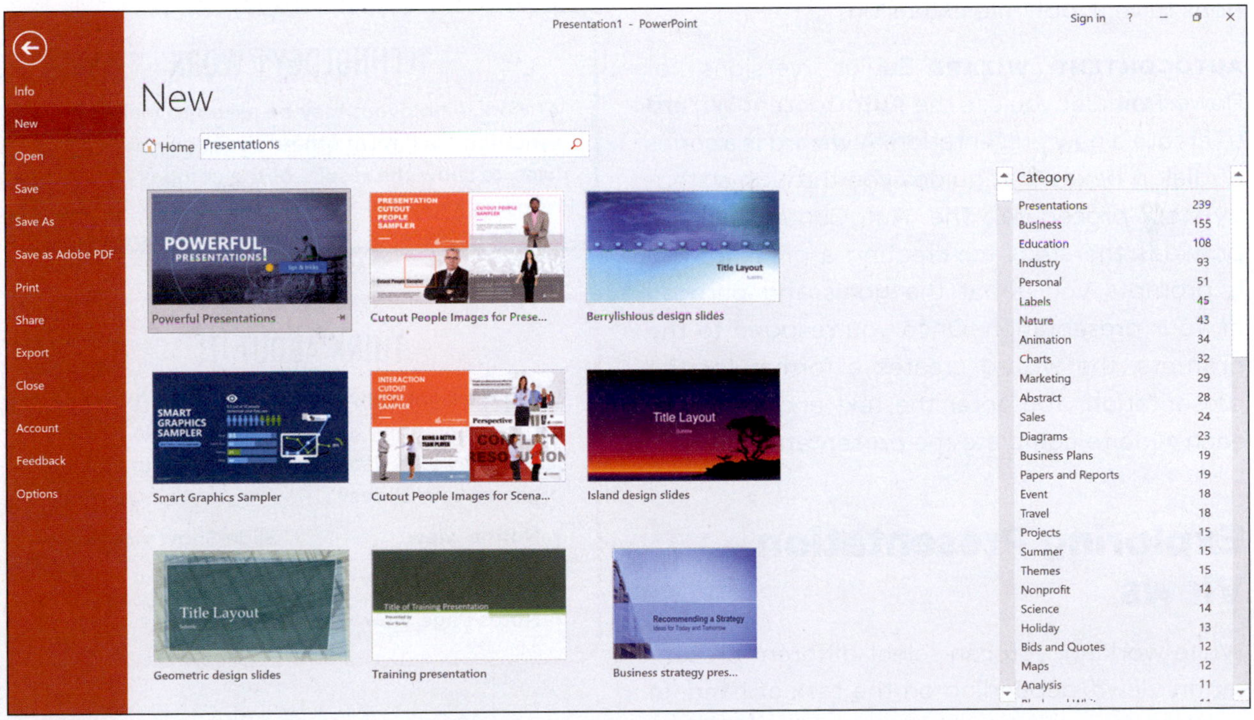

DID YOU KNOW?

Screen-reading programs that read text aloud can make working on a computer easier for people with visual impairments.

- Job Access With Speech, or JAWS, uses your computer's sound to read aloud what is displayed on the screen.

- Hal Screen Reader also converts what is on the screen to sound. It can be used with PowerPoint and even Braille text.

MICROSOFT CORPORATION

FIGURE 19.1.2 Create a new presentation based on a template.

BLANK PRESENTATION If you do not want to use a template, you can create a blank presentation. A blank presentation starts with one blank slide suitable for a title. You enter content, insert additional slides, and apply formatting to complete the presentation. While this option may require more work than using a template, it does have benefits. For instance, you can create a new presentation from scratch to make your work more original by selecting your own color scheme, art, fonts, and other design elements.

To create a blank presentation in PowerPoint, select File > New, select Blank Presentation.

SAVING A PRESENTATION No matter how you create your presentation, you must save it so it is available for use in the future. Use the File > Save As command to save a new presentation, or an existing presentation with a new name or in a new storage location. Use the File > Save command to save recent changes to an existing file.

By default, Microsoft PowerPoint 2016 presentations have a .pptx file extension.

AUTOCONTENT WIZARD Earlier versions of PowerPoint let you use the **AutoContent Wizard** to create a new presentation. A wizard is a series of dialog boxes that guides you through a step-by-step procedure. The AutoContent wizard provides the steps for creating a presentation. It prompts you about the goals and purpose of your presentation. Once you respond to the prompts, the wizard creates a format for the presentation. You enter the text and image on each slide to complete the presentation.

Exploring Presentation Views

While working, you can select different presentation views, depending on the task at hand. In most programs, you will find the View controls on the View menu or tab, and on the program's status bar.

Each view has its own strength. Depending on the program you use, you may be able to choose from a variety of views.

NORMAL VIEW Text and graphics can be inserted, deleted, or edited in **Normal view**. Normal view splits the screen to show the current slide in the main window, and **thumbnails** of each slide in a pane on the left. Thumbnails are small graphic representations of a page or slide. Below the current slide in the main window is the **Notes pane**, where you can enter speaker notes to use while delivering the presentation.

SLIDE SORTER VIEW **Slide Sorter view** displays thumbnails of all of the slides in a presentation. This view allows you to change the order of the slides by dragging them to different locations.

NOTES PAGE VIEW In **Notes Page view**, part of the screen displays the slide and the rest of the screen is a text box where you can enter notes that the presenter can use during a presentation or to print as handouts.

TECHNOLOGY@WORK

At work, employees may be asked to make presentations to inform others about company policies, to show the results of the company's latest research, or to sell a new product.

THINK ABOUT IT!

Using the right view in presentation software can make creating a presentation a little bit easier. Which views listed below would help you organize your slides?

- Normal view
- Slide Sorter view
- Notes Page view
- Slide Show view
- Reading view
- Master views

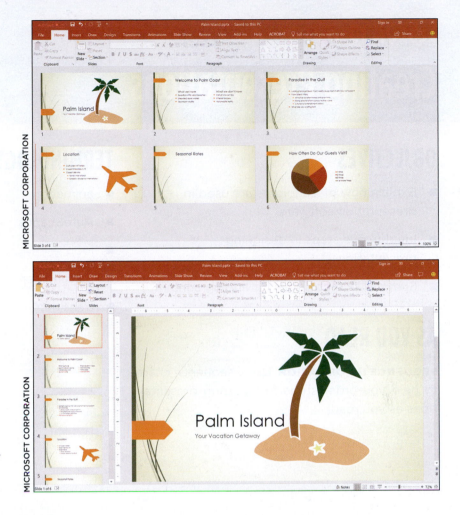

MICROSOFT CORPORATION

FIGURE 19.1.3 Slide Sorter view (top) and Normal view (bottom) in Microsoft PowerPoint.

SLIDE SHOW VIEW The primary on-screen method of previewing and displaying slides during a presentation is called **Slide Show view**. Slides are displayed full-screen, one after another, in order. A slide-show presentation can be set to automatically advance slides or to wait until the presenter, or person controlling the slide show, advances the slides manually. Notes do not display in Slide Show view.

PRESENTER VIEW Presenter view can be used at the same time as Slide Show view. It allows the presenter to see the notes during the slide show.

READING VIEW **Reading view** is similar to Slide Show view. It includes basic controls for navigating through the slide show. It is usually used when there is no presenter controlling the presentation.

MASTER VIEWS Many programs let you use **Master views** to make universal style changes to every slide, notes page, and/or handout pages.

OUTLINE VIEW In **Outline view**, an outline including titles and main text of all the text in the presentation displays in a pane on the left side of the window. The current slide displays to the right. You can enter and edit text in the outline pane or on the slide itself.

You may also be able to use Black and White and/or Grayscale views to see how slides will look if printed without color. This can be helpful for previewing handouts of slides that use dark backgrounds or thin fonts.

IC3✓ **Be able to use presentation views and modes.**

Creating Presentations

OBJECTIVES

- Explain how placeholders are used in presentation software.

- Identify five steps in designing presentations.

- Summarize techniques for adding content.

AS YOU READ

SEQUENCE INFORMATION Use a sequence chart to help you order steps for creating presentations as you read.

TERMINOLOGY

- animation

- AutoShapes

- loop

- placeholder

- transition

Designing Presentations

Following these five steps will help you plan, design, and save an effective presentation.

1. **Decide How Your Slides Will Be Formatted** To begin designing a presentation, choose an option for creating it. Choose either a blank presentation or a template. If none of the templates are exactly what you want, select the one that is closest. You can change much of its graphic content, format, and text. Graphics can be resized or deleted. Placeholders can be added, removed, or resized as well.

> IC3 ✔ **Know how to design slides.**

2. **Choose the Slide Layout** Every slide in a presentation has a slide layout. When you add a new slide, you select a layout that already has placeholders in position so you can add text and graphics in the most logical place on the slide. Some examples of slide layouts include bulleted lists, tables, grids, and flowcharts. Since each slide in a presentation can have a different layout, you can select a layout for each new slide you add, or change the layout of existing slides.

> IC3 ✔ **Identify presentation software options: layout.**

3. **Work with Placeholders** A **placeholder** is an area within a slide layout designed to hold data such as text or pictures. A placeholder automatically applies a format based on the type of content. For instance, selecting a text placeholder will position the insertion point so you can type text. Selecting a picture placeholder makes the insert and format pictures tools active.

4. **Insert Graphics and Sound** Make your presentations come to life by inserting sound, video, and graphics to support or illustrate the text. Always be mindful that the additions don't distract from the content.

5. **View and Organize the Presentation** It would, of course, be ideal to manage the development of a presentation so that you create every slide exactly the way you want it, in the sequence where it makes the most sense, without any errors. But, since that is unlikely to ever happen, you can use the tools in your presentation program to manage and organize the slides at any time.

As you work, save the presentation and preview it using Slide Show view. You can add and delete slides and edit and correct content as you work. If the presentation does not progress in a logical sequence, use Slide Sorter view to rearrange the slides.

> IC3 ✔ **Know how to manage slides.**

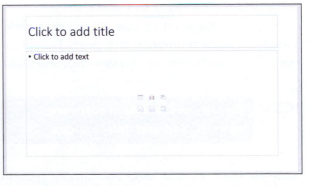

MICROSOFT CORPORATION

FIGURE 19.2.1 This slide layout in PowerPoint has placeholders for a title and content such as a bullet list, table, chart, or picture.

Adding Content to Presentations

When you create a new presentation, you must add as many slides as you need to display your content. As you add slides, you select the slide layout that will best present the content on that slide. You can delete slides you don't need, copy or import slides from other presentations, and change the slide layout as necessary.

To add a slide in PowerPoint, select the New Slide command on the Home tab, and then select the slide layout you want to use. To delete a slide, select the slide thumbnail and press Delete, or right-click the thumbnail and select Delete Slide.

IC3✔ Identify presentation software options: add and delete slides.

ADDING TEXT To add text, you simply type in a text placeholder or in an outline. Most slides have placeholders for titles. The main points are usually entered as a bulleted list, which is a neat and effective way to present information. Select the placeholder and begin typing. The program automatically formats the text to fit the area with a default font and alignment based on the template or theme.

ADDING NOTES You can add notes to each slide to use when you deliver the presentation. The notes may be a script you can read, or just important points you want to be sure to include. In PowerPoint, the default location for the Notes pane is below the slide area. If it is not displayed, select View > Notes.

ADDING GRAPHICS You can insert many types of graphics including clip art, pictures, drawings, charts, diagrams, and tables. In PowerPoint, use the buttons on the Insert tab of the Ribbon, or click the appropriate icon in a Content placeholder. PowerPoint drawing tools also include ready-to-use shapes, called **AutoShapes**. The list includes banners, arrows, borders, frames, and more. Save the file after every change.

Although using a placeholder helps position and size graphics on the slide, you do not need a placeholder to insert graphics. Select the desired tool and use it in a blank area of the workspace.

ADDING VIDEO AND SOUND A multimedia presentation combines text and graphics with sound and video. Both sound and animation, or moving images, are inserted using menu commands. For example, in PowerPoint you can choose to insert video or audio clips using buttons in the Media group on the Insert tab. You can use the Playback tools to control options such as the volume, whether the sound or video plays automatically or waits for a command from the presenter, and whether or not to **loop**, which means to replay continuously.

ADDING MOVEMENT TO SLIDES In most cases, there are two types of movement you can apply to slides:

- Apply a **transition** to control the change from one slide to the next. Most programs come with a large gallery of transitions such as fades, wipes, and cuts. Each transition has effects options such as whether the movement will be left to right or right to left. You can also set timing options

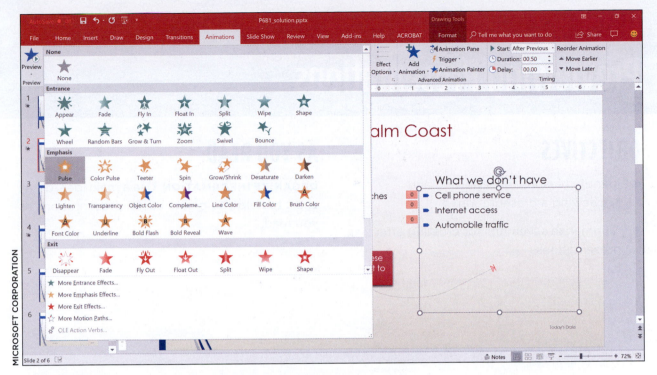

FIGURE 19.2.2 The Animations gallery in Microsoft PowerPoint 2016.

such as how long the transition will last and when it will start. You can apply a transition to one slide, selected slides, or to all slides. In PowerPoint, use the options on the Transitions tab of the Ribbon to apply and customize transitions.

- Apply an **animation** to control the way objects move on a slide. You can apply animations to graphics and text. For example,

you can set a bullet list so each bullet line displays in sequence, or all at once. Most programs come with a large gallery of animations, such as Fly in, Bounce, and Swivel. Each animation can be customized with effects that control how the object enters or exits the slide, or to add emphasis.

IC3✔ **Know how to add animations, effects, and slide transitions.**

Previewing Presentations

OBJECTIVES

- Identify reasons for reviewing and previewing a presentation

- Summarize seven tips for creating effective presentations.

AS YOU READ

ORGANIZE INFORMATION Use a main idea/detail chart to help you create useful presentations as you read.

Previewing a Presentation

Before finalizing a presentation, you should review it and preview it.

REVIEW Reviewing your presentation should include checking and correcting the spelling and grammar. Most programs include spell check tools that highlight possible errors and offer suggestions for correcting them. You can also send your presentation to a peer, such as a classmate or co-worker, for review. He or she can point out things that are unclear and suggest ways to improve the presentation. Many programs include tools to make peer review easier, such as the ability to insert comments.

PREVIEW Use Slide Show view to preview your presentation and check for inconsistencies such as incorrect fonts and spacing, poorly timed transitions, and animations that are out of order. During a preview, you can also practice delivering your presentation to an audience.

Creating Effective Presentations

Apply these seven tips to make your presentation effective.

ONE IDEA PER SLIDE Avoid crowding data onto a slide. Make as many slides as needed to present important information clearly.

KEEP IT SIMPLE The audience will be listening to your speech or narration while viewing your slides. Use simple words to emphasize key points. Include clear transitions from one topic to another.

DISPLAY KEY FACTS Your slides should serve as an outline for the audience. Your speech will fill in the gaps in that outline. Displaying too much information can make a presentation hard to follow.

FIGURE 19.3.1 In a well-designed presentation, each slide explains one key point or answers one key question.

ANDRESR/SHUTTERSTOCK

MIX IT UP Vary the layouts and content of your slides to help hold the audience's attention. For instance, switch between lists that appear on the right-hand and left-hand side, or break up text with illustrations.

USE COLOR CAUTIOUSLY Select colors that are pleasing to the eye. For instance, bright pink lettering on a bright blue background will be difficult to read. Avoid using too many colors on a slide.

WATCH THE FONTS Do not use more than two fonts on a single slide. This helps prevent a presentation from becoming too distracting to read. Also, be sure to use fonts that fit the tone. A presentation about the Civil War, for example, would not use fonts that seem playful or humorous.

MAKE IT READABLE Choose readable font and color combinations. Check that your text and images can be seen from the back of the room so your presentation can be viewed by your entire audience.

> ## TECHNOLOGY@WORK
>
> Before giving a presentation, test it with an audience such as co-workers, friends, or family.

> ## THINK ABOUT IT!
>
> Ask your test audience to point out slides that are hard to see or to understand. Which items listed below are concerns for presentation slides?
> - text too small
> - animation too fast
> - detailed information given
> - many colors used

REAL-WORLD TECH
DISTANCE LEARNING

Can you imagine creating presentations to show people who live hundreds of miles away? Distance learning teaches people at remote, or off-site, locations from the teacher. These students aren't seated together in a single classroom but are scattered around the globe watching the class online. Companies that develop distance-learning materials must create presentations students understand. It also means these presentations must keep students' interest. They may use slides, videos of actual lectures, and audio. Distance learning is offered by a large number of schools, colleges, and universities. Many people are now earning college degrees through distance learning by taking classes online. Some schools also offer classes that combine some face-to-face instruction with online presentations.

AFRICA STUDIO/SHUTTERSTOCK

Chapter 19 Review

REVIEW THE TERMINOLOGY

DIRECTIONS Match each vocabulary term in the left column with the correct definition in the right column.

1. presentation software
2. slide
3. wizard
4. template
5. Slide Show view
6. placeholder
7. AutoShapes
8. animation
9. thumbnail
10. Slide Sorter view

a. preformatted version of a certain type of document

b. list of ready-to-use drawing tools

c. allows you to change the order of slides by dragging them to different locations

d. single page in a presentation

e. creates and displays visual information

f. miniature versions of each slide image

g. area in a presentation that holds data

h. can automatically show a presentation in the correct order

i. images that show movement

j. a series of dialog boxes that provides a step-by-step guide

USE THE TERMINOLOGY

DIRECTIONS Complete each sentence with information from the chapter.

1. Graphics designed using _____ usually are accompanied by text.

2. Using _____ view lets you make universal style changes to every slide, notes page, and/or handout pages.

3. The _____ view provides information that only the presenter can see during a presentation.

4. An on-screen method of previewing a presentation's slides is called the _____.

5. Animation can be added to some PowerPoint presentations using the _____.

6. Bulleted lists, flowcharts, and grids can be included in a slide's _____.

7. You can create a multimedia presentation with _____.

8. In a presentation, only the most _____ should be included on slides, not everything you plan to say.

9. A(n) _____ presentation combines text and graphics with sound and animation.

10. To prevent a presentation from becoming too distracting, do not use more than two _____ on a single slide.

THINK CRITICALLY

DIRECTIONS Answer the following questions.

1. What are some benefits to using a template when creating a presentation?

2. What are disadvantages to adding clip art to PowerPoint presentations?

3. Why is it important to limit each slide in a presentation to a main concept or idea?

4. Why is it important to preview your presentation from the back of the room?

5. Which of the seven tips for creating effective presentations was the most meaningful to you? Why?

EXTEND YOUR KNOWLEDGE

DIRECTIONS Choose and complete one of the following projects.

1. In addition to PowerPoint, other software is available to create professional-looking presentations. Conduct research online or in software catalogs to find one other presentation program. Create a Venn diagram to compare and contrast the features of this program to those of PowerPoint.

2. Work in small teams, taking turns acting as team leader. Assign each team member one of the PowerPoint presentation views described in this chapter. Have each person create slides in his or her assigned view, summarizing the content of this chapter. As a team, present your slides to the class and watch their slides. Discuss the effectiveness of each view.

3. Work in small teams, taking turns acting as team leader. Plan and create a presentation that might be used in business, such as for training, marketing, or sales. Have each team member create at least one business-related element to include in the presentation, such as a table, embedded spreadsheet, chart, graph, organizational chart, or flowchart. Animate the elements, if appropriate. Deliver the presentation to the class.

IC3 PREP

1. For each line below, select whether the statement is True or False.

   a. Presentations are also known commonly as slide shows.

   b. A person who speaks over and controls a presentation is known as a slide-shower.

   c. Content in a presentation is arranged on individual pages, known as slides.

   d. Presentations can consist of text, graphics, sound, animation, and video.

2. Put the following steps for creating a presentation from a template in Microsoft Office into the correct order.

    a. Select the document category to view the available templates.

    b. Select File > New.

    c. Replace the sample text and fill in the placeholders.

    d. Find a template you like, select it, and select Create.

3. Which of the following is NOT a view in PowerPoint?

    a. Notes Page view   **d.** Image view

    b. Normal view   **e.** Reading view

    c. Outline view

4. For each line below, select whether the statement is True or False.

    a. When you create a new presentation, you must work with a limited number of slides to convey your ideas.

    b. The layout of each slide can be different, depending on how you would like that slide's information presented.

    c. You can select the layout of a slide as you add it to your presentation.

    d. It is difficult to delete unwanted slides.

5. What are some ways in which a slide can be altered or customized? (Select all that apply.)

    a. Slide text can be revised.   **c.** Different templates can be chosen.

    b. Graphics can be resized or deleted.   **d.** Fonts can be changed.

6. For each line below, select whether the statement is True or False.

    a. A placeholder automatically applies a format based on the selected type of content.

    b. Placeholders are able to hold content such as text or pictures.

    c. It is a good practice to load a presentation up with as many special effects, videos, sounds, animations, colors, and transitions as possible, to keep the audience engaged.

    d. Slides must be deleted if they are in the wrong order; they cannot be easily rearranged.

7. What are some common effects and transitions used in presentations? (Select all that apply.)

    a. one slide fading into the next

    b. each slide's background color is synced to the room's light system

    c. a bullet point list sliding in one point at a time

    d. a company logo animated to bounce around the slide

IC3 PROCEDURES

CREATING A BLANK PRESENTATION

1. Start PowerPoint.

   OR

   If PowerPoint is already open, select the **File** tab and then select **New**.

2. Select **Blank Presentation**.

CREATING A PRESENTATION BASED ON A TEMPLATE

1. Start PowerPoint.

   OR

   If PowerPoint is already open, select the **File** tab and then select **New**.

2. Type a keyword or phrase into the Search for online templates and themes box.

3. Press **Enter**.

4. Select a template.

5. If available, select a theme option from the Gallery.

6. Select the **Create** button .

SAVING A PRESENTATION AS A TEMPLATE

1. Open the presentation.

2. Select **File**.

3. Select **Save As**.

4. Select **Browse** .

5. In the Save As dialog box, from the Save as type list, select **PowerPoint Template (*.potx)**.

6. Enter a name for the template in the File name box.

7. Select **Save**.

CHANGING THE PRESENTATION VIEW

1. Select the **View** tab.

2. Select the desired View button:

   - **Normal**
   - **Outline View**
   - **Slide Sorter**
   - **Notes Page**
   - **Reading View**

   OR

Select a View icon on the status bar:

- **Normal** 🖼
- **Slide Sorter** ▦
- **Reading View** 📖
- **Slide Show** 🖥

CHANGING A SLIDE LAYOUT

1. Select the slide to change.
2. Select the **Home** tab.
3. Select the **Slide Layout** button Layout.
4. From the gallery, select the desired layout.

APPLYING A PRESENTATION THEME

1. Select the **Design** tab.
2. Select the theme to apply.

   OR

   Select the **Themes More** button.
3. Select the theme to apply.

INSERTING AN IMAGE FROM A FILE

1. Select the slide.
2. In the empty content placeholder, select the **Pictures** icon.

   OR

   a. Select the **Insert** tab.

   b. Select the **Pictures** button.
3. In the Insert Picture dialog box, browse to the location where the picture file is stored.
4. Select the picture file.
5. Select **Insert**.

INSERTING AN ONLINE PICTURE

1. Select the slide.
2. In the empty content placeholder, click the **Online Pictures** icon.

   OR

   a. Select the **Insert** tab.

   b. Select the **Online Pictures** button.
3. In the Insert Pictures dialog box, click in the search box and enter a search string that describes the picture you want.
4. Press **Enter**.
5. Select the desired image.
6. Select **Insert**.

SIZING A PICTURE

1. Select the picture.
2. Drag a sizing handle to resize the picture.

   OR

1. Right-click the picture.
2. On the shortcut menu, select **Format Picture**.
3. In the Format Picture task pane, select the **Size & Properties** button.
4. Select **Size**.
5. Set the height and width.

   OR

1. Select the picture.
2. Select the **Picture Tools Format** tab.
3. Use the **Shape Height** and **Shape Width** increment arrows to set the size.

POSITIONING A PICTURE

1. Select the picture.
2. Position the pointer a resize handle on the picture border.
3. When the pointer changes to a double-headed arrow, drag the picture to the desired position.

   OR

1. Right-click the picture.
2. On the shortcut menu, select **Format Picture**.
3. In the Format Picture task pane, select the **Size & Properties** button.
4. Select **Position**.
5. Set the horizontal and vertical positions.

ADDING A SLIDE USING THE PREVIOUSLY USED LAYOUT

1. Select the **Home** tab.
2. Select the **New Slide** button.

ADDING A SLIDE WITH A DIFFERENT LAYOUT

1. Select the **Home** tab.
2. Select the **New Slide** button down arrow.
3. From the gallery, select the desired layout.

DELETING A SLIDE

1. In the left pane, select the thumbnail of the slide to delete.
2. Press **Delete**.

APPLYING ANIMATIONS

1. Select a placeholder or object to which you want to apply the animation.
2. Select the **Animations** tab.
3. Select the **Animation More** button ⊡.
4. From the gallery, select the desired animation.

SETTING EFFECT OPTIONS

1. Select the placeholder or object to which you have applied the animation.
2. Select the **Animations** tab.
3. Select the **Effect Options** button ⬚.

   The graphic on your Effect Options button will depend on the animation already applied to the object or placeholder.

4. From the menu, select the desired effect.

APPLYING ANIMATION TO OBJECTS, CHARTS, AND DIAGRAMS

1. Select the graphic or object to which you want to apply the animation.
2. Select the **Animations** tab.
3. Select the **Animation More** button ⊡.
4. From the gallery, select the desired animation.

APPLYING SLIDE TRANSITIONS

1. Select the slide to which you want to add the transition.
2. Select the **Transitions** tab.
3. Select the **Transition to This Slide More** button ⊡.
4. From the gallery, select the desired transition.

ADDING TRANSITION EFFECTS

1. Select the slide with the transition.
2. Select the **Transitions** tab.
3. Select the **Effect Options** button ▨.
4. From the menu, select the desired effect.

CHANGING THE SLIDE LAYOUT

1. Select the slide.
2. Select the **Home** tab.
3. Select **Insert**.
4. Select the layout to apply.

CHAPTER 20
Enhancing Presentations

THE BIG MOMENT

You have worked hard to assemble all the necessary tools and information. The stage is now properly set. The colors and lighting are perfect, and the script is well written. The show is about to begin. Is this a Hollywood production? Is it a stage play? No, it's a computer presentation. Presentation software allows you to create a slide show with graphics, audio, text, animation, and more. Today, your computer screen is the stage. On other days, your show may be projected on a screen in a large auditorium or viewed on the internet.

Learning to use presentation software is an important skill for school and work. Learning to use it effectively will benefit you for years to come.

Presentation Options

OBJECTIVES

- Identify the purpose of presentation software.
- Explain the importance of knowing the output before developing a presentation.

AS YOU READ

ORGANIZE INFORMATION Use a spider map to organize tips for using presentation software effectively as you read.

TERMINOLOGY

- masters
- master slide
- viewable area
- visual aid

Using Presentation Software

One of the primary reasons for using presentation software is to create a visual aid for a speaker or presenter. A **visual aid** is something that illustrates a speech or narration. Having a visual aid helps the audience understand and remember the content. With presentation software, you can create slides and handouts to teach a concept or convey a message. Then, you can deliver the presentation on-screen in an office, in a conference room, or online.

CONNECTIONS

MATH Consider the cost if you are thinking of printing a presentation or presentation handouts. The more colors you use in your slides, the more it will cost to print them. For instance, a new color printing cartridge might cost about $45. It might print 100 pages using minimal color. That totals 45 cents per page. That same cartridge might only print 50 copies displaying a lot of color. That equals 90 cents per page, which can prove costly if you need several copies.

Most presentations use default settings suitable for creating and displaying a full color slide show to an audience on a monitor or screen, controlled by a live presenter. You can change the presentation options. For example, you can create a self-running presentation that does not require a live presenter, or that can be controlled by the viewer without the need for a presenter.

You can also make use of customization features such as designs and masters to create consistent and professional-looking presentations. For example, you can apply a design template or theme to your presentation to give it a uniform look and color scheme.

IC3 ✔ Identify presentation software options: presentations.

Working with Masters

Programs such as PowerPoint let you work with Slide, Notes, and Handout masters. **Masters** are default templates; changes you make to a master are applied to the components based on that master.

CREATIVA IMAGES/SHUTTERSTOCK

FIGURE 20.1.1 Presentations are used in many careers to share information with co-workers and customers.

A **master slide** is a default template that is applied to all slides. By editing a master slide, you are able to change fonts, sizes, colors, and layouts for all of the slides in a presentation. There are two different types of master slides in a presentation program such as PowerPoint:

- The Title Master controls the appearance of the title and subtitle of a title slide.

- The Slide Master controls the format for the slides.

For example, suppose you want to change the font used for the main heading at the top of each slide. You can open the Slide Master, select the heading placeholder, and make the change. When you change back to Normal view, all the slide headings in the presentation will have changed to match the new format.

Consider the Output

Presentation software programs offer options for optimizing the settings for printing a presentation, for displaying the slides on-screen, or for generating them as 35-mm slides. Other issues to consider are printer output and displays.

PRINTER OUTPUT If a presentation is to be printed and provided as a handout, the page setup should match the capabilities of the printer. A solid black background with green lettering might look fine on a computer screen. However, printing a colored background on every page for every person in the audience uses a lot of ink. In addition, simple color graphics lose their effect if they are printed in black. Also, dark backgrounds can make text hard to see on a printed page.

DISPLAYING THE OUTPUT For each presentation, it is important to anticipate how the slides will be viewed. Will it be displayed on a large monitor or on a smartphone or tablet screen? The display's **viewable area**, or portion of the screen where an image can be shown, affects what can be viewed. Different displays have different viewable areas. For instance, if the computer uses a television as an output device, some of the information may not be visible. This is also true when using an LCD (liquid crystal display)

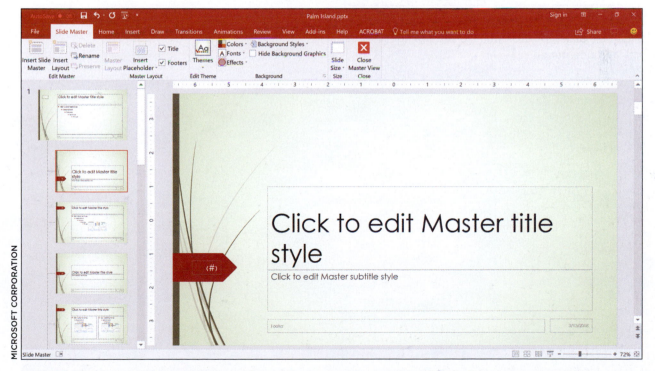

MICROSOFT CORPORATION

FIGURE 20.1.2 Use slide masters to set formatting and content options for all slides in a presentation.

455

monitor to project computer-screen images for large audiences. It is important to set up the slide show and adjust the slide size so that all content can be viewed properly.

In PowerPoint, by default slides are sized to the Widescreen setting, which has a 16:9 aspect ratio. Select Slide Size on the Home tab of the Ribbon to change to the Standard setting, which has a 4:3 aspect ratio, or select Custom Slide Size to open the Slide Size dialog box. Select the Slides sized for drop-down arrow to select a different output, such as On-screen Show or 35mm Slides, or set a custom size.

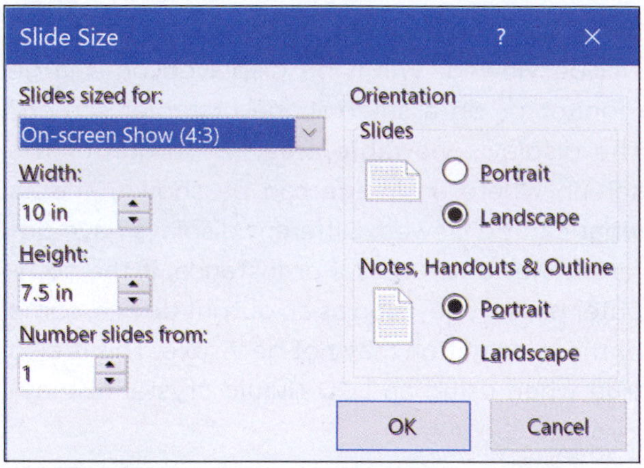

FIGURE 20.1.3 In Microsoft PowerPoint, use the Slide Size dialog box to optimize settings for slide size and orientation.

TECHNOLOGY@SCHOOL

When preparing a presentation for a class at school, it is a good idea to use Speaker Notes to help you remember what you want to say to the audience.

THINK ABOUT IT!

Entering notes can help remind you of details you want to share about your slides. For which of the ways listed below can Speaker Notes help you do this?

- help presenter remember dates and details
- organize layout of the slide show
- show thumbnails of the presentation
- prompt the punchline to a joke

Developing Presentations

OBJECTIVES

- Explain the use of a presentation outline.

- Identify slide layout options.

- Explain the benefit of designing the content of a slide before choosing the layout.

- Summarize the editing process that should occur after a draft presentation is complete.

AS YOU READ

SEQUENCE INFORMATION Use a sequence chart to sequence the steps to organize a presentation as you read.

TERMINOLOGY

- layout

- rehearsed presentation

- self-running presentation

- transition effect

Using a Presentation Outline

In most presentation programs you can use an outline to develop your presentation. You can type the outline to create slide titles and bullet items, or you can import an outline from a program such as Microsoft Word.

TYPING AN OUTLINE When you type a presentation outline, the first line you type displays as the slide title. From the title, you press Ctrl + Enter to start a bulleted list, or Enter to create a new slide. From the bulleted list, you press Enter to continue the bulleted list, or Ctrl + Enter to start a new slide. You can format and rearrange outline text and increase or decrease outline levels to change the way the text displays on the slide.

IMPORTING AN OUTLINE If you have an existing outline in a file created with a program such as Microsoft Word, you can import it into your presentation program. Each heading 1 level in the outline becomes a slide title, and the subheadings become bulleted lists.

TECHNOLOGY@WORK

Large companies often use organizational charts to identify the structure and responsibilities of employees. PowerPoint offers a template layout to help generate this information.

THINK ABOUT IT!

Which items listed below would be valuable to an organizational chart for a business?

- detailed job descriptions
- names of department heads
- telephone extensions
- work schedules

Choosing a Slide Layout

Each slide in a presentation can have its own slide layout. The **layout** is the way objects and placeholders are positioned on the slide. The first

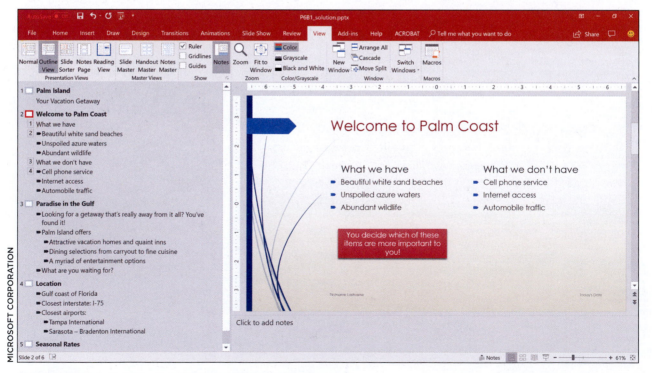

MICROSOFT CORPORATION

FIGURE 20.2.1 Outline view in Microsoft PowerPoint.

slide in a new blank presentation usually has the Title Slide layout, with placeholders for entering a title and a subtitle. By default, new slides you add have the Title and Content layout, with placeholders for a title and content such as a bulleted list, clip art, picture, chart, table, or media clip. Other layout choices include Two Content, Comparison, Title Only, Blank, Content with Caption, Picture with Caption, and Section Header.

Consider the content of a slide before you choose a layout. By deciding the slide's key points first, you can then select the most appropriate layout for it.

Editing Your Presentation

Good presenters preview and revise their presentations many times. Remember, the purpose of a presentation is to deliver a message to the audience. If there are errors, the message will not be received the way you want.

CHECKING ORGANIZATION Having the slides in the best order ensures the proper flow of ideas. You can use Slide Sorter or Outline view to rearrange slides. You can revise and reorganize bullet points of text in Normal view or Outline view.

CAREER CORNER

SALES REPRESENTATIVE Sales representatives often use presentation software to demonstrate or sell their company's products. Slides may show product features, compare products, explain costs, or give other information to customers or to people in the representatives' own organizations.

The ability to customize software presentations by reorganizing or replacing slides for different customers can help sales representatives better meet clients' needs.

IC3✔ Identify presentation software options: revise slide order.

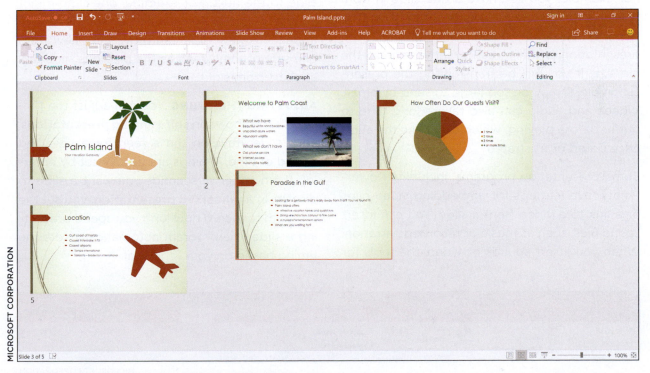

FIGURE 20.2.2 Rearranging slides in Slide Sorter view.

CHECKING ERRORS Presentation software can check spelling as you type text in a placeholder. If a red, wavy line appears under a word, it might be spelled incorrectly. If so, in Windows, right-click the word to open the suggested-spellings list and see other spelling choices, or run a spell check. You should still proofread your work, because spell check might not identify every spelling error.

Enhancing a Presentation

INSERTING IMAGES Text-only presentations can be dull. Insert clip art, photos, and other images to clarify and enhance key points. Use charts, shapes, and drawings to illustrate your ideas and to help your audience better understand the information in your slides.

ADDING ANIMATION, VIDEO, AND SOUND Sound, animation, and video can make a presentation more informative and interesting. Most presentation software can import and use standard animation formats, including animated .gif clips. You can also animate objects and text on a slide. For example, you can have a title slide in from the left, or set a picture to fade out or blink. One thing to keep in mind when adding media to a presentation is that it can greatly increase the file size. If you will be transmitting the presentation file, it may be too large to send by email. Videos and audio can also take a long time to buffer before playing, which can make the audience bored or frustrated.

Some presentation programs, including Power-Point, have features for embedding video clips or a link to a video from a slide. You can insert sound files, such as music or recorded narration. When you insert sounds or video, the tools for formatting the object and for selecting playback settings become available.

Playback settings include options such as when to start the playback, whether to loop or stop after playing, and whether to hide it when it is not playing. You can also trim the beginning or end of the video or audio clip, and select to have it fade in or out.

To insert a video in PowerPoint, select Insert > Video. If the file is stored online, select Online Video. If it is on your computer, select Video on My PC. Browse for and select the file to insert, and then select Insert. To insert an audio clip, select Insert > Audio. The options include selecting audio from your computer or recording audio.

IC3✔ **Know how to insert and manage media files.**

ADDING TRANSITION EFFECTS A **transition effect** is a multimedia feature that adds visual interest as your presentation moves from one slide to the next. For example, one slide might suddenly appear to fade out as the next slide appears. A new slide can move into view from one side of the screen as the previous slide disappears from sight.

ADJUSTING THE TIMING You can adjust the timing of slide shows. In **self-running presentations**, each slide stays on the screen for a specified period of time. Timings are usually set by entering the number of seconds you want a slide to display. In a **rehearsed presentation**, you set the program to record how long you spend presenting a slide; the program automatically sets the timing based on your rehearsal.

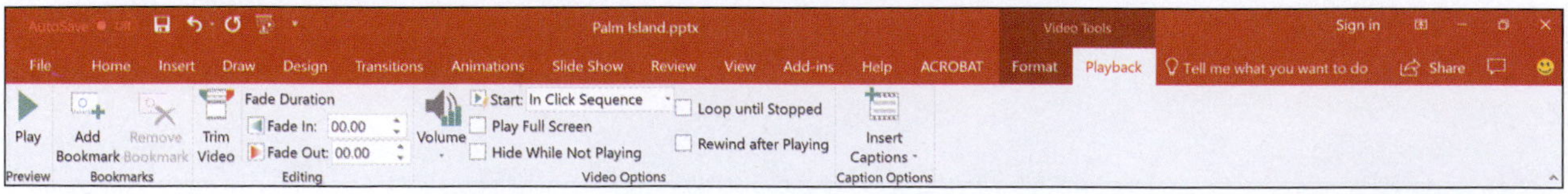

MICROSOFT CORPORATION

FIGURE 20.2.3 Use the commands on the Playback tab to set options for a video on a slide.

Enhancing and Finalizing Presentations

OBJECTIVES

- Identify strategies to enhance a presentation.
- Recognize options for publishing a presentation.
- Compare and contrast presentation delivery methods.
- Explain how to connect to external or extended monitors for displaying a presentation.

AS YOU READ

DRAW CONCLUSIONS Use a conclusion chart to draw conclusions about finalizing a presentation as you read.

TERMINOLOGY

- delivery method
- digital projector
- interactive presentation
- large-format display (LFD)
- on-screen presentation
- webcast

Making a Powerful Presentation

Presentation programs are effective tools for generating high-interest, engaging presentations. Here are ten tips for finalizing presentation slides so that they are easy to understand and help you meet your presentation goals.

REMEMBER YOUR GOAL. Keep your goal, and your main message, in mind as you outline your presentation. When finalizing your presentation, review your slides and the information they convey to ensure that your goal has been met.

SUPPORT YOUR MAIN IDEA. Start by stating your main idea or topic sentence. Follow it with details that are simply presented and that clarify or support your main idea.

KNOW YOUR AUDIENCE. Fewer words on a slide mean fewer words your audience has to read. However, make sure that you do not oversimplify the content on your slides or you run the risk of boring your audience. Finally, rehearse in clear language and make sure your slides are also clear to others.

PREVIEW AND REVIEW. A preview slide introduces the presentation for an audience. This slide usually appears after the presentation's title slide and before the first slide that addresses a point.

> **DID YOU KNOW?**
>
> A style guide is a list of standards to use for writing and designing documents. A style guide can be very helpful when a team of people is working on the same material. It can help prevent words, colors, and fonts from conflicting within a presentation, book, magazine, or newspaper. For example, one style guide might use the term *email* while another might use *Email*. Another style guide might state that all headings must be in a specific font.

A review slide usually restates the presentation's main points and may be identical to the preview slide. Used together effectively, a preview and review slide can help your audience remember the most important points of your presentation.

STAY ON POINT. The purpose of slides is to highlight key facts, so it is fine to leave out supporting details. Keep your text lively but to the point.

SELECT AND APPLY A CONSISTENT DESIGN. Too many different designs or too many colors and fonts can distract or confuse an audience.

BE SMART WITH ART. Use clip art, tables, charts, icons, and animations wisely to enhance a point. Don't add illustrations that do not contribute to your message.

STOCKFOUR/SHUTTERSTOCK

FIGURE 20.3.1 The more planning you do, the better your presentations will be.

PROOFREAD YOUR TEXT. Use spell check to help you eliminate typos from your work. Then, print your slides and ask someone to proofread them.

CHECK THE OUTPUT. Make sure the hardware on which you plan to display your work will be able to run your slide show. Incompatible machines can ruin your presentation.

WATCH THE CLOCK. Rehearse your presentation with a timer. Make sure any timed slides are sequenced with your verbal message.

Publishing a Presentation

Publishing a presentation means exporting or saving it in a format suitable for sharing with an audience. The format you use depends on how you want the audience to view your slides. You may want to be able to start a slide show automatically, or present it as a video, or distribute it on a CD. In most cases, you select a presentation format using the File > Export or File > Save As command. For example, in PowerPoint, the File > Export command gives you the following options:

CREATE ADOBE PDF Select this option to convert the presentation into PDF format.

CREATE PDF/XPS DOCUMENT Select this option so the document can be displayed using a free viewer on the web.

CREATE A VIDEO Select this option to save the presentation as a video that you can save on a DVD, upload to the web, or send via email.

PACKAGE PRESENTATION FOR CD Select this option to distribute the presentation on a CD, which can be used on most computers that have a CD drive.

CREATE HANDOUTS Select this option to export the slides and notes to a Word document.

CHANGE FILE TYPE Select this option to save the presentation in a variety of file types, including:

- The default Presentation format (.pptx)

- The format used for older versions of PowerPoint (.ppt)

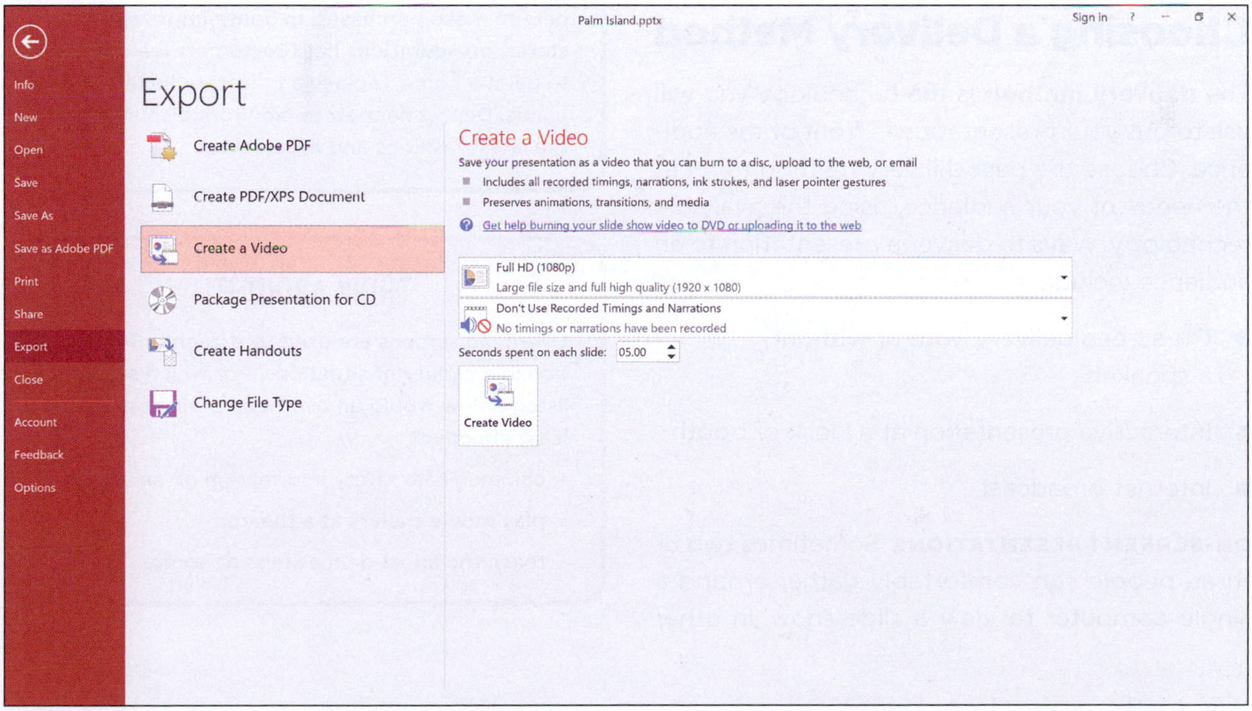

MICROSOFT CORPORATION

FIGURE 20.3.2 In PowerPoint, use the File > Export options to select a format for sharing or publishing your presentation.

- OpenDocument Presentation format (.odp)

- PowerPoint Show (.ppsx), which automatically opens the file in Slide Show view

- Template (.potx)

- PowerPoint Picture Presentation (.pptx), which converts each slide to a picture

- .png format to save print quality image files of each slide

- .jpg to save web quality image files of each slide

- Save as Another File Type to use the Save as type list in the Save As dialog box to select a file type

IC3 ✔ Understand how to share a presentation as a show or a video.

IC3 ✔ Understand how to publish a presentation in different formats, including .pptx, .pdf, .jpg, .show, and .png.

Choosing a Delivery Method

The **delivery method** is the technology you will use to put your presentation in front of the audience. Choose the best delivery method to meet the needs of your audience, using the available technology. Ways to deliver a presentation to an audience include:

- On-screen delivery, with or without a speaker

- Interactive presentation at a kiosk or booth

- Internet broadcast

ON-SCREEN PRESENTATIONS Sometimes two or three people can comfortably gather around a single computer to view a slide show. In other cases, large groups may view a presentation on an overhead or video monitor, a presentation projector, or a "jumbo" screen. This is called an **on-screen presentation**, or a screen display of the slides.

Most of the time you will use a **digital projector** connected to your computer or device to play the presentation on a large monitor or screen. Digital projectors project an image directly from the computer through a lens and onto the screen. The projector and speakers connect to your computer with cables.

A **large-format display (LFD)** is a flat-screen monitor ranging from 32″ to more than 90″ in size. You can connect your computer to an LFD to display your presentation in a large space. In large settings, other equipment is often required, such as a microphone, amplifier, and speakers, which allow the audience to hear the speaker and any sound that plays during the presentation.

TECHNOLOGY@WORK

Retailers use presentations in many ways. On-screen displays are often used to entice shoppers to make purchases. In home-improvement stores, presentations help customers learn how to paint a home, replace a faucet, or install blinds. Department-store monitors display the latest fashions and accessories.

THINK ABOUT IT!

Overhead screens are used to present information in a variety of situations. For which settings listed below would an overhead presentation be least effective?

- communicate safety information on an airplane
- play movie trailers at a theater
- teach the latest dance steps at home

USING TWO MONITORS Most presentation programs allow you to use more than one monitor to display a presentation. This is useful if you want two monitors showing the same presentation, or if you want one monitor showing the presentation to the audience while using Presenter View on the second monitor so the presenter can see the speaker notes.

In order to use two monitors, you must configure Windows to identify which monitor is primary and which is extended. You can do this using the Display Settings.

You can also use PowerPoint to configure the monitors. First, make sure both monitors are connected to your device. Then, in PowerPoint, select the Slide Show tab and then select Use Presenter View in the Monitors group. In the Display Settings dialog box, on the Monitor tab, select the monitor to use to display speaker notes, and then select the This is My Main Monitor check box. Select the monitor that the audience will view and then select the Extend my Windows Desktop onto this Monitor check box.

To deliver the presentation using two monitors, select the Slide Show tab and select Set Up Slide Show. In the Set up Show dialog box, under Multiple Monitors, select Automatic from the Slide Show monitor drop-down list, and then select OK. When you are ready to run the show, select Slide Show > From the Beginning or just change to Slide Show view.

IC3✔ **Understand how to connect external and extended monitor cables for audio and video to display a presentation.**

INTERACTIVE PRESENTATIONS PowerPoint allows users to create an **interactive presentation** in which a viewer can make selections and control the presentation. For example, to help promote a product at a conference sales booth or a shopping mall kiosk, you can set animation effects to play when a customer clicks a specific object on-screen. Depending on the object selected, the customer is routed to a specific part of the presentation and receives different information.

INTERNET DELIVERY If the audience is in a remote location, the presentation can be exported for broadcast on a website. Each user can then view the slide show at any time using a web browser. This method is useful for

PAVEL L PHOTO AND VIDEO/SHUTTERSTOCK

FIGURE 20.3.3 Most presentations are delivered using a projector connected to a computer with cables.

long-distance education, video conferences, and online meetings. Group size is not an issue, and interactivity and animation are both possible presentation features. When the presentation is live and controlled by a presenter over the internet, it is called a **webcast**.

AUDIENCE HANDOUTS AND OUTLINES You can help your audience remember important or complex information by providing printed handouts or outlines of the presentation. When you print an outline, you print the title and text of every slide. Handouts show thumbnails of each slide. Most programs, including PowerPoint,

have a Handout Master view you can use to set up the handout pages. For example, you can enter a header or footer.

When you are ready to print the handouts or outline, you use the File > Print command. In PowerPoint, on the Print tab in the Backstage view, you can select to print the presentation as handouts in a variety of layouts, or select to print just the outline.

IC3✓ Understand how to share presentation handouts and outlines.

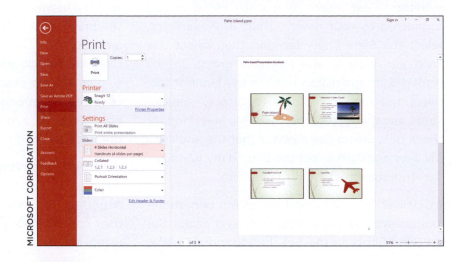

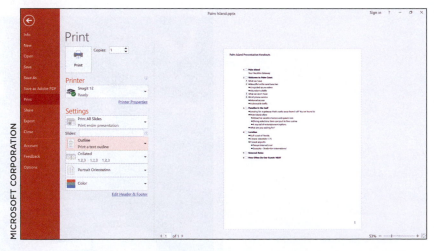

FIGURE 20.3.4 Use PowerPoint's Print options to select to print presentation handouts (top) or the presentation outline (bottom).

REVIEW THE TERMINOLOGY

DIRECTIONS Match each vocabulary term in the left column with the correct definition in the right column.

1. visual aid
2. digital projector
3. master slide
4. viewable area
5. transition effect
6. self-running presentation
7. rehearsed presentation
8. on-screen presentation

a. device used to display an image directly from a computer through a lens and onto a screen

b. changing the format of this slide changes all slides of this type

c. automatically switches from one slide to the next

d. uses a counter to help determine how long a slide should stay on the screen

e. graphic that is used to assist in communicating a topic

f. a display of slides on a monitor or screen

g. technique for switching from one slide to another during a presentation

h. portion of a screen on which an image can be seen

USE THE TERMINOLOGY

DIRECTIONS Determine the correct choice for each of the following.

1. What is the primary purpose of presentation software?
   a. show images to large audiences
   b. provide visual aids for speeches
   c. provide a way of creating art
   d. replace human presenters

2. Which color combination is best for printed handouts?
   a. white background with black letters
   b. black background with green letters
   c. dark blue background with red letters
   d. pale yellow background with white letters

3. Which slide usually restates the presentation's main points?
   a. title slide
   b. master slide
   c. review slide
   d. blank

4. Which slide layout is best for adding a two-column bulleted list?

   a. Title and Content

   b. Blank

   c. Two Content

   d. Picture with Caption

5. What kind of presentations are timed in a specific sequence?

   a. self-running

   b. rehearsed

   c. transition effect

   d. slide sorter

6. Which presentation delivery method is useful for long-distance education?

   a. on-screen delivery with a speaker

   b. internet broadcast

   c. interactive presentation at a booth

   d. printed handouts

THINK CRITICALLY

DIRECTIONS Answer the following questions.

1. What are some benefits to displaying a presentation on more than one monitor? Give examples.

2. Why should you know your method of output before preparing a presentation?

3. What choices does a presenter have for adding a graph, table, or spreadsheet to a slide?

4. How can the use of colors, fonts, font styles, and font sizes affect the design of a presentation?

5. Identify the functions of presentation software.

EXTEND YOUR KNOWLEDGE

DIRECTIONS Choose and complete one of the following projects.

1. There are many ways to add graphics to a presentation. You can download images from the internet; export images from digital files or paint or draw programs; or use clip art stored on your computer or on CD. Access to premade images makes adding images to slides easy. Start a presentation program, and create and save a new presentation file. Set up slide masters for a title slide and for a presentation slide that will display text and one image. Using the masters, create a title slide and three presentation slides. On each of the presentation slides, insert an image captured in a different way and a text description. Modify the masters to change the presentation format and design. Present your slides to the class, and explain the process you followed to create them. Document your sources.

2. Design, create, and distribute a survey to ten people of different ages to find out what kinds of presentations they have seen in the past 12 months. In your survey, include questions about the type of delivery method and the effectiveness of the presentation. Draw conclusions from the results of your survey about the use of presentation software to convey information to an audience. With a partner, compare and discuss the results of your surveys and your conclusions.

IC3 PREP

1. Which of the following are possible to achieve through the setting of presentation options? (Select all that apply.)

    a. a presentation that self-runs, without the need for a presenter

    b. a presentation that creates itself from information gathered from the cloud

    c. a presentation that can be controlled by its viewer

    d. a presentation using an online template to provide a professional theme

2. Which of the following are views suitable for revising the order of slides in a presentation? (Select all that apply.)

    a. View

    b. Outline

    c. Slide Sorter

    d. Arrange

3. A word in your presentation has a red, wavy line under it. What does this probably mean?

    a. The word is not interesting.

    b. The word is too long.

    c. There is no significance to the wavy red line.

    d. The word is spelled wrong.

    e. The word is on the wrong slide.

4. For each line below, select whether the statement is True or False.

    a. Presentations can include images, text, animation, video, and sound.

    b. It is not possible to animate the transition between the title slide and the next slide.

    c. When adding video to a slide, only a video available offline may be used.

    d. Sound playback in a presentation can be triggered at specific times, looped, or faded in and out.

5. Which statements are true for the PowerPoint Show (.ppsx) or video format? (Select all that apply.)

    a. These options are designed to be non-editable.

    b. These options will look better than other file options.

    c. These options help your presentation reach a wider audience.

    d. These options will automatically open in a Slide Show view.

6. Which of the following is NOT a valid file type for exporting or saving a presentation?

    a. PDF

    b. Word document

    c. Excel file

    d. Video file

    e. JPEG

7. For each line below, select whether the statement is True or False.

   a. Providing your audience with printed handouts or outlines of your presentation is considered unnecessary.

   b. Printed outlines show thumbnails of each slide in a presentation.

   c. Handout pages can be viewed and set up in the Handout Master view.

   d. The Print option in PowerPoint requires that you print both the presentation handouts and outline at the same time.

IC3 PROCEDURES

REVISING SLIDE ORDER

1. In the status bar, select the **Slide Sorter** button ⊞.

2. In Slide Sorter view, select the slide you want to move.

3. Drag the selected slide to its new position.

   OR

1. In the left pane in Normal view, select the thumbnail of the slide you want to move.

2. Drag the selected thumbnail to its new position.

INSERTING AN AUDIO FILE

1. Select the slide on which you want to insert the audio.

2. Select the **Insert** tab.

3. Select the **Insert Audio** button 🔊.

4. On the menu, select **Audio on My PC**.

5. In the Insert Audio dialog box, browse to the location where the audio file is stored.

6. Select the audio file.

7. Select **Insert**.

HIDING THE AUDIO ICON

1. Select the audio icon on the slide.

2. Select the **Audio Tools Playback** tab.

3. Select the **Hide During Show** check box.

SETTING AUDIO TO PLAY CONTINUOUSLY

1. Select the audio icon on the slide.

2. Select the **Audio Tools Playback** tab.

3. Select the **Loop until Stopped** check box.

SETTING AUDIO TO REWIND

1. Select the audio icon on the slide.

2. Select the **Audio Tools Playback** tab.

3. Select the **Rewind after Playing** check box.

SETTING THE AUDIO PLAYBACK VOLUME

1. Select the audio icon on the slide.

2. Select the **Audio Tools Playback** tab.

3. Select the **Volume** button .

4. Select the volume level.

TRIMMING AN AUDIO CLIP

1. Select the audio icon.

2. Select the **Audio Tools Playback** tab.

3. Select the **Trim Audio** button .

4. Drag the green handle on the left to trim the beginning of the audio.

5. Drag the red handle on the right to trim the end of the audio.

6. Select **OK**.

INSERTING A VIDEO FROM A FILE

1. In the slide's content placeholder, select the **Insert Video** icon .

   OR

   a. Select the **Insert** tab.

   b. Select the **Insert Video** button .

2. Select **Video on my PC**.

3. In the Insert Video dialog box, browse to the location where the video file is stored.

4. Select the video file.

5. Select **Insert**.

INSERTING AN ONLINE VIDEO

1. Select the slide on which you want to insert the video.

2. Select the **Insert** tab.

3. Select the **Video** button drop-down arrow .

4. Select **Online Video**.

5. In the Insert Video dialog box, type keyword(s) in the Search YouTube box to describe the video you want and press **Enter**.

6. Select the desired clip.

7. Select **Insert** to insert it on the slide.

   OR

   In the Insert Video dialog box, paste the embed code for the video you want to insert in the Paste embed code here box and press **Enter**.

PREVIEWING A MOVIE IN NORMAL VIEW

1. Select the video on the slide.
2. Select the **Video Tools Playback** tab.
3. Select the **Play** button ▶.

   OR

   Select the **Play/Pause** button ▶ on the video itself.

VIEWING A VIDEO IN A SLIDE SHOW

1. In the status bar, select the **Slide Show** button ⬒.
2. Hover the mouse pointer over the video.
3. Select the **Play** button ▶.

TRIMMING A VIDEO

Not available for most online videos.

1. Select the video.
2. Select the **Video Tools Playback** tab.
3. Select the **Trim Video** button.
4. Drag the end point arrow to the desired end time.
5. Select **OK**.

HIDING A VIDEO

1. Select the video.
2. Select the **Video Tools Playback** tab.
3. Select the **Hide While Not Playing** check box.

SETTING START OPTIONS FOR A VIDEO

1. Select the video.
2. Select the **Video Tools Playback** tab.
3. Select the **Start** button drop-down arrow ▶.
4. Select desired option.

SETTING A VIDEO TO PLAY CONTINUOUSLY

1. Select the video.
2. Select the **Video Tools Playback** tab.
3. Select the **Loop until Stopped** check box.

SETTING VIDEO TO REWIND

1. Select the video.
2. Select the **Video Tools Playback** tab.
3. Select the **Rewind after Playing** check box.

CHAPTER 21
Multimedia Basics

MEDIA MAKES A POWERFUL STATEMENT

For centuries, people have shared their thoughts and ideas by speaking, drawing pictures, or using written words. When you talk or write words on paper, you use one medium, or means of expressing information. Today, however, computers allow people to use many different media (the plural of *medium*) at the same time.

Video games, movies, and websites make use of all types of media, including text, graphics, audio, video, and animation. A few years ago, it took expensive equipment and a lot of experience to create and integrate different media. Today, PC software and smartphone apps make it possible for everyone to create entertaining and useful presentations, websites, interactive programs, games, videos, and more using a combination of media types.

Introducing Multimedia

OBJECTIVES

- Define multimedia and interactive multimedia.

- Explain how multimedia is used in various fields.

- Identify tools used to work with audio and video.

AS YOU READ

ORGANIZE INFORMATION Use a main idea/detail chart to help you identify details about multimedia applications as you read.

TERMINOLOGY

- frame rate

- interactive multimedia

- media

- medium

- multimedia

- sound card

- video capture board

- video editor

Defining Multimedia

A **medium** is a way to communicate information or express ideas. Talking is a medium, as is writing or drawing. The plural of medium is **media**. Different types of media can be combined in many ways. An animated cartoon, for example, combines moving graphics (one medium) with sound and music (other media). This is what is meant by the term **multimedia**—combining different media to express information or ideas.

MULTIMEDIA EVENTS Because multimedia can take so many forms and be used in so many ways, terms such as *event* or *experience* are often used to describe it. Although a feature film or television program usually involves multiple types of media, most multimedia events are on a smaller scale, such as a YouTube video, a website, a video game, or a PowerPoint presentation. And while many kinds of computer programs use multimedia, from games to encyclopedias, a teacher displaying slides or using a low-tech chalkboard is also creating a multimedia event.

INTERACTIVE MULTIMEDIA Many, though not all, examples of multimedia are interactive. **Interactive multimedia** allows the user to make choices about what is displayed. Computer and video games, educational computer software, and websites that let you decide what you see and how you interact with information are all examples of interactive multimedia.

To be interactive, a multimedia event must provide more than audio or video. It must also give the user a way to control the action and make choices that determine what happens next. Think of a video game that lets you direct the actions of an avatar. Or think of multimedia social networking websites that let you update your status, watch videos posted by others, and tag photos.

Using Multimedia

Multimedia applications are widely used today in business, education, and entertainment.

BUSINESS Multimedia technologies help businesses communicate with their customers and employees. Most corporate websites, for example, use sound, video, or animation to demonstrate products to customers.

Businesses also use multimedia to train employees. For example, many companies create custom multimedia programs that workers can access on a network or online. These programs use audio and video to demonstrate products and explain procedures. These programs can be interactive, which allows workers to jump to different areas of the content at will or take tests that provide feedback about their knowledge.

EDUCATION Multimedia can make learning more fun for students and provide extra tools for teachers. Interactive software can teach lessons, automate quizzes, and give students immediate feedback to help them track their progress.

TECHNOLOGY@SCHOOL

The sales catalogs that are sent to schools these days don't just include books. They also offer a large number of multimedia programs that can be used in teaching various subjects.

THINK ABOUT IT!

Which benefits listed below might a school gain from purchasing multimedia programs?

- easier material
- providing immediate feedback to students
- capturing students' attention
- reinforcing printed text
- matching students' learning styles to material

Multimedia programs offer audio and video to enhance learning in ways that printed text alone cannot. For instance, instructional software may use audio to teach languages. Social studies courses can include video clips from historical events.

ENTERTAINMENT Video and computer games are multimedia programs. Video, graphics, and sound combine to simulate different environments and situations. But interactivity is what gives these games their true appeal. Using a game controller or keyboard and mouse, you can direct the action from start to finish. Multimedia technologies are used in many products besides games. Movies use 3D animation and computer-generated effects. Concerts, documentaries, and television programs also incorporate multimedia.

Tools for Working with Audio and Video

Audio (sound) and video (movies and animations) are essential components of multimedia. You will need these three components to create multimedia.

SOUND CARD Recall that a **sound card** is a special expansion board that allows the computer to input, edit, and output sounds. Audio of all types is entered into the computer through the input jacks on the sound card. Once audio is captured on the computer's hard drive, you can edit and work with it. You can then play it through the computer's speakers or headphones, or save it to a disc. You can also send it to another audio device using the sound card's output jack. Full-featured cards even include optical inputs and outputs for digital sound and special software for mixing sound.

VIDEO CAPTURE BOARD Video signals, such as those from television programs or movies, have to be converted into a format that computers understand. This is done with a **video capture**

ALICE MCBROOM/PEARSON EDUCATION AUSTRALIA PTY LTD

FIGURE 21.1.1 Multimedia programs and courseware are available to teach all kinds of subjects to people of all ages.

board, a special card that plugs into a computer. You can transfer video through the capture board from video cameras, digital cameras, and other sources.

VIDEO EDITOR After video and audio are saved as digital files, you can combine them in new ways. You do this work with a video editor. A **video editor** is a program that allows you to cut and paste sound and video segments and change the order in which segments appear. Video editors also allow you to define the **frame rate**, or how many still images are displayed in one second, and specify the speed at which video should be displayed.

CAREER CORNER

CAMERA OPERATOR The people who operate the cameras that record movies, television shows, and other multimedia events are creative people, but they are also knowledgeable about the equipment they use and able to adapt to rapidly changing technology.

Camera operation is a competitive field, but it is expected to grow as multimedia applications expand in many areas. Interested candidates should take related courses in college or at a vocational institute and try to get experience working in related fields.

Multimedia File Formats

OBJECTIVES

- Identify video file formats.

- Summarize audio file formats and the platforms on which they run.

- Identify programs used to play multimedia programs on a computer or the internet.

AS YOU READ

OUTLINE INFORMATION Use an outline to help you understand multimedia tools as you read.

TERMINOLOGY

- browser plug-in

- encoder

- streaming

- synthesize

Video File Formats

Multimedia can combine text, audio, graphics, video, and animation. To do such complicated work, designers choose from a number of file formats, each suited for a specific task.

MPEG MPEG is a family of formats developed by the Moving Picture Experts Group. MPEG is commonly used to display video such as movie clips, animations, and recorded television broadcasts. MPEG files offer full-motion video that provides a very realistic effect.

Different versions of the basic MPEG format have been developed. MPEG-2 is generally used for regular television, DVDs, and high-definition television (HDTV). The MPEG-4 format is used for portable devices and internet streaming.

QUICKTIME™ Designed by Apple Inc., QuickTime is the basic file format for showing animation and video on Macintosh computers. QuickTime videos also can be viewed on Windows computers, but a special player must first be installed.

TECHNOLOGY@WORK

Have you heard of elevator music—that soothing background music that plays in elevators, hallways, and offices? Well, now there's *elevator multimedia*, too—small digital display screens in elevators, taxicabs, and other public locations.

THINK ABOUT IT!

Think about the kinds of multimedia productions that might be appropriate in public places. Which statements below are usable ideas?

- an online multimedia news service
- a dramatic short story
- illustrated readings of poems
- a pattern of colors and shapes synced to music
- a series of violent action scenes

AVI Audio Video Interleave, or AVI, is another name for Microsoft Video for Windows format. Some AVI videos are not of the best quality, but they can be played on any Windows computer. Many businesses create their multimedia in AVI format to tap into the huge market of Windows users.

Audio File Formats

While formats like MPEG, QuickTime, and AVI capture both pictures and sound, other formats can be a better choice when sound quality is a priority.

MP3 MPEG audio layer 3 (MP3) files are very common today, thanks to the ease of downloading music from the internet. The MP3 format takes a large audio file and makes it very small. It does this using regular compression methods and also by removing data from the music file that the human ear cannot hear. This results in a much smaller file, with little or no loss of sound quality.

WMA WMA is the music format of Microsoft. It stands for Windows Media Audio®. WMA files are also compressed from larger audio files but do not have information removed. WMA files can be converted back to the original uncompressed files while MP3s can only be uncompressed into approximations of the original files.

AU AU, or audio, is the standard format for audio files for the UNIX operating system.

WAV The waveform audio (WAV) format is built into the Microsoft Windows operating system. WAV files can be played on almost any computer system. WAV and WMA files can be converted into MP3 files using a hardware device or special software programs called **encoders** that convert the files from one format to another. Unlike MP3 and WMA files, WAV files are not compressed.

MIDI Musical Instrument Digital Interface, or MIDI, is a standard that allows a computer to control a musical instrument. MIDI sounds are **synthesized**. This means that sounds imitative of musical instruments are generated by the computer when they are played; no actual recorded sound is stored in the file.

Multimedia Players

You use a media player program to play multimedia content on your computer, media device, smartphone, or on the internet. This can be a stand-alone media player or a browser plug-in that you download for free from the internet.

MEDIA PLAYERS There are a multitude of media players available for computers, smartphones, and other devices. Some come preinstalled, like Apple iTunes on iPhones and Macs and Windows Media Player on Windows-based devices. Others can be downloaded from an app store. Some basic players are available for free while premium versions require a fee.

When selecting a media player, consider how you will use it. Do you want to play **streaming** audio and video—that is, play content that is broadcast in a continuous feed from the internet? Do you want to play music from your own library, or from a radio station? Will you watch news and weather reports, check out movie trailers and music videos, or watch YouTube or Vimeo videos? Most players can handle a wide variety of audio and video formats, although some have their own unique format. Many people have more than one player installed on their computer.

BROWSER PLUG-INS A **browser plug-in**, which may also be called an extension or add-on, is software that adds functionality to a web browser. Multimedia developers can use Adobe Animate (previously known as Flash) to create interactive multimedia content, such as animated games. Animate programs can accept user input, use high-quality audio and graphics, and are very small so they can be downloaded quickly. To view content created in these programs you need the Flash Player browser plug-in, which is available for free.

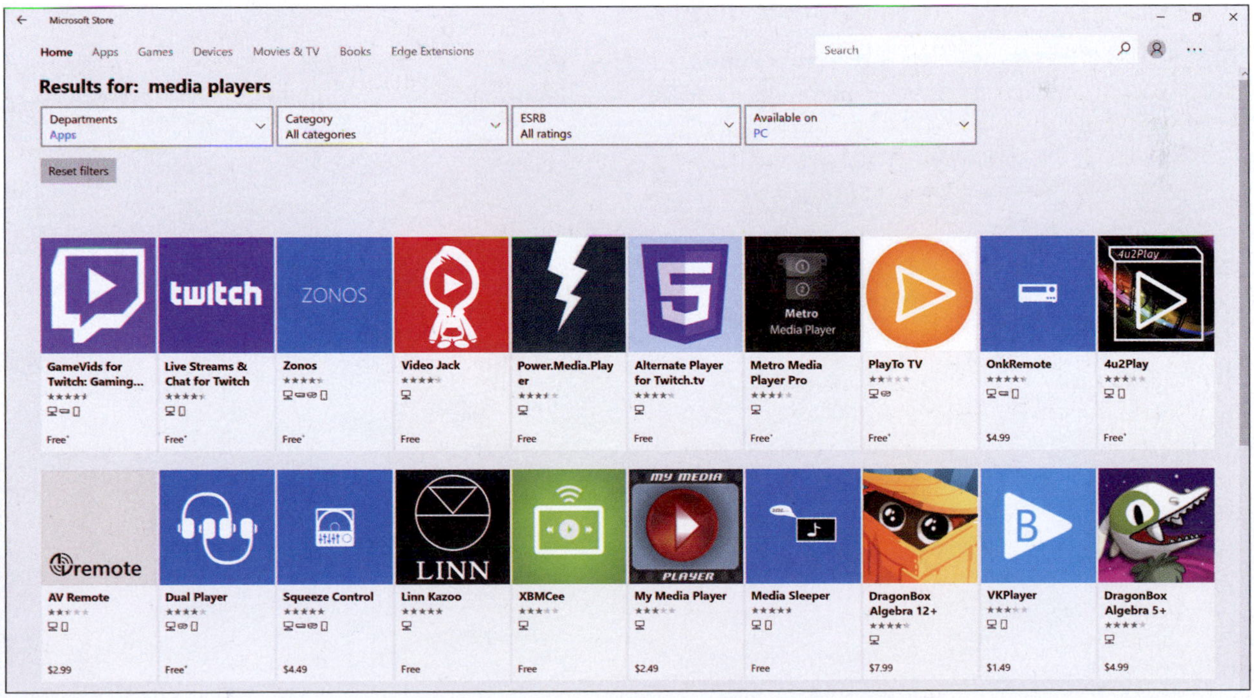

FIGURE 21.2.1 A variety of media players are available in the Microsoft Store.

Introducing Virtual Reality

OBJECTIVES

- Explain what virtual reality is, and describe some methods of presenting it.

- Discuss computer and video games.

AS YOU READ

ORGANIZE INFORMATION Use a concept web to help you organize details about virtual reality as you read.

TERMINOLOGY

- augmented reality

- Cave Automatic Virtual Environment (CAVE)

- head-mounted display (HMD)

- virtual reality (VR)

Forms of Virtual Reality

Virtual reality (VR) is a three-dimensional computer-generated environment that you can explore by using special hardware and software. Such environments simulate spaces, such as the flight deck of an airliner or the inside of an underwater cave. The purpose of all VR environments is the same: to let users explore and manipulate a computer-generated space. Users feel as if they are moving in the space and interacting with objects in the space as if in real life.

Sophisticated hardware and software are needed to create large-scale, detailed VR environments. Users can explore such environments in several different ways.

HMD A **head-mounted display (HMD)** is usually a helmet or a set of goggles that wraps around the head, blocking out light. A tiny computer monitor is located in front of each eye. Using these two separate monitors gives the illusion of three dimensions. HMDs often have headphones to provide audio to the user.

In some HMDs, tiny sensors can tell when the user's head tilts in any direction. The image on the monitors then shifts accordingly, in order to create a convincing illusion of being part of the action, rather than a spectator of it. HMDs can use liquid crystal display monitors to display images.

HMDs are now available for use with some smartphones, video game consoles, and computers. For example, Sony PlayStation VR works with the Sony PlayStation and Samsung Gear VR works with certain Samsung phones.

HMDs come in two categories: mobile and tethered. Mobile headsets are designed for use with a smartphone. You install an app on the phone and place your phone into the headset. There is no need for connecting any wires. The Samsung Gear VR is an example of a mobile VR headset. Tethered headsets are connected to the computing device using cables. Sony PlayStation VR is an example of a tethered headset.

ALEXEYBOLDIN/123RF.COM

FIGURE 21.3.1 Head mounted displays have a tiny computer monitor located in front of each eye to give the illusion of three dimensions.

CAVE The **Cave Automatic Virtual Environment (CAVE)**, is a room-sized, interactive VR environment used in a few businesses for research, training, and product development. It is an expensive and advanced form of VR. Images of a virtual world are displayed using LCD panels on the walls of a room. Visitors wear special goggles that create the illusion of three dimensions. The result is so realistic and so convincing that most "explorers" cannot tell where reality ends and virtual reality begins without reaching out and touching something.

In many CAVEs, users wear special gloves (called data gloves) or hold special wands, either of which can detect hand movements. These devices allow users to interact with objects in the virtual world, by opening doors, for example, or picking up the pieces in a virtual chess game.

AUGMENTED REALITY An emerging category of virtual reality is called **augmented reality**. Cameras in mobile devices are used to layer virtual digital information onto real information. The devices may be a smartphone or specially-developed glasses or headsets.

One of the first augmented reality applications to gain popularity is Pokemon Go by Niantic. The smartphone app displays Pokemon characters in

AKEI150/123RF.COM

FIGURE 21.3.2 Augmented reality overlays the real word with computer-generated information.

real locations. Augmented reality can also be used for self-guided tours in museums and cities by displaying information over real-world locations.

Computer and Video Games

The first electronic games displayed only simple, two-dimensional images with limited sounds. Today, you can choose from hundreds of games with detailed graphics, lifelike characters, and realistic environments.

COMPUTER GAMES Today's PCs, with their fast processors, powerful sound and graphics cards, and large displays, let you get the most from your games. Games for PCs can be installed using compact discs or downloaded from the internet.

GAME CONSOLES A game console is a device that uses a television to display a game. You interact with the game by using one or more controls, which are connected to the console. The most popular consoles in recent years have been the Nintendo Switch®, Microsoft Xbox One®, and Sony Playstation®.

While consoles used to be just dedicated to game playing, some are now used to stream videos. Consoles now have games like Sony's Just Dance that track the user's physical movements using sensors, and sometimes with VR headset components.

CONNECTIONS

SCIENCE Many educators believe virtual reality is having a major impact on science classrooms. Students can now "visit" and explore various ecosystems—take a stroll in a rainforest, for example, or shiver on the Alaskan tundra. Students studying anatomy can get a 3-D view of the respiratory system, the digestive system, and so on. Students opposed to dissecting animals can cut apart a virtual frog, making that experiment less distasteful.

ONLINE GAMES Many games, such as World of Warcraft (WoW), are available on the internet and allow multiple players to compete and cooperate in real time. To have the best gaming experience, you often need a high-speed internet connection and a game console, or a PC with multimedia features. Sometimes players must pay a monthly fee to play online, and all online multiplayer games require you to abide by a set of rules, called an End User Licensing Agreement (EULA). These rules prevent conflicts between players, and players who violate them are banned from playing.

BLEND IMAGES/SHUTTERSTOCK

FIGURE 21.3.3 Video games may be played on a wide variety of devices including television monitors, PCs, and smartphones, using a wide range of controller types.

Chapter 21 Review

REVIEW THE TERMINOLOGY

DIRECTIONS Match each vocabulary term in the left column with the correct definition in the right column.

1. multimedia
2. video capture board
3. video editor
4. frame rate
5. encoder
6. synthesize
7. virtual reality
8. head-mounted display
9. CAVE
10. interactive multimedia

a. allows the user to make choices about what is displayed

b. very realistic form of virtual reality that is displayed in a room

c. hardware that lets a computer work with video data

d. software that changes a WAV file into MP3 format

e. using more than one medium to express information or ideas

f. program that lets users manipulate sound and video

g. realistic, but simulated, 3-D world

h. number of still images displayed in one second

i. helmet or goggles used to display a virtual reality environment

j. the process in which a computer generates sounds

USE THE TERMINOLOGY

DIRECTIONS Determine the correct choice for each of the following.

1. What kind of multimedia lets users make choices about the direction a program may take?
   a. graphic multimedia
   b. animated multimedia
   c. interactive multimedia
   d. technical multimedia

2. What hardware allows a computer to input, edit, and output audio?
   a. a sound card
   b. a video editor
   c. AU
   d. 3-D

3. Which audio file format does a computer use to produce synthesized sounds?

   a. CAVE

   b. CD-ROM

   c. MIDI

   d. AVI

4. Which of the following allows you to view interactive multimedia games on your computer?

   a. .MIDI

   b. Flash Player plug-in

   c. CAVE

   d. Net video

5. Where are the monitors in an HMD located?

   a. on the wall

   b. in a helmet or a set of goggles

   c. in a room

   d. online

6. Which of the following layers virtual information with real information?

   a. CAVE

   b. virtual 3-D

   c. World of Warcraft

   d. augmented reality

THINK CRITICALLY

DIRECTIONS Answer the following questions.

1. For what purpose might a business want to hire a computer specialist who knows QuickTime and AVI?

2. What equipment and software would you need to develop your own multiplayer online game?

3. What two file formats are commonly used for interactive games found on websites?

4. Why is a virtual reality simulation used to train fighter pilots an example of interactive multimedia?

EXTEND YOUR KNOWLEDGE

DIRECTIONS Choose and complete one of the following projects.

1. In groups of four students, work cooperatively to choose a topic you are studying in language arts, social studies, science, math, art, or music. Plan a two-minute multimedia presentation on that topic that includes at least one example of each of these media: audio, video, text, and graphics. Assign one medium to each member to complete. Use groupware or collaborative software to review one another's work. Then, use a video editor to combine the pieces into a smooth, logical sequence.

2. Some adults believe that young people spend too much time playing video and computer games. Conduct online or library research to identify some specific objections that people have to these games. Then, debate the pros and cons of electronic games, using your research and your own gaming experiences as resources. Which argument was the most persuasive? Why?

3. With a partner, plan a one-minute audio advertisement on a topic approved by your teacher. Write a script that delivers the desired message. Rehearse and record it. Use audio editing software such as Audacity to edit it to the desired length. Share it with the class.

CHAPTER 22

Understanding Multimedia

USING YOUR SENSES

Human beings are sensory creatures—that is, we operate not just through what we know, but through what we see and hear and feel. Reading about something brings us understanding, but our senses of sight, hearing, and touch deepen that understanding.

Multimedia—combinations of words, sounds, images, video, and animation—can provide that sensory input. Multimedia productions can take many forms, including internet streaming, a television commercial, a full-length movie, a short video within a presentation, or an animated introduction to a website. Multimedia techniques are also used to create virtual worlds for us to explore, worlds that can test medical procedures, preview new buildings, and tap our imagination.

Exploring Multimedia

OBJECTIVES

- Describe the forms of multimedia.

- Describe how to access online multimedia.

AS YOU READ

OUTLINE INFORMATION Use an outline to help you organize details about multimedia as you read.

TERMINOLOGY

- information kiosk

- internet radio

- internet video

- stream

Delivering Multimedia

Multimedia combines text, graphics, video, animation, and sound. Television programs and movies are one-way multimedia—you are a passive viewer. Interactive multimedia lets you interact with the multimedia content.

Methods for delivering multimedia to an audience range from streaming television and internet programs to playing video games to watching a movie on a DVD.

STREAMING Multimedia presentations and events aren't limited to files stored on your computer. With an internet connection, you have access to an unlimited number of multimedia experiences. Many websites **stream** video and audio data—that is, transmit it across a network without interruption. You don't have to wait until the entire file is downloaded for it to play. The file begins playing as soon as it starts to download from the website to your device.

INTERNET RADIO **Internet radio** is a method for listening to music, talk, and information over the internet. Internet radio doesn't actually use radio waves. Instead, audio is converted to a digital format and streamed over the internet. Streaming radio places a temporary audio file on your hard drive. This is what is heard—not the actual stream. The audio stream continually updates the data as it plays.

INTERNET VIDEO Like internet radio, **internet video** uses streaming, but it delivers pictures as well as sound. News sites use online video to deliver the latest news. Movie sites preview upcoming releases and offer short films and animations. Subscription video sites, like Netflix and Hulu, stream TV shows and videos. In the business world, internet video is used for videoconferencing. In a videoconference, small cameras are used to allow people in different places to see and hear one another. Live streaming is when content is put onto the internet in real time.

DVDS DVDs can be used for multimedia experiences. Using a computer, game console or DVD player, you can watch a movie, play a game, learn a new skill, or integrate multimedia content into your daily exercise. For example, a DVD used with a stationary bike and your computer can give you 18 different "rides" and check your speed and heart rate while you pedal.

INFORMATION KIOSKS An **information kiosk** uses an automated system to provide information or training. In effect, this is a PC-in-a-box, usually with a touch screen allowing input. At the Museum of Science in Boston, Massachusetts, for example, you can create artificial fish and watch how they behave when you release them into a simulated fish tank.

FIGURE 22.1.1 A headset with earphones and a microphone is essential for experiencing multimedia such as video games.

SEZER66/SHUTTERSTOCK

GAMES Computer games, home video game consoles, gaming apps, and arcade games offer dramatic examples of multimedia. They create an interactive experience that uses many different media. Many video games create immersive worlds in which the player must clear objectives to win. The games can be educational, like a typing training program, or for entertainment, like a flight simulator or a fantasy adventure. Many modern video games involve an online component. Online gaming allows players to interact with each other in real time.

HELEN SUSHITSKAYA/SHUTTERSTOCK

FIGURE 22.1.2 A flight simulator game provides multimedia entertainment.

LESSON 22-2
Developing Multimedia

OBJECTIVES

- Identify specialized tools used to produce multimedia.

- Explain the term "authoring" as it relates to multimedia.

- Discuss the use of authoring tools.

AS YOU READ

ORGANIZE INFORMATION Use a spider map to help you categorize information about online multimedia as you read.

TERMINOLOGY

- authoring

- authoring tool

- pen-based graphics tablet

Hardware for Creating Multimedia

Certain hardware devices are used to create and make use of the elements of a multimedia presentation including the following:

PEN-BASED GRAPHICS TABLETS When creating still or animated graphics for use in a multimedia program, many artists find it easier to draw and sketch using a **pen-based graphics tablet** rather than a mouse. To use the tablet, you move a stylus, or electronic pen, across a sensitive touchpad or a touchscreen, and your movements are recorded by your graphics software. The images can then be saved and edited.

MICROPHONES Audio can be recorded into a conventional recording device and then imported through a sound card. Audio can also be recorded directly into the computer using a microphone. Most sound cards have a special plug for a microphone. Using the software that comes with the sound card, you can assign a file name, click "record," and start speaking into the microphone. The sounds will be recorded to a new audio file.

DIGITAL CAMERAS Digital cameras and camcorders are an easy way to acquire images and video for use in multimedia. These cameras do not require film. Images and video are stored in the camera and can then be transferred to the computer through a special cable or disk. Once on the computer, the pictures and video can be edited and used in presentations, movies, websites, and other applications.

Software for Creating Multimedia

Authoring is the term used to describe the creation of multimedia programs. To combine audio, video, graphics, and text, you use software called authoring tools.

USING AUTHORING TOOLS **Authoring tools** let you import, sequence, and modify the sounds, video clips, animations, text, and graphics you want to include in your multimedia product. You also control timing, transition effects, and volume. Most authoring tools save data in a format for use only by the software developers and authorized users. You use a media player program to view the finished piece.

FIGURE 22.2.1 Authoring programs let you create and edit multimedia projects.

STANISLAV POPOV/SHUTTERSTOCK

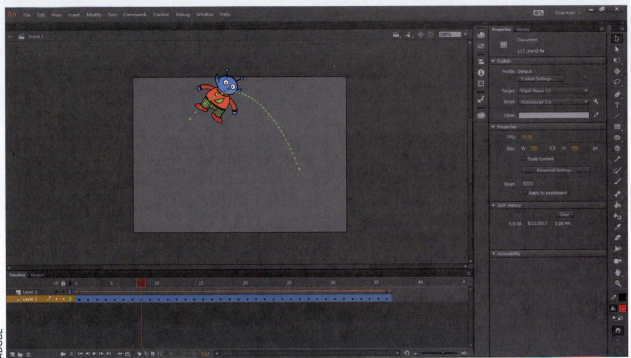

FIGURE 22.2.2 Animations created with Adobe Animate can integrate sound, graphics, and video.

CHOOSING AUTHORING TOOLS The authoring tool you choose depends on how complex your project will be, the type of computer system you have, and how much time you have to spend learning the program. Some sophisticated authoring tools are for media professionals; others are simple enough that they can be used on a smartphone to create multimedia videos and presentations. For example, iMovie is available for Apple iPhones; Movie Maker is available for Samsung Android phones.

Adobe offers a number of programs in its CC suite for working with different types of media. For example, Animate lets you integrate graphics, video, and audio to create animations.

Sometimes, basic multimedia authoring tools are built in to other programs. For example, Microsoft PowerPoint includes tools for inserting and controlling audio and video on slides. Office Sway, from Microsoft, is an online presentation program that lets you create presentations containing multiple types of multimedia to be viewed across many devices from personal computers to tablets and smart phones.

Exploring Virtual Reality

OBJECTIVES

- Explain what is meant by immersive virtual reality.

- Identify virtual reality equipment and language.

- Discuss real-world uses of virtual reality.

AS YOU READ

ORGANIZE INFORMATION Use a concept web to help you understand the practical applications of virtual reality as you read.

TERMINOLOGY

- data glove

- simulations

The Technology of Virtual Reality

Virtual reality works by making a computer-generated scene feel as it would in the real world. It does this by using three-dimensional, or 3D, graphics, video, color, texture, and sound.

In some cases, VR worlds are displayed on regular computer screens. A 3D video game is one example. Another example is a flight simulator, which is valuable in pilot training.

Virtual reality's main potential, however, lies in immersive technologies that surround a viewer with the VR world. With immersive VR, the user feels part of the virtual environment. For example, gaming consoles such as Sony PlayStation use VR headsets to immerse the player in a game.

VR GADGETS In addition to head-mounted displays, virtual reality often uses a device called a **data glove**. A data glove is a basic glove equipped with sensors that measure movements of the hand and fingers. One use of the data glove is to operate equipment from a distance.

Some VR products use sensors to track your movements. For example, the Occulus Rift VR headset comes with two sensors that can track your movement in place, and there is an additional sensor for tracking your movement around a room. The HTC Vive includes scanners that you attach to the walls of a room to track your movement.

VR LANGUAGE To create virtual worlds on the internet, programmers use a language called X3D. X3D allows programmers to describe objects that appear in the virtual world, such as shapes, buildings, landscapes, or characters.

Practical Applications of Virtual Reality

Virtual reality has become very useful for **simulations**. Simulations are virtual reality programs that mimic a specific place, job, or function. Virtual reality is used in many design and architectural businesses. It is also used in the military to train fighter pilots and combat soldiers without the risks of live training. In medicine, virtual reality is used to simulate complex surgery for training surgeons without using actual patients.

EASING PAIN At the University of Washington's Harborview Burn Center, virtual reality is being used to help severe burn victims deal with their pain. Patients are immersed in a virtual reality environment. There, they imagine that they are flying through icy canyons and cold waterfalls, building snowmen, and throwing snowballs. By focusing on things that are pleasant and cold, patients can focus less on their pain.

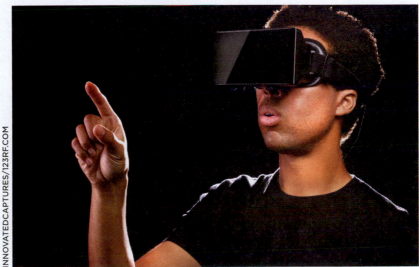

FIGURE 22.3.1 A head-mounted display is an important tool in immersive virtual reality.

INNOVATEDCAPTURES/123RF.COM

OVERCOMING FEAR A study by Walter Reed Army Hospital and Emory University School of Medicine showed that patients placed in virtual reality flight simulators overcame their fear of flying as successfully as patients treated using other techniques. But the VR method offers additional benefits: It is cheaper and easier than taking the patients on real airplane flights.

SAVING LIVES Heart surgeons often need to replace portions of a heart and its valves with artificial pieces. Designing replacement valves is very tricky, because even minor flaws can cause major problems.

Scientists at the University of Sheffield in England have developed a way to use virtual reality to test new heart valves before they are manufactured, using a computer to simulate how blood will flow through them. This software lets doctors predict whether or not the valve will work properly after it is in the body.

Virtual reality is also used to train doctors to perform surgery. Software can simulate open heart surgery, for instance, allowing doctors to practice without the risk of harming a patient. Virtual reality programs allow for doctors to control robots to perform surgery. Someday, doctors using virtual reality interfaces may be able to operate on actual patients halfway around the world!

TECHNOLOGY@WORK

VR applications can help in many fields. CAD software, for example, is used by architects and building supply stores to show customers how a kitchen might look with new cabinets.

THINK ABOUT IT!

Think about which professions might benefit from using virtual 3D worlds. Which professions listed below do you think would find this technology useful?

- museum exhibit organizer
- landscape designer
- art teacher
- flower arranger
- construction worker

FIGURE 22.3.2 Pilots can use virtual reality to train for helicopter flight.

PAVEL L PHOTO AND VIDEO/SHUTTERSTOCK

Chapter 22 Review

REVIEW THE TERMINOLOGY

DIRECTIONS Match each vocabulary term in the left column with the correct definition in the right column.

1. information kiosk
2. pen-based graphics tablet
3. stream
4. simulation
5. authoring tool
6. data glove

a. computer program that mimics a specific place, job, or function

b. transmit audio or video data across the internet without interruption

c. equipment with sensors that measure hand movements

d. automated system used for information or training

e. equipment that lets users draw images for animation and multimedia

f. software that helps in the production of multimedia

USE THE TERMINOLOGY

DIRECTIONS Determine the correct choice for each of the following.

1. Which input device is usually used on an information kiosk?
   a. DVD
   b. data glove
   c. keyboard
   d. touch screen

2. Which device allows you to input your voice directly into a computer?
   a. digital camera
   b. microphone
   c. CD-ROM drive
   d. media player

3. What kind of internet video starts playing as soon as you start to download it?
   a. graphic video
   b. virtual video
   c. streaming video
   d. ripping video

4. Which of the following is NOT accomplished using authoring tools?
   a. fading one video clip into the next
   b. setting the length of time an image will display on-screen
   c. setting the price of a multimedia program
   d. setting the volume for an audio clip

5. Which of the following CANNOT be produced using an authoring tool?

   a. web page

   b. head-mounted display

   c. multimedia presentation

   d. CD-ROM

6. Which VR application is sometimes used in pain-control therapy?

   a. simulations

   b. X3D

   c. CAD

   d. internet video

THINK CRITICALLY

DIRECTIONS Answer the following questions.

1. What special effects might you create for a multimedia presentation if you use a stylus and a digital camera?

2. What are three ways your computer can offer you interactive multimedia experiences?

3. Why might a business want to hire someone who is skilled in using authoring tools?

4. What piece of VR equipment might be useful in training surgeons? Why?

5. How might landscapers use VR technology to plan their work and attract customers?

EXTEND YOUR KNOWLEDGE

DIRECTIONS Choose and complete one of the following projects.

1. Digital video cameras are popular consumer items. Also popular are easy-to-use home-movie editing programs like iMovie® for Macintosh computers. Conduct research in the library, at a store, or online to find several cameras in the same price range, and compare their features. Repeat this process with several home-video editing programs. Create a chart in which to record your findings. Then, conclude which camera and which editing program you would recommend.

2. In small groups, use basic video production equipment and video editing software to create a one-minute video on a topic approved by your teacher. Use a storyboard to plan the shots. Use proper lighting. Edit the video, inserting, cutting, and erasing frames as necessary to achieve the desired message and length. Upload the completed video to a class website or social media page. As a class, discuss the video production process and the qualities of effective communication in a video.

PART 3
Living Online

CHAPTER 23

Telecommunications

HOW DO WE COMMUNICATE?

Communicating is how people connect with others. At its most basic, communication is an exchange between a sender and a receiver. The sender transmits the message with a specific intent. The receiver interprets the message and responds. There are many ways to communicate, with the most common being talking and writing, but we also use body language, sign language, and visual images such as pictures.

When we use technology to communicate we call it *telecommunications.* We depend on networked devices to make telecommunications possible. Wired and wireless technology let us have conversations using voice and text, exchange pictures and video, and post our thoughts on social networking sites.

These ways of sending and receiving messages and information are valuable to individuals, businesses, communities, and schools. And they all rely on networks.

Telephone Systems

OBJECTIVES

- Explain hard-wired telephone systems.
- Compare and contrast analog and digital connections.
- Explain cellular telephone systems.
- Identify the technologies for hard-wired and cellular telephone systems.

AS YOU READ

ORGANIZE INFORMATION Use a spider map to help you organize ways in which telephone systems operate as you read.

TERMINOLOGY

- 3G
- 4G
- analog
- broadband
- cable modem
- cell site
- cell tower
- cells
- cellular phone
- circuit
- coaxial
- digital
- duplex
- fiber-optic cable
- half-duplex
- landline
- leased line
- local loop
- real-time communication
- sat phone
- telecommunications
- telephone
- twisted pair
- Wi-Fi

The Development of the Real-Time Communication

Once upon a time, people had to be in the same room for live communication, or **real-time communication**, to occur. To communicate across distance, they had to write and send letters that were physically transported and delivered. Long-distance communication could take days or even weeks.

The electrical telegraph system, developed in the early 1800s, was the first technology that made it possible for people to communicate in near real-time across long distances. The first telephone message was sent in 1876 over a line connecting two rooms. A **telephone** is basically a system for transmitting sound by converting vibrations into electrical signals. Other technologies for sending information over a distance include cable and radio broadcasting. When we use technology to communicate, we call it **telecommunications**.

Telecommunications can be **duplex** or **half-duplex**. With duplex communication, the people on both sides can communicate at same time, like on a phone call. In half-duplex communication only one side can communicate at a time, like through walkie-talkies.

Hard-wired Telephone Systems

Recall that a **landline**, or hard-wired telephone, is a phone that is connected directly to the wiring that transmits the audio between the caller and the recipient. Landline phone calls are made through the Public Switched Telephone Network (PSTN). This network is built from copper wires and other cables and forms a **circuit** between the caller's telephone and another telephone.

LOCAL CALLS For local calls, the phone company provides directly wired services between the homes and businesses that belong to the local network. Within your neighborhood, landline telephones connect to a common network for telephone service. This common network, called the **local loop**, connects to the phone company's central office. The local loop from the central telephone office to the user is still an **analog** system. An analog system sends electrical signals that carry voice and other sounds.

LONG-DISTANCE CALLS Outside the local loop, the long-distance telephone system today is mostly digital. **Digital** connections use computer code and can carry voice, data, and video on a single line. When you dial a long-distance number on a landline, computers figure out how to complete your call. To connect analog and digital networks, special equipment changes analog signals into digital signals. Digital landline phones connect to a cable or fiber-optic system through a router.

Analog vs. Digital Communications

People often confuse the terms "analog" and "digital" when they are talking about communications or computers. The difference is important but easy to understand.

- In analog communications, sounds such as a person's voice or music start as waves or vibrations in the air. The vibrating air varies in frequency or pitch, which is how high or deep the sound is, as well as strength or loudness. A small microphone in the telephone converts the sound waves into varying patterns of electrical signals or radio waves. The pattern of electrical signals or radio waves is similar to the pattern of the sound waves. These signals are converted back into sound waves by a small loudspeaker in the receiver.

- In digital communications, sounds are converted into binary data (a series of 1s and 0s) at the caller's end. The stream of 1s and 0s is transmitted without any variation in the pattern of electrical or radio waves. The receiver converts the binary data back into sound waves.

Cellular Systems

Recall that a **cellular phone** is a mobile phone that uses radio waves to communicate. Cell phones bypass part of the wired system, using a cellular system instead.

LOCATING CELLS Cell phone systems are divided into **cells**, or geographic areas to which a signal can be transmitted. Each cell has a **cell site**, also called a base station, for all the cellular phones in that area. Each cell site has a radio tower, called a **cell tower**, that receives radio signals from other towers and sends them on to still other towers. As a caller moves from one area to another, a new cell site automatically picks up the call to keep the signal strong and clear. Ultimately, the signal gets to individual cell phones.

MANAGING LOCATIONS Each geographic area is assigned to a central base station, or Mobile Telephone Switching Office (MTSO). It, in turn, is connected to the standard Public Switched Telephone Network (PSTN) telephone system. The MTSO has several responsibilities:

- Directs cellular activities at base stations

- Locates cellular users in the area

- Tracks users as they roam, or move, from cell to cell

- Connects cellular phones to land-based phones

MAKING A CALL When you turn on a cellular phone, it searches for a signal from the service provider's base station in the local area. When you place a call, the MTSO selects a frequency for your phone and a tower for you to use, and identifies the tower you are using. Each tower sends and receives signals to and from the individual cell phones within its cell. The MTSO is connected to the local telephone network, usually by telephone cable. Cell phones are connected to the telephone network through the cell site.

If you dial a long-distance number from your cell phone, the MTSO connects the call through

FIGURE 23.1.1 Telephone wires on telephone poles connect landline phones across the U.S.

JERRY HORBERT/SHUTTERSTOCK

503

JAKELV7500/SHUTTERSTOCK

FIGURE 23.1.2 Cell towers receive and transmit radio signals to complete cell phone calls.

a leased line. A digital **leased line** is a permanent connection allowing the MTSO to interact with long-distance providers.

RECEIVING A CALL When someone calls your cell phone, the cellular service provider locates the phone by cell. Moving from one cell into another, the phone transmits this information to the service provider's base station. The base station reports this information to the MTSO so it knows where to find you.

DID YOU KNOW?

Cell phones have location tracking and Global Positioning System (GPS) technology built in. Your phone may have settings that let you turn these services off. However, it is still possible for operating systems to track your phone using the location of the cell towers your phone connects to. That means it is possible to collect data about the location of phones every time the phone connects to a cell tower, even if the GPS in the phone is off.

Transmitting with Wires and Without

Cellular phones use radio waves for transmission. For homes that have landlines, wires connect the phone jack in the wall to an interface box outside. Outside wires may be above or below ground. Wires also connect the local loop with distant places. The connection from the phone to the wires may be made at a phone jack, or it may be to a **cable modem**. The cable modem is usually the same modem that connects to **broadband** internet service. Broadband is high-capacity transmission that enables a large number of messages to be communicated simultaneously.

Traditional hard-wired landline phone services use twisted copper wires as the core of the cables that transmit the voice information, but newer, higher-quality systems, such as coaxial and fiber-optic cable, are used as well.

TWISTED PAIR At first, the entire telephone system depended on twisted pair technology. **Twisted pair** refers to a pair of copper wires that are twisted together to reduce interference, or outside noise. In the U.S. today, most homes and business buildings still have twisted pair wiring. Twisted pair wiring can be either shielded (STP) or unshielded (UTP). Twisted pairs may be shielded to prevent electric interference from other sources.

COAXIAL Another type of copper cable is called **coaxial**. A coaxial cable, or coax, is a traditional analog wire used to transmit cable television. These copper wires connect a cable in the home to a neighborhood node, and from there to the service provider. The cable modem sends and receives an electrical signal over the wires.

FIBER-OPTIC CABLES **Fiber-optic cables** are strands of fiberglass that transmit digital data by pulses of light. These cables can carry large quantities of information. They work faster and more efficiently than copper wires. As they get lower in price, it is likely that fiber-optic cables will eventually replace copper completely.

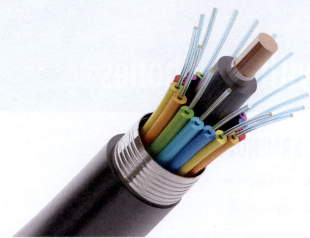

DESTINACIGDEM/123RF.COM

FIGURE 23.1.3 Fiber-optic cables are faster and more efficient than copper wires.

3G AND 4G Wireless communication frees users from traditional telephone lines. Messages are sent on radio or infrared signals. Cell phones use radio signals. Cell phone networks are usually referred to as **3G** (short for third generation) or **4G** (for fourth generation). These are references to the mobile communication standard that lets mobile phones access the internet.

WI-FI **Wi-Fi** networks use radio signals to connect computers. If a cell phone has a Wi-Fi adapter, it can transmit calls and provide other services using the internet. Wi-Fi makes cellular calls possible in areas that have internet access but are out of range of cell towers. Access to the internet through wireless networks also allows smartphones to run online apps, including text messages, video calling, instant messaging, and more.

SATELLITES A satellite telephone, or **sat phone**, transmits signals using communications satellites orbiting Earth. The caller phone transmits a signal to a satellite, which sends the signal to a land-based center, which then sends the signal to the receiving phone. The receiving phone can be a landline, a cell phone, or another satellite phone. Because satellite phones do not rely on cell towers, they are useful in remote areas, including at sea.

> ### DID YOU KNOW?
> In late 2017, the wireless industry released the first official 5G standard. 5G is not a replacement for 3G or 4G, but it does offer some improved capabilities. For example, it can transmit more data, respond faster, and connect more devices at the same time.

Competition Brings Choices

For more than 100 years, telephone service was provided only by telephone companies. The Telecommunications Act of 1996, however, introduced competition into the telecommunications market. Now, satellite companies, cable television companies, and businesses offering wireless services compete with telephone companies to provide high-bandwidth digital telecommunications. This competition has created new, affordable methods for transferring voice, video, and data.

People are no longer bound to a single choice for their telecommunications needs. Think of the different choices available to consumers at home and at work for sending and receiving voice, text, and images quickly and reliably. In addition to analog phones and DSL services, choices include:

- Digital satellite systems
- Cable systems
- Wireless networks

Integrating Computers with Telephones

OBJECTIVES

- Explain computer telephony integration.

- Sequence the steps in a modem transmission.

- Explain the purpose of a fax machine.

- Describe VoIP.

AS YOU READ

COMPARE AND CONTRAST Use a Venn diagram to help you compare and contrast modems and fax machines as you read.

TERMINOLOGY

- bits per second (bps)

- call center

- computer telephony integration (CTI)

- demodulation

- dial-up modem

- fax machine

- modem

- modulation

- router

- Voice over Internet Protocol (VoIP)

Using Computer Telephony Integration

By working together, computers and telephones can increase the power of communications. Linking computers to telephone systems is called **computer telephony integration (CTI)**.

While uses of CTI have expanded in recent years, one of the most traditional uses is when the computer takes the place of a human and acts as a **call center**, a central place where an organization's inbound and outbound calls are received and made. A call center CTI helps businesses and other organizations become more efficient. Suppose you call your favorite pizza restaurant for a delivery order. If this restaurant uses CTI, the modem and computer software work together to identify your name and your last delivery order. It will locate your house on an area map. Many organizations use CTI including the following:

- Emergency response centers in police and fire stations

- Hospitals

- Telemarketers (who conduct surveys or sell products or services by telephone)

- Voicemail services

- Banks, manufacturers, and small businesses

> ## TECHNOLOGY@HOME
>
> Many of us use a combination of technologies to communicate at home. We use phones, computers, and televisions to send and receive messages.

> ## THINK ABOUT IT!
>
> Conduct a class survey to identify how many of each tool below your class uses at home. Write your own answers and then compare your responses with those of your classmates. What conclusions can you draw?
>
> - analog telephones
> - cell phones
> - ISDN or DSL connections
> - digital satellite systems
> - cable systems
> - wireless networks
> - other

Using Modems

A device called a **modem** makes it possible for your computer and telephone lines to communicate, and for your computer and TV cables to communicate. Your computer is a digital device. The local loop that connects you to the

FIGURE 23.2.1 The 911 emergency telephone system is a great example of how computers and telephone systems can be integrated.

GRAHAM TAYLOR/SHUTTERSTOCK

507

telephone system is analog. The word *modem* actually names the work the device does: modulation and demodulation. Through **modulation**, the modem changes the digital signal of the computer to the analog sounds used by telephones. Then, the data—in the form of pictures, audio, or video—can travel over the telephone wires. When the data gets to its destination, the receiving modem changes the analog signals back to digital. This process is called **demodulation**. Modem speed is measured in **bits per second (bps)**, which is the amount of data that can be sent in one second.

DIAL-UP CONNECTIONS Back in the early 1990s, most people used phone lines and a device called a **dial-up modem** to connect to the internet for data transmission. The basic process for connecting via a dial-up modem is the same as for a cable or standard modem. You connect your phone to a computer or **router**, which is a networking device that forwards data packets between computer networks. This device connects to the modem. The difference is that you use a telephone to dial a phone number for an internet service provider. Once the connection is established, the modem encodes and decodes the audio frequency signals to transfer data.

Today, fewer than 10% of U.S. households connect to the computer using the local phone line loop, and they are generally located in rural areas where there is no other option. One problem with using dial-up is that you cannot be on your computer and use your telephone simultaneously, so the computer modem requires a dedicated phone line. Another drawback is slow speed. Dial-up modems can only transmit 56,600 bps, which has been surpassed by other technologies.

NORMAN CHAN/SHUTTERSTOCK

FIGURE 23.2.2 A modem like this changes digital signals into analog signals that can travel over telephone lines.

Sending Faxes

While dial-up is usually a thing of the past, there is one machine that still uses telephone lines to send printed messages or visual images. A facsimile machine, or **fax machine**, is a device that allows you to send pages of information to another fax machine anywhere in the world. Using an older stand-alone fax machine, or a multi-purpose printer with fax capabilities, users can transmit the content on hand-written documents, printed text, pictures, blueprints, or anything else on a page. Yet, even these machines are largely being replaced by email, by which you can send documents and scanned pages over the internet as attachments.

As a document enters a fax machine (or in a printer with fax capability), a sensor scans it. The data is converted to a digital signal. An internal modem in the fax machine changes the digital signal to an analog signal. The receiving fax machine accepts the analog signal, changes it back to digital, and prints a copy of the original document.

FIGURE 23.2.3 While a stand-alone fax machine like this may be obsolete, many businesses still use fax machines to transmit important documents.

VORONIN76/SHUTTERSTOCK

CAREER CORNER

TELEMATICS Blending telecommunications technology with computers to control the electric, electronic, and mechanical tools we use is a relatively new field known as telematics. Requirements for success in this industry include programming, engineering, and telecommunications training and experience. Telematics professionals will find a growing demand for their services as the field develops.

Voice over Internet Protocol

Just as you can use your telephone to send and receive messages over the internet, you can use the internet to send and receive messages over the telephone. **Voice over Internet Protocol (VoIP)** technology allows you to have a telephone connection over the internet. VoIP uses data sent digitally, with the Internet Protocol (IP), instead of analog telephone lines. People use VoIP to talk to each other from across the globe, sometimes for free. Most VoIP applications, such as Skype and Facetime, integrate cameras so callers can see each other during their calls.

REAL-WORLD TECH
FINDING YOUR WAY BY SATELLITE

SCANRAIL/123RF.COM

Some of the satellites that circle Earth can pinpoint any spot on the ground or at sea. Using signals from these satellites, a Geographic Positioning System (GPS) receiver can show maps and directions on a screen. GPS is widely used by the military, but it is also used by drivers, boaters, hikers, tourists, and others who may rely on directions. How is GPS used in cars?

Exploring High-Speed Telecommunications

OBJECTIVES

- Explain the importance of bandwidth.

- Describe the use of broadband transmissions.

AS YOU READ

ORGANIZE INFORMATION Use a chart to help you identify broadband technologies as you read.

TERMINOLOGY

- asymmetric DSL (ADSL)

- bandwidth

- broadband

- cable modem

- Digital Subscriber Line (DSL)

- fixed broadband

- mobile broadband

- SONET

- symmetric DSL (SDSL)

Working with Broadband Transmission

Broadband is the general term for all high-speed digital connections that transmit at least 1.5 megabits per second (Mbps). Broadband technology is able to send multiple signals at the same time. Several broadband technologies are available, including Digital Subscriber Line, cable, fiber optic, and 4G, and more are on the horizon.

- **Fixed broadband** refers to wired networks, such as fiber optic and Digital Subscriber Line (DSL), which are used for television and internet access.

- **Mobile broadband** refers to networks like 3G and 4G, which are used by cellular phones and other mobile devices.

Broadband transmission speed is affected by distance from the local telephone switching station, condition of the wiring and other equipment, and the number of people using the service. Generally speaking, a fixed broadband download speed of at least 10 Mbps is fast enough for someone to stream a high-definition video while someone else in the house is surfing the internet. In 2017, the average broadband download speed in the U.S. was about 55 Mbps; the average upload speed was just under 23 Mbps. The average mobile download speed in 2017 in the U.S. was about 22 Mbps and the average upload speed was about 8.5 Mbps.

DSL One of the most common fixed broadband services is **Digital Subscriber Line (DSL)**. DSL uses the same copper wires telephones use, but transmits data in digital form rather than analog. Voice calls and DSL can exist simultaneously on copper lines, because each service has its own frequency band.

DSL allows for very fast connections to the internet and features an "always-on" connection. DSL service also requires a modem, which translates the computer's digital signals into voltage sent across phone lines to a central hub. There is one drawback to DSL: A user must be within a few miles of a local telephone switching station for a connection to be made.

Different companies offer DSL at different levels of service and price. There are also two basic types: **asymmetric DSL (ADSL)**, which has faster download speeds than upload speeds, and **symmetric DSL (SDSL)**, which can send and receive data at the same speed. ADSL is more common. SDSL is generally used by businesses, while ADSL is used in private homes and businesses.

SONET Telephone companies that offer DSL and other internet connection methods rely on a digital network called **SONET**. SONET stands for *Synchronous Optical Network*. It uses fiber optics to provide faster connections and greater bandwidth—from 52 Mbps to up to a whopping 40 gigabits per second (Gbps).

FIGURE 23.3.1 In a videoconference, users in different locations transmit and receive audio, video, and computer data in real time. This kind of activity requires a great deal of bandwidth.

BLEND IMAGES/SHUTTERSTOCK

Internet and Television Access

If your family has cable television, the cable that provides your favorite television shows probably also lets you connect to the internet and make landline-based telephone calls. Connections usually are fast and reliable.

CABLE AND SATELLITE TV CONNECTIONS To connect your computer to a cable service, you need a **cable modem**. Like analog modems, cable modems can be internal or external. A cable modem connects your computer to the local cable TV line and supports data transfer rates of up to 30 Mbps—over 500 times faster than the old dial-up modem. However, this number can be misleading because most internet service providers (ISPs) cap subscribers' transfer rates to less than 6 Mbps to conserve bandwidth.

Cable modems download the signal from the internet and upload data to the internet. Not all cable modems allow two-way communication and some two-way communications work at different speeds. For example, downloading information may be faster than uploading. Cable modems also require an analog phone line and an analog modem.

If you have satellite television, your family subscribes to a digital satellite system called a Direct Broadcast Satellite (DBS) service. Satellites receive signals from a central broadcast center and then rebroadcast them around the globe. Most DBS systems also offer internet access and data transfer services, but do not transmit telephone calls. Because satellites can only transmit data to a subscriber, a modem and telephone line are needed to send data, such as a pay-per-movie request, to the provider.

The Importance of Bandwidth

Recall that **bandwidth** is the amount of data that can be sent through a modem or network connection. The more bandwidth, the faster the connection. It is usually measured in bits per second (bps) or in megabits per second (Mbps). The more bandwidth, the more information can be transferred in a given amount of time. If you are online watching a movie on a tablet while someone else in your family is online researching a topic for a report, and someone else is using IM to communicate with friends, you may notice a drop in speed or interruption in a download. That's because each device requires a lot of bandwidth, but there is only a fixed amount available.

The demand for bandwidth is always growing. People want increased bandwidth for video streaming, VoIP calls, web-based conferences, and online learning. Some ways companies are addressing the demand is to make more bandwidth available using satellites, adopting 5G technology, and investing in telecommunications infrastructure.

IC3 ✔ **Understand the importance of bandwidth.**

TECHNOLOGY@SCHOOL

With all the ways that schools use technology these days, they need a lot of bandwidth to send and receive information electronically.

THINK ABOUT IT!

Think about who in your school might benefit from increased bandwidth. Which tasks listed below could use bandwidth?

- students participating in a class teleconference
- a teacher researching Mars
- a librarian helping a student find a book
- a counselor checking student records
- a principal answering email

Chapter 23 Review

REVIEW THE TERMINOLOGY

DIRECTIONS Match each vocabulary term in the left column with the correct definition in the right column.

1. telecommunications
2. analog
3. digital
4. fiber-optic cable
5. modulation
6. demodulation
7. bits per second
8. bandwidth
9. broadband
10. cellular phone
11. cell
12. cell site
13. leased line
14. cable modem

a. the measure of how much data can be sent through a network connection

b. system using computer code to carry different kinds of data

c. changing digital signals to analog

d. system using electrical signals that match the human voice and other sounds

e. strand of fiberglass that transmits data by pulses of light

f. using a telephone network to send information

g. high-speed digital connection of at least 1.5 Mbps

h. measurement of the speed at which data can be sent in one second

i. changing analog signals to digital

j. permanent connection for long-distance cell phone calls

k. geographic area to which radio signals are sent

l. phone that uses radio waves to communicate

m. base station for handling cell calls

n. device that enables a computer to access the internet through a cable television connection

USE THE TERMINOLOGY

DIRECTIONS Complete each sentence with terminology from the chapter.

1. The _____ consists of the local loop and long-distance lines that handle data and voice communications.

2. In the long-distance telephone system, _____ largely have replaced twisted pair copper wire.

3. Radio and infrared signals make _____ communication possible.

4. Within a neighborhood, telephones connect to a common network called the _____.

5. A fax machine sending a document transmits data into a(n) _____ signal and changes it into a(n) _____ signal.

6. _____ offers a way for people across the globe to call each other over the internet free of charge.

7. DSL stands for _____.

8. Cell phones use _____ to communicate.

9. As a caller moves from one point to another, a new _____ relays the signal from MTSO to MTSO.

10. Linking computers and telephones to work together is called _____.

11. A wireless network, which may be called _____, is a short range network with high bandwidth for data transfer.

12. All cable modems allow downloading of data, but not all offer the ability to _____ information through the cable television connection.

13. _____ allow computers to communicate with each other without being physically connected.

THINK CRITICALLY

DIRECTIONS Answer the following questions.

1. Why is a modem needed to access the internet?

2. Why is faxing an order to a company an example of telecommunications in action?

3. For what types of documents might a fax machine be a better method of transmission than email?

4. Why might it be important for a home-office computer to have internet service that offers a lot of bandwidth?

5. Why are mobile phones called cell phones?

6. What common communications tools do you think use CTI to send and receive information?

EXTEND YOUR KNOWLEDGE

DIRECTIONS Choose and complete one of the following projects.

1. With your teacher's permission, research, compare, and contrast different methods for network connectivity, such as broadband, wireless, Bluetooth, and cellular. Take notes and keep track of your sources. Only use information from reliable and accurate sources. Make a table showing your findings, and present it to a partner or to the class.

2. Some states and industries have developed policies to guide cell phone use. Select one of the following topics: (1) states that have banned or restricted drivers from using handheld cell phones or (2) airlines that restrict cell phone calls at certain times. With your teacher's permission, conduct online research to identify the reasons for the rules or laws, using appropriate strategies to locate the information on the internet. Then, conclude whether or not the desired results have been achieved.

IC3 PREP

1. What is bandwidth?

    a. the speed of an internet connection, in bits per second

    b. the type of cable used to transmit data over a network

    c. the amount of data that can be sent through a modem or network connection

    d. the maximum number of applications that can run on a device without slowdown

2. Which of the following would take up bandwidth on a network? (Select all that apply.)

    a. watching a show on YouTube

    b. playing an online video game

    c. communicating with others with a VoIP client

    d. defragmenting a hard drive

    e. downloading updated video card drivers from the internet

3. For each line below, select whether the statement is True or False.

    a. Larger bandwidth equals a faster internet connection.

    b. Bandwidth can determine a device's speed with both online and offline tasks.

    c. In recent years, demand for higher bandwidth has leveled off.

    d. Bandwidth is usually measured in bits per second (bps) or in megabits per second (Mbps).

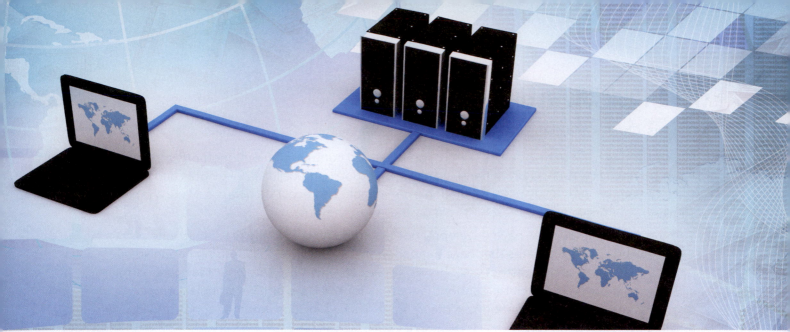

CHAPTER 24

Networking Basics

WHAT IS A COMPUTER NETWORK?

In the simplest terms, a computer network is a group of computers and devices connected to each other so they can exchange data. The smallest network may only connect two computers; the largest—the internet—connects millions. In this chapter you are introduced to the concepts and terminology associated with computer networks, including the difference between local area networks and wide area networks.

Introducing Computer Networks

OBJECTIVES

- Explain what a computer network is.
- List media commonly used in networks.
- Identify three key benefits of using a network.
- Discuss how computers communicate.

AS YOU READ

ORGANIZE INFORMATION Complete an outline to help you identify the details that support the main idea of the lesson.

TERMINOLOGY

- computer network
- data network
- gateway
- network
- network interface card (NIC)
- network traffic
- node
- open protocol
- physical media
- proprietary protocol
- protocol
- protocol suite
- synergy
- terminal
- Transmission Control Protocol/Internet Protocol (TCP/IP)
- wireless access point (WAP)
- workstation

Introducing Networks

If your family owns two computers, can they both use the same printer? If your computers are networked, they can.

Recall that a **network** is a group or system of connected things. A computer network, which may be called a **data network**, is two or more computing devices connected to each other so they can share data, devices, and other resources. Networks allow users to share files and programs, as well as printers and other equipment. They allow people to work together and to access the internet. A network may be small, with just a few connected devices, or it may be large, with thousands. The technology functions the same way, no matter how many devices are connected.

PHYSICAL MEDIA To create a computer network, each device must be able to communicate with the network. This requires establishing the physical connection using **physical media**. The medium can be any type of telecommunications connector: twisted pair telephone lines, coaxial cable, fiber-optic cable, or a microwave, radio, or infrared system. Working together, the network media and the computing device determine how much data can be sent through the connector.

NETWORK INTERFACE CARDS Some computing devices are designed with the ability to connect to networks. Others need a **network interface card (NIC)**, which handles the flow of data to and from the device in both wired and wireless networks. If the network is put together by actual cables, those cables connect to the NIC. NICs often have a light that blinks green and amber to alert you to any activity it may be experiencing. If the network is wireless, the NIC is usually built in to the device, such as a phone, tablet, or laptop. There are also standalone wireless network interface cards that can connect through a USB port.

WIRELESS ACCESS POINTS Even wireless networks require physical media. In addition to a wireless NIC in the device, the network needs a wireless transmitter, or hub, called a **wireless**

DESERG/SHUTTERSTOCK

FIGURE 24.1.1 Network interface cards enable PCs to connect to a network.

access point (WAP). The WAP is the central transmitter for sending and receiving wireless signals. It may be built in to the wireless router, or it may be a separate device that connects to the router using an Ethernet connection.

Organizing Users

If you have more than one computing device at home, you probably identify them by each user's name—your laptop, Mom's tablet, and so on. In businesses, schools, and other organizations, a network is usually organized into workstations, each with its own name and address. In both home and larger networks, pieces of equipment connected together must be able to locate and communicate with one another.

NETWORK MEMBERS A **workstation** is a computer connected to a computer network. It is often set up with the same operating system, applications, and access to resources as the other computers in the network. In a large network, a workstation may also be called a **node** by the people who take care of the network. A node is anything connected to the network that can receive, create, store, or send data along distributed network routes. A **gateway** is a node on your network that enables communication with other networks, such as the router on a home network that lets you connect to the internet.

Smartphones, tablets, and other devices equipped for networking can be part of a network.

WORKSTATION ALTERNATIVE Sometimes, in large organizations, network users work at a **terminal**, which usually includes a keyboard, a monitor, and a pointing device, such as a mouse. A terminal can feel as if the computer is local, but it's not. Users are actually sharing time on a central computer, with their own work displayed on their terminal's monitor.

Using terminals can save on the cost of purchasing workstations. They are also useful in situations with limited need for a workstation, such as a public computer in a library.

Ensuring Communication

Once a network is created, the computers and other connected equipment can communicate with one another. The communication on a network is called **network traffic**. Network traffic is the electronic pulses of information sent by the network cards to carry data through the network wires to its destination. Specifically, computers communicate with languages called protocols.

A **protocol** sets a standard format for data and rules for handling it. There are many different protocols available to use on networks. For computers to speak with one another, they must use the same protocol.

CONNECTIONS

LITERATURE With ebooks, your next reading selection could come from a network instead of a bookstore! Today, readers download their selections onto eReaders, laptops, PCs, tablets, and smartphones. Aside from convenience, there are practical advantages to ebooks. Many schools are making textbooks available as ebooks, so students don't have to lug around heavy backpacks filled with books. And senior citizens and people with disabilities can buy books or borrow them from the public library without leaving home.

GEORGE DOLGIKH/SHUTTERSTOCK

FIGURE 24.1.2 Workstations in a computer lab.

THINK ABOUT IT!

Think about the benefits of a network. Sequence the value of each possible benefit using a scale of 1 (lowest) to 4 (highest). What conclusions can you draw?

- a joint science experiment conducted by two schools
- a school newspaper file to which each computer user can contribute
- one version of a program installed on all computers
- one expensive printer shared among 20 computers

KINDS OF PROTOCOLS There are two protocol categories: open and proprietary. An **open protocol** is available for anyone to use. For example, the most common open protocol is the **Transmission Control Protocol/Internet Protocol (TCP/IP)**, which is used by computers on the internet.

A **proprietary protocol**, however, is not open to everyone. Instead, only people who buy certain equipment, services, or computers can use it. Some personal digital assistants, digital cameras, and even dial-up internet services use proprietary protocols. Overall, however, open protocols are more common. Both manufacturers and consumers benefit from open protocols that allow a broad range of connections.

A STACK OF PROTOCOLS The protocols networks use to communicate are often called a **protocol suite**. A protocol suite is the stack, or collection, of individual protocols that determines how the network operates. For example, TCP/IP is not just one network language, but many smaller ones. Each small protocol in this suite has a specific job to do in a specific order. Working together, protocols allow computers to communicate.

Working with Others

Everyone on a network has the ability to access programs and data stored anywhere on the network. You might use an application like Google Docs, which is stored on a network rather than on your own computer, or you might print a document on a printer that is located on a different floor than your computer. Of course, for security, you can specify sharing levels for folders and files to control who can access the stored data. Publicly shared folders allow anyone access. Shared folders may be shared only with authorized users. Sometimes shared folders are accessed using shared links. That means you send a link to someone to allow them to access the folder.

Networks also let people work together in new and exciting ways. People on a network can collaborate more easily than those working on standalone systems. **Synergy** is the effect a group effort can create. People working together on a network can sometimes accomplish more than people working alone on unconnected computers.

ROCKETCLIPS/123RF.COM

FIGURE 24.1.3 Using a network can make collaboration easier.

Using a Network

The steps you use to access network resources are basically the same as those you use to work on your own computer. Your actions may seem simple enough, but behind the scenes, the network's hardware and software are performing complex tasks.

Some tasks you can accomplish using a network include:

- Scheduling a meeting

- Instant messaging

- Sending email

- Videoconferencing

- Exchanging documents

- Playing games

Local Area Networks

OBJECTIVES

- Describe how local area networks work.

- Define how local area networks allow information sharing.

- Compare peer-to-peer and client/server networks.

AS YOU READ

ORGANIZE INFORMATION Complete a spider map to help you identify the basics of local area networks as you read the lesson.

TERMINOLOGY

- client

- client/server network

- collaborative software

- file server

- file sharing

- groupware

- local area network (LAN)

- network operating system (NOS)

- peer-to-peer (P2P) network

- remote resource

Introducing LANs

A school lab with its ten computers networked together is an example of a **local area network (LAN)**. A LAN is a network in which all the workstations and other equipment are near one another. LANs can be set up in any defined area, such as a home, a school, an office building, or even a cluster of shops.

A LAN can have just a few or several hundred users. Small or large, a LAN lets its members share equipment and information, resulting in lower costs. Some of the key functions that benefit LAN users include sharing files, using collaborative software, and sharing peripherals.

SHARING FILES Through a computer's operating system, people connected to a LAN can participate in **file sharing**. File sharing is making files available to more than one user on the network. The file is stored on a network server so anyone with permission rights may access the file from any location.

USING COLLABORATIVE SOFTWARE **Collaborative software** enables the network to help people work together more closely. With collaborative software, users can share calendars, work on a document together, or even hold meetings through the network. Collaborative software is also called **groupware**.

SHARING PERIPHERALS In addition to sharing files and software, a LAN allows users to access **remote resources**, such as printers, fax machines, or any other equipment, that is not connected directly to your computer, but is connected to the network.

Using a Peer-to-Peer Network

Your peers are your equals. In a **peer-to-peer (P2P) network**, all the computers are equals. Peer-to-peer networks are usually small, having anywhere from two to ten computers.

SHARING FILES In a P2P network, each user decides whether any files on his or her computer will be shared. You can share the files with one person, a few people, or everyone on the network. The reverse is true, too. Other workstations may have files you'd like to access through the network—and you can if you have permission.

CREATING A P2P NETWORK A P2P network is easy to create, since all of the workstations are equals. The operating system of each computer typically has built-in file-sharing abilities. The workstations are connected to each other through the network cable. In some systems, the network cables all connect to a central device called a hub. A hub handles the flow of traffic from computer to computer.

EVALUATING P2P NETWORKS A P2P network is ideal for small offices and homes. In a large business, however, peer-to-peer networking has some drawbacks:

- Security problems can arise.

- Data can be hard to back up.

- With many users, file sharing can become difficult.

- Finding shared files can be difficult.

- Managing resources can be complicated.

These problems occur because resources are scattered across many computers. If one computer fails or is turned off, its resources are no longer available to the network.

Using a Client/Server Network

Large businesses usually use a **client/server network**. With this system, one powerful computer provides information and management services to the workstation computers, which are called **clients**.

CREATING A CLIENT/SERVER NETWORK The main computer in a client/server system is called the **file server**, or the server. It contains the network operating system, other programs, and large data files. The **network operating system (NOS)** manages and secures the entire network. It controls access, permissions, and all aspects of network use, and provides a directory, or list, of all resources available on the network. Only those who provide a username and a password can use the network. It centralizes and protects data and controls what users can do with files. Thus, a client/server network is far more secure than a P2P network.

EVALUATING A CLIENT/SERVER NETWORK For a large office, file servers are better than peer-to-peer networks, for several reasons:

■ They offer a central location for files.

■ Data is easy to back up and easy to recover.

■ Servers are faster than workstations.

■ Servers are rarely turned off, although they can be offline for maintenance.

■ Security is easier to maintain.

TECHNOLOGY@WORK

Shared files and databases are extremely useful in many office situations. If the office is networked, any employee on the network can access the data.

THINK ABOUT IT!

Think about what information might be useful at a magazine publishing house. Which databases below do you think should be networked for any employee to access? Which should not?

• a collection of photographs of famous people

• a list of employees' salaries

• a directory of all subscribers and their addresses

• a dictionary and a thesaurus

• a series of notes on recent historical events

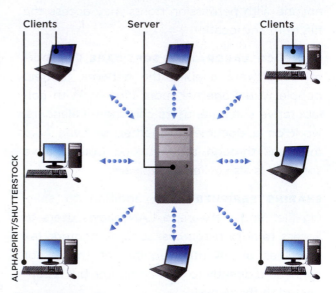

FIGURE 24.2.1 In a client/server network, the client devices access the network through the server.

Wide Area Networks

OBJECTIVES

- Identify the purpose and components of a wide area network.

- Compare methods organizations use to connect to a point of presence.

- Compare and contrast packet-switching networks and circuit-switching networks.

- Describe three types of WANs.

AS YOU READ

ORGANIZE INFORMATION Complete an outline to help you note key facts about wide area networks as you read the lesson.

TERMINOLOGY

- backbone

- circuit-switching

- congestion

- firewall

- frame relay

- intranet

- packets

- packet-switching

- permanent virtual circuit (PVC)

- point of presence (POP)

- port

- public data network

- router

- T1 line

- virtual private network (VPN)

- wide area network (WAN)

What Is a WAN?

A **wide area network (WAN)** connects computers and other resources that are miles or even continents apart. A business with offices in many places can use a WAN to link its LANs in different cities. Then, users from any of the locations can, with the proper permissions, access the network. The company can maintain a centralized information technology infrastructure, while each user can access files, printers, and other resources as if they were local. As far as users are concerned, working on a WAN is no different than working on a LAN.

Once a WAN is created, users may not even realize the files they are sharing are remote. And that's the way it should be. Users should not worry about the physical location of the shared files, just that the files are available.

How Is a WAN Controlled?

Like a client/server LAN, a WAN is controlled by a network operating system (NOS). A NOS is especially helpful on a WAN because there are so many users and resources to manage. The NOS also helps network administrators secure the resources throughout the network.

Creating WANs

To create a WAN, LANs are connected through high-speed data lines called **backbones**. Organizations attach to the backbone at a **point of presence (POP)**. But how do they get to the POP? There are several options.

ISDN AND DSL These technologies use ordinary telephone lines to attach to the backbone. Special adapters or modems provide ways to deal with digital data.

LEASED LINES Some companies rent a private end-to-end connection, called a leased line or dedicated line, from a telecommunications company. Leased lines are always active, and guarantee a single open circuit will be available between two points at all times. The data transfer rate of a leased line varies depending on the type of line, but is usually about the same as a symmetric DSL line.

T1 LINES Larger companies and many school districts lease **T1 lines**. T1 lines can be either copper or fiber optic, and they allow data to be sent at more than 1.5 million bps.

PERMANENT VIRTUAL CIRCUITS A **permanent virtual circuit (PVC)** allows multiple users' data to travel the line at once. Thus, they are cheaper than private lines. Most PVCs use a technology called **frame relay**. Frame relay allows voice, data, and video to travel on the same line and at the same time.

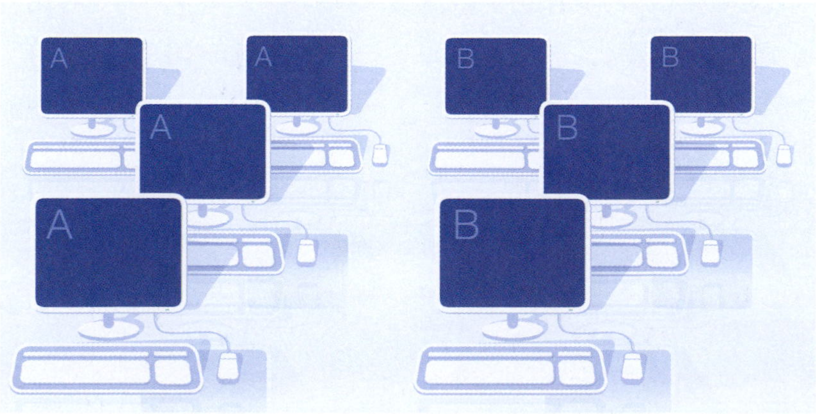

ALEX DVIHALLY/SHUTTERSTOCK

FIGURE 24.3.1 A WAN can be made up of multiple connected LANs.

NETWORKING THE NAVAJO NATION

FRONTPAGE/SHUTTERSTOCK

The Navajo Nation spreads across 26,000 square miles in Arizona, New Mexico, and Utah. The Nation's Diné College has seven campuses that are hundreds of miles apart. Only about half of the Nation's households have phone lines. How could the educational system take advantage of the internet? The solution was to create a WAN using a variety of technologies. Small satellite dishes receive information while phone and dedicated data lines send messages out. The Navajo Nation's wide area network has expanded to overcome the wide open spaces in which its people live.

What group or institution do you think would benefit from a WAN? Why?

Sending Data Long-Distance

PACKET-SWITCHING NETWORKS Most networks use **packet-switching** technology. The sending computer divides information into tiny segments called **packets**. Each packet is marked with a delivery address, so packet transfers are quick and accurate. When you transfer a file, send an email, or even browse a website, you're sending and receiving packets.

CIRCUIT-SWITCHING NETWORKS Some WANs use circuit-switching technology to transmit messages. **Circuit-switching** happens on a real, end-to-end connection between the sending computer and the receiving computer, which make up the circuit. There's no delay on circuit-switching networks, so they are ideal for sending voice messages and for teleconferencing. A telephone network uses circuit-switching.

Routers are network devices or programs that choose the best pathway for each packet. If there is **congestion**, or too much traffic, on the network, the router can delay some of the packets. The receiving computer puts the packets back together in the right order.

Types of WANs

Businesses and other organizations use three basic types of WANs.

PUBLIC DATA NETWORK A **public data network** allows a company to set up its own network. Telecommunications companies own the public data network and charge fees for the use of the network.

PRIVATE DATA NETWORK Some companies set up a private data network that cannot be accessed by outsiders. Having a private data network costs more than using a public data network.

VIRTUAL PRIVATE NETWORK A **virtual private network (VPN)** is a private network set up through a public network. VPN users connect to an internet service provider (ISP) to access the network.

Network Security

Recall that a network can be secured or unsecured. On an unsecured network, anyone within the network can access information. Secured networks, however, limit access and protect the computing devices and users.

SECURE AND UNSECURE NETWORKS Unsecure networks allow for free flow of information but leave little protection from hacking for the individual computers. Unsecured networks may be called public networks, although your home network may also be unsecured. An unsecured wireless network can be accessed by anyone within range of the wireless signal. It does not require a login or password and does not use encryption to protect data. Your neighbor may be able to access your unsecured Wi-Fi network to read files or access email, thereby learning personal information. Connecting to an unsecured network exposes your data and hardware devices to risks.

One way secured networks prevent unauthorized access is by requiring users to enter an ID and password. Another way is by using a firewall. You can secure a wireless network by using an encryption protocol such as Wi-Fi Protected Access 2 (WPA2).

PUBLIC AND PRIVATE NETWORKS Computing in a network can be private or public. When you use the computers in your local library, you are on a public network that anyone can access. The networks in your school or home, are private and usually require an ID and password for access.

There are also public and private IP addresses. Public IP addresses are used by all computers connected to the internet by a modem, including your home network computers. Private IP addresses are used on internal networks, such as a company **intranet**. Private IP addresses cannot be contacted directly over the internet the way a computer with a public IP address can be. This provides an extra layer of security for the internal network.

FIREWALLS Networks also use firewalls as a level of security. A **firewall** is a filtering system that opens or blocks programs and ports to keep outside data from entering the network. In networking, a **port** is an endpoint used by the communications protocol to identify the specific location on a computer where data transferred on the internet is sent or received.

Firewalls are usually located on a gateway, such as a router, that lets a network access the internet. The firewall examines the packets trying to get into the network and determines whether or not to let them through. Some firewalls are built into a computer's operating system, such as Windows. You or the system administrator can control what the firewall blocks and what it lets through by maintaining lists of allowed or blocked programs and ports.

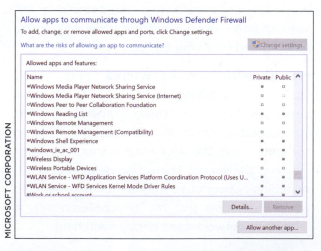

MICROSOFT CORPORATION

FIGURE 24.3.2 Use the Windows Defender Firewall Allowed Apps settings to allow or block programs and ports.

Chapter 24 Review

REVIEW THE TERMINOLOGY

DIRECTIONS Match each vocabulary term in the left column with the correct definition in the right column.

1. network
2. workstation
3. protocol
4. local area network
5. collaborative software
6. peer-to-peer network
7. file server
8. backbone
9. point of presence
10. virtual private network

a. network in which all computers are equal
b. computer connected to a network
c. local connection to a WAN
d. standard format and rules
e. set up on a public network
f. two or more computers linked together
g. program that lets people work together closely
h. high-speed line that carries network traffic
i. network set up in a limited area
j. the central computer in one kind of network

USE THE TERMINOLOGY

DIRECTIONS Determine the correct choice for each of the following.

1. Which of the following is NOT an example of a physical medium used to connect a network?
   a. telephone wires
   b. electric cords
   c. fiber-optic cables
   d. radio signals

2. Which of the following is sometimes used in place of workstations on a large network?
   a. a file server
   b. nodes
   c. a point of presence
   d. terminals

3. Which of the following is another name for collaborative software?
   a. groupware
   b. network operating system
   c. local area network
   d. backbone

4. Which of the following do users of a client/server network have to provide in order to use the network?

   a. a client name and password

   b. a file

   c. a protocol

   d. a username and password

5. Which of the following is used to control a WAN?

   a. NIC

   b. VPN

   c. NOS

   d. POP

6. Which of the following is used to provide a local connection to a WAN?

   a. NIC

   b. VPN

   c. NOS

   d. POP

THINK CRITICALLY

DIRECTIONS Answer the following questions.

1. How are a LAN and a WAN similar? How are they different?

2. Why might a P2P network be a good choice for a small network? Why might a client/server model be a good choice for a large network?

3. Why is the internet an example of a WAN?

4. What kinds of wires and wireless lines can be used as the backbone of a WAN?

5. Why are protocols important to LANs and WANs?

EXTEND YOUR KNOWLEDGE

DIRECTIONS Choose and complete one of the following projects.

1. With your teacher's permission, research, compare, and contrast a server, workstation, host, and client. Take notes and keep track of your sources. Create a chart showing your findings, and share it with a partner or with the class.

2. With your teacher's permission, research the differences, advantages, and disadvantages of standard protocols. Take notes and keep track of your sources. Only use information from reliable and accurate sources. Use the information to create a chart, and present it to a partner or to the class.

CHAPTER 25

Building Networks

DOES NETWORK DESIGN AFFECT ACCESS?

From your smartphone, to your school's computer lab, to the wireless network at the coffee shop, access to a network is everywhere. People are using networks for work, education, and entertainment every hour of the day.

Networks, and the science of network design, are becoming more important in our lives than ever before. In this chapter, you will learn about the different designs used to create networks, and how networks are used by businesses and individuals.

Connecting Computers

OBJECTIVES

- Explain what is meant by network architecture.

- Explain OSI.

- Define network topology.

AS YOU READ

ORGANIZE INFORMATION Use a main-idea chart to help you identify the details that support the main idea of the lesson.

TERMINOLOGY

- collision

- contention

- network architecture

- network layer

- Open Systems Interconnection (OSI)

- topology

Network Architecture

Network architecture is the science of designing a network. In many cases, a systems engineer is hired to find out what the network will be used for, and to design a network the operating system can handle.

Small networks are generally not very complicated. The network administrator first connects the network card of each workstation to the network cable, and then usually connects the cable to a hub. The administrator also has to make sure the operating system of the computer is set up to participate in the network. On larger networks, however, the job becomes more complicated.

FOLLOWING RULES Recall that all network communication, large or small, is based on and must follow common rules, called protocols. These rules were developed by the International Standards Organization (ISO).

The rules specific to computer networks are called the **Open Systems Interconnection (OSI)** model. These rules define what happens at each step of a network operation and how data flows through it. The OSI model has seven layers.

- Layer 7, the application layer, is at the top. Layer 1, the physical layer, is at the bottom. Each layer communicates with the layer above and below it to ensure that networking takes place. During transmission, on the sending computer, data flows from the application layer, down through each layer in the model, and out through the network. On the receiving computer, data flows back up through the model.

- Sometimes layers 1, 2, and 3 are called the lower layers. They define rules for how information is sent between computers over a network. The upper layers, or layers 4, 5, 6, and 7, define how applications interact with the network.

CAREER CORNER

SYSTEMS ENGINEER Systems engineers have enormous responsibility in working with networks. They design and install them, but they also continue working to improve the network and troubleshoot to solve problems. Systems engineers aim for maximum performance and security in the networks they deal with. They are knowledgeable about both hardware and software.

LAYERS OF THE OSI MODEL

Layer	Purpose
7. Application	Communicate with the operating system to do an actual job
6. Presentation	Package data from the operating system so the lower layers can understand it
5. Session	Create and end communication between two devices on the network
4. Transport	Manage the flow of data within the network and check for errors
3. Network	Route and address data traffic
2. Datalink	Choose the right physical protocols for the data
1. Physical	Define the actual network hardware, such as cabling and timing

■ Each layer has a job to do to prepare outgoing data for the network and incoming data for the operating system. All layers are important, but layer 3, the **network layer**, deserves special attention because that is the stage of the process when data is transferred from one router to another.

Network Topology

If you were to create a map of your neighborhood, you might include streets, lakes, and hills. A map of a network shows the physical structure of the network, including servers, workstations, and other network devices. The network's layout is called the network **topology**.

Topology isn't only concerned with where to put equipment, however. The design of a network must also solve another problem: Only one computer on a network can transmit at a time. When two computers try to access the network at the same time, they're in **contention**. If both sent their data at the same time, there could be a **collision**, and the data could become all mixed together.

To avoid such collisions, each computer divides its data into very small, fast-moving packets. Network equipment or software transmits these packets. Users typically are not affected by the tiny delays as each computer waits its turn to transmit data.

TECHNOLOGY@WORK

The word *contention* has more than one meaning. It can mean a state of rivalry or a statement that one supports.

THINK ABOUT IT!

Think about the various meanings of the word *contention*. Which sentence(s) below do not use the word correctly?

- Sally and Tom are in contention for the job of manager.
- Ralph did not apply for that position because he feels contention in his present job.
- It is Sally's contention that her skills are ideal for the job.

REAL-WORLD TECH
NETWORKING THE HOME

A smart house is one that connects systems to a network. It offers benefits such as wireless security systems and baby monitors, as well as central control of heat, lighting, and home entertainment systems. Even refrigerators can be connected. When home systems connect to the internet, homeowners can monitor and control them using a smartphone, tablet, or smart speaker device such as Amazon Echo or Google Home. Which high-tech feature would you most like to have in your home?

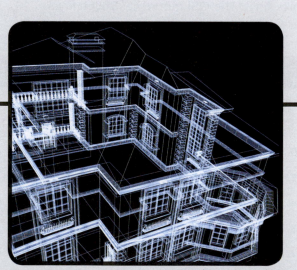
3DDOCK/SHUTTERSTOCK

OBJECTIVES

- Compare and contrast LAN topologies.
- List the pros and cons of different network topologies.
- Describe the operation of an Ethernet.

AS YOU READ

ORGANIZE INFORMATION Use an outline to help you identify types of LANs as you read the lesson.

TERMINOLOGY

- backbone
- bus topology
- CSMA/CD
- Ethernet
- hub
- mesh topology
- ring topology
- star bus topology
- star topology
- tokens
- token rings
- wireless token rings

Choosing a Network Topology

Each LAN can have a different combination of computers, printers, and other equipment. The LAN designer chooses a network type to connect the components. Each type of network can be described by its topology: bus, ring, star, star bus, and mesh.

BUS TOPOLOGY An older network design, **bus topology** is rarely used now. In a bus, devices are connected to a single network line like a string of holiday lights. When one network device fails, the entire network fails, and adding new devices to the network can also be tricky.

RING TOPOLOGY As its name suggests, **ring topology** connects all the network devices in a circle. To control collisions, such networks pass **tokens**, or special units of data, around the ring. Only the workstation that has control of the token can send other data onto the network. Because of the token-passing technique, these networks are also called **token rings**, or, if the network is wireless, **wireless token rings**. Like bus topology, one fault can disrupt a ring network, but this network type has the advantage of not requiring a network server.

STAR TOPOLOGY **Star topology** design connects each network device to a central hub. A **hub** is a connection point for all the computers,

FIGURE 25.2.1 In a bus topology, all computers connect to a single cable.

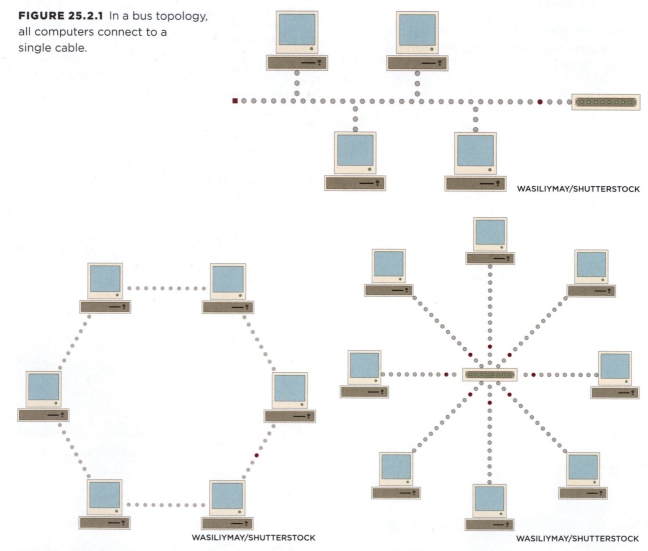

WASILIYMAY/SHUTTERSTOCK

WASILIYMAY/SHUTTERSTOCK

WASILIYMAY/SHUTTERSTOCK

FIGURE 25.2.2 A ring topology connects all the network devices in a circle.

FIGURE 25.2.3 A star topology design connects each network device to a central hub

printers, and other equipment on the network. Adding and removing devices to a star network is easy. If the hub loses power or fails, however, the network devices will not be able to communicate. Star topology avoids collisions by using strategies that manage contention.

STAR BUS TOPOLOGY **Star bus topology** connects multiple star networks along a bus. It is the most common design used in LANs today. Suppose each classroom in your school had its own network with its own hub. The hub in each classroom could then be connected to a common line, called a **backbone**. A backbone is a fast network medium that provides communication among all of the networks. It links all the hubs in the school, for example, expanding the reach of each network.

MESH TOPOLOGY In **mesh topology** the components are all connected directly to other components. Because this topology connects devices with multiple paths, redundancies exist. But, because all devices are cross-connected, the best path from one to another can be taken at any time. The drawback to mesh topology is that needing at least one and a half connections for each computer makes it very expensive to construct. This topology is usually used in the internet structure.

IC3✔ **Understand network topologies.**

Exploring Ethernet

Recall that **Ethernet** is the most common networking technology used on LANs. To create the network, Ethernet cables plug into Ethernet ports on computers, LANs, and cable or DSL modems. Ethernet and star bus topology work together to ensure fast data transfers, logical network design, and fewer collisions. Ethernet uses a rule called Carrier Sensing Multiple Access/Collision Detection, or **CSMA/CD**. This protocol governs how network devices communicate and what happens if they break the rules.

TECHNOLOGY@SCHOOL

Which topology would you use if you were in charge of networking a classroom with five computers, one printer, and one scanner?

THINK ABOUT IT!

Sequence the value of each topology below using a scale of 1 (lowest) to 5 (highest) to indicate which you believe would be best in the classroom.

- bus topology
- ring topology
- star topology
- star bus topology
- mesh topology

ETHERNET COMMUNICATIONS Like a well-mannered conversation, CSMA/CD requires each network device to take turns transmitting, or speaking. A device will tune in to the network to determine whether another device is speaking. If not, it will transmit the data. Every workstation on the network receives the data. However, only the device the data is intended for actually accepts it.

ETHERNET COLLISIONS If two devices transmit at the same time, a collision occurs. In that case, each of the conflicting devices waits a random number of milliseconds and then attempts to transmit again. The random waiting time helps prevent another collision.

Star bus topology expands a network's reach. As more devices are added to a single network and as more networks are connected, the chance of multiple collisions increases. To solve this problem, Ethernet often uses bridges, switches, or routers to divide the network into segments. To reduce congestion, messages are routed to the proper segment rather than to the entire network.

Connecting Remote Networks

OBJECTIVES

- Summarize the purpose of WANs.
- Specify WAN technologies.
- Identify common uses for WANs.
- Explain the use of intranets.

AS YOU READ

ORGANIZE INFORMATION Complete a concept web to identify different WAN applications.

TERMINOLOGY

- application programming interface (API)
- cloud computing
- electronic data interchange (EDI)
- extranet
- intranet
- point-of-sale (POS)
- telecommute

Overview of WANs

Recall that a wide area network, or WAN, is a network that links resources that are far apart from one another, while maintaining a centralized information technology infrastructure. Usually, a WAN connects two or more LANs into one large network. Suppose a company has networks in Chicago, Illinois; Indianapolis, Indiana; and St. Louis, Missouri. A high-speed data line between Chicago and Indianapolis can connect those two networks. From Indianapolis, another high-speed data line is connected to St. Louis. Now, all three networks are connected, and the company has a WAN.

PROTECTING A WAN In the example network described above, the company has a problem. If the data line between St. Louis and Indianapolis fails, users in St. Louis cannot communicate beyond their LAN. Companies can solve this problem by adding more high-speed lines. For example, a data line between St. Louis and Chicago would ensure connectivity to resources in all three LANs even if one line fails.

CONNECTIONS

SOCIAL STUDIES Who was that man? What made that woman famous? History examines many stories of people who made a difference. And the internet is making a difference in how you can learn about people in history. Specialized networks and networks maintained by universities, scholarly groups, and professional organizations provide rich sources for historical and biographical information. Check out www.biography.com for tons of biographical information about all types of famous people.

WANs in the Business World

The introduction of WANs allowed individuals to communicate, access resources, share data, and collaborate on projects across large distances. And as people became accustomed to working on a WAN, they developed new forms of personal and business communications.

GROUPWARE When the science of networking was applied to the need for collaboration, groupware was born. Groupware is another name for collaborative software.

FIGURE 25.3.1 WAN networks allow people spanning a large geographic area to share resources and communicate.

SHAMLEEN/SHUTTERSTOCK

EDI Companies can also use WANs for **electronic data interchange (EDI)**. EDI is an older technology that lets businesses communicate with other businesses over a WAN. EDI is typically used in the supply chain. For example, a company can use EDI to order equipment from a supplier quickly and accurately. It helps the supplier, too, because it automatically creates a bill and sends it to the buyer. Although EDI is expensive to set up, it saves both buyers and suppliers money: It saves paper and employee time, and it helps companies avoid having to stock large inventories.

API A newer alternative to EDI is called an **application programming interface (API)**. An API is a set of programming instructions and standards used to access an existing web-based application. It is a software-to-software interface that lets applications communicate with each other without user intervention. So, a company can have an API that communicates with a supplier's website. When a purchasing manager clicks a link in her inventory system, it goes directly to the supplier's website to check pricing or place an order.

WANs in Your World

You are likely exposed to WANs every day. Many of the retail stores you visit, such as grocery stores, shoe stores, or coffee shops, use WANs to track sales, inventory, and profits. You are also involved with WANs every time you use the internet.

THE POS SYSTEM One example of a WAN in action is a **point-of-sale (POS) system**. Here's how it works:

1. The cashier at a retail outlet, such as a grocery store, scans the barcode on the item you purchase. That bar code is linked to a central database.

2. The POS system allows the store to order more of the product automatically, learn which day of the week customers are likely to buy the item, and compare its sales with other stores.

3. Once a store has collected information on its sales, it can predict trends. Knowing these trends lets the store managers stock the shelves and set prices sensibly.

THE INTERNET The internet is the most common example of a WAN. You and others access the internet through an internet service provider (ISP). The ISP is connected to a backbone in order to reach other networks where web servers are located.

Cloud Computing

Recall that **cloud computing** is the use of remote network servers to store data and resources, such as applications. Cloud resources are shared, so users do not actually own them. Instead, they pay to use server space. Cloud computing is a cost-effective option for many businesses, because they do not have to build and maintain their own network.

With cloud computing, users with access to the cloud can retrieve data from multiple computers. Multiple users can also retrieve the same information, allowing for easy collaboration. Another benefit is that cloud-based applications, such as Microsoft Office 365 and Adobe Creative Cloud, are updated automatically. Users always have access to the most current software.

What Is an Intranet?

Many companies, universities, and other organizations install intranets. An **intranet** is a private network that uses the same TCP/IP protocols as the internet.

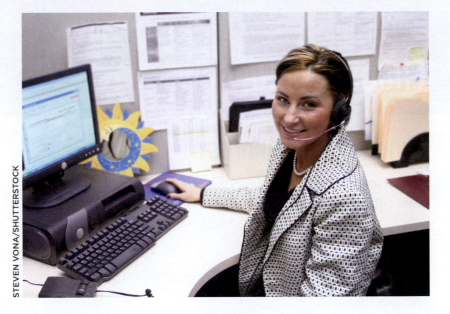

FIGURE 25.3.2 Company intranets enable employees to access information such as human resources forms, shared databases, and information about company policies.

STEVEN VONA/SHUTTERSTOCK

COMPARING INTRANETS AND THE INTERNET Intranets offer many of the same services the internet does, such as email and access to websites. Intranets are different from the internet in that they are not meant for public use. Firewall software prevents outsiders from accessing the intranet.

CREATING AN EXTRANET An intranet can also be converted to an **extranet**, which allows for limited public access. Companies often use extranets so employees can access the network while they travel or **telecommute**, which is when employees work from home while linked to the office by computer. Extranets are also used to share information with other businesses.

TECHNOLOGY@HOME

Often, an employee who is connected to the office through a network can work from home, or telecommute.

THINK ABOUT IT!

Think about the advantages and disadvantages of telecommuting for a company. Which items below do you think are advantages? Which are disadvantages?

- You do not have to dress up to go to work.
- You do not travel to get to work.
- You can avoid people very easily.
- You can work at your own pace.
- You can take breaks whenever you want.

Chapter 25 Review

REVIEW THE TERMINOLOGY

DIRECTIONS Match each vocabulary term in the left column with the correct definition in the right column.

1. network architecture
2. topology
3. contention
4. bus topology
5. hub
6. token
7. star topology
8. firewall
9. cloud computing

a. science of designing a network

b. network designed around a hub

c. software that prevents outsiders from accessing an intranet

d. layout of a network

e. two messages trying to travel at once on a network

f. use of a remote network for data storage

g. unit of data that prevents collisions in ring topology

h. network connected to one line

i. a connection point for all the computers, printers, and other equipment on the network

USE THE TERMINOLOGY

DIRECTIONS Determine the correct choice for each of the following.

1. All networks follow rules developed by the _____.
   a. ISO
   b. POP
   c. EDI
   d. LAN

2. The OSI model defines how data travels through _____.
   a. a collision
   b. backbones
   c. seven layers
   d. groupware

3. Early LANs were designed with _____.
   a. bus topology
   b. ring topology
   c. star topology
   d. star bus topology

4. Ethernet deals with contention by _____.
   a. storing messages in the session layer
   b. assigning messages to a POP
   c. dumping messages that collide
   d. delaying messages that collide

5. Groupware makes all of the following possible EXCEPT _____.

   a. videoconferences   c. electronic bulletin boards

   b. email   d. protocol stacks

6. A _____ topology is used in the internet structure, and it is the most expensive.

   a. tree   c. mesh

   b. star bus   d. ring

THINK CRITICALLY

DIRECTIONS Answer the following questions.

1. What is a mesh network topology? What are some of its benefits and drawbacks?

2. What equipment do you think employees need to telecommute?

3. For what purposes might a big bank use both LANs and a WAN?

4. Do you think LANs and WANs will become more or less standardized in the future? Why?

5. How has networking changed the way many companies do business?

EXTEND YOUR KNOWLEDGE

DIRECTIONS Choose and complete one of the following projects.

1. Work with a partner to find out more about Ethernet, which many schools use in their networks. With your teacher's permission, use a search engine and the keyword *Ethernet* to research three websites that describe this technology. Take notes and keep track of your sources. Next, outline and create a chart to help you evaluate the three sites. Identify the source of each. Then, develop a scale and rank each on completeness, clarity, organization, and overall value.

2. With your teacher's permission, research, the characteristics of backbones and segments. Take notes and keep track of your sources. Only use information from sites that are reliable and accurate. Compile the information into a report and present it to a partner or to the class.

3. With your teacher's permission, select, research, and analyze the directory services of two or three major network operating systems. Take notes and keep track of your sources. Only use sources that are reliable and accurate. As part of the research, identify clients that work well with each of the network operating systems and their resources. Write a paragraph summarizing your findings, and include a chart. Read your paragraph to a partner or to the class.

IC3 PREP

1. Which of the following should be considered when selecting a network topology? (Select all that apply.)

   a. placement of equipment
   b. contention
   c. lighting
   d. contact

2. Which of the following network topologies breaks down completely when a single network device fails? (Select all that apply.)

   a. star bus topology
   b. star topology
   c. ring topology
   d. bus topology

3. Which network topology is most frequently used in LANs?

   a. bus topology
   b. ring topology
   c. star topology
   d. star bus topology

4. To control potential collisions while transmitting data, a ring network employs special units of data known as _____.

   a. signals
   b. tokens
   c. bitcoins
   d. rings

5. In a star bus network, each network's hub is connected along a _____.

   a. backbone
   b. web
   c. star
   d. gate

6. In a _____ topology, the components are all connected directly to other components.

   a. bus
   b. ring
   c. mesh
   d. star bus

CHAPTER 26
Internet Basics

A NETWORK OF NETWORKS

The internet connects people all over the world through a huge network of computer systems and devices. The U.S. government and university researchers began the internet to share information. Since then, it has turned into one of the most exciting inventions in history.

As more and more people use the internet, the demand for user-friendly online services has also grown and created new business opportunities. Additionally, electronic mail, texting, and photo and video sharing services have changed the way people meet and communicate.

What Is the Internet?

OBJECTIVES

- Explain the organization of the internet.
- Discuss the history of the internet.
- Identify organizations responsible for setting standards for the internet.

TERMINOLOGY

- domain names
- internet
- internet client

AS YOU READ

ORGANIZE INFORMATION Use a spider map to organize information about the internet as you read.

Organization of the Internet

The **internet** is a global WAN, or network of networks. It connects everything from a single smartphone to a data center housing hundreds of servers. The internet can even connect devices that run different operating systems. This ability to share information with almost any computing device makes the internet a powerful tool for communication. The internet is made up of three important parts: servers, clients, and protocols.

SERVERS Internet servers are the computers that provide services to other computers by way of the internet. These services include processing email, storing web pages, or hosting cloud-based data.

CLIENTS AND PROTOCOLS **Internet clients** are the devices that request services from a server. When you connect to the internet, the device you use is considered a client. Like other networks, the internet uses protocols—the sets of rules that allow clients and servers to communicate.

Is the Internet a WAN?

Technically, the internet is a very large WAN. However, there are key differences between the internet and other WANs.

TYPE OF ACCESS The internet is public, while WANs are typically private. That means anyone can use the internet, while access to other WANs is controlled by the owner, which is usually a business or organization.

DEGREE OF SECURITY The internet is generally not as secure as a private WAN connection. Snoops and eavesdroppers on the public networks the internet uses to transmit information may try—and succeed—to access the data. A private WAN is more secure because it is more likely that only the organization that owns it has access to it. Internet users must take security measures on their own, such as installing firewalls and using antivirus and antimalware programs.

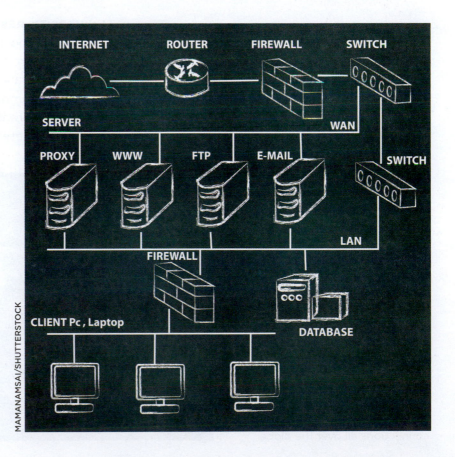

FIGURE 26.1.1 Like many networks, the internet is made up of connected client and server computers, which use protocols to communicate.

MAMANAMSAI/SHUTTERSTOCK

TECHNOLOGY@HOME

Staying current with changing technology is not always easy.

THINK ABOUT IT!

Listed below are other technologies invented since research for the internet began in the mid-1960s. Which item(s) listed below do you have in your home?

- food processor
- virtual reality gaming
- streaming television
- smart speakers
- cellular phone

TYPES OF INFORMATION On the internet, information is transmitted in the form of web pages and other types of files. A WAN is used for more than just browsing web pages. It provides access to network resources, such as printers, file servers, and databases.

Inventing the Internet

In the 1960s, people were working on ideas that later became the internet. In 1969, the first four major computer centers in the United States were linked. By 1973, the network was international. In 1983, the Internet Protocols went online for the first time. Two major groups worked on the development of the internet: the United States military and university researchers.

UNITED STATES MILITARY In the 1960s, the United States government wanted to find a way to communicate in the event of a disaster or military attack. The military began to work on a system that would operate even if some communication connections were destroyed. The Defense Advanced Research Projects Agency (DARPA) of the U.S. Department of Defense focused on computer networking and communications. In 1968, this research led to a network of connected computer centers called the Advanced Research Projects Agency Network (ARPANET).

UNIVERSITY RESEARCHERS With the military's leadership and funding, DARPA formed computing research centers at universities across the United States. From 1969 through 1987, the number of computers on the network increased from 4 to more than 10,000. These connections created the networks that became the internet.

FIGURE 26.1.2 The internet includes millions of servers and connections all over the globe.

LIGHTSPRING/SHUTTERSTOCK

Internet Management

Who owns the internet? The truth is that no specific organization or government does. Many organizations are responsible for different parts of the network. Here are some examples:

- The World Wide Web Consortium (W3C) is an international community of organizations, employees, and the public that develops standards for the web.

- Internet Engineering Task Force (IETF) is a large international community of network designers, operators, vendors, and researchers. This group is concerned with the future structure and smooth operation of the internet. Like many organizations that set computing standards, the IETF is "open," meaning any interested person can participate.

- Internet Corporation for Assigned Names and Numbers (ICANN) is a nonprofit corporation with a variety of responsibilities, including the management of **domain names**. The domain name is the part of an internet address that identifies the location where a web page is stored.

- Web Standards Project (WaSP) is a coalition that supports standards for simple, affordable access to web technologies.

FREEDOM OF THE INTERNET One advantage to the open quality of the internet is the ability to share information. Anyone can make an idea or opinion accessible to anyone else.

PITFALLS OF THE INTERNET However, there are pitfalls to this open organization. People can post whatever point of view or information they want, even if it is misleading or false. It is up to the users of the internet to think critically about the information they read online. If you have a question about anything you find on the internet, ask an adult you trust about it.

DID YOU KNOW?

Did you know that you can get a traffic report about the internet? Like the traffic reports you may hear on television or on the radio during rush hour, the Internet Traffic Report monitors the flow of data around the world. Visit www.internettrafficreport.com to see how the traffic is in your neighborhood.

REAL-WORLD TECH
VOTING ON THE INTERNET?

According to the Federal Election Commission, the internet is not ready for U.S. citizens to vote on it. Safeguarding the privacy, security, and reliability of the voting process is important to ensuring a free democratic election.

GUBH83/SHUTTERSTOCK

While there have been some experiments with internet voting, experts agree that it will be a long time before it is used in general elections. The internet, however, can improve some parts of the election process. For example, the technology is in place for secure overseas military voting. Also, registration databases and vote totals can be sent over the internet, saving time and money.

In what other ways might you use the internet to find out more about politics?

Connecting to the Internet

OBJECTIVES

- Identify ways to connect to the internet.

- Explain the purpose of internet service providers.

- Discuss the purpose of online services.

- List common internet connection problems.

AS YOU READ

OUTLINE INFORMATION Use an outline to organize information about connecting to the internet as you read.

TERMINOLOGY

- browse

- internet service provider (ISP)

- navigate

- online service

- Point-to-Point Protocol (PPP)

- username

Connecting to the Internet

Recall that there are different ways to connect to the internet. The reasons for various options are availability, location, speed, and price.

DIAL-UP, ISDN, AND DSL ACCESS The least expensive way to get online is to use a dial-up connection between a standard phone line and a modem. These connections are called "dial-up" because your computer must connect to the internet by using a telephone number to contact a server. Fewer than 10% of households in the U.S. still use dial-up access.

Recall that this type of access uses **Point-to-Point Protocol (PPP)**. In addition to the slow speed, a drawback of dial-up is that your computer is assigned a temporary IP address; you can't run server software without a permanent IP address. When the session is over, the connection is broken.

Some Digital Subscriber Lines (DSL) require a special telephone line. Integrated Services Digital Network (ISDN) lines require a special ISDN adapter and modem. As a result, both services cost more than regular phone service. Furthermore, DSL and ISDN are not available in all areas. One drawback of DSL is that service does not extend more than a few miles from telephone switching stations, so this service is unavailable in some areas.

CABLE AND SATELLITE Cable television companies offer internet access through cable modems. This access is at speeds much faster than dial-up modems. You need a network card in your computer, a cable modem, and cable access. Satellite access is also very fast for downloading files to your computer, but it requires a phone line and a modem for sending files to outside users.

LAN ACCESS If your school or library has a local area network (LAN) that is connected to the internet, you access the internet through the network. Likewise, if you have a wireless network at home, you are using a LAN. LAN access usually uses a high-speed connection, but the performance depends on how many LAN users are trying to access the internet at the same time. In most cases, you have a permanently assigned IP address on a LAN.

FIBER OPTICS An organization that needs a high bandwidth might use a T1 line, which stands for trunkline, for internet access. Internet service providers, who are responsible for maintaining backbones, need even faster connections, such as a T3 line. T1 and T3 lines use fiber-optic cables that are capable of handling huge amounts of data. This technology is popular for internet backbones and LANs.

Understanding Transmission Speeds

To get an idea of just how fast a modern backbone is, compare the speed of an old-fashioned dial-up modem to the speed of different types of fiber-optic lines. At one time, home computers came equipped with a 56K modem, which could transmit about 50,000 bits per second, or approximately 5,000 characters per second. The table below illustrates the amount of data that can travel across DSL, cable, and fiber-optic lines. You can find the connection speed of your computer in the Network and Sharing Center in Windows or the Network Utility on macOS.

LINE TYPES AND SPEEDS	
Type of Line	**Transmission Speed**
ADSL (Asymmetric digital subscriber line)	16 to 640 kilobits per second sending data
	1.5 to 9 megabits per second receiving data
SDSL (Symmetric digital subscriber line)	Up to 3 megabits per second
T1	1.544 megabits per second
T3	43.232 megabits per second

MEASURING DATA TRANSFER Sometimes people confuse measurements for data transfer speed with measurements for data storage or memory.

- Bits, kilobits, and megabits are used to measure data transfer. A cable modem might download data at 240 kilobits per second (Kbs).

- Bytes, kilobytes, and megabytes are used to measure data storage. A kilobyte, or 1 KB, is 1 thousand bytes. A megabyte, or 1 MB, is 1 million bytes. A gigabyte, or 1 GB, is 1 billion bytes. A terabyte, or 1 TB, is 1 thousand billion bytes. A petabyte, or 1 PB, is one million gigabytes. Most PCs have anywhere from 4 to 16 gigabytes (GB) of random access memory, and hard drives can store over a terabyte (TB).

In theory, you could measure data transfer speed using bytes. Recall that each byte is made up of eight bits of data. That means your 240 Kb download would transfer 30 KB of data per second.

Outside of the context, you can usually tell which is which by the abbreviation. Bytes are abbreviated with a capital B and bits are abbreviated with a lowercase b. So, Mbs is measuring megabits per second, and MBps is measuring megabytes per second.

IC3 ✔ Understand data sizes.

DID YOU KNOW?

You can use your operating system to check whether or not your computer is correctly connected to the internet. On most systems, a network or connectivity icon displays on the status bar. If there's a problem, it might be marked with an X or an exclamation mark. Right-click the icon to display a menu of options, including Troubleshoot Problems and Open Network and Sharing Center.

You can also check connectivity by opening your browser and trying to access a site such as Google or Amazon. If you can access the site, your computer is connected to the network.

Accessing the Internet

After you have a physical connection to the internet, you must select a way to get online. Internet service providers offer a way to access the internet, while online services deliver content to your device.

INTERNET SERVICE PROVIDERS An **internet service provider (ISP)** is a company that provides a link from your computing device to the internet. For a fee, an ISP provides its subscribers with software, a password, an access phone number, and a username. A **username** identifies who you are when you access the internet. An ISP does not usually provide online services; it only provides an easy-to-use connection to the internet. However, some ISPs now offer cloud-based storage and email. You can use either a local ISP or a national ISP.

ONLINE SERVICES Traditional **online services,** such as Microsoft Network (MSN), AOL, and Google, provide information and internet-based services such as email, newsfeeds, and social networking. They may also offer tools that help you **navigate**, or **browse** online, including a home page portal that you can customize with the content you want. Online services may also offer additional services, such as cloud storage space.

More recent online service providers include any business that offers services over the internet—from Amazon to banks offering online banking, to entertainment sites like YouTube. Online services are accessed via the company's website, and basic content is usually free. If you want to access premium content or services, you will have to register and have an account.

Common Connection Problems

There are some common problems that can interfere with an internet connection. Typical problems include loose connections, a power outage, interference from other devices, blocking from a firewall, and ISP service problems. You can try basic troubleshooting steps to isolate and solve the problem, including resetting devices, reconnecting cables, and temporarily turning off the firewall.

FIGURE 26.2.1 Connection problems may be caused by loose or disconnected cables.

BESTSHORTSTOP/SHUTTERSTOCK

Programs for Using the Internet

OBJECTIVES

- Explain the organization of the World Wide Web.

- Identify the difference between a desktop email client and web-based email.

- List benefits and drawbacks of using email.

- Explain File Transfer Protocol.

- Discuss issues related to transferring files.

AS YOU READ

IDENTIFY MAIN IDEA/DETAILS Use a main idea/detail chart to identify the main idea and details of internet programs as you read.

TERMINOLOGY

- binary files

- downloading

- email

- email client

- file compression

- file transfer protocol (FTP)

- hyperlink

- hypertext

- Hypertext Transfer Protocol (HTTP)

- linear

- non-linear

- portal

- search engine

- uniform resource locator (URL)

- uploading

- virus

- web-based email

- web browser

- web server

Accessing Information on the Web

The World Wide Web, or web, is a subset of the internet that includes all documents and other resources that use the **Hypertext Transfer Protocol (HTTP)**. HTTP sets the rules for how web servers and web browsers will respond to commands. A **web browser** is a software application that you use to view and navigate between web pages. A **web server** is a program that uses HTTP to manage files for the web. It also sometimes refers to the computers used to run that software. Popular web browsers are Mozilla Firefox, Google Chrome, Microsoft Edge, and Microsoft Internet Explorer.

The web is a huge collection of hypertext documents called web pages. In a **hypertext** document, certain words or pictures can serve as hyperlinks. A **hyperlink** is a link to another document on the web.

Standard pages of text are considered **linear**, which means you read through the page from top to bottom. Hypertext, however, is **non-linear**. You don't have to read a web page from top to bottom. You click on hyperlinks to navigate through multiple layers of information.

URLS Every document on the web has a unique address, called a **uniform resource locator (URL)**. To display a web page in a browser, you enter the URL in the address bar. You can also click a hyperlink which is set to connect to that URL.

HYPERLINKS Usually, you can tell when text is a hyperlink because it is underlined, in a different color, or highlighted. Sometimes there are buttons or images that can be clicked. When you move your mouse over a hyperlink—text or graphic—the pointer changes to an icon of a hand with a pointed finger. When you select a hyperlink, the destination that the hyperlink connects to is displayed. This can be a location on the same page, a different web page, or even an email address.

Internet and Web-based Services

An internet service provider supplies the connection you need so your computing devices can access the internet. You also need programs to find the information you need, communicate with others, and share information. The list of internet services grows daily. It includes everything from email, to online shopping and banking, to online learning, videoconferencing, and social networking. Many of the services are web-based, which means the software you need for the service is stored on a web server, not on your device. Some of the services use software that must be installed on your device.

EMAIL You use an **email** application to send and receive email messages. Usually, you can enter text and graphics in an email message. You can also attach files to messages for transmission.

There are two basic ways to access email: **email clients** and **web-based email**. Email clients, which are sometimes referred to as desktop email applications, are installed on your computer. The most well-known email client is Microsoft Outlook, but there are others, such as Mozilla Thunderbird and Mailbird. Web-based email, such as Outlook.com and Gmail, is accessed using a web browser.

Both email clients and web-based email offer many of the same features, including integration with a calendar and contacts list and the ability to search for messages or contacts. The main difference is that when you use an email client, you can store your messages on your computer storage drives, and you can compose email when you are not connected to the internet.

IC3✔ **Identify desktop and web-based email applications.**

Benefits of using email include cost and speed. You can send an email to anyone in the world who has an email account. You do not pay to send each email, as you would a letter. The cost of your email service is included in the fee you pay your internet service provider. Some web-based email services are free, although they might display advertisements. Email is not as fast as texting, but it is fast. In most cases, it takes less than a minute for an email message to reach its destination.

There are drawbacks to using email. The receiver may not open the email, so there is no guarantee it will be read. Criminals often hide viruses in email attachments. And, although there are not usually limits to the amount of text you can include in an email, there are limits to the size of attachments.

PORTALS A web or internet **portal** is a web page that pulls in and presents information in an organized way. Most web portals are customized by the user. For example, a web portal might display the weather, breaking news, a stock ticker, and a list of new email messages. It might have links to a search engine and a favorite magazine. Common web portals include Yahoo, AOL, and MSN.

SEARCH ENGINES A **search engine** is software that finds and lists information that meets a specified search. You begin searching by typing a keyword or phrase into a blank field. Then, the search engine will give you the results of that search as a list of links. Popular search engines include Google, Yahoo, and Bing.

Transferring Files

File Transfer Protocol (FTP) lets you transfer files on the internet. With an FTP client, you can transfer files from an FTP server to your computer in an operation called **downloading**. In **uploading**, you transfer files from the client to the server.

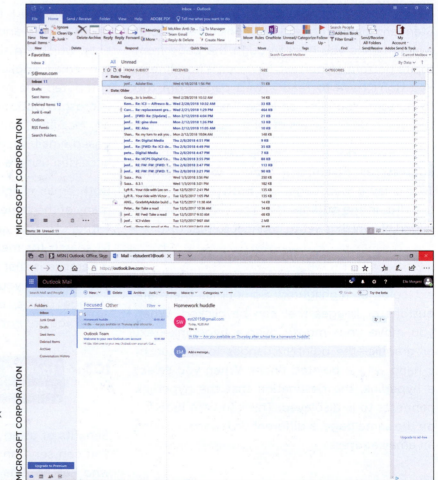

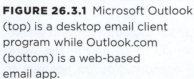

FIGURE 26.3.1 Microsoft Outlook (top) is a desktop email client program while Outlook.com (bottom) is a web-based email app.

THINK ABOUT IT!

Which item(s) listed below do you think would be appropriate for use of the internet at school?

- research a book report
- solve math problems
- email a friend
- play video games
- create a database of your favorite books

FTP can transfer both text files and binary files. **Binary files** are program files and non-text files such as, graphics, pictures, music or video clips. Once you've stored a file on an FTP server, you can share the URL so that others can download the file from the server, as well. The file remains on the server until you delete it. When you transfer a file as an email attachment, you must save the file on your computer or it will be deleted when you delete the message. Email is considered a more secure method of transfer, however, because only the recipient of the email message has access to the attached files.

Telnet is an older protocol that lets users access files on remote computers. Telnet has largely been replaced by the SSH and SSH2 protocols, which are encrypted and therefore more secure than Telnet. Of course, when you upload or download files you are transferring them between your computer and an internet, or cloud, server. Most websites have buttons or links to make it easy to upload and download files, or you may use your browser's File > Open and File > Save As commands.

Another way to share files over the internet is to share the online folder in which the files are stored. If you grant unlimited access, others can not only view and edit the online files, but also download them to their own computers.

File Transfer Issues

COMPUTER VIRUSES It's important to exercise caution when downloading files from the internet, especially program files. Files are commonly used to transmit viruses. Recall that a **virus** is a program created to damage computers and networks. The damage caused may be minor or serious, often altering or destroying data. It's a good idea to check all downloaded files for viruses before opening them. Most antivirus programs will do this for you automatically. You should update your antivirus program regularly to be protected from the newest viruses.

The Windows operating system helps by giving a security warning when a download is about to begin so you can confirm whether or not to continue with the download. You may want to review the advice provided by clicking the *What's the Risk?* link in the security warning.

FILE COMPRESSION The larger a file is, the more time it takes to travel over a network. **File compression** is a way of reducing file size so it can travel more quickly over a network. If you are sending a large file, it is beneficial to compress it. It can also be convenient to compress multiple files into one when you are sending them to someone in an email attachment. Some compressed files are set to decompress automatically. Others must be decompressed using decompression software. Two widely used compression software programs for Windows and Mac devices are WinZip® and 7-Zip.

Chapter 26 Review

REVIEW THE TERMINOLOGY

DIRECTIONS Match each vocabulary term in the left column with the correct definition in the right column.

1. internet
2. internet client
3. internet service provider
4. username
5. search engine
6. portal
7. hyperlink
8. uniform resource locator
9. download

a. highlighted text or graphic in a website that directs a browser to another URL

b. software that finds and lists information that matches criteria

c. computer that requests services from a server

d. identification while on the internet

e. address of documents on the web

f. vast network of connected computers

g. a company that provides access to the internet

h. to transfer a file from a server to a client

i. internet service that provides a guide to internet content

USE THE TERMINOLOGY

DIRECTIONS Complete each sentence with information from the chapter.

1. A network that covers a large area is called a(n) _____.
2. The three main parts of the internet are _____, servers, and protocols.
3. The two main groups responsible for inventing the internet are the U.S. military and _____.
4. A(n) _____ is the least expensive way to access the internet.
5. A(n) _____ enables someone to search for a website with a keyword.
6. In a(n) _____ document, certain words or pictures serve as hyperlinks.
7. File _____ is a way of reducing file size.
8. A(n) _____ is used to view web pages.
9. You can send a(n) _____ to someone by attaching it to an email message.
10. _____ are businesses that provide special software to guide users through internet content and activities.

THINK CRITICALLY

DIRECTIONS Answer the following questions.

1. What are some benefits to using an email client versus a web-based email?

2. What are two ways to distinguish between a reference to storage capacity and a data transfer rate? Give at least one example.

3. Why might someone use an online service?

4. Explain problems that might interfere with network connections. Select one of the problems and describe the troubleshooting steps you would take to solve the problem.

EXTEND YOUR KNOWLEDGE

DIRECTIONS Choose and complete one of the following projects.

1. With your teacher's permission, research and evaluate the wireless standards, protocols, and procedures for configuring a wireless device to a network. If possible, set up and configure a network—such as a home network—using standard protocols. Describe the experience to a partner or to the class.

2. With permission from your teacher, in small groups, conduct online research to learn what kinds of internet access are available in your area. Find out how much the services cost and the benefits of each. If possible, locate information from companies competing for the same services so you can compare prices. Compile your research in a chart. Then, summarize your findings as a class.

IC3 PREP

1. _____ are typically used to measure data transfer over time.

   a. Bytes

   b. Bits

   c. Blocks

   d. Bills

2. _____ are used to measure data storage.

   a. Bytes

   b. Bits

   c. Blocks

   d. Bills

3. How many bytes are in one megabyte?

   a. 1,000

   b. 100

   c. 1,000,000

   d. 10,000,000

4. Put the following data sizes in order from smallest to largest.

   a. 2 terabytes

   b. 6,000 megabytes

   c. 14,000 kilobytes

   d. 4 gigabytes

   e. 10,000 bytes

5. Which of the following is an example of a web-based email service? (Select all that apply.)

    a. Microsoft Outlook

    c. Gmail

    b. Outlook.com

    d. Thunderbird

6. For each line below, select whether the statement is True or False.

    a. Email clients are also known as desktop email applications.

    b. Web-based email services cannot be used while offline.

    c. Emails can consist of text and graphics; additional files cannot be attached.

    d. Depending on where in the world you are sending an email, you may be charged extra fees.

CHAPTER 27

Using the Internet

EXPANDING OUR HORIZONS

Are you interested in Japanese animation? Hiking trails in the Australian Outback? Sending pictures of your family to a pen pal in another country? Each day more resources are available on the internet. The ability to send data faster allows people to more easily share ideas, information, and entertainment with people all over the world.

Every day more people connect to the internet, using whatever form of technology is available to them. As demand for internet access increases, even remote areas of the globe are being connected to the internet and contributing to the ever-changing, diverse collection of information and services that can be found online.

Internet Structure

OBJECTIVES

- Sequence how information travels through the hierarchy of networks on the internet.

- Summarize the advantages of a cross-platform network.

TERMINOLOGY

- cross-platform

- Internet2 project

- platform

AS YOU READ

IDENTIFY KEY INFORMATION Use a concept web to help you identify key components of internet structure as you read.

Internet Infrastructure

Every computer on the internet has a unique Internet Protocol (IP) address. Any computer can communicate with any other computer on the internet by contacting the other computer's IP address.

When you use a computing device to connect to the internet, the device is called a client. A client uses a browser to request access to a web page stored on an internet server computer. Your request travels by local connections to your ISP's local point of presence (POP). From there, your ISP sends your request to a regional backbone, which uses high-speed lines that connect your city to a larger metropolitan area. Your request then travels to a network access point, or NAP.

On the internet, dozens of large ISPs connect with one another at NAPs in various cities. Trillions of bytes of data flow between the individual networks at these points. This is how your computer at home connects to another computer in a completely different region.

Requesting Data on the Web

To understand how a data request is sent on the internet, it might be helpful to compare the process to taking a road trip. Recall that when you request a web page through your web browser, the request travels by local connections—like streets in a town—to your ISP's local POP. From there, your ISP sends your request to a regional backbone—a type of data highway.

Your web page request then travels to a NAP, which is like a freeway. As your request nears its destination, it moves off the information freeway. It travels back through other regional highways and local roads until its trip is complete and the web page you requested is displayed on your computer screen.

CONNECTIONS

SCIENCE Vinton Cerf, one of the developers of TCP/IP protocols, has worked with scientists on parcel transfer protocol, which could be used for communicating on an interplanetary internet in outer space. It is hoped that this new technology will help pave the way for manned missions to Mars. The plan for wiring Earth to Mars would include using an existing international antenna system, a six-satellite constellation around Mars, and a new protocol for transferring data between the planets.

Cross-Platform Network

One amazing thing about the internet is that you can exchange information with computing devices using any platform. As long as all of the devices are using the same protocols, they can communicate. That means that it doesn't matter if the client is running Windows, iOS, Linux, or Android. They can all communicate over the internet.

Recall that a **platform** is a kind of computer that uses a certain type of processor and operating system, such as an Intel-based Windows PC. Software or hardware is said to have **cross-platform** capability when it can run the same way on more than one platform. When you are using the internet, you don't know which type of computer platform you are accessing, and it doesn't matter. This is because all computers on the internet use TCP/IP protocols. As a result, they all look and behave the same way online, regardless of their platform.

Many organizations, such as schools, use computers that run on different platforms. They may use computers running macOS in one part of the school and computers running Windows in another. Yet, they still need to share information. After the computers are connected with the

FIGURE 27.1.1 All kinds of computers can communicate with one another through the internet, as long as they use the same protocols.

MAXX-STUDIO/SHUTTERSTOCK

internet's TCP/IP protocols, the computers can exchange data and even control one another's operations. For instance, someone could create a file on a Mac and then send it to a printer connected to a computer running Windows.

The internet has revolutionized access to data. Anyone with an internet connection can find information on virtually any topic. Many local governments ensure access to all citizens by making internet access available at public locations such as libraries. That means even those who are disabled or disadvantaged have the same access as everyone else.

Internet Growth

Over the next decade, millions of new users will connect to the internet. Can the internet handle this kind of growth? Internet experts say that improvements must take place to make certain the internet doesn't become overwhelmed by its own success.

MORE INTERNET ADDRESSES The original internet addressing system, Internet Protocol version 4 (IPv4), allows for about 4 billion IP addresses. Surprisingly, that is not enough. One solution lies in a new version of the Internet Protocol called IPv6. However, the problem with this solution is that existing internet equipment must be modified to work with the new protocol.

MORE BANDWIDTH With growing internet use, new technologies to increase bandwidth must be developed. The **Internet2 (I2) project** will develop and test high-performance network and telecommunications techniques. These improvements will eventually find their way to the public internet, allowing faster access for all users.

TECHNOLOGY@HOME

In the United States, one employment benefit on the rise is telecommuting, or working from home on a computer.

THINK ABOUT IT!

Networks are needed to allow employees to work efficiently between their home and their office. Which type(s) of networks listed below would a telecommuter likely use to conduct work from home?

- LAN
- WAN
- internet

The Internet Domain Name System

OBJECTIVES

- Distinguish between Internet Protocol addresses and domain names.

- Explain the difference between second-level and top-level domain names.

- Identify different domain types.

- Explain how the DNS works.

AS YOU READ

OUTLINE INFORMATION Use an outline to organize information about the internet domain name system as you read.

TERMINOLOGY

- domain name

- domain name system (DNS)

- Internet Corporation for Assigned Names and Numbers (ICANN)

- Internet Protocol (IP) address

- second-level domain

- top-level domain

- top-level domain country code

- WHOIS database

Domain Names

Each computer that connects to the internet has to be uniquely identified. To do this, every computer is assigned a four-part number separated by periods called the **Internet Protocol (IP) address**. For example, the IP address for your computer might be 123.257.91.7. The administrator of the network to which your computer connects assigns your IP address. You can locate your computer's IP address by looking at its network settings.

IC3✔ Understand how IP addresses work.

A **domain name** uses plain language to identify one or more IP addresses and is used by others to locate information on the internet. For example, an internet server computer's domain name might be whitehouse.gov, but its numeric IP address might be 206.166.48.45. The domain name and the IP address are simply two ways to identify the same computer on the internet.

SECOND- AND TOP-LEVEL DOMAINS Every domain name includes a second-level domain name and a top-level domain name. The **top-level domain** identifies which registry—or part of the internet—where the name is registered. The top-level domain starts with the last period in the address—called dot—and includes the suffix that displays to the right of the dot. The **second-level domain** name usually identifies a specific company, organization, or even individual. It displays to the left of the last dot. So, in the address whitehouse.gov, *whitehouse* is the second-level domain and *.gov* is the top-level domain.

Top-level domain names usually identify the type of domain the website resides in. The most common top-level domains are .com (commercial), .edu (education), .org (nonprofit organizations), .gov (government), .mil (military), and .net (network organizations). Other top-level domain names include .biz (business) and .museum (arts and culture). New top-level domains are added as the need arises.

TECHNOLOGY@WORK

In February of 1996, Alex Jarrett started a nonprofit organization called the Degree of Confluence Project to have people visit each of the latitude and longitude markers in the world. They then send his company pictures of each location to post on a web page.

THINK ABOUT IT!

Any company, individual, or organization can create a website. But first it has to get a domain name. Which top-level domain name(s) listed below do you think would be most appropriate for Jarrett's company?

- .org
- .gov
- .edu
- .com
- .mil

Top-level domain country codes are two letter codes that identify the country where the site is located. For example, .us is the country code for the United States.

IC3✔ Understand domain types.

FIGURE 27.2.1 .com might be the most common top-level domain, but there are many others, including .edu and .org.

566

The Domain Name System

Internet domain names and addresses are tracked and regulated using the **Domain Name System (DNS)**. A special server called a DNS server matches each domain name to the correct IP address. Within DNS, each computer on the internet must have a unique name.

To acquire a domain name, you pay an accredited domain name registrar to insert an entry into a directory of all the domain names and their corresponding computers on the internet. Registrars are organizations that are authorized to reserve and give out domain names. Many of them are responsible for specific DNS registries. For example, the Public Interest Registry is responsible for maintaining the .org registry. If you want to register a .org domain name, you would contact the Public Interest Registry. To keep your domain name, you must pay a renewable registration fee. If you do not pay the fee, the domain becomes available for someone else to register in his or her name.

The central database of domain names is called the **WHOIS database**. You can look up information about the owner and servers of a certain domain on this database. The organization responsible for maintaining the database of registered domain names is the **Internet Corporation for Assigned Names and Numbers (ICANN)**. ICANN also maintains an Accredited Registrar Directory that provides a listing of accredited domain name registrars.

IC3✓   **Understand how DNS works.**

CAREER CORNER

BRANDING CONSULTANT Branding consultants work with businesses to define their image to their target customers. Everything from the colors on a logo to the domain name communicate a company's personality to a customer. Brand consultants use both research and creativity in the building of a company's brand.

REAL-WORLD TECH

THE INTERNET OF THINGS

Once, you needed a computer to access the internet. Today, smart objects that can connect online are everywhere. Your phone, television, car, and even household appliances may be connected to the internet. For example, you can install a smart thermostat in your home and then set the temperature using an app on a tablet or smartphone, or by talking to a smart speaker. The connection of all these devices to the internet is called the "Internet of Things." How many smart devices do you have in your home? Which ones would you like to have?

CHESKYW/123RF.COM

Chapter 27 Review

REVIEW THE TERMINOLOGY

DIRECTIONS Match each vocabulary term in the left column with the correct definition in the right column.

1. domain name
2. IP address
3. WHOIS database
4. Domain Name System
5. platform
6. Internet2 (I2)

a. domain name lookup

b. responsible for tracking and regulating internet domain names and addresses

c. project that tests new network technologies

d. identifies one or more IP addresses and is used to locate information on the Internet

e. a kind of computer that uses a certain type of processor and operating system

f. a four-part number separated by periods used to identify a computer connected to the Internet

USE THE TERMINOLOGY

DIRECTIONS Complete each sentence with information from the chapter.

1. After your web page request goes to your ISP's POP, it goes to a(n) _____.

2. Software or hardware is said to have _____ platform capability when it can run the same way on more than one platform.

3. The _____ domain identifies which type of organization registered the domain name.

4. _____ is a service organization that maintains a central database of domain names in the United States.

5. When you use your computer to connect to the internet, the computer is called a(n) _____.

6. The _____ of the network to which your computer connects assigns your IP address.

7. In the Domain Name System, each name has to be _____.

8. You can search the _____ database for the owner and servers of a particular domain.

9. In the future, the internet will need to increase bandwidth and create more _____.

THINK CRITICALLY

DIRECTIONS Answer the following questions.

1. Why is it important that the internet be cross-platform compatible? How is this accomplished?

2. How might the increasing popularity of the internet become a problem?

3. What is the goal of the Internet2 project? Do you think its achievements leave the public internet behind?

EXTEND YOUR KNOWLEDGE

DIRECTIONS Choose and complete one of the following projects.

1. With your teacher's permission, examine the networks used in your school. Or, ask your parents if you can examine your home network. Identify how many different types of computer platforms are used. Draw a diagram of at least one cross-platform connection, labeling the different devices and platforms. Write a paragraph explaining how the network works. Share your diagram with a partner or with the class, or hang the diagrams in the classroom and have a gallery walk to look at them all.

2. With your teacher's permission, use the internet to locate a website with a domain name that includes an international country code. Copy the URL to a word-processing document. Write a brief paragraph explaining the different parts of the domain name, including the country code. Share your paragraph with a partner or the class.

IC3 PREP

1. Which of these might be valid IP addresses? (Select all that apply.)

   a. 123.257.91.7

   b. 84.163.197

   c. 216.27.61.137

   d. 2A.15.107.9

2. The plain language equivalent of an IP address is commonly known as a _____.

   a. database

   b. domain name

   c. ICANN

   d. registry

3. The _____ domain name usually identifies a specific company, organization, or individual.

   a. top-level

   b. third-level

   c. second-level

   d. primary-level

4. What does the top-level domain .com stand for?

    a. common
    c. communication

    b. corporate
    d. commercial

5. For each line below, select whether the statement is True or False.

    a. The Domain Name System (DNS) server matches each domain name to its correct IP address.

    b. Within DNS, some computer names can overlap.

    c. Keeping a domain name registered requires a one-time payment for the life of the individual.

    d. The central database of domain names is called the WHOIS database.

6. Which top-level domain is the Public Interest Registry responsible for maintaining?

    a. .edu
    c. .net

    b. .org
    d. .museum

7. Where can you find your computer's IP address?

    a. address settings
    c. network settings

    b. domain settings
    d. identification settings

CHAPTER 28
Web Basics

A GLOBAL SOURCE OF INFORMATION

Imagine a library filled with all the books, magazines, journals, videos, slides, music, and other sources of information in the world. How big would the building be? How would the information be organized? How could you quickly locate the specific bit of information you need without being distracted by everything else?

Luckily, you don't need a building to house all of that knowledge. You've already got the web. Anyone with an internet connection can access this vast storehouse of data. You can turn to the web to research products, get help with schoolwork, catch up on current events, and much, much more. In this chapter, you will explore ways to identify and find the information you need, without getting sidetracked.

Understanding the Web

OBJECTIVES

- Explain the creation of the World Wide Web.

- Contrast the internet and the World Wide Web.

- Explain the parts of a URL.

AS YOU READ

ORGANIZE INFORMATION Use a summary chart to help organize details as you read.

TERMINOLOGY

- Cascading Style Sheets (CCS)

- graphical browser

- home page

- hyperlink

- hypertext

- Hypertext Markup Language (HTML)

- Hypertext Transfer Protocol (HTTP)

- style sheet

- tag

- web page

- web server

- website

- World Wide Web

Creating the Web

As early as 1980, a few people were trying to connect documents stored on different computers by means of a private network on the internet. These connected documents, it was thought, could someday create a "web" of information that would be instantly available to anyone.

In 1989, Tim Berners-Lee developed a way to retrieve one computer's internet address while working on another computer. The resulting programs and protocols led to the creation of the World Wide Web. Recall that the **World Wide Web**, or web, is a subset of the internet that includes all documents and other resources that use the **Hypertext Transfer Protocol (HTTP)**. Berners-Lee made this new technology freely available to everyone and pleaded with other researchers to help develop ways to expand it and make it more accessible.

In 1992, Marc Andreessen and other students at the National Center for Supercomputing Applications (NCSA) developed a web browser called Mosaic®. Recall that a browser is a program that enables users to navigate the web and locate and display web documents. Mosaic was the first **graphical browser** that could display graphics as well as text.

In 1994, Andreessen introduced Netscape Navigator. A year later, Microsoft released Internet Explorer, and that same year the web was opened up to public and commercial use.

The Internet and the Web

Many people use the terms *internet* and *web* as synonyms. In fact, the web is just one part of the internet. Recall that every computer on the internet has a unique IP, or Internet Protocol, address. Every document on the web also has a unique address, called its uniform resource locator, or URL.

Like email, newsgroups, and file transfer, the web is a service supported by the internet. Although these services share the internet and many of its resources, each is different, with its own set of protocols and applications.

A WEB OF DOCUMENTS The web is a vast collection of documents linked by hypertext. **Hypertext** is text that links to other information using **hyperlinks**. Web page developers format

FIGURE 28.1.1 The web gets its name from the web of connections it creates between computers all over the world.

VLAD KOCHELAEVSKIY/123RF.COM

documents and add the hyperlinks by using **Hypertext Markup Language**, or **HTML**. People all over the world create and format web documents by using standardized HTML codes called **tags**. These documents are saved, or published, to a server on the internet. When you use a web browser program to access a web document, each element on the page—text, images, sound, or animation—displays with its intended format.

FORMATTING THE WEB The graphical appearance of websites is one of the key features of the web. Web designers take care to make the pages appealing and easy to read. Instead of setting HTML tags for every element on every page, programmers use **style sheets**. A style sheet is a separate document that describes rules used to define how the elements of the pages in a website will look. **Cascading Style Sheets (CSS)** are style sheets that are used for HTML. The term *cascading* is used because CSS describes a hierarchy of style rules. Rules with a higher priority are applied over rules with a lower priority. This insures that the formatting will be consistent.

IC3✔ Understand browser functionality: HTML and CSS.

CAREER CORNER

WEB DESIGNER Web design is a growing field. Web designers consult for individuals and small businesses, work for companies with a strong presence on the web, and plan and teach programs in web design. Strong candidates in this field develop skills in fine arts, such as photography, filmmaking, and animation. They also need skills with computer graphics; digital video and audio; design software; and design languages such as HTML or Java.

Understanding Websites

A **web page** is a document on the web. A **website** is a collection of related pages, which are connected using hyperlinks. To help readers identify the relationship between pages in a website, they may use consistent formatting. For example, each page might have the same layout and use the same fonts and colors.

You select a hyperlink to browse, or move, from one web page to another. When you enter a URL in your browser, or select a link on a page, it sends a request to the computer on the internet

EXAMPLES OF HTML TAGS

Start Tag	End Tag	Result
\<html\>	\</html\>	Identifies an HTML document
\<h1\>	\</h1\>	Identifies a top level heading
\<p\>	\</p\>	Identifies a paragraph
\<a href = "name"\>	\</a\>	Inserts a hyperlink to the named location
\<ol\>	\</ol\>	Identifies a numbered list
\<ul\>	\</ul\>	Identifies a bulleted list
\<br /\>		Inserts a line break
\<img src ="name" alt="alternate text" /\>		Inserts the named image file and specified alternative text

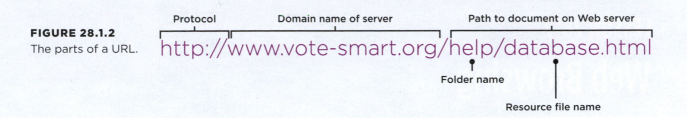

FIGURE 28.1.2
The parts of a URL.

that stores the page identified by the URL. That computer is called a **web server**. It stores web pages and responds to requests from web browsers. When the server receives your request, it sends the necessary information for the document to your computer, where it displays in your browser window.

Most websites have a primary page called the **home page**, or index page, which appears when you first enter the site's URL. A URL can also identify a specific page on a website.

Parts of a URL

PROTOCOL The first part of a URL specifies the protocol required to access the document. Web documents use http://, indicating that the file should be retrieved using Hypertext Transfer Protocol. Some URLs might have other protocols, such as FTP, which shows that the file should be retrieved with file transfer protocol. Another protocol, telnet, allows for access to remote computers. Still another protocol, mailto, lets you select an email address link on a web page to automatically start your email client with the address entered in the To: field.

DOMAIN NAME The next part of a URL, such as www.fbi.gov, is the domain name. Recall that the domain name is the part of the URL that identifies the server that hosts the website. This part of the URL usually takes you to the site's home page.

PATH The remainder of a URL, if any, defines a path to the document's location on the web server. Like any computer, a web server stores files in folders, so the path lists the folder and subfolders, if any, containing the desired document. Thus, a URL such as http://www.fbi.gov/employment/ identifies a folder named *employment* on the site's web server.

RESOURCE FILE NAME At the end of a URL, you may see the name of a file—the specific web resource for which you are looking. The resource may be an HTML document or a web page, a video clip, a text file, or another type of resource. The filename extension identifies the type of resource.

TECHNOLOGY@WORK

Companies and organizations try to obtain a domain name that will easily lead people to their website's home page. The address of specific pages is not as important because the home page can provide navigation aids, such as a row or column of subject buttons.

THINK ABOUT IT!

Below are parts of the URL for the Public Broadcasting System (PBS) program Nature. Sequence from 1 (first) to 4 (last), the order in which the parts of the URL should be listed.

- www.pbs.org
- /index.html
- http://
- wnet/nature

575

OBJECTIVES

- Explore web navigation tools.
- Discuss browser functionality.
- Demonstrate common website navigation conventions.

AS YOU READ

ORGANIZE INFORMATION Use an outline to organize ways of accessing and evaluating web pages as you read.

TERMINOLOGY

- add-on
- address bar
- authentication cookie
- Back button
- Bookmarks
- browsing history
- cookie
- extension
- Favorites
- Forward button
- History
- hover
- in-app browser
- in-browser app
- knowledge base
- mouse over
- navigation buttons
- plug-in
- popup
- popup blocker
- Refresh button
- Reload button
- search engine
- subject guides
- tabbed browsing
- tracking
- widget

Browsing the Web

You use a web browser application to display web pages on your computer. Most web browsers, including the popular Mozilla Firefox, Google Chrome, and Microsoft Edge, share some common features. For example, most have an **address bar** where you can enter a URL, and scroll bars for moving up and down and left and right through the page.

IC3✔ **Understand browser functionality: different browsers.**

NAVIGATION BUTTONS Located on the browser's toolbar, **navigation buttons** let you perform certain operations quickly. When you select the **Refresh** or **Reload button**, the browser downloads the page you are already viewing again, which may update certain features. When you select the **Back button**, the browser reloads the previous page. The **Forward button** moves ahead to pages previously viewed before you selected Back.

ADDRESS BOX If you type a URL in the address bar and press Enter, the browser will display the web page located at that URL in the current tab, or a new tab depending on the setting. In most browsers, if you type a search phrase and press Enter, the browser displays a page of search results using the default search engine applications. Select a link in the search results to open that page.

IC3✔ **Understand browser functionality: navigating with URLs, scroll bars, and navigation buttons.**

TABBED BROWSING By default, most browsers support **tabbed browsing**, which means they can display more than one web page in a single window. Each page displays on a separate tab so you can switch back and forth from one page to another without opening a new browser window. You can enable or disable this feature, if you want. If you disable tabbed browsing, each web page you visit will open in a new browser window.

IC3✔ **Understand browser functionality: new windows and tabs.**

FAVORITES, BOOKMARKS, AND HISTORY Most browsers also have tools for helping you get back to pages you use often, or have visited recently. **Favorites** or **Bookmarks** let you create a list of frequently visited web pages. Then, rather than retyping the URL, you can return to any bookmarked or favorite page by selecting its name in the list. Most browsers let you sync your favorites across all of your devices, so if you add a page to Favorites in Chrome on your laptop, it will be available on the Favorites list in Chrome on your smartphone. Some, including Edge and Chrome, let you import your Favorites from a different browser. You can delete a page from the Bookmark or Favorites list when you no longer need it.

Browsers also track your **browsing history**, which is all the pages you visit, and make them available for viewing in a **History** list. You can select a page from the list, or clear the list to remove the record of sites you have visited.

IC3✔ **Understand browser functionality: bookmarks, favorites, and synchronization.**

FIGURE 28.2.1 Most browsers feature navigation buttons, an address bar, and tools for creating a list of frequently visited websites.

Customizing a Web Browser

Browsers start with default settings, but usually you can customize the settings to suit your preferences. Most customization options can be found in a dialog box such as Settings or Internet Options.

CHANGING THE START PAGE You can customize your browser by making any web page your start page. You can also set your browser to display a blank page when it launches, so you don't have to wait for a start page to load before you begin to browse.

SECURITY AND PRIVACY You can select different levels of security and privacy. For example, you could increase system security by disabling all internet file downloads. You may also increase your browsing privacy by blocking the small files that store identification information, called **cookies**, from being automatically stored on your computer. Most browsers include options for preventing **tracking**, which is when a website gathers information about your web browsing activity.

ORGANIZING FAVORITES OR BOOKMARKS You can use the browser's organization tools to create folders and subfolders to organize your preferred links. You can also add to and remove from your Favorites or Bookmark list.

Navigating a Website

You use a browser to navigate among various websites, but you use the website navigation tools to move within the site. Most websites use basic navigation principles, similar to other applications. For example, they use mouse clicks and right-clicks—or taps and holds on a touchscreen—to select options and links. Some elements on a web page respond to a **hover**, or **mouse over** action, which is when you rest the mouse pointer over an object. The mouse over might trigger an event such as a popup window or a movement.

On a web page, some elements respond to a click-and-hold action, which may be called a delayed click. For example, following a link in most browsers requires a single click. Using a click-and-hold, or delayed click, might produce a different response, such as a popup Help window, or the ability to drag-and-drop an element to a different location. These types of actions might also be used on gaming websites for specific actions within the game.

IC3✔ **Understand how to use common website navigation conventions: click, delayed click, double-click, mouse over, and drag-and-drop.**

Most well-designed sites use common website navigation conventions to make it easy for visitors to find what they are looking for. Among the most common are the following:

- Navigation bars are placed across the top of the page, or along the left side. They include links to the main pages of the site, such as Home and Contact Us. Home is linked to the site's home or main page. The Contact Us page lists the information visitors need to contact the business behind the website. If there is a hierarchy to the site, there are usually drop-down menus from the navigation bar. You might click the Contact Us page and see a menu of choices such as By Email, By Phone, and By Chat.

- Text links are formatted so visitors know they are links. This usually means they are a different color than the surrounding text, and may be underlined.

- Buttons are used as links. If something looks like a button, chances are you can click it to follow the link. For example, a button with a left-pointing arrow is used as a link to go back to the previous page.

- Icons should represent what you expect. For example, an envelope means email; a shopping bag or cart means a shopping bag or cart.

- Site maps may be used to display an alphabetical list of links to all pages in the site.

- Search boxes may be used to let you search the site for specific content.

IC3 ✔ **Understand how to use common website navigation conventions: basic web navigation principles.**

DID YOU KNOW?

You can use a browser's Reading List feature to save a page to read later, even if you are offline. Safari, Chrome, and Edge all let you add a page to a Reading List. The browser caches the page, so when you are ready to read, simply open the Reading List and click the page, with or without an internet connection.

Web Page Features

You use a browser to interact with web pages, and web pages interact with your browser. Web pages and websites make use of your browser software to provide interactive content and multimedia. They also keep track of your actions while you have the page open. Some of the features and tools that web pages use to interact with you include cookies, popups, plug-ins, and in-browser apps. Most browsers have settings you can use to control the use of these features.

COOKIES Some websites use cookies to keep track of you, your preferences, and your browsing history. Cookies are small files that the website generates and stores on your computer. When you visit the site again in the future, the site uses the cookie to identify you. One type of cookie, called an **authentication cookie**, is a piece of data that allows your computer to log in to a secure website through a secure account.

Most browsers include a tool that you can use to delete cookies from your system. This can free up some disk space and help guard your privacy. It can also cause some inconvenience because websites you visit frequently will not recognize you, and may require you to sign in each time. To delete cookies in Microsoft Edge, open the Settings pane. Under the Clear browsing data heading, select Choose what to clear. Select Cookies, and then select Clear.

IC3 ✔ **Understand browser functionality: cookies**

POPUPS A **popup** is a window that opens—or pops up—unexpectedly on a web page. Popups are usually advertisements. They may include text, video, or audio. Popups may display even if you do not select anything on the screen. A popup might appear if you spend a set amount of time on a page or if you hover the mouse over an image, video, or text. For example, if you are reading a news article, a popup asking you to subscribe to the site might display.

Most popups are positioned in front of the page you are trying to view, obscuring the content. You must take some kind of action to get the popup to close. For example, you may have to click a Close button or select a Skip This Ad link. This action may result in a cookie or other tracking tool being installed on your system. Most browsers include a **popup blocker** tool that you can enable to stop popups. For example, in Edge, open the Settings pane and select View advanced settings. Drag the Block pop-ups toggle into the On position.

IC3✔ | **Understand browser functionality: popups.**

WIDGETS, PLUG-INS, AND ADD-ONS Many websites have interactive elements such as popup windows, buttons, and pull-down windows. These components are called **widgets**. You use widgets to perform a function or access a service, such as checking the weather in your home town, or viewing a Twitter feed.

Similar to widgets are **plug-ins**. Plug-ins are mini programs embedded in a website to add a feature or function, such as a search engine or video player. One of the most well-known plug-ins is Adobe Flash Player, but there are many others, including Java Virtual Machine, Microsoft Silverlight, and Adobe Acrobat Reader.

Plug-ins are complete programs and can even be installed on computers or other devices without a browser. An **add-on**, however, is code designed specifically to add a feature to a web browser, modify a web page, or integrate your browser with other services. For example, you might use an add-on to share or sync your list of bookmarked pages across different browsers, or display a button you can use to link directly to your Twitter account. Add-ons may also be called browser **extensions**.

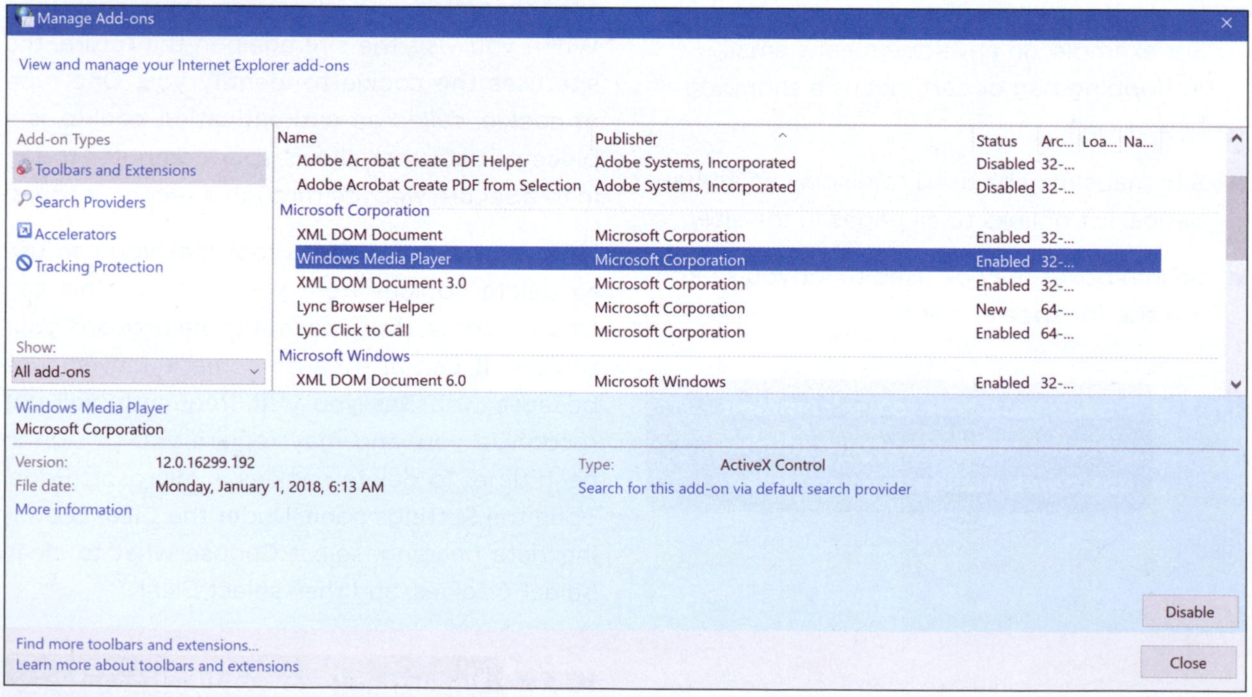

FIGURE 28.2.2 The Manage Add-ons dialog box in Windows 10.

There are some risks with using add-ons. Hackers can use them to track your online movements and even collect personal information. They may also slow down your system performance. In most browsers you can view, enable, and disable add-ons.

IN-BROWSER APPS Some browsers support the integration of websites and apps by allowing certain sites to open associated apps. This is called an **in-browser app**. For example, Windows 10 defaults to a setting that allows the Groove Music app to open when you visit a Groove Music web page in a browser such as Edge or Chrome. Usually, the browser will display a prompt confirming that you want to open the website before doing so. By changing to the associated website, the app may run more efficiently and you may be able to access additional features.

Some browsers include a tool you can use to allow or block the ability to open a site within an app. In Edge, open the Settings pane and select View advanced settings. Drag the Open sites in apps toggle into the On or Off position. You can also use the Apps for websites settings page in Windows 10 to associate an app with a website.

Some people might confuse *in-browser apps* with *in-app browsers*. An **in-app browser** is a navigation tool built in to some applications or websites. Many social networking sites include in-app browsers. For example, you can use Facebook's in-app browser to navigate the Facebook site without using a stand-alone browser, such as Chrome or Edge.

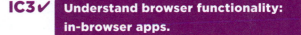

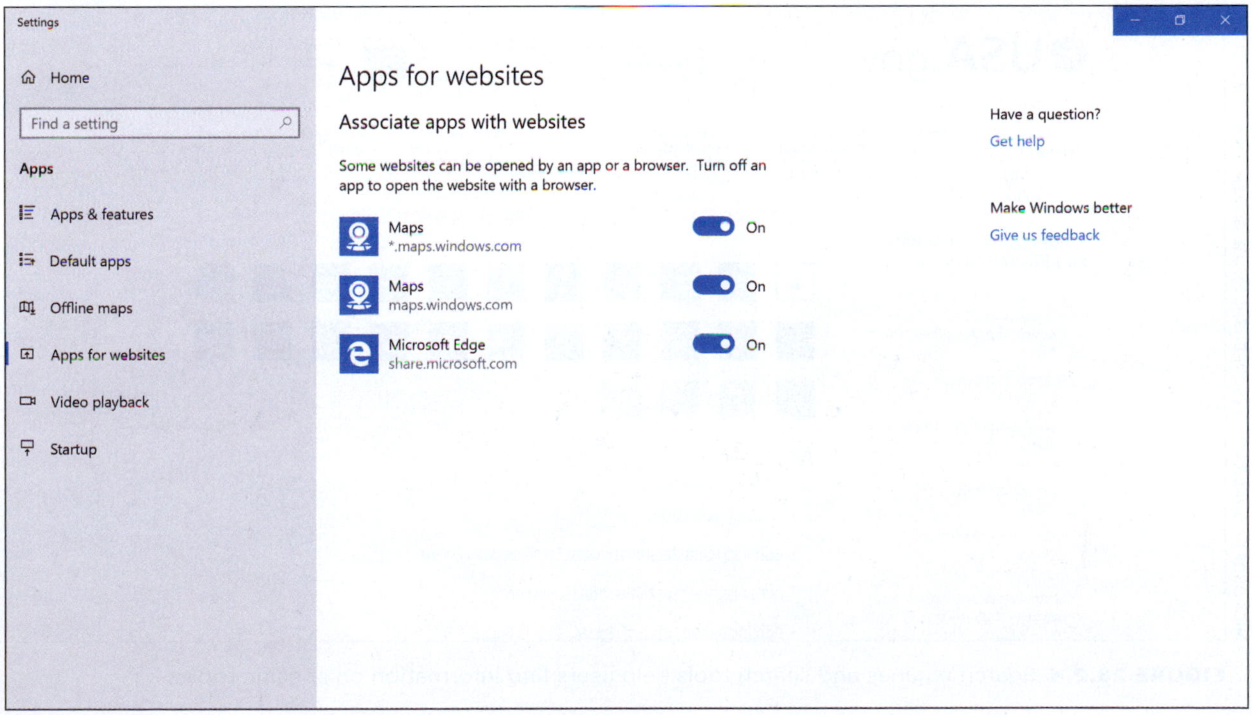

FIGURE 28.2.3 The Apps for websites settings in Windows 10.

Finding Information on the Web

The web is an amazing tool for acquiring information, but because it is so large, it can be hard to locate the information you need. Subject guides and search engines can help.

SUBJECT GUIDES Many websites offer **subject guides** to help you navigate the web. These are pages grouped together under headings like Careers, News, or Travel. These guides include links only to articles and pages that provide useful information about the subject.

KNOWLEDGE BASE A **knowledge base** is a searchable collection or database of information related to a specific subject. For example, a law library might have a knowledge base of law articles, cases, and other relevant information. Companies often maintain a knowledge base of helpful information that customers can use to solve problems on their own.

SEARCH ENGINES A **search engine** is a program or website designed to search the web looking for documents that match specified criteria, such as keywords. In a matter of moments, the search engine displays a list of links to pages that match. General search engines, such as Google, Yahoo, or Bing, search throughout the web to find matches. Some search engines are customized for a certain topic. For example, the website USA.gov lets you search all .gov websites for topics related to the U.S. government.

Some search engines support advanced searches that let you search for files based on file type, size, category, and other properties. For example, you can search for picture files, videos, or music.

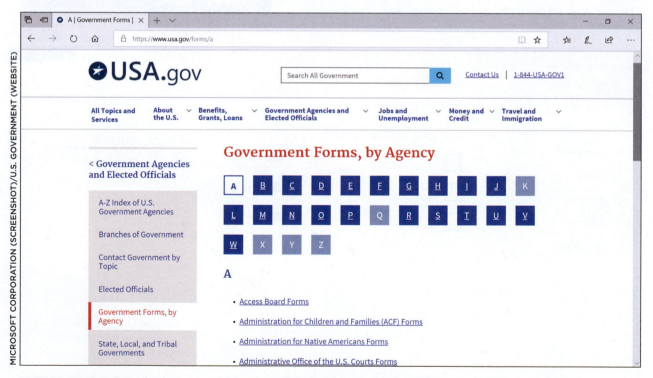

MICROSOFT CORPORATION (SCREENSHOT)/U.S. GOVERNMENT (WEBSITE)

FIGURE 28.2.4 Search engines and search tools help users find information on specific topics.

Exploring E-Commerce

OBJECTIVES

- Compare and contrast methods of e-commerce.

- Identify reasons for the success of online shopping.

- Recognize the purpose of government websites.

AS YOU READ

ORGANIZE INFORMATION Use a spider web to help you organize ways to use e-commerce as you read.

TERMINOLOGY

- e-commerce

- online banking

- online presence

Electronic Commerce

Recall that electronic commerce, or **e-commerce**, is the use of telecommunications networks or the internet to conduct business. E-commerce is not new; companies have used wide area networks, or WANs, to do business for years.

Thanks to the internet and affordable computers, e-commerce has become accessible to anyone who has an internet connection and a web browser. More and more internet users are researching products, shopping, opening bank accounts, and trading stocks online. Many businesses realize that they may lose customers if they do not have an **online presence**, or website, where people can learn about the business and usually do business, as well.

Online Banking

In **online banking**, customers use a web browser to access their accounts, balance checkbooks, transfer funds, and pay bills online.

PERSONAL FINANCE PROGRAMS Programs such as Intuit's Quicken® have features that can help you budget your money, analyze your spending habits, balance your checkbook, and make account transactions. Many of these programs can be linked to actual accounts to automatically track your transactions. One drawback to these programs is that anyone with access to your password can access this data.

WEB-BASED BANKING Web-based banking allows users to access their accounts in financial institutions. All the data is stored on the bank's computer, not your own, so you can access your account from any computer that has an internet connection. You can learn about different types of services and interest rates, transfer funds, check your statements, reconcile your accounts, or even pay bills online. This service allows you to set up accounts for the businesses you want to pay. When you receive a bill in the mail, you log on to your bank account, enter the amount to be paid, and pay online instead of writing a check and mailing the payment.

Online Shopping

When many people think of e-commerce, they think of shopping online. Online shopping has grown in popularity due to convenience, choice, and security features built into popular web browsers.

THE BUYER'S POINT OF VIEW The web is an excellent resource for researching products, services, and prices. At many sites, buyers can read product reviews posted by other buyers. At other sites, they can find vendor and product ratings.

THE SELLER'S POINT OF VIEW One of the main advantages of online business is low startup cost. For a small investment, a vendor can set up a website and sell products online to a wider variety of customers than one physical location offers. Vendors may not even need a website if they use an existing site, such as eBay or Etsy.

TECHNOLOGY@HOME

Almost anyone with financial resources can set up a checking or savings account at an online bank.

THINK ABOUT IT!

Think about the advantages an online bank account offers. Which of the following would be an advantage?

- lets you check your account any time
- lets you make deposits anytime
- helps you avoid math mistakes
- helps you plan your spending
- prevents overspending

FIGURE 28.3.1 e-Commerce websites have benefits for both shoppers and sellers.

ANDREY_POPOV/SHUTTERSTOCK

Amazon.com, for example, was launched by Jeff Bezos in 1995. Rather than visit a bookstore that stocks 10,000 to 40,000 titles, consumers around the globe can log on to Amazon and search a database of millions of titles. What started out as "The Earth's biggest bookstore," has morphed into the Earth's biggest store—period. The website not only offers millions of books, music, and movies, but it also sells everything from auto parts, toys, and electronics to cosmetics, prescription drugs, and groceries. In 2017 the company was responsible for 44 percent of all U.S. e-commerce sales, or about 4 percent of the country's total retail sales figure.

DID YOU KNOW?

As you follow interesting links on the web you are setting up a *clickstream*—a record of every website and every web page that you visited. Your internet service provider and the websites track your clickstream and sell it. Internet marketers and advertisers use the information to target you with certain ads. You can minimize this by turning on the tracking protection or private browsing features of your web browser.

Government Websites

The United States government makes services available online through websites using the top-level domain .gov. On government websites you can find important information about how the government functions and government policies. There are websites for all levels of government, from the federal legislative and executive branches to your state and local governments.

Government agencies have websites as well. On the Internal Revenue Service's website you can find information about paying taxes. Through your state's Department of Motor Vehicles website you can find information about registering a car, or obtaining a driver's license. There are also sites for other permits and licenses, such as those for hunting or entering national parks.

The United States Postal Service website allows you to renew your passport and purchase stamps. You can even buy e-stamps to print at home, saving a trip to the post office.

Chapter 28 Review

REVIEW THE TERMINOLOGY

DIRECTIONS Match each vocabulary term in the left column with the correct definition in the right column.

1. graphical browser
2. HTML
3. web server
4. web page
5. website
6. navigation button
7. cookie
8. e-commerce
9. tracking
10. style sheet

a. tool that lets users perform routine operations with a browser

b. a small file that stores identification information

c. computer that houses websites and sends documents to users

d. a collection of related documents on the web

e. document that describes rules used to define how the elements of the pages in a website will look

f. conducting business through a network on the internet

g. web navigation program that shows pictures and text

h. when a website gathers information about your web browsing activity

i. single document on the web

j. markup language used to format web documents

USE THE TERMINOLOGY

DIRECTIONS Determine the correct choice for each of the following.

1. Which was the first browser that could display graphics as well as text?
   a. Internet Explorer
   b. Mosaic
   c. Firefox
   d. Chrome

2. Which of the following is NOT part of a complete URL address?
   a. protocol
   b. server
   c. path
   d. author

3. Which of the following browser tools will most easily help you revisit a website you enjoyed?

   a. Favorites or Bookmarks   c. Refresh or Reload

   b. Forward   d. Address box

4. By which of the following does a search engine search?

   a. URL addresses   c. Bookmarks

   b. Favorites   d. keywords

5. Which of the following has contributed the most to the growth of e-commerce?

   a. traditional stores   c. affordable computers

   b. advanced web browsers   d. personal finance programs

6. Which of the following is the language used to create web pages?

   a. FTP   c. HTML

   b. HTTP   d. LINUX

THINK CRITICALLY

DIRECTIONS Answer the following questions.

1. What are Cascading Style Sheets, and how are they used to consistently format HTML?

2. What is the benefit to deleting cookies after browsing the web? If cookies are used by browsers to track your history, why wouldn't you always immediately delete them?

3. Which web browser features or tools do you find most useful? Why?

4. Identify the protocol, domain name, path to the document on the server, and the resource file name in the following URL: http://www2.ed.gov/nclb/choice/index.html.

5. Explain the purpose of the HTML elements tags, style sheets, and hyperlinks.

EXTEND YOUR KNOWLEDGE

DIRECTIONS Choose and complete one of the following projects.

1. Browsers provide other features and functions in addition to those listed in this lesson. For example, as you begin to type an address, most browsers reveal a list of sites you've already visited that begin with the same letters. With your teacher's permission, work with a partner and explore the functions of a browser. Position the mouse over other buttons to see what appears. Select the buttons to see what happens. Visit the online Help feature to find out more about it. Create a chart in a word-processing program and enter your findings.

2. Work with a partner or small group. With your teacher's permission, use a web browser to view the websites of one online-only retailer and one retailer that also has stores. Create a chart comparing and contrasting the two sites. Are the sites visually appealing? Are they easy to navigate and use? Share your chart with another team or the class.

3. The web has been praised for the wealth of knowledge it provides for users around the world. It is also criticized for the dangers it makes possible and for the temptation it offers some people. With your teacher's permission, conduct online or library research to learn the praises and objections people have for the web. Take notes and keep track of your sources. Be sure to evaluate the information you find and only use it if it is accurate, relevant, and valid. Participate in a debate on the advantages and disadvantages of the web as a resource.

IC3 PREP

1. The web is a vast collection of documents linked by _____.
   a. hypertext
   b. tags
   c. keywords
   d. CSS

2. _____ are standardized HTML codes used to create and format web documents.
   a. Hyperlinks
   b. Style sheets
   c. Tags
   d. Rules

3. Mozilla Firefox, Google Chrome, and Microsoft Edge are all examples of what?
   a. search engines
   b. web browsers
   c. social media
   d. HTML

4. Which of the following is a common feature of a web browser? (Select all that apply.)
   a. scroll bars
   b. address bar
   c. back button
   d. volume slider
   e. tabs

5. For each line below, select whether the statement is True or False.
   a. If you previously selected the Back button, the Forward button will return you to the page you navigated away from.
   b. Typing a search phrase into a browser's address bar and hitting Enter will usually return search results.
   c. The Refresh or Reload button can fix a previous page load error, but it will not update any new page information.
   d. Scroll bars allow you to navigate up, down, left, and right in most websites.

6. _____ allow a browser to display more than one web page in a single window.
   a. Navigation buttons
   b. Scroll bars
   c. Tabs
   d. Popups

7. You are browsing the web and need to open a new page, but would like to stay on the current page too. What should you do? (Select all that apply.)
   a. Open a new browser window.
   b. It is not possible for a browser to have two pages open at once.
   c. Open a new browser tab.
   d. Use a split screen view.

8. For each line below, select whether the statement is True or False.

    a. You can return to any bookmarked or favorite page by selecting its name in the list.

    b. It is possible for many browsers to sync bookmarks across a user's devices.

    c. It is important to be sparing with bookmarks, as browsers can only store a few at a time.

    d. Browsers only remember your bookmarks as long as you visit the page every day.

9. Like traditional files on a computer, a Favorites list can be organized into _____.

    a. folders   **c.** size

    b. file types   **d.** tabs

10. What action is typically used to select a link or option in a browser, using a mouse?

    a. delayed click   **c.** double-click

    b. mouse over   **d.** single click

11. What are some likely outcomes to performing a delayed click action (or click-and-hold) on a website element? (Select all that apply.)

    a. The element in question may be hidden.

    b. The ability to drag-and-drop the element to a different location.

    c. A popup Help window may appear.

    d. Nothing will happen. It is not a valid action.

12. A "Home" link on a typical website will likely lead you where, when clicked?

    a. A map website showing the location of the Webmaster's house.

    b. The home page you have set in your browser.

    c. The home page your browser has set as the default.

    d. The main page of the site you are on.

13. What are some good contact methods to put on a website's Contact Us page? (Select all that apply.)

    a. by email   **c.** chat online

    b. in person   **d.** by phone

14. Put the following steps in order for deleting cookies in Microsoft Edge.

    a. Under the Clear browsing data heading, select Choose what to clear.   **c.** Select Clear.

    d. Select Cookies.

    b. Open the Settings pane.

15. A _____ is a piece of data that allows your computer to log in to a secure website through a secure account.

    a. padlock icon   **c.** hyperlink

    b. popup   **d.** authentication cookie

16. For each line below, select whether the statement is True or False.

    a. Popups are usually advertisements.

    b. Popups can only display if you select something in your browser.

    c. Closing a popup may install a tracking tool on your system.

    d. Popup blockers are available for web browsers, but they must be installed separately.

17. Which of these elements may be used in a popup advertisement?

    a. video   **c.** sound

    b. audio   **d.** links to another website

18. Interactive elements on a website, such as popup windows, buttons, and pull-down windows, are often known as _____.

    a. plug-ins   **c.** add-ons

    b. widgets   **d.** extensions

19. What is the main difference between a plug-in and an add-on?

    a. Plug-ins and add-ons provide the same functionality.

    b. Add-ons are not able to slow down a browser's functionality.

    c. Plug-ins can be installed without a browser.

    d. Plug-ins offer full encryption during web browsing.

20. What are the potential benefits to running an in-browser app? (Select all that apply.)

    a. An app will often run more efficiently.

    b. An app will respect your privacy.

    c. An app may have access to more features.

    d. An app usually allows for paid transactions.

IC3 PROCEDURES

VIEWING A WEB PAGE IN A BROWSER

1. Start the browser.

2. Position the insertion point in the Search or enter Web address box and type the web page address.

3. Press **Enter**.

NAVIGATING WEB PAGES

■ Select the **Back** button ← to return to the previously viewed page.

■ Select the **Forward** button → to go to the page you were on when you clicked the Back button.

USING A WEBSITE'S NAVIGATION BAR

1. Locate the navigation bar, typically located at the top of the web page or along the left side.

2. Select a link within the navigation bar to go to that page.

3. Select the **Home** link or **Home** button ⌂ on the navigation bar to return to the website's home page.

FINDING SPECIFIC INFORMATION ON A WEBSITE

■ Use the website's navigation bar to go to pages with more specific information.

■ Position the insertion point in the site's Search box, and type the keyword(s) for which you are searching.

■ Press **Ctrl + F**, type the text you want to find, and then press **Enter**.

REFRESHING A WEB PAGE

Select the **Refresh** button ↻.

OR

1. Right-click the page's tab.

2. On the shortcut menu, select **Refresh all**.

OPENING A NEW TAB

Select the **New tab** button ⊞.

CLOSING A TAB

Select the **Close** button ✕ on the tab of the page you want to close.

SHOWING HISTORY OF RECENTLY VISITED WEBSITES

1. In Edge, select the **Hub** button ☆≡.

2. In the Hub task pane, select the **History** button ↻ to display the History pane.

NAVIGATING TO A RECENTLY VISITED SITE

1. Select the desired time frame in the History pane to list the sites visited during that time.

2. Select a site to list the web pages visited at that site.

3. Select a page to display it.

DELETING AN ITEM ON THE HISTORY LIST

1. Right-click the item you want to delete.

2. On the shortcut menu, select **Delete**.

CLEARING THE HISTORY LIST

1. In the History pane, select **Clear all history**.

2. Select the checkbox next to the items you want to clear.

3. Select **Clear**.

USING A SEARCH ENGINE

1. In the Address bar, type the address for the desired search engine and press **Enter**.

2. In the Search box, type the subject for which you are searching and press **Enter**.

3. In the list of websites that meet the search criteria, select the site you want to visit.

ADDING A PAGE TO FAVORITES IN MICROSOFT EDGE

1. Display the desired web page in Edge.

2. Select the **Add to favorites or reading list** button ☆.

3. Select the **Favorites** button ☆, if necessary.

4. In the Name box, enter a name for the favorite.

5. If desired, select the **Save in** drop-down arrow and select a folder in which to store the page address.

6. Click **Add**.

USING FAVORITES IN MICROSOFT EDGE

1. In Edge, select the **Hub** button ☲ on the toolbar.

2. In the Hub task pane, select the **Favorites** button to display the Favorites pane.

3. If necessary, select the folder where the page you want is stored.

4. Select the page you want to view.

DISPLAYING THE FAVORITES BAR IN THE EDGE WINDOW

1. In Edge, select the **Hub** button ☲ on the toolbar.

2. In the Hub task pane, select **Settings**.

3. Toggle the **Show the favorites bar** setting to On.

   Only items stored in the Favorites folder display on the favorites bar.

BOOKMARKING A WEB PAGE IN GOOGLE CHROME

1. Display the desired web page in Chrome.

2. Select the **Bookmark this page** button ☆.

   OR

   Press **Ctrl + D**.

3. In the Name box, enter a name for the favorite.

4. If desired, select the **Folder** drop-down arrow and select a folder in which to store the page address.

5. Select **Done**.

SYNCHRONIZING BOOKMARKS AND FAVORITES ACROSS WINDOWS DEVICES

1. In Windows 10, enter **Sync** in the Search box on the Taskbar.

2. Select the **Sync your settings** link.

3. Turn on **Sync your settings**, and the individual sync settings you want to enable.

4. In Edge, select the **Settings and More** button ⎸···⎸ and then select **Settings**.

5. Turn on **Sync your favorites, reading list, top sites, and other settings across your Windows devices**.

6. Repeat steps on all devices.

SYNCHRONIZING BOOKMARKS AND FAVORITES USING CHROME

1. In Chrome, select the **Customize and control Google Chrome** button ⋮ and then select **Settings**.

2. Sign in, if necessary.

3. Under People, select **Sync**.

4. Turn on the **Bookmarks** option.

5. Repeat steps on all devices.

USING HYPERLINKS ON A WEB PAGE

- Select a hyperlink to display its destination.

- Hover the mouse pointer over an element to reveal hidden content, if available.

- Move the mouse cursor again to make the tooltip disappear.

DRAGGING AND DROPPING TO UPLOAD FILES TO A WEBSITE

1. Start your browser and navigate to the web page where you want to place the file(s).

   For example, go to Dropbox or Google Drive and open the folder.

2. Open the File Explorer folder where the file(s) to move is stored.

3. Resize and arrange the windows so you can see both the File Explorer and the browser window at the same time.

4. Select and drag the file(s) from the File Explorer folder and drop them on the web page window.

CHAPTER 29

Using the Web

FINDING YOUR WAY AROUND THE WEB

The web is quickly becoming the preferred source for information on news, weather, products, and much more. It is also a tool for conducting business, ranging from shopping to investing, and for keeping in touch with friends, colleagues, and family. Knowing how and where to find useful and accurate resources is the key to successfully using the web.

As a student, you might search for information to help with schoolwork, to learn more about things you are interested in, or decide which products you want to own. Some people look for information about careers, places where they might want to live or visit, or about current events. Learning how to find your way around the web will prepare you to take advantage of the variety of resources it offers.

Understanding Hypertext

OBJECTIVES

- Discuss how hypertext has changed the way people read.

- Compare and contrast traditional writing methods and writing for the web.

- Explain the use of breadcrumbs.

AS YOU READ

ORGANIZE INFORMATION Use a table to help you organize what hyperlinks do as you read the lesson.

TERMINOLOGY

- breadcrumbs

- dead link

- hypermedia

- web cache

A New Way to Read

Recall that documents displayed on the web are created using hypertext and hyperlinks that you use to navigate from one location to another on the web. The new location might be another part of the page you are on, another page on the same website, or another website entirely.

The most common links are underlined or highlighted words, but graphic images can also be links. Graphic links aren't always highlighted, so watch the mouse pointer. If it changes to a pointing hand icon, it's positioned over a hyperlink.

The web supports **hypermedia**, which extends hypertext to multimedia content, such as audio and video. When you select a video icon on a web page, the video clip opens in a media player app.

Dead links are links to pages that have been moved or deleted from the internet. If you select a dead link, you may see a message that the page no longer exists in that location or you may reach a page that obviously is not one you want. Select the Back button to return to the document you were viewing.

A New Way to Write

Well-designed web pages usually are not crammed with information. Designers generally break the information into shorter segments and use hypertext to link the segments.

USING LINKS FOR EXPLANATION Hypertext authors don't have to explain everything on one page. Instead, they can define links to other documents containing additional information. If readers want to know more about the topic, they can use the links. When they're done exploring the new page, they can navigate right back to the original document.

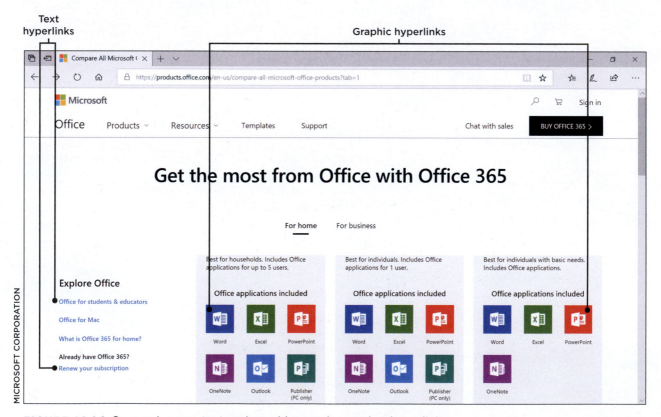

FIGURE 29.1.1 On a web page, text and graphics can be used as hyperlinks.

USING LINKS FOR REFERENCE Have you ever had to write a research paper using footnotes? Web page authors cite references differently. Rather than identifying the source at the bottom of a page, they set up a link to the original source. Likewise, bloggers include links to related pages on their posts.

Browsers Navigate the Web

Hypertext allows for documents to be linked on the web, but your browser software program is the tool you use to move from one document to the next. Recall that in order to help you effectively navigate the web, your browser has many functions. You can enter a web page address and the browser displays that page. Most browsers let you search for a page if you don't know the address, and you can use navigation buttons to move forward and back through pages you have been looking at. Browsers also maintain a History list of sites you have visited in the past, and you can create your own Favorites or Bookmarks list for sites you visit frequently.

BREADCRUMBS Many browsers now also use **breadcrumbs** for navigation. Breadcrumbs are links that help you keep track of what page you are viewing in a website or on a server by displaying the path you followed to get there. Usually, breadcrumbs are near the top of the browser window or in the address bar, displaying links back to each previous page you viewed while navigating to the current page. Each link is separated by a greater-than symbol, like this: *Home Page > Topic Page > Subtopic Page*. You can click any link to go directly to that page.

IC3 ✔ | **Understand browser functionality: breadcrumbs**

CAREER CORNER

WEB ADVERTISING Web advertising is a growing field. Candidates for jobs in online advertising still need traditional art, marketing, and advertising skills. But they also need strong business and technical skills that will let them use the powerful tools of the web to attract customers' attention to the product's message, and a savvy knowledge of how to use the web to find and target their audience.

WEB CACHE When you open a web page, your computer temporarily stores the document in a **web cache** on a storage device, such as a hard disk. The cache allows you to quickly display pages you have already viewed. You might notice that when you select the Back button in your browser, the web page loads much faster than it did originally. That's because it is being loaded from the cache on your storage disk, not from an internet server. The cache can also be used to identify and track your online activity. It also takes up storage space on your device. Most browsers include a tool that lets you clear the cache.

IC3 ✔ | **Understand browser functionality: cache**

Designing for the Web

OBJECTIVES

- Discuss web page design tools.

- List six major steps in creating a website.

- Identify advanced design and browser tools.

AS YOU READ

ORGANIZE INFORMATION Use an outline to help you organize details about web page design as you read.

TERMINOLOGY

- applet

- Dynamic Hypertext Markup Language (DHTML)

- GUI editors

- JavaScript

- storyboard

- web host

- Webmaster

- WYSIWYG

Choosing Web Page Design Tools

To publish documents on the web, you must use Hypertext Markup Language, or HTML, to format the text and define links to other documents. Each section of text is enclosed in tags that mark it as a heading, a paragraph, a link, and so on. Several kinds of programs allow you to work with HTML tags. You may use other programming languages, like JavaScript, along with HTML while programming a website.

TEXT EDITORS Programs like Notepad and TextEdit are simple tools you can use to enter both text and codes. Using these programs can be tedious, though. If you want your web page to include a menu, for example, you have to write the HTML code for each detail of that menu.

HTML EDITORS These programs feature text editing and an easier way to add HTML tags. Examples include HomeSite™ and BBEdit™. These kinds of programs require the user to do most or all of the HTML coding manually.

WORD-PROCESSING PROGRAMS You can use a word-processing program to create a web page. However, it must be a program such as Microsoft Word that allows you to save your work as an .htm or .html file.

GUI EDITORS **GUI editors** are the sophisticated editing programs that let you create a page without entering tags yourself. Sometimes still called **WYSIWYG** (What You See Is What You Get) editors they are almost as easy to use as a word processor, and feature many of the same editing and formatting tools. The difference is that these programs automatically apply the HTML coding for you. You set up the page to look the way you want, including graphics or hyperlinks, and the program adds the HTML codes. Adobe® Dreamweaver® is an example of a program that automates the process of formatting documents for the web.

CONTENT MANAGEMENT SYSTEMS (CMS) These programs let you create blogs and simple websites. Sometimes called a Web Management System, they are software or a suite of tools and applications that allow an individual or organization to create, edit, review, and publish electronic text. Most of these systems provide a web-based GUI, which allows you to use a web browser to access the CMS online. Examples of CMS include Tumblr and Wordpress.

Creating a Website

Anyone can have a website nowadays. Other than the design and content, all you need is a domain name and a place on the web where you can store your pages. A **web host** is a company that provides space on a web server for websites, either for free or for a small monthly fee. The following list describes the main steps for creating a website:

1. Plan the website. Some designers use a **storyboard** for this. A storyboard is a map or plan that defines the layout, organization, and navigational structure of the site. Think about your purpose and audience. Consider that the purpose of the website may influence the domain you will use. For example, if you are creating a website for your school, you will probably use an .edu domain. If you are creating a website for a business, you will probably use the domain .com.

2. Choose your design tools. Do you want to learn HTML and code the site manually? Can you use a GUI editor? Or, is a CMS such as Wordpress the way to go?

3. Design and create the website. Do you have the web design skills to build your own site? Otherwise, a fast way to build a website is to use a pre-coded template that includes titles and navigation bars.

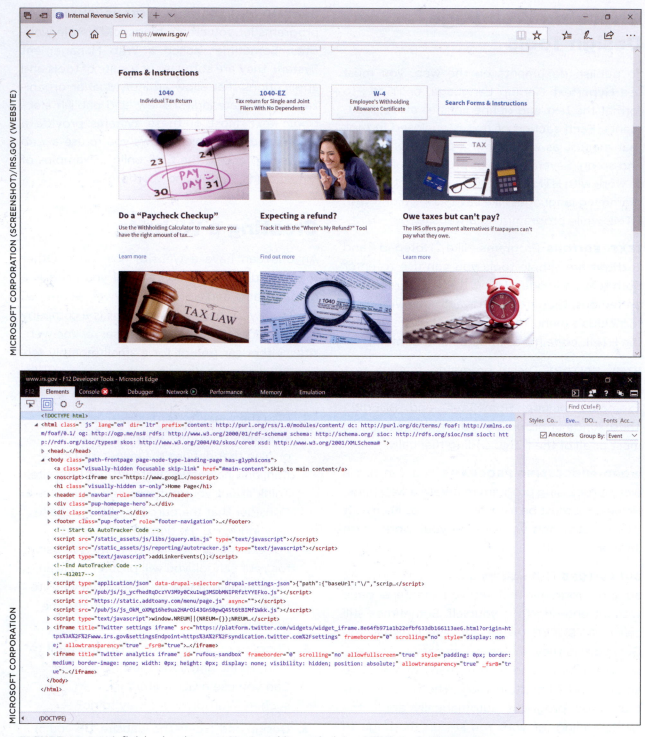

FIGURE 29.2.1 A finished web page (top) and its underlying HTML code (bottom).

You can find website templates online, and many CMS sites let you choose from a wide variety. All you have to do is insert text, graphics, and links based on your storyboard or map.

4. Upload the website. To put your website on the internet, you have to upload, or publish, your files to the server of your web host. This is usually done through a utility program provided by your web host.

5. Test the website. This means viewing your pages in a web browser and testing all links to see if they look and work as you intended.

6. Maintain the website. Don't just build a website and forget about it. You are the **Webmaster**—the person responsible for the look and maintenance of the site. Keep your site up-to-date and accurate so visitors will keep coming back.

TECHNOLOGY@SCHOOL

Today, many schools have their own websites, with a Webmaster who makes the site useful for students, teachers, and families.

THINK ABOUT IT!

If your school or school district has its own website, which features listed below does it offer? If your school does not have a website, which features listed below do you think would be helpful in your school community?

• school calendar
• a showcase for student
• work bulletin board for school-related discussions
• homework schedule for each class
• lunch menus
• campus tours

Website Design

The principles of design and color theory used in graphics are also an important part of web-page design. Successful web pages use design principles such as balance, unity, scale, contrast, and harmony.

■ The entire page should have a unified theme, helping viewers recognize and respond to the page content.

■ To emphasize different parts of the page, there must be contrast between images, colors, titles, and text.

■ Design elements such as typeface, color, and space help you make sure the text is easy to read. Imagine trying to read green text on a web page with a red background!

■ It is also important to use the space on the web page wisely.

■ Design elements such as shape, texture, space, and form help you create a page that is appealing and easy to use.

Web pages should be easy to navigate. This means designers must consider the types of links that will display, and where they will be located.

■ The content should be easy to read and links should be clearly marked.

■ Many sites have a header or footer with important links and information. Home is almost always a link to the site's home or main page.

■ Some sites use Navigation bars to list links to the major topics or sections, including a Contact Us page listing the information viewers need to contact the business behind the website.

■ Some larger sites include site maps, which usually display an alphabetical list of links to all pages in the site.

■ Some sites have built-in search engines so users can more quickly find the content they are interested in.

Exploring Advanced Tools

To create some of the dramatic effects you see on the web, designers use advanced design tools and upgraded browsers to display the pages as they intended.

ADVANCED DESIGN TOOLS Designers can use **Dynamic Hypertext Markup Language (DHTML)** to add interactivity and animation to web pages. You might see butterflies flying across a screen or a personal greeting when you visit an online store. Some designers use **JavaScript**, a cross-platform programming language, to create **applets**, or small applications for the web.

These and similar tools make it possible to have internal search engines, animation, download-able audio and video clips, and streaming audio and video on the web.

ADVANCED BROWSER TOOLS Web users may like to access splashy features, but their browsers must be able to process them. Browsers can be upgraded with plug-in programs and extensions. RealPlayer® and Windows Media® Player play streaming media. Shockwave®/Flash™ support interactive documents and animation, and Adobe® Acrobat® Reader makes it possible to view documents on-screen in the same format as they appear when printed.

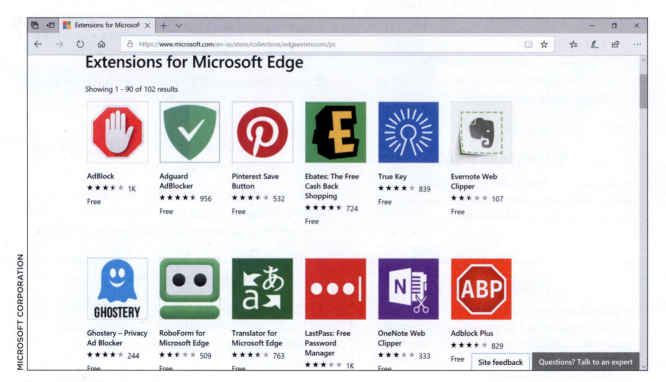

MICROSOFT CORPORATION

FIGURE 29.2.2 Use extensions to add functionality to a browser.

Working on the Web

OBJECTIVES

- Demonstrate how to use inclusion or exclusion operators and wildcards to find information on the web.

- Demonstrate how to search the internet using keywords, hashtags, and other advanced methods.

- Explore methods to critically evaluate the validity of online resources.

AS YOU READ

IDENTIFY INFORMATION Use an outline to help you identify effective ways to use the web as you read.

TERMINOLOGY

- assumption
- Boolean search
- digital misinformation
- exact-phrase search
- hashtag (#)
- inclusion operator
- exclusion operator
- objective
- propaganda
- proximity operator
- wildcard

Getting More from Web Searches

Search engines index words in web pages and maintain a database of those words. You can search for websites, pages, people, and hashtags by typing one or more keywords in the search engine; the engine then displays a list of pages that contain your key words.

You can improve search effectiveness by using advanced search tools, such as a **Boolean search**, which lets you use special terms and characters called Boolean operators.

INCLUSION OPERATORS An **inclusion operator** is a plus sign (+) or the word AND. It indicates that you want to find only pages that contain a match for all the specified words. Searching for *dog+husky* finds only pages that contain both words.

EXCLUSION OPERATORS An **exclusion operator** is a minus sign (–) or the word NOT. Use it to find pages that contain certain words but not

others. Searching for "*dog AND husky NOT sled*" returns a list of pages with the words *dog* and *husky* but not *sled*.

PROXIMITY OPERATOR NEAR is a **proximity operator**. Use it to search for words that appear close together in a document.

EXACT-PHRASE SEARCH Use quotation marks around a phrase to conduct an **exact-phrase search**. The search engine will find the phrase exactly as typed. For example, searching for "*Austin, Texas*" finds only pages that contain that exact phrase. It won't find pages with just *Austin* or just *Texas*.

PARENTHESES Use parentheses to nest one expression within another. For example searching for (*growth OR increase*) NEAR (*internet OR web*) finds documents that mention the words *growth* or *increase* within a few words of *internet* or *web*.

WILDCARDS Many search engines let you use **wildcards**, or symbols that stand for other characters. The most common wildcard is the

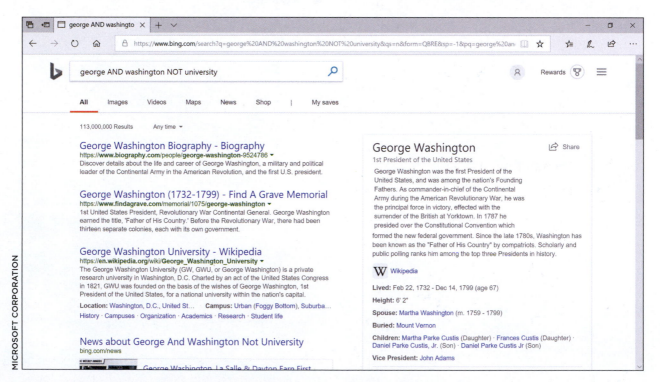

FIGURE 29.3.1 Conducting a search using the Boolean operators AND and NOT.

asterisk (*). A single asterisk can represent one or more characters. If you search for *harvest**, you get pages with variations on the word, such as *harvests* and *harvester*.

Another common wildcard is the question mark (?). A single question mark represents a single character. If you search for *to?*, you get pages containing words such as *top* or *toy*.

ADVANCED SEARCH FORMS Many search engines and web pages feature special pages with tools for advanced searches. These pages often appear as forms; instead of constructing complex keyword searches yourself, you can use the form's text boxes and options to create very sophisticated searches. Nearly all such advanced search pages support Boolean operators, special symbols, and wildcards. You can also search for files by type, category, size, date, or other properties.

SEARCHING ON A WEB PAGE Many web pages, apps, and social media sites have a search box located near the top of the window that you can use to search that page. You can also use your browser's Find command to search the current page for specific information. In most browsers, press Ctrl + F to display a search box, or select the command on the Edit or Customize menu. Type the search term and press Enter to highlight each occurrence of the term on the page.

HASHTAG SEARCH All over social media, **hashtags (#)** are added to the beginning of key words or phrases to call attention to a topic or idea. You can use the hashtag system to search for related messages and subject threads that are identified using hashtags. You can conduct a hashtag search using the search feature on the social networking site, or in a standard search engine. There are also apps designed specifically for hashtag searches.

IC3✔ | **Know how to search the internet using keywords, hashtags, and other advanced methods.**

Saving the Information You Find

One of the most powerful uses of the web is to conduct research. Once you find the information you need, you may want to save it so you can refer to it again, or, if you have legal permission, use it in a report or presentation. You can use many standard application procedures to save, copy, and paste information from a web page.

- Use the File > Save As command in your browser to save the web page on your computer.

- If you only need some text, you can select it and then use the Copy and Paste commands or drag-and-drop to copy it into a word processing document.

- You can save an image by right-clicking it and using the Save Image As command, or you can drag it from the web page into an open document or folder on a storage device.

- You can also use the File > Print command in your browser to print a web page.

Evaluating Information on the Web

Whether you're doing schoolwork or pursuing your own interests, it is important to use critical thinking to evaluate the information you find on the web for accuracy before you use it. Many sites may cover the same information but you are responsible for determining which sites are more accurate.

One example is news. Before the internet, most news was covered by news organizations such as newspapers and television. With the internet's easy access and global reach, citizen journalists have emerged. Citizen journalists are not professional journalists, but instead are just everyday people who take the time to post articles, photos, and videos online on sites other than those run by major media outlets. These journalists can often give accurate reports of world events and fact-check the news in newspapers. However, they can also make things up. Unofficial reporting must be evaluated by the accuracy of the information given. When evaluating information on the web consider these criteria:

AUTHOR The author should be identified on the site. If you can't locate this information, there may be a reason the author chooses to remain anonymous. If you do locate a name, conduct a search to find out more about the person or organization responsible for the site's content.

LANGUAGE AND PURPOSE Always evaluate the content to determine if it is presented in a balanced manner and is supported by facts, or if it is biased or argumentative. This can help you determine the author's purpose. **Objective** information is balanced and fair. Information designed for a purpose is presented to achieve a desired result, such as to promote a particular viewpoint, to mislead, or to support preconceived assumptions. An **assumption** is something that is accepted as being true even if there is no factual proof.

Many people try to twist information or use it out of context in order to influence thinking. This type of misleading information is called **propaganda**. Even worse, digital misinformation is now everywhere online. **Digital misinformation** refers to actual content that has been deliberately changed so that it represents something very different from its original form. The ability to alter text, photos, videos, and sound makes it almost impossible to identify when content is real or just something that has been manipulated somehow, or presented out of context. The best way to determine if something is real or fake is to evaluate the source of the information and to seek out multiple viewpoints on the same topic.

CONTENT VALIDITY Does the author indicate the sources of the information? Do those sources appear to be respected, valid, and authoritative? Run a search on the references or other sources to see what you can learn. Determine if

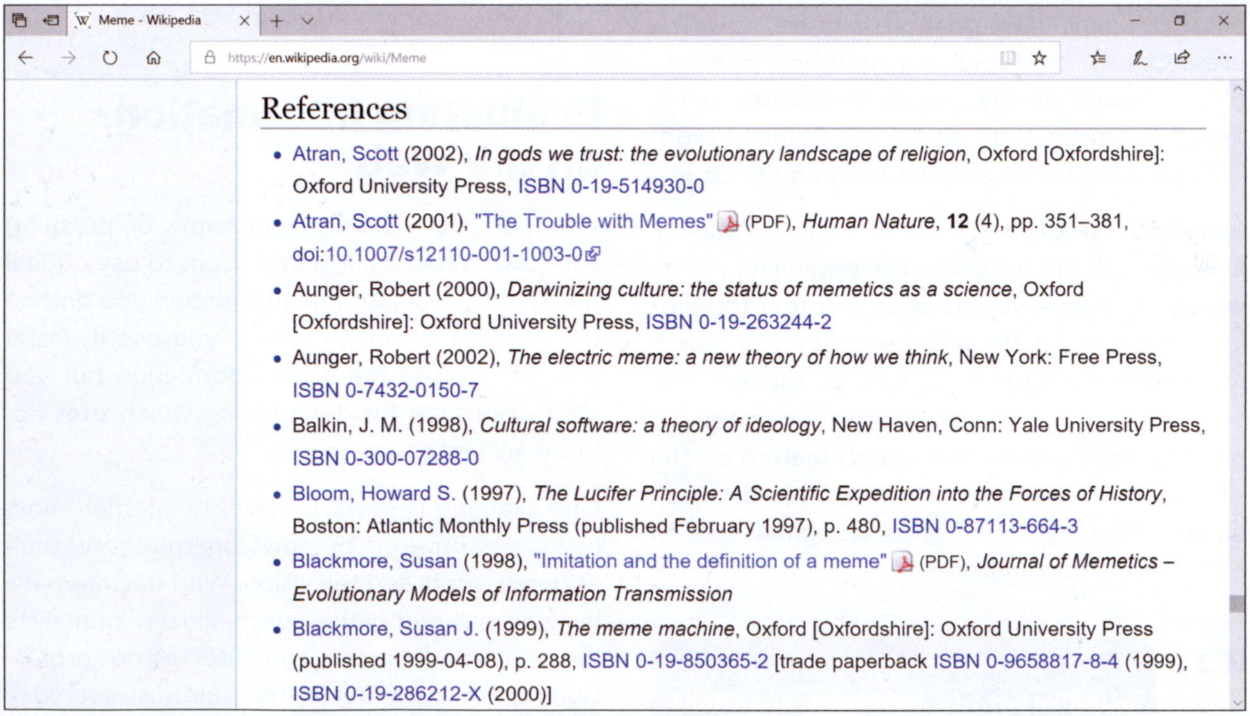

References

- Atran, Scott (2002), *In gods we trust: the evolutionary landscape of religion*, Oxford [Oxfordshire]: Oxford University Press, ISBN 0-19-514930-0
- Atran, Scott (2001), "The Trouble with Memes" 📄 (PDF), *Human Nature*, **12** (4), pp. 351–381, doi:10.1007/s12110-001-1003-0
- Aunger, Robert (2000), *Darwinizing culture: the status of memetics as a science*, Oxford [Oxfordshire]: Oxford University Press, ISBN 0-19-263244-2
- Aunger, Robert (2002), *The electric meme: a new theory of how we think*, New York: Free Press, ISBN 0-7432-0150-7
- Balkin, J. M. (1998), *Cultural software: a theory of ideology*, New Haven, Conn: Yale University Press, ISBN 0-300-07288-0
- Bloom, Howard S. (1997), *The Lucifer Principle: A Scientific Expedition into the Forces of History*, Boston: Atlantic Monthly Press (published February 1997), p. 480, ISBN 0-87113-664-3
- Blackmore, Susan (1998), "Imitation and the definition of a meme" 📄 (PDF), *Journal of Memetics – Evolutionary Models of Information Transmission*
- Blackmore, Susan J. (1999), *The meme machine*, Oxford [Oxfordshire]: Oxford University Press (published 1999-04-08), p. 288, ISBN 0-19-850365-2 [trade paperback ISBN 0-9658817-8-4 (1999), ISBN 0-19-286212-X (2000)]

MICROSOFT CORPORATION (SCREENSHOT); WIKEPEDIA (WEBSITE)

FIGURE 29.3.2 Look for references and links when evaluating an online article.

the information given is fact or just opinion. Also take note of spelling and grammatical errors. They can indicate that the author is not professional and is not concerned by publishing errors.

RELEVANCY Most search engines list results in the order of hits received. Thus, search engines sometimes place popular sites before relevant sites. Don't be fooled into thinking that a page is relevant simply because it appears at the top of a list of results. Also, commercial search engines allow advertising and sponsored links, which are paid for by companies hoping to get your business. Don't assume the first link on a results page is the best. It might just be from the company that paid the most.

IC3✓ Know how to research topics and evaluate the validity of online resources.

TECHNOLOGY@HOME

Home-computer users often search the web for information they need to finish a project or draw a conclusion.

THINK ABOUT IT!

For which of the reasons listed below might you or a family member conduct online research at home?

- research doctors in your community
- determine a reason for a rash
- find a babysitter
- learn to roast a turkey
- locate a local air-conditioning repair service
- compare product prices at local stores

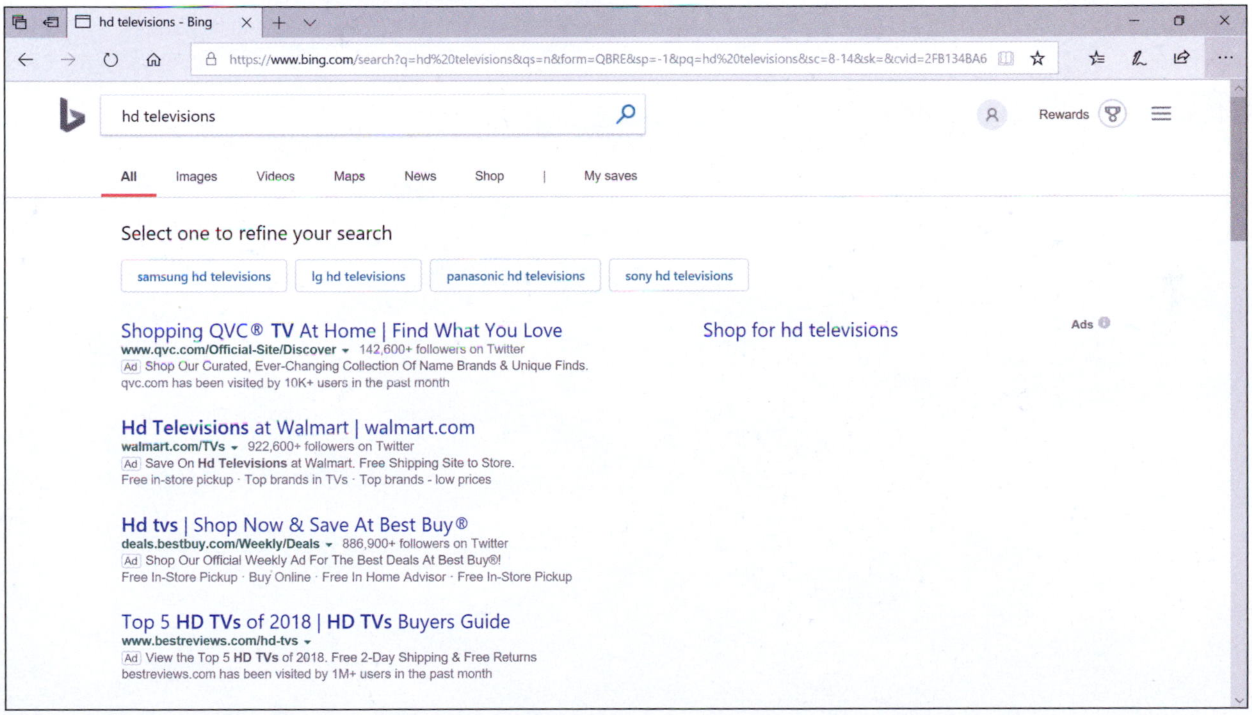

MICROSOFT CORPORATION

FIGURE 29.3.3 Searching for HD television returns a list that's almost all advertisements.

FIGURE 29-4

Conducting Business Online

OBJECTIVES

- Analyze online shopping.

- Compare and contrast online and traditional stores.

- Explain the process of securing online transactions.

AS YOU READ

ORGANIZE INFORMATION Use a chart to help you organize main ideas and details about e-commerce as you read.

TERMINOLOGY

- click-and-mortar store

- digital wallet

- encryption

- e-tailer

- Near Field Communication (NFC)

- secure electronic transaction

FIGURE 29-4 CONDUCTING BUSINESS ONLINE

Online Shopping

The web has become a global market. Most things are available for sale online, and most people shop online at least some of the time. Some of the reasons for the popularity of online shopping are convenience, the number of products, and the ability to compare features and price.

WHAT SELLS ONLINE Merchandise that sells successfully online ranges from clothing to jewelry, electronics to vacations, and furniture to homes and cars. Amazon.com is a successful, high-profile company that started out selling books and moved into many other product lines. The company tries out new products to see if they will sell well. If they don't, that link is shut down.

Most shopping websites offer search features and filters to help you locate items and check the latest prices. Buyers can also access a directory of online vendors, or **e-tailers**, organized by category.

CHALLENGES OF SELLING ONLINE Not every business can successfully sell products online, and some who do face unique challenges. For example, there are very few successful online knitting and yarn stores, because knitting and crochet enthusiasts like to see and feel the yarn before they buy it. Companies that sell perishable items, such as fresh fruit or baked goods,

must have a system in place that lets them deliver products quickly and safely. A book can travel for days without suffering any quality problems, but red velvet cupcakes must be delivered before they become stale. While grocery store consumers like to talk to the butcher or squeeze the melons to see if they are ripe, some online grocers have found a niche by tailoring their offerings to hurried consumers who don't want to take the time to shop in a traditional store. They also do well targeting people who may have a hard time getting to the store, or carrying items home, such as senior citizens and the disabled.

THE ONLINE SHOPPING EXPERIENCE Online shopping is similar to in-store shopping in many ways. When you are buying a pair of jeans in the mall, you are able to browse from store to store comparing the prices at different locations. You might also shop at a store your friends recommend. Online, you can browse many different retail websites to find the best deals. You can also read reviews to learn if a site is respectable and secure. Most sites have rating systems or customer comments that you can use to learn about other consumers' experiences with the seller. These reviews can help you make an educated decision on which websites to use. When you shop online, you are giving your personal and financial information to a third party. It is important to be savvy and responsible while shopping online.

Click-and-Mortar Versus Brick-and-Mortar

A traditional retail outlet is known as a brick-and-mortar store. Businesses that also sell products online are called **click-and-mortar stores**. Some online businesses have brick-and-mortar counterparts, while others only exist online.

ONLINE-ONLY STORES Online shopping sites like eBay and Etsy do not operate in traditional stores. This saves the company money on salaries and overhead, so prices can be lower.

KASPARS GRINVALDS/SHUTTERSTOCK

FIGURE 29.4.1 Shoes and clothing sell successfully online.

FIGURE 29-4 CONDUCTING BUSINESS ONLINE

Although online shopping is convenient, if you have a problem with your purchase, you cannot talk to someone about it face-to-face. If you want to return something, you will have to ship it back and sometimes pay for shipping costs, too.

CLICK-AND-MORTAR Online stores that also have brick-and-mortar locations have an advantage over companies that do business only online. If you are not satisfied with a product, you may be able to take it back to a store location for an immediate refund or replacement. You can speak with someone face-to-face and get the problem resolved right away. Some click-and-mortar stores also let you order online, and then pick products up at a store. This lets you see the item before you actually take it home.

Secure Electronic Transactions

One of the keys to the growth of e-commerce is **secure electronic transactions**. Originally a standard that relied on digital signatures, secure electronic transactions now refer to a variety of measures e-tailers use to secure online transactions so customers can bank and shop online. Without safeguards, private information can be misused, lost, or stolen, which could result in identity theft and fraud.

SECURE SITES A secure website uses **encryption** and authentication standards to protect online transaction information. Encryption converts the information into code so your personal information, including debit card numbers and personal identification numbers (PINs), are safe when you shop online. You can tell that you are viewing a secure website because the letters "https" display to the left of the website name in the Address bar of your browser. On an unsecured site, there is no "s." Also, a small lock icon displays in your web browser's status bar. You can select the lock icon to display details about the site's security system.

SECURE PAYMENT SERVICES As online shopping has increased in popularity, so have secure online payment services. These services are

LMILIAN/123RF.COM

REAL-WORLD TECH
E-PINIONATED ONLINE SHOPPERS

Word- of-mouth spreads fast on the internet. In fact, when it is unstoppable, we say that a product, a video, or phenomenon has gone "viral." One way to get reliable word-of-mouth opinions of products you want to purchase online is to go to epinions.com, which offers unbiased reviews of products and services. They are written by average people of all ages so you can research the latest electronic gadget or piece of clothing. Most e-commerce sites, however, offer customer reviews and a five-star rating system for all products. Check them out before you put items into your virtual shopping cart.

Which would be more likely to prompt you to write a product review online: a good or a bad product experience?

FIGURE 29-4 CONDUCTING BUSINESS ONLINE

linked to an account and credit card so you do not have to enter your data for each transaction. Sometimes called a **digital wallet**, these services may be associated with a specific site or may be accepted on multiple sites. To use a secure online payment service, you sign up directly and provide your payment information only once. The service keeps your records secure and handles payments to online vendors for you, using only secure methods.

PayPal®, which started out as a service for eBay buyers and sellers, is one of the most popular secure online payment services. It is used by millions of buyers and sellers on thousands of e-commerce sites. Users can designate an amount to be used for PayPal purchases, and, when you make an online purchase, the money is deducted directly from your bank account.

Apple has a payment service app called Apple Pay that lets you use an iPhone, iPad, or Apple Watch to pay in stores and online. Google Pay is another digital wallet app for use with mobile devices, as is Samsung Pay. When these devices are equipped with one of these apps and a wireless technology called **Near-field communication (NFC)**, you can use them to make a payment simply by placing your phone or watch near a contactless payment terminal.

NFC uses encryption and a special processor to ensure security. The fact that communication is limited to very short distances also adds security by reducing the risk of someone intercepting the exchange and stealing the data.

SHAO-CHUN WANG/123RF.COM

FIGURE 29.4.2 NFC makes it possible to pay with a smartphone or smartwatch.

TECHNOLOGY@SCHOOL

Schools, too, can place orders for merchandise online.

THINK ABOUT IT!

Which item(s) listed below do you think your school might order online?

- costumes for a school play
- school supplies
- textbooks
- electronic equipment
- athletic equipment

CONNECTIONS

THE ARTS Like stores, museums and art galleries may offer both an online and a virtual presence. Google's Art Project (googleartproject.com) offers visitors an online tour of seventeen of the world's most famous art museums. Visitors can view hundreds of works of art in the privacy of their own homes, tour the museums, and even create and share their own collection of masterpieces.

Chapter 29 Review

REVIEW THE TERMINOLOGY

DIRECTIONS Match each vocabulary term in the left column with the correct definition in the right column.

1. hypermedia system
2. dead link
3. WYSIWYG
4. e-tailer
5. encryption
6. exclusion operator
7. wildcard
8. web cache
9. web host

a. lets users retrieve audio and video online

b. symbol that stands for another character

c. sophisticated web page editing programs

d. temporarily stored web pages on a personal computer

e. someone who primarily uses the web to sell goods or services

f. connection to a document that no longer exists or has been moved

g. minus sign or the word NOT

h. coding used to protect data

i. a company that provides space on a web server for websites

USE THE TERMINOLOGY

DIRECTIONS Determine the correct choice for each of the following.

1. Which of the following indicates that a particular graphic on a web page is actually a link?

   a. The mouse pointer turns into a pointing hand.

   b. The mouse pointer changes color.

   c. The graphic moves across the screen.

   d. The graphic is underlined.

2. Which of the following can you use to upgrade a browser to add new features to an application?

   a. plug-in program

   b. cookie

   c. DHTML program

   d. WYSIWYG program

3. Which of the following is NOT an indicator that a website is an accurate source?

    a. author is identified on the site

    b. information is balanced and factual

    c. the link displays at the top of a list of search results

    d. spelling and grammar are correct

4. Which of the following might yield a list of pages with *travel*, *travels*, *traveled*, and *traveling*?

    a. wildcard

    b. database

    c. inclusion operator

    d. exclusion operator

5. What term is used to describe a traditional retail outlet that does not sell products online?

    a. online stores

    b. test stores

    c. brick-and-mortar store

    d. click-and-mortar store

6. Which of the following is a secure payment service that consumers can use to complete online transactions?

    a. eBay

    b. Secure Payment Service

    c. PayPal

    d. ASCII

THINK CRITICALLY

DIRECTIONS Answer the following questions.

1. What are some ways to preserve a website or its elements for you to use for research or other purposes? Give specific examples.

2. Why is it not always a good idea to take the "top hit" of a search result at its word?

3. What are several ways to find information quickly on the web?

4. Identify at least six design elements, and explain how their use can help you create an effective web page.

5. Compare and contrast writing HTML with a text editor and developing a web page using a GUI editor.

EXTEND YOUR KNOWLEDGE

DIRECTIONS Choose and complete one of the following projects.

1. Identify a click-and-mortar store and explore the differences in how they sell products online vs. in a storefront building. Do they sell the same merchandise? Do they use the same pricing? What are the advantages and disadvantages for the company? For the customer? Write your findings in a report, and share it with a partner or with the class.

2. With your teacher's permission, with a partner, try using several web browsers. Look for and test features such as opening and closing multiple tabs, History, and the Bookmarks or Favorites list. Explore customization options such as how to enable or disable multiple tabs, plugins, and add-ons. Discuss the advantages, disadvantages, and features of each. Then, create and complete a Venn diagram to summarize your preferences.

3. With a partner or small group, plan, design, develop, and publish a website for a business. Look at available templates and use storyboarding techniques to help with the planning, navigation, and design. Select the tools you will use to develop the site. For example, will you use HTML, DHTML, or XML editors? Will you need to convert from one to another? When you are ready, select an available template to use to create the site. Insert text, graphics, and links. Use the principles of design and color theory to make sure the pages in the website are consistent, appealing, and readable. Modify the website template to achieve your design goals, if necessary. Optimize, edit, and test the pages, and then publish the website using FTP, or as instructed by your teacher.

IC3 PREP

1. For each line below, select whether the statement is True or False.

   a. All entries in a list of breadcrumbs are links that will take you to their respective pages when selected.

   b. Each link in a breadcrumb list is usually separated by a dash symbol.

   c. Breadcrumbs display the site you are on, as well as the pages you navigated through to get there.

   d. Breadcrumbs are usually listed near the top of the browser window.

2. Generally, hitting the Back button in a browser loads the previous page more quickly than the first time you loaded it. What causes this to be the case?

   a. Webmasters constantly optimize their pages to achieve quicker load times.

   b. Recently viewed sites are temporarily stored locally in a web cache, which allow for fast reloads.

   c. Machines learning algorithms in the cloud use your browsing history to anticipate your next page load.

   d. Recently viewed sites are stored in the computer's RAM.

3. What are some downsides to the use of a web cache? (Select all that apply.)

   a. A web cache uses local storage, which takes up space on your computer.

   b. A web cache cannot be cleared.

   c. Your cache can be used to identify and track you online.

   d. The more items that are stored in the cache, the slower your system will run.

4. Entering chili+dog into a search term makes use of which Boolean operator?

   a. inclusion

   c. proximity

   b. exclusion

   d. exact phrase

5. A symbol (such as an asterisk or question mark) that stands in for other characters in search terms is known as a _____.

   a. bool

   c. indicator

   b. hashtag

   d. wildcard

6. You are looking for specific information on a subject, and you know what you're searching for is somewhere on one particular page. How can you quickly find this information? (Select all that apply.)

   a. Use a built-in search bar on the page itself, if one exists.

   b. Enter your search terms and the name of the website into your search or address bar in your browser window.

   c. Use Ctrl+F to open a search dialog on the web page.

   d. Read the page slowly and carefully until you find what you are looking for.

7. What are some true points regarding the rise of citizen journalists on the web? (Select all that apply.)

   a. It is easier to spread misinformation or propaganda.

   b. Citizen journalists are overwhelmingly better than traditional news anchors.

   c. Mainstream news is able to be fact-checked by eyewitnesses.

   d. News of events can potentially reach an audience much faster.

8. What are some things that might indicate an article on the web may not be trustworthy? (Select all that apply.)

   a. multiple cited sources from respected authors

   b. multiple spelling errors

   c. objectivism

   d. an inability to find the author's name on the work

IC3 PROCEDURES

SEARCHING WITH KEYWORDS

1. Open the search engine.

2. In the Search box, type as specific a keyword as possible to help focus the search.

USING AN EXACT PHRASE SEARCH

1. Open the search engine.

2. In the Search box, type the search string enclosed in quotation marks to return only those pages with an exact match.

SEARCHING WITH BOOLEAN OPERATORS

■ Use the AND operator to find pages that include more than one search term; for example, type **dogs AND terriers** to find pages that contain both "dogs" and "terriers."

■ Use the OR operator to find pages that include one search term or another; for example, type **dogs OR terriers** to find pages that contain either of the terms.

■ Use the NOT operator to find pages that contain one search term but exclude other terms; for example, type **Harvard NOT University** to find pages that contain the word "Harvard," but not the word "University."

SEARCHING WITH WILDCARD CHARACTERS

- Use the asterisk (*) wildcard character to substitute for any number of characters.
- Use the question mark (?) wildcard character to substitute for a single character.

SEARCHING USING NATURAL LANGUAGE

In the search box, type a question or phrase describing what you are searching for; for example, type **conducting effective internet searches** to return pages that contain information on the topic.

SEARCHING USING SUBJECT DIRECTORIES

In the Address bar, type the address of the subject directory you want to search. If you do not know the web address, use a search engine to find a subject directory.

USING COMMON SEARCH OPTIONS TO NARROW A SEARCH

1. On a page that offers advanced search tools, select the **Advanced Search** link.
2. Select the options to narrow your search.
3. Select **Search**.

Additional Web Procedures

COPYING DATA FROM A WEB PAGE

Copying Text

1. Display the web page.
2. Select the text you want to copy.
3. Press **Ctrl + C**.
4. Click in the file where you want to paste the copied text.
5. Press **Ctrl + V**.

Copying Graphics

1. Display the web page.
2. Right-click the graphic you want to copy.
3. On the shortcut menu, select **Copy**.
4. Click in the file where you want to paste the graphic.
5. Press **Ctrl + V**.

PRINTING A WEB PAGE

1. Display the web page.
2. Press **Ctrl + P**.
3. In the Print dialog box, select the printing options as desired.
4. Select **Print**.

DOWNLOADING A FILE FROM THE INTERNET

1. Display the web page from which you want to download the file.
2. Select the file to download and then select the page's **Download** button ⬇.

   You may see a message box asking you to accept a service agreement concerning the download.
3. Follow the prompts to download the file, and install, if necessary.

   The file is stored in your default Downloads folder.

CHAPTER 30

Personal Communications Basics

STAYING IN TOUCH

How do you contact friends after school, on weekends, or during school vacations? Chances are you use telecommunications devices and software to stay in touch and keep up-to-date.

Computer technology makes it possible to stay connected with people who are close by or far away. You can chat, text, email, and even talk face-to-face. In today's wired and wireless world, there are many options to keep you communicating.

Using Email

OBJECTIVES

- Describe email systems.
- Identify the purpose of a unique identifier.
- Explain the parts of an email address.
- Identify the key components of an email message.
- Describe the process of creating, sending, and replying to messages.

AS YOU READ

SEQUENCE INFORMATION Use a sequence chart as you read to help you outline the process of receiving a message and responding to it.

TERMINOLOGY

- alias
- attachment
- email
- email body
- email client
- email header
- email server
- forward
- mailbox name
- reply
- server address
- thread

What Is Email?

Electronic mail, or **email**, allows people to send an unlimited number of messages quickly and easily to anyone with an email address. Messages sent through email can be casual, like a letter to a friend, or formal, like a memo for a business. It is also less expensive than standard mail and voice, fax, and telephone messages. To use email, all you need is a computing device with internet access, email software, and an email account.

Email also lets you attach files to a message. Any file sent along with an email message is called an **attachment**. Common attachments include word-processing documents, spreadsheets, photos, artwork, and movies.

Some email programs, like Microsoft Outlook, include features for managing a calendar and contact list, as well as taking notes and scheduling tasks.

Understanding Email Addresses

Like a computer on a network, every communication service user must have a unique identifier, usually called a username. The system uses the identifier to differentiate one user from another in order to deliver services, such as mail. For email, the identifier is the email address.

All email addresses have two parts. The **mailbox name** is the part of the address before the "at" symbol (@) that identifies the user. The **server address** follows the symbol. It gives the domain name of the email server where the mailbox is stored. An **email server** is a computer, operated

Mailbox name

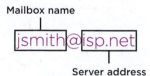

Server address

FIGURE 30.1.1 Every email address has two basic parts—a mailbox name and a server address.

by your internet service provider (ISP), that accepts and delivers incoming messages and sends outgoing messages.

Sending and Receiving Email

An **email client** is a program that you use to create, send, receive, and manage email messages. You may get the program from your ISP, as part of a productivity suite, or you may purchase one. For example, Microsoft Outlook is the email client that comes with the Microsoft Office productivity suite. There are also web-based email clients, such as Google's Gmail and Microsoft's Outlook.com.

COMPOSING EMAIL To compose a new message, you use the email client's command for creating—or composing—a new message. The client displays a form for you to complete. The form includes two main parts—the **email header**, which includes places for entering the recipient(s) and the subject, and the **email body**, which is where you type the message. The header is important because it identifies the particular routing information for the message, including the address of the person or people the message is going to and who is sending it. It is important to complete the header correctly so the message can be delivered.

IC3✔ | **Understand email etiquette: header.**

Start by entering the recipient's email address in the To: line of the message form. Depending on your email client's features, you may select someone's name from an address book, or type the email address. For example, Chris Rodriguez have the email address chris_rodriguez@isp.net or cjr615@isp.net. Instead of typing a complete address, you may be able to type an alias, or select it from a list. An **alias** is an easy-to-remember nickname for the recipient, such as Chris_R.

To send a copy of the message to other recipients, you can enter them in the To: field, separating each address with a semicolon, or add them in the Cc: line. Cc stands for *carbon copy*. To send a copy of the message without the recipient's email address appearing in the To: or Cc: line, enter it in the Bcc: line. Bcc stands for *blind carbon copy*. Recipients whose addresses are in the To: or Cc: line are not able to see whose address is in the Bcc: line when they open the message.

IC3✔ **Understand email etiquette: Cc vs. Bcc.**

Next, fill in the Subject line. The Subject line gives the recipient an idea of the message's content and may help the recipient decide whether to open it or delete it. Some email clients will not accept messages with blank Subject lines.

When the header is complete, type the message in the email body. Proofread the message for errors and make corrections. You can add an attachment by selecting the Attach file command and then selecting the file you want to attach. Finally, click Send. The message moves to your Outbox folder where it remains until the system sends it through the internet to the recipient's email server.

RECEIVING EMAIL When you receive an email message, it displays in your Inbox folder. Select the folder to display the Message list. Depending on the way you have your email software set, you may see just the header information, a few lines of the body text, or the entire message may display in a Reading or Preview pane. Open the message to view it in a separate window.

Replying to and Forwarding Email

REPLYING TO EMAIL You can **reply**, or respond, to the person who sent a message by selecting the Reply command. You can also select Reply All, which responds to all the people who received the original message. It is always a good idea to check the recipients when you

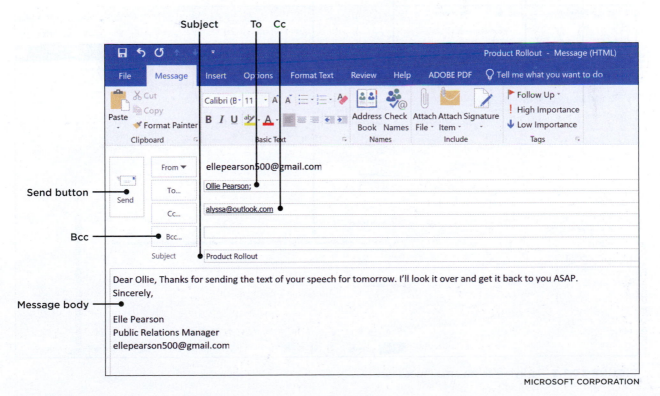

MICROSOFT CORPORATION

FIGURE 30.1.2 Composing an email message with Outlook 2016.

Reply All to make sure you really want everyone to receive your response.

Several things occur when you choose the Reply command:

- Your program displays a reply form with the original sender's address entered in the To: field.

- The subject field on the form usually includes the abbreviation *Re:* to the left of the subject text. *Re* stands for *regarding*.

- The original message may be included in the body of the reply, so the recipient can read the entire message **thread**, or conversation. Most email programs give you the option of excluding the original text from your reply, or to identify it as the original message using formatting. For example, you can indent it or change the color of the text.

- You can type your reply above or below the original text, and then click Send.

IC3✔ Understand email etiquette: Reply vs. Reply All.

FORWARDING EMAIL When you receive a message, you can **forward** it, which means pass it along to someone else. The Subject line of a forwarded email may include the abbreviation *Fw:* to the left of the subject text to show that the message has been forwarded. You can add comments in the body of the message above the original message text.

Before you send any email, it's good to remember that your email can easily be forwarded to others. Don't write anything that you don't want other people to see!

IC3✔ Understand email etiquette: Forward.

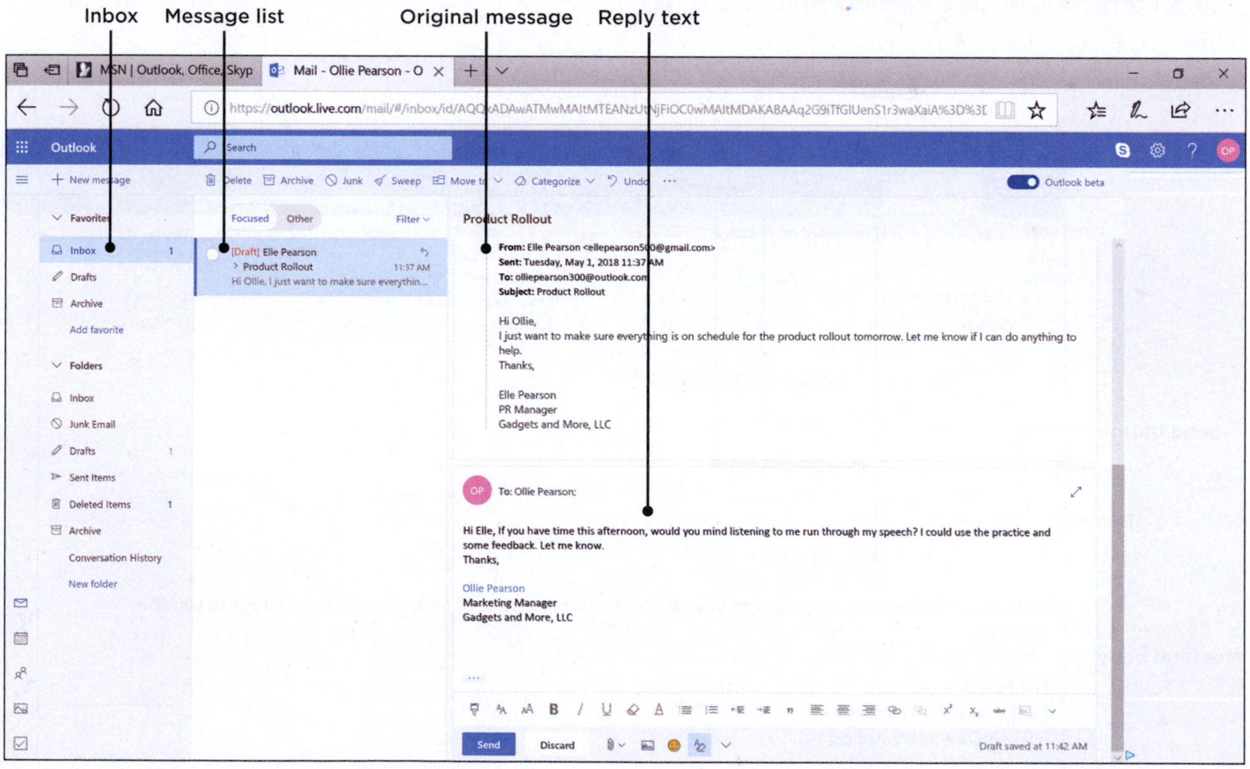

Inbox   Message list   Original message   Reply text

MICROSOFT CORPORATION

FIGURE 30.1.3 Replying to an email message.

CONFIGURE MESSAGE OPTIONS Most email programs let you set delivery options before sending a message. Typical delivery options include selecting when you want a message to send, specifying the level of importance or sensitivity, setting security options such as encryption, and requesting a confirmation that a message has been opened or read.

TECHNOLOGY@HOME

Netiquette is a term that describes polite online behavior.

THINK ABOUT IT!

Which of the following online rules help make email more useful?

- Type a lengthy description in the Subject line.
- Don't write in all caps.
- Vary fonts and type sizes in the message.
- Check and correct spelling.
- Edit the original message so only the part you are answering appears in your reply.
- Don't write in anger.
- Be brief, but be polite.
- Don't attach very large files.
- Reply promptly.

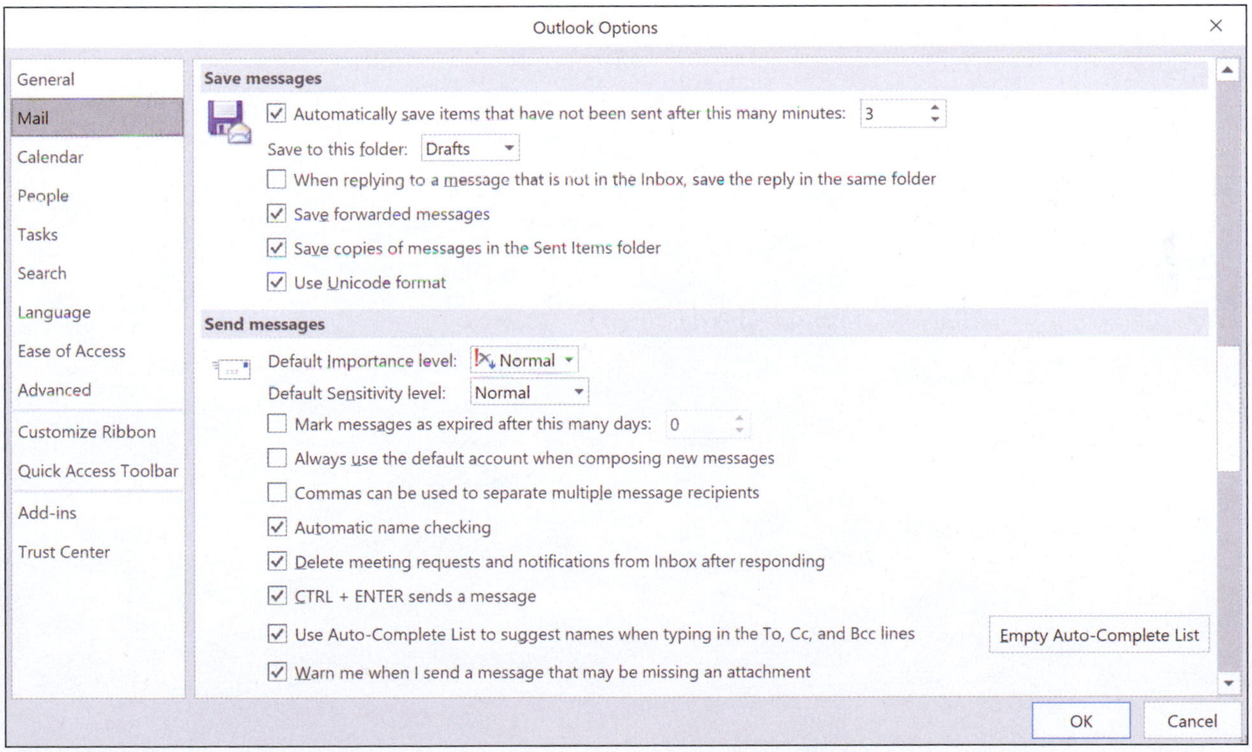

MICROSOFT CORPORATION

FIGURE 30.1.4 Options for sending and receiving email in the Outlook Options dialog box.

Avoiding Email Problems

OBJECTIVES

- Examine problems related to email.
- Define bounce messages and spam.
- Explain the use of digital signatures with email.

AS YOU READ

COMPARE AND CONTRAST Use a Venn diagram as you read to help you compare and contrast various email problems.

TERMINOLOGY

- bounce message
- digital signature
- junk mail
- spam

Failed Email

It is easy to send email messages, but it is also easy to make mistakes while doing it. What happens when you make a mistake?

USING THE WRONG ADDRESS One of the most common email mistakes is entering an incorrect address in the To: field. When you do this, one of two things will happen:

- Your message will go to the wrong person if the incorrect address is someone else's valid address. Unless that person replies, you may never know what happened to your message.

- The email server will return the email to you with a bounce message.

A **bounce message** is a notice from the email server telling you that your message could not be delivered. Bounce messages are often the result of an incorrect email address. You might also receive one if a message is not delivered because the recipient's mailbox is full. This happens because many ISPs limit the amount of server space available for each user's messages.

You sometimes see "MAILER-DAEMON@..." as the "From" address of a bounce message. Never reply to a bounce message. While most are valid, some are phishing messages used by scammers trying to collect personal information.

AVOIDING BOUNCE MESSAGES Check the address you enter in the message To: field before sending a message to make sure you have entered it correctly. Also, if you change your email address, be sure to notify people. If the old address no longer exists, your friends, family, and co-workers will receive a bounce message; if it does exist, their messages will sit in your unused Inbox and you will never receive them.

> ## TECHNOLOGY@WORK
>
> Bounce messages are a part of email use. But what should you do when you get one?

> ## THINK ABOUT IT!
>
> Suppose you email the school photographer to find out whether your class pictures are ready. However, you get a bounce message. Which actions listed below might then be helpful?
>
> - Retrieve the message from your Sent Items folder and check your typing.
> - Confirm the email address of the photographer.
> - Resend the message to the same address.
> - Send a reply to the bounce message asking for help.

Junk Email or Spam

Many email users complain about the flood of **spam** or **junk mail**. Spam and junk mail refers to any unwanted messages and advertisements. Like physical junk mail, spam usually tries to sell something to the recipient.

Sometimes you unknowingly sign up to receive the spam delivered to your Inbox. When you make an online purchase, you might agree to accept emails from the company about future sales. You might have signed up for email newsletters at many websites, or joined a group that lets you exchange messages about a topic. All of these actions are likely to result in spam. You might even be responsible for sending spam, if you actively forward unwanted mail to others.

Spam can cause several problems:

- The recipient wastes time reviewing and deleting spam.

- Spam clogs email servers, slowing internet traffic.

- Spam often contains incorrect or misleading information.

- Spam may contain links that install viruses or other malware on your computer.

IC3✔ **Understand email etiquette: spam and junk mail.**

BLOCKING UNWANTED EMAIL You can mark unwanted messages as junk or spam so your program automatically delivers them to the Junk or Spam folder instead of your Inbox. You can unsubscribe from email newsletters by selecting the "unsubscribe" link at the bottom of the page in tiny print. Yet, stopping spam from reaching email servers and clients is an ongoing battle. Some servers use technology to block "spammers." Most email clients provide special spam filters that users can configure to automatically delete junk mail. It is still worthwhile to check your spam folder regularly, however, as sometimes personal or important email can be mistakenly re-routed there.

IC3✔ **Understand email history and management: spam and junk mail.**

Email Risks

Because you cannot see who is actually sending you a message, email is often used to commit crimes. Someone can send you a message

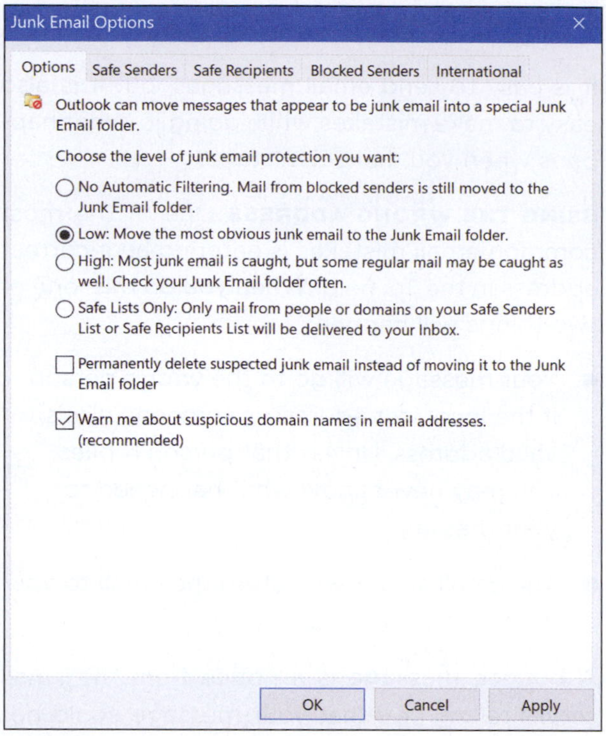

FIGURE 30.2.1 Setting Junk Email Options in Microsoft Outlook.

MICROSOFT CORPORATION

and pretend it is from someone else. The message could contain a virus or request personal information. If you trust the person or organization you believe sent the message, you open it or reply.

USING DIGITAL SIGNATURES One way to secure email messages is by using a **digital signature**—an electronic identifier which verifies that the message was created and sent by the person whose name appears in the From: field. Most email programs support digital signatures, which are purchased from a vendor, such as Symantec's VeriSign Authentication Services. Once the certificate is installed on your computer, you can use it to "sign" any message you send by embedding the certificate in the message. The signature proves that the message comes from you.

Remote Communications Tools

OBJECTIVES

- Compare and contrast methods of online conferencing.

- Explain tools used for telecommuting.

- Summarize the goals of web-based training.

- Explain distance learning.

AS YOU READ

ORGANIZE INFORMATION Use an outline as you read to help you organize information about remote communications tools.

TERMINOLOGY

- blended learning

- chat

- chat room

- Learning Management Systems (LMS)

- online conference

- screen sharing

- telecommute

- teleconference

- telepresence

- videoconference

- web-based training

- Voice over Internet Protocol (VoIP)

Online Conferencing

While the use of email is convenient, there are times when you need to speak with others directly. If you just need to speak to one person, you might place a direct phone call. If you need to have more than one other person on the call, you could use a conference call. Many phones have features that let you join multiple people into one telephone call just by pressing a button.

IC3✔ **Understand and identify online conference offerings: phone conferencing.**

In-person meetings and telephone calls are ideal, but in today's world people are spread over wide areas. Scheduling a call or a meeting can be difficult and expensive. Luckily, telecommunications provide lots of options for setting up an **online conference**, which is a virtual meeting using web-based software or apps. Options include teleconferences, videoconferences, and chat rooms.

Online conferences help companies in several ways:

- They save time and money.

- They are similar to in-person meetings.

- They are convenient.

- They allow all participants to communicate in real time.

FIGURE 30.3.1 Sometimes a telephone call is the best way to communicate with someone one-on-one.

TELECONFERENCE A **teleconference** is an online meeting of two or more people. A teleconference allows participants to communicate in real time, just as they would if they were sitting together in the same room. In a typical real-time teleconference, each participant sits at a computer. They see messages typed by the other participants and type responses for the others to see immediately. Most teleconferences include voice communication as well, using either a telephone call-in number or a microphone built into the computer.

There are apps and online services that enable teleconferencing, such as GoToMeeting and Cisco Webex. Usually, one person sets up the meeting and acts as the leader, or presenter. The leader invites others by sending a link. Participants click the link to join the meeting. There may be a telephone number to call for voice communication.

VIDEOCONFERENCE A **videoconference** is a teleconference that includes video as well as text or audio. Videoconferences require equipment such as cameras, a fast network connection, a microphone, and video screens or computer monitors. A web-based videoconference allows participants to connect to a web server, identify themselves, and then join the meeting. Google Hangouts, Skype, and FaceTime are all apps that support web-based videoconferencing, and can be run from any computing device.

IC3✔ **Understand and identify online conference offerings: videoconferencing.**

Videoconferences can serve many purposes. Depending on the goal, they are set up in one of three delivery methods:

- One-to-one videoconferences allow two people to see and talk to each other on their computers. This type of conference is easy to set up using **Voice over Internet Protocol (VoIP)**, which is technology that enables the delivery of voice and multimedia over the internet. Apps such as Skype, FaceTime, and Google Hangouts use VoIP so you can make voice or video calls using a smartphone, tablet, or computer.

- One-to-many videoconferences are similar to watching television programs. Many people can watch the presentation, but usually only one person speaks to the group. The conference can be accessed by each individual on their own device, or projected on a large monitor in a shared room.

- Many-to-many videoconferences are like a face-to-face meeting. Any of the participants can speak and be seen and heard at any time in the conversation. Like a one-to-many, participants may be working on their own devices, or some may be in one room using a shared monitor.

FIGURE 30.3.2 A many-to-many videoconference is like a face-to-face meeting, except some participants are in remote locations.

SCREEN SHARING An important feature of most videoconferences and teleconferences is the ability to share one's screen. **Screen sharing** is when you let others see what is displayed on your screen in real time. Most web-based video- and teleconferences allow screen sharing, which means everyone who logs in can view the presenter's screen. In this way, the presenter can demonstrate actions instead of just talking about them. The presenter can also pass control to anyone else on the call. This makes it possible to deliver a presentation, review a report, or demonstrate a product to a group of people who are not all in the same location. It can be used for training, marketing, and collaborating.

CHAT A real-time teleconference in which participants discuss chosen topics by typing is called a **chat**. Typed messages display in a window or pane in real time, so all participants can read them and respond. A chat is possible using a chat app, or chat platform technology. The app, or platform, provides the interface and organizes the topics. The space where the chat messages or threads display may be called a **chat room**. Google's Hangouts Chat is a chat platform for business users.

Chat platforms offer a variety of features. Most support both private and public chats. They usually use hashtags to identify topics and key points, so users can use the hashtags to find, join, and follow the chats that interest them. Other features may include drag-and-drop file sharing, direct messaging, and video chats.

Many businesses use chat apps so that teams of employees can communicate quickly and easily. They also use them to communicate with customers. Many websites include a chat tool so customers can contact customer support without waiting for an email or telephone response. Online learning platforms might include a chat feature for real-time discussion groups.

REAL-WORLD TECH
GETTING CAREER ADVICE ONLINE

JIANGHAISTUDIO/SHUTTERSTOCK

It's not too early to start exploring careers and find out what conduct, dress, and behaviors are acceptable in the workplace. You can find career advice online in news feeds, blogs, and other publications. Some might be geared toward specific careers and some to general career advice, like how to be a good team member, solve problems, or get organized.

Search for career question-and-answer forums available online. Look for ones that offer general advice on how to dress and behave in the workplace. Remember, as with all online resources, be cautious about where you send email and any information you share.

Not all chats are for conducting business. Amazon's live-streaming video platform, Twitch, includes a streaming chat on the right-hand side of the app window so users can discuss the current stream. It also has a chat room feature that allows subscribers to discuss specific topics, even when there is no video streaming.

Unlike business chats where the participants know each other, participants in chats on a platform such as Twitch may be strangers. Be careful about revealing personal or confidential information in a chat. You do not know how someone might use details from your conversation without your knowledge or permission.

IC3✔ **Know how to use chat platforms.**

Working from a Distance

Thanks to telecommunications, in 2018 nearly 4 million employees worldwide were able to telecommute instead of traveling to an office every day. **Telecommute** means to work from a remote location while accessing office resources using a network. Employees can work from a home office, a hotel room, or anywhere there is an internet connection. The trend to work remotely is growing, and some businesses have found it possible to succeed without a centralized office at all.

Telecommuting might sound ideal, but the challenges include staying up-to-date with co-workers and teammates, keeping project schedules on track, and being able to access data and applications when you need them. There are numerous remote workforce tools available to make telecommuting a success, including the following basic tools:

■ A secure reliable Wi-Fi connection

■ A chat platform, such as Google's Hangouts Chat, or Slack

■ An online meeting app with video chat, such as Google Hangouts, GoToMeeting, or Join.me

■ Cloud storage with sharing features, such as Google Drive, Dropbox, or Microsoft OneDrive

■ Calendar sharing for scheduling, such as those found in Outlook or Google Calendar

Other remote workforce tools that make the ability to work from anywhere possible include project management apps, a password manager, and a to-do list app.

IC3✔ **Know basic remote workforce tools.**

Learning from a Distance

Distance learning makes use of **telepresence** to let you to learn anytime, anywhere—as long as you are on a device connected to the internet. Telepresence refers to any technology that gives the user the feeling they are physically present in one location when they are actually somewhere else. Virtual classrooms are one such tool for online learning.

A **Learning Management System (LMS)** is an application designed for education that can manage records, report grades, and deliver subject matter content. You can complete high school courses or even earn a complete college degree online. Many schools offer classes via distance learning, and they use a variety of technologies. In many cases, the instructor provides lectures and displays slides through a one-to-many videoconference, which students can watch on their home computers. Tests and quizzes can be completed online, and students can work together via teleconference, instant messaging, and email.

WEB-BASED TRAINING One method of distance learning is **web-based training**. Schools, colleges, and businesses are using the speed and technology of the internet to deliver educational programs and activities. This method of education offers anytime, anywhere learning, as long as you have an internet connection.

BLENDED LEARNING Some students find the best method of learning combines traditional classroom education with web-based education. **Blended learning** offers opportunities for students to interact with others face-to-face and at a distance. Courses may include projects, discussion groups and chats, multimedia, and the opportunity to earn points and prizes by participating in and completing activities.

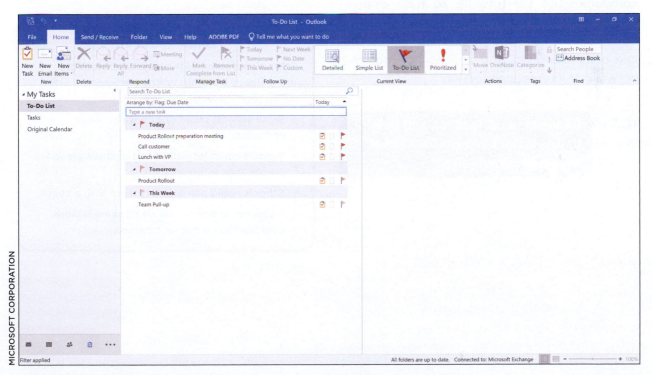

MICROSOFT CORPORATION

FIGURE 30.3.3 A to-do list and a calendar are useful tools for remote workers.

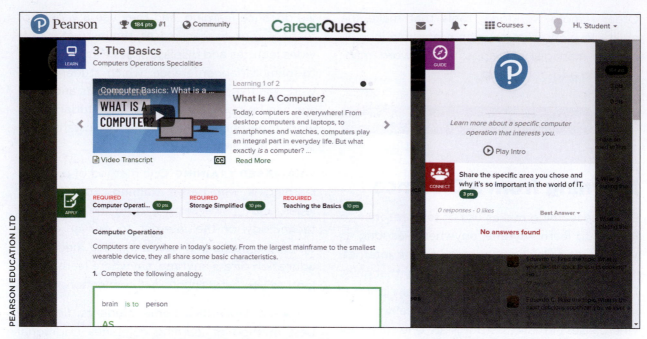

FIGURE 30.3.4 Online learning platforms engage students with multimedia, interactive activities, and discussions.

COMPUTER-BASED TRAINING Online instruction is one form of computer-based training, or CBT. But one of the oldest methods for delivering computer-based training—the CD—remains popular among teachers and students. Many companies use CD tutorials to train employees on policies, products, and procedures. The advantage of this type of CBT is that the user can carry it around, and it does not require a network or internet connection.

IC3 ✔ **Understand options for, and how to use, distant/remote/individual learning technologies.**

TECHNOLOGY@SCHOOL

Many students and teachers use distance learning.

THINK ABOUT IT!

Think about some of the ways schools might use distance learning. Which statement(s) listed below identify a sensible use?

- Small schools could offer a wider range of courses.
- Schools could let individuals or small groups pursue their interests.
- Schools could pair a sports team with a coach.
- A teacher in one school could share lessons with teachers on other campuses.

Chapter 30 Review

REVIEW THE TERMINOLOGY

DIRECTIONS Match each vocabulary term in the left column with the correct definition in the right column.

1. attachment
2. mailbox name
3. email client
4. alias
5. email server
6. bounce message
7. spam
8. digital signature
9. teleconference
10. videoconference

a. part of an email address

b. a meeting that provides audio and visual contact for people in different locations

c. a notice that email could not be delivered

d. junk email

e. anything sent with an email

f. a meeting via computers and a network or the internet, which lets participants talk or exchange text messages

g. an electronic identifier used to verify the identity of an email sender

h. an ISP computer that accepts, sends, and delivers email messages

i. software that lets you create, send, receive, and manage email messages

j. nickname by which an email user is known

USE THE TERMINOLOGY

DIRECTIONS Complete each sentence with information from the chapter.

1. In an email address, the symbol @ represents the word _____.

2. The _____ is an internet service provider's computer that routes email.

3. In an email message form, the _____ field identifies people other than the main recipient who should receive the message when it is sent.

4. When you _____ an email message you have received, you send it to another person.

5. You will not get a bounce message if you enter an incorrect but _____ address.

6. Some email clients have _____ that you can configure to delete unwanted email.

7. Sometimes, _____ can clog email servers, slowing internet traffic.

8. Online conferences save money because people don't have to _____ to attend a meeting.

9. One-to-one _____ allow two people to see and talk to each other on their computers.

10. Many schools now offer classes through the internet, a practice known as _____.

THINK CRITICALLY

DIRECTIONS Answer the following questions.

1. What is screen sharing, and what are some ways in which it is useful? Give some examples.

2. If you were part of a business considering telecommuting for your employees, what are some tools you would want to be sure your employees had to achieve success and productivity? Give some examples.

3. What advantages do email, teleconferences, and videoconferences offer to workgroups in different locations?

4. What is one way to avoid receiving a bounce message?

5. Could distance learning make use of a videoconference? How?

EXTEND YOUR KNOWLEDGE

DIRECTIONS Choose and complete one of the following projects.

1. In small groups, brainstorm the advantages and disadvantages of face-to-face communications, traditional letters, email, telephone calls, teleconferencing, and videoconferencing. Then, create a list of situations for which each of these media might be the most appropriate communications choice.

2. Working with a partner or small group, use the Calendar feature in your email program to schedule a meeting and send a meeting request to your partner or group members. Follow up the meeting request with an email that includes an attachment of an agenda in a document. When you receive the email from someone else, save the attachment and open it in a word-processing program.

IC3 PREP

1. Which of the following are part of an email header? (Select all that apply.)

   a. domain

   b. email address(es) to which the email will be sent

   c. email message

   d. subject line

2. Where should an email address be added when you would not like others in an email chain to know that address is receiving a copy of the thread?

   a. subject line

   b. To: line

   c. Bcc: line

   d. Cc: line

3. What is a valid method of sending an email to more than one person at once? (Select all that apply.)

  a. Enter multiple email addresses in the To: line, separated by semicolons.

  b. Add email addresses to the To: and Cc: Fields.

  c. Add email addresses to the top of the email body.

  d. Add email addresses to the To: and Bcc: fields.

4. When should you use Reply instead of Reply All in a group email thread? (Select all that apply.)

  a. You have a question for the message sender that does not concern the others.

  b. You want to share your thoughts with everyone in the thread.

  c. You want to share your thoughts with the message sender first, before sharing them with the others.

  d. You have a question for everyone in the thread.

5. What does it mean when you receive a message with Fw: in the subject line?

  a. The sender forwarded the message from someone else.

  b. The message is important.

  c. The email is a group message.

  d. The message is a reply to one you sent.

6. What is a true statement about spam email? (Select all that apply.)

  a. Spam is impossible to block.

  b. Spam clogs email servers, slowing internet traffic.

  c. Spam often contains incorrect or misleading information.

  d. Spam is always sent by robots.

  e. Spam may contain links that install viruses or other malware on your computer.

7. Why is it good to check your Spam folder periodically? (Select all that apply.)

  a. Spam filters can flag legitimate emails as spam.

  b. If you receive newsletters you do not want, you can unsubscribe so you no longer receive them.

  c. There is no reason to ever check your Spam folder.

  d. Newsletters typically are marked as spam.

8. Which statement describes a telephone conference. (Select all that apply.)

  a. It occurs in real time.

  b. It can only include two people.

  c. It requires VoIP.

  d. It requires typing.

9. Which of the following is NOT a web-based videoconferencing app?

  a. Skype

  b. Discord

  c. Google Hangouts

  d. FaceTime

10. For each line below, select whether the statement is True or False.

  a. VoIP enables the delivery of voice and multimedia over the internet.

  b. Voice and video calls are only available through expensive equipment.

  c. In a many-to-many VoIP conference, only two people are allowed to join.

  d. One-to-many videoconferences are similar to watching television programs.

11. What is screen sharing?

    a. When two users exchange screen names, or usernames, on an internet forum.

    b. When a user posts a screenshot of their computer desktop for other users to admire.

    c. When a user lets others see what is displayed on their screen in real time.

    d. When two people use the same monitor at the same time.

12. For each line below, select whether the statement is True or False.

    a. In a chat room, topics can be identified by hashtags.

    b. Chat rooms can be private or public.

    c. Chat is used exclusively for business.

    d. In a chat room, everyone knows who everyone else is.

13. Which of the following is NOT a common tool for successful telecommuting businesses?

    a. a chat platform, such as Slack

    b. a secure, reliable Wi-Fi connection

    c. cloud storage with sharing features, such as Dropbox

    d. expensive computer equipment

    e. calendar sharing for scheduling, through apps like Google Calendar

14. For each line below, select whether the statement is True or False.

    a. Online instruction has completely ended the use of CDs in computer-based training.

    b. It is possible to complete an entire college degree through online classes.

    c. Virtual classrooms are an example of telepresence.

    d. Blended learning combines online education with the use of textbooks.

IC3 PROCEDURES

CREATING A NEW MAIL MESSAGE WITH OUTLOOK

1. Select **Mail** in the Navigation Bar at the bottom of the Outlook window.

2. Select the **Home** tab.

3. Select the **New Email** button.

    OR

1. Select the **New Items** drop-down arrow.

2. On the menu, select **Email Message**.

CREATING AND SENDING A MAIL MESSAGE

1. In the email message window, position the insertion point in the To: box and type the recipient's email address.

2. If desired, click in the Cc: box, and type the email address of the copied recipient.

3. In the Subject box, type the subject of the message.

4. Position the insertion point in the message window and type the message text.

5. Select the **Send** button.

RECEIVING MESSAGES

1. Select the **Send/Receive** tab.
2. Select the **Send/Receive All Folders** button .

   OR

   Select **Send/Receive All Folders** button on the Quick Access Toolbar.

READING MAIL

1. In the Folder Pane, select Inbox.
2. In the message list, select the message you want to read to display it in the Reading Pane.

   OR

   In the message list, double-click the message you want to read to display it in a message window.

REPLYING TO MAIL

1. Select the message to which you want to reply.
2. Select the **Home** tab.
3. Select the **Reply** button .
4. Type your reply.
5. Select the **Send** button .

REPLYING TO ALL

1. Select the message to which you want to reply.
2. Select the **Home** tab.
3. Select the **Reply All** button .
4. Type your reply.
5. Select the **Send** button .

FORWARDING A MESSAGE

1. Select the message you want to forward.
2. Select the **Home** tab.
3. Select the **Forward** button .
4. In the message window, enter the email address in the To: and Cc: boxes of the recipient to which you want to forward the message.
5. Type a message if desired.
6. Select the **Send** button .

MARK A MESSAGE AS JUNK IN OUTLOOK

1. In the Message list, right-click the message to mark.
2. Select **Junk**.
3. Select **Block Sender**.

   OR

1. Select the message to mark.

2. Select the **Home** tab.

3. Select the **Junk** button 🚫.

4. Select **Block Sender**.

SET OUTLOOK TO BLOCK JUNK MAIL

1. In Outlook, select the **Home** tab.

2. Select the **Junk** button 🚫.

3. Select **Junk E-mail Options**.

4. On the Options tab, select the level of junk email protection you want.

5. Select **OK**.

START A SKYPE CHAT IN OUTLOOK.COM

1. Log in to your Outlook.com account.

2. Select the **Skype** button Ⓢ to open the Skype chat window.

3. Select the **New Conversation** button ⊞.

4. Select the contact.

   OR

   Enter the contact information in the Search box and then select the contact.

5. Select **Create**.

6. In the Type to chat box at the bottom of the chat window, type the chat message.

7. Press **Enter**.

   The message will display in the other person's chat window. Replies will display at the bottom of your chat window.

START A GOOGLE HANGOUTS CHAT

1. Start Chrome.

2. Select the **Google apps** button ⊞.

3. Select **Hangouts**.

4. Select the **New conversation** button ⊕.

5. Select the contact.

   OR

   Enter the contact information in the Search box and then select the contact.

6. In the Send a message box at the bottom of the chat window, type the chat message.

7. Press **Enter**.

   The message will display in the other person's chat window. Replies will display at the bottom of your chat window.

CHAPTER 31

Understanding Personal Communications

OUR NEED TO COMMUNICATE

Thanks to technology, people today have many communications options, from speaking face to face or talking on the phone to using computers and devices to exchange ideas and information. Technology also gives us more freedom in communicating. Your grandparents probably remember what it was like to sit at home waiting for a phone call, or to need a quarter to use a pay phone. Now, voice calls, texts, and email travel with us.

Understanding Email Systems

OBJECTIVES

- Describe how email travels through networks.

- Summarize the key email protocols.

- Explain authentication.

- List email options that you can customize.

- Discuss the proper use of signatures and headers in email.

- Explain the benefits and risks of email attachments.

AS YOU READ

ORGANIZE INFORMATION Use a concept web as you read to help you organize ideas about email systems.

TERMINOLOGY

- attachment

- authentication

- email signature

- email virus

- executable file

- Internet Message Access Protocol (IMAP)

- macro virus

- Multipurpose Internet Mail Extensions (MIME)

- Post Office Protocol 3 (POP3)

- replicate

- Simple Mail Transfer Protocol (SMTP)

What Happens When You Send and Receive Email?

When you send and receive email messages, even when you use web-based email, you participate in a client-server network. Your email software is the client. The computer that accepts and forwards messages for its users is the email server. Because email servers and clients use the same protocols, you can send messages to and receive messages from anyone with an email address, as long as the computers have access to the same network or the internet.

SENDING MESSAGES Internet service providers (ISPs), companies and institutions, and other mail services maintain the email servers. When you select Send, most messages travel first to your ISP's email server via **Simple Mail Transfer Protocol (SMTP)**. The email server then examines the recipient's address. If the person you are emailing uses the same server you do, the message is delivered instantly. A copy of the message is stored in your Sent Items folder, so you have access to it if you need it.

RECEIVING MESSAGES To receive a message, the email client retrieves the message from the server by using another protocol, and places it

FIGURE 31.1.1 A copy of each outgoing message is stored in the Sent Items folder in Outlook.com.

in your Inbox mail folder. The two most commonly used message retrieval protocols are **Post Office Protocol 3 (POP3)** and **Internet Message Access Protocol (IMAP)**. Another protocol is **Multipurpose Internet Mail Extensions (MIME)**, which translates files sent as email attachments.

With IMAP, messages you send and receive are stored on a server, and can be synced across multiple devices. With POP3, messages you send and receive are downloaded to a specific device. As soon as they are downloaded, they are deleted from the server. If you want to keep the messages on the server, you must change the default settings.

DIFFERENT SERVERS Often, the sender and the recipient use different ISP email servers. For example, you may use Outlook, while your friend uses Gmail. In this case, the Outlook server, using SMTP, sends your email message to the Gmail server via the internet. The Gmail server then delivers the message to your friend.

To handle your email, your client needs your username and password. The server also uses this information in a process called **authentication** to identify you and confirm that you are a valid user. Guard your username and password, and change your password frequently. It should be easy for you to remember but difficult for others to guess. If someone learns your password, change it. Never allow others to log on with your password.

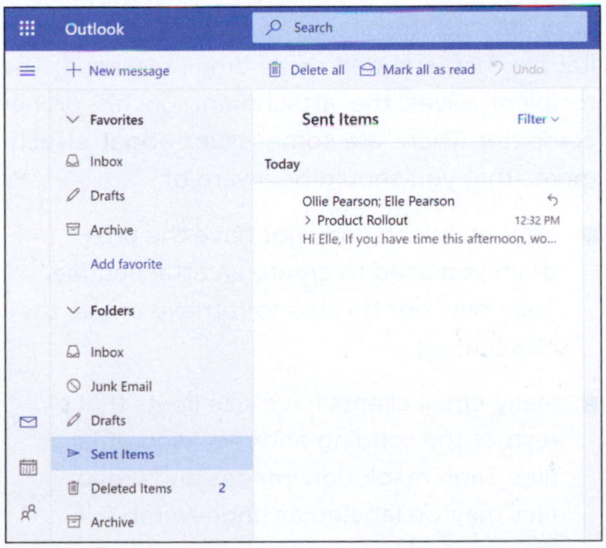

Configuring Email Options

All email clients allow you to customize your emails. You can usually do this by selecting Mail Options or Mail Settings. For instance, you can set how frequently you want to send and receive messages. Other options include how to display original message text when forwarding or replying and whether to track when messages are opened. Most programs let you set up an automatic reply or away message for when you are out of the office or otherwise not available. The reply is sent in response to any incoming message in order to politely tell the sender that you are unavailable, and when you will be back. Some systems even let you customize an automatic reply for specific addresses. Other options let you automatically forward messages and set your spam or junk filter to block mail from specific addresses.

EMAIL SIGNATURES AND HEADERS An **email signature** is information that displays after the message text in the message body, identifying you as the sender. It might be your name, or it might include your name and additional information, such as your title, contact information, and even an image. You can insert a signature every time you type a message, or you can use your email program's mail options to create one that the program will automatically enter in each new message. For example, in Outlook, choose File > Options > Mail and then select the Signatures button. Select New, enter and format the signature information, and select OK. You can create different signatures for different accounts, or for different uses. For example, you might have one for business and one for personal correspondence.

Just as in a formal business letter, it is proper to include a complete signature in an email so the recipient knows who wrote the message. It is also proper to include a complete salutation, or header, when typing an email message. Show respect for the recipient by starting the

FIGURE 31.1.2 Creating email signatures in Microsoft Outlook.

message with a greeting and a name, such as *Dear Mr. Johnson*, and ending with a closing, such as *Thanks*, followed by a signature.

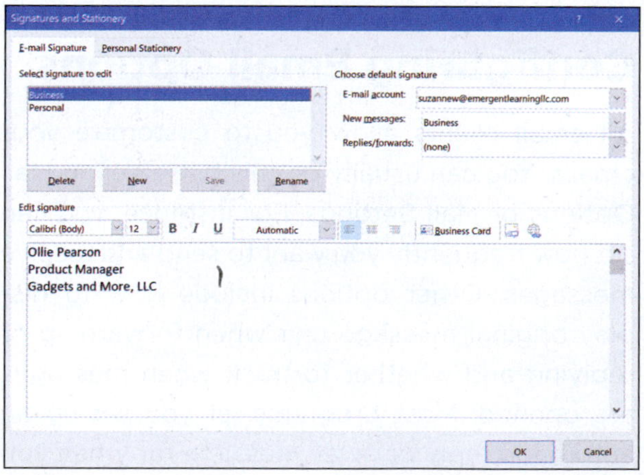

IC3✔ **Understand email etiquette: signature and header.**

EMAIL NOTIFICATIONS By default, most email programs notify you when you receive a message by playing a sound or displaying an envelope icon on your screen. You can customize the notifications so the icon does not display, or to make a specific sound or no sound at all. You can also turn notifications off completely so that you are not distracted by notification sounds or vibrations throughout the day.

Certain websites let you set up notifications or alerts that can be sent to you via email. For example, on a social networking site, you can select a setting to send you a notification when someone posts a new picture. On a news site, you can select a setting to send you a notification when there is breaking news about a topic that interests you, such as sports scores or weather.

Email Attachments

A useful feature of email is the ability to send attachments. Recall that an **attachment** is a digital file that is added to an email message. The recipient saves the attachment on his or her computer. There are some issues about attachments that you should be aware of:

- Your recipients may not have the program you used to create an attached file. They may not be able to retrieve or use the attachment.

- Many email clients have size limits that restrict the sending and receiving of large files. High resolution images and video files may be labeled as undeliverable if they exceed the size limit. Even if they can be delivered, they can take a long time to download and even cause the recipient's email software to crash. Be sure your recipients want to receive large files before you send them. One way to get larger attachments to your recipients is to use an online storage folder, such as Dropbox. You register at the site and can then store files on its server. You send a link via email that the recipient clicks to access the file. The recipient can make the choice to view the file online or download it.

IC3✔ Understand the size limits of email attachments.

COMMON USES OF ATTACHMENTS Attachments are a great way to transmit documents to a friend, family member, or colleague. You can send a report to a classmate you are working with, or transmit an expense worksheet to a manager. Companies no longer need to print, package, and ship documents. Instead, with just

a few clicks, documents can be sent as email attachments. This saves time and money.

The Dangers of Email Attachments

Some attachments can contain an **email virus**—a script or program that causes harm, such as changing or deleting files. The worst viruses **replicate**, or copy themselves. They locate your address book and send themselves to every address listed in it. Since your name appears in the message header, the friends and family who receive the message do not suspect a problem until they open the attachment and their devices become infected.

Email viruses can do great harm to businesses, too. Imagine that a virus replicated on the computers listed in employees' address books. The email servers would become overloaded, and files would be destroyed.

A paper clip icon in the message list.   The attachment in the message preview.

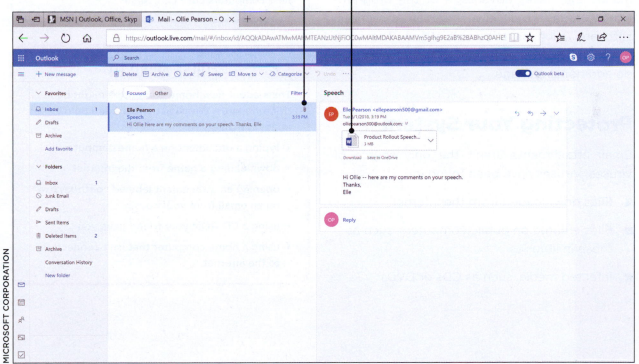

FIGURE 31.1.3 Receiving an email message with an attachment.

EXECUTABLE FILES One way of spreading a virus is through an executable file. An **executable file** is one that carries out instructions that might destroy files on your computer, change its settings, or cause internet traffic jams. You can recognize an executable file by the extension at the end of the file name: .com, .exe, .vbs, .bat. If you get an email message that has one of these files attached, beware. You may be asking for trouble if you open it.

MACRO VIRUSES Another type of virus is called a macro virus. A **macro virus** is a series of commands that takes advantage of the programming language built into everyday application software, such as Microsoft Word. The virus might add words or phrases to documents, or do additional damage.

Protecting Your System

Email attachments aren't the only source of viruses. Viruses have been found in:

- Files downloaded from the internet

- Files created on public computers, such as those in libraries

- Infected media, such as CDs or DVDs

ANTIVIRUS SOFTWARE A good antivirus software program will run all the time on your computer. It looks for any application or script that tries to manipulate the system. Some antivirus software can also scan incoming and outgoing email for viruses.

AUTOMATIC UPDATES Virus programmers continually try to create new viruses and make changes to existing ones, with a primary goal of making viruses more difficult to detect and eliminate. The developers of antivirus software, however, are never more than a step behind the virus programmers. Most good antivirus programs can be updated regularly via the internet. Some of the programs can update themselves automatically, without the user even knowing about it. By regularly updating your antivirus software, you can protect yourself against the most current viruses.

Organizing with Email and Digital Calendars

OBJECTIVES

- Explain the use of an address book.

- Recognize the purpose of email folders.

- Explain how to schedule appointments and events.

- Demonstrate the use of multiple calendars.

- Recognize the difference between sharing and syncing calendars.

- Explain how to subscribe to a calendar.

TERMINOLOGY

- address book

- archive

- digital calendar

- email folder

- recurring event

AS YOU READ

ORGANIZE INFORMATION Use an outline to help you identify ways to organize with email and a digital calendar as you read the lesson.

Managing Email

Email programs provide tools that you can use to keep your email organized. Two of the most important are an address book to keep track of your contacts and folders where you can store messages.

ADDRESS BOOK All email programs come with an **address book**, which is a database where you store the names and email addresses of frequent email contacts. Many programs automatically add each address you use to your address book. When you create a new message, you can select the recipient from the address book to quickly insert the information in the message header. Often, if you start typing an email address, the program displays a list of possible recipients in the address book, and all you have to do is click the one you want to enter their information.

When you receive a message, you can choose to add the sender's contact information to your address book.

Some programs provide more robust address books. They have tools for creating a contact card to store additional information about each person, such as phone number, company and title, mailing address, photo, and social networking links.

You may be able to create group contact lists in your address book. If you and several friends are working on a project, you might create a group list called *Project* and add the email address of each group member to the list. This feature lets you send a message to all the contacts in the group at once, saving you the time of typing each address separately.

IC3 ✓ **Understand contact management: address book.**

EMAIL FOLDERS The list of messages in your Inbox can grow quickly. You should delete unimportant messages after you read them. However, it is important to maintain a history of your email correspondence by saving important messages in an **email folder**. Email programs usually come with some folders already set up, such as the Inbox, Outbox, Junk, Sent, and Deleted Items, or Trash. You can create additional folders to store related messages. For example, you can create a folder to store messages relating to a specific topic, or which come from a specific person. The Folder list, usually on the left side of the email window, displays all the available folders.

> ## CAREER CORNER
>
> **EDUCATIONAL MEDIA TECHNOLOGY SPECIALIST** Computers and telecommunications are now everyday teaching tools. Schools, museums, and other educational institutions that offer programs to the public have a growing need for educational media technology specialists. Knowledge of effective education practices, hardware, software, and the principles of networking are requirements for applicants in this field.

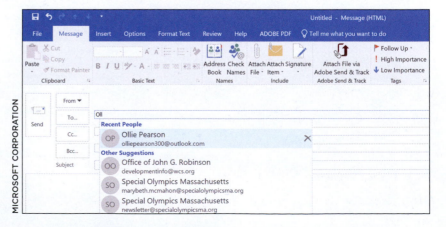

FIGURE 31.2.1 Using the address book in Outlook to enter an email address.

To see the contents of a folder, select it in the Folder list. To open a message, select it in the Message list, or use the Open command. To move a message from one folder to another, you can drag it, or use the Move command.

To store a message in a folder, drag the message from the Inbox to the desired folder. To open a message saved in a folder, select the folder in the Folder list, and then select the message in the Message list or use the Open command. Most programs also have tools for searching email folders. In Outlook, select a folder and then type a search term in the Search Current Mailbox field at the top of the Message list.

IC3✔ **Understand email history and management: folders.**

Organizing Email

VIEWING MESSAGES IN THE INBOX Incoming messages display in your Inbox. Depending on your setup, you may see just a list of messages,

the message header with a few lines of the message body, or the entire message in a preview or reading pane. Open the message to view it in a separate window. At the top of the message is the message header. Recall that the message header contains information that identifies the sender of the message, other recipients, the date sent, and the subject. The body of the message is the text that the sender wrote to you.

SORTING MESSAGES Most email clients allow you to sort the messages in the Message list—that is, arrange them in alphabetical or numerical order based on information in the header. For example, you might be able to sort by the sender's name, date received, and so on. To sort the messages by sender in Outlook, click the From heading. To sort by Subject or Date, click either of those headings.

Some programs also let you organize and display messages by conversation, which means the entire thread of sent messages and replies that have the same subject line are grouped together, similar to a text message thread.

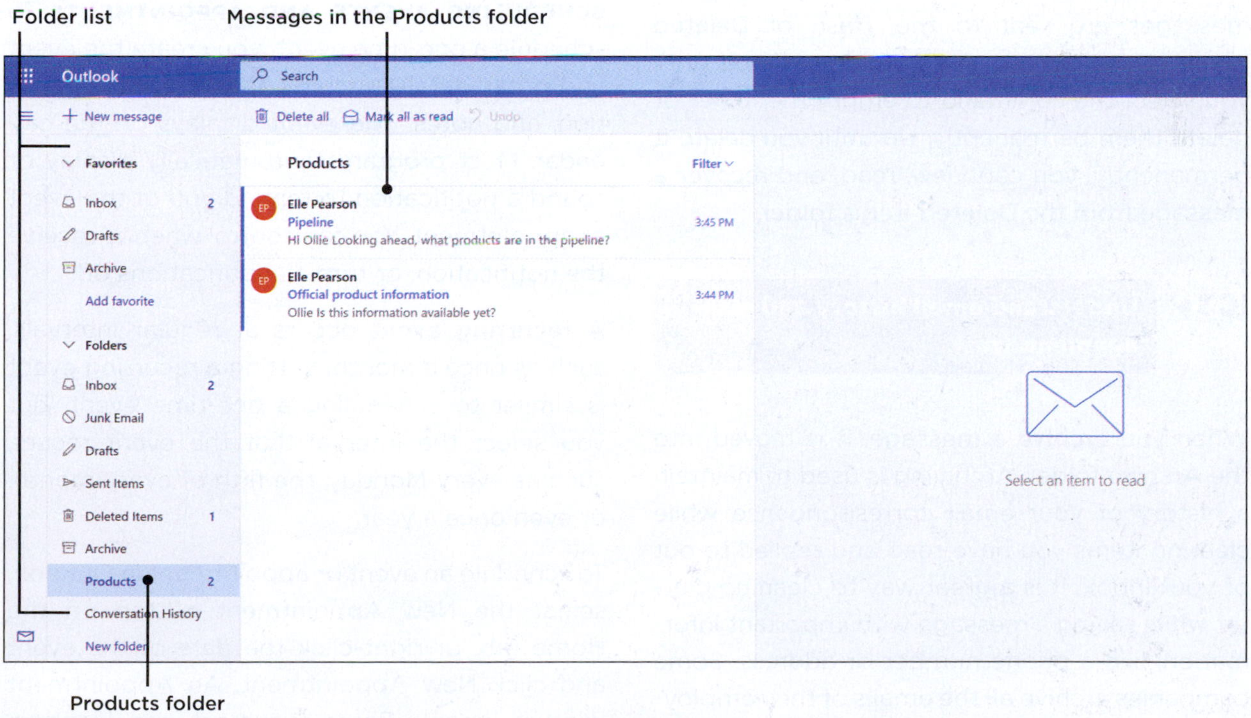

Folder list **Messages in the Products folder**

Outlook	Search	
+ New message	Delete all Mark all as read Undo	
⌄ Favorites	Products	Filter ⌄
Inbox 2	EP **Elle Pearson** Pipeline HI Ollie Looking ahead, what products are in the pipeline?	3:45 PM
Drafts		
Archive	EP **Elle Pearson** Official product information Ollie Is this information available yet?	3:44 PM
Add favorite		
⌄ Folders		
Inbox 2		
Junk Email		
Drafts		
Sent Items		
Deleted Items 1		
Archive		
Products 2		Select an item to read
Conversation History		
New folder		

Products folder

FIGURE 31.2.2 Use folders to keep your email organized.

MICROSOFT CORPORATION

THINK ABOUT IT!

Think about guidelines employees should follow when sending email on company time. Which statements listed below do you think describe good business "netiquette?"

- Use your company address for personal messages.
- Make sure the content of your messages is appropriate for your boss to read.
- To criticize someone, do it by email.
- Send your manager a message without proofreading it first.
- Do not open or respond to email from unknown senders.

REMOVING MESSAGES Often you do not want to keep a message in your Inbox. You can move it to another folder, delete it, or archive it. Deleted messages are sent to the Trash or Deleted Items folder but are not actually deleted until you select the command to empty the folder or delete them permanently. Up until you delete it permanently, you can view, read, and recover a message from the Deleted Items folder.

IC3✔ Understand email history and management: trash.

When you **archive** a message, it is moved into the Archive folder. Archiving is used to maintain a history of your email correspondence while clearing items you have read and replied to out of your Inbox. It is a great way to clean up clutter while saving a message with important information, like a phone number or address. Some companies archive all the emails of their employees. For legal reasons, it is important they have

a record of electronic communications. Using the Archive folder to retain messages you want to keep but do not want in your Inbox is useful because you can quickly search the Archive folder to find a message you need.

IC3✔ Understand email history and management: archiving.

Using a Digital Calendar

Many communications programs, such as Outlook, include a digital calendar that you can use to schedule one-time and recurring events and appointments. A **digital calendar** is an app that provides tools for scheduling and managing appointments, meetings, and events. There are also stand-alone calendar programs and online calendar apps, such as Google Calendar. Calendars can be used on any computing device, including a computer, tablet, or smartphone. Digital calendars can play an important role in helping you manage your time and stay organized and prepared.

SCHEDULING EVENTS AND APPOINTMENTS To schedule a one-time event, you create the event and enter details such as the date, time, location, and notes. The event displays on the calendar. Most programs automatically display or sound a notification to remind you of the event or appointment. You can control when to receive the notification, or turn all notifications off.

A **recurring event** occurs at regular intervals, such as once a month. Setting a recurring event is similar to scheduling a one-time event, but you select the interval that the event recurs, such as every Monday, the fifth of every month, or even once a year.

To schedule an event or appointment in Outlook, select the New Appointment button on the Home tab, or right-click the date of the event and click New Appointment. An Appointment window opens. Enter a subject and location.

Select a start date and time and an end date and time. Use buttons on the Ribbon to set options such as how far in advance you want a reminder. Click the Recurrence button to display options for creating a recurring event.

You can set an importance level, choose an option from the Show As drop-down for how to code the time on the calendar display, and even invite others, which means sending them an email with the event details so they can add it to their calendars. Enter notes in the body of the appointment window. For example, you might list the other people involved, or enter a call-in number for a teleconference. When the information is complete, select Save & Close on the Appointment tab of the Ribbon.

In Google Calendar, click on the date of the event or appointment to open the Event dialog box. Enter a title for the event, and then set the start date and time and end date and time. Click the Reminder button if you want to mark the appointment as an all-day or recurring event. Click More Options to add a location, set the notification reminder, add a conferencing option

such as Hangouts, enter notes, and more. When all the information is complete, select Save.

IC3 ✔ **Know how to create one-time and recurring events and appointments.**

INVITING OTHERS When you schedule an event or appointment, you can send invitations by text message or email to other people or contact groups that you want to attend the meeting or event. Your program will keep track of their replies. The button to Invite Attendees in Outlook is on the Appointment tab of the Appointment window. The command to Add guests in Google Calendar is in the More Options window. In both programs, you select contacts from your address book, or enter the contact information manually.

USING MULTIPLE CALENDARS Most programs allow you to maintain more than one calendar, so you can have one for work and one for personal appointments. Many programs even let you create calendars for specific types of

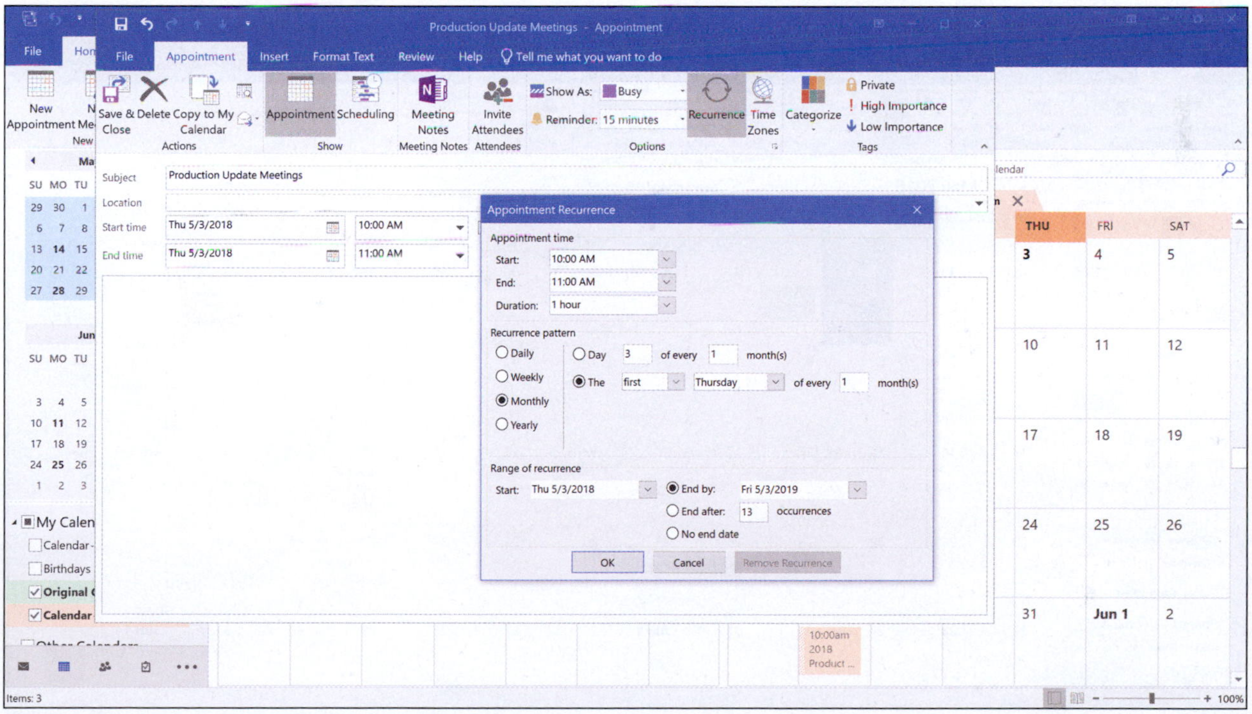

FIGURE 31.2.3 Creating a recurring event in Outlook 2016.

events, such as birthdays, holidays, or sporting events. Calendars are color-coded so you can tell them apart. The way you display multiple calendars depends on the program you are using. In Outlook, select the check box to the left of a calendar you want to view in the Navigation pane on the left.

In Google Calendar, by default, all scheduled events and appointments are shown on a single calendar display, but each event is color-coded to indicate which calendar it is on. For example, a teleconference with your co-workers would display in the color associated with your Work calendar, while lunch with your sister would display in the color associated with your Personal calendar. Clear the checkboxes next to calendars you do not want to view, or select Options to the right of the calendar you do want to view and select Display this only.

IC3✔ **Know how to view multiple calendars.**

SHARING CALENDARS You can share calendars with others so that you can see their schedule and they can see yours. This is particularly useful at work when you need to coordinate with a team, or when an assistant might maintain a calendar for a manager. When you share a calendar, you can select whether the other person can see all event details or just whether or not you have something scheduled. This can help protect your privacy, because others will know you are busy, but will not know what you are doing. You can also give other people permission to create, edit, or manage events and appointments.

In Outlook, select the calendar you want to share and select Share Calendar on the Home tab of the Ribbon. Or, right-click the calendar to share and select Share > Share Calendar. An email window opens. Enter the email address of each person you want to share with, select options, and then select Send. To change permissions, select the Calendar Permissions button on the Home tab of the ribbon, select options and then select OK.

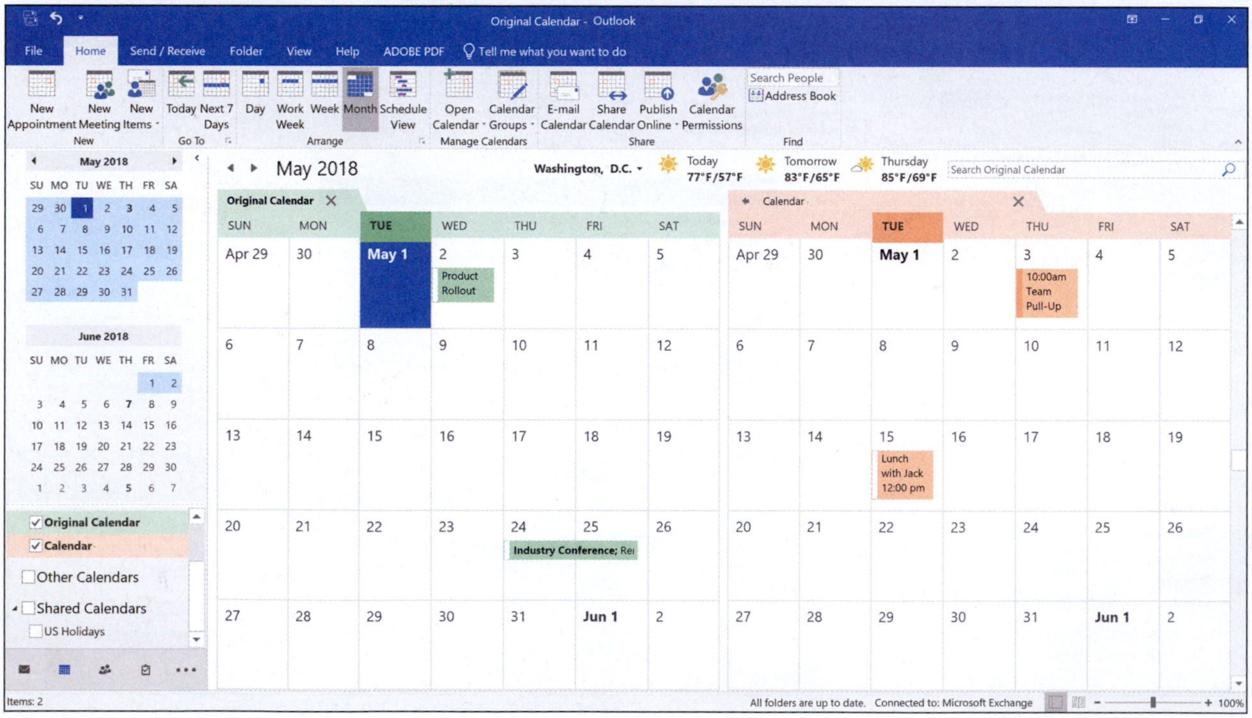

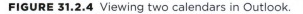

FIGURE 31.2.4 Viewing two calendars in Outlook.

In Google Calendar, select Options to the right of the calendar you want to share and then select Settings and Sharing. If you want anyone to share the calendar, select the Make available to public check box. To share the calendar with only specific people, under Share with specific people, select Add People and then select the people from your contacts list, or enter the contact information. Select a Permissions level from the Permissions drop-down list, and then select Send. The program sends an email notification to everyone you share it with, and adds the calendar to their Google Calendar Lists.

IC3✔ **Know how to share calendars.**

SYNCING CALENDARS By default, most calendar programs will sync across your devices, and even across compatible applications. For example, if you receive an email confirming an appointment, it may be automatically entered on your calendar. Sometimes, the email will display an option to add the event to your calendar, but other times the syncing may happen automatically. Things like dentist appointments, dinner reservations, or anything confirmed via email may suddenly appear on your calendar. There is usually a setting in the calendar app to block syncing, if you choose.

CALENDAR SUBSCRIPTIONS Many websites maintain calendars of events. You can subscribe to these calendars to have events added to your own calendar. Subscribing involves filling out an online form with your contact information, and selecting the types of events that interest you. The website will send you notifications when an event is scheduled or changed.

IC3✔ **Understand how to subscribe to calendars.**

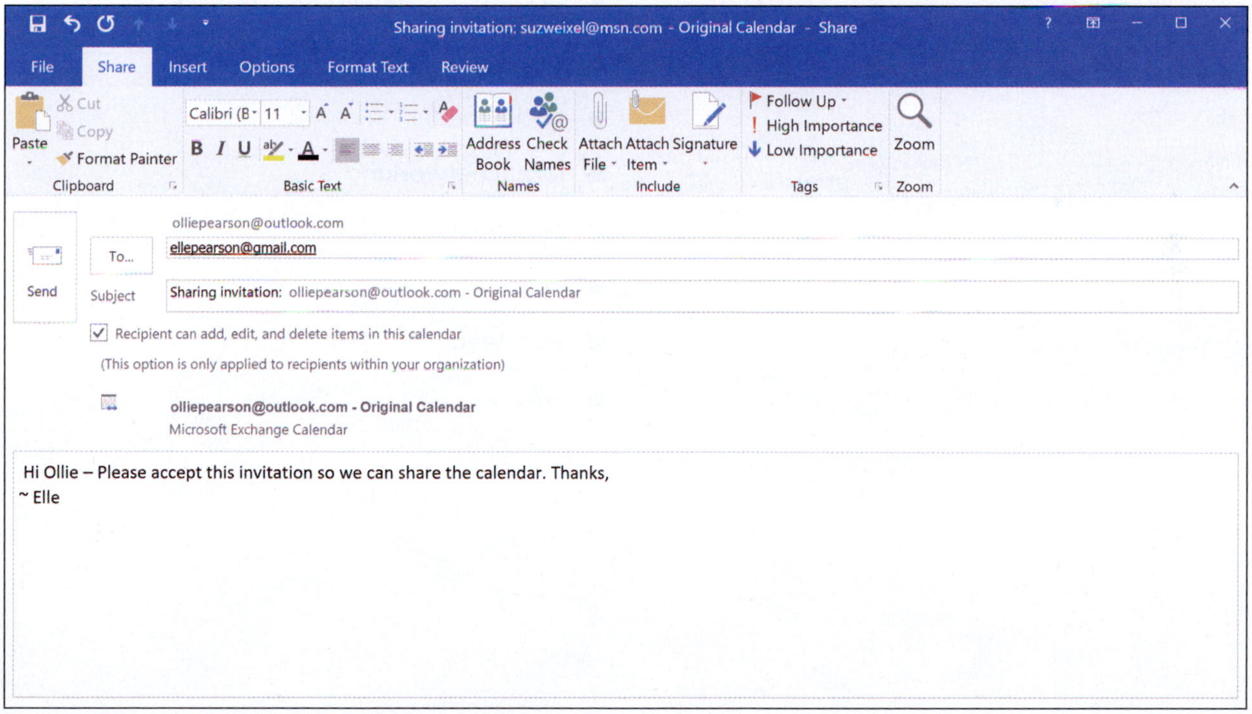

FIGURE 31.2.5 Sharing an Outlook 2016 Calendar.

MICROSOFT CORPORATION

Understanding Communications Tools

OBJECTIVES

- Compare and contrast communications tools.
- Explain the use of SMS text services.

AS YOU READ

ORGANIZE INFORMATION Use a column chart to help you compare and contrast communications tools as you read the lesson.

TERMINOLOGY

- blog
- digital identity
- flame
- internal social media site
- libel
- live streaming
- online forum
- podcast
- profile
- progressive download
- slander
- social media
- social networking
- streaming
- vlog
- web feed
- wiki

Internet Communications

The internet is a fast and easy way for people to communicate. If you have an internet connection and an account with a communication service, you have a wide range of options for sending and receiving text, images, video, and sound. Communication can be formal, such as through email or video conferencing, or it can be more informal, through online chat channels or forums, instant messaging, and social networking sites.

ADVANTAGES AND DISADVANTAGES Digital communication on the internet helps create and maintain bonds between people. It is also available around the clock, making it possible to communicate at any time of day. These same advantages also cause problems. Constant digital communication can get in the way of face-to-face communication and hurt personal relationships. It also leaves room for misunderstandings. Digital communication allows for large digital social networks to be formed, introducing people to new ideas and perspective. However, it is important to keep in mind that this should not be a replacement for real-life interactions.

Communications Standards

Whatever type of communication you use, it is important to abide by certain standards. Personal communication may be less formal than you use for business, but you should still be polite and respectful. You never know who will read it.

- Use correct spelling. Proofread before sending to make sure there are no errors.

- Using abbreviations may be fine for personal communications with your friends and family but not for professional communications.

- Using all capital letters is considered to be shouting. Be sure to use proper capitalization.

- Don't send messages or images that may embarrass you in the future. Take a minute to think about what you are saying before you send a message.

- Don't forward or send unwanted messages like spam.

- Don't **flame**, or insult, anyone, even as a joke. Sometimes written communication is misinterpreted as being serious, even if it was intended to be funny.

- Don't use electronic communication to bully others.

- Don't make false statements that might hurt someone's reputation. It's called **libel** or **slander**, and it's illegal. You may be sued for damages.

Choosing the Best Tool for the Job

Communicating is all about delivering and receiving messages. You want to know the message you send is received, and you want others to know you are receiving the messages they send. Even though there are many options for communicating socially and for business, you should always choose the method most appropriate for the situation. For example, is it appropriate to text your manager to request a day off, or would it be better to make a telephone call? Is it appropriate to send an email to a friend when you are running late for dinner, or should you text? Consider both the message and the recipient when selecting the best communication tool to use.

EMAIL Email is a good tool for a formal communication, similar to a handwritten and mailed letter. There are no limits on the length of an email message, so you can include as much information as you need. It is also easy to store emails so you can maintain a record of the conversation, and almost everyone has an email account. Emails can be forwarded, so do not assume messages you send will remain private. One drawback is that while messages are delivered almost instantaneously, there is no way of knowing when the other person will open and read the message, if at all.

IC3 ✔ Know the best tool for the various situations and scenarios: email.

SMS With a messaging app you can send text messages to any cell phone number. Text messages sent using Short Message Service (SMS) are received immediately. They are much less formal than email, but a good way to reach someone quickly. Like email, however, there is no way to know if someone reads the text, until you receive a response. Most apps place a character limit on each text, which causes some people to use abbreviations and omit punctuation. They are gaining acceptance for both personal and business communications as more people become comfortable using smartphones and messaging apps. Still, due to the informal nature of texting, it is best to limit its use to family and friends. Text messages can be forwarded, so they may not be private.

IC3 ✔ Know the best tool for the various situations and scenarios: SMS.

TWEETS A tweet is a form of text messaging that uses the Twitter app; you send the message to the Twitter internet site, where any registered user can read it. Twitter limits most messages to 280 characters. Twitter allows for short messages to be read by a much larger audience. When you send a tweet, remember that anyone can read it.

INSTANT MESSAGING Recall that instant messaging (IM) is a way for individuals and groups to communicate with their contacts in real time from device to device. IM is similar to a telephone call, because you know the other person is receiving the message and responding. IM is suitable for informal communication but may not be suitable for more formal interactions.

You and the people you are communicating with must all be using the same IM app, and you must be on each other's contact list, so it is best for communicating with people you know. IM is usually free, and is often built-into other platforms. For example, Facebook Messenger is built into Facebook, iMessage comes on Apple iPhones and iPads, and Gmail has a Chat feature called Hangouts. Other common IM services include Skype, Slack, and Jabber.

Instant messaging services may also provide video calling, file sharing, and device-to-device or device-to-phone calling. To use video calling, the device must have a working camera, microphone, and speaker.

IC3 ✔ Know the best tool for the various situations and scenarios: IM.

VOIP Recall that Voice over Internet Protocol (VoIP) is technology that enables the delivery of voice and multimedia over the internet. Apps such as Skype, Facetime, and Google Hangouts use VoIP, so you can make voice or video calls using a smartphone, tablet, or computer. VoIP can be used in any situation when you want to have a face-to-face conversation with someone who is far away. This could be a friend, family member, or colleague.

IC3 ✔ Know the best tool for the various situations and scenarios: VoIP.

TELEPHONE CALLS There are still times when making a telephone call is the best way to communicate. Almost everyone has a phone with them at all times, so you know when someone answers you will be able to deliver your message.

Telephone calls can be formal, such as a phone interview for a job, or informal, such as catching up with family or friends. Making a telephone call requires more of a time commitment than other forms of communication. You must stop other activities, and use a device to place the call. You

FIGURE 31.3.1 VoIP calls are best for face-to-face conversations across long distances, as long as you have an internet connection.

ROCKETCLIPS, INC./SHUTTERSTOCK

must then take the time to talk to the other person, or people, on the line. Tools such as hands-free dialing and headsets make it possible to take notes while you are on the call. Keep in mind that unless you record the call, there is no record of the actual conversation. In addition, the call may not be private. The use of a speakerphone enables others to hear the conversation.

IC3✔ **Know the best tool for the various situations and scenarios: telephone calls.**

TELECONFERENCE AND VIDEOCONFERENCE When you want to communicate with more than one person in real time, a teleconference or videoconference is your best option. Recall that a teleconference, such as one using the Cisco Webex service, is an online meeting of two or more people. A videoconference is a teleconference that includes video as well as text or audio. Both teleconferences and videoconferences must be scheduled in advance to make sure everyone involved is present and able to access the conference. These conferences can be formal or informal, depending on who is participating. Keep in mind that you may not always be aware of who is in the room during such a conference.

IC3✔ **Know the best tool for the various situations and scenarios: teleconference and videoconference.**

Using SMS and MMS

Recall that text messaging, or texting, allows you to use a smartphone or other mobile device to type a brief message and transmit it to another phone or as a group conversation to multiple phones. Text messages are sent using Short Message Service (SMS). Texts are uploaded to the service's server and then downloaded to the recipient's device. Most text messages are limited to 160 characters in length. If you exceed that limit, the messaging app will usually break the message into two or more messages, sent separately.

You must have a messaging app on your phone, but you can send messages to—and receive messages from—any cell phone number. You can even send texts to some landlines. The recipient does not have to use the same messaging app that you use. Text messages are usually sent using a cellular network, but may use Wi-Fi if it is available. Cellular service plans can place a limit on the number of text messages you can send and receive, and may charge you if you exceed that limit.

Text messaging is a great tool for sending a quick message to someone. Many businesses are starting to use it as a way to communicate with customers. For example, you might receive a text message from a restaurant confirming a reservation, or letting you know a table is ready. It is not ideal for conducting a detailed conversation.

Text messages can be distracting, and it is important not to let messages take your attention away from things happening in front of you, such as a class or face-to-face conversation with someone. As with all communication, you should always be polite and respectful when you text. You never know who will read the message. Messages can be forwarded and passed around. Text messages may be deleted from a device, but they remain stored on a server and can be retrieved. Do not text anything you might regret or be ashamed of.

IC3✔ Know how to use SMS texting.

MMS Digital messages that include photos, audio, and videos are sent using Multimedia Messaging Service (MMS). The process is basically the same as with SMS messages: the message is uploaded to a server and then downloaded to the recipient's device. There is not usually a size limit for an MMS message, but if it is too large the service may have trouble with the transmission, or the recipient may have trouble with the download. MMS messages usually use data and will count toward your cellular service plan's data limit. If you exceed the data limit, you will incur overage charges. Just because you can include images or videos with an MMS message does not mean you should. As with texts, the messages can be forwarded and passed around. They remain stored on the server even after they have been deleted from a device.

Using Social Networking

Social networking is a way to use **social media** tools on the internet to make connections with other people. Social media sites, such as Snapchat, Instagram, Facebook, and LinkedIn, provide the tools you need to connect family, friends, and business colleagues by linking your own personal **profile** to those of others. You can share pictures, videos, and text posts.

You can leave comments and ratings, and generally stay up-to-date and engaged with others in the online community. Most social networking sites are free, although you have to register an account to use them.

Your profile is like a web page about you. It is what people see when they look you up on the site. Your profile can include a lot of information, or just the bare essentials. Most social networking profiles can include a picture, education or work history, and a status. You can tailor your profile to add as much or as little personal information as you wish, as well as uploading photos, posting messages, and linking to other sites.

Social media and social networking sites are a great way to stay in touch with people you know, and to meet new people with similar interests or common friends. Some sites, like LinkedIn, help you make connections that can further your career. Some, like YouTube, provide entertainment, and, if other people like your posts, can become a career.

IC3✔ Know what a social network is, and how it is used.

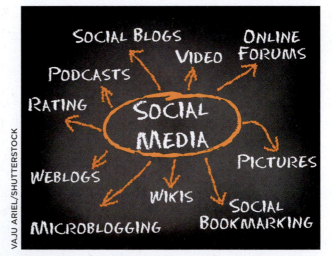

VAJU ARIEL/SHUTTERSTOCK

FIGURE 31.3.2 A social network can help you stay engaged and involved with friends, family, colleagues, and the community.

DIGITAL IDENTITY When using social networking, you must remember that everything you do and say is online for others to see. All of the information you post on social networking sites define your **digital identity**. It is what people learn about you when they look you up online, visit your pages, and read your posts. For better or for worse, it is what they assume is true. Colleges will search your digital identity when considering your application for enrollment. Employers will look you up before inviting you to interview for a position. Both might decide to reject you based on the information they find.

IC3✔ **Understand what a digital identity is.**

DRAWBACKS OF SOCIAL MEDIA Like beautiful people in advertisements, life on social media is not always what it seems. People have a tendency to share happy, positive facts and experiences that make it seem like everything is always wonderful. Looking at their profiles, pages, and posts, you might assume that nothing bad ever happens to anyone else. Some people end up depressed and unhappy because of this. Another drawback is that spending too much time on social networking sites can keep you from spending time with real people.

There is a lack of privacy on social media. Always think about what you are going to write before you post it. You do not want to post content that may embarrass you or hurt another's feelings. You may be able to set privacy settings to control who can see what you post. You should also consider how the website uses your information. By signing up for an account, you usually agree that they may collect and use at least some of your personal information. The site may sell it to advertisers or use it to track your interests.

Once you create an account, you are likely to receive a lot of messages from the site, or from people who use the site. Friends of friends of friends might want to connect with you just to increase their number of online friends. Criminals might want to trick you into giving out personal information, or even into meeting in person. It is okay to ignore messages from strangers.

INTERNAL VS. OPEN SOCIAL MEDIA SITES Many companies and schools create internal social media sites. An **internal social media site** is a private site that is accessed only by the organization's members, such as employees or students. For example, Pearson Corporation first launched an internal social media site called Neo in 2010. Your school might have an internal site. Like on other social media sites, employees create profiles and develop networks by linking to others. Unlike other sites, internal sites do not allow access to people outside the company. Internal sites are useful for creating contacts between employees working in offices in different locations. They can make it easier to collaborate, help new employees fit in, and provide a way for management to share information.

IC3✔ **Recognize the difference between an internal and an open media site.**

Other Digital Communications

PHOTO AND VIDEO SHARING Photo and video sharing is using the internet to send digital photos or video clips to another internet user. These photos and videos can be shared privately or publicly using MMS or on websites and apps, such as Instagram, Snapchat, and Youtube.

PODCASTS A **podcast** is an audio or video file that is created for downloading to any device equipped with an application that can play MP3 files. Podcasts come in many genres, from comedy and music, to gaming, and even history. Many radio stations create podcasts of popular programs or parts of them. College teachers create podcasts and upload them to a special Apple website called iTunes U or to other web locations. Students can download the podcasts to hear the lecture.

BLOGS AND WIKIS A **blog**—or weblog—is a type of web page diary. People create blogs to share their thoughts and opinions. A blog is stored on a web server, like a web page, and the owner usually updates it on a regular basis. Anyone with access to the internet can read a blog. Blogs are not restricted to only text. Photo blogs consist solely of digital photographs. **Vlogs** are video logs in which the vlogger appears on video. Often, blogs provide a way for readers to comment on the blog content.

A **wiki** is a collaborative web page. Anyone can edit or create content on the page. The most notable wiki is Wikipedia.org, an encyclopedia website with user-generated content. It is important to keep in mind that blogs and wikis reflect the opinions of the people who write or edit the content; they may not always be accurate or up-to-date.

ONLINE FORUMS An **online forum** is a site that allows users to engage in discussions by posting messages to each other. Forums usually focus on a specific topic. They may be built in to an app, such as a game, or be part of another site. For example, many companies have forums where users can ask questions about their products. Some education sites have forums where students can collaborate or where they can ask questions and discuss class work.

IC3✔ Know what blogs, wikis, and forums are and how they are used.

WEB FEED A **web feed** is a service that automatically downloads web page content that a user has signed up for. The content may include the text of news, opinions, or audio/video files. A site that offers a web feed has a symbol such as RSS to indicate that a feed is available. When a browser detects a feed on a web page, it may also display a special web feed icon. When you click on the button, the site asks the user to indicate how and where the content is to be downloaded.

Streaming Services

A growing number of people are using **streaming** services to watch movies and television shows and listen to music and other audio programming. Streaming media, including audio and video, is transmitted as a continuous stream of data that plays as it arrives, so the user does not have to wait for it to download. The file begins playing as soon as it starts to download from the website to your device. This is in contrast to a **progressive download**, which downloads completely to the local device before you can play it. When you purchase a song from iTunes, you must download it completely before playing it. When you stream a song from Spotify, it starts playing immediately.

Usually, media files for streaming are stored on a server where users can access them using a streaming app and an internet connection. When content is put onto the internet in real time—instead of being stored on a server—it is called **live streaming**. You can use a live streaming app such as Facebook Live to broadcast live streaming content. You can also watch live streaming events on a website, such as Twitch, or by using an app.

STREAMING APPS There are all sorts of video and audio streaming apps and sites available online. Some are free, and others charge a monthly or single-use fee.

- Audio streaming apps include Spotify, Amazon Music, Apple Music, Pandora, and iHeartRadio.

- Video streaming apps include Netflix, Amazon Video, Hulu, PlayStation Vue, Vevo, Twitch, and Microsoft Stream.

- Live streaming apps include Facebook Live, Livestream, Periscope, and YouTube Live.

STREAMING DEVICES Any device that can connect to the internet can stream, but the quality is affected by transmission speed, bandwidth, display quality, and speakers. Smart speakers, such as Amazon Echo or Google Home, are one way many people stream music, podcasts, and other audio.

Websites and online services that provide streaming content, such as Netflix, Amazon, and Spotify, post the minimum recommended transmission speed requirements. For example, Netflix recommends a minimum of 5 Mbs to stream good quality audio and video.

Some smart TVs come equipped for internet access, and others use devices such as Roku or Apple TV to provide streaming services. Usually, you pay a subscription fee to access streaming channels or apps, and then you can watch the programs you want, when you want.

IC3✔ Understand what video, audio, and live streaming are and how they work with devices.

Commenting Online

Many websites allow you to share and express your views on the site's content by commenting. Usually, once you register, you can type a comment which is linked to the content on the site. Others can click the link to read your comment.

For example, you can comment on many online newspaper articles. Online stores let customers review products on the website, or share their experiences about using the products. Content sharing sites, like YouTube, allow viewers to give feedback on uploaded content and videos. You can upload your own content to these sites, or just comment on something you viewed. Social media sites allow for a great degree of freedom in posting ideas and opinions. Posts can be commented on and then those comments in turn can be commented on, creating full conversations that can include many people from many locations.

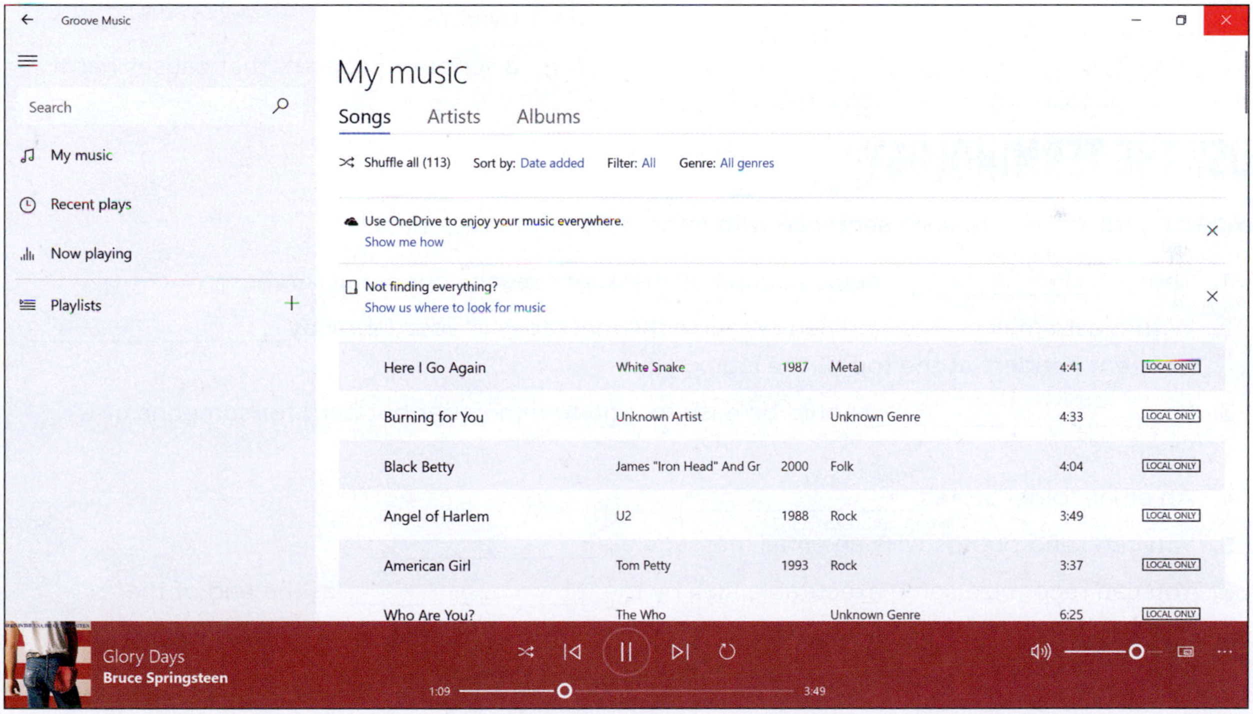

FIGURE 31.3.3 Streaming music in the Groove Music app.

MICROSOFT CORPORATION

Chapter 31 Review

REVIEW THE TERMINOLOGY

DIRECTIONS Match each vocabulary term in the left column with the correct definition in the right column.

1. message header
2. authentication
3. email folder
4. replicate
5. executable file
6. macro virus
7. email virus

a. part of an email that identifies the sender, among other information

b. series of commands hidden in a document

c. to copy or reproduce, as a virus makes copies of itself

d. process by which an email server identifies valid users

e. place to store saved messages

f. can launch a program; sometimes used by viruses

g. a script or program that causes harm

USE THE TERMINOLOGY

DIRECTIONS Complete each sentence with information from the chapter.

1. The _____ helps your email messages reach your email server.

2. With most email clients, you can organize the messages in your Inbox by _____ different headers at the top of the Inbox.

3. Your _____ should be easy for you to remember but hard for someone else to guess.

4. An email folder stores _____.

5. You can send photos with an email message as _____.

6. You can recognize some executable files by the _____ at the end of the file name.

7. _____ software checks for viruses and alerts you to them.

8. An email server uses _____ to confirm that you are a valid user.

9. Incoming messages are listed in your _____.

10. Some email servers or clients may reject attachments that are too _____.

THINK CRITICALLY

DIRECTIONS Answer the following questions.

1. What is the overall purpose of SMTP, MIME, and POP3?
2. How can you secure both your outgoing and incoming email?
3. How might your antivirus software help others?
4. Summarize the reasons for organizing email into folders.
5. Explain ways you can customize email options.

EXTEND YOUR KNOWLEDGE

DIRECTIONS Choose and complete one of the following projects.

1. Ransomware, such as WannaCry, is a type of virus that locks down computer systems until the owners pay a ransom fee. With your teacher's permission, research ransomware to learn how it spreads, and how it can be defeated. Present your findings in a report.
2. Email is one type of electronic communication, but there are many others, including texting, instant messaging, blogging, and social networking. Compare and contrast the advantages and disadvantages of different types of electronic communication. Summarize your findings in a report and present it to your class.
3. With your teacher's permission, practice using the configuration options for your email program. Learn how to block spam or junk mail, how to create a signature, and how to use automatic replies. Discuss these features with a partner, or as a class.
4. Start your email program. With your teacher's permission, create a distribution list or contact group of people in your class. Create a message and address it to the contact group. Set the importance level as high, and request a delivery receipt. With your teacher's permission, send the message.

IC3 PREP

1. "Dear Mr. Johnson" would be an example of an email _____.
   - **a.** signature
   - **b.** body
   - **c.** header
   - **d.** attachment
2. Put the following steps in order for creating a new signature in Outlook.
   - **a.** Choose File > Options > Mail.
   - **b.** Select New.
   - **c.** Enter and format the signature information and select OK.
   - **d.** Select the Signatures button.
3. Which of the following could be quickly and easily sent as an email attachment? (Select all that apply.)
   - **a.** a Word document
   - **b.** an MP3 file of your favorite song
   - **c.** a video game
   - **d.** a feature-length movie file

4. What can happen if a very large file is sent as an email attachment? (Select all that apply.)

   a. The sender's computer may become infected by a virus.

   b. The email client may not be able to send the email.

   c. The recipient's email client may crash.

   d. The email client may take a long time to deliver the email.

5. For each line below, select whether the statement is True or False.

   a. All email programs come with an address book.

   b. Email contacts must always be added manually to an address book.

   c. Some email programs let you add information about contacts, such as photos and social networking links, to an address book.

   d. Address books do not allow you to create groups.

6. Which of the following is NOT likely to be a default folder in an email program?

   a. Inbox

   b. Trash

   c. School

   d. Outbox

   e. Sent Items

7. For each line below, select whether the statement is True or False.

   a. Unwanted emails can be moved, deleted, or archived.

   b. Deleted messages are sent to the Trash or Deleted Items folder, where they can be recovered.

   c. Deleted messages cannot be recovered.

   d. Emails in a Trash or Deleted Items folder cannot be viewed without restoring them to the Inbox.

8. For each line below, select whether the statement is True or False.

   a. Archiving is a good way to clean up clutter while saving a message with important information.

   b. Companies are legally barred from archiving their employee's emails.

   c. Archiving an email is the same as deleting it.

   d. Once an email is archived, it is easy to search for it within the Archive folder.

9. Which of the following are valid parameters when setting an appointment in a typical calendar app? (Select all that apply.)

   a. importance level

   b. names and/or email addresses of invitees

   c. whether an event is one-time or recurring

   d. date and time for the event

10. In Outlook, what is the menu that allows you to switch or toggle between multiple calendars?

    a. View menu

    b. Calendar menu

    c. Toggle menu

    d. Functions menu

11. How does Google calendar identify different calendars shown at once?

    a. Different calendars have different icons.

    b. Different calendars are displayed in different colors.

    c. Different calendars use different fonts.

    d. Only one calendar can be viewed at one time.

12. For each line below, select whether the statement is True or False.

    a. Events in a calendar app can be set as either public or private.

    b. It is possible to notify others of your calendar events, but generally not through the calendar app itself.

    c. It is possible to share with others that you will be busy in your calendar, without divulging the specific details of your plans.

    d. Calendar privacy settings can be configured on a per-contact basis; you are able to share your calendar with some contacts without sharing with all of them.

13. What typically happens when you subscribe to a website's calendar of events? (Select all that apply.)

    a. You will be asked to maintain the website's calendar.

    b. You will be sent notifications when an event is scheduled or changed.

    c. The website's calendar will likely be displayed within your own calendar app.

    d. You will be redirected to an online form which will ask for your contact information.

14. When communicating with others, which of the following would be best suited to email?

    a. a quick, time-sensitive conversation

    b. formal communication, similar to a letter

    c. information you do not wish for others to see or learn

    d. a question or opinion for a large group on the internet

15. When communicating with others, which of the following would be best suited to SMS messaging?

    a. casual conversation between family and friends

    b. formal communication, similar to a letter

    c. a job interview

    d. news you wish to keep private

16. Which of the following does NOT contain an Instant Messaging platform?

    a. Facebook

    b. iPhones

    c. Outlook

    d. Gmail

17. Which of the following programs could a workplace use to make voice or video calls over VoIP? (Select all that apply.)

    a. Slack

    b. FaceTime

    c. Google Hangouts

    d. Skype

18. For each line below, select whether the statement is True or False.

    a. Telephone calls are no longer a useful means of work-related communication.

    b. Making a telephone call typically requires more of a time commitment than other forms of communication.

    c. Phone conversations can be applied to both formal and informal situations.

    d. Phone conversations are not automatically recorded as they occur.

    e. Phone conversations can include more than two people at a time.

19. When communicating with others, which of the following would be best suited to a teleconference or videoconference?

    a. casual conversation between family and friends

    b. information you would like kept private

    c. a workplace meeting with a remote office branch

    d. a one-on-one job interview

20. For each line below, select whether the statement is True or False.

    a. Text messages are usually sent using a cellular network, but may use Wi-Fi if it is available.

    b. All cellular plans offer unlimited text message.

    c. A text message is typically used for sending a quick message to someone.

    d. It is rude to let text messages distract from in-person conversation.

21. Social networks typically involve a person creating a _____, which allows others to find and connect with you.

    a. quiz

    b. collage

    c. list

    d. profile

22. All of the information you post on social networking sites defines your _____.

    a. avatar

    b. digital identity

    c. profile

    d. username

23. Which of the following is an example of an internal social media site?

    a. Facebook

    b. Myspace

    c. college-based networking site

    d. YouTube

24. Match the type of website to its intended use:

    1. Wiki

    2. Online forum

    3. Blog

    a. personal thoughts or opinions, similar to a diary

    b. a collection of information intended to be maintained by a group

    c. a page for posting discussion topics

25. Which of the following is NOT an example of a streaming app?

    a. Skype

    b. Hulu

    c. Spotify

    d. Twitch

26. What is the difference between streaming and progressive download?

  a. Progressive downloads are faster.

  b. Streaming is higher quality media.

  c. Progressive downloads are smaller in size.

  d. Streaming media plays as it continues to download.

IC3 PROCEDURES

CREATING AN EMAIL SIGNATURE IN OUTLOOK.COM

1. Log in to your Outlook.com account.
2. Select the **Settings** icon ⚙.
3. Select **View full settings**.
4. Select **Compose and Reply**.
5. In the Email signature area, enter and format the signature.
6. Select options, as desired.
7. Select **Save**.

CREATING AN EMAIL SIGNATURE IN OUTLOOK

1. In Outlook, select **File** and then select **Options**.
2. Select **Mail**.
3. Select the **Signatures** button.
4. Select **New**.
5. Type a name and select **OK**.
6. Enter and format the signature information.
7. Select **OK**.

   OR

1. Create a new email message.
2. On the Message tab, select the **Signature** button ✎.
3. Select **Signatures**.
4. Select **New**.
5. Type a name and select **OK**.
6. Enter and format the signature information.
7. Select **OK**.

MANUALLY ADDING A SIGNATURE TO AN EMAIL IN OUTLOOK

1. Create a new email message.
2. On the Message tab, select the **Signature** button ✎.
3. Select the signature to add.

ATTACHING A FILE TO A MESSAGE IN OUTLOOK

1. Compose the email message.
2. Click the **Message** tab.

   OR

   Click the **Insert** tab.
3. Click the **Attach File** button.
4. In the Insert File dialog box, navigate to the location where the file is stored.
5. Click the file, and then click **Insert**.

OPENING AN EMAIL ATTACHMENT IN OUTLOOK

1. Display the message in the Reading Pane.
2. Double-click the attached file in the message header to open the file in its native program.

PREVIEWING AN ATTACHMENT IN OUTLOOK

1. Display the message in the Reading Pane.
2. Click the attached file in the message header to display its contents in the Reading Pane.

SAVING AN ATTACHMENT IN OUTLOOK

1. Display the message in the Reading pane.
2. Click the attached file in the message header that you want to save.
3. On the Attachments tab, select the **Save All Attachments** button.
4. In the Save All Attachments dialog box, verify the file to save.
5. Select **OK**.
6. In the Save Attachment dialog box, navigate to the location where you want to save the file.
7. Enter a file name and set the file type, if desired.
8. Select **Save**.

CREATING A FOLDER FOR STORING MAIL IN OUTLOOK

1. Select the **Folder** tab.
2. Select the **New Folder** button.
3. In the Create New Folder dialog box, type the name of the new folder.
4. Select where you want to place the folder.
5. Select **OK**.

MOVING A MESSAGE IN OUTLOOK

1. In the message list of the mail window, select the message you want to move.
2. Drag the message to the desired folder in the Folder Pane.

   OR

1. Select the message.
2. On the Home tab, select the **Move** button.
3. From the menu, click the desired folder.

CREATING A SEARCH FOLDER IN OUTLOOK

1. Select the **Folder** tab.
2. Select **New Search Folder** button 🔍.
3. From the Select a Search Folder list, select the type of search folder you want to add.
4. Select customization options, as necessary.
5. Select **OK**.

DELETING A MESSAGE IN OUTLOOK

1. Right-click the message you want to delete.
2. Select **Delete**.

   OR

1. Select the message.
2. On the Home tab, select the **Delete** button ✖.

VIEWING A DELETED MESSAGE IN OUTLOOK

1. In Outlook, in the Folder list, select either the **Trash** or the **Deleted Items** folder.
2. In the message list, select the message to view.

RESTORING DELETED ITEMS IN OUTLOOK

1. In Outlook, in the Folder list, select either the **Trash** or the **Deleted Items** folder.
2. In the message list, select the message to restore.
3. Move the selected message to a different folder.

RECOVERING DELETED MESSAGES FROM THE SERVER IN OUTLOOK

1. In Outlook, in the Folder list, select either the **Trash** or the **Deleted Items** folder.
2. Above the message list, select the **Recover items recently removed from this folder** link.

   OR

   On the Home tab, select the **Recover Deleted Items from Server** button ♻.
3. Select the **Restore Selected Items** option button.
4. Select the message(s) to restore.
5. Select **OK**.

EMPTYING THE DELETED ITEMS FOLDER IN OUTLOOK

1. In Outlook, in the Folder list, right-click either the **Trash** or the **Deleted Items** folder.
2. Select **Empty folder**.
3. Select **Yes**.

   OR

1. Select either the **Trash** or the **Deleted Items** folder.
2. Select the **Folder** tab.
3. Select the **Empty folder** button 🗑.
4. Select **Yes**.

ARCHIVING A MESSAGE IN OUTLOOK

1. In the message list, select the message to archive.
2. On the Home tab, select the **Archive** button ⬚.

   If there is no Archive folder, Outlook prompts you to create one.

SETTING UP AUTOARCHIVE IN OUTLOOK

1. Select a folder in the folder list.
2. Select the **Folder** tab.
3. Select the **AutoArchive** button ⬚.
4. Set options.
5. Select **OK**.

ADDING AN ENTRY TO THE ADDRESS BOOK IN OUTLOOK

1. Select the **Home** tab.
2. Select the **New Items** drop-down arrow ⬚.
3. On the menu, select **Contact**.
4. Enter information into the contact form.
5. Select the **Save & Close** button ⬚.

   OR

1. On the **Home** tab, select the **Address Book** button ⬚.
2. In the Address Book dialog box, select **File**.
3. Select **New Entry**.
4. In the New Entry dialog box, select **New Contact**.
5. Select **OK**.
6. Enter information into the contact form.
7. Select the **Save & Close** button ⬚.

SCHEDULING AN ALL DAY EVENT WITH OUTLOOK

1. In Outlook, select the **Calendar** icon ⬚ at the bottom of the Navigation pane.
2. On the Home tab, select the **New Appointment** button ⬚.

   OR

   Select the **New Items** button ⬚ and then select **All day event**.
3. Enter a description in the Subject box.
4. Enter a location in the Location box, if necessary.
5. Enter a start date and time.
6. Enter an end date and time.
7. Select the **All day event** check box.
8. In the notes area, enter any additional information.
9. On the Event tab, select the **Save & Close** button ⬚.

SCHEDULING A RECURRING EVENT WITH OUTLOOK

1. In Outlook, select the **Calendar** icon ▦ at the bottom of the Navigation pane.

2. On the Home tab, select the **New Appointment** button ▦.

   OR

   Select the **New Items** button and then select **All day event**.

3. Enter a description in the Subject box.

4. Enter a location in the Location box, if necessary.

5. Enter a start date and time.

6. Enter an end date and time.

7. On the Event tab, select the **Recurrence** button ⟳.

8. In the Recurrence pattern area, select the recurrence interval.

9. Select other recurrence options, as necessary.

10. Select **OK**.

11. In the notes area, enter any additional information.

12. On the Event tab, select the **Save & Close** button.

SCHEDULING A ONE-TIME APPOINTMENT WITH OUTLOOK

1. In Outlook, select the **Calendar** icon ▦ at the bottom of the Navigation pane.

2. On the Home tab, select the **New Appointment** button ▦.

   OR

   Select the **New Items** button and then select **Appointment**.

3. Enter a description in the Subject box.

4. Enter a location in the Location box, if necessary.

5. Enter a start date and time.

6. Enter an end date and time.

7. In the notes area, enter any additional information.

8. On the Appointment tab, select the **Save & Close** button.

SCHEDULING A RECURRING APPOINTMENT WITH OUTLOOK

1. In Outlook, select the **Calendar** icon ▦ at the bottom of the Navigation pane.

2. On the Home tab, select the **New Appointment** button ▦.

   OR

   Select the **New Items** button and then select **Appointment**.

3. Enter a description in the Subject box.

4. Enter a location in the Location box, if necessary.

5. Enter a start date and time.

6. Enter an end date and time.

7. On the Appointment tab, select the **Recurrence** button ⟳.

8. In the Recurrence pattern area, select the recurrence interval.

9. Select other recurrence options, as necessary.

10. Select **OK**.

11. In the notes area, enter any additional information.

12. On the Appointment tab, select the **Save & Close** button 📤.

SCHEDULING A MEETING WITH OUTLOOK

1. In Outlook, select the **Calendar** icon 🔲 at the bottom of the Navigation pane.

2. On the Home tab, select the **New Meeting** button 👥.

    OR

    Select the **New Items** button 🗂 and then select **Meeting**.

3. In the To: box of the message header, enter the email addresses of the contacts you want to invite to the meeting.

4. Enter a description in the Subject box.

5. Enter a location in the Location box, if necessary.

6. Enter a start date and time.

7. Enter an end date and time.

8. Select or clear the **All day event** check box.

9. In the notes area, enter any additional information.

10. Select the **Send** button 📧.

SCHEDULING A RECURRING MEETING WITH OUTLOOK

1. In Outlook, select the **Calendar** icon 🔲 at the bottom of the Navigation pane.

2. On the Home tab, select the **New Meeting** button 👥.

    OR

    Select the **New Items** button 🗂 and then select **Meeting**.

3. In the To: box of the message header, enter the email addresses of the contacts you want to invite to the meeting.

4. Enter a description in the Subject box.

5. Enter a location in the Location box, if necessary.

6. Enter a start date and time.

7. Enter an end date and time.

8. On the Meeting tab, select the **Recurrence** button 🔄.

9. In the Recurrence pattern area, select the recurrence interval.

10. Select other recurrence options, as necessary.

11. Select **OK**.

12. In the notes area, enter any additional information.

13. Select the **Send** button 📧.

SHARING AN OUTLOOK CALENDAR WITH OTHERS

1. In Outlook, select the **Calendar** icon ▦ at the bottom of the Navigation pane.

2. In the Navigation pane, select the calendar to share.

3. On the Home tab, select the **Share Calendar** button ▦.

   OR

   Right-click the calendar to share and select **Share > Share Calendar**.

4. In the To: box of the message header, enter the email address of the person with whom you want to share the calendar.

   *To allow the person to modify your calendar, select the **Recipient can add, edit, and delete items in this calendar** check box.*

5. Select the **Send** button ▭.

SETTING OUTLOOK CALENDAR PERMISSIONS

1. In Outlook, select the **Calendar** icon ▦ at the bottom of the Navigation pane.

2. In the Navigation pane, select the calendar to share.

3. On the Home tab, select the **Calendar Permissions** button 👥.

4. Select the **Add** button.

5. In the address book, select the contact of the person to whom you want to assign permissions.

6. Click the **Add** button and then click **OK**.

7. Select or clear the permissions options.

8. Select **OK**.

CREATING AN EVENT IN GOOGLE CALENDAR

1. Sign in to your Google account and open Google Calendar.

2. Select the **Create event** button ➕.

3. Enter a description in the Add title box.

4. Enter a start date and time.

5. Enter an end date and time.

6. Select the **All day event** check box if it is an all day event.

7. Select an option from the Recurrence drop-down list, or select **Custom** and set recurrence options.

8. Enter a location in the Add location box, if necessary.

9. Select conferencing options from the Add conferencing drop-down list, if necessary.

10. Select **Add notification** to enter notification options.

11. Select the calendar on which to schedule the event, if necessary.

12. Select a color for the calendar, if necessary.

13. Select the status to display on the calendar.

14. Enter a description of the event.

15. To invite others, select **Add guests** and select the invitees from your contact list, or enter the invitees' email information.

16. Select **Save**.

17. Select **Send** to send invitations, if prompted.

SHARING A GOOGLE CALENDAR WITH EVERYONE

1. Sign in to your Google account and open Google Calendar.

2. To the right of the calendar you want to share, select the **Options** button ⋮.

3. Select **Settings and sharing**.

4. Select the **Make available to public** check box.

5. Select **OK**.

SHARING A GOOGLE CALENDAR WITH SPECIFIC PEOPLE

1. Sign in to your Google account and open Google Calendar.

2. To the right of the calendar you want to share, select the **Options** button ⋮.

3. Select **Settings and sharing**.

4. Under Share with specific people, select **Add people**.

5. Select or enter the contact information of the people whom you want to share the calendar.

6. From the Permissions drop-down list, select a permissions level.

7. Select **Send**.

SUBSCRIBING TO AN INTERNET CALENDAR WITH OUTLOOK

1. In your browser, browse to the page where the calendar is displayed.

2. Select the URL in the address bar, right-click the selection, and select **Copy**.

3. Switch to Outlook and select the **Calendar** icon ▦ at the bottom of the Navigation pane.

4. On the Home tab, select the **Open Calendar** button ▦.

5. Select **From Internet**.

6. Paste the URL of the internet calendar into the New Internet Calendar Subscription box.

7. Select **OK**.

8. Select **Yes** to add the calendar and subscribe to updates.

Additional Outlook 2016 Procedures

FORMATTING MESSAGE TEXT

1. In the email message window, select the message text you want to format.
2. Select the **Format Text** tab.
3. Select the button or its drop-down arrow to apply the desired format. Some common formats are:
   - Font `Calibri (Body)` ▾
   - Font Size `11` ▾
   - Bold `B`
   - Italic `I`
   - Underline `U`
   - Text Highlight Color `⠿` ▾
   - Font Color `A` ▾
   - Align Left `≣`
   - Center `≣`
   - Align Right `≣`
   - Justify `≣`
   - Bullets `≔` ▾
   - Numbering `≔` ▾

CHECKING SPELLING IN A MESSAGE

1. Select the **Review** tab.
2. Select the **Spelling & Grammar** button `✓`.
3. In the Spelling and Grammar dialog box, select the desired option to change or ignore the word.
4. When the spelling check is complete, select **OK** in the message box.

PRINTING AN EMAIL MESSAGE

1. Select the message you want to print.
2. Select **File**.
3. Select **Print**.
4. In Backstage view, set the print options as desired.
5. Select the **Print** button `🖶`.

MESSAGE HEADER TO DISPLAY IT'S COPYING A MESSAGE

1. In the message list of the mail window, select the message you want to copy.
2. Hold down **Ctrl** and drag the message to the desired folder in the Folder Pane.

   OR

1. Select the **Home** tab.
2. Select the **Move** button `📁`.
3. From the menu, select **Copy to Folder**.
4. In the Copy Items dialog box, select the folder to which you want to copy the message.
5. Select **OK**.

FLAGGING A MESSAGE FOR FOLLOW-UP

1. Select the message to flag.
2. Select the **Home** tab.
3. Select the **Follow Up** button `🚩`.
4. From the menu, select the desired follow-up deadline.

ENTERING AN EMAIL ADDRESS USING THE ADDRESS BOOK

1. Create a new email message.
2. Select the **To** button [To...].
3. In the Select Names dialog box, select the recipient's address.
4. Select **To**.
5. Select **OK**.

SEARCHING MAIL

1. In the Folder Pane, select the folder you want to search.
2. In the Search text box at the top of the message list, type the text for which you want to search.
3. Press **Enter**.

CREATING A DISTRIBUTION LIST

1. Select the **Home** tab.
2. Select the **Address Book** button [icon].
3. In the Address Book dialog box, select **File**.
4. Select **New Entry**.
5. In the New Entry dialog box, select **New Contact Group**.
6. Select **OK**.
7. In the Contact Group window, select in the **Name** box and type the name for the contact group.
8. Select the **Contact Group** tab.
9. Select the **Add Members** button [icon].
10. Select the resource from which you will add members.
11. In the Select Members dialog box, double-click member names.
12. When you have selected all the members, select **OK**.
13. Select the **Save & Close** button [icon].

IDENTITY THEFT

BRIAN A JACKSON/SHUTTERSTOCK

CHAPTER 32

Issues for Computer Users

COMPUTERS AND SAFETY

In the past, criminals needed to break into a building to steal money or goods. Today, criminals can steal data stored on a computer without going anywhere near a home or office building. They simply use an internet connection and special software to cover their tracks. With these tools, they can drain money out of a company's accounts or steal its secrets. They can steal a person's credit card information to sell or use.

Some people and many businesses have electronic security systems to prevent break-ins to homes and offices. Fortunately, there are also ways you can protect your computer systems and devices.

Privacy Online

OBJECTIVES

- Summarize the danger of sharing personal information on the internet.

- Explain how cookies and global unique identifiers endanger privacy.

- List ways to protect your data.

AS YOU READ

ORGANIZE INFORMATION As you read the lesson, use an outline to help you organize basic information about privacy issues.

TERMINOLOGY

- cookie

- global unique identifier (GUID)

- infringe

- power surge

- uninterruptible power supply (UPS)

Privacy in Cyberspace

Many consumers share personal information about themselves, their habits, and their finances. Sometimes, however, such information is gathered without a person's knowledge or approval.

HOW BUSINESSES OBTAIN PERSONAL INFORMATION Some businesses gather information from public records kept by the government. They may also access information that people volunteer about themselves.

- Website registration—Many websites require visitors to fill out registration forms.

- Online purchases—Some websites gather information about people who buy their goods or services.

- Warranty registration—To take advantage of a product warranty, you usually must register with the manufacturer. Some warranty registrations ask for a lot of personal information.

- Sweepstakes entries—Many people fill out sweepstakes entry forms hoping to win a prize. In doing so, they provide important personal information.

- Social networking sites—These sites gather information about their users from their profiles and posts, including where they live, what they like, and products they use.

- Search engines and messaging services— Some of these sites collect data about users and their online search history to learn what interests them.

Companies that gather personal information often sell it to other organizations, such as marketing companies, whose job it is to sell products and services to consumers. As a result, marketing companies have access to enormous quantities of data about people. This information is stored in large computerized databases.

PROTECTING PRIVACY Some people say that individuals should have the right to refuse to provide information about themselves, as well as the right to have information about themselves removed from a database. Although such a guarantee does not yet exist in the United States, you can protect your privacy by being careful to whom you give personal information about yourself. You can also select privacy settings on websites and social networks that limit who can access your personal information or view your posts. For example, you can select to only share your personal information with friends, or set your social networking status to invisible so other people do not know you are online.

RESPECTING OTHERS' PRIVACY You also need to make sure not to **infringe** or interfere with the privacy and rights of others. Do not post personal information about others online, via texts, or in emails.

EXPECTATIONS OF PRIVACY Remember that everything you post online or send by email is on record. Employees of a company have no right of privacy for their email when they use their employer's computer system. Although the employer may not say so, every message might be read by someone who alerts management if anything seems amiss. Employees may face serious consequences if they disclose inside information to competitors, threaten or harass other employees, or tell jokes.

In addition, when you apply to a college or university, or to a job, you should expect that the school or potential employer will look for you online. A simple search will let them see a history of what you have posted on almost every internet site. These are strong reasons why you should always be respectful and polite online, and why you should never post items that may be embarrassing to you in the future.

THINK ABOUT IT!

Think about what you might post online. Which statement(s) below might reveal too much personal information?

- "In my town, people often leave their doors unlocked."

- "We always go to the shore on weekends in the summer."

- "I don't like being alone."

- "Our porch light doesn't work."

- "My parents get home an hour after I arrive from school."

Technology and Your Privacy

The internet has generated new methods for tracking what people do. Even if you do not buy anything online, outsiders can use different hardware and software to learn about your habits and interests. Some people worry that these technologies—and your personal information—can be misused.

COOKIES Recall that a **cookie** is a small file that is saved to your hard drive when you visit some websites. Cookies give websites a way of storing information about you so it is available when you return. Cookies are meant to make your web experience more pleasurable by personalizing what you see. However, they can also be used to gather data on your browsing and shopping habits without your consent. If you wish, you can set your browser to reject cookies or warn you about them. Several programs and web browsers let users see what the specific purpose of a cookie is. Then you can decide whether or not to accept the cookie.

GLOBAL UNIQUE IDENTIFIERS A **global unique identifier (GUID)** is a unique identification number that is generated by a piece of hardware or by a program. Companies that place GUIDs in their products generally do not say so openly. Some people worry that GUIDs can be used to follow a person's online activity, invading his or her privacy.

GPS Mobile devices almost all have built-in global positioning system (GPS) services, which is handy when you need directions to a job interview, but can become invasive when used to track where you are, have been, and are thinking of going. Many websites and apps ask permission to use GPS to identify where you are, even if the information is not necessary for using the app. For example, just because you look up a restaurant website online does not mean you have to give that website access to your location. If you need directions to the restaurant, your mapping app, which already has GPS access, can provide them. You can turn off the GPS on your device when you are not using it.

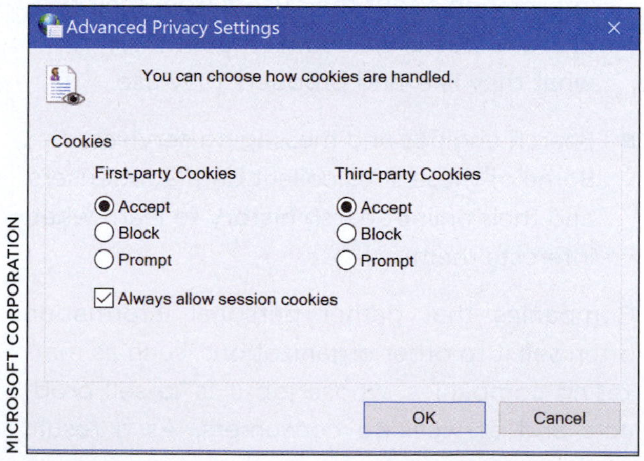

MICROSOFT CORPORATION

FIGURE 32.1.1 Use Privacy settings to control cookies.

Protecting Data

Recall that one of the simplest and most important methods of protecting data and keeping your computer running efficiently is to install and use an antivirus program or antimalware program to discover, quarantine, and remove viruses, spyware, and malware. These programs continually monitor your system for dangerous files. Once they find a virus, they delete it or quarantine it so it can do no harm.

Simply installing an antivirus program is not enough to protect your computer. New viruses are created every day. Software publishers update their antivirus programs to defeat each new attack, and you must make sure you keep the program on your computer up-to-date. The easiest way to do this is to set your antivirus program to update automatically using an internet connection.

FIREWALLS To help block unauthorized users from accessing your computer through a network, you can install and activate a firewall. Recall that a firewall is a program that restricts unauthorized network access to your computer. Most operating systems, including Microsoft Windows, come with a firewall, and so do many antivirus programs.

BACKING UP A hard drive crash is a problem, but it does not have to be a disaster as long as you have backed up your data. Backing up is simply creating a copy of the data on your hard drive that is stored separately in an off-site or remote location away from the hard drive. You can back up data manually or use a program that performs the backup automatically on a set schedule.

After a crash, the lost data can be restored from the backup. Some programs, such as Microsoft Word and Adobe Acrobat, automatically backup your files while you work. If the program crashes before you save your current changes, when you reopen it you will be prompted with a message asking if you want to restore your last session. By pressing "yes," you open the latest backed-up version of the document.

REMOVING DATA There may be a time when you want to permanently remove data from your storage devices. Just deleting a file is not enough. Hackers can easily find deleted files. To make sure information is not left on a drive, you must reformat or wipe the drive, which destroys all files. You can clear a smartphone or tablet by resetting it to its factory configuration.

POWER-RELATED PROBLEMS Just like any other device that runs on electricity, a computer can be affected by power fluctuations or outages. These problems can lead to the loss of data. A **power surge**, or a sharp increase in the power coming into the system, can destroy a computer's electrical components.

You can help protect your computer from power problems by attaching an **uninterruptible power supply (UPS)** between your computer and the power source. This battery powered device goes to work when it detects an outage or critical voltage drop. It powers the computer for a period of time. A UPS can also protect against power surges by filtering sudden electrical spikes. The unit offers surge protection and will prevent a spike in power from damaging your computer. In event of a power outage, the unit will keep your computer running long enough for you to shut it down properly. Some electrical power strips have surge protection, but do not include a battery.

All About Cybercrime

OBJECTIVES

- Identify techniques that intruders use to attack computer systems.

- Discuss different types of cybercrime.

- Summarize how computer crime costs businesses money.

AS YOU READ

IDENTIFY KEY POINTS As you read, use a conclusion chart to help you identify key points about computer-related crime.

TERMINOLOGY

- computer crime

- cybercrime

- downtime

- identity theft

- memory shave

- phishing

- scanning

- software piracy

- spoof

- superzapper

- time bomb

- trap door

- Trojan horse

- virus

- worm

Cybercrime Techniques

Many cybercrimes are based on the ability of people to tap illegally into computer networks. They may create a **virus**, **worm**, or **Trojan horse** program to infiltrate computers and damage or delete data. Or, they may use a variety of other criminal techniques.

SCANNING Some intruders develop programs that try many different passwords until one works. This is called **scanning**, or probing. Networks can be blocked from scanners by limiting the number of failed attempts to log onto the system. After three password failures, for instance, the network can refuse access.

SUPERZAPPING A program called a **superzapper** allows authorized users to access a network in an emergency situation by skipping security measures. In the hands of an intruder, a superzapper opens the possibility of damage to the system.

SPOOFING Some intruders **spoof**, or use a false Internet Protocol (IP) or email address to gain access. Intruders assume the IP address of a trusted source to enter a secure network and distribute emails containing viruses.

PHISHING **Phishing** criminals try to lure victims into giving them user names, passwords, bank account numbers, or credit card details, usually by using an email that looks like it comes from an official and legitimate source. For example, in a typical phishing scam, a thief sends an email message that looks as if it is from your bank, asking you to verify or update your account information. The thief captures the information you enter and can then steal from your account.

TIME BOMBS A **time bomb** is a program that sits on a system until a certain event or set of circumstances activates the program. For example, an employee could create a time bomb designed to activate on a certain date after he or she resigns from the company. Although a time bomb is not necessarily a virus, these malicious programs are often categorized or described as viruses.

TRAP DOORS Some employees may create a **trap door**, or a secret way into the system. Once they quit working for the employer, they can use this to access the system and damage it. Not all trap doors are viruses, but some viruses are trap doors. Many Trojan horse programs, for example, act as trap doors.

SCAMS Some criminals use advertisements and email messages to scam you into sending them money. For example, they might claim you have won a lottery, and if you pay a tax or fee, they will send you the winnings.

SOCIAL ENGINEERING A common criminal tactic is to use social engineering to trick you into clicking a link that will install a virus or capture your personal information. Social engineering is not technical. It relies on human nature and manipulation to convince someone to do something. A common social engineering hack would be an official-looking email notifying you about a problem with your bank account. When you click a link you are sent to a fake bank website.

DID YOU KNOW?

Spyware is software that sends information about you and your web-surfing habits to companies from whom you downloaded programs, or for whom you completed online registrations.

Spyware programs install themselves on your system without your knowledge. Most spyware claims that it tracks habits, without naming specific individuals. Its goal is to gather data and then draw conclusions about a group's web habits. It can also make your computer run more slowly than it should.

You can protect your computer from spyware by installing and using virus and malware protection software.

Types of Cybercrime

Crimes using the internet can take many different forms. They affect individuals, businesses, and government agencies.

FRAUD When someone steals your personal information, he or she can impersonate you and make credit card purchases in your name or access your bank accounts. This is called **identity theft**. The criminal leaves you with bills and a damaged credit rating.

PIRACY **Software piracy** is the illegal copying of computer programs. It is estimated that about one third of all software in use is pirated. Recall that most programs that people buy are licensed only to the purchaser. In other words, it is illegal for you to copy such a program and give it to a friend. It is also illegal to accept a copy of software from someone else. Software piracy affects software publishers. They lose money when people use illegal copies of programs to avoid paying for legitimate copies.

THEFT The vast majority of computer thefts occur "on the inside" (by employees), leaving no signs of forced entry. The hardest crime to detect is **memory shaving**. In this act, a thief steals some of a computer's memory chips but leaves enough so the computer will start. The crime might go unnoticed for days or weeks.

VANDALISM Some web servers are not properly secured. As a result, intruders can vandalize a website by replacing the real content with fake content.

The High Cost of Computer Crime

The internet has opened the door to new kinds of crime and new ways of carrying out traditional crimes. **Computer crime** is any act that violates state or federal laws and involves using a computer. The term **cybercrime** often refers specifically to crimes carried out by means of the internet. Computer crime causes businesses to lose money in the following ways.

STAFF TIME Even if intruders steal nothing from a business, they still cost companies money. Staff must take time to make the network secure again and consider how to stop security breaches.

MICROSOFT CORPORATION (SCREENSHOT); FEDERAL TRADE COMMISSION (WEBSITE)

FIGURE 32.2.1 The Federal Trade Commission offers information on how to avoid identity theft.

DOWNTIME Security breaches also cost a company in terms of **downtime**, or a temporary stop to work. System administrators sometimes shut a network down to prevent the loss of data. While the system is down, workers cannot do their jobs. A company can lose business if customers are affected by downtime.

BAD PUBLICITY When security problems become known, the public image of a company may suffer. Even if no personal information is lost, customers lose confidence that the company's security is trustworthy. Customers then take their business elsewhere, and, for publicly-traded companies, stock prices may fall.

Fighting Cybercrime

Law enforcement officials are using technology to catch cybercriminals. Several groups have taken part in this effort.

COMPUTER CRIME AND INTELLECTUAL PROPERTY SECTION (CCIPS) The Department of Justice created a special group known as CCIPS to advise and train federal prosecutors and local law enforcement on cybercrime. They review and propose new laws. They coordinate international efforts to combat computer crime and prosecute offenders.

COMPUTER HACKING AND INTELLECTUAL PROPERTY PROJECT (CHIP) In the CHIP project, law enforcement officials and prosecutors work closely together to pursue cybercrime. CHIP offices are in areas with a heavy concentration of computer companies.

NATIONAL INFRASTRUCTURE PROTECTION CENTER (NIPC) In 1998, government officials became worried about terrorist attacks on U.S. computer systems. Staffed by people from intelligence agencies and private companies such as internet service providers, the NIPC ensures that the nation's computer systems could continue to operate in the case of an attack.

REAL-WORLD TECH

CAMBRIDGE ANALYTICA

ALEXSKOPJE/SHUTTERSTOCK

In 2018, a voter-profiling company called Cambridge Analytica was discovered to have collected the personal information of nearly 87 million Facebook users, without their consent. The company began collecting the data in 2014, possibly with the intent of selling the information to clients interested in developing targeted advertising for candidates in the 2016 U.S. presidential election.

Cambridge Analytica accomplished the data grab by developing a personality-quiz app for Facebook. About 270,000 Facebook users downloaded the app, giving access to their data when they clicked the licensing agreement check box. The company was able to exploit weaknesses in Facebook's privacy and security controls and also access the data of those users' friends without their knowledge or permission.

Do you read the licensing agreement when you download an app? Do you know what information you are making available, or who will be using it?

Avoiding Cybercrime

OBJECTIVES

- Describe ways criminals obtain passwords.

- Discuss ways to protect your computer from being accessed by others.

- Explain the criteria of a strong password.

- Summarize ways to stay safe online.

AS YOU READ

SUMMARIZE As you read the lesson, use a chart to help you summarize ways to protect information on your computer.

TERMINOLOGY

- packet sniffer

Password Theft

Many computer crimes start when an unauthorized user hacks, or gains unauthorized entry, into a computer network. This often happens when the intruder learns the password to access the victim's computer and the network. Following are ways such criminals learn passwords.

GUESSING Too often, computer users choose passwords that are easy for them to remember, such as birthdates, names of pets, names of celebrities, and names of family members. Unfortunately, these passwords are also easy for intruders to guess. Surprisingly, the most common passwords used are "password" and "123456," both of which are extremely weak.

FINDING Sometimes people keep passwords written on pieces of paper near their computer. Other times, criminals simply look over someone's shoulder as he or she types the password and use it later. An intruder can also search the trash in the hopes of finding user IDs and passwords.

SNIFFING Some criminals may use **packet sniffers**. A packet sniffer is a program that examines data streams on networks to try to find information, such as passwords and credit card numbers.

PRETENDING Some intruders pretend to be network administrators. They call network users and ask for their passwords, claiming that the passwords are needed to solve a problem in the system.

MODIFYING Network software makes the people who administer a system into superusers. Intruders who have superuser access can modify virtually any file on the network. They also may change user passwords to ones that only they know, so the real users cannot log in.

Protecting Your Personal Data

It is in your best interest to protect your computer and its data. Here are some ways to help protect personal information.

USE STRONG PASSWORDS Whenever you create a password, don't use things like family names, nicknames, or birth dates. Random passwords are often the strongest, like S3nD3v. Use a combination of at least six upper- and lowercase letters, numbers, and symbols. Often the site will let you know if your password is strong enough. Remember to change your password every few months. Do not keep a record of your passwords on your computer or on a piece of

---

CONNECTIONS

LANGUAGE ARTS Where did all the unusual names for destructive software come from?

A computer virus is named for the kind of virus that causes infectious diseases like the cold and the flu.

A worm is named for a tapeworm, a kind of organism that lives in the intestines of another creature and lives off the food that creature eats.

A Trojan horse takes its name from an ancient Greek story about soldiers who entered a fortress by hiding inside the body of a giant replica of a horse, which the defenders allowed in. The soldiers hidden inside the horse attacked and defeated the defenders.

ANGELA WAYE/SHUTTERSTOCK

FIGURE 32.3.1 You may be required to provide a user name and password before accessing a computer network. Be sure to use a "strong" password.

paper near your computer. Never give out your passwords to anyone, and never type a password while someone is watching.

BROWSE ANONYMOUSLY When you go online, surf from sites that protect your identity. Anonymizer and IDZap are two sites offering this service. Some browsers offer anonymous browsing, including Chrome's Incognito or Edge's InPrivate. These modes affect your local privacy, meaning the privacy on your local device. They do not affect your online privacy. That means using Incognito or InPrivate will not hide your browsing from your employer, your internet service provider, or the websites you visit.

USE A DIFFERENT EMAIL ADDRESS Although you may not be able to do this at school, on a home computer you can sign up for a free email account from a website such as Outlook.com or Gmail. Use that address when you register at websites or participate in other public internet spaces. This will protect you from receiving unwanted mail, or spam, at your primary email address.

AVOID SITE REGISTRATION Be careful of websites that require you to register. Do not fill out a registration form unless the site clearly says that the data will not be shared with other people without your permission.

Be Smart Online

You can avoid most computer crime simply by being a smart computer user. You can make sure your browser settings are at the highest level for security and privacy, you can delete email from unknown senders without opening it, and you can be wary of offers that seem too good to be true. Make sure you do business only with established companies that you know and trust. No reputable company or bank will ever ask you to send them your username, password, account information, or social security number. You should never reveal financial or other personal information, even if the request sounds legitimate.

TECHNOLOGY@HOME

One way companies generate mailing lists for spam messages is by checking the email and social networking addresses of people online. If you use online services, you can minimize spam at your primary email address by using a secondary email address. You can then easily permanently delete the spam delivered to the secondary address.

THINK ABOUT IT!

Which contacts listed below would you give your secondary email address to?

- friend
- movie promotional site
- website from which you ordered a new pair of shoes
- chat room
- website where you receive support for your computer

SAFE SOCIAL NETWORKING Here are some safety tips for online social networking:

- Do not add just anyone as a "friend." This person will see everything you post, including pictures and status updates.

- Check your settings. If you don't understand how to manage your account, get an experienced adult to help you make sure you maintain your privacy.

- Learn how to change your status to invisible, so others do not know you are online, or visible when you want to be available to others.

- Give your parents or other trusted adult access to monitor your social networking activity.

FIGURE 32.3.2 Never give out private information online.

- Remember that your posts and profiles can be easily tracked online. Don't write or post anything online that you would not want your grandparents or teachers to see or that you would not want posted about yourself.

- Never give out private information such as your phone number or address.

- Never agree to meet a new online friend in person.

- If you feel uncomfortable about an online experience, immediately tell a trusted adult.

- Don't download or install programs without parental permission.

Chapter 32 Review

REVIEW THE TERMINOLOGY

DIRECTIONS Match each vocabulary term in the left column with the correct definition in the right column.

1. identity theft
2. phishing
3. global unique identifier
4. computer crime
5. cybercrime
6. downtime
7. software piracy
8. packet sniffer
9. scanning
10. spoof

a. using a program to try different passwords until one works
b. using a computer to break the law
c. using the internet to break the law
d. when workers cannot work because a network is temporarily not available
e. illegal copying of software programs
f. identification number generated by a piece of hardware or by a program
g. useing a false IP or email address to gain access to a network
h. impersonating someone in order to commit fraud
i. using an official-looking email to lure victims into providing personal data
j. method of finding another's password

USE THE TERMINOLOGY

DIRECTIONS Determine the correct choice for each of the following.

1. Which of the following should you do cautiously because it could result in sharing personal information without your approval?
   a. buying software
   b. copying software
   c. registering at a website
   d. getting warranty protection

2. Which of the following malicious programs is activated by an event or set of circumstances?
   a. worm
   b. email virus
   c. time bomb
   d. Trojan horse

3. Which of the following might cause a business to lose money as a result of computer crime?
   a. faulty product design
   b. downtime
   c. economic recession
   d. fire

4. Which kind of destructive computer program can move from one operating system to another?

    a. macro virus   **c.** virus

    b. Trojan horse   **d.** worm

5. What is an example of a password that is easy to guess?

    a. a combination of numbers and letters that makes no sense

    b. a four-letter nickname

    c. ten letters that do not spell a word

    d. eight randomly chosen numbers and symbols

6. Which of the following is NOT a law enforcement group for fighting cybercrime?

    a. CCIPS   **c.** CHIP

    b. FDA   **d.** NIPC

THINK CRITICALLY

DIRECTIONS Answer the following questions.

1. Why is it a good idea to keep personal information confidential?

2. Summarize the components of a strong password.

3. Give examples of computer crime and cybercrime that illustrate the difference between the two terms.

4. What are the consequences of software piracy? How can you help prevent piracy?

5. Which methods of protecting your privacy and your data do you follow?

EXTEND YOUR KNOWLEDGE

DIRECTIONS Choose and complete one of the following projects.

1. Create a poster illustrating one way you can be a smart computer user. Present your poster to the class, and then, with permission, display the poster in a public area of your school, such as a hallway or cafeteria.

2. With your teacher's permission, use the internet to investigate a cybercrime. Write a brief report outlining what happened, what damage resulted, and whether the criminal was caught. If he or she was caught, describe how. State what consequences the criminal must face.

3. Because the internet is so easily accessible, it is important to learn how to protect your identity and personal information when you are online. With permission from your teacher, conduct research using the internet to compile a list of web safety tips. Be sure to evaluate the information you find and only use that which is accurate, relevant, and reliable. Publish your findings, with permission from your teacher, on your school's website.

CHAPTER 33

Using Computers Responsibly

LESSON 33-1
COMPUTER ETHICS

LESSON 33-2
UNDERSTANDING COPYRIGHT LAWS

ETHICAL BEHAVIOR

Computers are tools, and, like other tools, they are controlled by the person using them. People can use computers to learn, to communicate, and to have fun. However, what makes computers useful also makes them dangerous. People can use computers to snoop into another person's private life or to commit crimes. Careless computer users can pass computer viruses from their devices to those of other users. Companies can collect and sell personal information, sometimes without a person ever knowing it happened.

Honest people respect others. They learn to use tools with care and to protect themselves and others from harm. Computer users must behave honestly and responsibly, too.

Computer Ethics

OBJECTIVES

- Give examples of rules in acceptable use policies (AUPs).

- Summarize netiquette.

- Discuss online identity management.

- Explain how to manage online profiles.

- Explain cyberbullying.

- Recognize factors affecting digital wellness.

AS YOU READ

ORGANIZE INFORMATION As you read the lesson, use a chart to help you organize details about privacy and ethics.

TERMINOLOGY

- acceptable use policy (AUP)

- brand

- censor

- cyberbullying

- digital wellness

- ergonomics

- ethics

- filter

- netiquette

- screen time

- trolls

Ethical Computer Use

How people use computers, including networks and email, can affect other people. People who practice **ethics** behave morally, which means respecting the principles of right and wrong behavior. Ethical computer users respect others, and make sure their actions do not harm anyone.

ACCEPTABLE USE POLICIES One way you can act ethically is to follow your school district's **acceptable use policy (AUP)**. These policies identify the responsibilities of internet use. They spell out certain rules of behavior and explain the consequences of breaking those rules. Many businesses use AUPs, too, to govern the way workers use company-owned computers. Some websites may also have AUPs that users must agree to in order to register an account. An AUP may include the following ethical guidelines:

- Do not visit websites that contain content that does not meet community standards.

- Do not use language, that is profane, abusive, or impolite.

- Do not copy copyrighted material.

- Do not damage computer equipment belonging to the school or business.

- Do respect the privacy of other people.

Schools and businesses may restrict the content that users can access from internal computers. For example, they may **censor**, or block, specific sites that they determine are inappropriate.

They may also use a **filter** to block access to sites. Disabling the filters or otherwise accessing blocked sites is considered breaking the AUP, and may result in punishment.

POSSIBLE PENALTIES People who do not follow these rules may face consequences. They might lose privileges or be suspended from school activities. Very serious violations, such as using a school or business computer to threaten someone, may require police involvement.

IC3✔ Know about censorship and filtering.

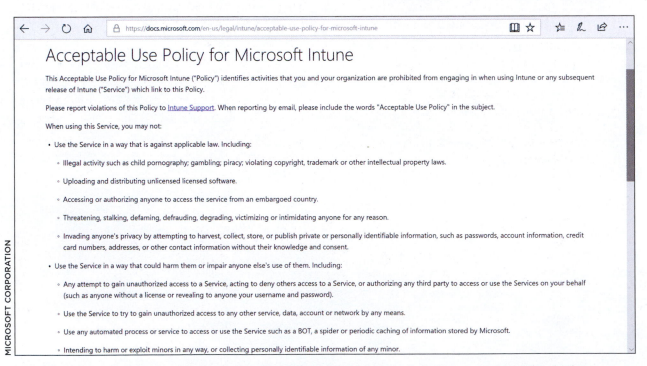

FIGURE 33.1.1 An AUP provides guidelines for using online resources including apps, browsers, and search engines.

Practicing Netiquette

There is an informal set of rules for online behavior called **netiquette**. As an ethical computer user, you have a responsibility to use netiquette at all times. Some ways to practice netiquette include:

- Send emails only to people who really need to see a message.

- Keep email messages short.

- Avoid sending extremely large files via email.

- Do not use impolite or rude language online.

- Do not pretend to be someone else online.

- Do not use someone else's work without citing the source.

- Do not share files illegally.

The rules of netiquette are similar to general standards for good behavior. If you go to a search engine and type "netiquette," you will find many websites on the topic.

TECHNOLOGY@WORK

A confidentiality agreement—also called a nondisclosure agreement—is a signed contract used to keep people from discussing secret, proprietary, or sensitive information. Sometimes employees must sign such an agreement regarding employer information, and sometimes companies sign one regarding client or customer information.

THINK ABOUT IT!

What type of information do you think might be protected by a nondisclosure agreement?

Managing Your Online Identity

Online, people learn about you by what you post and what sites you frequent. You can use your online profile, or digital identity, to both promote a positive image—or **brand**—of yourself, and to protect your identity. Building your brand means making sure everything you post or display online supports the reputation and character you want people to associate with you. You can accomplish positive branding by taking care to model ethical behavior when posting information online.

IC3 ✔ **Understand online identity management, including branding.**

You can protect your identity by making sure you effectively manage all of your online profiles, including on gaming sites and on social networking sites such as Twitter, LinkedIn, and Facebook. Know how to update your profile so the information is accurate and honest, without giving out too much that might identify you in real life. Be sure to limit the amount of personal information you include in your profile, and to use privacy settings to make sure outsiders cannot learn more than you want to share. Remember that websites want to collect as much information about you as possible to use or to sell. Also, there are individuals who might try to use the information to find you in real life, even if you do not want to meet them.

IC3 ✔ **Know how to manage profiles on gaming and social networking sites.**

It is possible to maintain more than one online profile. For example, you might maintain both a professional and a personal identity online. To accomplish this, you would set up different online accounts for different purposes. You

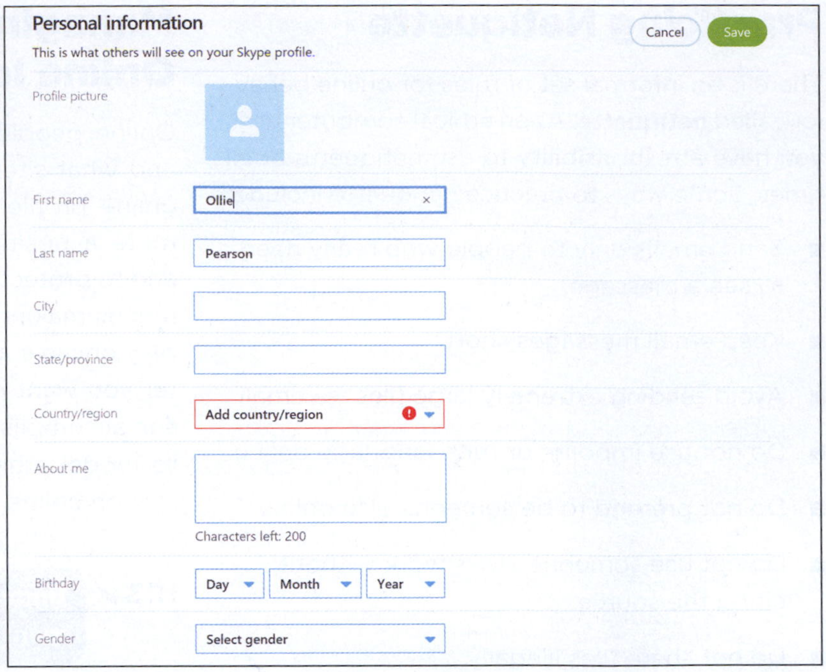

MICROSOFT CORPORATION

FIGURE 33.1.2 Managing profile settings in Skype.

might have one email account you use for professional and business communication such as a job search, and a separate email account for personal communication with your friends and family. You might have a LinkedIn account for professional contacts, an Instagram account for use with your friends, and a Facebook page for staying in touch with your grandparents and other family members.

IC3✔ Know the difference between personal vs. professional identity.

Cyberbullying

According to the Cyberbullying Research Center, "**cyberbullying** is when someone repeatedly harasses, mistreats, or makes fun of another person online or while using cell phones or other electronic devices." Cyberbullies hurt their victims by doing things like sending threatening or harassing messages or texts, posting private pictures online or via cell phones, and creating hurtful websites, like fake Instagram sites.

Cyberbullying is hard to fight, because usually it happens anonymously and away from school and home. However, it has led to many high profile cases of teen suicide, spreading unstoppable rings of grief through whole communities. If you are the victim of cyberbullying, you should tell someone you trust right away: your parents, your internet or mobile phone service provider, your school—or even the police.

If you engage in cyberbullying behavior, be aware that all 50 states have laws against bullying, and 48 of them include electronic harassment in those laws. Punishments vary by state, but may include expulsion from school, large fines, and jail time.

IC3✔ Know what cyberbullying is.

694

Don't Be a Cybercriminal

When you use the internet it can feel as if no one can identify who you really are. As a result, behavior online can often turn inappropriate, rude, and even illegal. Some users are internet **trolls**, which means they go on sites specifically to post rude, mean comments intended to upset people. Remember, you can be tracked; someone will figure out who you are.

Whether you are playing a game online or posting a comment on a website, it is important to behave in the online space as you would in the real world. Always be courteous and respectful. If you post a negative review of a product or service, make sure it is true and accurate and not mean or spiteful. Poor reviews can be damaging to a business. Never insult or bully an individual, or post comments that are untrue. Cyberbullying is a crime.

Sometimes it is not mean comments that can get you into trouble. Many people flirt using electronic communications. Messages can be forwarded or posted on social networking sites for all to see. Sending inappropriate text and pictures electronically is called sexting, and, in some circumstances, it is illegal.

TECHNOLOGY@HOME

Gestures, facial expressions, and tones of voice—which people use in conversation to add intent or meaning—are missing from email.

THINK ABOUT IT!

Which items listed below do you think would be clearly communicated through the text in an email? Which could be miscommunicated?

- fact
- sarcasm
- anger
- question
- joy

Digital Wellness

Digital wellness means using technology safely and appropriately. In addition to topics discussed previously, such as the ethical use of computers and protecting your personal information, it also includes physical health and safety.

SCREEN TIME While **screen time**, or the amount of time you spend using a computer screen, is important and provides many benefits, it also detracts from things like physical activity and face-to-face time with friends and family. So, how do you know how much screen time is enough? It depends on many factors, but here are a few indicators that you might want to cut back, or take a break:

- Does it make you sad when you visit other people's social networking pages?
- Is screen time interfering with a healthy diet?
- Are you losing sleep because you are online throughout the night?
- Do you get headaches looking at the screen?

IC3 ✔ **Understand the effects of screen time.**

ERGONOMICS Some problems that come from too much screen time have to do with the ergonomics of the environment. **Ergonomics** refers to the interaction of people and the objects or equipment they use. For example, a standard keyboard might result in wrist pain for someone who types a lot, but an ergonomically-designed keyboard might reduce that pain.

You can positively impact your digital wellness by following ergonomic best practices while using digital devices, including the following:

- Use proper posture when sitting and standing.
- Make sure there is sufficient lighting to see the screen.

DAVID SANDERSON/PEARSON EDUCATION LTD

DAVID SANDERSON/PEARSON EDUCATION LTD

FIGURE 33.1.3 Incorrect posture (left) can cause pain and injury, while correct posture (right) supports digital wellness.

- Take breaks to limit the length of time you spend looking at a screen.

- Switch between devices to avoid repetitive actions.

- Use ergonomic devices, such as keyboards and mice, but also chairs and desks.

IC3✔ **Understand ergonomic best practices.**

KNOW YOUR AUDIENCE As online technologies grow and change, it is important to maintain an awareness of how they impact individuals and society. In our online, digital world, you start a conversation by sharing an opinion, idea, or experience. Who is receiving that message? Is it being interpreted the way you intend? Consider that when you send a tweet, the whole world might be your audience. Social communication is interactive—you might send out a message, but your audience has the opportunity to react and reply. Always consider the audience—the people who will read your posts and view your pictures—as you navigate the online environment.

IC3✔ **Understand how to cope with changes in technology: audience awareness.**

696

Understanding Copyright Laws

OBJECTIVES

- Define copyright.
- Identify types of intellectual property.
- Explain intellectual property laws, rights, and usage.
- Give examples of plagiarism.
- Explain the fair use doctrine.
- Discuss the purpose of a software license.

AS YOU READ

ORGANIZE INFORMATION As you read the lesson, use a chart to help you organize details about copyright laws.

TERMINOLOGY

- citation
- copyright
- copyright infringement
- Creative Commons license
- derivative
- fair use doctrine
- intellectual property
- patent
- plagiarism
- public domain
- software license
- software piracy
- trademark

Copyright Laws

Copyright is the legal right to make copies, license, and otherwise use **intellectual property** such as a literary, creative, or artistic work. Federal laws that involve copyright protect individuals and companies from the theft or misuse of their intellectual property, including music, lyrics, literature, scripts, choreography, graphics, pictures, sculpture, videos, films, and architecture. They also extend to productions and performances that use these copyrighted materials.

Copyright exists as soon as a work is created. It is a crime to copy intellectual property without the permission of the person who owns the copyright to it. Someone who pretends that another person's work is his or her own has broken the law by committing **copyright infringement**. He or she has stolen another person's work. Penalties include paying a large fine and possibly jail time.

IC3 ✔ Know about copyrights.

PROTECTING COPYRIGHT If you create intellectual property, you are protected by copyright laws, including the following:

- The right to produce or reproduce the copyrighted work
- The right to prepare derivative works based upon the work
- The right to distribute copies of the work to the public
- The right to perform a copyrighted work publicly
- The right to display the copyrighted work publicly

The U.S. Copyright Act of 1976 clarifies the protections that are guaranteed to the owner of a copyrighted work. To protect a copyright or to simply clarify who created the work, the owner can register it with the U.S. Copyright Office.

The owner sends a copy of the completed work along with the fee, which depends on what type of work it is. If the owner must bring a lawsuit for infringement against another party for violating the copyrighted work, it helps to have a copy of the work on file with the U.S. Copyright Office.

IC3 ✔ Know about intellectual property rights and usage.

CITE YOUR SOURCE If you use information you find on the web in your work, you must give credit to the source. You do this by inserting a reference to the source, called a **citation**, in a footnote, endnote, or bibliography. A proper citation gives credit to the source, and provides the tools a reader needs to locate the source on his or her own. Some websites have features that automatically generate citation information for you.

As a general rule, you should always seek permission to use content from the intellectual property owner, even if the work is licensed in a way that suggests redistribution is permissible. Written permission may be required for long quotes, artwork, or videos, or if you use content for commercial use, such as advertising. Check the copyright restrictions before using any content you download from the internet. Even if a website advertises "free" clip art, there may be restrictions that could end up costing you a significant amount of money if you use the content without proper permission.

PLAGIARISM If you do not cite your sources you are guilty of **plagiarism**, which is the unauthorized and uncredited use of another person's ideas or creative work. Plagiarism is equivalent to stealing another person's work and passing it off as your own. The consequences of plagiarism can be quite significant. If you plagiarize work in school, you may have to redo the assignment or lose credit all together. Your school may also take disciplinary actions, such as detention. In the professional world, the consequences of plagiarism are even more significant. A professional who plagiarizes work suffers a loss to his or her reputation and may face legal ramifications, such as a lawsuit.

To avoid plagiarism you just need to properly cite your source. You should insert a citation when you quote, summarize, or paraphrase someone else, use someone else's idea, or reference someone else's work. In a works cited section or footnote, tell the reader the source of your credited information.

IC3✔ **Know about plagiarism rules and laws.**

TRADEMARKS AND PATENTS In addition to copyright, some intellectual property is protected by trademark or patent. A **trademark** is a symbol that indicates a brand or brand name is legally protected and cannot be used by other businesses. A **patent** is the exclusive right to make, use, or sell a device or process. Many types of inventions can be patented. Using trademarked or patented property without permission is called infringement. The penalty is usually a large fine and a court order to stop.

IC3✔ **Know about licensing rules and laws for intellectual property.**

THE FAIR USE DOCTRINE If intellectual property is protected by copyright, you must have permission from the copyright holder to use the work. However, part of copyright law called the **fair use doctrine** allows you to use a limited amount of copyrighted material without permission for educational purposes. For example, you can quote a few lines of a song or a passage from a book.

The fair use doctrine is important for media makers because it's the part of U.S. copyright law that permits the use of previously published materials, provided that a particular set of conditions are met. When you use previously published work in a new creation, it's considered to be a **derivative** of the original. Here are the four criteria that a judge or jury would use to determine if your use is legitimately fair:

- The purpose of the derivative work. For instance, a collage made by an instructor that will not be sold or distributed beyond the classroom is probably fair, while one inserted into a commercial publication is likely to be ruled in violation.

- The nature of the content of the original. Factual content can legitimately be reused, whereas creative content is considered to be intellectual property.

- How much of the original work is used in the derivative. For visual works, there is no set guideline for how much you are allowed to use. But, if the transformative quality (not quantity) of the new work is hard to recognize, your work may be so similar to the original that it seems to use "too much" of it.

- The effect of the new work on the actual or potential market value of the original. If the new work defames the original or lessens the value of the original work, the use would not be considered fair.

IC3✔ **Know about the fair use doctrine.**

PUBLIC DOMAIN AND CREATIVE COMMONS Not all works are protected by copyright laws. You are free to use images that are in the **public domain**. Public domain includes official media created by the U.S. government, much of the content in the Library of Congress (LOC), and works that have an expired copyright (the life of the author plus 70 years for U.S. authors).

In addition to the public domain and expired copyrights, some artists actively contribute to a growing collection of media licensed with alternative mechanisms to the traditional U.S. copyright. **Creative Commons licenses** allow artists to set specific guidelines in regard to how their work can be shared, transformed, or redistributed, both commercially and non-commercially.

Software Licensing

Recall that buying proprietary, copyrighted software comes with a **software license**, which allows the buyer to use and install the program, and sometimes entitles the buyer to receive free or reduced cost support and updates. Individuals might buy a single-user license for one copy of the program, or a single-seat license to install the program on a single computer. Organizations such as schools or businesses usually buy a volume or site license which lets them install software on multiple systems or a network for multiple users. Network licensing generally costs less per user and allows users to share resources.

SOFTWARE PIRACY People who copy copyrighted software to sell, give away, or install on other computers are guilty of violating federal copyright laws and stealing, called **software piracy**. Violating a copyright and pirating software are both morally wrong and illegal. These activities discourage the authors of good software from writing new and better programs because they may not get paid for their work. Pirated software cannot be registered, so users do not get the support services they may need.

IC3✔ Know about licensing rules and laws for software programs.

FIGURE 33.2.1 Downloading copyrighted software to sell, give away, or install on other computers is a crime.

DAVID TORDABLE/123RF

REVIEW THE TERMINOLOGY

DIRECTIONS Match each vocabulary term in the left column with the correct definition in the right column.

1. copyright
2. ergonomics
3. fair use doctrine
4. plagiarism
5. citation
6. ethics
7. trademark
8. derivative
9. patent
10. screen time

a. behaving morally

b. unauthorized use of another person's ideas or work without credit

c. exclusive right to make, use, or sell a device or process

d. interaction of people and the objects or equipment they use

e. laws that protect creative, literary, or artistic work

f. the amount of time spent using a computer screen

g. using previously published work in a new creation

h. legal protection of a brand or brand name

i. reference to a source material

j. allowed use of a limited amount of creative work without needing permission

USE THE TERMINOLOGY

DIRECTIONS Determine the correct choice for each of the following.

1. What is stolen in copyright infringement?
   a. back-up files
   b. GUIDs
   c. someone's work
   d. someone's identity

2. What should you use to give credit to a source?
   a. citation
   b. plagiarism
   c. infringement
   d. netiquette

3. Which of the following is used to identify the responsibilities of a user on an organization's computer system?

   a. copyright laws

   b. fair use doctrine

   c. acceptable use policy

   d. antivirus program

4. Why is copyright infringement a crime?

   a. It is illegal to make back-up copies of your work.

   b. It violates the rights of a software publisher to its own work.

   c. It results in identity theft.

   d. It is theft of another's work.

5. Which of the following can help protect your computer system from a power surge?

   a. power surge system

   b. universal serial bus supply

   c. device driver

   d. uninterruptible power supply

THINK CRITICALLY

DIRECTIONS Answer the following questions.

1. Explain the consequences of plagiarism.

2. Explain the concept of intellectual property laws including copyright, trademarks, and patents. What are the consequences of violating each type of law?

3. If a software program can be illegally obtained online for free instead of purchased legally, why should you purchase it?

EXTEND YOUR KNOWLEDGE

DIRECTIONS Choose and complete one of the following projects.

1. Review rules your school district may have for computer use as part of its acceptable use policy. Categorize policies based on appropriate use, vandalism or destruction, and consequences of violations. As a class, debate the benefits and drawbacks of items in the policy, such as censorship and filtering.

2. With your teacher's permission, examine the ergonomics of your school's computer workstations. Write a report recommending improvements.

3. In pairs or small groups, research, write, and produce a handbook or brochure explaining how to be a responsible user of digital technology.

IC3 PREP

1. How might a school or business keep users from accessing inappropriate web content? (Select all that apply.)

    a. Specific sites may be censored, or blocked, on internal devices.

    b. A filter may be employed to block access to specific sites.

    c. Any site a school or business finds objectionable can be immediately and permanently deleted from the web.

    d. Cookies may be used to track who accesses inappropriate content.

2. Which of the following can help you develop a positive online brand? (Select all that apply.)

    a. using comments to insult people online

    b. posting photos of yourself participating in illegal activities

    c. linking your profile to nonprofit agencies where you volunteer

    d. posting a video of your family celebrating a happy occasion

3. Which of the following is NOT a way to positively build your brand online?

    a. posting helpful information for another user in an online forum

    b. linking to thought-provoking articles on your social media

    c. complaining about the barista who served you that morning in your personal blog

    d. wishing your friend a happy birthday on Twitter

4. Which of the following are positive suggestions for managing social networking profiles? (Select all that apply.)

    a. Use privacy settings so only certain people can see sensitive personal information.

    b. Keep your personal information updated as it changes.

    c. Include false information that makes you sound successful.

    d. Limit the amount of information that is included to essentials.

5. How can separating your online presence into personal and professional identities help you maintain a positive digital identity with friends, family, and employers?

    a. It is not wise to separate your digital identities, as potential employers will not learn enough about you in their searches.

    b. Separating digital identities can help you maintain a professional image when searching for a job, while maintaining your personal social media with friends.

    c. It is not possible to have more than one digital identity online.

    d. Having multiple identities online is a good way to hide bad behavior.

6. Why is it hard to fight cyberbullying? (Select all that apply.)

    a. Cyberbullies are often digital programs, and thus cannot be prosecuted.

    b. Cyberbullies can create false digital content quickly and easily.

    c. There is no such thing as a cyberbully.

    d. Cyberbullies are able to operate anonymously, making them hard to track.

7. Which of the following is a problem associated with an excess of screen time? (Select all that apply.)

   a. headaches

   b. sleep loss

   c. chronic lateness

   d. depression from browsing social media

8. Which of the following are valid suggestions to improve ergonomics during computer use? (Select all that apply.)

   a. Keep proper posture while using a computer.

   b. Use a computer in a dimly-lit room.

   c. Take periodic breaks from looking at the screen.

   d. Periodically switch devices, if possible, to avoid repetitive actions.

9. Before someone posts information on social media, what should he or she consider? (Select all that apply.)

   a. Will the post make people laugh?

   b. Is the post true?

   c. How will the message be interpreted by others?

   d. How will the message affect the poster's digital identity?

10. For each line below, select whether the statement is True or False.

   a. Copyright is the legal right to make copies, license, and otherwise use intellectual property.

   b. Federal copyright laws protect individuals and companies from the theft or misuse of their intellectual property.

   c. Federal copyright law does not explicitly protect productions or performances of copy-righted materials.

   d. Using someone else's intellectual property is allowed as long as you change the title.

11. If you create intellectual property, you are protected by which of these copyright laws? (Select all that apply.)

   a. The right to produce or reproduce the copyrighted work.

   b. The right to distribute copies of the work to the public.

   c. The right to an attorney in small claims court.

   d. The right to prepare derivative works based upon the work.

   e. The right to display the copyrighted work publicly.

12. Failing to cite the sources of a piece of work is known as _____.

   a. copyright infringement

   b. intellectual fraud

   c. taboo

   d. plagiarism

   e. stealing

13. Where in a piece of written work is it common to place your citations? (Select all that apply.)

   a. footnotes

   b. header

   c. endnotes

   d. bibliography

   e. biography

14. To avoid plagiarism, it is important to:

    a. cite your sources

    b. hide the name of the property owner

    c. register with the U.S. Copyright Office

    d. claim the work as your own

15. Which of the following does NOT require a citation?

    a. summarizing an existing work

    b. quoting someone

    c. an original limerick

    d. paraphrasing someone

16. For each line below, select whether the statement is True or False.

    a. A patent legally protects a brand or brand name from misuse.

    b. Using trademarked or patented property without permission is called plagiarism.

    c. A patent is the exclusive right to make, use, or sell a device or process.

    d. The penalty for infringement is usually a large fine and a court order to stop.

17. Which of these would likely be considered legal under the fair use doctrine? (Select all that apply.)

    a. quoting a few lines from a song in a musical study

    b. a parody of a book passage made to defame the original author

    c. a collage made up of licensed material for a school art project

    d. a personal sequel to a popular work intended for retail sale

18. Why is it important to obtain licensed versions of any software you plan to use? (Select all that apply.)

    a. Unlicensed software cannot be registered, and is therefore not eligible for support services.

    b. Obtaining unlicensed software constitutes software piracy, which is illegal.

    c. Licensed software runs faster and works more efficiently than an unlicensed copy.

    d. Not paying for licensed software can discourage authors of good software from continuing their work, as they may not be paid for it.

IC3 PROCEDURES

MODIFYING A SKYPE PROFILE

1. Start Skype and log in to your account.

2. Press **Ctrl + I**.

   OR

   Select the user profile link, which is a circle with your initials or your account picture, in the upper-left of the window.

3. Select **Manage Account**.

4. Select **Edit profile**.

5. Enter the personal information you want to share, such as first name, and delete the information you do not want to share, such as Birthday.

6. Enter the Contact details you want to share, such as email address, and delete the details you do not want to share, such as Home phone.

7. Select the Profile settings you want to enable and clear the ones you do not want to enable.

8. Select **Save**.

ADDING OR CHANGING A SKYPE PROFILE PICTURE

1. Start Skype and log in to your account.

2. Select the user profile link, which is a circle with your initials or your account picture, in the upper-left of the window.

3. Select the user profile link.

    If the device has a camera, it opens so you can position your face in the frame.

4. Select the **Take a picture** icon 📷.

5. Adjust the zoom using the slider on the right of the image, and then select **Save**.

    *If you don't like the picture, click the **Delete the picture** icon 🗑, and try again.*

    OR

1. Start Skype and log in to your account.

2. Select the user profile link, which is a circle with your initials or your account picture, in the upper-left of the window.

3. Select the user profile link.

4. Select the **Choose a picture file** icon ⬚.

5. Browse to the location where the picture file is stored.

6. Select the file and select **Open**.

7. Select **Save**.

MODIFYING A TWITTER PROFILE

1. Start Twitter and log in to your account.

2. Select the **Profile and settings** link in the upper-right of the window (your profile picture).

3. Select **Edit profile**.

4. Enter or edit the profile content.

5. Select **Save changes**.

ADDING OR CHANGING A TWITTER PROFILE PICTURE

1. Start Twitter and log in to your account.

2. Select the **Profile and settings** link in the upper-right of the window (your profile picture).

3. Select **Edit profile**.

4. Select **Add a profile photo**.

    OR

    Select **Change your profile photo**.

5. Select **Upload photo**.

6. Browse to the location where the picture file is stored.

7. Select the file and select **Open**.

8. Drag the circle to position it over the part of the image you want to use, if necessary.

9. Use the zoom slider to zoom in or out on the picture, if necessary.

10. Select **Apply**.

11. Select **Save changes**.

ESB PROFESSIONAL/SHUTTERSTOCK

21st Century Skills

SKILLS FOR SUCCESS

LESSON 34-2
COMMUNICATING AND COLLABORATING

LESSON 34-3
LIVING WITH TECHNOLOGY

WHAT SKILLS DO I NEED TO SUCCEED?

We live in an exciting, fast-paced, complex world. As the future leaders of our families, communities, government, and workforce, it is critical that you acquire the skills you need to succeed in school, work, and life.

In addition to specific skills for using technology and applications in the career you choose to pursue, you will benefit from learning transferable skills that will help you no matter what life path you follow. In this chapter, you will explore key transferable skills you can use to succeed.

Skills for Success

OBJECTIVES

- Analyze the decision-making process.
- Compare and contrast short-term and long-term goals.
- Analyze problems and solutions.
- Discuss methods of time management.

AS YOU READ

ORGANIZE INFORMATION Complete an outline to help you identify key facts about skills for success as you read the lesson.

TERMINOLOGY

- consequences
- decision
- expenses
- goal
- income
- long-term goal
- problem
- process
- resources
- responsibility
- short-term goal
- solution
- time management

Making Decisions

Any time you make up your mind about something, or choose one option over another, you are making a **decision**. Some decisions are simple—what time will I leave for school? Some are more difficult—should I tell my friend I don't like her hair style? The results—or **consequences**—of your decisions affect you in big and small ways.

- If the consequences of a decision are positive and contribute to your well-being, it means you made a healthy—or good—choice.

- If the consequences are negative and interfere with your well-being, that means you made an unhealthy—or poor—choice.

SIX STEPS TO A DECISION You can turn decision making into a process. A **process** is a series of steps that leads to a conclusion.

1. Identify the decision to be made.
2. Consider all possible options.
3. Identify the consequences of each option.
4. Select the best option.
5. Make and implement a plan of action.
6. Evaluate the decision, process, and outcome.

After you have acted on your decision, you can look back and evaluate it, based on your values and standards.

THOUGHTFUL DECISION-MAKING We all make mistakes. Despite our best intentions, we make poor choices. Most of the time, it doesn't matter too much. If you cut your hair too short, it will grow back. Sometimes, though, we must live with the consequences of our actions for a long time—maybe even our whole lives.

Setting Goals

A **goal** is something you are trying to achieve. Goals help direct your actions and guide your decision-making because they give you something to work toward. They help give your life meaning, because you know that there is a purpose in what you do. When you achieve a goal, you can be proud and express satisfaction.

If all you do is think about a goal, it's just a dream. You make goals real by deciding what you want to achieve and then planning how to get there. While you should set goals that are within reach, there is nothing wrong with challenging yourself to push harder.

SHORT-TERM AND LONG-TERM GOALS When you want to achieve something quickly, you set **short-term goals**. You can accomplish short-term goals in the near future—maybe even today. For example, finishing your homework on time is a short-term goal.

FIGURE 34.1.1 Buying a car is a long-term goal.

CATHY YEULET/123RF.COM

A **long-term goal** is something you want to achieve in the more distant future—maybe a year from now, or maybe even more distant than that. Graduating from college is a long-term goal. So is buying a car.

FIVE STEPS TO A GOAL There's a process you can use to help identify, assess, and set goals:

1. Identify the goal.
2. Assess whether the goal is something you really want.
3. Make a plan for achieving the goal.
4. Write down your action plan for achieving the goal, being as specific as possible.
5. Every once in a while, reevaluate your goals.

Solving Problems

Any barrier or obstacle between you and a goal is a **problem**. Problems pop up all the time. Mostly, we come up with a solution without thinking too hard. Say you want to go to the movies Saturday night, but your mother says you can't go out until you clean your room.

- The problem: Your messy room is an obstacle between you and the movies.

- The solution: You clean your room.

Some problems sneak up on us over time, sometimes hidden by something else. You might want to do well in Social Studies, but you fall asleep in class every day. Is the problem that your teacher is boring, that your classroom is too warm, or is it that you are staying up late at night playing video games?

SIX STEPS TO A SOLUTION When problems are harder to identify, or harder to solve, you can use the decision-making process to figure out the best **solution**:

1. Identify the problem.
2. Consider all possible solutions.
3. Identify the consequences of each solution.

4. Select the best solution.
5. Make and implement a plan of action.
6. Evaluate the solution, process, and outcome.

Managing Time

Time management means organizing your schedule so you have time to complete tasks and meet your responsibilities. Combining goal-setting with time management is a very effective way to make sure you get things done.

- Create a time journal or log to figure out exactly how you currently spend your time.

- Set specific, realistic, and attainable goals using schedules. Scheduling helps you plan ahead, so you know when you will do something, and you can be ready for it.

- Create to-do lists, and rank list items in order of importance.

- Learn to say no. Some people may ask for too much of your time. They may expect you to take on more **responsibility** than you can handle. It is OK to say no. Be polite and respectful, but explain that your schedule is full.

- Ask for help. If you are having trouble completing tasks that are part of your assigned responsibilities, you will need to find a way to get them done. Ask your teacher, a counselor, a family member, or a friend to help you learn how to organize your time, or find ways to be more efficient.

Calendar programs on your computer and phone are an excellent way to organize your schedule for efficient time management. In the calendar, you can enter a one-time event, such as an appointment, or program recurring events, such as a weekly piano lesson. With each event, you can include details such as the location, or enter notes to help you remember important information.

FIGURE 34.1.2 There are apps that can help you manage your time and projects so you can meet your responsibilities.

Programs like Google Calendar and Outlook let you invite people to your events and even create group calendars that others can access online. You can even program notifications to remind you of important events, such as family birthdays or the ACTs. You can set up multiple calendars for business and personal use, or subscribe online to calendars for other organizations.

MANAGING RESOURCES Keeping your time and to-do list organized is critical, but if the **resources** you need are not organized, you will not succeed at the task at hand. For example, if you complete the research for a project on time, but cannot find it in order to write the report, you will be unable to complete the assignment. Set up a system of folders—both on your computer and, if you deal with paper, in a filing cabinet—that you keep organized so that you can always find the resources that you need.

One important resource you need to manage is money. Many people track their finances by creating a spreadsheet of the **income** they earn and the **expenses** they spend. There are also financial and banking apps that you can use.

Keeping track of your finances helps you plan your budget and make sure you are not spending more than you are earning. It also helps you understand where and how to spend your money. Budgeting shows you how much you should allocate, or put aside, for necessities like housing and food. Then, you will see how much you have left over to spend on other things, like entertainment. It is also important to remember a portion of your earned income is taxed by the government. This money must be deducted from your budget. Finally, a frugal money manager saves and invests. You need savings for emergencies and eventually for retirement.

OBJECTIVES

- Explain critical thinking.
- Describe the key features of effective communication.
- Recognize the importance of teamwork and leaders.
- Describe bullying.

AS YOU READ

ORGANIZE INFORMATION Complete an outline to help you identify key facts about communication and collaboration as you read this lesson.

TERMINOLOGY

- active listening
- critical thinking
- effective communication
- nonverbal communication
- verbal communication

Thinking Critically

Critical thinking can help you evaluate your options in many situations. You can use it when you are making decisions, setting goals, and solving problems. When you think critically, you are honest, rational, and open-minded about your options. You consider all possibilities before rushing to judgment.

- Being honest means acknowledging selfish feelings and preexisting opinions.

- Being rational means relying on reason and thought instead of on emotion or impulse.

- Being open-minded means being willing to evaluate all possible options—even those that are unpopular.

Communicating Effectively

Communicating is how people connect with others. Communication prevents misunderstandings. It gives you a way to share ideas. It even makes it easier for you to appreciate and respect other people's opinions.

At its most basic, communication is an exchange between a sender and a receiver. The sender transmits the message with a specific intent. The receiver interprets the message and responds. **Effective communication** is when the receiver interprets the message the way the sender intended. Ineffective communication is when the receiver misinterprets the message.

Sometimes barriers get in the way of effective communication. When you recognize any potential communication barriers, you can take steps to overcome them—both when you listen and when you speak.

VERBAL COMMUNICATION **Verbal communication** is the exchange of messages by speaking or writing. Talking is usually a very effective form of verbal communication. When you speak clearly and use language the receiver understands, he or she almost always gets the message the way you intend it.

FIGURE 34.2.1 Communicating with people of different backgrounds helps you build global awareness and understanding.

SZEFEI/SHUTTERSTOCK

NONVERBAL COMMUNICATION Nonverbal communication helps put words into context. This form of communication includes visual messages that the receiver can see, such as a smile when you are talking. It also includes physical messages, such as a pat on the back.

ACTIVE LISTENING Active listening is an important part of effective communication. When you are an active listener, you pay attention to the speaker, and make sure you hear and understand the message. Active listening is a sign of respect. It shows you are willing to communicate and that you care about the speaker and the message. When you listen actively, the other person is more likely to listen when you speak, too.

Cooperating and Collaborating

Any group that works together to achieve a common goal is a team. When you are part of a team, you have access to all the knowledge, experience, and abilities of your teammates. Together you can have more ideas, achieve more goals, and solve more problems. A successful team relationship depends on all team members working together. They depend on each other. They trust one another. If one team member does not do his or her share, the entire team suffers. The challenges of a team relationship come from having different people working together. Even if everyone agrees on a common goal, they may not agree on how to achieve that goal.

BEING A LEADER Teams benefit from strong leadership. Leaders exhibit positive qualities that other people respect, such as self-confidence. They use skills such as goal setting and critical thinking to make healthy decisions for the benefit of the team.

Being the leader does not mean you are always right. The leader's opinion does not count more than the opinions of the other team members. An effective leader keeps the team on track and focused on achieving its goals.

BEING A TEAM MEMBER While a strong leader is important to the success of a team, team members must also be committed to the group's success. An effective team member helps teammates if they need help, does not blame teammates for problems or mistakes, and offers ideas and suggestions instead of criticism.

BULLYING A bully is someone who tries to hurt others on purpose, not just once but over and over. Bullies can be boys or girls, big or small, young or old. Bullies can be found at school, but

FIGURE 34.2.2 Cooperating with others makes it easier to achieve your common goals.

STEPHEN COBURN/SHUTTERSTOCK

they can also turn up in other areas of your life, including in your neighborhood, at work, and even at home.

Some of the things bullies do include:

- Physically hurting others by tripping, pushing, kicking, pinching, or punching

- Calling people names

- Teasing people about the way they look, the way they act, or their values

- Excluding someone—leaving someone out

- Spreading rumors

- Stealing or breaking personal belongings

- Using threats or violence to make people do things they don't want to do

If you are being bullied, you need to take action right away.

- Tell someone!

- Avoid the bully as much as you can.

- Refuse to do what the bully says.

- Stand up for yourself!

Recall that cyberbullies are bullies who use technology such as the internet, cell phones, and interactive gaming devices to hurt others. They might:

- Send threatening or harassing messages

- Steal passwords and pretend to be someone else online

- Use blogs or social networking sites to spread rumors

- Send private pictures through email or cell phones

- Create hurtful websites

- Distribute someone else's personal information

Victims of cyberbullying may be depressed, anxious, lonely, and may consider suicide, while perpetrators, or cyberbullies, often are more likely to be aggressive, skip school, and abuse illegal drugs. Cyberbullying can be tricky to stop, because often it is anonymous and takes place away from school. If you are being cyberbullied you can take many of the same steps you would take with a face-to-face bully.

FIGURE 34.2.3 The best way to stop a bully is to tell someone about the bullying.

GRAHAM OLIVER/123RF.COM

Living with Technology

OBJECTIVES

- Identify the impact of technology.

- Compare and contrast the benefits and drawbacks of technology.

- Discuss the relevance of technology.

- Recognize the risks of technology.

AS YOU READ

CLASSIFY INFORMATION Use a two-column chart to help you compare the benefits and drawbacks of technology as you read this lesson.

Using Technology

Technology is a varied resource that impacts all areas of your life. It makes everyday life easier, more fun, and more rewarding. As with any resource, knowing when and how to use technology can help you be more productive. Using technology just because it's there or seems cool might be fun; it can also end up wasting other resources, such as time, energy, or money.

For example, the internet is a technology we use all the time. It can provide many benefits when you use it wisely. You can find information to complete a homework assignment, communicate with friends, and research a product before you buy it. If you don't use the internet wisely, you might waste time looking at websites that provide incorrect or misleading information. You might spend so much time online that you put your real-life relationships at risk. Or, you might accidentally send personal information to identity thieves.

Critical thinking can help you recognize how best to use technology in your own life. You can decide whether technology will be a resource you use to achieve your goals, or if it will cause new problems.

IMPACT OF TECHNOLOGY Throughout history, technology has had an impact on every aspect of life, including how you learn and what you study. You might use or encounter the following common types of technology.

- Information technology is likely to be the type of technology you use and that impacts your daily life the most. It refers to the use of computers to collect, store, and distribute information.

- Communications technology is part of information technology. It refers to the use of technology to make communication easier and more efficient. It includes cell phones, as well as videoconferencing, Voice over Internet Protocol (VoIP), and social networking.

- Agricultural technology is the use of technology to control the growth and harvesting of animal and plant products. It includes a wide range of areas, such as soil preparation, harvesting and planting techniques, and the use of chemicals for growth or pest control.

FIGURE 34.3.1
Videoconferencing is a technology that makes face-to-face communication across distance possible.

ANDREY_POPOV/SHUTTERSTOCK

- Medical technology is the use of technology to improve the management and delivery of health care. It includes areas such as medical imaging technology, nuclear medicine technology, and veterinary medical technology.

- Banking technology also stems from information technology. It includes areas such as software for managing online banking, controlling access to accounts, and technology for automated teller machines, as well as debit and credit card readers.

RELEVANCE OF TECHNOLOGY Understanding and using technology is important in all aspects of your life. The more you know about technology the more prepared you will be for college, career, daily living, and life-long learning.

- In school you will need technology to research and write papers and communicate with peers and instructors.

- Whatever career you choose, you will need to use technology. Skills such as using application software and troubleshooting hardware are transferable to most jobs.

- Throughout your life you can use technology to keep up with current events and stay informed.

You use technology every day. You will be more productive if you have a basic understanding of how technology works, and what it can do.

BENEFITS AND DRAWBACKS OF TECHNOLOGY Is it always better to use technology? There are obvious benefits to using technology, but there are also drawbacks. Most new technologies have both positive and negative effects.

- Manufacturing is faster when you use assembly lines, robots, and automated management systems, than when you build products by hand. But, manufacturing processes may release chemicals into the environment causing pollution, and experienced craftsman may lose their jobs.

- Water filtration systems, access to electricity, and advancements in medical care are a few ways technology has improved health and the quality of life. Technology also creates ethical dilemmas, such as testing medical products on animals or genetically modifying food products.

Some newer technologies can help reverse problems caused by older technologies. For example, pollution caused by technology brought some animals to the brink of extinction. Genetic technology is helping animal breeding programs to restore some animal populations. Understanding the positive and negative effects can help you make choices about how best to use technology.

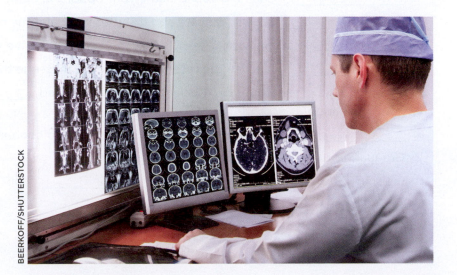

FIGURE 34.3.2 Almost all career fields use some type of technology.

BEERKOFF/SHUTTERSTOCK

Chapter 34 Review

REVIEW THE TERMINOLOGY

DIRECTIONS Match each vocabulary term in the left column with the correct definition in the right column.

1. goal
2. decision
3. problem
4. process
5. solution
6. consequences
7. responsibility
8. income

a. results that happen in response to a decision or action

b. something people expect you to do or that you must accomplish

c. a series of steps that leads to a conclusion

d. something you are trying to achieve

e. the amount of money you earn for a job

f. the process of choosing one option over one or more alternative options

g. the way to solve a problem

h. a barrier or obstacle between you and a goal

USE THE TERMINOLOGY

DIRECTIONS Complete each sentence with information from the chapter.

1. _____ can help you evaluate your options in many situations.

2. _____ shows you care about the speaker and the message.

3. Combining goal-setting with _____ is an effective way to get things done.

4. _____ is when the receiver interprets a message the way the sender intended.

5. The exchange of messages by speaking or writing is called _____ communication.

6. _____ communication helps put words into context.

7. Graduating from college is a _____ goal.

8. Finishing your homework on time is a _____ goal.

THINK CRITICALLY

DIRECTIONS Answer the following questions.

1. What does it mean if the consequences of a decision are positive? What if the consequences are negative?

2. List the five steps you can use to identify, assess, and set goals.

3. How can you use the decision-making process to solve problems?

4. Why might it be easier to misinterpret a text message or email than a face-to-face conversation?

5. List four areas of study that have been impacted by technology.

EXTEND YOUR KNOWLEDGE

DIRECTIONS Choose and complete one of the following projects.

1. Write down three decisions you have faced in the last two days. As a class, discuss the decisions. If more than one of you faced the same decision, discuss the different—or similar—choices you made and why. Compare the outcomes of the choices made by different people.

2. With a partner, practice effective communication skills. Think of something you would like to tell your partner, and then use verbal, nonverbal, and active listening techniques to deliver the message and to receive the message delivered by your partner. Would you use different methods to communicate with people in the workplace such as a co-worker, supervisor, or customer? What if there was a conflict? Try the exercise again pretending to be in a work situation. Discuss the experience with the class.

CHAPTER 35
Career Skills

WHY SHOULD I PLAN FOR A CAREER?

Planning for a career is a job in itself. It takes time, energy, and careful management. So why do it? Putting effort into career planning can help you set realistic and attainable goals for education. It can help you identify your strengths and weaknesses, so you focus your resources on finding a career that you will enjoy.

Spending time exploring career opportunities can also be fun and exciting, because you experience new situations and activities. This chapter will help you understand things you can do now that will lead to a successful career in the future.

Identify Career Opportunities

OBJECTIVES

- Explain the difference between a career and a job.

- Describe the importance of values, interests, and abilities in a self-assessment.

- List sources for occupational research.

- Identify nontraditional occupations.

AS YOU READ

ORGANIZE INFORMATION Use an outline to help you organize information about identifying types of careers as you read the lesson.

TERMINOLOGY

- abilities

- career

- economics

- interests

- job

- job outlook

- nontraditional occupation

- trend

- values

Identifying Types of Careers

A **career** is a chosen field of work in which you try to advance over time by gaining responsibility and earning more money. Another word for career is occupation. A **job** is any activity you do in exchange for money or other payment. A job does not necessarily lead to advancement.

Even if you have no idea what career you want in the future, you can start now to identify different types of careers and the tasks and duties you would be expected to perform. Learning about careers now will help prepare you to recognize job opportunities and choose the career that is right for you.

Individual Assessment

The first step in identifying a career is self-assessment. That means taking a close, objective look at your **interests**, **values**, and **abilities**. Knowing this information will help you identify the types of tasks and duties you will find rewarding. You then use that information to select careers or career clusters to investigate further.

INTERESTS Your interests tell what you like to do and what you do not like to do. They are the subjects or activities that attract your attention and that you enjoy doing or learning about. There are six general interest categories: the arts, business, crafts, office operations, science, and social. Knowing your interests helps you identify a career that you will find interesting.

VALUES A value is the importance that you place on various elements in your life. Knowing what values you feel most strongly about helps you avoid compromising the things that are most important to you. Recognizing your values also helps you prioritize what matters most to you in a career. Money might be more important to you than leisure time. Working with people might be more important to you than what shift you work.

ABILITIES An ability, or skill, is something you do well. You have many abilities. For example, you may work well with your hands, or you may be very good at mathematics. It is much more pleasant to work in an occupation that uses your abilities.

There are fourteen general categories of abilities: artistic, clerical, interpersonal, language, leadership, manual, mathematical/numerical, musical/dramatic, organization, persuasive, scientific, social, visual, and technical/mechanical. You might have abilities in more than one category.

FIGURE 35.1.1 The interests and values of a firefighter might be different from those of an architect or chemical engineer.

T-DESIGN/SHUTTERSTOCK

Occupational Research

Occupational research can help you identify job opportunities and the accompanying job duties and tasks required by a career. It can also help you learn about the education and job skills you would need for career success. By conducting occupational research, you learn details about a career, including tasks performed, duties, the **job outlook**, the education and job skills required, the working environment, the type of experience an employer looks for, and many other things. It requires time and effort to research the occupations that interest you and to prepare for a specific career. Remember, your efforts allow you to find a job that gives you satisfaction.

There are many resources you can use in your research. A good way to get started is to interview individuals who are already working in an occupation that you are interested in.

THE CAREER CLUSTERS The U.S. Department of Education organizes careers into 16 clusters. The careers in each cluster are in related industries or business areas. Each cluster is organized into pathways. Each pathway leads to a set of specific careers. The careers in a cluster require a similar set of skills and the same core training and education. You can narrow your career search by identifying a cluster that interests you. You can investigate the career clusters and pathways at www.careertech.org. The sixteen career clusters are:

- Agriculture, Food & Natural Resources
- Architecture & Construction
- Arts, Audio/Video Technology & Communications
- Business Management & Administration
- Education & Training
- Finance
- Government & Public Administration
- Health & Science
- Hospitality & Tourism
- Human Services
- Information Technology
- Law, Public Safety, Corrections & Security
- Manufacturing
- Marketing
- Science, Technology, Engineering & Mathematics
- Transportation, Distribution & Logistics

FIGURE 35.1.2 Careers in information technology are on the rise due to our growing reliance on technology at home and in the workplace.

DOTSHOCK/SHUTTERSTOCK

TECHNOLOGY@WORK

Local and global trends can impact career plans and life goals in almost all career fields. You can use the internet to monitor trends to help you stay prepared so you can adjust your plans and goals.

THINK ABOUT IT!

With your teacher's permission, research local and global trends that you think might impact your choice of career. Which of the following trends would most likely impact a career in information technology?

- population shifts from rural areas to cities
- local food movements
- new wireless networking systems
- discovery of a new planet

EMPLOYMENT TRENDS Employment trends influence the number of available jobs in a certain industry as well as where the jobs are. A **trend** is a general move in a certain direction. An employment trend is one way the job market is changing over time. Many factors influence employment trends, including economic factors and even cultural trends. For example, a shift from using personal computers to using smartphones impacts employment in the information technology industry.

Technology itself has a strong influence on employment and job outlook. It creates new jobs, replaces old jobs, and changes the way some people perform their existing jobs. Understanding the function and use of technology in the modern workplace is an essential skill in many professions.

- The development of new technology, such as mobile phones and handheld devices, creates new jobs in areas such as application development, sales, and research and development.

- The trend toward smaller computers has shifted the manufacturing of systems from desktops to notebooks and tablets.

- Improvements in robotics have made it possible to use robots in positions that people once held, such as on automobile assembly lines.

- Electronic record keeping in health care has changed the way medical professionals enter patient information, order prescriptions, and access patient records.

- The trend toward storing information and applications on the internet instead of on local computers has eliminated the need for some information technology managers at large companies.

- The trend toward using video conferencing instead of traveling to meetings impacts travel agents, hotel workers, and people who work in restaurants where travelers might eat.

A good source for information about employment trends is the *Occupational Outlook Handbook*, which is published by the Bureau of Labor Statistics. It describes more than 200 occupations, including responsibilities, working conditions, education requirements, salary ranges, and job outlook. Look it up at bls.gov/ooh.

ECONOMICS Economics and the government also impact job opportunities and the information technology industry. **Economics** is the study of how people produce, distribute, and use goods and services. An economic system is a country's way of using limited resources to provide those goods and services. In the United States, the free enterprise system encourages people to use their resources to invent products, start companies, and compete for business. The government also imposes regulations and standards that can limit or expand free enterprise.

NONTRADITIONAL OCCUPATIONS A **nontraditional occupation** is any job that a man or woman does that is usually done by someone of the other gender. Try not to rule out a nontraditional career because you associate it with one gender or another; it might be a good match for your skills and abilities.

NONTRADITIONAL OCCUPATIONS	
Men	**Women**
Nurse	Construction worker
Administrative assistant	Auto mechanic
Flight attendant	Detective
Hair stylist	Architect
Childcare worker	Chemical engineer
Elementary school teacher	Pilot

BLEND IMAGES/SHUTTERSTOCK

FIGURE 35.1.3 More people are finding success in nontraditional occupations than ever before.

Employability Skills

OBJECTIVES

- Compare and contrast hard skills and transferable skills.
- List professional qualities.
- Describe job application materials.
- Explain why education is important.

AS YOU READ

ORGANIZE INFORMATION Complete an outline to help you organize information about employability skills as you read this lesson.

TERMINOLOGY

- application form
- cover letter
- employability
- hard skills
- job interview
- life-long learning
- personal academic plan
- portfolio
- professionalism
- references
- resume
- transferable skills

Employability Skills

Employability means having and using skills and abilities to be hired and stay hired. Once you recognize the skills that make you employable, you can practice and develop them in school and at home, so you are ready to use them on the job.

TYPES OF SKILLS Employability skills can generally be placed into two groups: **hard skills** and **transferable skills**. Employers often look for people with hard skills to fill specific jobs. For example, a software development company looks to hire people skilled at writing code.

Transferable skills can be used on almost any job. They are called transferable skills because you can transfer them from one situation or career to another. The foundation skills you use to succeed in other areas of your life, such as decision-making and problem-solving, are transferable skills. You can practice and develop these skills in school and at home.

ELENA ELISSEEVA/SHUTTERSTOCK

FIGURE 35.2.1 Knowing how to present yourself in a positive way is an important employability skill.

Some computer skills are also transferable. There are very few jobs today that do not require basic computer use. If you have these basic skills, you can take them wherever you go:

- Turn a computer on and start a program

- Type on a computer keyboard without making many mistakes

- Access the internet and navigate from one location to another

- Use a search engine to do basic internet research

- Write and send email

PROFESSIONAL QUALITIES **Professionalism**, or work ethic, is the ability to show respect to everyone around you while you perform your responsibilities as best you can. It includes a basic set of personal qualities that make an employee successful. These qualities include:

- Integrity

- Courtesy

- Honesty

- Dependability

- Punctuality

- Responsibility

- Cooperative

- Positive

- Open-minded

- Flexibility

Professionalism also means you demonstrate positive work behaviors, such as regular attendance. A professional also maintains a clean and safe work environment, performs tasks effectively, shows initiative, and takes pride in his or her work accomplishments. These behaviors lead to advancement at work, in school, and in everyday life.

PROFESSIONAL APPEARANCE A professional appearance is a positive work quality that enhances your employability and can help you advance in your career. Dress standards vary depending on the career that you choose. For example, you wouldn't expect your car mechanic to be wearing a suit and tie, and you wouldn't want your lawyer to be wearing grease-covered clothing. However, good grooming habits are required in all professions. The following are recommendations for maintaining a well-groomed, professional appearance:

- Wear clothes that are clean, neat, and in good repair.

- Wear clean and appropriate shoes.

- Keep your hair neat and clean.

- Brush your teeth at least twice a day.

- Floss daily.

- Use mouthwash or breath mints.

- Bathe daily.

- Use unscented deodorant.

- Keep makeup light and neutral.

- Keep jewelry to a minimum.

- Do not use perfume or cologne.

- Keep nails clean.

Career Search Skills

Employability skills also include the ability to prepare and organize the materials you will need for a job search. Every job search requires the following:

- A **resume**, which is a written summary of your work-related skills, experience, and education. It introduces you to the prospective employer by presenting a snapshot of your qualifications. It should be brief and to the point, printed on white paper, true and accurate, and have no typographical,

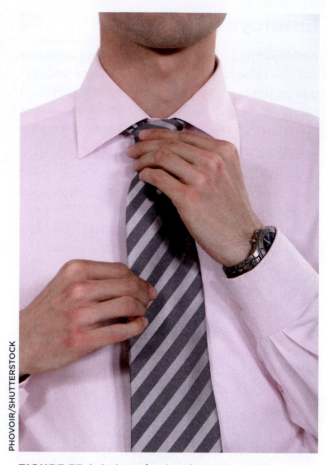

FIGURE 35.2.2 A professional appearance is a positive work quality.

grammatical, or spelling errors. A good resume attracts the interest of the reader so he or she wants to learn more about you.

- A **cover letter**, which is a letter of introduction that you send with a resume.

- A list of **references** that includes the names and contact information of people who know you and your qualifications and who are willing to speak about you to potential employers.

You may also be expected to fill out an **application form**—sometimes online and sometimes on paper. Application forms require you to enter specific information about your education and past employment, including dates and locations. As with your resume, it is important to be truthful and accurate.

If an employer thinks you have the qualifications for the job, you will be invited for a **job interview**. A preliminary interview may be by phone, but almost all employers will expect a face-to-face meeting. The interview is an opportunity for you and the interviewer to ask questions and decide if the position is right for you. You should prepare for the interview by researching the company and the position and practicing the answers to questions you think the employer might ask. You should also prepare a few questions that you can ask the employer.

After an interview, it is important to write a thank-you note to the employer to show your interest in the position. You should also be prepared to follow-up with a phone call or email.

Recognizing the Value of School

Finishing school is an investment in your future. Most companies will not hire an employee who has not graduated from high school, and many will not hire an employee who has not graduated from college. If a company does hire dropouts, it usually pays them less than it pays graduates.

School also provides an opportunity to prepare for a career. Core subjects such as reading, writing, and math are vital for the career search process.

Science, social studies, music, art, technology, and sports all help you gain knowledge and build skills you will need to succeed at work, such as teamwork, problem-solving, and leadership. School clubs and organizations such as SkillsUSA also help you build skills for future success.

PERSONAL ACADEMIC PLAN A **personal academic plan** is a document that you use to set goals for the things you want to accomplish in school. Some schools call it a personal career plan. Some things that you might put in your plan include:

- Yearly academic goals

- Assessment of your skills, knowledge, and experience

- Assessment of factors that will contribute to your success

- Assessment of factors that might interfere with your success

- Basic skills assessment

FIGURE 35.2.3 Employers value employees who graduate from high school and earn a college degree.

SIRTRAVELALOT/SHUTTERSTOCK

MONKEY BUSINESS IMAGES/SHUTTERSTOCK

DID YOU KNOW?

In addition to completing an application form, some employers require applicants to take a test as part of the application process. For example, a personality test might help identify if someone is honest. Other tests are used for specific jobs.

- A cashier might be asked to take a basic math test.

- A customer support representative might be asked to take a problem-solving test.

- A computer technician might be asked to demonstrate a repair.

You can ask a potential employer if you will be expected to take any tests so that you can be prepared.

DEVELOPING A PORTFOLIO Some academic plans include a portfolio. A **portfolio** is a collection of information and documents that show the progress you make in school and in your career planning. It helps you stay on track to achieve your educational and career goals. A portfolio may be an actual folder that holds printed documents and other materials, or it may be electronic and stored on a computer. Some things to include in a portfolio are examples of achievement, such as an essay you are proud of, and awards or certificates of accomplishment.

LIFE-LONG LEARNING Life-long learning means continually acquiring new knowledge and skills throughout the course of your life. Education and training are not limited to learning new skills for the workplace. You should consider educational opportunities to enrich your life at home, with friends, and in your community. Understanding and using technology can help you achieve life-long learning. It provides access to online information and helps you stay informed about current events and other topics.

FIGURE 35.2.4 Continuing education can lead to many rewards.

Workplace Environments

OBJECTIVES

- Discuss workplace safety.
- Recognize ethical work behavior.
- Analyze workplace rules and procedures.
- Define customer service.

AS YOU READ

IDENTIFY INFORMATION Use an outline to help you identify aspects of a workplace environment as you read this lesson.

TERMINOLOGY

- customer service
- employee handbook
- organization structure
- work ethics

Workplace Environments

Every workplace is different. Fitting in to a workplace will help ensure your career success. A first step is to understand the **organization structure** of the workplace. An organization structure is the system that assigns work, authority, and responsibility within a company.

The organization structure defines the chain of command, which is the path of authority and supervision among employees. It identifies the responsibilities of each employee, the relationships between employees, and the relationship between departments within the company. By understanding the organization structure of the place where you work, you will better understand your role in the workplace.

WORKPLACE STRUCTURE There are many different ways a business can be organized. A business can have one or many owners. A single owner has sole propriety over his or her business. The owner is personally responsible for the business. When more than one person owns a company, they are partners in ownership. Large businesses called corporations are owned by shareholders, or people who own a certain portion of the company. The shareholders are not responsible for the corporation. In fact, the corporation is its own legal entity.

> ### DID YOU KNOW?
>
> Many companies pair new or younger employees with older, more experienced mentors. A mentor is someone who can provide career advice and guidance to help you achieve your career goals. Having a mentor is one way to build positive relationships in the workplace.

Businesses are complex and require many different people with a large range of skills. Within a business there is a hierarchy, or order, to the employees. Not everyone can be in charge, so there is an order of command and responsibility. For example, in a sandwich shop the owner is in charge of the business. He directs the managers who in turn direct the staff. A large business may have multiple departments with varying responsibilities. For example, a large corporation will have administrative, accounting, marketing, and sales departments. If the company is in a large building, it may have a mail room, custodial services, security, and human resources, as well.

SAFETY IN THE WORKPLACE In 1970, the federal government passed a law called the Occupational Safety and Health Act. This law requires all employers to provide a safe and healthful workplace. Workers must be provided with safe equipment, protective clothing when needed, and education about safety practices. The Occupational Safety and Health Administration (OSHA) was formed to inspect companies and enforce safety laws. Even so, more than 5,000 Americans die from on-the-job accidents every year. As a worker under the Occupational Safety and Health Act, you have the following rights and responsibilities:

- Right to know. You have the right to know about hazards in your workplace, as well as the right to training to learn how to identify workplace hazards and what to do if there is an incident.

- Right to refuse unsafe work. If you have reasonable grounds to believe the work you do or the piece of equipment you use is unsafe, you can stop work immediately. You cannot be laid off, suspended, or penalized for refusing unsafe work if you follow the proper procedures.

- Responsibility to follow safety rules. It is your employer's responsibility to teach you the safety rules; it is your responsibility to follow the rules.

- Responsibility to ask for training. If you feel that you need more training than your employer provides, it is your responsibility to ask for it.

- Responsibility to speak up. It is your responsibility to report incidents and unsafe work practices as well as unsafe conditions.

Part of your responsibility as a worker is to make sure that you keep your work environment safe for yourself and for others. You can practice this at school and at home. You have to take some responsibility for your own safety. That means using equipment properly, according to instructions, and being aware of safety hazards.

ETHICS AT WORK Ethics are a set of beliefs about what is right and what is wrong. **Work ethics** are beliefs and behaviors about what is right and wrong in a work environment. Ethical behavior includes treating people with respect and also following the law. For example, taking home office supplies is not ethical—it's stealing. Employers value employees who behave ethically at work. It shows that you are honest and respectful, so others will trust and respect you in return.

Behaving ethically at work also means following the company rules, regulations, and processes. Usually, when you start a new job you are given an employee handbook. An **employee handbook** describes company policies and procedures, such as how to request vacation time, and the different benefits that are available. It should also list all rules and policies that you are expected to obey. These might include:

- Maintaining confidentiality of information

- Respecting copyrights and patents

- Respecting co-workers' and customers' rights

REAL-WORLD TECH
ONLINE FORMS

WORKER/SHUTTERSTOCK

Instead of having applicants fill out paper application forms, many businesses use online forms. In many ways, online forms are similar to analog, written forms, in that they are a mechanism for collecting specific information. However, with information entered online, businesses can quickly compile it into a database, which makes it easier to organize and manage. Also, information entered in an online form is always clear as there is no illegible handwriting.

Online forms provide fields for entering text, drop-down menu options, and check boxes for marking a selection. Online forms may also be easier to use than printed forms. For example, you can only enter information where you are supposed to, and it is easy to delete an error and enter the correct information.

Ethics extends beyond the actions and behaviors of individual workers. It also applies to companies and organizations as a whole. A company that ignores the safety of workers, or hides information customers need to make an informed purchasing decision, is not behaving ethically.

CUSTOMER SERVICE An important part of the workplace environment is how a business treats its customers. **Customer service** is the way a business meets the needs and wants of each and every customer. A happy customer will return; an unhappy customer will not. And many unhappy customers will post negative comments and reviews about the service, which will impact the business.

If you interact with customers as part of your work responsibilities, your employer will expect you to behave in a polite and professional manner at all times. Even if you do not directly interact with customers, you will be expected to present yourself to co-workers and other businesses in a way that reflects positively on the company.

ESB PROFESSIONAL/SHUTTERSTOCK

FIGURE 35.3.1 Positive customer service is always good for business.

Chapter 35 Review

REVIEW THE TERMINOLOGY

DIRECTIONS Match each vocabulary term in the left column with the correct definition in the right column.

1. career
2. job
3. trend
4. portfolio
5. ability
6. interests
7. professionalism
8. personal academic plan
9. transferable skill
10. work ethic

a. once you learn this, you can use it at any job

b. things that attract your attention and that you enjoy doing

c. the ability to show respect to everyone around you while you perform your responsibilities to the best of your ability

d. a collection of information and documents that shows the progress you make in school and in your career planning

e. a chosen field of work in which you try to advance over time by gaining responsibility and earning more money

f. beliefs and behaviors about what is proper in a workspace

g. any activity you do in exchange for money or other payment

h. a skill or something you do well

i. a general move in a certain direction

j. a document that you use to set goals for the things you want to accomplish while you are in school

USE THE TERMINOLOGY

DIRECTIONS Complete each sentence with information from the chapter.

1. Recognizing your _____ helps you prioritize what matters most to you in a career.

2. _____ can help you evaluate your options in many situations.

3. By conducting occupational research, you learn details about a career, including tasks performed, the job _____, the education required, and the working environment.

4. A(n) _____ occupation is any job that a man or woman does that is usually done by someone of the other gender.

5. _____ means having and using skills and abilities to be hired and stay hired.

6. Employers often look for people with _____ skills to fill specific jobs.

7. A business with good _____ will meet the needs of its customers.

8. A(n) _____ is a document that you use to set goals for the things you want to accomplish while you are in school.

9. At a(n) _____, the employer asks questions to determine if you are right for the job.

CRITICAL THINKING

DIRECTIONS Answer the following questions.

1. What is the first step in identifying a career?

2. What is the function of a resume?

3. Describe three ways technology has influenced employment and job outlook.

4. List at least six work behaviors and qualities that enhance employability and job advancement.

5. Select and explain one of the rights and responsibilities a worker has under the Occupational Safety and Health Act.

6. How might planning and time-management skills such as project management and scheduling help you prepare for and obtain employment?

EXTEND YOUR KNOWLEDGE

DIRECTIONS Choose and complete one of the following projects.

1. Use a personal assessment to identify a career that interests you, and then record your personal career goals. Use the internet, library, or your school's guidance resources to learn more about that career, including specific job duties and tasks. Alternatively, interview someone who has that career. Use these career resources to develop a list or database of businesses that hire people in that career and of opportunities for continuing education or workplace experience in that field. Identify the education, job skills, and experience you will need to achieve your career goals. Create a timeline showing how you will achieve these goals, and present it to a partner or to the class.

2. Using effective reading skills, find an advertisement for a job opening that interests you. Using effective writing skills, use a word-processing program to prepare a resume, cover letter, and list of references for that position. With a partner, practice filling out an application form and interviewing for the position. During the interview, demonstrate positive workplace behaviors and qualities, such as flexibility and initiative. After the interview, write a thank-you note. With your partner, play-act how you might make a follow-up phone call to find out if you got the job. Remember to demonstrate positive work behaviors and qualities while talking on the phone.

APPENDIX A

Web Page Development and Computer Programming

LESSON A-1
WEB PAGE DEVELOPMENT

LESSON A-2
COMPUTER PROGRAMMING

THE VALUE OF LOGIC

Even if you don't plan to pursue a career in web development or computer programming, understanding the logic and processes that go into designing effective websites and building functioning programs can help you succeed. These skills rely on problem solving, attention to detail, and analysis, all of which are useful in any career you choose. In this appendix, you will explore the requirements for using HTML to create a web page. You will also learn some of the basic processes for designing a computer program.

Web Page Development

OBJECTIVES

- Compare and contrast HTML text editors with GUI editors.

- Demonstrate the ability to design, create, and revise a website.

AS YOU READ

ORGANIZE INFORMATION Use a main idea/detail chart to help you identify details about web page development as you read.

TERMINOLOGY

- attributes

- Cascading Style Sheets (CSS)

- end tag

- Graphical User Interface (GUI)

- singletons

- start tag

- style sheet

- syntax

Designing and Developing for the Web

An effective website not only looks good, but also conveys a message and is easy to use. A successful web developer uses the principles of design, color theory, and organization to communicate useful information quickly and efficiently. Knowing how to use web development tools will help you plan, design, create, publish, and maintain a successful website.

Hypertext Markup Language

Recall that Hypertext Markup Language (HTML) is the most common language used to define how a web page should look. A markup language requires marks, called tags, to provide the instructions for formatting the page and the page content. You can type them manually using an HTML text editor such as Notepad, or you can use an authoring tool which writes the HTML code automatically. Other common markup languages include Extensible Hypertext Markup Language (XHTML), that is HTML in XML syntax, and Dynamic Hypertext Markup Language (DHTML), which is a combination of HTML and other technologies used to add interactivity and animation to web pages.

Tags

Tags are words or abbreviations enclosed in angle brackets (< >). There are strict rules, called **syntax**, that control how you enter tags. If you follow the rules, your page will look the way you want. You use most tags in pairs to surround the content you want to format. The **start tag**, or open tag, is placed at the beginning, and the **end tag**, or close tag, is placed at the end. The end tag must have a slash (/) between the tag name and the left bracket. HTML5 requires tags to be entered in all lowercase, so, the HTML5 start tag for applying bold formatting is <bold>, and the end tag is </bold>.

SINGLETONS Some tags are called **singletons** because they do not work in pairs, generally because they do not surround anything. For example, tags used to insert something like an image, video, or horizontal line only require one tag. For singletons, the syntax has a slash between the tag name and the right angle bracket. So, the tag for inserting a horizontal line is <hr/>.

ATTRIBUTES Some tags have **attributes**, which you combine with values to provide additional information about how you want the page to look. For example, you might want to use a width or height attribute with the tag for inserting an image to control the size of the image, or a color attribute to set the font color. The syntax for an attribute is the attribute name, followed by an equals sign (=), followed by the value enclosed in quotation marks. So, the start tag for changing the font color to red is <font color="red">.

REQUIRED TAGS There are a few required tags for all HTML documents. These include the following:

- <!doctype html> This singleton is the document type declaration for HTML5, and must be the first tag entered. It tells the browsers that the document is an HTML5 file.

- <html> The HTML tag surrounds everything else in the document.

- <head> The head tag surrounds the tags that describe the characteristics of the page, such as the character set used and the title.

- <body> The body tag surrounds the rest of the web page content.

Cascading Style Sheets

Originally, HTML was developed to define the organization of content on a web page, not format it. In HTML 3.2, formatting tags such as <font> </font> were added. Although formatting tags made it possible to add color and other formatting to a web page, it also made writing HTML more time-consuming. In HTML 4 and 5, **Cascading Style Sheets (CSS)** are used

COMMON HTML TAGS

Start Tag	End Tag	Result
<title>	</title>	Identifies a title
<h1>	</h1>	Identifies a top level heading
<h2>	</h2>	Identifies a second level heading
<p>	</p>	Identifies a paragraph
<b>	</b>	Applies bold
<i>	</i>	Applies italic
<ol>	</ol>	Identifies a numbered list
<ul>	</ul>	Identifies a bulleted list
<li>	</li>	Places a number or bullet at the start of a line in a list
<img src="name">		Inserts the image file identified by the src attribute "name" value (src stands for source)
<a href="name">	</a>	Inserts a hyperlink to the location identified by the href attribute "name" value (href stands for hyperlink reference)
<table>	</table>	Identifies a table
<table border="n">		Sets the width of a border around table cells to the value "n"
<table width="n">		Sets the width of a table, in pixels, to the value "n"

for all HTML formatting. A **style sheet** is a separate document that describes the styles, or rules, that define how the elements look on the page. CSS are called *cascading* because they describe a hierarchy of style rules. Rules with a higher priority will be applied over rules with a lower priority. This insures that the formatting will be consistent. Because the CSS is stored in a separate file, you can attach it to more than one page. You can also change it and have the change affect all pages attached to it.

The syntax for a CSS rule is a little more complex than an HTML tag. It includes a selector, which identifies the HTML element you are going to format, and a declaration block enclosed in curly braces, which specifies the formatting. The declaration block can include one or more declarations, separated with semicolons. Each declaration includes a property name, such as color, a colon, and a value, such as red. It is a good idea to put each declaration in a block on a separate line just to make it easier to read. The CSS rule for formatting a heading with bold and blue is:

```
h1 {

color: blue;

font-weight: bold;

}
```

MELODY SMART/SHUTTERSTOCK

FIGURE A.1.1 Use HTML5 with cascading style sheets to define web-page content.

Using a GUI Authoring Tool

Although you can type HTML tags, it is much easier to use a **Graphical User Interface (GUI)** authoring tool or editor. Adobe Dreamweaver is a popular HTML GUI authoring tool. There are also many that are available free for downloading or for use on web hosting sites. Also called a "What You See Is What You Get" (WYSIWYG) authoring tool or editor, these programs let you enter text and content as if you are working in a word-processing document. The program automatically writes the HTML code to create the web page. Most GUI editors today include both a text editor for entering the text and tags, if you want, and a WYSIWG, or visual, editor, which lets you drag-and-drop objects to build the site.

GUI authoring tools include features to make it easy for you to create and publish a web page, or even a website. Most come with built-in templates that include page and text formatting as well as placeholders for graphics and other elements. Some templates even include navigational elements. You can use a template to quickly create a professional-looking web page, and you can edit the template to suit your own needs. Most GUI authoring tools also let you create your own web page template and save it to use to create consistent pages.

Other features include spell check, automatic line numbering, web page preview so you can see how your page would look in a browser, support for CSS, and automatic publishing so you can upload your web page files to your web server. They may integrate an FTP client so you can upload the files using FTP.

DID YOU KNOW?

Many website developers use the three-click-rule when designing the navigation scheme for a site. The three-click-rule states that visitors should be able to find the information they need with no more than three clicks. It is based on the belief that people will become frustrated or angry after three clicks and leave the website to try to find the information somewhere else. Recently, however, studies have shown that in fact, people are willing to go as high as 25 clicks before abandoning a site.

Navigation

A single web page might look nice, but the purpose of the web is to enable browsing from one page to another. To accomplish this, you use hyperlinks that let a visitor navigate to a different location on the same page, to a different page within the site, and to a page at an external site. A website's navigation scheme should be logical, simple, and consistent, so visitors can find what they need quickly and easily.

Two of the most effective navigation schemes are simply highlighting text and graphic hyperlinks so they are easily identified, and using a navigation bar, which presents a series of links across the top or along the side of the page. For both, using descriptive text or images to identify links is important, so visitors know where the link will take them. With HTML, you use the anchor tag, <a> </a>, to surround the text or insert image tag you want to use as the link. You add the href attribute to the anchor start tag to identify the destination that will display when the visitor clicks the link. (href stands for hyperlink reference.) So, this code will result in the word HOME that links to a site's home page:

<a href=http://www.sitehomepage.com> HOME</a>.

Computer Programming

OBJECTIVES

- Explain basic programming logic structures.
- Demonstrate the ability to use a high-level programming language.

AS YOU READ

ORGANIZE INFORMATION Use an outline to help you organize details about computer programming as you read.

TERMINOLOGY

- algorithms
- binary
- bytecode
- decision
- high-level programming languages
- iteration
- loop
- object code
- pseudocode
- sequence
- source code
- variable

Introduction to Computer Programming

A computer program is the software instructions, or **source code**, that tells a computer what to do. Some programs stand on their own, like a calculator or contact list. Others are part of a larger system, such as one that imports records into a database, or plays a video in a web browser.

Computer programming means writing **algorithms**, which are the specific steps the computer must follow in order to solve a problem or complete a specific task. The steps must be exact, so the computer can follow them over and over and always get the desired result. They must also take into consideration all possibilities that might occur, and still allow the computer to get the desired result.

The algorithms must be written in a language the computer can understand, and that means following the rules, or syntax, required by that language. There are many, many computer programming languages available. Most programming languages used today are **high-level programming languages**, which means they are not dependent on a particular type of computer. They often use natural language, or English elements, that are more intuitive and easier to understand and use.

Compiled vs. Interpreted Languages

A compiled language uses source code that cannot be executed by a computer until it has been translated by a compiler program into **binary** form. Binary code uses only two possible values: 0 and 1. The result, called **object code**, can be read and acted on by a computer. C++ is a compiled language.

An interpreted language does not need a compiler program to translate the code. Instead, it uses a program called an interpreter to translate the source code directly into actions. Perl, Python, and HTML are interpreted languages.

Some languages, such as Java, are compiled into bytecode. **Bytecode** is an object code that can be processed by a virtual machine program instead of by a computer's processor, enabling it to be used on any computer platform. That is why Java programs can be transmitted across a network and run on any computer that has the Java Virtual Machine program installed.

Programming Variables

In computer programming, a **variable** is a symbol or name that stands for a value. They are important because programmers can write code using variables, which are replaced by real data when the program is executed. This lets the same program be executed multiple times, using different data.

Variables have a name and a data type. Some common data types include string, which is a sequence of characters that does not contain numbers used for calculations; numeric, which is numbers or amounts that are used in calculations; character, which is text; integers, which represent whole numbers; and date, which is the method of coding dates.

Basic Logic Structures

The three basic logic structures in computer programming are **sequence**, **decision**, and **loop**. The sequence is the order of operations. The decision, which may also be called the selection or branch, is the choice made at the end of each step. The loop is a repeated action that occurs until the desired result is achieved.

Each occurrence of a loop is called an **iteration**. In computer programming, iteration statements are used to repeat code using different variables. The code uses a variable to set a condition, and then instructs the computer to start a sequence, check for a certain condition, and, based on the condition, either start another iteration or exit the loop. Some common iteration statements include:

- **for** The for loop is a control statement that is usually used when there is a finite, or limited, number of iterations you want. For example, a for loop might be used in a customer database to total outstanding payments. The program would instruct the computer to start with the outstanding payment for customer record 1, add the outstanding payment for customer record 2, and so on. After the last customer record, the program exits the loop.

- **while** A while loop causes the program to repeat the code if a particular condition is true. If the condition is false, the program exits the loop. If the condition is false at the beginning of the loop, the loop is never executed.

- **do-while** A do-while loop is similar to a while loop except that the condition is not checked until the end of the first iteration, so the sequence is always executed at least once.

The Software Development Process

Every computer program solves a problem, usually by turning input into output. There are seven basic steps in the software-development process.

1. Identify the problem.
2. Identify the solution. This includes identifying the criteria for achieving a successful solution as well as any constraints or limitations.
3. Design and document an algorithm showing all of the steps required to solve the problem.
4. Code the program.
5. Test the program.
6. Debug the program.
7. Repeat steps 1 through 6 until the problem is solved.

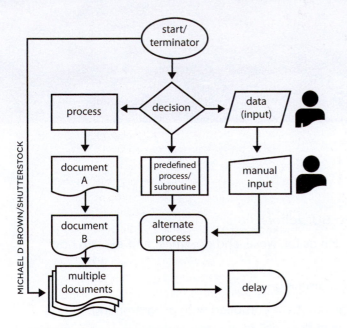

MICHAEL D BROWN/SHUTTERSTOCK

FIGURE A.2.1 A flowchart is one way to document a program algorithm.

Program Design

In order to design a computer program, you need to know and document the following:

- What will the output of the program be? This involves analyzing the problem to determine everything that the user will see while using the program, such as screens, fields, buttons, and even printed reports. You will create lists of these items and even draw or create samples.

- What data is needed to produce that output? This also involves analyzing the problem to determine everything that the user will enter while using the program, such as information typed in a field. Again, you will create lists and samples.

- How will the computer process the input in order to produce the output? This is the logic you will use to write your code to

produce the desired result, and you can document it using algorithms in the form of flowcharts or **pseudocode**. Pseudocode lets you write logic using specific words instead of flowcharts. It relies on structural conventions used when coding software, but since it doesn't have to be executed by a computer, it omits details such as variable declarations. It simply spells out how the program is going to work in a language that is easier to understand than code or a flowchart. You may also use a storyboard to model the program flow and functionality.

Testing and Debugging

After you code your program, you must make sure it works the way you designed it. The tools for this are testing and debugging. Testing usually refers to checking that the syntax in your program code is correct, and debugging usually means identifying and correcting logic errors. You must test, debug, evaluate, and repeat until the program runs correctly and produces the desired result.

The most basic way to test your code is to read it. You can do this at stages while you are writing the code, or all at once at the end. By reading the code, you can find and correct problems with the syntax. There are also automated testing procedures, such as running the code through a compiler to identify syntax errors.

To debug your program, you run it using test data. It is important to make sure your test data is comprehensive so that it will test every part of the program. If something does not work the way you planned it, you must figure out why, and modify the program to solve the problem. Then, you start the testing and debugging process again.

Appendix A Review

THINK CRITICALLY

DIRECTIONS Answer the following questions.

1. Compare and contrast HTML text editors with GUI editors.

2. Describe iterative programming structures, such as for, while, and do-while, and explain how they are used in programming.

3. Explain the types and uses of variables in programming.

4. Compare and contrast programming languages that are compiled with programming languages that are interpreted. Explain why Java does not fit in either category.

EXTEND YOUR KNOWLEDGE

DIRECTIONS Choose and complete one of the following projects.

1. Use an HTML text editor to create a web page using basic HTML tags. Include the required tags as well as tags for elements such as lists and tables. Use formatting tags to apply character styles and text alignment. Insert at least one image and a link to an external website. Test your web page, and make corrections as necessary so that it looks the way you want in a browser. Share your page with a partner or the class, and discuss the process of writing HTML.

2. Use a GUI authoring tool to create a website based on a template. Modify the template as necessary to achieve an effective look and feel for your site. Use the principles of design and color theory to make the web pages attractive, engaging, and efficient. Create a well-organized navigation scheme so visitors will be able to find the information they need. Create hyperlinks using text and images. Publish the site using FTP. Present your site to a partner or to the class, explaining why you chose the colors, design, and navigation structure.

3. Plan, design, and create a program using a high-level programming language. Start by identifying the problem your program will solve and the steps you will take to achieve the solution. As part of the design process, use pseudocode that uses structured programming to document the program flow you are going to use to solve the problem. Check the logic in your pseudocode, and correct it as necessary. When you are ready, convert the pseudocode into the programming language. Analyze and test the code to identify and troubleshoot errors, and then use debugging procedures to make the changes necessary to insure the program will run correctly and produce the desired result. Demonstrate your program to a partner or to the class.

Glossary

3-D REFERENCE A reference to a cell or range on a specific worksheet in a 3-D spreadsheet.

3-D WORKBOOK A workbook that includes multiple worksheets in the same file.

3G A cellular network that uses the third generation of wireless mobile telecommunications technology.

4G A cellular network that uses the fourth generation of wireless mobile telecommunications technology.

A

ABILITIES Skills that you do well.

ABSOLUTE REFERENCE The method of copying or moving a formula that keeps its cell references exactly as they are.

ACCEPTABLE USE POLICY (AUP) A policy—published by a school district, business, or other organization—that identifies rules of behavior that must be followed by anyone using that organization's telecommunications equipment, computers, network, or internet connection.

ACCESS TIME The amount of time required for a disk drive's read/write head to locate data on the surface of a disk.

ACTIVE CELL The current, or selected cell in use in a spreadsheet application.

ACTIVE LISTENING Paying attention to the speaker in order to hear and understand the message.

ADD-ON Code designed specifically to add a feature to a web browser, modify a web page, or integrate a browser with other services. Also called an extension.

ADDRESS BAR The area in a web browser where you can enter a URL.

ADDRESS BOOK A simple database for storing names and content information for use with an email program.

ALGORITHM A sequence of instructions. In programming, the specific steps the computer must follow in order to solve a problem or complete a task.

ALIAS An informal name by which an email user is known.

ALIGN The tool in a draw program that determines how images will be placed in relation to one another.

ALIGNMENT In word processing, the way a paragraph lines up between the pages' left and right margins. In graphic design. The placement of text and objects so they line up within a space.

ALTERNATING CURRENT (AC) The flow of electricity that travels in one direction through a wire and then reverses direction.

ANALOG A type of system that sends electrical signals that match the human voice and other sounds.

ANIMATION The process of showing many images in rapid sequence to make them appear as if they are in motion. In presentation design, a feature used to control the way objects move on a slide.

APPLET A small application with limited features and functions.

APPLICATION FORM A form for entering information about yourself, your education, and your work history when applying for a job.

APPLICATION SOFTWARE A program or group of programs designed to perform specific tasks, such as create documents, store information, or edit videos.

APPLICATION WORKSPACE The large area of a program's window that displays the document in use.

APPLICATION PROGRAMMING INTERFACE (API) A set of programming instructions and standards that lets web-based applications communicate without user intervention.

APPS Third-party software programs developed specifically for smart phones, tablet computers, and some PCs.

ARCHIVAL STORAGE DEVICE A storage device for information that is not frequently used.

ARCHIVE Move email to an Archive folder so it is out of the way but available if needed.

ARGUMENT The data that a function will use.

ARITHMETIC OPERATORS Symbols used in mathematics to identify the process to use in a calculation.

ASCENDING ORDER The sorting of data by increasing value.

ASCII A system that uses eight-bit codes to represent 256 characters.

ASSUMPTION Something that is accepted as being true even if there is no factual proof.

ASYMMETRIC DSL (ADSL) Has faster download speeds than upload speeds.

ATTACHMENT A digital file transmitted with an email message.

ATTRIBUTES Modifiers used with HTML tags to provide additional information about how to format the content.

AUGMENTED REALITY An emerging technology in which cameras and mobile devices are used to layer virtual information onto real information.

AUTHENTICATION The process of confirming the identity of a valid user.

AUTHENTICATION COOKIE A piece of data that allows a computer to log in to a secure website through a secure account.

AUTHORING The process of creating multimedia programs and content.

AUTHORING TOOL A program that includes tools for creating multimedia programs.

AUTOCOMPLETE A feature of some programs that automatically completes an entry as you type, based on data entered previously.

AUTOCONTENT WIZARD In some applications, a series of dialog boxes that helps the user create a new presentation.

AUTOCORRECT A feature that fixes common spelling mistakes as they are typed.

AUTOFILL A spreadsheet command that automatically enters related, sequential data (such as the days of the week) into a connected set of cells.

AUTOFIT A feature in some spreadsheet programs that automatically adjusts the available space to fit the data in a column.

AUTOSAVE The feature in an application program that saves the current file after a specified amount of time has elapsed.

AUTOSHAPES A list of ready-to-use shapes in the Draw tool.

B

BACK BUTTON A tool that lets users reload the previously viewed page in a browser.

BACKBONE High-speed lines that carry data through a network.

BACK UP To create a copy of programs and/or data for safe-keeping. Also, the copy or backup of a file.

BACKUP UTILITY A program that automatically copies data from the hard drive to a backup storage location.

BALANCE The way objects are arranged in an image or on a page; symmetrically arranged objects are evenly balanced; asymmetrically arranged objects are unevenly balanced.

BANDED COLUMNS Shading applied to every other column in a table, to help distinguish the table data.

BANDED ROWS Shading applied to every other row in a table, to help distinguish the table data.

BANDWIDTH The amount of data that can travel through a network connection.

BANDWIDTH LIMIT A limit to the amount of data you can download, set by internet service providers.

BASIC INPUT/OUTPUT SYSTEM (BIOS) A set of programs, built into a PC's ROM chips, that controls the function of the computer's keyboard, disk drives, monitor, and several other components; the programs also help the computer start itself when the power is turned on.

BATCH PROCESSING A way of changing a database that delays updates until a group of data is ready to process.

BETA VERSION A working copy of a program from early in the development, used for testing prior to release.

BINARY A format that has only two possible values: 0 and 1.

BINARY FILES Files stored in binary format, including program files and other non-text files such as graphics, pictures, music, or video clips.

BIT The smallest unit of information with values of either 0 or 1; a number that is a building block for computer languages; short for binary digit.

BITMAP An image formed by a pattern of dots; also called raster graphic or a bitmapped graphic.

BITS PER SECOND (BPS) The amount of data that can be transmitted in one second.

BLENDED LEARNING A method of learning that combines traditional classroom and web-based training.

BLOG Short for "web log," a web page that a writer updates regularly with news or opinions.

BLUETOOTH Wireless technology that uses radio signals to allow communication between devices over short distances.

BOOKMARKS A tool in a web browser that lets users store links to frequently visited web pages.

BOOLEAN ALGEBRA Math that uses only the numbers 0 and 1.

BOOLEAN SEARCH A type of search that uses an operator to link keywords.

BOOT To start a computer.

BORDERS The visible gridlines that define columns, rows, and cells in a spreadsheet or table.

BOUNCE MESSAGE A message from an email server stating that a message could not be delivered.

BRAND An image or reputation developed to influence the opinions of others.

BREADCRUMBS Links that help you keep track of what page you are viewing in a website or on a server by displaying the path you followed to get there.

BROADBAND The general term for all high-speed digital connections that transmit at least 1.5 megabits per second (Mbps), though transmission speeds may be much higher.

BROWSE To move through a network or program to find resources or files. In a database, to look through one record at a time.

BROWSER HISTORY Information about websites a browser user has visited that is stored on the computer.

BROWSER PLUG-IN Software that adds functionality to a website or browser. Also called an extension or add-on.

BROWSING HISTORY A chronological list of web pages a user has visited, stored in a web browser.

BUS TOPOLOGY A network design that connects the network to a single line.

BYTE A group of bits combined into groups of eight or more.

BYTECODE An object code that can be processed by a virtual machine program instead of by a computer's processor, enabling it to be used on any computer platform.

C

CABLE MODEM A device that allows a computer to access the internet through a cable television connection.

CACHE A hardware or software component where recently accessed data is stored so it can be accessed again more quickly in the future.

CALL CENTER A central place where an organization's inbound and outbound calls are received and made.

CAREER A chosen field of work in which you try to advance over time by gaining responsibility and earning more money.

CASCADING STYLE SHEETS (CSS) A hierarchy of style rules used with HTML to define the elements of a web page.

CATHODE RAY TUBE (CRT) An older type of monitor that produces images by using electrons to make phosphors glow.

CAVE AUTOMATED VIRTUAL ENVIRONMENT (CAVE) A virtual reality environment where images of the virtual world are projected on the walls of a real room.

CELL The box in a table or worksheet where a column and row meet; also, a geographic area to which a signal can be transmitted.

CELL ADDRESS A unique name by which each cell on a worksheet is identified.

CELL IDENTIFIER An area in a worksheet that displays the cell address of the active cell.

CELL REFERENCE The shorthand command that tells a spreadsheet program to use the information entered in a certain cell.

CELL SITE The location of the radio tower that sends and receives radio signals for a particular cellular phone.

CELL STYLE A set of formats, such as a font and font style, shading, and borders, that you can apply to cells in a spreadsheet.

CELL TOWER Receives radio signals from other towers and sends them on to still other towers.

CELLS Geographic areas to which a cell phone signal can be transmitted.

CELLULAR NETWORK SYSTEM A communications network system that uses cells and cell sites to transmit and receive radio signals, usually for the purpose of making a phone call.

CELLULAR PHONE A mobile phone that uses radio waves to communicate.

CELLULAR SERVICE CONTRACT An agreement between a consumer and a cellular service provider that specifies how much the consumer must pay for specific services.

CELLULAR SERVICE PROVIDER A company that provides cellular service.

CENSOR To ban or block.

CENTRAL PROCESSING UNIT (CPU) A piece of the computer's hardware that processes and compares data, and completes arithmetic and logical operations.

CHARACTER SET A system for coding letters and numbers.

CHART A graphical image, such as a pie or a set of columns, used to visually display numerical data, making it easy to understand and analyze.

CHAT A real-time teleconference in which participants discuss chosen topics by typing.

CHAT ROOM A pane or window in a chat application where the chat messages or threads are displayed.

CHECK BOX Small squares to the left of each item in a list of options.

CIRCUIT In electronics, a path between two or more points along which an electrical current can be carried; in telecommunications a specific path between two or more points along which signals can be carried.

CIRCUIT BOARD An insulated board on which microchips and other components are mounted or etched.

CIRCUIT-SWITCHING A technology that provides an unbroken connection between two computers, enabling them to exchange data quickly; also used in telephone networks to open a dedicated line (a circuit) for a phone call and leave the circuit open for the duration of the call.

CITATION A reference to a source that gives credit to the source and provides the tools a reader needs to locate the source on his or her own.

CLICK-AND-MORTAR STORE A business that offers products online.

CLIENT A workstation computer attached to a network, which is controlled by a server.

CLIENT/SERVER NETWORK A network system that uses a central server computer.

CLIP ART A graphic that has already been created for use by others.

CLIPBOARD A tool in many application programs that temporarily stores cut or copied data.

CLOUD APPS Applications that are stored on cloud servers so you do not have to install them on your computer.

CLOUD COMPUTING Using the internet and central remote servers to host, or store, data and/or applications.

CLOUD STORAGE Space on internet servers where data and applications can be stored and accessed.

CMOS Complementary Metal-Oxide Semiconductor. A battery powered memory chip on the motherboard that stores information about the computer components.

COAXIAL A traditional analog wire used to transmit cable television.

COLLABORATE Work together with others to set and accomplish goals.

COLLABORATIVE SOFTWARE Application software designed to be used by a group of people working together.

COLLISION A problem in networking that occurs when two computers try to transmit data across a network at the same time, causing data packets to collide and both transmissions to fail.

COLOR The way the eye sees light.

COLOR DEPTH The number of colors that can be displayed on a monitor at one time.

COLOR PALETTE A display of options that allows the user to choose a color.

COLUMN A vertical series of cells in a spreadsheet or table.

COMMAND An instruction that tells a software program what action to perform.

COMMAND BUTTON An icon on a toolbar, dialog box, or Ribbon that tells the computer to perform an action when the icon is clicked.

COMMA-SEPARATED VALUES (CSV) A file format in which commas are used to identify where a new column begins.

COMMERCIAL SOFTWARE Copyrighted software that must be purchased before it can be used.

COMPATIBILITY The ability to share files between two different application programs or operating systems.

COMPILER A program used to translate the source code of a computer program into binary form using only 0s and 1s.

COMPRESS To reduce the size of a file.

COMPUTER A machine that changes information from one form into another by performing input, processing, output, and storage.

COMPUTER CONFIGURATION The arrangement of the hardware, software, and peripherals that comprise a computer system.

COMPUTER CRIME Any act that violates state or federal laws involving use of a computer.

COMPUTER NETWORK Two or more computing devices connected to each other so they can share resources and information.

COMPUTER SYSTEM The parts of a computer that perform the four basic functions of computing: input, processing, output, and storage.

COMPUTER TELEPHONY INTEGRATION (CTI) Linking computers to telephone systems.

CONDITIONAL FORMATTING Formatting that is applied to spreadsheet cells only when certain conditions are met.

CONGESTION Delay caused by too much traffic on a network.

CONNECTOR A plug used for connecting a device to a computer port.

CONSEQUENCES Results that happen in response to a decision or action.

CONTENTION The condition that occurs when two computers try to access a network at the same time.

CONTIGUOUS Adjacent, as in a range of cells that are all in one, contiguous block.

CONTRAST A principle of design that uses differences in shape and color to create a comparison.

COOKIE Small files that store identification information, stored on a hard drive by a website that the user visits.

COPY To place a duplicate of a selection on the Clipboard.

COPY PROTECTION A physical device or software tool that keeps users from making unauthorized copies of the software.

COPYRIGHT The right to control the use of creative, literary, or artistic work.

COPYRIGHT INFRINGEMENT Someone who pretends that another person's work is his or her own has broken the law by committing copyright infringement.

CORRUPTED The state of a file that has been damaged so it cannot be used.

COVER LETTER A letter of introduction that you send with a resume.

CRASH To suddenly stop working.

CREATIVE COMMONS A license that lets copyright holders make some of their work available for public use while letting them retain other parts of their work.

CRITERIA Details usually used to identify specific information.

CRITICAL THINKING The act of thinking in an honest, rational, and open-minded manner.

CROP To trim the edges from a graphic to make it fit a space or to remove an unwanted part of the image.

CROSS-PLATFORM A type of software or hardware capable of running the same way on more than one platform.

CROSS-PLATFORM COMPATIBILITY The ability to share files across operating systems.

CSMA/CD A rule that governs how Ethernet network devices communicate.

CURRENT The flow of electricity through a wire.

CUSTOMER RELATIONSHIP MANAGEMENT (CRM) A system for managing customer data and interactions.

CUSTOMER SERVICE The way a business meets the needs and wants of each and every customer.

CUT A command used to remove a selection from a document and place it on the Clipboard.

CYBERBULLYING To use electronic communications to threaten or harass someone.

CYBERCRIME The use of the internet or private networks to violate state or federal laws.

CYLINDER The same track location on the platters of a hard drive.

D

DATA Raw, or unprocessed, information such as text, audio, video, and images entered into a computer.

DATA ACCESS PAGE A form in HTML format that can be viewed and used in a web browser.

DATA DECAY The loss of information due to the gradual wearing down of a storage medium.

DATA GLOVE A glove equipped with sensors to measure movements of the hand and fingers.

DATA INTEGRITY The quality, availability, and usability of data stored on a computer.

DATA LOSS When data on a storage device is damaged or made unusable.

DATA MAINTENANCE The upkeep of a database that includes regular updates, modifications, and deletions.

DATA MINING To find valuable information by examining trends in large amounts of data.

DATA NETWORK Two or more computing devices connected to each other so they can share resources and information.

DATA PROJECTOR A device that shows a computer's video output on a screen.

DATA SERIES A set of data that changes by a constant value.

DATA SOURCE A file containing variable data used for customizing a mail merge document.

DATA STRUCTURE The way a database is organized.

DATA TRANSFER RATE The number of bits per second at which data is transferred.

DATA TYPE Settings applied to a database field, which allow the field to store only information of a specific type and/or format.

DATABASE An organized collection of information that may or may not be stored in a computer.

DATABASE MANAGEMENT SYSTEM (DBMS) A software program used to manage the storage, organization, processing, and retrieval of data in a database.

DATASHEET A table in a database.

DEAD LINK A connection to a web document that no longer works.

DECISION The process of choosing one option over one or more alternative options. In computer programming, one of the three basic logic structures. Decision refers to the choice made at the end of each step.

DECREMENT The number by which each value in a series decreases.

DEFAULT The preset options in a program.

DEFAULT FACTORY SETTINGS The preset options set up when a device is first built and sold.

DELIVERY METHOD The technology used to deliver electronic content such as a presentation to an audience.

DEMODULATION The process that changes the analog signal received by a modem to the digital signal used by a computer.

DERIVATIVE Based on another source, such as the use of a published work to create a new work.

DESCENDING ORDER The sorting of data by decreasing value.

DESKTOP The workspace on a Windows-based computer screen.

DESKTOP COMPUTER An individual's personal computer that resides on a desk or table.

DESKTOP PUBLISHING A program with expanded design options to create documents for publication.

DESTINATION FILE The file in which you place shared or pasted data; also, the file that displays when a link is clicked.

DEVICE A hardware component installed for use with a computer system.

DEVICE DRIVERS The programs that enable peripherals and devices to communicate with computer hardware through the operating system.

DIALOG BOX A window that provides options that let you customize the command.

DIAL-UP MODEM An analog modem used to connect to the internet over a standard telephone line.

DIGITAL A method of expressing signals or data as a series of the digits 0 and 1.

DIGITAL CALENDAR An app that provides tools for scheduling and managing appointments, meetings, and events.

DIGITAL CAMERAS A camera that records and stores photos in a digital format that the computer can work with.

DIGITAL GRAPHICS Images created or modified using computer hardware and software.

DIGITAL IDENTITY The impression created about a person based on the information that person posts online.

DIGITAL MISINFORMATION Actual digital content that has been deliberately changed so that it represents something very different from its original form.

DIGITAL MULTILAYER DISCS (DMDS) A disc that contains multiple layers of a fluorescent material that stores information on each layer. A disc can hold up to 1 terabyte of data.

DIGITAL PROJECTOR A projector that displays digital information on a projection screen.

DIGITAL SIGNATURE A method of verifying the source and content of an email message or application file.

DIGITAL SUBSCRIBER LINE (DSL) DSL uses the same copper wires telephones use, but transmits data in digital form rather than analog.

DIGITAL VIDEO CAMERA A camera that records moving images in digital form.

DIGITAL VISUAL INTERFACE (DVI) A video display interface used to connect a video source to a display device.

DIGITAL WALLET Secure online payment services linked to an account and credit card so users do not have to enter payment data for each transaction.

DIGITAL WELLNESS Using technology safely and appropriately.

DIRECT CURRENT (DC) A constant flow of electricity through a wire.

DIRECTORY A hierarchical filing system.

DISCUSSION BOARDS A type of web app that allows users to exchange comments and ideas, usually on a specific topic. Sometimes called forums or message boards.

DISK SCANNER Utility which checks magnetic disks for errors.

DISTRIBUTE A tool that moves objects to distribute, or space, them from each other.

DOCUMENT MAP An outline of a word-processing document that can be seen in a separate pane.

DOCUMENTATION Instructions on how to install a program, use the application, and troubleshoot any problems.

DOMAIN NAME The phrase used to identify one or more internet protocol (IP) addresses.

DOMAIN NAME SYSTEM (DNS) The system by which internet domain names and addresses are tracked and regulated.

DOT MATRIX PRINTER An impact printer that uses hammers or pins to press an ink-covered ribbon to create characters on paper.

DOWNLOAD To transfer copies of files from a remote computer to a local computer by means of a modem or network.

DOWNTIME A temporary stop to all work on a network.

DRAFT VIEW A basic view used in word-processing applications.

DRAW PROGRAM A program used to create and edit vector images.

DRIVER UTILITY Software that contains information needed by application programs to properly operate input and output devices.

DROP-DOWN MENU A list of options.

DUPLEX People on both sides can communicate at same time, like on a phone call.

DVD-RAM A high-capacity read/write storage device.

DYNAMIC HYPERTEXT MARKUP LANGUAGE (DHTML) A programming language that adds interactivity to a web page.

E

EBOOK An electronic version of a book, newspaper, magazine, website, or other printed content that can be viewed on an eBook reader or on a device with an eBook reader app.

EBOOK READER A device or app used to display and manage eBooks. Also called an eReader.

E-COMMERCE The use of telecommunications networks or the internet to conduct business.

ECONOMICS The study of how people produce, distribute, and use goods and services.

EFFECTIVE COMMUNICATION Communication in which the receiver interprets the message the way the sender intended.

ELECTRONIC DATA INTERCHANGE (EDI) A business-to-business wide area network.

EMAIL A communication system for transmitting messages to anyone with an email address and internet access.

EMAIL ATTACHMENT A file sent along with an email message that can be stored or opened by the recipient.

EMAIL BODY The main area of an email message form where the message is entered.

EMAIL CLIENT A program installed on a user's computer, that enables the user to create, send, receive, and manage email messages.

EMAIL FOLDER A folder used to store and organize related email messages in an email application.

EMAIL HEADER The fields at the top of an email message form for entering the recipient(s) and the subject.

EMAIL SERVER A program, on an internet service provider's server computer, that sends, receives, and delivers email messages to client computers.

EMAIL SIGNATURE Information that displays after the message text in the message body, identifying the sender.

EMAIL VIRUS A malicious program sent in an email message to deliberately cause computer problems for the recipient.

EMBED To copy an object into a document; both the object and the document remain independent when changes are made to either one.

EMERGING TECHNOLOGY A new and innovative technological development.

EMPHASIS In graphic design, creating a visual focal point.

EMPLOYABILITY Having and using skills and abilities to be hired and stay hired.

EMPLOYEE HANDBOOK A document that describes company policies and procedures.

ENCODER A software program that converts a file.

ENCRYPTION The process of encoding data so that it cannot be used without first being decoded.

END TAG In HTML coding, the word or abbreviation enclosed in brackets with a slash between the tag name and the left bracket, used to mark the end of formatted content.

END USER LICENSE AGREEMENT (EULA) A set of rules provided by a business or organization that all users must abide by.

ENTERPRISE STORAGE SYSTEM Technology that allows networked computers to access one or many different types of storage devices.

EREADER A device or app used to display and manage eBooks. Also called an eBook reader.

ERGONOMIC Designed to provide comfortable use and avoid stress or injury.

ERROR MESSAGES Information displayed when something happens to prevent a command from executing.

E-TAILER A retailer that primarily uses the web to sell goods or services.

ETHERNET A networking technology used for local area networks.

ETHICS Moral principles.

EVOLVING TECHNOLOGY An existing technology that changes to be more efficient or to meet a different need.

EXACT PHRASE SEARCH A web query used to search for a phrase exactly as it is typed.

EXCLUSION OPERATOR A minus sign or the word NOT used to search for web pages that do not contain certain words.

EXECUTABLE FILE A file that carries out instructions as part of a program.

EXPENSES Money that is spent.

EXPORT To format data so it can be used in another program.

EXTENSIONS Code designed specifically to add a feature to a web browser, modify a web page, or integrate a browser with other services. Also called an add-on.

EXTRANET A wide area network designed to look and work like the internet, that allows for limited public access.

EYEDROPPER A tool that picks up and works with a specific color from an image.

F

FAIR USE DOCTRINE The use of copyrighted material in a review, in research, in schoolwork, or in a professional publication, which does not necessarily require permission from the material's owner.

FAVORITES A list of frequently visited web pages stored in a web browser for quick access.

FAX MACHINE A device that makes a digital copy of a document, then transmits the data to another device, such as a computer modem or other fax machine.

FIBER-OPTIC CABLE Strands of pure glass that transmit digital data by pulses of light.

FIELD The part of a database that holds an individual piece of data.

FIELD NAME Identifier for a database field.

FIELD SEQUENCE The order in which the fields will appear in each record.

FIELD SIZE A limit on the size of a field, which is typically the number of characters in the largest expected data value.

FIELD WIDTH Maximum number of characters a field can contain.

FILE A unit or grouping of information that has been given a unique name.

FILE COMPRESSION A way of reducing file size so that large files can travel more quickly over a network or consume less disk space.

FILE COMPRESSION UTILITY A software program that reduces the size of a file for storage or transmission purposes.

FILE EXTENSION Letters following a period in a file name that indicate the application a file was created in.

FILE FORMAT Standards used to write data to a disk.

FILE FRAGMENTATION The allocation of a file to noncontiguous sectors on a floppy disk or hard drive.

FILE NAME A series of characters that gives each document in a folder a unique name.

FILE SERVER The main computer in a client/server system.

FILE SHARING Making files available to more than one user on a network.

FILE TRANSFER PROTOCOL (FTP) A standard network protocol used for the transfer of computer files between a client and server on a computer network.

FILTER To select or display items based on whether they meet or match specific criteria; also, a feature in some email programs that can delete certain messages or file messages in folders. In graphics, preset features that apply specific effects to images. Also, to block access to websites, web pages, or applications.

FIND AND REPLACE A feature in some applications used to locate a word or word combination and then change it to a different word or combination.

FIREWALL A filtering system that opens or blocks programs and ports on a computer to keep data from entering a network.

FIRMWARE Permanent instructions stored in read-only memory (ROM) that control computer components.

FIXED BROADBAND Wired networks, such as fiber optic and digital subscriber line (DSL), which are used for television and internet access.

FLAME To insult online in a text message, an email, or other communication.

FLASH DRIVE A small storage device that uses flash memory and connects to the computer through a USB port; also called a pen drive, jump drive, or thumb drive.

FLASH MEMORY Storage medium that has no moving parts and stores data in electronic cells.

FLAT-FILE DATABASE A database that can work with only one file at a time.

FONT A specific typeface with a certain size and style that is used for characters in a document or on a screen.

FONT COLOR The color used to display the font.

FONT SIZE The height of characters, measured in points.

FONT STYLES Characteristics such as bold and italic applied to text.

FOOTER Information placed at the bottom of every page in a document.

FORM An on-screen window for users to view, enter, and edit data.

FORMULA A mathematical expression used to link and perform calculations on numbers in worksheet cells.

FORMULA BAR The area in a spreadsheet where you enter data and formulas and where you can view the contents of the active cell.

FORMULA IDENTIFIER A symbol that identifies a spreadsheet entry as a formula or function, such as an equal sign (=).

FORWARD To send a received message to a third party by selecting the Forward command.

FORWARD BUTTON A tool that lets users move ahead to previously viewed pages in a browser.

FRAME An empty section in a document that will eventually hold text or graphics; or a section of a web page window; also, an individual still image in an animated sequence. In a spreadsheet, it is the element that forms the top and left border of the worksheet grid, where the column letters and row numbers display.

FRAME RATE The number of still images displayed every second in a full-motion video or animation.

FRAME RELAY A communications technology used by most permanent virtual circuits that allows voice, data, and video to travel on the same line at the same time.

FREEWARE Copyrighted software given away for free.

FRICTION The action of one surface or object rubbing against another.

FULL SYSTEM RESTORE The process of using the restore command to restore all data from a full system backup.

FULL-DUPLEX Communication that uses one frequency for talking and a second, separate frequency for listening.

FUNCTION A commonly used formula that is built into a spreadsheet program.

FUNCTION KEY A shortcut key at the top of a keyboard that is labeled with the letter F and a number.

G

GAME CONTROLLER A handheld device that lets you input commands and interact with video and computer games.

GARBAGE IN, GARBAGE OUT (GIGO) A phrase that stresses the importance of inputting accurate data in a database.

GATEWAY A node on a network that enables communication with other networks.

GENRE A category or classification.

GLOBAL UNIQUE IDENTIFIER (GUID) A unique identification number generated by hardware or by a program.

GOAL Something you are trying to achieve.

GRAMMAR CHECK A word-processing tool that identifies problems with verb tense, sentence structure, pronouns, punctuation, and capitalization.

GRAPHIC Anything that can be seen on a computer's screen. Also, drawings, photographs, charts, and other objects that you can insert into a document or file.

GRAPHICAL BROWSER A web navigation program that shows pictures and text.

GRAPHICAL USER INTERFACE (GUI) A visual display that allows the user to interact with the computer by using graphical objects on the screen.

GRAPHICS TABLET A hardware device used for drawing.

GRID An advanced graphics tool that displays a grid onscreen to assist with alignment.

GROUP To combine separate vector images into one image; also part of a Microsoft Ribbon tab that displays related tasks.

GROUPWARE Software that supports multiple users working on related tasks.

GUI EDITORS A software development tool for creating web pages with graphical user interfaces by arranging graphic control elements instead of entering tags.

GUTTER The margin along the side of the page closest to the binding in a printed and bound publication.

H

HALF-DUPLEX Communication in which only one side can communicate at a time.

HANDHELD COMPUTER A small palm-size computing device.

HANDWRITING-RECOGNITION SOFTWARE Software that converts handwritten text to digital format.

HARD DRIVE The most commonly-used type of secondary storage device, which stores bits of data as aligned particles on the surface of a magnetic disk.

HARD REBOOT Turning off all power to a device by pushing the power button or unplugging the system.

HARD SKILLS Skills used for a specific job that do not transfer to other jobs.

HARDWARE The physical parts of a computer.

HARD-WIRED TELEPHONE A telephone that is connected directly to the wiring that transmits audio from a caller to a recipient. Also called a landline.

HARMONY When elements of a graphic come together as a complete idea.

HASHTAGS (#) The hash or pound sign (#) added to the beginning of a word or phrase to call attention to a specific topic or idea.

HEADER Information placed at the top of every page in a document.

HEADER ROW The top row of a spreadsheet or table that contains column labels.

HEAD-MOUNTED DISPLAY (HMD) A helmet that wraps around the head; used for virtual reality experiences.

HEXADECIMAL VALUE A six-digit code used to represent the red, green, and blue values of a color.

HIBERNATE MODE A power state in which data from RAM is saved to the hard disk and then power is shut down.

HIERARCHICAL Multilevel.

HIGH-DEFINITION MULTIMEDIA INTERFACE (HDMI) A digital cable standard for audio and video transmission.

HIGH-DEFINITION TELEVISION (HDTV) A type of television that produces a sharper image than regular television.

HIGH-LEVEL PROGRAMMING LANGUAGES Programming languages that are not dependent on a particular type of computer.

HISTORY A chronological list of web pages a user has visited, stored in a web browser.

HOLOGRAPHIC DATA STORAGE SYSTEM (HDSS) A future storage technology in which data is stored in images called holograms on optical cubes.

HOME PAGE The front or main page of a website.

HORIZONTAL APPLICATION A type of application software that is designed to meet the needs of many different users.

HOVER To rest the mouse pointer over an object on a web page or other program screen. Sometimes called a mouse over.

HUB A connection point for computers, printers, and other equipment on a network.

HYPERLINK An electronic link providing direct access from a marked place in a hypertext or hypermedia document to another place in the same or a different document.

HYPERMEDIA An extension to hypertext that supports links to resources in different types of media, including text, audio, and video.

HYPERTEXT Text that links to other information using hyperlinks.

HYPERTEXT MARKUP LANGUAGE (HTML) The code that describes the format, layout, and structure of a document for publication on the web.

HYPERTEXT TRANSFER PROTOCOL (HTTP) The protocol that controls how web pages are transmitted and displayed on the web.

I

ICON An on-screen picture that represents an object, resource, or command.

IDENTITY THEFT The taking of another person's identity for the purpose of committing illegal acts.

IF STATEMENTS In programming, a statement that defines conditions that must be met for the program to move on to the next step.

IMAGE EDITOR An advanced paint program that edits bitmapped images.

IMPACT PRINTERS A printer that uses keys or pins to strike an ink ribbon to create an image on paper.

IMPORT To bring information into a program from another program.

IN-APP BROWSER A navigation tool built in to some applications that allows users to browse the web.

IN-BROWSER APP An app that can be opened and run by a website, rather than running in a browser window.

INCLUSION OPERATOR A plus sign or the word AND; used to search pages to find a match for specified words.

INCOME Money that is earned.

INCREMENT The number by which each value in a series increases.

INDENTATION Added space between a margin and the text.

INFORMATION KIOSK An automated system that provides information or training; usually has a touch screen to allow input.

INFORMATION OVERLOAD The result of a computer user being overwhelmed by the amount of information generated by his or her computer.

INFRINGE Undermine or interfere with; also, to actively break the terms of a law or agreement.

INKING The task of finishing and enhancing preliminary drawings, usually for comics or animation.

INKJET PRINTERS A printer that works by spraying a fine stream of ink onto paper.

INPUT Raw information, or data, that is entered into a computer; also, to enter data into a computer.

INSERTION POINT A mark that indicates where entered text will be placed in a document.

INSTALL Prepare a computer to run a specific program or use a specific device, usually by copying the necessary instructions to the computer's hard drive.

INSTANT MESSAGING (IM) A system on the internet that allows two people who are online to communicate by typing messages.

INTEGRATED SOFTWARE A program that combines the basic features of several applications into one package.

INTELLECTUAL PROPERTY Someone's creative, literary, or artistic work.

INTERACTIVE MULTIMEDIA A program that uses different types of media (such as text, sound, animation, and others) to convey its message, and which allows the user to choose the content that will be displayed next or direct the flow of the content.

INTERACTIVE PRESENTATION A presentation that responds to input entered by the user.

INTERESTS Subjects and activities that you enjoy doing and learning about.

INTERFACE A means for users to control or operate a computer.

INTERNAL SOCIAL MEDIA A private social media site that is accessed only by the organization's members, such as employees or students.

INTERNET A vast, public wide area network that links computing devices around the world.

INTERNET CLIENT The computer and related software that requests a service on the internet.

INTERNET CORPORATION FOR ASSIGNED NAMES AND NUMBERS (ICANN) The organization responsible for maintaining the database of registered domain names.

INTERNET MESSAGE ACCESS PROTOCOL (IMAP) A message retrieval protocol that stores email messages on a server so they can be synced across multiple devices.

INTERNET PROTOCOL (IP) ADDRESS A four-part number separated by periods that identifies each computer connected to the internet.

INTERNET RADIO Radio that can be accessed through the internet.

INTERNET SERVICE PROVIDER (ISP) A company that provides the actual link between a computer and the internet.

INTERNET VIDEO Video that can be accessed through the internet.

INTERNET2 (I2) PROJECT A project conducted by Internet2 (I2), a not-for-profit U.S.-based computer networking consortium, to develop and test new internet technologies.

INTERPRETER A program used to translate source code directly into actions.

INTRANET A private network set up internally by a business or organization.

IR WIRELESS One of the earlier wireless technologies that allowed computers to exchange data. It uses infrared radiation to transmit data. Infrared is electromagnetic energy at a wavelength slightly longer than that of a red light.

ITERATION In computer programming, each occurrence of a loop.

J

JAVASCRIPT A cross-platform programming language used to create applets, or small applications for the web.

JOB Any activity you do in exchange for money or other payment.

JOB INTERVIEW A meeting in person or on the phone between a job applicant and a potential employer to discuss the position and the candidate.

JOB OUTLOOK A prediction of future opportunities for a particular occupation.

JOYSTICK An input device that uses a lever to move objects on the screen.

JUNK MAIL Unwanted messages and advertisements.

K

KEY FIELD An element that links tables in a relational database.

KEYBOARD SHORTCUT A combination of keys that carries out a specific action.

KEYWORD In a spreadsheet function's syntax, the name of the function; also, text or a phrase used in a search.

KNOWLEDGE BASE A database of information usually related to a specific subject.

L

LABEL Text or a combination of numbers and text typically used for titles or explanation in a worksheet.

LABEL PREFIX A character entered in a spreadsheet cell that identifies a number as text.

LAND A flat, reflective area on the surface of an optical disc.

LANDLINE A hard-wired telephone connected directly to the wiring that transmits audio from a caller to a recipient.

LANDSCAPE ORIENTATION Positioning a page so that content is displayed down the page's short edge, resulting in a page that is wider than it is tall.

LAPTOPS Small portable computers.

LARGE-FORMAT DISPLAY (LFD) A flat-screen monitor ranging from 32" to more than 90" in size.

LASER PRINTERS A non-impact printer that uses an electrostatic digital printing process.

LASER SENSOR A laser-operated tool in an optical drive that reads information.

LASSO The tool in an image editor program that selects complex or freehand shapes.

LAUNCH To start an application program.

LAYERING To stack parts of a bitmapped image on top of another level.

LAYOUT An on-page arrangement of text, graphics, backgrounds, images, and other design elements on a page, slide, or other document.

LEADING Line spacing.

LEARNING MANAGEMENT SYSTEM (LMS) An application designed to deliver subject matter content, manage records, and report grades in an educational environment.

LEASED LINE A permanent connection between the mobile telephone switching office (MTSO) and the long-distance providers that will complete the call.

LIBEL False statements that might hurt someone's reputation.

LIFELONG LEARNING Continually acquiring new knowledge and skills throughout the course of your life.

LINEAR Progressing from one step to the next sequentially, or in order.

LINES An element of design that defines form.

LINK To create a connection between an object's source application (the program in which an object was created) and a destination application (a program into which the object is copied), allowing the object to be edited in either program.

LIQUID CRYSTAL DISPLAY (LCD) Monitor panel that produces color by using an electric field to combine crystals of different colors.

LIST BOX A scrollable list of choices.

LIVE STREAMING Content uploaded live to the internet instead of being stored on a server so that users can access it as it happens in real time.

LINE SPACING The amount of space between the lines of text in a paragraph.

LOCAL APPLICATIONS Programs installed on the user's local computer. Sometimes called desktop applications, perpetual applications, or non-subscription applications.

LOCAL AREA NETWORK (LAN) A network in which all workstations and equipment are near each other.

LOCAL LOOP The network that connects to a telephone company's central office.

LOCK SCREEN A screen that displays on a device until a user enters a password.

LOGIC GATE A device that performs a logical operation on one or more binary inputs and produces a single binary output.

LONG-TERM GOAL Something you want to achieve in the more distant future.

LOOP To replay continuously. In computer programming, one of the three basic logic structures. Loop refers to an action that is repeated until the desired result is achieved.

LOSSLESS COMPRESSION A method of reducing the size of a file so that it can be returned to its original state without losing any data.

LOSSY COMPRESSION A method of reducing the size of a file so that some data may be lost when the file is decompressed.

M

MACRO A set of mouse actions, keystrokes, or commands recorded for repeated use.

MACRO VIRUS A series of commands that is hidden in a document.

MAGIC WAND The tool in an image editor program that selects all the touching pixels of a similar color.

MAIL MERGE A process that inserts variable information into a standardized document to produce a personalized or customized document.

MAILBOX NAME The part of an email address before the "at" sign (@).

MAINFRAME A type of computer used by many people at the same time to allow access to the same secure data.

MAINTENANCE RELEASE A minor revision to correct errors or add minor features to a software program.

MALWARE A program designed to damage or disable your system or data.

MARGINS The space between the edges of the page and the text.

MARQUEE A tool in an image editor program that highlights a simple shape.

MASTER PAGE The pattern that sets the basic features of a document's look for all the other pages to follow.

MASTER SLIDE A default template that is applied to all slides of a certain type.

MASTER VIEW A view in a presentation program that you use to make universal style changes.

MASTERS Default templates applied to all slides of a certain type.

MAXIMIZE To make an application window as large as possible.

MEDIA The plural of medium.

MEDIUM Something used to communicate information or express ideas.

MEMORY Specialized chips, connected to the computer's motherboard, which store data and programs as they are being used by the processor.

MEMORY CARD A storage device often used with mobile devices and digital cameras.

MEMORY SHAVE To steal some of a computer's memory chips.

MEMORY SPEED The amount of time that it takes RAM to receive a request from the processor and then read or write data is called memory speed.

MENU A list of commands.

MENU BAR The bar generally located below an application's title bar where a set of commands is listed.

MERGE Combine into one.

MERGE AND CENTER A spreadsheet command that merges selected cells and centers the data at the same time.

MESH TOPOLOGY A network design in which all components are connected directly to other components.

MESSAGE HEADER The fields at the top of an email message form for entering the recipient(s) and the subject.

METADATA Data about data.

MINIMIZE To make an application window as small as possible.

MOBILE APPS Applications designed to download and use on a mobile device such as a smartphone or tablet.

MOBILE BROADBAND Networks such as 3G and 4G, which are used by cellular phones and other mobile devices.

MOBILE DEVICE A wireless computer that is small enough to use when it is held in your hand.

MOBILE INTERNET SERVICES Internet services made available on mobile devices.

MOBILE TELEPHONE SWITCHING OFFICE (MTSO) An operation center where the landline public switched telephone network system connects to the mobile phone system.

MODEM A device that allows a computer to transmit data to other computers through telephone lines.

MODULATION The process that changes the digital signal from a computer to the analog signal of a telephone.

MONITORING SOFTWARE Software that can track desktop and online activities that occur on a computer system.

MOTHERBOARD The primary circuit board to which all devices are connected and through which all data passes.

MOUSE OVER To rest the mouse pointer over an object on a web page or other program screen. Sometimes called hovering.

MULTICORE PROCESSORS Single integrated circuits with two or more CPUs.

MULTIMEDIA Using different types of media (such as text, graphics, video, animation, or sound) at the same time.

MULTIMEDIA MESSAGING SERVICE (MMS) The technology used to transmit messages containing multimedia content from one mobile device to another.

MULTIPLE SELECTION LIST A scrollable list of choices.

MULTIPURPOSE INTERNET MAIL EXTENSIONS (MIME) A protocol used to translate email attachments.

MULTITASK To work with more than one computer application at a time.

MUSICAL INSTRUMENT DIGITAL INTERFACE (MIDI) An interface that connects a computer to electronic musical instruments, to control the instruments and record their output.

N

NAVIGATE To move through a network or program to find resources or files.

NAVIGATION BUTTON The name for a type of button, or tool, in a web browser used to move from one web page to another.

NEAR-FIELD COMMUNICATION (NFC) A short-distance wireless technology that uses encryption and a special processor to ensure security.

NEST Include an item such as a function or a table, within another, similar item.

NETIQUETTE An informal set of rules for how to behave online.

NETWORK Two or more computers connected to each other to share resources.

NETWORK ARCHITECTURE The science of designing a network.

NETWORK INTERFACE CARD (NIC) A hardware device that physically connects a computer to a network.

NETWORK LAYER A subset of protocols that govern how data is handled and transmitted over a network.

NETWORK OPERATING SYSTEM (NOS) A set of programs that manages and secures a network.

NETWORK TRAFFIC The electronic pulses of information that carry data through a network to its destination.

NEWSPAPER-STYLE COLUMNS In word processing, a feature used to divide a section into multiple columns so that the text flows from the bottom of one column to the top of the next column.

NODE Anything connected to a network, such as a computer, printer, or fax machine.

NONCONTIGUOUS Not adjacent or next to one another.

NONIMPACT PRINTERS Printers that do not create an image by striking an ink ribbon against paper.

NON-LINEAR Progressing in a random, or non-sequential order.

NONTRADITIONAL OCCUPATION Any job that a man or woman does that is usually done by someone of the other gender.

NONVERBAL COMMUNICATION Using visual and physical messages such as a smile or handshake to help put words into context.

NONVOLATILE MEMORY Memory that stores data permanently, even when the computer is turned off.

NORMAL VIEW The view in many applications that is used most often.

NOTEBOOKS Small computers that can be easily transported.

NOTES PAGE VIEW A view in a presentation program that is used to view and edit notes.

NOTES PANE An area in a presentation program where the user can enter speaker notes to use while delivering the presentation.

NOTIFICATION A visual or audible reminder used by an application or device to inform that user that something has happened, or is about to happen.

O

OBJECT A piece of data such as an image, chart, video or sound clip, or a section of text.

OBJECT CODE Readable instructions created by compilers translating the source code into binary form.

OBJECTIVE Balanced and fair. Also, a goal.

OBJECT-ORIENTED DATABASE A database that stores objects, such as sound, video, text, and graphics.

OBJECT-ORIENTED PROGRAMMING A method of programming that provides rules for creating and managing objects.

OBJECTS The elements used to store, enter, and manage data in a database program.

OHM'S LAW A scientific rule that describes how electricity will behave as it travels through circuits.

ONLINE ANALYTICAL PROCESSING (OLAP) A form of analytical processing used for storing and analyzing historical information.

ONLINE BANKING An app that allows users to log in to a bank to pay bills and access accounts online.

ONLINE CONFERENCE A virtual meeting using web-based software or apps.

ONLINE FORUM A site that allows users to engage in discussions by posting messages to each other.

ONLINE PRESENCE A website that provides information about a business and provides online access to the company's services.

ONLINE SERVICE A business that provides access to the internet as well as to custom content, discussion groups, news, shopping services, and other information that is available only to its paying subscribers.

ONLINE STORAGE Data that is stored and accessed on a remote internet server instead of on a local storage device.

ONLINE TRANSACTIONAL PROCESSING (OLTP) A form of analytical processing in which data is updated immediately, used to immediately approve internet credit card purchases.

ON-SCREEN PRESENTATION A display of slides on a computer screen.

OPEN PROTOCOL A standard that anyone can use.

OPEN SYSTEMS INTERCONNECTION (OSI) Rules that define what happens at each step of a network operation and how data flows through it.

OPEN-SOURCE SOFTWARE Software for which the source code is made available to the public.

OPERATING SYSTEM (OS) A system that allows hardware devices to communicate with one another, run efficiently, and support software programs.

OPERATORS A symbol used in mathematics to identify the process to use.

OPTICAL CHARACTER RECOGNITION (OCR) Software used by most scanners that turns text into a digital file.

OPTICAL STORAGE DEVICE A storage device that uses laser beams to read the information stored on the reflective surface of a disc.

ORDER A tool that changes the position in which objects are stacked or layered.

ORDER OF OPERATIONS The rules that specify which operation to execute first in a mathematical expression.

ORGANIC LIGHT EMITTING DIODE (OLED) A technology used for monitors and screens that is made from sheets of organic material that glows when an electrical field is applied; OLED monitors do not require backlighting or diffusers.

ORGANIZATION STRUCTURE The system that assigns work, authority, and responsibility within a company.

ORIENTATION The position or direction in which a page is displayed or printed.

OUTGOING VOICEMAIL MESSAGE A recorded message that plays when a phone is not answered, instructing the caller to leave a message.

OUTLINE VIEW A view in some applications that reveals the hierarchical structure of a document, including headings, subheadings, and text.

OUTPUT The result of a computer's processing, displayed on-screen, printed on paper, or heard through a speaker.

OUTPUT DEVICE Any piece of hardware that shows the result of computer processing.

P

PACKET A tiny segment of information transmitted over a network.

PACKET SNIFFER A program that examines data streams on networks to find information such as passwords and credit card numbers.

PACKET-SWITCHING A method of transmitting data across a network by breaking it into tiny segments called packets.

PAGE LAYOUT The arrangement of text on a page.

PAGINATION The automatic division of a document into pages.

PAINT PROGRAM A basic program for working with a raster or bitmapped image.

PANE A section of a document after the window has been split.

PAPER SIZE The size of the paper used to display or print a document.

PARAGRAPH Any amount of text up to a forced new line.

PARAGRAPH SPACING The amount of space between the last line of one paragraph and the first line of the next paragraph.

PARALLEL PORT A connector for a device that sends or receives several bits of data simultaneously by using more than one wire.

PARSE A spreadsheet feature that breaks down data into parts that will fit into the spreadsheet cells.

PASSWORD A word, or a string of letters and/ or numbers, that is used to gain access to a computer system or network and that is usually known only to the user and an administrator.

PASTE A command used to insert an item copied or cut to the Clipboard.

PATENT The exclusive right to make, use, or sell a device or process.

PATH A string of characters used to identify the specific location of a folder or file within the directory system.

PEER-TO-PEER NETWORK (P2PN) A small network that usually includes from two to ten computers but no server.

PEN-BASED GRAPHICS TABLET A touchpad that uses a stylus to create images.

PERIPHERAL Input, output, and storage devices that can be connected to a computer.

PERMANENT VIRTUAL CIRCUIT (PVC) A circuit that allows multiple users' data to travel at the same time on the same line.

PERSONAL ACADEMIC PLAN A document that you use to set goals for the things you want to accomplish in school.

PERSONAL DIGITAL ASSISTANT (PDA) A small, highly portable handheld computer that is used for taking notes or keeping track of appointments.

PERSONAL INFORMATION MANAGER (PIM) A program responsible for storing phone numbers and addresses and creating schedules.

PERSONAL PRODUCTIVITY PROGRAM A horizontal application used to help people work more effectively.

PERVASIVE COMPUTING Microprocessors embedded in everyday objects, allowing them to communicate with users and other devices. Also called ubiquitous computing.

PHISHING A method by which cybercriminals lure users into revealing account codes and passwords by pretending to be a legitimate website.

PHYSICAL CONNECTION A connection created by using physical media.

PHYSICAL MEDIA The wires, cables, or wireless transmitters and receivers used to connect the computers in a network.

PIT An indented area on the reflective surface of an optical disc that scatters light from a laser.

PIXEL A single point in a bitmapped graphic.

PLACEHOLDER An area within a slide layout designed to hold data, such as text or pictures.

PLAGIARISM Illegal copying of creative material owned by another person.

PLATFORM A kind of computer that uses a certain type of processor and operating system.

PLATTER One of a stack of metal disks that store information in the hard drive.

PLAYER SOFTWARE A program that plays audio or video files.

PLUG AND PLAY (PNP) The capability of Windows-based PC operating systems to detect new, compatible devices.

PLUG-IN PROGRAM A program that adds new features to an application on the computer.

PLUG-INS Mini programs embedded in a website to add a feature or function, such as a search engine or video player.

PODCAST An audio or video file that is created for downloading to an iPod or an MP3 player.

POINT A unit used to measure the height of characters in a font. One point equals 1/72 of an inch.

POINT OF PRESENCE (POP) A local connection to a wide area network.

POINTER The icon that represents the position of the mouse on a computer screen.

POINTING DEVICE A device such as a mouse used to input commands by moving a pointer on a screen and making selections.

POINT-OF-SALE (POS) SYSTEM Hardware and software used for processing sales transactions.

POINT-TO-POINT PROTOCOL (PPP) A method of connecting to the internet in which Transmission Control Protocol/Internet Protocol (TCP/IP) packets are sent from a computer to a server that puts them on the internet.

POPUP A window that opens—or pops up—unexpectedly on a web page.

POPUP BLOCKER A tool that is used to stop popup windows from opening.

POP-UP MENU A list of shortcut commands that appears when an area of the screen is right-clicked or the mouse button is held down.

PORT A connection, either hardware or software, between a computer and an external device. In networking, an endpoint used by the communications protocol to identify the specific location on a computer where data transferred on the internet is sent or received.

PORTAL An internet service that provides an organized subject guide to internet content such as news, weather, sports, and email.

PORTFOLIO A collection of information and documents that show the progress you make in school and in your career planning.

PORTRAIT ORIENTATION Positioning a page so that content is displayed or printed down the long edge, creating a page that is taller than it is wide.

POST OFFICE PROTOCOL 3 (POP3) A message retrieval protocol used to transmit email from a server to a specific device.

POWER SURGE A sharp increase in power coming into the computer system.

POWER-ON SELF TEST (POST) A series of tests a computer performs while starting up.

PREFERENCE A choice that specifies how a user wants a program to operate.

PREMIUM APPS Apps that cost money.

PRESENTATION A visual display of information, often in a slide show format.

PRESENTATION SOFTWARE A specialized software that is used to create and display visual information.

PRESENTER The person who narrates and controls a presentation in front of an audience.

PRIMARY STORAGE Memory chips that are built into a computer, such as random access memory (RAM).

PRINT AREA A portion of a worksheet intended to be printed.

PRINT LAYOUT VIEW The view of a word-processing document that shows how the document will appear when printed.

PRINT PREVIEW The feature in a program that shows how a document will look when printed.

PRINTER A peripheral hardware device that produces a paper copy of the display shown on a monitor.

PROBLEM Any barrier or obstacle between you and a goal.

PROCEDURAL PROGRAMMING A method of programming that uses step-by-step instructions.

PROCESS A series of steps that leads to a conclusion.

PROCESSING A task a computer carries out with data in response to a command.

PRODUCT KEY A string of characters that certifies that a user is authorized to install a program.

PRODUCTIVITY SUITE A program that combines several programs and all of their features.

PROFESSIONALISM The ability to show respect to everyone around you while you perform your responsibilities as best you can.

PROFILE Information about a person stored on a website or social media site.

PROGRAM The coded instructions that tell a computer what to do; also to write the code for a program.

PROGRAMMER An expert who writes the instructions for software.

PROGRAMMING LANGUAGE A coded language used to write instructions for a computer.

PROGRESSIVE DOWNLOAD Media that downloads completely to the local device before the user can play it.

PROPAGANDA Misleading information used out of context in order to influence thinking.

PROPERTY A piece of data attached to or associated with a file, folder, program, or device; also called metadata.

PROPORTION The size and location of one object in relation to other objects.

PROPRIETARY PROTOCOL A protocol standard that only certain people can use.

PROPRIETARY SOFTWARE Copyrighted software that you must buy before using.

PROTECT To block accidental changes in a file or on a device.

PROTECTED VIEW A read-only mode in which most editing features are disabled.

PROTOCOL The rules that define how data is transmitted and formatted on a network.

PROTOCOL SUITE A collection of individual protocols that determines how a network operates.

PROXIMITY In graphic design, using the closeness between objects to indicate a relationship.

PROXIMITY OPERATOR A web query that searches for words that appear close together.

PSEUDOCODE A way to write logic using specific words instead of flowcharts.

PUBLIC DATA NETWORK A network that allows different companies to set up their own networks.

PUBLIC DOMAIN A category of intellectual property not subject to copyright laws.

PUBLIC DOMAIN SOFTWARE A program distributed for free without a copyright.

PUBLIC SWITCHED TELEPHONE NETWORK (PSTN) The global system that uses copper wires to carry analog voice data.

Q

QUARANTINE To disable and remove a virus.

QUERY A request to search a database to find records matching specific criteria.

QUERY LANGUAGE A set of characters, terms, symbols, and rules used in the construction of database queries.

QUERY-BY-EXAMPLE (QBE) To request information from a database by providing an example.

R

RADIO BUTTONS Small circles to the left of each item in a list of options. They may be called option buttons.

RANDOM ACCESS MEMORY (RAM) Special chips that store data and instructions while the computer is working.

RANDOM ACCESS STORAGE DEVICE A storage device that lets the computer go directly to the needed information.

RANGE In a spreadsheet, a selected group of cells.

RASTER GRAPHIC An image formed by a pattern of dots; also called bitmapped graphic.

READ MODE A view customized for reading rather than for writing.

READ/WRITE DEVICE A storage device that allows users to access information and save it to the device.

READ/WRITE HEAD In a disk drive, the component that writes data to and reads data from the surface of a disk.

READING VIEW A view in some applications designed to make it easier to read content on the screen.

READ-ONLY DEVICE A storage device that allows users to access information but not save or change it.

READ-ONLY MEMORY OR (ROM) Chips on the motherboard that contain the instructions that start the computer and control some input and output devices.

READ-ONLY VIEW A view in which users can read the content but cannot edit or otherwise manipulate it.

REAL-TIME COMMUNICATIONS Communication that is occurring live.

REBOOT To restart the computer.

RECORD A part of a database that holds data about a particular individual or item.

RECURRING EVENT An event that occurs at regular intervals.

REDO A command that puts a change back in effect after it was cancelled with Undo.

REDUNDANT ARRAY OF INEXPENSIVE DISKS (RAID) A term used to describe a collection of drives or disks that run together to store data.

REFERENCES The names and contact information of people who know you and your qualifications and who are willing to speak about you to potential employers.

REFORMAT The command used to erase all data from a disk and prepare for use as if it was new.

REFRESH BUTTON A tool in a web browser used to download the page you are already viewing again, which may update certain features. Also called the Reload button.

REHEARSED PRESENTATION A slide show timing method that changes from one slide to the next according to the will of the creator so that the presentation moves at the exact desired speed.

REINSTALL Install a program or device again.

RELATIONAL DATABASE A database in which shared key fields link data among tables.

RELATIVE REFERENCE In a spreadsheet, a method of copying or moving a formula that changes the values in the formula depending on its new location.

RELOAD BUTTON A tool in a web browser used to download the page you are already viewing again, which may update certain features. Also called the Refresh button.

REMOTE RESOURCE Information and components available via a network.

REPETITION When color, shape, or pattern is repeated throughout a graphic.

REPETITIVE STRAIN INJURY (RSI) Nerve damage in the hand caused by continued use of a keyboard or mouse.

REPLICATE To copy.

REPLY To respond to the person who sent a message by selecting the Reply command.

REPORT An ordered list of selected database records and fields in an easy-to-read format.

REPORT TEMPLATE A pattern that controls how data will be displayed in a database report.

RESISTANCE A force caused by an obstruction or blockage.

RESOLUTION For a raster image, the number of pixels in a certain section of the image; for a monitor, the number of pixels that are displayed on the screen at any given time, used as a measure of sharpness of picture quality.

RESOURCES Things used to get something else.

RESPONSIBILITY Something people expect you to do or that you must accomplish.

RESTORE Replace or recreate data using backup files.

RESTORE DOWN The command to return a program window to the size and position it had before it was maximized.

RESTORE POINT A marker that identifies the configuration settings in effect at a specific point in time.

RESUME A written summary of your work-related skills, experience, and education.

RIBBON A toolbar area in Microsoft Office applications since 2007.

RING TOPOLOGY A network design that connects all devices into a circle.

ROOT DIRECTORY The main storage location in a hierarchical filing system.

ROUTER A networking device that forwards data packets between computer networks.

ROW A horizontal series of cells in a spreadsheet or table.

S

SAFE MODE A method of starting a computer with a limited set of files and drivers so you can identify and fix problems.

SANS SERIF FONT A font that has no serifs, or lines, projecting from its ends.

SAT PHONE A satellite telephone that transmits signals using communications satellites orbiting Earth.

SCANNER A device that converts printed images into a digital form.

SCANNING A type of cybercrime that uses programs to try different passwords until one works.

SCREEN SAVER A utility program that changes the screen display after a preset period.

SCREEN SHARING A feature of some videoconference and teleconference applications that lets the participants view the presenter's computer screen.

SCREEN TIME The amount of time you spend using a computer screen.

SCREEN-MAGNIFIER SOFTWARE Software that makes images larger and changes colors to make text easier to see on a monitor.

SCROLL To move from one part of a document to another on the screen.

SEARCH ENGINE Software that finds a list of websites that meet a specified search.

SECONDARY STORAGE Computer disk drives such as the hard drive and CD-ROM drive used to store large amounts of data.

SECOND-LEVEL DOMAIN The part of a domain name to the left of the dot that identifies a specific company, organization, or individual.

SECTION A part of a document that contains specific format settings.

SECTOR A section of a track on a computer disk.

SECURE ELECTRONIC TRANSACTIONS (SET) A standard that uses digital signatures to protect buyers and sellers online.

SELECT A feature that allows the user to highlight, or select, data such as text or objects on-screen.

SELECTION TOOL A tool that can select a portion of an image to be moved, enlarged, or edited.

SELF-RUNNING PRESENTATION A slide show timing method that changes from one slide to the next at a given increment of time.

SEQUENCE In computer programming, one of the three basic logic structures. Sequence refers to the order of operations.

SEQUENTIAL STORAGE DEVICE A storage device that requires a computer to scan from the beginning to the end of stored information.

SERIAL PORT A connector through which information transfers in or out of the computer system one bit at a time.

SERIF FONT A font that has serifs, or lines, projecting from its ends.

SERVER A computer that manages data and programs used in a network.

SERVER ADDRESS The part of an email address after the "at" sign (@).

SHADING Color applied to fill a cell.

SHAPE Forms that comprise graphics.

SHARABLE LINK A direct link to an online file or folder made available so others can access the information.

SHARE Allow multiple users access to the same online storage folder and its contents.

SHAREWARE Copyrighted software that can be sampled before it is purchased.

SHEET TAB A spreadsheet element that identifies each worksheet in the file.

SHORT MESSAGE SERVICE (SMS) The technology that allows brief text messages to be transmitted from one mobile device to another.

SHORT-TERM GOAL Something you want to achieve quickly.

SIMPLE MAIL TRANSFER PROTOCOL (SMTP) The protocol used to transmit email from a client to a mail server.

SIMULATION A virtual reality program that mimics a specific place, job, or function.

SINGLE-SEAT LICENSE License to install and use software on only one computer.

SINGLETONS HTML tags that are not required to work in pairs.

SINGLE-USER LICENSE A license to use one copy of a commercial software program.

SITE LICENSE A license that allows a group to install software on a specific number of computers for internal use only.

SLANDER False statements that might hurt someone's reputation.

SLEEP MODE Power state in which power is shut off to non-essential components but some power is used and data remains in RAM.

SLIDE A separate page in a presentation program on which information is organized.

SLIDE SHOW A presentation in which slides are displayed on a screen or monitor in sequential order to an audience.

SLIDE SHOW VIEW A view in a presentation program used to display the slide show presentation.

SLIDE SORTER VIEW A view in a presentation program used to display thumbnail-sized versions of all slides at once.

SLOW RETRIEVAL The lengthy time it takes for some storage devices to locate stored information.

SMALL COMPUTER SYSTEMS INTERFACE (SCSI) A set of parallel interface standards used for connecting and transferring data between a computer and peripheral devices.

SMART TV A television that has built-in Ethernet and Wi-Fi capability so it can connect to the internet through a local area network.

SMARTPHONE A small computing device that includes telephone, text, and data capabilities.

SOCIAL ENGINEERING Ways of influencing someone to do something that may not be in their best interest.

SOCIAL MEDIA Websites that provide tools for connecting with family, friends, and colleagues by linking profiles, and exchanging comments and messages.

SOCIAL NETWORKING Virtual online communities that facilitate communication between users.

SOFT REBOOT Using the computer's own software to allow your computer to shut down properly.

SOFTWARE Programs that tell a computer what to do and how to do it.

SOFTWARE AS A SERVICE (SAAS) Purchasing a subscription for software that is stored on a network instead of installed on the user's computer.

SOFTWARE LICENSE The document that contains permission for a buyer to install and use a program.

SOFTWARE PIRACY The illegal copying of computer programs.

SOLID STATE DISK (SSD) A high-capacity storage device that contains high-speed random access memory.

SOLUTION Actions for overcoming a challenge or problem.

SONET A standardized digital communication protocol (Synchronous Optical Network) that is used to transmit a large volume of data over relatively long distances using a fiber optic medium.

SORT To arrange data in a specific order.

SOUND CARD A circuit board chip that converts sounds in analog form into digital form and vice versa.

SOURCE CODE The software instructions that tell a computer what to do.

SOURCE FILE The location from which data was collected.

SPACE The distance between objects in a graphic or on a page.

SPAM Unrequested email messages and advertisements.

SPEECH SYNTHESIS SOFTWARE A type of software that lets a computer read text files aloud.

SPEECH-RECOGNITION SOFTWARE Software used for inputting text or commands by speaking into a microphone.

SPELL CHECK A tool that checks the spelling of each word against a dictionary built into the program to identify potential errors.

SPOOF To use a false IP or email address.

SPREADSHEET A software program used for processing numbers that are stored in tables, such as budgets or financial statements.

STAND-ALONE PROGRAM Application software that specializes in one task.

STAR BUS TOPOLOGY A network design that connects multiple star networks in a local area network.

STAR TOPOLOGY A network design that connects each network device to a hub.

START TAG In HTML coding, the word or abbreviation enclosed in brackets used to mark the beginning of formatted content.

STATUS BAR The area below the application workspace that shows information about the program or document.

STORAGE The action by which a computer saves information so the information is available for use and reuse.

STORAGE AREA NETWORK (SAN) A network of storage devices that can be accessed by multiple computers.

STORAGE DEVICES Computer components that retain data even after the power is turned off.

STORAGE MEDIA The material that retains the stored information in a computer storage device.

STORAGE SERVICE PROVIDER (SSP) A company that leases storage space on a network or cloud server.

STORYBOARD A map or plan that defines the layout, organization, and navigational structure of a website.

STREAM To transmit data over a network or internet connection without interruption.

STRUCTURED QUERY LANGUAGE (SQL) A standard database query language.

STYLE A set of formats for similar elements in a document.

STYLE CHECK A word processing tool that suggests ways to improve the writing style in a document.

STYLE SHEET A collection of predefined formats that can be applied to a document.

STYLUS A pointing device used for drawing on a graphics tablet.

SUBDIRECTORIES Folders stored within the root or other folders.

SUBJECT GUIDES Web pages grouped together under topic headings that include links only to articles and pages that provide useful information about the topic.

SUBROUTINE In programming, a sequence described in a single line of code.

SUBSCRIBER IDENTIFICATION MODULE (SIM) CARD A small piece of plastic with an integrated chip that fits inside a cell phone and stores information used to verify that the owner is a network subscriber.

SUPERCOMPUTER A large and powerful scientific computer that can process large amounts of data quickly.

SUPERZAPPER A program that accesses data by avoiding security measures.

SYMMETRIC DSL (SDSL) Digital subscriber lines that can send and receive data at the same speeds.

SYNC Update data so that it is the same in multiple locations.

SYNCHRONOUS SCROLLING A feature in some applications that allows two documents to be displayed and scrolled at the same time.

SYNERGY The combined effect group effort can create.

SYNTAX Rules for specifying something precisely, such as the rules for wording a spreadsheet function, or for entering software code.

SYNTHESIZE To create sounds imitative of actual musical instruments using a computer.

SYSTEM ADMINISTRATOR The person responsible for maintaining a computer system.

SYSTEM IMAGE The result of a full system backup.

SYSTEM REQUIREMENT The minimum equipment a computer needs to run an application.

SYSTEM SOFTWARE Software programs that help the computer work properly.

T

T1 LINE Copper or fiber-optic lines that allow data to be sent at more than 1.5 million bits per second.

TAB A part of the Ribbon in Microsoft Office applications since 2007 that contains related groups of commands. Also, a separate page within a web browser window.

TABBED BROWSING A function in most web browsers that lets users open each web page on a separate tab so more than one web page may be displayed in a single browser window.

TAB-DELIMITED TEXT Text that has tab characters at every point where a spreadsheet program should break for a new column.

TABLE Data organized into rows and columns.

TABLET COMPUTER A computer that combines the features of a graphics tablet with the functions of a personal computer; sometimes called a tablet PC.

TABS Stops placed along a line in a word-processing document used for aligning text.

TAB-SEPARATED VALUES FILES Text files that have tab characters at every point where a spreadsheet program should break for a new column.

TAG A code used in HTML for formatting web pages.

TASK PANE A dockable window in some programs that displays options for customizing commands.

TELECOMMUNICATIONS The process of sending information over a telephone network.

TELECOMMUTE To work from home by communicating with a workplace through a network.

TELECONFERENCE A live meeting using computers and telecommunications equipment that allows two or more people in different locations to participate.

TELEPHONE A system for transmitting sound by converting vibrations into electrical signals.

TELEPRESENCE Any technology that gives the user the feeling they are physically present in one location when they are actually somewhere else.

TEMPLATE A file that already includes layout, formatting, prompts, and some text suitable for a specific document type.

TERABYTE A unit of measure equal to 1024 gigabytes.

TERMINAL A keyboard and monitor attached to a shared, central computer.

TEXT MESSAGING A brief message transmitted from one mobile device to another.

TEXT ORIENTATION The rotation of text within a cell in a table or spreadsheet.

TEXTURE In graphics, the quality of the surface of a shape.

THEME A collection of formatting settings including colors, fonts, and effects.

THERMAL TRANSFER PRINTER A printer that uses heat to transfer color dyes or inks onto paper.

THREAD A series of related messages generated by replying and forwarding from one recipient to another.

THREE-DIMENSIONAL (3D) PRINTER A device that interprets a model as 2 dimensional layers, which they output one on top of the other in an additive process to produce a 3D object.

THUMBNAIL A small, representative version of a graphic.

TIME BOMB A computer virus programmed to perform a task (often a destructive one) at a specific date and time.

TIME MANAGEMENT Organizing a schedule so there is time to complete tasks and meet responsibilities.

TIME-LIMITED TRIAL A type of software that stops working after a certain number of uses or days.

TITLE BAR The top row of an application window where the program name and often the name of the document is shown.

TOKEN A unit of data used in ring topology to prevent collisions; or a handheld electronic device that generates a log-on code.

TOKEN RINGS A network design that connects all devices into a circle, and controls collisions using a unit of data called a token.

TOOLBAR A row of icons that represent the program's most commonly used commands.

TOP LEVEL DOMAIN The suffix of an internet domain that identifies the type of organization that registered the name.

TOP-LEVEL DOMAIN COUNTRY CODES A two letter code that is part of a domain name that identifies the country where the site is located.

TOPOLOGY The layout of the physical structure of a network.

TOUCHSCREEN A display device that allows a user to interact with a computer by touching areas on the screen.

TRACE To convert pixels into lines.

TRACING A process used to convert raster graphics to vectors.

TRACK One of a set of uniform circles made on a disk.

TRACK CHANGES A feature in a Microsoft Office application that marks each editing change made by one or more members of a group working on the same document.

TRACKING A method used by some websites to gather information about a user's browsing history.

TRADEMARK A symbol that indicates that a brand or brand name is legally protected and cannot be used by other businesses.

TRANSACTIONAL PROCESSING A way of changing a database that keeps its records up to date at all times.

TRANSFERRABLE SKILLS Skills that can be transferred from one situation or career to another.

TRANSFORMER A device that transfers electricity from one circuit to another.

TRANSISTORS Switches that use electricity to complete tasks.

TRANSITION A presentation graphics feature that controls the change from one slide to the next.

TRANSITION EFFECT In a presentation program, a special effect that adds visual interest when the current slide disappears and the next slide appears on the screen.

TRANSMISSION CONTROL PROTOCOL/INTERNET PROTOCOL (TCP/IP) The set of rules for formatting and transmitting data over the internet, used by every computer that is connected to the internet.

TRAP DOOR A type of virus that enables an unauthorized user (such as a hacker) to secretly gain access to a computer.

TREND A general move in a certain direction.

TROJAN A type of malware designed to look harmless but that allows unauthorized access to your computer.

TROJAN HORSE A program disguised as useful but that is destructive to the data on a hard drive.

TROLLS People who go on websites specifically to post rude, mean comments intended to upset others.

TROUBLESHOOTING Diagnosing and attempting to correct a problem with a piece of hardware or a software program.

TRUNCATED Appear cut off.

TWEEN The ability of a graphics program to determine in-between frames.

TWEET A text message created, sent, and received using the Twitter app. Also to send a tweet.

TWISTED PAIR A pair of copper wires used for transmission that are twisted together to reduce interference, or outside noise.

U

UEFI (UNIFIED EXTENSIBLE FIRMWARE INTERFACE) A firmware interface that supports fast startup, large capacity storage drives, and strong security features.

UNDO A command that reverses the previous action.

UNGROUPING Separating grouped vector images into individual images.

UNICODE A system using 16 bits to encode characters, creating more codes for foreign languages.

UNIFORM RESOURCE LOCATOR (URL) The unique address given to a document on the internet.

UNINSTALL To remove a program from a computer.

UNINTERRUPTIBLE POWER SUPPLY (UPS) A device that aims to prevent interruption of power to a computer.

UNITY In graphic design, when a third object is used to establish a connection between two other objects.

UNIVERSAL SERIAL BUS (USB) A standard that allows communication between devices, such as between a flash drive and a computer.

UNMERGE Divide merged cells back into their original structure.

UPDATE To install a fix or repair for an operating system or program; also, the software used to update.

UPGRADE To install a new and improved version of an operating system or program.

UPLOAD To send data from a client computer to a server computer through a network or internet connection.

USB FLASH DRIVE A small storage device that uses flash memory and connects to the computer through a USB port; also called a pen drive, jump drive, or thumb drive.

USER ACCOUNT A collection of information used to identify a person and grant him or her access to a computer system or network.

USER PROFILE Software settings associated with a specific user account.

USER RIGHTS Settings assigned to a user account to limit or allow access to a computer system.

USERNAME The online identity of a person who is accessing a system or network.

UTILITY SOFTWARE Programs that are used to maintain and repair the computer.

V

VALUE A number, such as a whole number, a fraction, or decimal; also, a numerical representation of a color in a graphics program.

VALUES The importance that you place on various elements in your life.

VARIABLE A symbol or name that represents a value that may change.

VARIETY In graphic design, the use of different colors and shapes to create visual interest.

VECTOR GRAPHIC An image that is created using paths or lines.

VERBAL COMMUNICATION The exchange of messages by speaking or writing.

VERSION A release of a software program, usually identified by a unique number to distinguish it from previous releases.

VERSIONING Saving previous or incremental versions of programs or files.

VERTICAL APPLICATION A type of application software that is designed for a very limited purpose in a field or business.

VIDEO ADAPTER A circuit board that creates the images seen on a monitor.

VIDEO CAPTURE BOARD A circuit board chip that converts analog video images into a digital file. Also called a video capture card.

VIDEO EDITOR A program that combines and edits video and audio files.

VIDEO GRAPHICS ARRAY (VGA) A standard for connecting video devices such as monitors, televisions, and projects to a video adapter card in a computer.

VIDEO MEMORY (VRAM) The memory in a video adapter, used to store video images.

VIDEOCONFERENCE A meeting that provides audio and visual contact for participants in different locations.

VIEWABLE AREA A portion of the screen where an image can be shown.

VIRTUAL MEMORY Storage space on the hard disk that can function as memory when needed.

VIRTUAL PRIVATE NETWORK (VPN) A private network set up through a public network.

VIRTUAL REALITY (VR) A computer-generated, realistic, three-dimensional world.

VIRTUALIZATION Physical storage pooled from multiple network storage devices into what seems to be one single storage device managed from a central console.

VIRUS A type of malware, or harmful code, that can copy itself and spread through software.

VISUAL AID A graphic that helps convey information to an audience.

VLOGS Video logs in which the vlogger appears on video.

VOICE OVER INTERNET PROTOCOL (VOIP) Technology that sends digital voice data over the internet to enable internet-based telephone calls.

VOICEMAIL Technology that allows callers to leave a recorded spoken message that the recipient can play back using a telephone, cell phone, or other device.

VOLATILE MEMORY Memory which does not retain data when the computer is turned off.

VOLTAGE Electric pressure.

VOLUME LICENSE A license that allows a group to install software on a specific number of computers for internal use only.

W

WEARABLE COMPUTER A mobile computing device designed to be worn on the body, leaving the hands free for other tasks.

WEB APPS Applications that reside on a web server and run in a web browser; sometimes called online or Cloud applications, they are not copied to the local storage device.

WEB BROWSER A program used to view web pages.

WEB CACHE A hardware or software component where information about recently accessed web pages is stored for future access.

WEB FEED A service that automatically downloads web page content that a user has signed up for.

WEB HOST A company that leases storage space for websites.

WEB LAYOUT VIEW The view in a word-processing program that shows how a document will appear when published on the web.

WEB PAGE A single document on the web.

WEB SERVER A program that uses HTTP to manage files for the web. Also, the computers dedicated to using HTTP to store and manage web documents.

WEB-BASED EMAIL Email applications that are accessed via the internet instead of installed on your computer.

WEB-BASED TRAINING Educational courses available via the internet.

WEBCAM A small camera that attaches to the computer monitor, sits on your desk, or is built into the computer.

WEBCAST A live broadcast of audio and video over the internet.

WEBMASTER The person responsible for the creation and maintenance of a website.

WEBSITE A location on the internet where a collection of related web pages is stored.

WHOIS DATABASE The central database of domain names.

WIDE AREA NETWORK (WAN) A network that connects computers and other resources over great distances.

WIDGETS Interactive elements on a website, such as pop-up windows, buttons, and pull-down windows.

WI-FI A wireless technology that uses radio signals over a distance up to 300 feet to connect devices to the internet.

WIKI A website that contains information created and updated by anyone who has access to the site.

WILDCARD A symbol that stands for one or more characters; used to search pages with variations of a word in the search.

WINDOW A rectangular, on-screen frame used to view a program or document.

WIRELESS ACCESS POINT (WAP) A central transmitter for sending and receiving wireless signals.

WIRELESS CONNECTION A transmission via radio waves.

WIRELESS DATA PLAN A contract that identifies how much a user must pay to access, upload, and download internet data using a wireless connection.

WIRELESS TOKEN RINGS A wireless network design that connects all devices into a circle, and controls collisions using a unit of data called a token.

WIZARD A series of dialog boxes that gives a step-by-step guide through a procedure.

WORD WRAP In an application program, the automatic starting of a new line of text when the previous line is full.

WORD-PROCESSING PROGRAM A program used to create documents through typing, editing, formatting, and printing functions.

WORK ETHICS The beliefs and behaviors about what is right and wrong in a work environment.

WORKBOOK A spreadsheet program file.

WORKSHEET A grid made of vertical columns and horizontal rows in a spreadsheet program.

WORKSPACE The blank area where a graphic will display in a paint or draw program.

WORKSTATION A computer connected to a computer network.

WORLD WIDE WEB (WEB) Part of the internet comprised of linked documents.

WORM A computer virus that spreads over a network without user execution.

WRITE The process of storing information on a storage device.

WRITE-PROTECT SWITCH A sliding bar on a USB flash drive that can be set to prevent changes to the data stored on the drive.

WYSIWYG Behind-the-scenes programming that stands for "What You See Is What You Get."

Z

ZOOM To increase or decrease the magnification of content on a screen.

Index